PRAISE FOR *AMERICAN-MADE*

"Comprehensive...impassioned." —*Seattle Times*

"Provides a succinct survey of the Great Depression
and particularly its consequences for workers...A warm glow
of history enshrouds the WPA." —*Washington Post*

"Launched in 1935, at the bottom of the Great Depression, the
Works Progress Administration (WPA) served as a linchpin of FDR's
New Deal....Nick Taylor vividly and painstakingly paints the full
story of the WPA from its inception to its shutdown....A splendid
appreciation." —*Publishers Weekly* (starred review)

"Vastly informative, popular history at its finest."
—*Dallas Morning News*

"[A] well-considered account of the Works Progress Administration,
the New Deal's signature jobs program...Colorful,
compelling...Readable and vividly rendered—a near-definitive
account of one of the most massive government interventions
into domestic affairs in American history."
—*Kirkus Reviews* (starred review)

"An important book, reviving memories not only of the WPA but
of human perseverance in the face of hardship, and a government
that acted with rare wisdom and compassion."
—Gay Talese, author of *A Writer's Life*

"A vivid, engagingly written book." —*San Francisco Chronicle*

"Grade A...Taylor's book is filled with both insight and wisdom.
It is highly readable, absolutely terrific and highly recommended."
—*Tucson Citizen*

"Nick Taylor has done a superb job of restoring to our national
memory an experience that changed literally millions of lives.
The chapters on the WPA writing, art, and theater groups are
especially fascinating—and remarkably relevant."
—Thomas Fleming, author of *The New Dealers' War: F.D.R.
and the War Within World War II*

"A classic textbook of lessons from the past, animated by dramatic
narrative. Nick Taylor has achieved a rarity of the historian's
craft—a masterwork of scholarship that consistently entertains with
portraits of the diversity and vitality of our American character."
—Sidney Offit, curator, George Polk Awards in Journalism

AMERICAN-MADE

THE ENDURING LEGACY OF THE WPA:
WHEN FDR PUT THE NATION TO WORK

Nick Taylor

BANTAM BOOKS

AMERICAN-MADE
A Bantam Book

PUBLISHING HISTORY
Bantam hardcover edition published March 2008
Bantam trade paperback edition / March 2009

Published by
Bantam Dell
A Division of Random House, Inc.
New York, New York

All rights reserved
Copyright © 2008 by Nick Taylor
Cover design by Tom McKeveny
Excerpt from Ernie Pyle column on p. 215:
courtesy of Scripps-Howard Foundation

Book design by Glen M. Edelstein

Library of Congress Catalog Card Number: 2007034563

Bantam Books and the Rooster colophon are registered trademarks
of Random House, Inc.

ISBN 978-0-553-38132-0

Published simultaneously in Canada

www.bantamdell.com

147028622

For Barbara

CONTENTS

AMERICAN-MADE

PROLOGUE

The human toll of the Great Depression of the 1930s is almost impossible for us to fathom. When Franklin D. Roosevelt took office as president of the United States in March 1933, as many as 15 million people—a quarter of the nation's workers—had no jobs and no hope of finding one. Factoring in their families, this meant that in a nation of 130 million, perhaps 34 million were literally without support: no money for rent, no food to feed their children, no coats against the wintry cold. Factories lay idle, storefronts vacant, fields plowed under. State governments, cities, and towns had exhausted their meager relief funds. The desolation knew no boundaries: the skilled and the unskilled alike stood on the breadlines, waited their turns in soup kitchens, scavenged in town dumps; when they were evicted from their homes they built impromptu shacks to house their families until the police came and knocked the shantytowns down.

When Roosevelt took over the reins of government from Herbert Hoover and worked to gain a foothold in the struggle against starvation and homelessness, his first step was to provide direct relief—the dole. The handouts ranged from cash payments to surplus food and clothing, but these were emergency measures to fill basic necessities. They did not alter the underlying problem of unemployment, nor did they address the singular—and vital—human need: the urgency of maintaining dignity.

The president's instinct that it was far better to give people work than handouts was shared by Harry Hopkins, the shrewd and savvy former social worker Roosevelt chose to administer the relief program. Even in this era of remarkable characters, Hopkins stood out. He had no patience with foot-dragging politicians who mouthed good intentions but didn't back their words with votes—and he said so. He was a lightning rod for action, fiercely honest, hated by conservatives, reviled by the anti–New Deal press, and adored by the people who worked for him. He created jobs in the initial relief programs but it was not until the Works Progress Administration—the WPA—was established by presidential act in 1935 that jobs became the focus of relief and gave genuine hope to formerly jobless workers.

In turn, they shouldered the tasks that began to transform the physical face of America. They built roads and schools and bridges and dams. The Cow Palace in San Francisco, La Guardia Airport in New York City and National (now Reagan) Airport in Washington, D.C., the Timberline Lodge in Oregon, the Outer Drive Bridge on Chicago's Lake Shore Drive, the River Walk in San Antonio—all these accomplishments and countless others are WPA creations. Its workers sewed clothes and stuffed mattresses and repaired toys; served hot lunches to schoolchildren; ministered to the sick; delivered library books to remote hamlets by horseback; rescued flood victims; painted giant murals on the walls of hospitals, high schools, courthouses, and city halls; performed plays and played music before eager audiences; and wrote guides to the forty-eight states that even today remain models for what such books should be. And when the clouds of an oncoming world war eventually shadowed Europe in darkness and loomed over the United States, it was the WPA's workers who modernized army and air bases and trained in vast numbers to supply the nation's military needs. In fact, there was scarcely anything they did not do.

The WPA lasted for eight years. Its accomplishments were enormous, yet during its lifetime it was the most excoriated program of the entire New Deal. Its workers were mocked as shiftless shovel leaners. Its projects gave rise to a mocking new word: "boondoggles." Red-baiting congressmen called it a hotbed of Communists. Its very initials became a taunt; WPA, said its critics, stood for "We Piddle Around."

And at the end of its life, amid the global fight to save democracy that was World War II, the WPA sank virtually unnoticed. On July 1, 1943, as the United States and the Allies fought against the Axis forces of Nazi Germany, fascist Italy, and Imperial Japan that had conquered much of Europe and the Pacific Rim of Asia, the WPA's obituary was buried on page 9 of the *New York Times,* along with the news that a San Francisco jury had found bandleader Gene Krupa guilty of contributing to the delinquency of a minor for having his young valet carry marijuana cigarettes. "WPA Pays Up and Quits" read the single-column headline, followed by four brief paragraphs. These described the Work Projects Administration, as it was known then, in skeletal statistics. Unnamed officials said that the "WPA spent about $10,500,000,000 and employed 8,500,000 persons since its inception in 1935," and that it had sent back $105 million in unspent funds and $25 million worth of supplies and materials to the U.S. Treasury.

Like the spiritless obituary of a forgotten celebrity, the perfunctory notice gave no hint of the passions its subject once inspired. It barely suggested the WPA's sweeping, nation-changing mission. It said nothing at all about its incalculable value in rebuilding—and often actually building—the country's infrastructure and training vast numbers of workers to meet the demands of wartime. It left unmentioned its place in the national consciousness: the turmoil it generated, the vitriol hurled at it, the controversies that swirled around it. Politicians had grown hoarse in attack and just as hoarse in its defense; yet after consuming miles of newsprint and vats of ink, the WPA was reduced at its death to numbers on a balance sheet.

It died because it no longer had reason to exist. War production had America's factories turning out planes, warships, and cargo vessels; guns big and small, and ammunition to feed them; Jeeps, tanks, and troop carriers; tires, clothing, and boots; medical supplies. Refineries were working to capacity. With men fighting overseas, labor of all kinds was in short supply. Women put on coveralls and safety goggles, riveting and welding to help meet the industrial labor shortage; what seemed like novelty at the start quickly became the norm. The 25 percent unemployment rate of a decade earlier would reach 1.9 percent in 1943. The next year it would fall below 1 percent. Breadlines and shantytowns were a bad memory, now that the WPA had made it possible to forget them.

World War II raged on for two more years, and when it was over, rather than look back at an anguishing past, Americans were ready to move on. They stored their memories of the depression in a dim corner of the attic and passed along its traumatic residues to new generations in the form of ludicrous habits of thrift. My parents rinsed off aluminum foil and reused it, spread out wet paper towels to dry. Only recently, in a newly "green" world, have practices such as these taken on new credence.

In the same way, the contributions of the WPA have gradually emerged from unawareness. They are drawing renewed attention now, not only for the program's arts and brick-and-mortar legacies but also for its example. The Roosevelt administration placed an extraordinary bet on ordinary people, and the nation realized a remarkable return. The story of the WPA reminds us that the backbone of the United States is the strength, the patience, and the underlying wisdom of its people when they are called upon to face a crisis and are given the means to overcome it.

That story starts in a country that was on its knees.

PART I

IN EXTREMIS

The cure for unemployment is to find jobs.
—HERBERT HOOVER, DECEMBER 5, 1929

Oh, why don't you work
Like other men do?
How the hell can I work
When there's no work to do?
—"HALLELUJAH, I'M A BUM," ANONYMOUS

1. THE END OF JOBS

In 1932, the United States faced the greatest crisis in its history short of war. The American industrial powerhouse that had emerged at the end of the Great War in Europe had fallen still. The stillness had progressed from the stock market, which had lost almost 90 percent of its value since the awful crash of October 1929, to the nation's factories, and from the factories to city avenues, small-town streets, and out across the countryside, where it reached farmers who were mired in a crisis of their own, caused by debt and drought. Workers from every walk of life were idle, one-quarter of the workforce—13 million men and women, though some estimates ranged to 15 million and above. As their resources dwindled, they descended a spiral from belt-tightening to despair to destitution. Millions lost their homes, wore their clothes into rags, and had to forage like animals for food: city dwellers fought for scraps in garbage cans and dumps, while in the country, the hungry scratched for roots and weeds.

For all of the physical suffering, the greatest loss was to the spirit. People felt fear, shame, despair; the suicide rate soared, and the nation trembled at the prospect of a dark, uncertain future. The optimism that Americans had distilled from the promise of the Constitution and learned to take as their birthright—their dreams—had disappeared with their access to work.

This did not have to happen. That it did was dictated by a revered American political philosophy that denied the central government a role in addressing social problems. In the so-called New Era, which began in 1921 and spanned the Republican presidencies of Warren G. Harding, Calvin Coolidge, and now Herbert Hoover, business interests effectively ran the country with some friendly advice from Washington, primarily in the form of useful information. The right data, gathered by the government, would allow banks to adjust their loan portfolios and manufacturers their production schedules, thereby achieving greater efficiencies than they had attained on their own. Labor was a commodity, like iron ore or cotton, to be purchased on the open market at the cheapest price. It was outlandish to think that employers would have any interest in their employees beyond their productive capacity, and even odder to think that the federal government would interfere by telling them how to treat their workers. As for human health and welfare, these were private matters. Society understood that there would always be a few unfortunates who could not— or chose not to—work and take care of themselves, and for these stragglers local governments and private charities were expected to lend a helping hand. It was certainly not Washington's job to feed and clothe people or give them employment. The government had an interest in promoting social goals, since a healthy, well-fed, stable nation provided a good business climate, but that was all.

"The sole function of government," Hoover had said in the fall of 1931, two years after the crash, "is to bring about a condition of affairs favorable to the beneficial development of private enterprise." His predecessor, Coolidge, had put it more succinctly (a practice for which he was famous; his nickname was "Silent Cal"): "The chief business of the American people is business."

But the New Era had failed, and Hoover's efforts to revive it had been fruitless. Babe Ruth had put the president's performance into harsh perspective. Early in 1930, the New York Yankees slugger was holding out for a contract that would pay him $80,000 a year. When sportswriters reminded him that the president made $75,000, Ruth responded, "What's Hoover got to do with it? Besides, I had a better year than he did."

And conditions were not improving. Businesses continued to fail at an unprecedented rate, more than 50,000 since the crash, and the pace of these failures was accelerating. By 1932, more than 3,600 banks had closed, robbing millions of depositors of their life's savings. Every time a bank or business shut its doors, men and women lost their jobs and their buying power, which meant more business failures. As a result, industry was operating at a fraction of capacity, with production lines slowed or shut down entirely. In Birmingham, Alabama, 25,000 of the steel town's 108,000 salaried workers had no jobs at all, and another 75,000 were working reduced hours, for an average pay of $1.50 a day. Thirty percent of workers were jobless in Detroit, 40 percent in Chicago, 50 percent across the state of Colorado. New York City had 800,000 workers without jobs. Skilled laborers in the construction industry—carpenters, plumbers, and electricians—saw their jobs disappear as new construction vanished. White-collar professions were equally hard hit. Only half the nation's engineers had work. With few new homes, or commercial or public buildings, to design, architects' practices were decimated; only one in seven had jobs. Nationally, unemployment had doubled in a year.

After the prosperity of the late 1920s, the widening epidemic of joblessness sent shock waves through the nation. Before the crash, almost every non-farmer who could work and wanted a job had one. The unemployment rate in 1929 had been just 3.2 percent. Flush times had begun to seem permanent, a notion supported by the nation's leaders. Hoover, accepting the Republican presidential nomination in June 1928, said, "Unemployment in the sense of distress is widely disappearing.... We in America today are nearer to the final triumph over poverty than ever before in the history of any land. The poorhouse is vanishing from among us."

When it was jobs, not unemployment, that vanished, people found it impossible to believe at first. They never thought it could happen to them. Office workers who got pink slips went home and circled newspaper want ads at the kitchen table, then went out the next morning with the paper tucked under their arms, full of expectation, only to return at night disappointed. Factory men gathered day after day in union halls, in employment offices, and at the gates of the factories where they used to work. Bulletin boards bristled with "No Help Wanted" signs. Barkers bellowed "No jobs today, men" over bullhorns at the factory gates. Each day hope flaked away like layers of old paint. And when the reality that there were no jobs finally sank in, the job seekers continued to leave their homes each morning, but now sat on park benches and in the reading rooms of public libraries. They haunted the counters of cheap coffee shops and stood in sheltered doorways. Anything was better than returning home and admitting defeat to a wife whose eager hope shone on her face as she opened the door—and to children who sensed the desperation in their parents' whispered conversations.

The hardships that followed came on slowly. Those who hadn't lost their savings when a bank failed spent them down to nothing. Then they borrowed. They put off paying rent, bought on credit at the grocery store, skipped the installment payments on their furniture. When their credit was gone, they leaned on relatives and friends. When their clothes wore out, they darned and patched until the fabric couldn't hold new thread. When the soles of their shoes wore through, they stuffed them with cotton, cardboard, or old newspapers. When they couldn't pay for electricity or coal and suppliers cut them off, they huddled together in the dark and chased coal trucks down the street to pick up the odd lumps that fell onto the pavement. When they found the eviction notice nailed to their front door, they tore it down and hoped the sheriff would forget them.

Food was the last necessity to go. Parents skipped meals so their children could eat. Siblings ate on alternate days. Teachers watched skinny, ill-clothed, malnourished children nodding at their desks until the day came when they dropped out of school and vanished. Foster homes and orphanages swelled with youngsters whose parents could not afford to feed them, 20,000 in New York alone. At night people lurked behind restaurants and grocery stores waiting for the refuse cans to be set out, and fought others for the chance to claw through the garbage. They followed sanitation trucks to city dumps. They stared at the food displayed in grocery store and bakery windows and wished they had the nerve to hurl the brick that might let them satisfy their children's hunger for a night.

By 1932, the situation of city dwellers had finally fallen to a par with the nation's farmers, who for the past ten years had not been able to sell their crops and livestock for what these cost to grow. The farm troubles had started in the aftermath of the world war. Food from

America had sustained Europe when its own farms were idled by the war, but once those farms regained their productivity America's export markets disappeared, and suddenly its farmers were producing more food than the domestic market could absorb. Protective tariffs, which sheltered American manufacturers from inexpensive imports, had never been erected on behalf of farmers. While the nation's overall economy recovered from the brief postwar depression of 1920–21, when manufacturing output fell 25 percent, the farmers never regained their buying power. Subsequent years of drought had made matters even worse. Eleven million farm families continued to live in unremitting poverty, and the banks' hold on their mortgaged land grew ever tighter.

And no matter where they lived, those who had a roof at all were lucky, because the sheriff could not forget those struggling in arrears, even if he wanted to. When the eviction notice was hammered to the door a second and a third time, the dispossessed were likely to steal away in the middle of the night to find space where they could, sometimes in apartments where landlords who were also desperate were offering terms of free rent to fill their empty space, sometimes doubling up with the same relatives and friends they had already pressed for loans, sometimes even in their cars. But for many who lost their homes through eviction or foreclosure, including farmers who had been turned out or simply walked away from barren and unproductive land, there was no place to go. Following rumors or blind hope that jobs waited at the next crossroad or rail junction, thousands upon thousands became nomads. Old farm trucks driven by grim men plied the roads, overloaded with mattresses and furniture, pots and pans, suitcases and chests, wives and children and sometimes parents crowded together in the cab or huddled under canvas in the back. Others rode in—or under—empty freight cars or hitchhiked, wandering between hobo jungles where they might find a crude meal and temporary shelter. Most though not all of them were men. Women and even children were also on the roads and rails, their days spent in a twilight world of fear and want. The homeless numbered as many as 2 million. They collected in city doorways, in railway freight yards, under bridges. They lived in squalid migrant camps and shantytowns cobbled together from abandoned cars, discarded tarpaper, sheets of tin, scraps of wood.

Yet even the most impoverished families were slow to turn to charity. Americans' deep-rooted belief in work came with a catch: failing to find it, it was not in their blood to ask for help. Campaigning in 1928, Hoover had extolled "the American system of rugged individualism," a system, he said, that "has come nearer to the abolition of poverty, to the abolition of fear of want, than humanity has ever reached before." But even when the system failed in 1929, bringing them face-to-face with poverty and want—and fear itself—Americans clung to its assumptions. If they couldn't make their own way in the world, the fault must be with them.

"Oh, don't bother," a laid-off Texas teacher who had been forced to seek assistance told a social worker who was trying to cheer her up. "If, with all the advantages I've had, I can't make a living, I'm just no good, I guess."

The growing evidence of suffering brought no change in the philosophy that ruled government and business. The United States clung to a tradition of poor laws that harked back 350 years to Elizabethan England. The burden of caring for the poor fell on local governments and private charities. In recent years a few state governments, led by New York, had set up formal systems to administer what was called "relief," as in relief of want by way of cash payments, vouchers for necessities such as food and rent, and—where work could be created—paying jobs. But Washington remained aloof. Business and banking interests insisted on maintaining this alignment of responsibilities, which had been in place under the Republican administrations that with few exceptions had been in power since the Civil War. When the United States Chamber of Commerce polled its members in December 1931, they responded 2,534 to 197 that "needed relief should be provided through private contributions and by state and local governments."

But these governments were now as broke as the people who needed their help, and as the depression deepened they were unequal to the task. City tax collections had shrunk with the contraction of the economy. Many local governments were on the verge of bankruptcy. Charitable donations had also shriveled, and with them the ability to provide relief to families in need.

Those charged with the burden of the poor sought solutions with growing desperation. Winslow Township, New Jersey, an area of small farm communities with about 5,000 people, mirrored the country as a whole. One worker in five was out of work. On January 2, 1932, the eight members of the Winslow Township Committee convened in Blue Anchor, a crossroads halfway between Philadelphia and then-sleepy Atlantic City. The committee voted to dismiss the five-member police force it no longer could afford to pay. Then, led by its aptly named chairman, Herman Priestley, the committee called for a week of prayer to ask God's help in solving the township's unemployment crisis.

Prayer was all many jobless Americans had left in 1932.

2. THE PEOPLE ON THEIR OWN

The lack of jobs created desperate carnivals of stunts and pleading. With the government refusing to address the crisis, Americans were left to their own considerable ingenuity. In New York City, a thirty-one-year-old mechanic asked a judge to let him break the law to work. Thomas Bell said he had been offered a job tending bar in a speakeasy, illegal in those days of Prohibition. "The missus and kids ain't had a decent thing to eat in a week, only scraps of garbage," Bell told the judge.

"I'm sorry for you," said Judge Alfred C. Coxe, "but I cannot promise you immunity if you violate the law."

In Los Angeles, a philanthropist named Louis Byrens mounted a "slave market" to auction off the services of jobless Angelenos. Bidders bought the services of a law student, a waitress, a truck driver, an electrician, a cook, a mason, a garage worker, and a stenographer for prices ranging from 33⅓ cents to 50 cents an hour. But efforts like these were the exception; while eight workers were landing jobs at Byrens's auction, hundreds of out-of-work men jammed the counter of the American Legion Employment Bureau in downtown Los Angeles, shouting and waving for attention when an occasional job opening was announced. The scene repeated itself daily: too many people scuffling and shouting in pursuit of too few jobs. Los Angeles, which was preparing to host the 1932 Olympic Summer Games, had—if the statewide rate was any guide—unemployment close to 28 percent.

One woman wrote the *New York Times* to suggest that homeowners should spruce up their houses to give decorators and tradespeople badly needed jobs. Another proposed that people who had steady jobs give their clothes away and buy new ones. In a similar vein, Hoover urged new-car buyers to place their orders early. "There is nothing that provides widespread employment more than automobile construction," he said.

A Tudor sedan with Ford's new V-8 engine cost about $450 in 1932. The nation's per capita income was $400, and not a single state boasted a per capita income over $1,000. The per capita income of the District of Columbia, however, was $1,061, which perhaps accounted for the president's difficulty in recognizing the hardship that gripped the nation.

Hoover's willingness to ignore reality could be genuinely startling. In the fall of 1930, an apple surplus in the Pacific Northwest had prompted apple distributors to try a new marketing technique: they would offer apples by the box on credit to individuals who would sell them by hand, apple by apple, on city streets around the country. As if by magic, a desperate new profession bloomed. In New York alone, 6,000 men trudged to fruit distributors each morning, picked up boxes of apples on credit, and made for street corners with signs that advertised both their plight and their goods: "Unemployed. Apples 5¢." At best, given a box of perfect apples, a man could pay the $1.75 they had cost him and take home $1.85 for the day. Then the International Apple Shippers Association, which had devised the program, raised the price per box to $2.25, reducing the potential profit by 50 cents. Some years later, Hoover wrote in the volume of his memoirs that dealt with the depression that the sudden appearance of the apple sellers had nothing to do with unemployment. Rather, it was the apple growers who used public sympathy for the unemployed to inflate their prices. "Many persons," he contended, "left their jobs for the more profitable one of selling apples." He appears to have actually believed it.

Shoeshine boys—and men—appeared by the thousands with the same unnerving suddenness. So did door-to-door salesmen, with the result that the Fuller Brush Company was one of the few business models to improve during the depression.

The efforts of local governments to create jobs were equally haphazard. The suburban village of Larchmont, New York, in Westchester County, north of New York City, was accustomed to seeing businessmen board the commuter trains for city office jobs each morning. Now the crowds on the train platforms were sparse, and Larchmont put some of its unemployed to work clearing woods and vacant lots, burning brush, and sawing logs into cordwood. The outdoor work was considered healthy, and citizens with fireplaces could warm themselves with inexpensive firewood.

In nearby White Plains, the emergency work bureau arranged with local country clubs to have unemployed men work as caddies. At the exclusive Century Country Club, however, this arrangement lasted only as long as it took the club's women golfers to realize that the elderly men and laborers carrying their golf clubs had no idea of the rules of the game. They talked at the tees and on the greens, tossed balls from the rough back onto the fairway, and didn't know which clubs to offer. The women protested, and the system was suspended until the men had been properly trained in golf rules and etiquette. Golfers as a class were not ungenerous, however. St. Louis golfers donated so many of their out-of-fashion plus-four trousers, bloused at the knee, that the Citizens' Committee Clothing Bureau appealed for donations of knee-high golf socks to complete the outfits.

Arizona revived gold prospecting as a job-creation tool. With dude ranch tourism dead in the depression, cowboys traded their ten-gallon hats and woolly chaps for working gear, loaded burros with picks, spades, and pup tents, and headed for the hills along with old-time prospectors hoping to find gold. California planned its own gold-mining revival. The mining committee of the Los Angeles Chamber of Commerce predicted jobs for 50,000 men once the mining process was refined to prevent hydraulic mine tailings from damaging farms. In the state of Washington, according to testimony before a House labor subcommittee, farmers and unemployed loggers had created jobs for themselves as firefighters by setting forest fires.

Hay fever sufferers in Illinois could thank the unemployment crisis for relief. Officials there deployed 8,000 men on highway roadsides to pull up ragweed as the August pollen season approached. Weed pullers in East St. Louis objected to the average $2 weekly they were being paid, and went on strike. In Missouri, the Pittsburgh Plate Glass company took back 650 employees it had laid off, gave them four hours' work a week, and paid them in food and movie tickets. Miami, Florida, imposed a $1 tax on the city's auto drivers in order to assist the unemployed, a measure expected to raise $100,000 a year. "All of it will go into the pockets of Miami's six thousand unemployed," said Mayor R. B. Gautier, failing to add that the money involved would amount to less than $1.40 per man per month.

A Needham, Massachusetts, woman divided her estate into garden plots so those without jobs could raise their own food. In Illinois, the International Harvester company marked off some of its property into half-acre "farms" for its unemployed. An appeal to New Yorkers to "adopt" needy families resulted in 550 adoptions, reducing the number of families on the rolls of the city's Home Relief Bureau to 132,513. The Savannah, Georgia, welfare association asked fishermen who caught more fish than they could eat to donate the excess to feed people without jobs. A speaker at the garden meeting of the Women's National Republican Club announced a plan to place baskets at Grand Central and Pennsylvania Stations in New York so that commuters with gardens could contribute vegetables and fruit to the city's soup kitchens. Before his conviction for tax evasion the previous fall, gangster Al Capone had sponsored a soup kitchen in Chicago that fed 3,000 men a day. A jobless airplane mechanic who turned in a lost watch at the West 47th Street police station in New York was rewarded with a permanent place at the head of a charity food line. This was no small reward; the soup kitchen sponsored by William Randolph Hearst's *New York American* at the north end of Times Square—one of eighty-two soup kitchens throughout the city—had a line that was regularly two blocks long, even though there was another Hearst-sponsored kitchen nearby, at the south end of the square.

Obviously, none of these sincere but paltry efforts stemmed the tide of unemployment or relieved the general suffering. The numbers of the jobless continued to rise. Almost 1.3 million Pennsylvanians were out of work in August 1932. St. Louis, with a population just over 800,000, had 125,000 on relief. Almost 200,000 New Yorkers lost jobs between January and October, putting the rolls of the jobless in the city at 985,034; one in seven city residents was on relief. On nationwide radio, nurse and social worker Lillian Wald pleaded for young women thinking of seeking their fortune in the city to stay home. Girls are "nearly starving here," she said, blaming rosy scenarios in novels and movies for bringing a stream of hopeful young people to a city where a million of its own residents could not find work. Labor forecasters predicted that 13 million Americans would be out of work by winter.

Even those who had work had too little of it. With American industry operating at a fraction of its capacity—in 1932 U.S. Steel was producing 19.1 percent of the steel it was capable of making—many employees were working two days a week or less and were paid accordingly, as was the case in Birmingham, Alabama. Even at plants that were relatively busy, a share-the-work movement, conceived of by Hoover and business leaders that August, promised added deprivation to workers who were lucky enough to still have jobs. The plan, headed by Standard Oil of New Jersey president Walter C. Teagle, was supposed to create 1 million new jobs by cutting hours for those who were employed and giving those hours to workers who had been laid off. Sharing their jobs meant that workers shared poverty as well, all of them working and earning less, while employers were unaffected.

But some work was better than none—and none was more and more the case. One 1932 estimate placed the number of men, women, and children with no income whatsoever at 34 million, a figure amounting to almost 28 percent of the United States population.

3. PLEAS ON DEAF EARS

Agrowing chorus of voices was saying that as a matter of humanity, government could not stay uninvolved. As the Winslow Township Committee voted in New Jersey, a Roman Catholic priest in Pittsburgh decided that it would take more than prayer to sustain the unemployed miners and steelworkers of western Pennsylvania. These industries were among the hardest hit by the depression. Across the state, a quarter of the working population, nearly 1 million people, was jobless. Although Governor Gifford Pinchot had initiated a state road-building program that employed 25,000 workers, he had written Hoover in August 1931 to say that "hundreds of thousands will go hungry next winter unless the Federal Government steps in."

Next winter had now arrived, and Father James R. Cox was marshaling an army of the unemployed to begin a march—or, more accurately, a motorcade—to Washington. Cox was forty-five, a florid, paunchy millworker's son for whom the needs of the jobless were a calling as insistent as his ministry. His parish was Pittsburgh's oldest, St. Patrick's, centered in a rundown section of produce warehouses along the Allegheny River called the Strip. At Pitt Stadium in

December, 60,000 people had answered his call to a rally of the unemployed. Now he urged them on to Washington, to confront Hoover with the human evidence of massive unemployment. He hoped they would embarrass the president into dropping his opposition to a large-scale program of government-funded public works that would employ the jobless in road and street construction, building repairs, and other infrastructure improvements such as water and sewer systems.

Fifteen thousand people showed up for Cox's motorcade in the cold first week of January. Many of the jobless men were accompanied by their families. The Pennsylvanians piled into 2,000 cars and trucks and set out for Washington in a convoy eight miles long. They arrived in the capital on January 6 and camped overnight on government-owned lots in southwest Washington. The next day the "haggard, unshaven" marchers gathered outside the Capitol while Cox went inside to deliver their petition for a federal jobs program to Pennsylvania's representatives in Congress. Then, as the marchers ate a meal of wieners and sauerkraut dished out at army field kitchens set up by the District of Columbia police, Cox received a White House audience with Hoover.

By all accounts, the president gave Cox his full attention. He was not without compassion. He had risen to prominence on the strength of his efforts at relieving want, the first time in Europe during and after the Great War, when he headed programs that supplied food to millions in Belgium and northern France. The Russian writer Maxim Gorky had credited him with saving the lives of 3.5 million children and 5.5 million adults. As commerce secretary for eight years under Harding and Coolidge, Hoover had studied the 1920–21 recession and devoted himself to trying to design cures for business downturns while holding fast to fundamental laissez-faire assumptions. When the Mississippi River broke its banks in the spring of 1927, flooding the Mississippi Delta and making refugees of almost a million people, Coolidge placed Hoover in charge of the response. He organized everything from rescue fleets and refugee camps to the delivery of food, clothing, and medical supplies, and launched the rebuilding effort afterward. His brilliance at the job—and his equal brilliance at publicizing it with personal appearances, news releases, and radio broadcasts—made him a national hero and helped win him the Republican nomination for president in 1928. His sincerity was not an issue when Hoover, after Cox had finished his appeal, expressed "intense sympathy for your difficulties."

But words of sympathy were one thing, action another. The rest of the president's comments were as predictable as his expression of concern. The fundamentals of the economy were strong, he insisted, and a balanced budget ensuring the sound credit of the government was the only sure way to bring about recovery. He had been echoing the same refrain ever since the crash, to the point that it often seemed as if optimism was his only policy. "I am convinced we have now passed the worst," he had told the United States Chamber of Commerce on May 1, 1930. "There is one certainty in the future...—that is prosperity." A month later, when a delegation came to press him to start a program of public works, he greeted them by declaring, "Gentlemen, you have come sixty days too late. The depression is over." Now, in January 1932, Hoover told Cox that a government-sponsored work program would not only violate tradition but cost too much. "The real victory," he said, "is to restore men to employment through their regular jobs."

Cox's army did not leave entirely empty-handed. Senator James J. Davis of Pennsylvania gave the marchers $100 and a local Catholic charity donated $300, the contributions forming a gasoline fund to take them back to Pennsylvania. Before they turned their wheezing vehicles toward home, they detoured to Arlington National Cemetery to visit the Tomb of the Unknown Soldier. Cox addressed the men and their families as they shivered on the marble plaza in the winter cold, the monuments of Washington visible across the Potomac through the naked trees. "Today you have asked only for your God-given right to work," he said.

Home again in Pittsburgh, Cox dismissed Hoover's response to unemployment as "utterly inadequate," announced the formation of the Jobless Party, and later became its presidential candidate. It was the dawn of an election year, and as the 1932 campaign took shape, no issue would prove to be more potent than the lack of jobs. Among the major parties, congressional Democrats had long been raising the government's inaction as an issue, led by House Speaker John Nance Garner, who was supported by publishing baron William Randolph Hearst for the presidential nomination. And he was not alone. Democrats were salivating over the chance to face a vulnerable Hoover and contrast themselves with him.

4. THE PHILOSOPHY OF "RUGGED INDIVIDUALISM"

Hoover's beliefs were shaped at the nexus of business and technology. An Iowan by birth and a Californian by migration, he had graduated from Stanford with a degree in geology and gotten rich in far-flung mining ventures. By the time he was forty, at the beginning of the war in Europe in 1914, he owned pieces of mines and oil fields on four continents and was considered, according to a London mining publication, "a wizard of finance." At that point he was a millionaire and making money had receded as a goal, so his ambition turned to applying the lessons of engineering to society. All forms of engineering were then a rising science, and if they could tame and bring order to the natural world, they might also benefit the world of men. And since the world of men was ruled by business, Hoover believed the scientific application of enlightened business principles could improve the lot of workers and still leave room for profits at the top. As a Quaker, he believed in social responsibility. As an engineer, he believed it could be achieved according to a blueprint.

Finally, as a lifelong Republican, he saw little role for the government in this design. Business and industry, organized under the proper influences, could do it all provided they had the information on which to act. The national government waged war and conducted foreign and economic policy, but virtually its only domestic role was to compile the necessary information for business and industry and bring it to the attention of leaders in the private sector and in state and local governments. It became their job, from then on, to act in response to business trends—in the case of recession, for example, to increase spending on plants and public works to counteract the downturn. Hoover had urged the adoption of such countercyclical spending to smooth out hiccups in the business cycle since his days as commerce secretary. Never before had the government taken even this small hand in guiding the economy, a role Hoover, a baseball fan, likened to umpiring rather than playing in the game. But when the depression struck, as president he gave himself few options otherwise, either to attack unemployment or to alleviate the hardships it caused. If federal money could not be spent to create jobs or provide food, clothing, and shelter, the money had to come from somewhere else. And if the state and local governments had tapped all their taxing power and were too broke even to pay their own employees, which was the case in Chicago with its teachers, the only source of money left was voluntary givers. This is where the president now turned.

Persuasion was another of his beliefs. Hoover had great faith in the power of words, assurances, appearances. Like engineering, the art of advertising was also on the rise, and brand names such as Camel cigarettes, Maxwell House coffee, and Coca-Cola were increasing their market share with popular slogans such as Maxwell House's "Good to the last drop." None of this was lost on the president; he had once told the *Saturday Evening Post* that "the world lives by phrases." In a later era, he would have been noted for his belief in "spin." As jobs kept disappearing, he judged language by its potential for encouragement.

In the fall of 1930, he had appointed an Emergency Committee for Employment. A dispatch from Washington at the time reported that "President Hoover has summoned Colonel Arthur Woods to help place 2,500,000 persons back to work this winter." Woods, the committee chair, was a former New York City police commissioner and an officer in the army's air corps during the world war; he had worked in relief during the 1920–21 depression, when a drop in manufacturing triggered a jump in joblessness. Hoover instructed him to approach unemployment as a local problem, but Woods could find no local solutions. He decided it required action on a national scale and, as

Father Cox and others were also to do, urged the president to submit a plan of federally funded public works to the Congress. Hoover dismissed the idea, Woods resigned, and the committee dissolved.

By March 1931, half a year later, unemployment had worsened drastically. Eight million people were now out of work, double the number just one year earlier. And the numbers of the unemployed kept rising. In August, Hoover replaced the first committee with another, the President's Organization on Unemployment Relief (POUR). Its chair was American Telephone and Telegraph president Walter S. Gifford, who also chaired the Charity Organization Society of New York; like Hoover, Gifford believed in voluntary private action. POUR mounted an advertising and publicity campaign to encourage private giving. This was more to Hoover's liking, and the president himself launched the campaign in a nationwide radio address on October 18, in which again he left no room for a federal program: "No governmental action, no economic doctrine, no economic plan or project can replace that God-imposed responsibility of the individual man and woman to their neighbors." The depression, he said, was "a passing incident in our national life," and "the number who are threatened with privation is a minor percentage."

The next morning's report in the *New York Times* said the president was "depending on the efforts of individual communities to preclude the appropriation of relief funds by Congress."

From October 19 to November 25, 1931, Americans were bombarded with ads from every conceivable source: newspapers, magazines, billboards, and the radio trumpeted "the thrill of a great spiritual experience. In those few weeks millions of dollars will be raised in cities and towns throughout the land, and the fear of cold and hunger will be banished from the hearts of thousands." But humorist Will Rogers, recruited to draw listeners to the initial broadcast, had placed the campaign's challenge in perspective with typical barbed wit: "You have just heard Mr. Gifford, the biggest hello man in the world, a very fine high-caliber man, but what a job he has got! Mr. Hoover just told him, 'Gifford, I have a remarkable job for you; you are to feed the several million unemployed.'

" 'With what?' says Gifford.

" 'That's what makes the job remarkable. If you had something to do it with, it wouldn't be remarkable.' "

POUR's campaign aimed to raise $12 million, or about $1.20 for every person who then was unemployed, but Gifford did little beyond promoting the idea that giving was spiritually uplifting. In January 1932, as Cox's haggard Pennsylvanians were descending on the capital to plead for a government jobs program, Gifford was testifying before a Senate committee studying unemployment. He did not have much to say. He told the senators he had no idea how much money the campaign had raised. Nor did he know how many people were unemployed, how many were receiving charity, how relief needs differed from place to place, or how local governments were supposed to raise money to provide relief. Nevertheless, he assured the senators, local resources could meet the need. Federal intervention, he said, would only reduce the amount of private giving and make the problem worse.

To be fair, Gifford was not the only idiot. Many business and industry leaders, surveyed for a New Year's Day story on their outlook for the year ahead, had predicted that 1931 would bring a business recovery. The main reason for this optimism appeared to be the conviction that 1931 couldn't possibly be as bad as 1930. It "is a new year," said Alfred P. Sloan, the president of General Motors. "We should enter it with new ideas, new measures, new confidence, new hope...if our attitude toward the new problems of the new year is constructive, rather than critical, we shall make greater progress in 1931 than we did in 1930." Colonel Michael Friedsam, the founder and head of the upscale New York department store B. Altman & Co., said, "I firmly believe that business in general is now in a good position to begin reconstruction, and that good management, vision, and courage, which are inherent in American business, will now start things moving in the right direction." National Steel Corporation chairman Ernest T. Weir concurred: "I think there is assurance that we are close to the turning point and can confidently expect 1931 to be a year of more normal general business."

What else could the captains of industry and the business leaders say? But their predictions proved to be as wrong as Hoover's each time he asserted that recovery was "right around the corner." The fine qualities that Friedsam attributed to his fellow executives had deserted them. No one in business or government, bound to the framework of their beliefs, had a clue about how to solve the crisis.

And unemployment kept rising, inexorably, remorselessly. Yet the president still treated the problem as a crisis of confidence, something to be talked away, or joked or rhymed or sung about. "What this country needs is a good big laugh," he had said early in 1931. "There seems to be a condition of hysteria. If someone could get off a good joke every ten days, I think our troubles would be over."

In fact there were jokes aplenty about the hard times, but Hoover was frequently the butt of them. One had him asking his treasury secretary, banker Andrew Mellon, "Can you lend me a nickel? I want to call a friend," and Mellon responding, "Here's a dime. Call both of them."

On another occasion, Hoover said the country needed a good poem. But when he told crooner Rudy Vallee that he would give him a medal if he could sing a song "that would make people forget their troubles and the depression," Vallee responded by recording a song from a musical, *Americana,* that opened on Broadway in the fall of 1932. The musical's theme, largely reprised in Hollywood's *Gold Diggers of 1933* a year later, evoked the hard times, nowhere more poignantly than in Yip Harburg and Jay Gorney's "Brother, Can You Spare a Dime?"

> They used to tell me I was building a dream, with peace and glory ahead.
> Why should I be standing in line, just waiting for bread?

The writers said they got the idea for the song as they walked past the breadlines in Times Square. This anthem of the penniless forgotten man is the song Vallee chose to record. Bing Crosby released his own version of "Brother, Can You Spare a Dime?" at almost the same time, and both went to number one on the charts. But rather than distracting people from the depression, its sweeping popularity reminded Americans that millions of their fellow citizens were out of work, and that for many the indignity of begging for handouts was their only recourse.

5. HOOVERVILLES AND HUNGER

The ripples of joblessness kept widening, engulfing the laboring and middle classes alike. In New Concord, Ohio, eleven-year-old John Glenn, who would later become the first American to orbit the earth in the Cold War space race, overheard his parents in whispered conversation one day in 1932; his father, a plumber whose new business had dried up in the general construction falloff and whose repair clients couldn't afford to pay their bills, told his mother he was afraid they would lose their house. "The conversation struck terror in my heart," Glenn wrote. He experienced fears shared by many depression children: Where would they move? Did they have relatives or friends who would take them in? Would the family break up, with John and his sister parceled out to relatives or, worse, to foster homes?

The Glenns managed to hold on to their house, but many didn't. As family budgets went from black to red and rents and mortgages fell into arrears, foreclosure and eviction followed. Homeowners, renters, and farmers and their families were turned out with the clothes on their backs, and bank auctioneers sold property, furniture, machinery, and implements for pennies on the dollar. Philadelphia saw

1,300 evictions a month in 1931. New York had some 200,000 for the year. The secret humiliation of the jobless became a public shame when their household goods were stacked on city sidewalks, on small-town lawns, and in farm lots.

Comedians treated evictions with the same defiant humor that tinged most depression jokes. "Who was that lady I saw you with last night at the sidewalk café?" asked the straight man. "That was no lady, that was my wife," came the expected retort, and then the new punch line: "And that was no sidewalk café, that was my furniture."

In cities, tenant organizers devised rent strikes to try to ward off evictions. In the country, farmers petitioned for moratoriums on mortgage foreclosures, and when that failed, they tried direct confrontations. Buyers attending a foreclosure auction might think twice about bidding for farm land or equipment when surrounded by a band of twenty or more glowering farmers, who appeared even more threatening because their long beards made them look like avenging Old Testament prophets. When they could, farmers took up collections to keep the property of their fellows out of the hands of banks.

But efforts such as these had no wide effect, and shantytowns filled with the homeless became the most visible signs of the nation's distress. Areas of cities and pockets of countryside resembled war zones where civilians took shelter in the rubble. Depression humor had given these places a name, "Hoovervilles," just as the president's name was attached to other signs of destitution for which, as people saw it, Hoover bore the blame. Empty pockets pulled inside out were Hoover flags. Jackrabbits or other small game that could add substance to a meager stewpot were Hoover hogs. Hoovervilles sprang up almost overnight, at railroad junctions, alongside city dumps, on riverfronts, and in parks and other vacant lands. When empty and abandoned buildings were available, the homeless occupied them, too.

The Hooverville in Seattle, Washington, sprawled over nine acres of a defunct shipyard near the docks south of downtown. City officials burned it down twice when it sprang up in the fall of 1931, but relented after the squatters rebuilt it a third time. It eventually grew to 479 acres with 639 residents; an unemployed lumberjack named Jesse Jackson kept the peace and was the colony's liaison with the city and nearby businesses. More than a thousand people lived in a Hooverville alongside the Mississippi River in St. Louis, where they built a church from orange crates. Two hundred men lived in the Youngstown, Ohio, dump, some in huts burrowed into the refuse. The incinerator provided winter warmth, and they got some of their food from the dump's garbage house, where they competed for the rotting scraps with local women foraging for their families. Connie Eisler Smith, whose father had invented a way to mass-produce radio tubes and incandescent lamps and thus was spared the ravages of the depression, remembered at age five riding in the family's chauffeur-driven car past the city dump in Newark, New Jersey, and seeing shacks of tin and cardboard built in the garbage piles. Pittsburgh's shantytown, by the railroad yards five minutes from downtown, spread over a city block and housed 300 residents who proclaimed Father Cox, of the January march on Washington, their "mayor."

In New York, where the legally elected mayor, "Gentleman Jimmy" Walker, was a corruption-tainted playboy unsuited to governing the city in hard times, these impromptu communities popped up in every corner. The *New Yorker* magazine suggested that anyone "wanting to see civilization creaking" should visit a shantytown near the Hudson River piers. Some of the city's homeless took up residence in Central Park. An unemployed carpenter named Hollinan made a home out of a cave and lived there with his wife for almost a year. Another man converted a baby buggy into a makeshift shelter. A group of out-of-work tradesmen set up near the obelisk behind the Metropolitan Museum of Art, building shanties out of bricks and egg crates that were made to withstand the ravages of winter. They called it Hoover Valley. The place grew from a handful of shacks in December 1931 to seventeen the following summer. Its residents could look west above the tree line and see the towers of Central Park West's luxurious apartment houses, or east to the elegant buildings on Fifth Avenue, many now half empty as even the rich downsized to save money. City police and parks department workers tolerated the inhabitants of Hoover Valley and generally treated them with respect, bantering with them on their patrols through the park but otherwise leaving them alone. Eventually the health department ordered the colony shut down for lack of sanitation, but new arrivals were building foundations for their own shacks even as the department was preparing its written notice of eviction.

Efforts to solve homelessness were the same haphazard, uncoordinated mess as those meant to create jobs. In Connecticut, the Unemployed Citizens League petitioned the U.S. Shipping Board to use a condemned ocean liner, the *George Washington,* as housing. The Los Angeles Street Railway Company donated fifty of its old streetcars to be used as living quarters. Some of the unemployed of New Orleans lived in houseboats on Lake Pontchartrain. The Detroit Department of Public Works borrowed 300 tents from the Michigan National Guard and planned a tent city to house homeless families. The city was a step behind the twenty families who had already formed a tent colony in the city's Clark Park in August 1931. In New York, proposals for emegency housing included piers on Staten Island; the Bronx Terminal Market on the Harlem River, where fruits and vegetables were received into the city; and vacant warehouses and lofts.

Except for miserable and scattered schemes such as these, the homeless were largely on their own. In the cities, police regularly rousted them from vacant lots, fire escapes, abandoned buildings, and subway platforms. Invariably, these sweeps picked up someone with a hard-luck tale that caught the attention of sharp-eyed police reporters, and readers opened their newspapers to learn of British heirs and formerly well-paid professionals among the indifferent depression's victims. But romanticizing the homeless did nothing to ease their squalor, malnutrition, disease, and brutal exposure to the weather.

"Nobody is actually starving," said Hoover, for whom seven-course meals and black tie were customary whether he was hosting an official dinner or dining alone in the White House with his wife, Lou. "The hoboes, for example, are better fed than they have ever been. One hobo in New York got ten meals in one day."

The evidence contradicted him. New York City health authorities recorded twenty deaths by starvation in 1931, ninety-five in 1932. Numerous others were barely averted. Police in Danbury, Connecticut, found a mother and her sixteen-year-old daughter huddled in a makeshift shelter in the woods, where they had been eating apples and wild berries to survive. The same week, constables in North Babylon, Long Island, came upon a forty-four-year-old woman starving in a maple grove, where she had been sleeping in a pile of old clothes and eating scraps she had begged from local restaurants. Interviewing her, the police learned she was a registered nurse who had served in France during the world war but had been unable to find work for several months.

But even hunger was subject to spin. The nation's health was better than ever in 1931, said the Metropolitan Life Insurance Company, because less money and less food meant people were no longer overeating.

Food was not scarce. If anything, it was too plentiful. Farmers continued to utilize the productive capacity they had developed when Europe needed their food, but crops rotted in the fields now because there was no one to buy them and the farmers could not afford to harvest them. Wheat and corn could not be sold for what they cost to produce. Breadlines in the Midwest snaked past stuffed grain silos. Ranchers shot livestock rather than ship them to market; it cost $1.10 a head to transport a sheep that would sell for $1, while at the consumer end of the food chain, the many without jobs went hungry because at 16 cents a pound for bacon, 15 cents for a dozen eggs, 23 cents a pound for butter, and 13 cents a pound for beef chuck roast, food cost too much to buy. The same was true of wool and cotton. Bales of fabric for coats and dungarees and dresses piled up in warehouses, but at $7.50 for a child's coat, $1.50 for a pair of overalls, and $1 for a woman's dress, families all across the country could not afford to put even basic new clothes upon their backs.

The extent of hunger, if not actual starvation, was highlighted when New York State's Temporary Emergency Relief Administration, the first state agency set up to aid the unemployed, arranged for jobless men on relief to get free fishing licenses. The rush of applicants overwhelmed town clerks and state conservation officers, who turned the free license trade over to local welfare offices.

And the health authorities had more to deal with than malnutrition and exposure. For many, medical and dental care were unattainable luxuries. Tuberculosis was the biggest preventable killer of adults. Infant deaths were commonplace because pregnant women could not afford prenatal care. For youngsters already weakened by lack of food, childhood diseases such as measles, mumps, whooping cough, and chicken pox could be lethal. Nor were any of these conditions equal-opportunity afflictions. In cities from Denver to New York, the death rate for white adults was 55 per 100,000 population, while among blacks it was almost six times higher. Even outside the South, where the term "Jim Crow" described a system of overt brutality against them, blacks faced not only abysmal health conditions but also job discrimination, official neglect, and police abuse.

6. THE PROBLEM WITH LAISSEZ-FAIRE

The economic crisis had exposed grotesque disparities between the rich and poor. There were two Americas, and they were vastly different. The assets of the rich had swelled to unbelievable levels during the boom of the late 1920s. One percent of the people owned 59 percent of America's wealth by 1929, yet simultaneously more than half the country's population of 123 million struggled in poverty, trapped below a minimum level of subsistence.

These millions had little recourse if they had no work. There was nothing of what would later be called a "safety net." In this Darwinian struggle for survival, there were always more workers waiting to take the place of those who dropped from illness, frayed nerves, or exhaustion. There were a few rules governing child labor, life-threatening working conditions, job safety, and workdays that stretched human endurance: Oregon had passed a law limiting women in laundries and factories to a ten-hour workday, Massachusetts set a minimum wage for women, and all but nine states barred factory workers under the age of fourteen. But laws such as these specifically applied to women and children, and even so, they often worked for less than $2.50 a week. There were no such protections for men, nor was there job security or insurance against unemployment. In the view of John E.

Edgerton, the longtime head of the National Association of Manufacturers, attempts to impose social goals through legislation were nothing more than meddling jealousy: "Society in general continues through political processes to unload its obligations upon industry, penalizing at every opportunity the silently rebuking superiorities of accomplishment."

Edgerton owned woolen mills in Tennessee, which like other industries were working below capacity and had slashed the hours of employees. Testifying before a committee of the U.S. Senate, he said it concerned him not at all that families could not live on one or two days' wages a week. "Why, I've never thought of paying men on the basis of what they need. I pay for efficiency," he said.

Efficiency meant work practices such as the speedup and the stretch-out. On the Ford production lines, where men made $4 for a ten-hour workday, it was common practice for supervisors to increase the speed of the belts that moved the cars past the men assembling them. This made their jobs a trial of endurance, a whirlwind of bolting, riveting, and welding that left workers shaken and spent at the end of the day. Those who couldn't keep up were fired. Henry Ford believed that "the average man won't really do a day's work unless he is caught and cannot get out of it."

The stretch-out was favored by textile mill owners in New England and the South. Its essence was the same as the speedup—making workers do more work in less time for the same amount of money. Textile workers were paid even more poorly than autoworkers, and their numbers included children physically too small to work in the heavier industries. Whereas Ford's security force monitored the time workers spent on bathroom and lunch breaks, in the textile mills the enforcer was the stopwatch. Weavers, carders, and strippers were timed doing their jobs. Then they were told to do a little more. Before long, weavers—many of them teenage girls—worked two and four looms for every one they had worked before, yet received the same meager wage. Like the auto workers, they paid the price in elevated stress levels and deteriorating health.

Since the turn of the century, the Supreme Court of the United States had helped business withstand almost every effort to reform practices such as these. Following its 1905 ruling in *Lochner v. New York* against a New York State law limiting bakery workweeks (for men) to sixty hours and workdays to ten hours, the Court cited liberty of contract under the Fourteenth Amendment to strike down state minimum wage laws. Liberty of contract meant that employers and employees were free to engage in working arrangements without government interference, a relationship that obviously favored the employer. The commerce clause of the Constitution gave Congress authority to regulate aspects of the production of goods sold in interstate commerce. But after the 1916 Keating-Owen Act used the clause to ban the sale of goods produced by factories that employed children under fourteen, mines that employed children younger than sixteen, and any facility where children under sixteen worked at night or more than eight hours daily, the court ruled in *Hammer v. Dagenhart* in 1918 that Congress had overstepped its bounds. Justice Oliver Wendell Holmes dissented in the five-to-four ruling. "[I]f there is any matter upon which civilized countries have agreed...it is the evil of premature and excessive child labor," he wrote. "I should have thought that...this was preeminently a case for upholding the exercise of all its powers by the United States." Another child labor law, passed in 1918, was also declared unconstitutional. Under Chief Justice William Howard Taft, the former president and fellow Republican appointed by President Harding in 1921, the court's pro-business stance solidified. Among the consequences were shop clerks working for 10 cents an hour, brick and tile makers for 6, and lumbermen for a nickel; as many as 7 million children between the ages of ten and fifteen were still in the labor force.

Labor was seen as an annoying and easily abused necessity not only by industry but also by the highest levels of the government. When a cut in the prime interest rate spurred a brief rebound in the stock market early in 1930, treasury secretary Andrew Mellon forecast a recovery. "Liquidate labor, liquidate stocks, liquidate the farmers, liquidate real estate," he advised. "People will work harder, live a more moral life. Values will be adjusted, and enterprising people will pick up the wreck from less competent people."

Yet it hadn't happened quite as Mellon had predicted. Liquidating labor, by which he meant wholesale layoffs as industries cut production, forced perfectly competent millions out of their jobs and onto breadlines. Union leaders and reformers increasingly questioned the unrestrained laissez-faire capitalism that had allowed this to happen.

They questioned tariffs that protected American manufacturers from cheap imports but prompted foreign governments to throw up tariffs of their own that halted U.S. exports, especially of farm products.

As the crisis worsened, and as the impoverished farmers and the unemployed and their advocates grew more outspoken, there was unheard-of talk of revolution. Frustrated officials kept warning Washington that people were running out of patience. As A. N. Young, the president of the Wisconsin Farmers Union, said when he appeared before the Senate Agriculture Committee in January 1932: "The farmer is naturally a conservative individual, but you cannot find a conservative farmer today....I am as conservative as any man could be, but any economic system that has in its power to set me and my wife in the streets, at my age—what can I see but red?" Edward F. McGrady of the American Federation of Labor (AFL) also told a Senate committee, "If something is not done and starvation is going to continue, the doors of revolt in this country are going to be thrown open." In June, three weeks after the Illinois Emergency Relief Commission telephoned the White House to say that half a million people in Chicago faced starvation if its relief stations had to close, Mayor Anton Cermak told the Senate it would be less expensive to lend his city $150 million to provide relief and pay teachers and city workers who had gone for months without paychecks than to send troops later.

The anger and frustration were indeed rich ground for agitators. All across the country, Socialists and Communists looked for advantage among the jobless and hungry, a toehold for their radical political goals. They organized rent strikes, rallies, marches for jobs and against hunger. As the protests swelled, the forces of law and order struck back, their arsenals fully loaded with guns as well as words.

7. RUMBLES ON THE LEFT

If Communism had never had broad appeal in the United States, it was not for lack of trying. But the Socialists had been far more successful; they had their ideological origins in worker-oriented European craft guilds, and the waves of immigrants that arrived in America in the nineteenth century brought this ideology with them. The belief that government control of the means of production and distribution could save workers from the boom-and-bust cycles of unregulated economics found a political voice in 1901, when railway union leader Eugene V. Debs adopted Socialism and founded the Socialist Party of America. He was a charismatic speaker and the party grew rapidly, responsive to his appeals for worker rights and his condemnations of injustice and poverty. In the 1912 election, won by Woodrow Wilson, Debs polled a startling 900,000 votes as his party's presidential candidate—6 percent of the popular vote. That same year Berkeley, California; Schenectady, New York; and Milwaukee, Wisconsin, were among fifty-six municipalities that elected Socialist mayors. Noted authors Jack London and Upton Sinclair embraced Socialism, and intellectuals and students eagerly discussed the utopias it would foster. By then the party had enrolled 125,000 members, and was considered to be in the leftmost column of the Progressive movement, which advocated reforms in society and industry and opposed the corporate conglomerates, called trusts, that monopolized markets and restrained competition.

But after the 1912 election, a hardening left wing split the Socialist ranks. The more radical joined the Industrial Workers of the World—the IWW, or "Wobblies." Their aim was to unite all workers into a single union to bring about a Socialist government, which they meant to do through labor strikes and protests rather than political or military action. Then came 1917 and the Communist revolution in Russia. When the Bolsheviks overthrew centuries of czarist rule, increasing numbers of young American Socialists turned from reform to issue calls for revolution. They saw themselves re-creating the Marxian class struggle that pitted workers against the bourgeoisie, the middle class, and in 1919 they broke away to form the first Communist Party in the United States. At the same time, the Bolsheviks themselves, led by Vladimir I. Lenin and now officially the Communist Party, had determined to export their revolution and were flooding the United States with propaganda attacking Western capitalism and democratic institutions. They were also sending out feelers and making contacts among American Communists.

In addition to their noisy complaints about the American system and calls to overturn it, the Socialist and Communist parties in the United States both took up anti-war positions. Together these factors isolated the parties and made their members targets of laws against espionage and sedition that had been enacted amid the surge of patriotism surrounding America's entry into the world war in 1917. Before the war ended in November 1918, Debs was arrested and jailed for giving speeches against the military draft, and federal agents prowled his audiences arresting young men who could not produce draft cards. His conviction on espionage charges was upheld by the Supreme Court in March 1919.

A month later, on the eve of Socialist May Day celebrations (which in Cleveland, the site of Debs's original conviction, would descend into widespread rioting), a package labeled to look like a sample from Gimbel's department store arrived at the Atlanta home of former U.S. senator Thomas W. Hardwick. When a maid opened it, it exploded, blowing off her hands, and in the days to come postal authorities uncovered a nationwide plot in which "infernal machines," as such stealth bombs were known, had been sent in the mail to political, legal, and corporate leaders including Supreme Court Justice Oliver Wendell Holmes, John D. Rockefeller, and J. P. Morgan. Many of the addressees had investigated the spread of Communist propaganda through the mails, or prosecuted or presided over cases involving IWW anti-war activities and bombings. On June 2, a bomb exploded outside the Washington home of U.S. attorney general A. Mitchell Palmer, killing the apparent bomber and blowing out windows in the home of assistant secretary of the navy Franklin D. Roosevelt, who lived across the street. There were bombings in seven other eastern cities the same night, and all these were linked to the IWW, partly by the anarchist leaflets calling for class war using dynamite and guns that were scattered, along with body parts, outside Palmer's home.

Palmer had already been calling for new laws against radical activities. Now he threw the full force of the Justice Department against the Wobblies and any and all anarchists, Communists, and Socialists, radical and otherwise, conducting raids across the country and detaining aliens and any suspected sympathizers. Over a matter of months in 1919 and 1920, Palmer's agents arrested some 10,000 radicals and labor agitators and deported 800, including the noted anarchist Emma Goldman, in what famously became known as the Red Scare. His campaign failed to stop the most lethal bombing of all, however. On September 16, 1920, a bomb packed with shards of iron window-sash weights exploded outside the Wall Street offices of J. P. Morgan, killing 30 people instantly and more in the days to come, and injuring 300.

In the wake of the Red Scare, the left was effectively marginalized. The revolution-preaching Communists went underground, while the Socialists lost half their party membership as a result of Palmer's crackdown and the appearance in the upper Midwest of the new Farmer-Labor Party, whose platform mimicked their own call for reforms. Although Debs polled almost 914,000 votes in the 1920 presidential election, it was a far smaller percentage than he had received eight years earlier, since the total vote had grown from 15 million to almost 27 million. Debs died in 1926 and Norman Thomas inherited his mantle, becoming the Socialist Party's perennial candidate. It was Thomas, a Princeton-educated Presbyterian minister from New York, who completed the party's transition from its worker-oriented roots to a party of utopia-minded middle-class intellectuals.

The prosperity of the late 1920s seemed to signal a death knell for the anti-capitalist parties; in 1928 both William Z. Foster, the first Communist candidate for president, running on the Workers Party ticket, and Norman Thomas, on the Socialist line, did poorly. Yet a strong current for reform remained. In the 1924 election almost 5 million votes had gone to Robert M. La Follette of Wisconsin and Burton K. Wheeler of Montana, running on the new Progressive Socialist ticket. Those votes shifted to the Democrats four years later, and although the Republicans won, the shift showed that Americans preferred to seek change through the ballot box, not revolution.

But the depression revived the moribund radicals, especially the Communists, and gave them a recruiting tool. Anger over the economic devastation and the government's inaction spanned both the cities and the farm belt, and the Communist Party, directed by Moscow, was active in both places. Although the party had only 8,000 members in 1931, their impact far outweighed their numbers. As A. N. Young of the Wisconsin Farmers Union had testified at the beginning of 1932, "The fact is today that there are more actual reds among the farmers in Wisconsin than you could dream about....I almost hate to express it, but I honestly believe that if some of them could buy airplanes, they would come down here to Washington to blow you fellows all up."

In the cities, the party organized locally based Unemployed Councils made up of the jobless, and staged marches and demonstrations to protest unemployment, evictions, and racial discrimination. Solving these problems was beside the point; the party's organizers designed the events to provoke confrontations with the police and show the proletariet under attack by ruling reactionaries in order to encourage revolution. More often than not, they were successful. Police threw tear gas bombs to break up a demonstration outside the White House on March 6, 1930. On the same day, a crowd of 35,000 gathered in New York's Union Square to listen to a roster of Communist speakers. Uniformed police and plainclothes detectives stood by until Foster, the party's presidential candidate of two years earlier, exhorted the audience to march on city hall. At that the police waded in, swinging nightsticks and bloodying scores of men and women. Ample press coverage of even the smallest local demonstrations fed the impression that the Communists were a larger force than they actually were.

Nonetheless, they were indeed growing. In November 1931, the National Committee of Unemployed Councils called members to a National Hunger March on Washington. Fewer than 2,000 signed up, but the city prepared for agitation. Small groups, most from the Midwest and Northeast, headed for the capital, staging rallies and demonstrations along the way and occasionally clashing with police. But Pelham D. Glassford, the District of Columbia's capable new police superintendent, remained low-key, saying that the marchers were "just tourists coming to Washington, but with a lot of publicity." When they arrived in two columns of backfiring cars on a cool, clear Sunday in early December, curious Washingtonians outnumbered them. The marchers were a mix of blacks and whites, women and men, all of them weary and bedraggled. Spectators were struck by how thin the women's coats were and by the fact that most of the men wore no coats at all, only sweaters. Most of them seemed hungry first and revolutionary a distant second.

Glassford, a retired brigadier general whose army nickname had been "Happy," proceeded to co-opt the visitors. He provided cots for the men, lodging for the women, and food for everybody. He had also mustered a force of 1,369 police and made sure they were prepared for trouble, but he let the marchers sing Communist anthems, orate from soapboxes, and parade around with banners. When they approached the Capitol on Monday to press their demands on Congress, an army of police armed with rifles, riot guns, and tear gas bombs stood guard, with machine gun emplacements added for good measure, but by then Glassford had already defused much of the marchers' potential to do violence.

The Unemployed Councils had a bundle of demands; oddly, none of them included jobs. They wanted unemployment and old-age insurance; free rent, gas, and electricity for the unemployed; bread and clothing made from surplus wheat and cotton; and $50 in cash to see each unemployed worker through the winter, plus $10 for each dependent. Congress refused to hear directly from the marchers, and they were also rebuffed at the White House. When they heard this, they marched and sang "The Internationale" again. Two days after they arrived, the police amiably gassed up their cars and trucks, helped crank them to life, and pointed them toward the District limits, which the marchers crossed peacefully. Those who returned to New York, where the national committee was headquartered, reached their destination at Union Square in a driving rainstorm. Surveying the rainswept square, they abandoned their plans to hold a rally, paraded once around the square in the comfort of their cars, and drove farther downtown for dinner and more songs and speeches.

But locally, the councils continued to agitate and confront police. Three thousand council-organized protesters in St. Louis converged on city hall in July 1932. When they charged the doors, they were met with police bullets and tear gas, and four were shot; in all, six policemen and thirty-five protesters were injured. In another council action in September, jobless workers in Toledo, Ohio, looted a grocery store of flour, sugar, and canned goods. In Cleveland, a crowd of between 800 and 900 was tear-gassed as it rushed a branch office of Associated Charities to protest inadequate relief. Later that fall, unemployed workers tried to storm the office of the mayor, Ray T. Miller, and were ridden down by police on horseback. In New York City, where Communist protests focused on the Home Relief Bureaus that had been placed at public schools throughout the city, riots and demonstrations brought arrests, fines, and jail terms.

Rivaling the Communists was the Unemployed Citizens League, an organization of the jobless that had grown from its beginnings in Seattle in 1931 to a nationwide presence. Its chapters stressed self-help and bartering, and direct appeals to local governments rather than provocation. Both groups pressed Philadelphia in the summer of 1932 for action against evictions and utility cutoffs, but only the Unemployed Council's demonstrations at city hall drew police reaction and arrests.

Spontaneous, home-grown anger also erupted into confrontations. Marion Stull, the Floyd County, Iowa, supervisor of the poor, arrived at her office in Charles City one Monday morning to find fifty to seventy-five jobless men waiting to confront her. Seven of them snatched her and drove her to a town thirty miles away, where they held her prisoner for several hours and then knocked her unconscious before fleeing. When they were arrested, the men protested that Stull had played favorites with the town's relief fund: she had moved some men from $2-a-day road repair and gardening jobs to woodcutting jobs that paid only $1.25. The town's chief of police was later charged with conspiracy in aiding Stull's abduction. In Elizabeth, New Jersey, homeless men armed with axes, saws, and crowbars swarmed over a dock of the Carbonic Manufacturing Company on Staten Island Sound and chopped it up for firewood. In Copper Hill, Tennessee, an architect named Charles Grimwood inexplicably ran help-wanted ads in papers from the East Coast to California seeking bricklayers, carpenters, electricians, plumbers, steel riggers, mill hands, timekeepers, and bookkeepers. A thousand men descended on the tiny mountain copper-mining town. When they learned no jobs were available, some of the men stormed Grimwood's house, mauled him, and tore his clothes before police arrived and chased them off.

At the heart of all the protests was the lack of work and the Hoover administration's refusal to consider a jobs program. In San Francisco, George Bratt, an Amherst College graduate and actor who had turned to furniture making, was evicted with his family for non-payment of rent. With his household goods piled on the sidewalk and his wife and four children milling about in confusion, Bratt walked away, declaring that he could take care of himself but the institutions of society should provide for his dependents. His wife agreed. "I glory in his spunk," she said. "He is fighting for a principle. As long as society has deprived him of his means of making a living, society must house and feed his family."

Few corporate leaders shared such views about the obligations of society. One who did was seventy-year-old Daniel Willard, president of the Baltimore and Ohio Railroad. In a commencement address the year before at the University of Pennsylvania, Willard had anguished over a system that could not provide work yet would not provide relief, and asserted feelings not that different from those of the homeless and jobless. In their circumstances, he said, "I would steal before I would starve."

Congressman Kent Keller of Illinois echoed him; responding to testimony that people in two West Virginia counties were breaking into warehouses to steal supplies, he said that he would do the same thing if he were starving.

The palpable desperation and widespread protests kept authorities on edge. When six shabbily dressed men entered the Irving Trust Company branch in the Chamber of Commerce Building on Court Street in Brooklyn, New York, a guard drew his gun and ordered them to put their hands up. Three did, but the others fled, triggering rumors of an attempted holdup. Then the three who had run returned to the bank, accompanied by officials of the American Legion. They explained that the "holdup men" were veterans who had been looking for an office in the basement where the Red Cross was distributing free flour. The men had allotment tickets and had come to pick up their supplies of flour when they entered the bank door by mistake.

Fear like this was easily exploited. Prosecutors, police, and politicians blamed Communist agitation for almost every protest, as if the breakdown in society could have no other cause. It was better to blame outside provocateurs than the government's own stubbornness. And with anger rising, public order had to be maintained at any cost. Two singular incidents, in March and July of that bleak year, painted vivid pictures of a country straining at the seams.

8. THE GUNS OF DEARBORN

On Monday, March 7, 1932, 1,300 laid-off Ford Motor Company workers hunched into the collars of their coats and braved a bitter wind as they assembled at a spot just inside the southwest city limits of Detroit. They had come to march to Ford's massive River Rouge plant in nearby Dearborn. Detroit's Unemployed Council had been planning the march for weeks, though if the marchers had known the temperature would be pegged at zero with a stiff wind blowing, they might have picked another day. William Z. Foster, the Communist leader, had spoken at a rally the night before, although he was not among the marchers.

The marchers wanted jobs, even at Ford's $4 workday. They also wanted workdays reduced to seven hours from Ford's ten, a slower production line, and the right to organize. The company opposed all these demands.

They set out at 2:00 P.M., walking in close ranks against the cold. Others, women as well as men, joined the line of march along the way, clambering off trolley cars and out of automobiles that they left parked along Fort Street. When the marchers reached the city limits where Detroit abutted Dearborn to the west, their numbers had grown to about 3,000, and they now faced their Rubicon. Detroit had given them permission to march, but Dearborn, the home of Ford's corporate and manufacturing headquarters, had denied it. Dearborn police always worked closely with the Ford security force, which had even spied on workers' bathroom breaks to keep the production lines moving and union conversations down.

A line of forty Dearborn police, with Ford's private enforcers in the background, blocked the marchers' path across the city line. Behind them lay the Ford complex, a colossus of looming buildings and towering smokestacks spread over 2,000 acres, served by its own rail system and deepwater port. It was the largest factory complex in the world. The marchers halted and spread out facing the police line. Dearborn's chief of police shouted a demand to see their marching permit. "We don't need one," a voice shouted back, and the marchers surged across the line, heading for the plant's Gate Number 3, the employment gate where new hires were announced.

The police fired a barrage of tear gas, which blew away in the stiff wind. The marchers responded by picking up chunks of slag and frozen mud and hurling them at the police. The policemen drew their guns. Although several of them were hit and knocked down by the projectiles, they held their fire, and the marchers reached the factory gate, pooling into a milling crowd while police, Ford security, and a squad of firemen looked on.

More firemen were stationed on an overpass above the crowd that led from the car park to the plant. Wielding high-pressure hoses, they began blasting the marchers with cold water. Then Harry Bennett, the notorious chief of Ford security, arrived on the scene and grappled with one of the marchers, Young Communist League leader Joseph York. Someone threw a piece of slag that hit Bennett on the head, and he and York went down together. When York broke free and stood up, the sudden rattle of a submachine gun sounded from the overpass.

Bullets raked the marchers as they scrambled for their lives. York took a bullet in the stomach and fell, mortally wounded. Three other marchers, including a sixteen-year-old boy, also died in the rain of gunfire. Marchers and police were joined in hand-to-hand fighting as gunshots raked cars along the street, shattering glass and piercing doors and fenders. Inside the Ford employment building, bullets and rocks exploded through the windows, and workers hit the floor. Ten more marchers were shot and scores injured. The bombardment of slag wounded fifteen policemen. A call went out for reinforcements. Detroit police, Michigan state troopers, sheriff's deputies, and National Guard troops arrived with machine guns, shotguns, tear gas bombs, and pistols. They swept up dozens of marchers on riot charges, sent the most seriously injured to hospitals, where they were chained to their beds, and took the rest to jail to be chained to cots inside their cells.

The press put the bulk of the blame on Foster and the Communist Party. "Responsibility is not hard to fix," claimed the *Detroit Free Press.* "The inciters were William Z. Foster and the other Red agitators." Police put out an all-points bulletin for Foster, whose speech the night before, according to the *New York Times,* had been "inflammatory." Detroit prosecutor Harry S. Toy said there was no evidence that the march was "a hunger march or an unemployment march." "A small group of plotters or agitators" was responsible and "criminal syndicalism" was involved.

Still, the conservative *New York Herald Tribune* ran an editorial that condemned the Dearborn police "for using guns on an unarmed crowd, for viciously bad judgment and for the killing of four men." And an assistant Detroit prosecutor who interviewed the hospitalized marchers reported that all but one denied any Communist connection.

The four dead lay in state in Workers' Hall in Detroit, under a red flag and a portrait of Lenin. Ten thousand people joined their funeral procession, and 30,000 watched their burial in a shared plot that had a view of the Ford plant.

The Ford incident hardened views at both ends of the political spectrum. The right could claim that Communists were intent on turning workers against their employers, causing strikes, and halting production, while the left could charge that the ruling industrialists would go to any end to keep their workers down and prevent them from organizing.

But the vast majority of Americans, those in the middle, recognized that the real issue was the lack of jobs, and neither marching Communists nor gunslinging corporate security forces could be blamed for that. And very few people, even those who attended Communist-organized rallies and walked in Unemployed Council marches, actually wanted to overthrow the government. They were impatient by now and they wanted change, but it was change within the framework of a system they knew, respected, and in most cases loved. They simply wanted their government to address their problems.

9. THE BONUS MARCH

Jobless veterans of the world war were also increasingly restive. They had trouble finding work because they were older—not old, but in their thirties and forties—and in 1932 employers looked to younger men to endure the stresses of the speedup, the stretch-out, and other rigors of the American workplace. The Veterans Bonus Act of 1924, enacted in gratitude for their war service and over Calvin Coolidge's veto, had promised them $1 a day for time spent stateside and $1.25 a day for service overseas. But while payments of $50 or less were made immediately, those owed more than that could not collect until 1945, when what were actually insurance policies established in their names would mature. In the desperate conditions they and their families were now enduring, thirteen years was an impossible length of time to wait for payments that would average around $1,000. Veterans who were out of work and out of money reasoned that their country could better express its gratitude by paying them immediately, even if the amount fell short of what it would be at maturity.

A Texas congressman and veteran, Wright Patman, took up the immediate-payment cause and Congress passed a bill in 1931, but Hoover vetoed it. Patman kept trying, but the issue languished until an army sergeant from Portland, Oregon, who had been in the world war had a stroke of genius in what today would be called product branding. Walter W. Waters, who had been laid off from his cannery job, decided that personal lobbying by veterans would turn the tide. In the late spring of 1932, he assembled 300 Portland-area veterans for a "march" on Washington. The genius was in their name; he called his men the Bonus Expeditionary Force (BEF), after the doughboys who had set out for Europe in the spring of 1917 as the American Expeditionary Force. Waters's Bonus Army, as it became known, left for Washington in May in stock cars commandeered at a Union Pacific railyard.

As word spread, veterans from across the nation packed their bags, assembled their families, and joined the move on Washington. They found widespread sympathy along the way. Railroad yard workers hitched empty boxcars onto freight trains for the veterans to ride in. Towns assembled bands and parades to cheer them on. Restaurants donated food, and local posts of the American Legion, whose national office opposed immediate payment of the bonus, took up collections. By the time the Oregon veterans crossed the Mississippi, local police and politicians were helping them move east, first in private vehicles and then in National Guard trucks that took them through Indiana, Ohio, West Virginia, Pennsylvania, and finally Maryland and into the District of Columbia.

By the end of May more than 3,000 men and their families had reached the nation's capital. Police superintendent Pelham Glassford was again prepared, and directed most of them to a campsite in southeast Washington next to the Anacostia River. From their bivouac across the 11th Street drawbridge, they could see two national icons—the masts of the USS *Constitution*, "Old Ironsides," the legendary nineteenth-century warship that was visiting the Washington Naval Yard; and beyond it to the north, the dome of the U.S. Capitol, which was the focus of their bonus hopes. Glassford had procured some National Guard tents. These were quickly filled, so the camp expanded with makeshift huts in the manner of Hoovervilles around the nation—and the veterans kept on coming until the Bonus Expeditionary Force numbered almost 20,000 men, women, and children.

The administration's response was to ignore them.

The veterans settled in. Waters, who had assumed the title of "commander," ran the camp in semi-military fashion. Bugle calls echoed across the rows of tents and shacks, calling the veterans to drill. Medics staffed a first-aid tent where they treated mosquito bites, stomachaches, and other ailments. Provisional MPs kept order, and the *B.E.F. News* provided weekly information updates. A well-known Washington radio preacher, Lightfoot Solomon Michaux, conducted worship services, and the Salvation Army set up a library. A mess tent provided by Glassford served up meals of bread and stew washed down with coffee for 6 cents a day per person, which was raised from donations. The bonus marchers were so taken by their treatment that they named their bivouac Camp Marks, a salute to police captain S. J. Marks, the commander of the district's Eleventh Precinct, which adjoined the camp.

On June 15, the House of Representatives passed Congressman Patman's newest bonus bill, but it would have cost almost $2 billion, a figure that frightened budget balancers. When the Senate killed it two days later, some of the veterans responded with a three-day "death march" around the Capitol. Waters vowed to stay in Washington until the bonuses were granted, and called for reinforcements.

The influx of new arrivals overflowed Camp Marks, and many of them moved into a former commercial tract along Pennsylvania Avenue three blocks west of the Capitol. Others occupied abandoned buildings on the Mall near the Washington Monument. The Pennsylvania Avenue buildings, owned by the Treasury Department, had been scheduled for the wrecking ball to make way for a new government complex that would become the Federal Triangle. Indeed, demolition had already started, with the building fronts knocked down, exposing the interiors, when the veterans started to arrive back in May. Glassford had allowed some of them to occupy these buildings, which they called "bonus forts," and the new men and their families took over the surrounding area until about 2,000 people were encamped there. On July 5 the veterans massed on the Capitol steps, waving signs signaling their determination to wait the Congress out. "No Pay, All Stay," read one placard.

The summer lengthened. Humidity and heat blanketed the low-lying capital, fraying nerves and shortening tempers. But in general, the veterans were orderly, and the few Communists among them spent their days haranguing sparse audiences in a large meeting tent that had been set up in Camp Marks. It was on these few that General Douglas MacArthur, the army chief of staff, focused. His loathing of Communism dated back a dozen years to the Red Scare, and although the veterans represented no threat to Washington, he added troops to the city's army garrison, ordered additional troops at Fort Myer, Virginia, into anti-riot training, and made sure tanks were standing by.

And by now the veterans were beginning to test the city's patience. Downtown businesses complained that the ragged campers moving through the streets, and their shantytowns, river bathing, and fly-blown latrines, were hurting sales as well as the image of the nation's capital. It did not help that Waters was now strutting around in boots and jodhpurs and talking of forming an organization of "Khaki Shirts" to fight "the sordid scheme of special privilege." Congress scolded Glassford, who had taken funds from his own pocket to help feed the veterans, for admitting them to the District and letting them camp on government property. Meanwhile, the veterans staged boxing matches at Griffith Stadium (home of the Washington Senators base-ball team) to raise money, wandered about, and waited, hoping that the visible evidence of their distress would finally move a majority in Congress.

The president continued to ignore them. He said meeting with them wasn't possible; he didn't have the time. He had found time, however, to meet with National Geographic Society president Gilbert Grosvenor and flyer Amelia Earhart, to whom he awarded a gold medal. Meanwhile, barricades went up around the White House, impeding traffic and pedestrians alike.

On July 11, Hoover vetoed a $2 billion public works jobs plan that might have sent the veterans home, calling it "a squandering of public money." He signed another bill eagerly, however. This provided $100,000 in interest-free travel loans to the veterans, to be repaid when they finally got their bonuses. The bill imposed a July 15 dead-line to accept the loans, so it was clearly designed to encourage them to leave the capital before Congress adjourned the following day. Those who did apply had their fingerprints taken, which the United States Bureau of Investigation, later to become the FBI, used to probe for criminal records and evidence of Communist involvement. They took their travel money, and began to trickle out of Washington by rail and road. But several thousand stayed, and new arrivals continued to roll in.

When the final gavel fell on the congressional session, it left the veterans with no rationale for staying on. Their reservoirs of public sympathy were spent. Editorial pages that had supported them now called them ungrateful squatters thumbing their noses at authority. The administration spread suggestions that they were dominated by criminals and Communists and that the "better elements" had all gone home. Attorney General William D. Mitchell charged that they had "practically levied tribute" from small merchants. Finally, on July 28, Hoover directed that the "bonus forts" along Pennsylvania Avenue be cleared.

It was an oppressively hot day. A pair of treasury agents appeared in the morning, ordered the veterans to leave, and went away when they refused. An hour later Glassford roared up on his big blue motorcycle and repeated the order, backed by police with nightsticks. After conferring with Waters, the veterans and their families began bundling up their clothes and cooking pots and taking down their faded flags, preparing to depart.

When word of the evictions reached Camp Marks, some of the veterans there dashed across the 11th Street drawbridge before the police could raise it and converged on Pennsylvania Avenue and 3rd Street. Even so, the evictions proceeded peacefully for several hours. Then a new group arrived that pushed its way through police ropes and started hurling bricks and rocks pulled from the debris of the half-demolished buildings. Bricks struck Glassford, but he shook them off and headed for a vantage point on the second floor of one of the buildings, two policemen behind him. Those two were attacked with bricks, a loaded garbage can, and their own nightsticks, and at that point several policemen started shooting. One veteran fell dead and another collapsed with mortal wounds. Glassford shouted, "For God's sake, stop shooting! Put your guns away and don't shoot again!" His officers obeyed, but word of the clash reached the White House. Hoover ordered Secretary of War Patrick J. Hurley to send in the army.

MacArthur was ready, his troops and tanks on call at Fort Myer on the other side of the Potomac. At about four-thirty in the afternoon, the 200-man Third Cavalry, mounted and with sabers drawn, moved from the staging area at the Ellipse below the White House past the Treasury Building to Pennsylvania Avenue. Behind the cavalry came machine gun carriages and trucks carrying six small tanks, followed by some 400 infantrymen with bayonets fixed to their rifles and blue tear gas bombs hanging from their belts. MacArthur, in full dress uniform, sat in one of two staff cars bringing up the rear. It was the end of the workday, and as they neared the bonus forts in the evacuation zone thousands of office workers filled the streets. At first both the veterans and the civilians, on the north side of the avenue across from the roped-off forts, thought the military display was a parade and started to applaud. Then the cavalry, led by Major George S. Patton, wheeled into the crowd.

The civilians scattered one way and the veterans another as cavalrymen swung the flats of their sabers. Some were ridden down and trampled, including Senator Hiram Bingham of Connecticut. Spectators and veterans began to boo and jeer the troops. At the buildings they were supposed to be evacuating, veterans now formed a line and raised flags. The cavalry focused on them, driving at the points in the line where the flags were waving.

Behind the cavalry, the infantrymen put on gas masks and policemen tied handkerchiefs over their noses and mouths. Then the soldiers entered the gaping buildings and threw tear gas bombs to clear the rooms. Gasping for breath, veterans and their wives streamed out clutching their children and what possessions they could carry. The troops drove them in the direction of the 11th Street Bridge and Camp Marks across the river, the cavalrymen hurrying them along. "It was like sons attacking their fathers," one of the marchers recalled.

MacArthur paused on the north side of the river while his forces ate at a field kitchen and darkness fell across the capital. Hoover sent explicit orders that they were not to cross the river, but MacArthur ignored this; he was, he said, too busy to be bothered by "people coming down and pretending to bring orders." At 9:22, he led a column of infantry toward the bridge. The cavalry followed.

The veterans had already started to evacuate their makeshift shelters, but some families still remained when the foot soldiers arrived, hurling tear gas bombs and driving the residents toward the edges of the camp. A seven-year-old boy was trying to save his pet rabbit when a soldier laced into him, shouting, "Get out of here, you little son of a bitch!" and stabbed his bayonet into the boy's leg. Ambulances sped to carry away the casualties. Two infants died, apparently from the tear gas. At 10:14 the troops doused the tents and shacks with gasoline and started torching them. Patton's cavalry moved into the camp at 11:15 to finish them off. By midnight the glow of flames could be seen from the White House, where Hoover was just learning that MacArthur had ignored his orders.

As the Bonus Army scattered toward the city limits and into the countryside, the White House began the job of blaming the marchers. Hoover claimed most of the "real veterans" had gone home when they were offered travel loans and that "a considerable part of those remaining are not veterans; many are Communists and persons with criminal records." He blamed them for leading the others into "violence which no government can tolerate." He repeated the charge in a September letter while releasing a U.S. Bureau of Investigation report on the events on July 28. It referred to "the extraordinary proportion of criminal, communist, and non-veteran elements amongst the marchers." MacArthur, meanwhile, had already said that only one in ten of the ousted men were "real" war veterans.

In fact, a Veterans Administration survey of the bonus marchers showed that 94 percent of them had army or navy records, that 67 percent had served overseas, and that 20 percent were disabled.

Editorial pages around the country supported Hoover in calling out the army. The *New York Times* charged the bonus marchers with "defying decency," with "insolent lawlessness," and with insubordination "almost amounting to insurrection." The *Boston Herald* called the march a holdup by "the undeserving," and the New York *Daily News,* in a photo caption, described them as "B.E.F. reds." But on the following morning, photos of the routed veterans, the soldiers torching their camps, and the smoldering remains told a different story. It seemed to many that the Bonus Army's major crime had been to embarrass the administration by calling attention to the poverty and unemployment that had occurred on Hoover's watch. One decorated veteran, headed back to Pennsylvania after the rout from Washington, was given a ride by journalist Malcolm Cowley. "If they gave me a job, I wouldn't care about the bonus," he said.

Unleashing the army on jobless men who had fought for America in the world war left a sour taste that would last through an election season already well under way.

10. ROOSEVELT ONTO THE STAGE

The Democrats *were* talking about jobs. Prominent among them, in addition to House Speaker Garner, was Franklin Delano Roosevelt, the governor of New York. He had announced his candidacy for the Democratic presidential nomination on January 21, 1932, after a year or more of work by his team of political operatives, raising money, making new contacts, and wooing the party regulars who controlled wards in major cities. As he approached the Democrats' nominating convention, scheduled for Chicago in late June, Roosevelt was campaigning as the anti-Hoover. He advocated a federally funded program of public works jobs and federal relief for the unemployed, while at the same time courting conservatives by distancing himself from the League of Nations.

Now fifty-three, Roosevelt had been a politician most of his adult life. He had won his first elective office, a seat in the New York State Senate, when he was twenty-eight, in 1910. Reelected two years later, he soon resigned to accept an appointment as assistant secretary of the navy in the administration of the new president, Woodrow Wilson, the New Jersey governor and former head of Princeton University whose candidacy he had vigorously supported in the 1912 election. Family wealth had eased Roosevelt's journey into politics and shaped his profile: he was a patrician with a common touch, a reformer, a conservationist, and a pragmatist given to testing the political winds to see where opportunities might lie. Former President Theodore Roosevelt, whose niece Eleanor had married Franklin in 1905, was a distant cousin, but where "Teddy" was direct and blustery, Franklin was oblique and rhetorically eloquent. Wilson was reelected in 1916, and again Roosevelt made a significant contribution. After helping manage naval affairs through the United States' eighteen-month involvement in the world war in Europe, he was rewarded with the Democratic vice presidential nomination in the campaign of 1920. Although he and Ohio's James M. Cox, the presidential nominee, lost badly to the Republican ticket of Harding and Coolidge, Roosevelt proved an enthusiastic and able campaigner, laying the groundwork and whetting his ambition for another bid at national office.

Those ambitions came to a grievous halt the following summer when Roosevelt, now thirty-nine, was stricken with polio at his family's summer home at Campobello, an island in Canadian waters off the northern coast of Maine. Severely crippled, he began his lengthy rehabilitation in the magnesium-salted thermal baths of Warm Springs, Georgia. There he learned to walk again, and he stepped back onto the national stage in the summer of 1924, using two canes and braces on his legs to walk fifteen perilous feet before a crowd at Madison Square Garden to nominate Alfred E. Smith, then the governor of New York, as the Democratic candidate for president. The hall burst into a standing ovation when he reached the podium and gripped its edges for support. Although Smith lost the nomination to John W. Davis (and Republican Calvin Coolidge was to win the presidency in November), Roosevelt had rekindled his own political career. Four years later, in 1928, he won his first two-year term as New York's governor, succeeding Smith, and during his second term launched a series of measures to combat the depression in New York.

Roosevelt had always been a natural politician. He was gregarious, laughed easily, and was quick to smile. And after his rebound from polio, he had acquired a deeper and more subtle quality of confidence: nothing seemed to faze him. He communicated a forceful serenity, an attitude that no crisis was too great to overcome. One pose in particular would become iconic—his head thrown back, face creased in a grin, cigarette holder jutting at a jaunty angle from his teeth; it imparted a joy of combat and the certainty of winning. Here was a man who believed in himself, it said, and if you took his side in a fight, he would reward your belief in him.

It was this quality that resonated with Americans whose radios were tuned to the National Broadcasting Corporation on the night of April 7, 1932, when Roosevelt made the first nationwide broadcast of his campaign from the state capital in Albany. In his speech, listeners heard what many had not heard for a long time: that America's people and their problems mattered as much as the difficulties faced by bankers and industrialists.

"It is said that Napoleon lost the battle of Waterloo because he forgot his infantry," he said. "He staked too much upon the more spectacular but less substantial cavalry. The present administration in Washington provides a close parallel. It has either forgotten or it does not want to remember the infantry of our economic army.

"These unhappy times call for the building of plans that rest upon the forgotten, the unorganized but the indispensable units of economic power; for plans...that build from the bottom up and not from the top down, that put their faith once more in the forgotten man at the bottom of the economic pyramid."

"The forgotten man" was the memorable phrase. Its powerful impact and populist overtones struck fear in Roosevelt's rivals for the nomination. They accused him of firing the first salvo in a class war. Al Smith, his former ally, was the loudest.

Nominating Smith in 1924, Roosevelt had called him the "Happy Warrior," and the nickname stuck. Smith was to finally win the nomination in 1928 but go on to lose to Hoover in a general election landslide that he attributed in part to prejudice against him as a Roman Catholic. In that same election year, Roosevelt had succeeded Smith as New York's governor, and afterward, Smith, a charismatic figure in New York, could never understand Roosevelt's failure to ask him for advice, accept his suggestions on appointments, or include him in his political calculations. Over the next four years, he came to resent Roosevelt's swift rise to national prominence.

Smith, the grandson of Irish immigrants, had grown up poor on New York's Lower East Side. After his father died when he was thirteen, he dropped out of parochial school to help support his mother and his younger sister by working at various menial jobs. But he had one notable skill, a gift for public speaking, and this gave him his entry into politics, by way of the Tammany Hall organization that pulled the strings of New York City's government. Tammany was corrupt but effective; voters got favors and Thanksgiving turkeys for their loyalty, and the politicians who benefited sealed the bargain by parceling out public jobs.

Smith's base was the Fourth Ward, an irregular patch of lower Manhattan squeezed between the East River piers and Chatham Square, overshadowed by the Brooklyn Bridge, and so full of saloons and bars that it was also known as the Whiskey Ward. Its tenements were packed with immigrants: Irish and Italians, Germans, Russian and eastern European Jews, and assorted other nationalities. Some had fled tyranny; all sought work. They baked, they pickled, they picked rags, they worked in factories, and they heaved cargo, and when they were tired and broken, like Smith's father when he died, there were few options open to them. Widows who could not support their children placed them in foster homes and orphanages, as Smith's mother almost did. The reformer Jacob Riis had focused on the Fourth Ward in his famous exposé, *How the Other Half Lives*, published in 1890, when Smith was seventeen. It still remained an area where children as young as seven worked in factories, teenagers walked the streets as prostitutes, and charity workers tried to keep the elderly and disabled who couldn't work from starving. Smith used his wit and charm to solve small problems Tammany leaders delegated to him, and his public speaking skills came to their attention. With a reputation for being incorruptible, he rose through the organization until he won a seat in the State Assembly in Albany, where he emerged as a leader among the minority Democrats. Assembly members of both parties gathered for his speeches, roared at his jokes, and deferred to his sharp eye for spotting bills whose fine print rewarded special interests. When the Democrats won the majority in 1911 they chose Smith, eight years after he was first elected, as majority leader.

In March of that year, 146 young immigrant women, most between the ages of thirteen and twenty-three, died in a fire at the Triangle Shirtwaist Company factory in lower Manhattan's Greenwich Village. Many were trapped behind locked or inward-opening doors. Others jumped down the elevator shaft, and more than sixty were driven by the heat to jump from the ninth floor to the sidewalk. The only safety measures in the factory had been twenty-seven buckets of water and a fire escape that collapsed.

The disregard for workers' safety angered Smith, and he lobbied for a place on the factory investigation commission that was formed in the wake of the fire. The rest of his time in the Assembly was marked by his eloquence on behalf of exploited workers. He fought for state pensions for widows, disability insurance, and workers' compensation, and against child labor. Tammany steered him to election as New York County sheriff and later as president of the city's governing body, the Board of Aldermen, and in 1918, he became the first Tammany candidate to be elected governor of New York. He lost a 1920 bid for re-election but won again in 1922, and began three consecutive two-year terms that were marked by an avid populism on behalf of ordinary people and against entrenched interests.

But after leaving the governorship following his unsuccessful presidential campaign, Smith found that he missed the perks and authority of office. He had relished knowing men with money and power, chief among them John J. Raskob, a former General Motors executive who, after running Smith's failed campaign, had built the Empire State Building and made him its president with a $50,000-a-year salary. Smith now seemed blind to the tenement dwellers for whom he once had fought. He bragged of the lease on his Fifth Avenue apartment, rode in a chauffeured limousine, and served as a corporate director. After his defeat, Smith had vowed not to run for president again. But seeing Hoover vulnerable to any Democrat, even a Catholic, probably wishing for revenge, and judging Roosevelt's populism a threat to his new patrons' interests, he jumped into the race for the Democratic nomination just two weeks after Roosevelt declared his candidacy.

Now, at the Democrats' traditional Jefferson Day dinner in April, held a week after Roosevelt's radio address and attended by all the party's candidates for the nomination except Roosevelt, Smith accused him of demagoguery. "At a time like this," he said, "when millions of men and women and children are starving throughout the land, there is always the temptation to stir up class prejudice, to stir up the bitterness of the rich against the poor, and of the poor against the rich." It would delude and ruin the poor, he said, sounding very much like

Herbert Hoover, "to make them believe that they can get employment before the people who would ordinarily employ them are also again restored to conditions of normal prosperity."

But Roosevelt had found the people receptive to his talk of change. On May 22, he reached another rhetorical high. It came in Atlanta, where he had stopped after a visit to Warm Springs to accept an honorary degree from Oglethorpe University and speak at its commencement. Standing on the stage of the Moorish-themed Fox Theatre under a ceiling of winking lights designed to imitate a starry night, he began with familiar commencement greetings but quickly found his campaign voice. Again speaking in populist themes, he addressed the irony of America's unaffordable abundance, caused not "by any natural calamity—by drought or floods or earthquakes or by the destruction of our productive machine or our manpower. Indeed," he said, "we have a superabundance of raw materials, a more than ample supply of equipment for manufacturing these materials into the goods which we need, and transportation and commercial facilities for making them available to all who need them. But raw materials stand unused, factories stand idle, railroad traffic continues to dwindle, merchants sell less and less, while millions of able-bodied men and women, in dire need, are clamoring for the opportunity to work."

To address what he called this "awful paradox," Roosevelt said, some preached that the business cycle would eventually return the country to prosperity, while others found the problems confronting society so complex that people who shared common goals could not agree on how to reach them. In each case, he said, the result was inaction—doing nothing, drifting.

Then came the words that Americans were to seize on as they had "the forgotten man": "The country needs and, unless I mistake its temper, the country demands bold, persistent experimentation. It is common sense to take a method and try it: If it fails, admit it frankly and try another. But above all, try *something*."

This call to action was not broadcast, so reaction was delayed. But it generated newspaper headlines the next day, and the *New York Times* and the *Atlanta Constitution* ran the text in its entirety. Some of his advisors worried that the speech would be perceived as radical, since he had called for "a wiser, more equitable distribution of the national income" in which "the reward for a day's work will have to be greater . . . and the reward to capital . . . will have to be less." The *Times* criticized its failure to lay out a specific plan. But as news of the speech spread, its message struck home. Americans were ready to experiment, were ready for actions that would break the stranglehold of *in*action that had left them helpless.

11. THE BATTLE IS JOINED

The Oglethorpe commencement speech was Roosevelt's last major policy statement before the Democratic National Convention. He and his politically savvy staff had been preparing for this occasion for many months, and he approached the convention with a lead in delegates, though not the two-thirds majority he would need to win the nomination.

The Republicans preceded the Democrats to Chicago. On June 16, they nominated Hoover, as expected, in a convention noted primarily for what it lacked: debate, new ideas, and any sense of optimism. He made no acceptance speech to the delegates. According to a tradition followed by both parties, the nominee-designate would wait to accept the nomination until he was formally notified of it, a span of several weeks; no candidate of either party had ever accepted at the convention itself. The Democrats who arrived on June 27 and filled the tiers of Chicago Stadium were a different crowd, boisterous and sanguine, younger, freer-spending. The change in tone prompted Anne O'Hare McCormick of the *New York Times* to write, "To the Republicans politics is a business, while to the Democrats it's a pleasure."

Roosevelt's operatives would have called it not a pleasure but very hard work. His longtime aide Louis McHenry Howe plotted strategy behind the scenes even when laid low by asthma and bronchitis, and two New York Irishmen, big, bald James Farley and suave Edward J. Flynn, worked the delegates. Roosevelt had about 551 votes, 200 short of nomination, and there were powerful forces aligned against him. House Speaker John Nance Garner, "Cactus Jack" from Uvalde, Texas, was also seeking the nomination, and he was backed by newspaper baron William Randolph Hearst. Backing Smith was Raskob, who in addition to being a financier was chairman of the Democratic National Committee. The shift of a single state's delegates could produce an avalanche of defections, so Flynn and Farley's task was to keep delegations pledged to Roosevelt on board while convincing others to shift in his direction. The job required a poker face, a steady hand, and a horse trader's sense of possibilities.

Smith continued denouncing Roosevelt, but he could not dent the front-runner's delegate count. Indeed, Roosevelt added to it. The first vote, completed at six-thirty the morning of July 1 after an all-night session, left him just a hundred votes short of nomination. Then his momentum stalled and a compromise candidate seemed likely to emerge. However, nobody wanted a repeat of the 1924 convention, which had cast an astonishing 103 ballots before it decided on John W. Davis as the nominee. The break came when Garner signaled his willingness to join Roosevelt on the ticket as the vice presidential candidate. This moved the Texas delegation to Roosevelt and brought Hearst and California with it. The logjam was broken, and Roosevelt was nominated on the fourth ballot with only Smith's delegates refusing to support him. Smith himself left the convention bitter and angry as word circulated that Roosevelt would break with tradition and come to Chicago to personally accept the nomination.

Roosevelt boarded a Ford Trimotor airplane the next morning, July 2, for the flight from Albany to Chicago. It was a rough flight that required two refueling stops, and he arrived two hours late. But this did not faze the delegates. Excited by the unprecedented appearance of their nominee, they were poised to respond, and the instant Roosevelt took the stage, a red rose in the lapel of his navy suit, they leaped to their feet in a thunderous standing ovation. As Arthur Krock of the *New York Times* wrote, "The great hall seemed to surge upward."

Roosevelt immediately expanded on the theme of change. The "unprecedented and unusual times" demanded unprecedented acts, he

said. "Let it from now on be the task of our party to break foolish traditions. We will break foolish traditions and leave it to the Republican
leadership...to break promises."

He quickly turned to the depression and renewed his populist campaign themes. "There are two ways of viewing the government's
duty," he said. "The first sees to it that a favored few are helped and
hopes that some of their prosperity will leak through, sift through, to
labor, to the farmer, to the small business man. That theory belongs to
the party of Toryism, and I had hoped that most of the Tories left this
country in 1776."

The Democrats, by contrast, "must be a party of liberal thought, of
planned action, of enlightened international outlook, and of the greatest good to the greatest number of citizens."

He recounted the events of the depression: the piling up of surpluses
that had flooded markets without reducing prices, the flow of profits
into excess plant capacity and stock speculation, the crash, the plant
shutdowns, the loss of jobs and purchasing power, the bank failures
and contraction of credit, the inexorable rise of unemployment. To
produce change, the top and the bottom of the economic pyramid had
to be treated together. "Statesmanship and vision," he said, "require
relief to all at the same time."

Roosevelt called for emergency public works to provide jobs. He
had said early in his campaign for the nomination that such a plan was
a "stopgap," and he gave no specifics other than the reforestation of
millions of acres of marginal and unused land, which he said would
employ a million men. He also called for an end to Prohibition and to
tariffs that had choked world trade, but it was to the theme of jobs
that he returned. "What do the people of America want more than
anything else?" he asked the delegates packing the convention floor
and the galleries above. "To my mind, they want two things: work,
with all the moral and spiritual values that go with it, and with work,
a reasonable measure of security—security for themselves and for their
wives and children. Work and security—these are more than words.
They are more than facts. They are the...true goal to which our efforts at reconstruction should lead."

He blamed the Republicans for clinging to "sacred, inviolable, un-
changeable" economic laws while "men and women are starving."
They gave the people no hope. He would give them hope again, he

said, his confident voice ringing through the hall as he uttered one more phrase for the ages: "I pledge you, I pledge myself, to a new deal for the American people. . . . This is more than a political campaign. It is a call to arms. Give me your help, not to win votes alone, but to win in this crusade to restore America to its own people."

The delegates drowned Chicago Stadium in their applause. They shouted and cheered, jumped on chairs and wept, and from beneath the din rose the notes of the organ sounding yet another note of hope, the Roosevelt campaign song: "Happy Days Are Here Again."

12. A NEW DIRECTION

The stock market reached the end of its long, slow slide that summer, bottoming out on July 8 when the Dow Industrials hit 41.22, down from 381.17 in September 1929. But jobs still disappeared, and those without them belonged more than ever to a new order: the former middle class. As local governments continued to exhaust their dwindling resources, the chaos of relief efforts grew worse. The mayors of twenty-eight cities, meeting in Detroit, had urged Hoover to treat the problem with wartime urgency and create a $5 billion loan fund for public works. Detroit had already issued emergency rations of bread and milk to jobless families and was scraping for money to pay the grocers who supplied the rations and who were now threatening to cut off credit to the city unless it paid its bills. New York was paying relief families an average of $2.39 per week, and welfare officials figured they were reaching only half the families hit by unemployment. Fully half of Chicago's workers had no jobs.

Nationally, only a fourth of unemployed families were receiving any relief at all. Government funds, state and local, were a minuscule portion—1.5 percent—of what was being spent, averaging $1.67 a month per citizen. The rest came from a haphazard conglomeration of private charities and help givers, including community chests and the

Salvation Army, soup kitchens and food banks, and relatives and friends who still had something left to give.

At last, and reluctantly, Hoover made one concession to conditions. Early in the year, he had allowed the creation of the Reconstruction Finance Corporation (RFC), a $2 billion agency whose purpose was to shore up weak banks, railroads, and insurance companies by making loans to them. New York congressman Fiorello La Guardia called it "a millionaire's dole." He had proved to be right; most of the loans made during the agency's first months, when its activities were kept secret to avoid panicking depositors, went to big banks. On July 21, however, Hoover expanded the pool of loan recipients to include states and cities and set aside $300 million of the RFC funds so that they could provide relief and jobs. He also cut his own salary 20 percent, and Vice President Charles Curtis and nine cabinet officers all took 15 percent pay cuts to promote government economy, a savings of $37,500 a year.

But these gestures signaled no real change in the president's thinking. On the night of August 11, he put on the white pants and blue blazer of a summer yachtsman and got in his limousine for the short trip to the Daughters of the American Revolution's new Constitution Hall, two blocks from the White House grounds. There, Republican National Committee chairman Everett Sanders formally notified the president of what he and the rest of the country had known for almost two months—that he was the party's presidential nominee. He opened his campaign for reelection with his acceptance speech to 4,000 in the auditorium and a nationwide radio audience on CBS and NBC.

Hoover called his management of the economy "the most gigantic program of economic defense and counterattack ever evolved in the history of the Republic," and insisted that no more should be done. "It is not the function of the government," he said, "to relieve individuals of their responsibilities to their neighbors, or to relieve private institutions of their responsibilities to the public, or the local government to the states, or the responsibilities of state governments to the federal government." These were "the fundamental principles of our social and economic system." He tried to tie Roosevelt to the agitators of the left, saying that "the solution of our many problems...is not to be found in haphazard experimentation or by revolution." He spoke again and again of national ideals and "eternal principles" to justify his administration's inaction of the past three years. These had caused him, he said, to reject "the temptation…to resort to those panaceas and short cuts which…would ultimately undermine" those principles.

Ultimately, he acknowledged one prescient truth. "Today millions of our fellow countrymen are out of work," he said. "Prices of farmers' products are below a living standard. Many millions more who are in business or hold employment are haunted by fears for the future. No man with a spark of humanity can sit in my place without suffering from the picture of their anxieties and hardships before him day and night. They would be more than human if they were not led to blame their condition upon the government in power."

In October, a month before the election, Hoover and his wife, Lou, embarked on a campaign trip, a series of railroad whistle stops that would take the beleaguered president from Washington back to his home state of Iowa. This was a courageous plan, for at the far end lay a deepening farm crisis, sporadic violence, and talk of revolution from both left and right.

Farmers had withheld their products from the market in order to force prices higher, and those efforts were growing increasingly militant. To keep farm products from moving, they were blockading roads with telephone poles and logs bristling with railroad spikes, brandishing pitchforks and clubs for emphasis as they ordered drivers bound for market to turn back. Bankers were the target of the Farmers' Holiday Association, as its unofficial theme song made clear:

> Let's call a farmer's holiday
> A holiday let's hold;
> We'll eat our wheat and ham and eggs
> And let them eat their gold.

In an apparently spontaneous action, Iowa dairy farmers blocked all ten roads leading to Sioux City. They waylaid milk trucks and dumped the milk they carried into roadside ditches. Only trucks that supplied hospitals were allowed through. The movement spread to Council Bluffs, Des Moines, and across state lines, leaving authorities helpless. When the sheriff at Council Bluffs arrested sixty farmers for picketing the roads, a thousand of their supporters threatened a mass march on the jail, and the picketers were released.

Throughout the Midwest, county sheriffs, judges, lawyers, and farm foreclosure auctioneers were facing the fury of the farmers. A lawyer who had foreclosed on a farm in Kansas was found murdered. As they did at foreclosure auctions, farmers massed in courtrooms to intimidate judges and lawyers. One hung a hangman's noose from his barn in case prospective buyers missed the point. Campaigning for the governorship of North Dakota, William "Wild Bill" Langer suggested farmers treat the banker "like a chicken thief" and shoot him if he set foot on their farms.

As Hoover's train steamed through the fall landscape, making the stops in small towns that were a campaign tradition, the president could see just how far his political capital had ebbed. Whistle stops usually meant cheers and applause from the audiences who gathered around the rear platform of the last car to greet campaigning politicians, but cold stares and silence were what faced Hoover when he emerged with his wife to stand behind the Pennsylvania Railroad logo. Aides noticed that the men in the Secret Service detail guarding him were growing increasingly nervous with each stop. When he finally reached Des Moines, the militant farmers of Milo Reno's Farmers' Holiday Association were waiting there by the thousands, brandishing signs that read, "In Hoover we trusted; now we are busted." Republican officials turned out 100,000 spectators for the presidential parade, but the Iowa National Guard, warned to expect trouble, stationed troops along the four-mile route.

Hoover's speech that night was yet another recitation of the steps he had taken to battle the depression, without which "things would be infinitely worse." He defended balancing the budget, ensuring the sound credit of the government, continuing protective tariffs, and maintaining the gold standard that tied the money in circulation to the nation's gold reserves. For the Republicans these were absolutes, as fundamental as the Constitution. He attacked the Democrats for advocating federal spending to create jobs and relieve want when these were not the government's responsibility, and charged that the source of the depression lay outside the United States, in the worldwide economic turmoil. It was a speech heavy with detail presented without flair. For a man who was fundamentally shy and introverted, who preferred the meetings and conferences of governance to the tumult and spontaneity of campaigning, it was a brave performance. But the

gloom surrounding him only one month before the election was inadvertently captured in a *Des Moines Register* headline the next day. It
referred to an unusual occurrence at a send-off party just before the
Hoovers left Des Moines: "Hoover Smiles at Reception."

In that final month, the president threw himself fully into the campaign, traveling to the Midwest, Maryland, and West Virginia. He
seemed desperate to explain himself, to convince the country that his
position was the right one. There could be no departure from tradition, no change in thinking. What the government had always done, it
would keep doing. What it had never done (beyond measures he had
already tried, such as the RFC), it should not attempt. The Democrats
meant revolution, the end of the American way of life. But the people
had lost patience. A crowd waiting at the station booed him in Detroit,
and on the route to the auditorium where he was to speak people
brandished signs that read "Down with Hoover." In St. Paul, he called
the Democrats "the party of the mob." When he went on to say,
"Thank God we still have a government in Washington that knows
how to deal with a mob," apparently a reference to the eviction of the
Bonus Army, his audience stirred with disapproval.

Meanwhile, Roosevelt moved forward, progress that was based less
on what he said than on how he said it. His proposals were still vague,
but in contrast to Hoover's grim defensiveness, he projected confidence. The battered fedora, the grin, the upthrust chin, the cigarette
holder pointing skyward like an exclamation point, the words that
embraced the people's yearnings—all this rebutted Hoover's baleful
accusations. The "new deal" of his acceptance speech had captured
what the country sought; specifics could wait. Three years of depression were enough.

The people spoke on election day, November 8. Roosevelt compiled
a massive victory, 22,825,016 votes to Hoover's 15,758,397: a 57 to
39 percent margin in the popular vote. The margin was even more
pronounced in the electoral college, where he won 472 votes to
Hoover's fifty-nine. Democrats also rolled up big majorities in both
the House and Senate.

Voters had paid scant attention to the candidates of the far left.
Socialist Norman Thomas, still the favorite of many intellectuals,
failed to break 900,000 in the count. William Z. Foster, the
Communist Party candidate, lost by a much wider margin. His feeble

showing of just 102,221 votes belied the concern, expressed in countless headlines and official statements after the Ford and Bonus Army debacles, that Communism was eating at the country's very foundations.

Clearly Americans wanted no part of a government that ran their lives, but in sweeping Roosevelt to victory, they were demanding that it pay attention to their needs. For the millions of the unemployed, that meant one thing only: jobs.

But these would not come soon. Roosevelt would not be inaugurated president until March 4, 1933. This four-month lag between November and March was the vestige of a long-vanished time, before airplanes permitted half the country to be traveled in a day and the telephone, telegraph, and radio transmitted information instantly from coast to coast. Thus for these endless months Hoover remained in the White House, sullenly defending his rejected policies, even as vast numbers of people with no work and no resources faced the deepening winter with impatience, anxiety, and hunger.

PART II

HOPE ON THE RISE

Work-Is-What-I-Want-and-Not-Charity.
Who-Will-Help-Me-Get-a-Job.
—SIGN HELD BY A JOBLESS WORKER

Our greatest primary task is to put people to work.
—FRANKLIN D. ROOSEVELT IN HIS INAUGURAL ADDRESS,
MARCH 4, 1933

1. JOBS FROM THE SKY
(AND NOWHERE ELSE)

On December 7, 1932, one month after the election, the temperature in New York City reached a springlike 62 degrees. Better-off New Yorkers undoubtedly enjoyed the unexpected warmth, but men without jobs at the approach of winter prayed for snow. Two days later it appeared their prayers were answered. The temperature dropped to 30 degrees, and on December 10 the season's first real snow began to fall. Fifteen thousand jobless men waited for the call to clean the city's streets, but the uncooperative skies dropped a mere two inches and left them disappointed. The next week, things improved. A daylong blizzard dropped half a foot of snow and this time, street bosses handed out shovels to 20,000 men for two days' worth of work at 50 cents an hour. Men in suits and overcoats joined laborers in work clothes, all bending to their shoveling not just in New York but in cities up and down the snow-blessed eastern seaboard.

Across the country in Los Angeles, the city council was trying to pry money from the Reconstruction Finance Corporation to create some public works jobs. It had been almost six months since Hoover had reluctantly opened the business loan program to state and local governments. Many had filed applications, but most of these were tied up in Washington red tape; of the $300 million set aside for public sector relief loans, a mere $30 million had been granted. But even if they had been approved quickly it would not have made much difference, for the money was inadequate. The Los Angeles application, for example, would cover only ten days' work for 14,000 men.

For most jobless workers, there were not even these faint glimmers of hope. Several states, following New York's fall 1931 initiative, had begun relief programs, but while these improved on what local governments had done, they barely dented the need. The Seventy-second Congress convened in a lame duck session on December 5 and debated work-relief spending, but with Hoover still holding veto power, it decided not to act. Nor did it act on Hoover's measures, including a national sales tax that Roosevelt opposed because it would hit the poor harder than the rich. The new Congress would not take office until inauguration day, March 4. The private sector had nothing new to offer. Indeed, hearings into banking practices begun by the Senate Committee on Finance and Currency in 1932, and resumed in January 1933, were producing a parade of bankers confessing to gross ethical lapses, on one hand, and on the other, a parade of business leaders admitting they still had no clues about how to revive the economy. Three full years of depression had failed to generate solutions to the idle factories, the crops rotting in the fields, and the millions of jobless men and women without money for bare necessities for themselves and their families.

And still the crisis deepened. Through the gray days of late winter, more factories shut down and more shops and offices closed their doors, putting still more people out of work. Unemployment climbed to new heights, rising until one in every four employable workers had no job and no prospect of finding one. It was a jobless rate of 25 percent.

On the first day of the outgoing Congress's final session, the Communists mustered protests and marches that echoed their hunger march on Washington; 1,200 descended on the Capitol to chant, "Feed the hungry, tax the rich," while locally the Unemployed Councils organized rent strikes and agitated for relief payments. Each new incident and headline increased the fear that Communism might find a wider audience, and nervous voices called for public order at all costs. Kansas governor Alfred M. Landon said, "Even the hand of a national dictator is in preference to a paralytic stroke." Republican senator David A. Reed of Pennsylvania looked with admiration at the order fascism had imposed on Italy. "If this country ever needed a Mussolini, it needs one now," he said. Indeed, his colleagues in the Congress seemed ready to confer dictator-like powers upon Roosevelt. New York representative Hamilton Fish wrote the president-elect in February to say that he and his fellow Republicans were ready to "give you any power you may need."

And as the country waited for the new administration and whatever it had to offer, fear also attacked the banking industry, driving depositors to tellers' windows to withdraw their funds and pushing the nation's monetary system toward collapse and with it, what remained of the economy.

Louisiana, concerned that a run of withdrawals would accelerate, closed its banks in early February. Such closures were euphemistically called bank "holidays." The withdrawal fever subsided in Louisiana and its banks reopened. But at the end of the second week in February, Henry Ford's troubled Union Guardian Trust, one of two big bank holding companies in Michigan, was reduced to begging for an RFC loan in order to stay open. But it didn't have the collateral to support the $50 million loan it wanted, and Ford himself refused a compromise that would have subordinated his claim to certain assets. His version of rugged individualism was at least consistent; he scorned government assistance just as he scorned the workers who toiled on his assembly lines.

On Valentine's Day, after Ford refused to rescue his own bank, Michigan governor William A. Comstock introduced the concept of the bank holiday to his state, ordering the banks closed for eight days. Frightened depositors made their way to Indiana and Ohio, then to Illinois and Pennsylvania, trying to withdraw cash or preferably gold. Bank closings rippled outward, spreading as depositors panicked. Before the Michigan action, they had been taking gold out of banks at the rate of $20 million a day, their right under the gold standard that promised the dollar's convertibility to gold. But after Michigan acted, the rate of gold withdrawals almost doubled, and currency was flying out of the banks at the rate of $122 million daily. By that point, more than 5,500 banks had failed. Millions of citizens had lost their life's savings. The Senate finance committee hearings, revealing that bank owners and officers had routinely protected their own interests at the expense of their customers, eroded depositor confidence still further. Those people who still had assets to protect headed for the exits, taking their cash with them. The rich sought shelter overseas, but the vast majority hid their money within reach: under mattresses, behind a brick in a corner of the basement, or in coffee cans that they buried beneath the bushes in their backyards under the cover of darkness.

As William Gibbs McAdoo, the treasury secretary under Woodrow Wilson, two-time candidate for the Democratic presidential nomination, and newly elected senator from California, said, "Our entire banking system does credit to a collection of imbeciles."

2. AN AGONY OF WAITING

In the meantime, Roosevelt was assembling his cabinet. He sought a mix of the familiar and the new that would offer the same qualities that he himself projected—reassurance that he would not stray too far from the mainstream, and promise that he would push an agenda of reform. He did, however, tell a representative of William Randolph Hearst that the cabinet would be "radical" in that no one in it would know the way to the New York Stock Exchange. And he avoided making cabinet posts quid pro quos for early political support.

Senator Thomas J. Walsh, a craggy Montanan who had uncovered the Teapot Dome bribe-taking scandal in the Harding administration, was Roosevelt's choice for attorney general. For secretary of state he turned to Senator Cordell Hull of Tennessee, who had fought for lower tariffs and might be able to repair the mistrust and damage generated by protectionism. William Woodin, a Pennsylvanian whose long career in business included heavy manufacturing, banking, railroads, and shipping, was one of the rare businessmen who supported the new president's ideas, and despite concerns about his health he agreed to serve as secretary of the treasury after Virginia senator Carter Glass declined the job. Henry A. Wallace of Iowa, whose father had been agriculture secretary in the Harding and Coolidge adminis-

trations, was a progressive farmer who argued for limiting crop production through his popular family journal, *Wallace's Farmer.* When
Roosevelt floated his name among farm leaders for secretary of agriculture, the response was so positive that he asked him to serve even
though, or perhaps because, he was a Republican. For secretary of war
and secretary of the navy, Roosevelt chose Utah governor George
Dern and Virginia senator Claude A. Swanson, respectively. Commerce went to Daniel C. Roper, a South Carolinian who had served as
commissioner of internal revenue in the Wilson administration. The
one obvious patronage appointment was James Farley, his longtime
political advisor, as postmaster general.

Aside from Farley, none of these were people Roosevelt knew well,
but he dipped again into his pool of close acquaintants for the sensitive post of secretary of labor. Frances Perkins, a well-born Bostonian
who had risen through the ranks of social work, had helped make Al
Smith an advocate for labor reforms and worker protections when she
worked as an investigator for the Factory Investigating Commission,
formed after the Triangle Shirtwaist fire. During Roosevelt's governorship, she had headed the New York State Industrial Commission that
oversaw relations between labor and employers, and proved herself a
skilled political maneuverer. She protested that the secretary of labor
should be a union leader, but Roosevelt, urged on by a letter campaign
organized by reformer and Democratic women's organizer Mary
Williams (Molly) Dewson, insisted that Perkins take the appointment.
She did, and in the process became the first female cabinet member in
history.

If Roosevelt knew Perkins well, he did not know Chicagoan Harold
L. Ickes at all. But his initial choices for interior secretary had not
worked out, and as time drew short Ickes's credentials came to his attention. He was a lawyer, a longtime advocate of better government,
and a passionate Progressive. Loosely defined, a progressive was anyone who favored an agenda of social and political reforms aimed at
improving the lot of factory workers and slum dwellers. The name fit
social workers such as Jane Addams, the founder of Hull House in
Chicago, who with her supporters pushed protective laws for women
and children through the Illinois legislature at the turn of the twentieth
century. In its more formal sense, it identified a Midwest-centered
movement, largely Republican, that championed urban and industrial

reforms, trust-busting, and natural resource conservation, of which Ickes was a part. He was among the reform-minded Republicans who had split from the national party and formed the Progressive Party in 1912. It was the Progressives who nominated former president Theodore Roosevelt, and Roosevelt who gave the party its more colorful nickname when, asked if he was fit to serve, he pronounced himself "fit as a bull moose." The Bull Moose Party outpolled the Republican ticket but lost to Woodrow Wilson and the Democrats in the 1912 presidential race. However, state-level Progressives were more successful at putting through reforms, as in Illinois and in Wisconsin under Governor Robert M. La Follette, whose legislative successes included workers' compensation and a number of progressive tax laws. Nationally, the Progressives had felt by 1932 that they had no alternative but to get behind the Democratic ticket, and Ickes had served on the national committee of the National Progressive League for Roosevelt. When the president-elect summoned him to New York to look him over and subsequently offered him the job, he did not have to be asked twice.

But as the negotiations and arm-twisting with the various nominees proceeded, Roosevelt could do little that was substantive other than wait for his March 4 inauguration, so on February 3, in Jacksonville, Florida, he boarded the yacht of his Hudson River neighbor Vincent Astor for a vacation cruise. The 264-foot *Nourmahal* worked its way down the coast and docked in Miami on the fourteenth, the day after the Michigan bank closings, and Roosevelt came ashore for a reception at Bayfront Park on Biscayne Bay that evening.

He rode to the park in an open car and, from a perch on the top of the back seat, addressed the crowd of 20,000 gathered at the amphitheater, saying he had enjoyed the fishing and hoped to return next year. In the crowd was Chicago mayor Anton Cermak, who had made the trip to Miami hoping to mend fences with Roosevelt after delaying the delivery of Illinois delegates at the convention. He was also planning to appeal for federal money for Chicago teachers, who were owed months of back pay but had continued working, in some cases mortgaging their homes to stay in the classroom despite the city's inability to pay them. He approached the car and asked for a meeting. Roosevelt, who was leaving later in the day, agreed to see Cermak on the train before he left.

At that moment, a nine-year-old girl in the waiting crowd, Leona Merrill, noticed a small dark man fidgeting nervously on the park bench next to her. As she screamed, "That man has a gun!" he fired a .32 revolver at the presidential car, shouting, "Too many people are starving to death!" But the child had cried out just in time, and a woman jostled the shooter. He missed Roosevelt, but Cermak and four others were less lucky. "I'm all right! I'm all right!" Roosevelt called out quickly, assuring the crowd that he was safe, and had Cermak lifted into his car. A police escort brought it to Jackson Memorial Hospital as Roosevelt held the wounded mayor and comforted him.

The assailant was an out-of-work bricklayer named Giuseppe Zangara. He had no personal grudge against the president-elect; he was an angry, ailing, unemployed anarchist who was to say later, "I hate all officials and everybody who is rich." In the annals of speedy trials, his murder conviction must have set a record. Zangara was found guilty after Cermak died on March 6, two days after the presidential inauguration, and was executed in the electric chair at the Florida State Prison at Raiford on March 20.

Lulled by the three months of waiting following the election and numbed by the drumbeat of bad news, the nation shook itself awake at the assassination attempt. The inauguration was only three weeks away, and the United States had almost been robbed of its clear choice of leader. Emotions resurfaced now—the respect for Roosevelt's courage in fighting his way back from polio now renewed by his performance when literally under fire, as well as a realization of what the country had come close to losing.

But not everybody felt this way. Business moguls still believed dark hours lay ahead, when Roosevelt's radical "new deal" would come into being. And in the bunker-like atmosphere of the White House, his days there dwindling, Hoover clung to his conviction that a failure of public confidence was all that was wrong with the nation. Recovery was right around the corner if only people would believe it and act accordingly. He was still looking for that emblematic song, that poem, that joke that would inspire them to forget their troubles. So certain was he that the country could persuade itself out of the gloom of 25 percent unemployment that with only two weeks remaining in his term, he tried to induce Roosevelt to voice support for his economic policies. He handwrote a ten-page letter telling the president-elect he should "restore confidence and cause a resumption of the march of re-covery" by stating his rejection of inflationary programs, his support of a balanced budget at all costs, and his pledge to maintain the credit of the government. He sent similar suggestions to Republican senator Simeon D. Fess of Ohio, also recommending that Roosevelt should re-ject federally funded public works and government-backed mortgage insurance. And he warned Senator Reed of Pennsylvania in a third let-ter that unless Roosevelt embraced his policies and abandoned the promises of the "so-called new deal," "a complete financial debacle" would result.

It was bizarre even to imagine that the new president might accede to Hoover's program and repudiate his own. But Roosevelt did recog-nize that the fear consuming the nation was real, and he knew he had to address it. As he sat in his study at Hyde Park, drafting his inau-gural speech in pencil on a yellow legal pad, he sought words that would give Americans fresh courage and restore their belief in the country and its future. He felt the weight of history, and he strove to keep the speech close in length to the seven or so minutes of Abraham Lincoln's second inaugural address. That biblically infused speech, de-livered as the Civil War was in its final weeks, was almost literally a prayer, in which Lincoln fervently condemned slavery and prayed that the nation be reunited under "a just and lasting peace" with "malice toward none" and "charity for all." But Roosevelt, driven by the need to explain complex events, kept making additions to the draft until it stretched to almost fifteen minutes.

As he wrote, the bank panic continued to spread. The days leading to March 4 were as harrowing as any the country had experienced since the Civil War. By the end of February, Arkansas, Indiana, Maryland, and Ohio had declared bank holidays to halt the bank runs and another twenty states were considering the move. On March 1, the head of the Federal Reserve Bank of New York informed the Federal Reserve Board that its reserves of gold had fallen below the le-gal limit of 40 percent of the value of paper currency the bank had is-sued.

That day, Roosevelt and his party left Hyde Park and drove to New York City in an eight-car motorcade. Cheering crowds lined the streets of every town and village they passed through, and filled the sidewalks of New York on the route to his East 65th Street townhouse. Security was tight after the assassination attempt in Miami three weeks earlier. At around four the next afternoon, the door of the townhouse opened and Roosevelt and his wife emerged at the head of a party that descended to the street as police held back the throngs of onlookers. Minutes later, a motorcade of fifteen cars, followed by a luggage van, carried the Roosevelt party through Manhattan to the West Side Elevated Highway and downtown to a ferry slip at the end of Liberty Street. There, they boarded a ferry that took them across the Hudson to Jersey City, where a train was waiting to bring them to Washington.

They arrived that night and checked into the Mayflower Hotel. Flags in the capital were flying at half-staff for Senator Tom Walsh, the attorney general–designate, who had died aboard a train on his way to the inauguration, and Roosevelt named Homer S. Cummings of Connecticut, a trial lawyer and former chairman of the Democratic National Committee, to replace him.

Meanwhile, the newspapers were tracking the ever-spreading bank closings. California, Alabama, Oklahoma, and Louisiana declared bank holidays, and Mississippi limited withdrawals. Pressure was mounting on Hoover to close the banks nationwide. The departing president, however, would not act on his own. But even when New York declared a statewide banking holiday effective March 4, inauguration day, and Illinois, Massachusetts, New Jersey, and Pennsylvania followed suit, Roosevelt declined to join him. He wanted his actions to stand apart from Hoover.

3. ACTION AT LAST

A Hollywood director would have rejected the weather on inauguration day as overkill. Added to the dominant plot element—that the nation was careening into the abyss of fiscal disaster—a cold wind scythed out of the northwest and drove bursts of rain before it. Saturday, March 4, 1933, was as ugly in weather as in national outlook. Across the country, all twelve Federal Reserve banks were closed, and commercial banks in forty-three states either were closed, were limiting withdrawals, or had placed other restrictions upon normal banking. Even on his final day in the White House, Hoover had thrown himself into a flurry of work, still trying to gain acceptance of his program. Reporting on his last full day in office, the *New York Times* wrote, "That he leaves office reluctantly and with a feeling of not having had a fair opportunity is obvious."

Wrapped in overcoats and huddling under umbrellas, people began to fill the pine benches set up before the Capitol, where the inauguration would take place. One hundred thousand spectators crowded into the sodden forty-acre tract to witness the transfer of power. Others shivered in bleachers on the roof of the Capitol portico. Four hundred thousand more lined Pennsylvania Avenue between the White House and the Capitol. Many spectators climbed up into trees and

onto rooftops, and some stood in the open fronts of the partially demolished buildings where the Bonus Army had camped the previous
summer. Bunting hung from the lampposts, and Roosevelt's image
smiled from posters mounted in store windows. But the mood was
grave, reflective rather than jubilant, as if the great crowds recognized
that the nation stood at a crossroads. Machine gun cages guarded the
corners of the Capitol, and policemen and soldiers stood watchfully
along the avenue.

The open presidential limousine set out from the White House a
little before noon. The atmosphere within the car was strained. Hoover
had not been gracious about relinquishing the reins of government,
nor about the customary protocols. He was packing his bags the day
before when his friend Leland W. Cutler, a fellow Stanford graduate
who was then president of the San Francisco Chamber of Commerce
and lobbying for money to build a bridge across San Francisco Bay,
dropped by the White House. Hoover asked if he was staying over for
the inaugural festivities, and Cutler replied that a Democratic inauguration was not his idea of a festivity. "Nor mine," said Hoover, and in
that vein, he had chosen not to invite the Roosevelts for the traditional
inaugural eve dinner. They had come for tea instead, and even then he
had tried to persuade his successor to join him in a statement about the
banking crisis. Roosevelt again declined, and the meeting had ended
badly, with Hoover haughtily dismissing the normal courtesies of the
transition. The tension lingered even now, as the car made its way
along Pennsylvania Avenue toward the Capitol, the two men seated
side by side in the back.

Hoover stared straight ahead, ignoring the applauding crowds and
Roosevelt's efforts to make conversation. At first the president-elect
followed his lead in not responding to the crowds, but it must finally
have seemed foolish not to acknowledge the applause, so Roosevelt
began to smile at last and waved his top hat as they passed along the
avenue.

At the Capitol, he waited in a committee room while John Nance
Garner took the vice presidential oath in the Senate chamber. Then
those in attendance moved from the chamber to the inaugural stand
outside and a bugle call announced the beginning of the ceremony.
Roosevelt, bareheaded and without an overcoat, walked to the
podium on the arm of his son James. He raised his right hand, placed

his left on the old Dutch family Bible open to the thirteenth chapter of 1 Corinthians—"And now abideth faith, hope, charity, these three; but the greatest of these is charity"—and repeated the oath of office after Supreme Court chief justice Charles Evans Hughes. Then he turned to the crowd, gripped the podium, and began to speak, his first words invoking an almost religious urgency: "This is a day of national consecration."

As the new president continued, the sun found openings in the clouds and threw shafts of light on the spectators. The words he had chosen with such care were eloquent, and they resonated with people hungry for hope. "This is preeminently the time to speak the truth, the whole truth, frankly and boldly," he said. "This great Nation will endure as it has endured, will revive and will prosper. So, first of all, let me assert my firm belief that the only thing we have to fear is fear itself—nameless, unreasoning, unjustified terror which paralyzes needed efforts to convert retreat into advance."

With that, Roosevelt began to spell out his vision for America. He scorned "the unscrupulous money changers" for their "false leadership" and lack of vision while "a host of unemployed citizens face the grim problem of existence, and an equally great number toil with little return." He spoke of rebalancing the scales, returning ethics and unselfishness to business, and embracing anew "social values more noble than mere monetary profit." Among those values, he asserted, was "the joy and moral stimulation of work," which "no longer must be forgotten in the mad chase of evanescent profits." Providing work lay at the center of his plan. "This nation asks for action, and action now," he said. "Our greatest primary task is to put people to work. This is no unsolvable problem if we face it wisely and courageously. It can be accomplished in part by direct recruiting by the government itself, treating the task as we would treat the emergency of a war, but at the same time...accomplishing greatly needed projects to stimulate and reorganize the use of our natural resources."

He provided few details, but that hardly mattered. Reassurance was the key, and reassurance lay in his words and the sound of his voice. Across the nation, everywhere there was a radio, Americans listened. They gathered by the tens of millions on the farms and in the cities, around stoves in country stores, in the kitchens of apartments where the rent was overdue and in homes threatened by foreclosure, in restaurants and hospitals and offices; and in the combative thrust of Roosevelt's Jacksonian address they found glimmerings of the hope they so sorely needed.

"The people of the United States have not failed," he reminded them as he drew toward the end. "In their need they have registered a mandate that they want direct, vigorous action. They have asked for discipline and direction under leadership. They have made me the present instrument of their wishes. In the spirit of the gift I take it."

If the people wanted action now, action is what they got. As the president and first lady led the inaugural parade back along Pennsylvania Avenue to the White House and emerged after a quick lunch to view it from an open reviewing stand, during the three hours it took the 18,000 marchers to pass before them, his aides were finalizing a pair of proclamations. One put a national banking holiday into effect on Monday, the first business day after the inauguration, and halted gold and silver exports and foreign exchange transactions. The other called an emergency session of the Congress for the Thursday that followed. He signed them both on Sunday afternoon.

The start of the new workweek was like nothing the country had experienced. With the banks closed, Washington didn't know what to do with out-of-towners who had come to the inauguration and now wanted to go home. Hotel cashiers refused out-of-town checks, and guests who wired home for money could get, at most, $100. Merchants across the country devised strategies to cope with the cash shortage. Some sent runners armed with $20 bills to make small purchases at other stores and collect the change, until those stores caught on and sent runners of their own. Others turned to barter. At the Golden Glove boxing matches in Madison Square Garden, the sponsoring New York *Daily News* accepted anything worth the 50 cent admission fee, including food, clothes, books, and tools. By the night of Thursday, March 9, hours after it convened, the brand-new Congress had passed and the president had signed emergency banking legislation. To those depositors who had withdrawn gold or gold certificates, the Federal Reserve Board offered a grace period to redeposit what they had taken out. After that, said the board, the hoarders' names would be released.

At ten o'clock on the night of March 12, eight days after his inauguration, Roosevelt sat before a microphone as a young radio reporter named Robert Trout, with the Washington CBS affiliate WJSV, prepared to introduce him. Trout had worked up two openings with his manager, an Iowan named Harry Butcher. The president had liked the more folksy of the two, and thus Trout entered radio history, launching not only an enduring term but a new twist in political communication, the use of the airwaves to bypass hostile newspapers and speak directly to the people. "The president," he said, "wants to come into your home and sit beside your fireplace for a little fireside chat."

Roosevelt spoke for fourteen minutes, explaining the banking system, his actions in dealing with the bank closures, and the phased reopenings that would follow. He spoke in clear and simple terms; as Will Rogers wrote, the president had "stepped to the microphone... and knocked another home run," taking a dry subject and making "everybody understand it, even the bankers." He closed by asking the people to overcome their doubts. "Confidence and courage are the essentials of success in carrying out our plan," he said. "You people must have faith; you must not be stampeded by rumors and guesses. Let us unite in banishing fear. We have provided this machinery to restore our financial system, and it is up to you to make it work. It is your problem, my friends, your problem no less than it is mine. Together we cannot fail."

The banks started reopening on Monday, March 13, and, as if people had been waiting for this signal from their president, money started flowing in again.

4. WINDS OF CHANGE

Official Washington itself had changed in those few days. Within the White House, where Hoover had ignored the servants and kept attendants standing at motionless attention while he ate his meals, a new atmosphere prevailed. The gloom and stiffness had been swept away; now the place vibrated with energy and informality and a sense of purpose. Government offices and the Capitol, accustomed to dreary recitations of reasons why things could not change, were already filling up with decisive young lawyers and academics. Many of them were available only because the depression had shrunk private opportunities in their professions, and they carried the message that change was not only possible but mandatory. Reporters who were used to rebuff and to printed statements found themselves ushered into the Oval Office and invited to ask questions.

Roosevelt had intended to dismiss the Congress from its special session once the banking legislation was enacted. But with the majority Democrats clearly in a mood to act and his advisors urging him to take advantage of their eagerness, he decided to push forward on all fronts. The government was no longer sitting on its hands.

His first target was Prohibition. Since 1919, when the states ratified the Eighteenth Amendment to the Constitution prohibiting the manufacture, transportation, and sale of alcoholic beverages and the Volstead Act set up provisions for enforcement, much of the country had played a charade of temperance. Fifteen thousand legal pubs and saloons in New York City had closed, to be replaced by more than double that number of illegal speakeasies. Congress had its own bootlegger in the person of George L. Cassidy, known as the "Man in the Green Hat," who bragged that he had the keys to more Capitol Hill desks and offices than anyone in history. Rumrunners crossed the borders from Canada to the United States by land and sea, moonshiners flourished in the hills of Appalachia, and organized-crime gangs fought for pieces of the illegal liquor market, resulting in some 500 gangland murders in Chicago alone. The lame duck Congress had passed the Twenty-first Amendment, repealing the Eighteenth, before Roosevelt took office, but while it awaited ratification by the states he decided to ease the national thirst. He proposed amending the Volstead Act to legalize beer and wine with an alcohol content of 3.2 percent, and Congress passed the measure easily. It also passed reductions in veterans' pensions and federal and congressional salaries that were aimed at cutting the budget by half a billion dollars, an economy measure on which the president would soon reverse himself.

Americans were drinking publicly again on April 7, albeit beverages that were officially "non-intoxicating." By then, barely a month into his presidency, Roosevelt had placed before the Congress a wide array of legislation designed to attack the farmers' woes, regulate Wall Street's issuance of new securities, create an army of young men to improve the national parks and forests, and spend $500 million to meet human needs through the creation of a new position, that of federal relief administrator—all intended to ease the worst effects of the depression. In process were other far-reaching proposals: to bring electricity to a large part of the rural South through a series of hydroelectric dams in the Tennessee River valley; provide mortgage protection for small homeowners; separate commercial from investment banking and insure private savings accounts; take the country off the gold standard; stabilize the economy, especially industrial production, through planning; and create a huge program of public works. This great surge of lawmaking, to be famously known as the "Hundred Days," symbolized the new administration's activism and its willingness to experiment.

Of all the problems these proposals were intended to address, the farm problem was perhaps the worst. Anger in the farm belt continued to grow, and the lynch mob sentiments stirred by foreclosures were getting worse. Farmers in Le Mars, Iowa, dragged a judge from his courtroom when he refused to halt foreclosure proceedings, tied a noose around his neck, and crowned him with a greasy hubcap before they left him praying in a roadside ditch. After farmers in Denison, Iowa, attacked deputies and foreclosure agents at a farm sale, Governor Clyde L. Herring declared martial law in six counties and armed National Guard troops moved in. Sheriff's deputies in White Cloud, Michigan, had to resort to tear gas to scatter 400 farmers gathered to protest a foreclosure sale at the Newaygo County courthouse.

And these were people who still had the vigor to protest. Many of the ragged jobless workers in cities and small towns, the wandering homeless, and the denizens of the nation's many Hoovervilles had been crushed to apathy by their bleak prospects. Millions of people had not only no money but no food, clothing, or shelter, and the situation was growing more desperate by the day. On average, families who were on relief were getting only 50 cents a day, far too little to put together a subsistence diet. Still worse, the greatest need existed in the poorest states. In some states, four people in ten were on relief, and there were counties in which relief families constituted 90 percent of the population. The existing relief system had already proven its inadequacy. Now it was crumbling under the weight of need.

Members of Congress and his own advisors had urged Roosevelt to rescue the system with a federal appropriation. But none of these entreaties offered a structure to go with it and neither, when he took office, did the president. He lacked a design that would unify the scattered existing relief efforts, varying from state to state, into a single central agency that could put the money where the need was. That changed midway through his second week in office, and the plan laid out before him must have been familiar, for it was modeled after the state relief agency set up in New York when he was governor. The architect of both was a transplanted Iowan named Harry Lloyd Hopkins.

5. THE PASSION OF HARRY HOPKINS

E ven in a town newly populated by go-getters, Hopkins stood out. Forty-two years old, lanky and slumped, with large, bright brown eyes animating a thin, almost concave face, he disdained the normal courtesies of politics and cared not a whit about the trappings of bureaucracy or status. His singular talent was for creating organizations on the fly, organizations free of complicated charts and tangles of responsibility. He worked to exhaustion and inspired others to do the same. And he believed with a fiery passion in the rights of the poor to decent treatment, rights that he expounded with sharp-tongued, impatient wit.

He had been poor himself, though not deprived. His father, David Aldona Hopkins, was a Sioux City harness maker when Harry was born in August 1890. When the harness shop failed two years later, Al Hopkins moved his wife, Anna, and four children, of whom Harry was the youngest, to Chicago, where he worked as a traveling salesman for a Milwaukee harness maker. In 1901, after the birth of a fifth child—there were now one daughter and four sons—the family returned to Iowa and settled in Grinnell, which Anna chose because of the college there. She was a sober and religious woman, active in Methodist church work that focused on helping the less fortunate. Al

Hopkins, on the other hand, was a free spirit who indulged himself in luxuries and entertainments during his sales trips around the Midwest; good times were had when Al Hopkins was in town. In 1910, an accident settlement allowed him to stop traveling. He set up a new harness shop in Grinnell, became active in civic affairs, and pursued a passion for bowling, which also gave him an income in side bets. This was something he couldn't talk about at home; Anna forbade it, and once Al had to sneak into the basement with Harry to show him $500 in bowling alley winnings. He also enjoyed taking self-important people down a peg; this and his taste for the good life were his chief legacies to his son.

Grinnell College solidified the egalitarian instincts Hopkins had learned from both his parents. The school, founded by Congregational ministers in 1846, was a fountain of Social Gospel Christianity, which taught that the greatest sin was selfishness. When he graduated from Grinnell in 1912, Hopkins left for New York to begin a career in social work. He had a job with Christodora House, one of the city's settlement houses that ran various social, relief, and job placement programs, and he spent that summer in New Jersey overseeing a youth program. Then he hit New York. By night, he joined a claque of opera fans who traded their loud applause for free seats, and also guided out-of-town friends on tours of the city's racy neighborhoods. By day, he got serious. As a "district visitor" at Christodora House, he went to the homes of poor people to assess their worthiness for aid. In the squalid tenements and teeming streets within his Lower East Side territory, the same neighborhoods that had produced Al Smith, Hopkins found a level of poverty he had never known existed. Over time, his understanding deepened. He began to bristle when he heard the jobless referred to as malingerers; obviously some were, but far more craved the opportunity to work. He also realized that forcing people to reveal just how poor they were in order to qualify for aid abused their dignity. He developed a low tolerance for the assumptions many people made about the poor, the conditions in which they lived, and the ways society treated them.

Bright, committed, and in a hurry, Hopkins moved quickly. He left Christodora House after nine months to work for the Association for Improving the Condition of the Poor (AICP), New York City's oldest social welfare agency. The AICP administered a wide range of programs, and in less than three years Hopkins moved from its employment bureau to relief supervisor for the Lower East Side to supervisor of the agency's Fresh Air Hospital, a tuberculosis clinic. In 1915, New York's Progressive mayor, John Purroy Mitchel, appointed Hopkins's boss at the AICP, John A. Kingsbury, to be commissioner of public charities. Kingsbury brought Hopkins into city government as executive secretary of the new Board of Child Welfare, and there, still in his twenties, he built from scratch an effective organization to deliver relief to mothers with dependent children.

When Tammany Hall ousted Mitchel two years later, Hopkins left the city to work for the Red Cross. During five years there, he headed disaster relief in the middle Gulf states, and then civilian relief focused on the families of men serving in the world war. He worked long hours and gained a reputation both for delivering relief and for inspiring those under him. By the time he was thirty, he was heading the relief program in the Red Cross's ten-state southern division. In 1922, he returned to New York, and the next year was appointed director of the New York Tuberculosis and Health Association. In the meantime he helped found the American Association of Social Workers and served as its president. And when the depression hit and began to take its toll on jobs in New York City, he volunteered his free time to help his friend Bill Matthews, with whom he had worked at the AICP, try to find jobs for the unemployed through the city's Emergency Work Bureau.

During this time another of Hopkins's characteristics came to the fore: he outspent his income. He earned $10,000 a year, a handsome salary at a time when most Americans were making less than a third of that, but he maintained a suburban home and a summer cabin in the Catskills for his family, booked first-class hotels and train compartments when he traveled, ate and entertained his friends at expensive restaurants and speakeasies, and was beginning to indulge an interest in collecting rare books. His first marriage, to a social worker he had met at Christodora House named Ethel Gross, began to fall apart from both financial strain and a new romance, this with a secretary at the Tuberculosis and Health Association named Barbara Duncan. After fitful efforts to patch up his marriage, he and Ethel divorced in May 1931, with Ethel receiving custody of their three sons, and he married Barbara a month later.

That August, Governor Roosevelt called a special session of the New York legislature to address the effects the depression was having in the state. "Our government is not the master but the creature of the people," he told the legislators. "The duty of the state toward its citizens is the duty of the servant to its master. One of these duties of the state is that of caring for those of its citizens who find themselves the victims of such adverse circumstance as makes them unable to obtain even the necessities for mere existence without the aid of others. To these unfortunate citizens aid must be extended by government—not as a matter of charity but as a social duty." A month later, the legislature appropriated $20 million for unemployment relief in the form of grants to local governments. The money came from doubling the state income tax. Jesse Isidor Straus, president of the R. H. Macy department stores, headed a three-member board overseeing the organization set up to administer the relief funds, and he persuaded the Tuberculosis Association to give Hopkins a leave of absence to get the program under way as its executive director. Hopkins started work on October 8, 1931, and by November 1, New York's Temporary Emergency Relief Administration (TERA) was up and running.

From the start, he demonstrated a capacity for which he later would be famous: he was extraordinarily efficient at spending public money. By the end of January 1932, 1.2 million New Yorkers, nearly 10 percent of the state's population, were receiving TERA aid. Its funds were gone by the end of the winter, and Roosevelt had gone back to the legislature for another $20 million to carry the program until November, when a $30 million bond issue for further funding would be on the ballot.

The agency was divided into two components. One, the Home Relief Bureau, oversaw direct relief in the form of chits for immediate needs, from food, clothing, and heating fuel to rent and medical care. Recipients submitted their chits to doctors and landlords, brought them to local retail stores and took away the goods, or turned them in at relief commissaries for surplus foodstuffs or donated clothing. The other component, the Emergency Work Bureau, envisioned creating jobs for employable but jobless workers.

Hopkins much preferred work to direct relief. It cost more; the pay had to approach prevailing local wage rates, and except for make-work jobs such as raking leaves, there were added costs for equipment and materials. But all of his experience had shown him that most people would rather work than take handouts. A paycheck from work didn't feel like charity, with the shame that it conferred. It was better still if the work actually built something. Then workers could retain their old skills or develop new ones, and add improvements to the public infrastructure like roads and parks and playgrounds.

By March 1932, Hopkins had managed to put 80,000 people into jobs. Straus resigned as head of the TERA board the same month, and in April the governor appointed Hopkins to replace him while continuing to run the agency itself. That summer, Hopkins reported to the legislature that after nine months of operation, TERA's work program had "prevented the starvation of 130,000 families" and "produced many lasting improvements." Eighty-five cents of every dollar had gone for wages, with the rest for materials and maintenance. He said he needed another $11.5 million to carry the program into the fall, speaking of the "renewed morale many of [the unemployed] have felt in earning bread and butter for themselves and their children."

Road construction accounted for 40 percent of TERA's work relief spending, but men had also worked on sanitation and water supply systems, parks and playgrounds, utilities, schools and other public buildings, and general public improvements. Hopkins had also put clerical and professional workers and teachers into TERA jobs, and a number of these workers were women who were heads of households. And when he learned that members of the artists' colony at Woodstock were in danger of starving, he stretched the limits of TERA to create an arts program. In the same November balloting that elected Roosevelt president, New Yorkers approved the issuance of $30 million in TERA bonds by a four-to-one margin, allowing a further expansion of the work program.

All of these experiences formed components of the relief plan Hopkins took to Washington after the inauguration. He was becoming a familiar face in the capital by then, having first shown up just after the election to lobby for an RFC loan for New York. After the first of the year, members of Congress, anticipating federal relief, had sought his expertise as the head of the first, and largest, state relief program. In staff conferences and committee testimony, he had urged a federal appropriation of up to $1 billion to give grants, not loans, to states. (He had proposed something similar to Roosevelt in a letter he

had written back in December.) There was of course no chance
Hoover would sign such a measure even if it passed, but Hopkins was
helping to lay the foundation for quick action after the transition.

The new administration was in its second week when Hopkins arrived on a train from New York on March 13. With him was William
Hodson, head of the New York City Welfare Council. The two men
had brought a relief plan on which they had collaborated and then refined during the three-hour train ride, with the intention of placing it
before the president when they got to Washington. But Roosevelt was
too busy to see them, so they sought out fellow New Yorker Frances
Perkins, the new secretary of labor.

The three met at the Women's University Club. Hopkins and
Hodson told Perkins that the widespread poverty caused by unemployment was brewing revolution; the government had to intervene.
Federal money should be granted to the states, and the grants should
be managed by a single agency, acting on an emergency basis, that was
charged with the dual role of parceling out direct relief and creating
jobs. These were the main points Hopkins had made in his December
letter to Roosevelt.

Perkins was impressed by the precision of the facts and figures laid
before her. Here were both a grasp of the problem and a seemingly
workable plan. She got them in to see the president, and as Hopkins
and Hodson laid out their ideas in the White House, Roosevelt saw
how the relief program he had championed in his home state could be
expanded nationally. It gave shape to the vague calls for federal relief
and was a plan that he could call his own.

Just one week later, on March 21, the president sent the plan for
federal relief to Congress. It asked to place $500 million in unspent
Reconstruction Finance Corporation funds in the hands of a federal
relief administrator, who would head an agency to distribute the funds
among the states. The Senate approved the plan over Republican objections before the month was out, the House followed suit a few
weeks later, and the Federal Emergency Relief Act became law on May
12, 1933.

Roosevelt chose Hopkins as the relief administrator. The two had
not had a close relationship in Albany; they had conferred perhaps a
dozen times, by telephone more often than in person, but the agency
had been successful, it had given Roosevelt no headaches, and he knew

Hopkins was fast and energetic and bursting with ideas, all invaluable criteria for dealing with the national crisis. He called Hopkins to offer him the job on Friday, May 19. Hopkins's secretary noted in his datebook, "Received telephone call from President Roosevelt requesting Mr. Hopkins to come down to Washington—on a temporary basis— to organize the Federal Relief Administration."

Hopkins was eager to accept, but first the president had to wrest him from New York, which took some sleight of hand. "Very difficult to find a man fitted for this special work and felt Hopkins could get away for a month or two without interfering your state program," Roosevelt telegraphed Herbert H. Lehman, his successor as governor. He had also to contend with a rich offer from Jesse Straus, who was trying to lure Hopkins to Macy's. Both the state and Macy's jobs paid more than the $8,000 federal relief administrator's salary—in Straus's case the offer was $25,000, and Hopkins needed money, since half his salary went to child support. But his social conscience was not susceptible to money, and he knew the federal relief job would let him apply on a grand scale the lessons he had learned at TERA. He accepted the job, taking an almost 50 percent cut from his $15,000 state salary, the minute Lehman agreed to let him go. The Senate confirmed his appointment the next day and his datebook closed out his New York career. "Took train to Washington on Sunday," he wrote.

6. "MONEY FLIES"

Hopkins started work the next day, Monday, May 22. Space had been cleared in one of the RFC offices for the new relief operation, but before heading there he dropped by the White House at Roosevelt's request. Behind the invitation lay the president's concern that while his new relief administrator knew as well as anybody in the country how to put the necessities of life into hands that needed them, he knew less well, if at all, the demands that were about to descend on him for jobs and patronage. He wanted to brief Hopkins about the realities of political pressure and to reassure him that he could ignore politicians who wanted to swap jobs for votes or campaign support. The meeting lasted only about five minutes. Roosevelt said that relief had to be immediate, adequate, and dispensed without regard for politics, and that Hopkins was never to "ask whether a person needing relief is a Republican, Democrat, Socialist or anything else."

Hopkins was pleased to have an ally in the president, whose directives reflected his own views. He objected on principle to the mutual backscratching that was the norm in politics, and he also knew that political interference would make it harder to build the decentralized, professionally run relief structure he envisioned.

Minutes after leaving the White House, he reached 1734 New York Avenue and the Walker-Johnson Building, situated between the Corcoran Gallery and the Washington Girl Scouts' Little House, as the organization called its local meeting places. The place seemed appropriate to the needs of a relief agency, given its exposed steam pipes and an odor of poverty that to one visitor smelled like "a combination of hospital, locker room and stable." There was also a cockroach problem, so it smelled of insecticide as well. At his tenth-floor office, no polished mahogany desk or other symbols of a grand bureaucracy awaited him. In fact, the office lacked any desk at all; it was still in the hall outside, together with chairs and cabinets, waiting for workmen to move it in. Without waiting for them, he pulled a chair up to the desk, sat down amid the scattered furniture, and composed a telegram to be fired off to the governors of all forty-eight states. Washington would henceforth be paying attention to their needs, he told them, and he instructed them to set up organizations for administering relief. Once the telegrams were dispatched, he started to throw together the beginnings of a staff. He drank coffee, chain-smoked Lucky Strikes, and moved through his duties like a sheriff in a Tom Mix western, leaving swirls of smoke to mark his progress. Before that first day was over, he had reviewed requests for RFC loans and under the aegis of the new agency, the Federal Emergency Relief Administration, or FERA in the rapidly evolving alphabet soup of the New Deal, issued $5,336,317 in grants to eight states: Colorado, Georgia, Illinois, Iowa, Michigan, Mississippi, Ohio, and Texas.

Hopkins's swift, almost hungry grasp of his new position stunned a capital still getting over the inaction of the Hoover years. "Money Flies" read the *Washington Post*'s headline the next morning. The story under it predicted that the half-billion-dollar relief appropriation "won't last a month if Harry L. Hopkins, relief administrator, maintains the pace he set yesterday in disbursing more than $5,000,000 during his first two hours in office."

"I'm not going to last six months here, so I'll do as I please," Hopkins retorted.

Assembling his staff, he chose his closest aides from among a lifetime of social work contacts. One of them was Frank Bane, the head of the American Public Welfare Association, which Bane had organized just two years earlier. The two men had met when they were doing Red

Cross relief work in Mississippi during the world war; they had stayed in touch, and Bane agreed to come to the Emergency Relief Administration as an unpaid consultant. As his chief deputy, Hopkins hired American Public Welfare Association fieldworker Aubrey Williams, an Alabaman who had grown up poor, fought in the world war, and stayed on in France to earn a doctorate at the University of Bordeaux. Alan Johnstone, a Harvard law school graduate, headed the South Carolina Relief Administration before he came to FERA as a field representative for the Southeast, and other aides included holdovers from the RFC's Emergency Relief Division and workers from the Community Chest and other private social agencies. But experience in social work was not a strict prerequisite. Jacob Baker, a former high school teacher, personnel and engineering consultant, and founder of the Vanguard Press, was hired to head the work division. Corrington Gill, with a degree in economics and statistics, had tracked hiring and unemployment data for Hoover's Federal Employment Stabilization Board before becoming a reporter and later business manager of the Washington Press Service. He visited Hopkins one day to offer his help, and Hopkins promptly hired him to compile the vast array of statistics on relief cases, unemployment, and other evidence of need he would use to guide the work of FERA. Thus, backgrounds varied; what mattered was that Hopkins's top staff all shared his commitment to federal relief and his capacity for crushingly long hours.

They were few in number. Hopkins rejected the bureaucratic tendency to multiply just as he spurned the corner office and the big desk. He wanted a handful of people he could trust, and he refused to shoehorn them into an organizational chart to satisfy other bureaucrats. "I don't want anybody around here to waste any time drawing boxes," he told inspectors from the Bureau of the Budget when they came to look at the way his agency was organized. During FERA's first year, he ran it with a Washington staff of 121 people whose combined salaries totaled $22,000 a month.

RFC transfers made up the bulk of FERA's field staff. Since they had already been working with state and local officials on loan requests, they gave Hopkins a quick way to prepare these governments to handle the flow of federal money to the poor. He divided the nation into ten districts and dispatched field representatives to introduce the new structure to state and local workers. Few states had highly evolved welfare organizations staffed with professional social workers. Most were outmoded agencies filled with political hacks whose attitudes echoed those of the Elizabethan poor laws: they believed they were serving lazy individuals who didn't deserve the charity they got. This was where Hopkins's impatience flared hottest, and when he encountered resistance to putting relief into the hands that needed it, he had the option, with Roosevelt's approval, of federalizing a state's relief structure and appointing his own administrators.

FERA's first charge was to drag families back from the edge of starvation, put clothes on their backs, and give them shelter. "In more places than could be believed," Hopkins wrote later, "families had been asked to live on two dollars a month."

Half of the $500 million relief appropriation was to be spent as matching funds, one federal dollar for every three state and local dollars spent on relief during the previous three months. Because some states and many cities had exhausted their resources, the other $250 million was for outright grants, but Hopkins also recognized that some states might say they were broke even if they weren't, so from the start he dispatched teams of public finance experts to scour their books for hidden funds. Despite such precautions, however, spending continued at the frantic pace suggested by his first hours on the job. By the end of June, he had parceled out $51 million in grants and matching funds to forty-five states, the District of Columbia, and the Territory of Hawaii, and family subsistence levels were rising toward an eventual $15 a month.

Those first federal dollars undoubtedly saved lives. But Hopkins wanted to move quickly from providing handouts to providing jobs. Logic and his own experience had given him strong feelings about this. The memories of more than twenty years earlier, when he was working for Christodora House, stayed with him. In one family in his caseload, a young boy was shot and killed while stealing milk to feed his sister. He had seen lines of people with their feet wrapped in rags shuffling their way along to receive their single daily meal of crude soup dipped out of a garbage can; entire families sickened by the damp, cold basements that were the only places they could afford to live in and from which they were cast out onto the street when they couldn't afford them any longer. Nonetheless, most people sought charity only as a last resort. In the soup lines and the dank basements, they were at least anonymous. Asking an agency for help was different; thus identified by name, they themselves were devalued.

It was as true now as when Hopkins had been a beginning social worker. The application offices run by local relief boards, which determined eligibility, lined the needy up in open rooms to confess their poverty to clerks who assumed they were lying. They could own nothing that had any value. Survival was parceled out in bits and pieces— food from a surplus commissary, chits for groceries from a store, donated clothes, a check given to the landlord, a bucket of coal for heat. The attitude of the time was that a person getting relief "must be made to feel his pauperism," wrote Hopkins in his account of his federal relief work, *Spending to Save*. "Every help which was given him was to be given in a way to intensify his sense of shame."

What was worse, it was a relief investigator's job to share what he found with the community. Relief boards reported to schoolteachers, clergy, public nurses, and any other group that might provide assistance to the poor. The poor had no secrets.

Hopkins hated the paternalism of telling people what they needed and the ignominy of exposing their plight. If people on relief got handouts, he preferred that it be straight cash, with no strings attached. That, at least, gave them the freedom to spend part of a relief check on beer and cigarettes if that was what they wanted; the human spirit suffered more from loss of choice than loss of vitamins. But the truth was Hopkins didn't like any form of direct relief at all. He wanted to give people jobs.

One federal work program—the Civilian Conservation Corps (CCC)—was already in place. This was the reforestation initiative Roosevelt had first spoken of in his speech accepting the Democratic nomination. He had proposed it to Congress on March 21, and it was approved so swiftly that the president signed it into law only ten days later. The CCC enlisted the cabinet departments of Agriculture, Labor, War, and the Interior in coordinating a greater range of jobs than he had originally envisioned. The young men Roosevelt was sending to work on federal lands would upgrade the national parks and forests, improve flood control, and fight soil erosion. They would live in military-style camps that would be administered by the army.

Not everyone embraced the CCC at first. The American Federation of Labor objected on grounds that the proposed $30 monthly pay was too low. Socialist Norman Thomas feared that placing young men in outdoor work camps was a step toward the kind of fascism that was beginning to emerge in Europe. Only a few short weeks had passed since the end of February, when a fire had destroyed the German Reichstag and given Adolf Hitler the opportunity to claim dictatorial powers and proclaim the Third Reich, and one component of his power was "Hitler Youth," bands of goosestepping teens who engaged in physical and military training. Roosevelt neutralized labor's objections by appointing a vice president of the machinists union, Robert Fechner, to head the program, and worries about an American version of Hitler Youth emerging from the CCC camps never took hold. The first enrollee, Henry Rich, was inducted on April 7, a week after the program was approved, and the first camp opened ten days later in the George Washington National Forest near Luray, Virginia. It was named Camp Roosevelt, in honor of the president.

The CCC was limited to unmarried men between eighteen and twenty-five from families on relief, and $25 of the $30 monthly pay they earned had to be sent home. As they assembled at the quasi-military camps, the men encountered conditions that soldiers have always complained about: the food was bad, or at least monotonous; sleep was impossible in the tents and prefabricated barracks, which were either stifling or too drafty; city men ganged up against their country cousins and vice versa.

But despite these gripes, the CCC was popular from the start. A sense of camaraderie emerged as men from Chicago, New York, and San Francisco got to know their counterparts from small towns, farms, and ranches. Many corpsmen from the cities had never been out of earshot of the rumble of trucks and trains or the clatter of horsecarts. They had never slept out of doors, swum in running streams, or seen beyond the city lights to the stars of the Milky Way splashed across the night sky. They discovered a different country and a different world as they built fire observation towers, cleared firebreaks, planted trees by the millions to halt erosion, thinned overgrown forests, stocked fish, cleaned up and improved historic battlefields, and built shelters, paths, and camping areas. Most of them put on weight and added muscle. All this, plus money in the pocket and in the paychecks the government sent home, overwhelmed any complaints.

The CCC shared its one conspicuous failure with the nation as a whole. While almost one enrollee in ten was black, a number reflecting their percentage of the population, black Americans had been harder hit by the depression and were thus underrepresented in the CCC as a percentage of the poor. And while the CCC tried at first to integrate camps outside the South, this effort gave way to complaints from the communities where camps were located and to the army's institutional racism. In 1935, Fechner would resegregate blacks into some 150 camps of their own and write Thomas L. Griffith, president of the National Association for the Advancement of Colored People, who had complained to Roosevelt, that because blacks did equal work in the same conditions as whites, "this segregation is not discrimination."

The CCC was barely a month old when over a thousand world war veterans, the remnants of the Bonus Expeditionary Force, returned to Washington to press their case with the new administration. For budgetary reasons, Roosevelt also opposed paying the bonuses immediately, but he gave the veterans a better welcome than Hoover had. Where Hoover had barricaded the White House, Roosevelt welcomed their leaders. Using his longtime political guru Louis Howe as an emissary, he provided them with tents, showers, and latrines at Fort Hunt, an abandoned army base across the Potomac River in Virginia. Army cooks manned a mess tent where three meals a day were served without charge, along with endless cups of coffee. Army doctors and dentists attended to medical and dental needs. A big tent was raised for meetings, and the navy band played for them. Eleanor Roosevelt went to visit them one muddy spring day, and they sang camp songs together. As one veteran said, "Hoover sent the army; Roosevelt sent his wife." When new arrivals swelled their numbers to 3,000, Roosevelt offered them jobs in the CCC. Twenty-six hundred accepted once it was clear the bonuses weren't going to be paid, and the rest took an offer of free rail transportation home.

Roosevelt's estimate of a million jobs, however, had been wildly optimistic. More than 100,000 of the "CCC boys" were in the woods by June, with additional men signing up every day. August would see 1,500 camps and upward of 300,000 enrollees, but that would hardly dent the ranks of 15 million unemployed. Far more jobs were needed, and the administration was pushing to create them, directly through public works and indirectly through an engineered business revival. In mid-May, the president had presented a monumental two-part piece of legislation that was now working its way through the Congress. One part, Title I, attacked the vicious industrial Darwinism that had glutted the market with goods, shut down plants, and killed jobs even as it turned factories into sweatshops with child labor, seventy-hour workweeks, and wages as low as 15 cents an hour. In its place, the administration proposed a version of economic planning. It would regulate production by forming industries into voluntary trade associations exempt from antitrust laws. These would follow preset production levels, and adopt common standards—called codes—for wages, hours, and working conditions, and a minimum age for workers. The codes had force as penal statutes, although a system of government sanctions was expected to enforce compliance.

With private industry thus stabilized and, it was hoped, expanding and adding jobs, a flood of federal money into public works would add fuel to the economy as well as help enforce the voluntary standards in private industry. Title II, the second part of the legislation, proposed borrowing $3.3 billion to put into dams, bridges, and other large-scale projects that would both provide jobs and enhance the country's infrastructure.

This legislation was called the National Industrial Recovery Act, and Congress passed it on June 13. Roosevelt signed it three days later, marking the end of the Hundred Days, the New Deal's first thunderous volley of change. Its fifteen major pieces of legislation brought new protections to homeowners, farmers, and investors, provided necessities of life to those without them, established the Tennessee Valley Authority (TVA) as the instrument that would electrify the rural South, created new work programs, and attempted to force restraint on the inhumane world of industrial and agricultural laissez-faire. It was a stunning record, and it sent a message of hope to many across the nation and consternation to a few.

7. THE DESIRE TO WORK

The hope for jobs, however, lay largely in the future. Through FERA, subsistence aid had begun to reach the starving, but except for the young CCC men planting trees and cutting firebreaks in the parks and forests, systematic efforts to create a large-scale work program had not yet begun to mesh. Title II of the National Industrial Recovery Act envisioned massive and ambitious public works. So did the TVA, which would build forty-seven dams in six states—all of Tennessee and parts of Kentucky, North Carolina, Georgia, Alabama, and Mississippi—to provide flood control, river navigation, and, most important, affordable electricity to a neglected region. These programs would eventually reshape the lives of millions, but in the short run they would provide no jobs.

Roosevelt wanted to short-circuit this delay, and he talked with Harry Hopkins about creating more jobs immediately under FERA. In mid-June, the White House assembled a conference of state officials, including eight governors, to explain the agency's policies and procedures. The president himself addressed the delegates, suggesting that they initiate practical projects such as road and street repair. It was important to put people to work quickly, said Roosevelt, but "there is no intention of using the public works funds to build a lot of useless projects disguised as relief. It is the purpose to encourage real public works."

Three days later, on June 17, Hopkins addressed the National Conference of Social Work meeting in Detroit. He predicted that "between now and October first at least two million men are going to be put to work" under his emergency relief appropriation. He also hinted that the jobs to be created would employ not just unskilled laborers, the first casualties of the depression, but professionals as well. "We are now dealing with people of all classes," he said. "It is no longer a matter of unemployables and chronic dependents, but of your friends and mine who are involved in this. Every one of us knows some family of our friends which is or should be getting relief. The whole picture comes closer to home than ever before."

Hopkins made an additional point as well. He said—and it was the first time any federal official said it—that the people's welfare was a direct federal obligation, that the government should provide relief without the artificial pretense of sending it through local governments and private charities. It was a pronouncement that would dictate welfare policy, for better or worse, for the next sixty years.

FERA's first projects were inherited. These were mostly temporary and haphazard jobs originally launched by state and local governments using Reconstruction Finance Corporation loans. They continued while FERA's Division of Research, Statistics, and Finance struggled to get a clear picture of the range of work needs; prior studies, such as the one done under Colonel Arthur Woods's direction while Hoover was still president, were badly out-of-date. Indeed, a truly comprehensive picture of poverty and joblessness in the United States had never been possible under the previous patchwork of local governments and charitable agencies. The picture that was now emerging showed unemployment in almost every job category, which to Hopkins and his aides at FERA meant an opportunity to attack a wide range of social needs.

"Here is the chance of a lifetime to do something about some of these things if we have any brains at all," he had said in Detroit. "I am for experimenting... trying out schemes which are supported by reasonable people and see if they work. If they do not work, the world will not come to an end."

There were, for example, vast numbers of teachers out of work, at the same time that there were still greater numbers of illiterate or semi-literate adults whose lack of education shut them off from jobs. Hopkins saw this as a prescription for adult education, a prescription whose final component fell into place because cash-strapped school districts, unable to offer full curriculums, had space to spare. As he wrote later in *Spending to Save,* "It might be all right to give groceries or cash relief to an unemployed textile worker, and let his former customer go without sheets. Sheets are private, and it is a matter of taste and nobody's business whether you use them or not." On the other hand, "to feed the school teacher and dispense with his services was not enough. With more leisure, there was a greater demand for education, both to while away the boredom, and to acquire and improve skills for a constantly more critical labor market."

Thus teachers became the first white-collar workers hired under FERA; indeed, the agency would eventually put tens of thousands of teachers to work. They primarily conducted classes for unemployed adults in literacy and general education, vocational education, and vocational rehabilitation—but they also made it possible to reopen nursery schools that had been closed for lack of funds.

Unemployed textile workers fit the same prescription, despite Hopkins's breezy—and utterly inconsistent—dismissal of their importance to consumers. Sheets may have been a matter of choice, but FERA's field reports confirmed that millions of families were literally living in rags, and many needed blankets and mattresses as well as clothing. Completing this equation were countless vacant storefronts and unused factory buildings. FERA began renting these spaces and setting up sewing operations, hiring workers who had been thrown out of textile jobs to cut, stitch, stuff, and sew. Commercial garment and bedclothes manufacturers objected that these relief goods would steal their markets, but Hopkins begged to differ. He argued that the families receiving goods produced by the sewing rooms could not afford to buy them, so nobody was losing any business; and as he pointed out, once the sewing room workers started getting paid, they might start buying clothes and sheets again.

But even an innovator such as Hopkins could not have imagined some of the work that FERA proposals led to. The central Louisiana town of Marksville applied for funds to build a park and a swimming pool on some city-owned land alongside the Old River. The project would employ more than a hundred laborers, and it was quickly approved. But Indian mounds on the park site had already attracted the attention of archaeologists from the Smithsonian Institution, who knew that remains of an early native American culture called the Hopewell had been excavated nearby. FERA workers were already digging the swimming pool when they turned up Hopewell artifacts, and local amateur archaeologists persuaded the town to switch the project to an archaeological dig. The Smithsonian's assistant curator of archaeology, Frank M. Setzler, arrived in Marksville in late August to supervise the revamped project. He and his assistant had worried that untrained laborers would destroy vital pieces of the early culture, but their fears were unrealized. The local diggers excavated the site just as well as trained workers could have done it, and as potsherds, stone knives, spear and arrow points, and pipes emerged from the mounds and the outlines of a native village became visible, the archaeologists found themselves with the rare luxury of workers to spare on a dig that covered several acres.

Both the projects FERA inherited and those it initiated under Hopkins eventually put some 2 million people to work, most in local road building and street repair. But as the summer of 1933 stretched into the fall, none of the new programs was creating enough jobs. The biggest laggard was the Public Works Administration (PWA), the agency designated to build large-scale public works under Title II of the National Industrial Recovery Act. Roosevelt had placed interior secretary Harold L. Ickes in charge of the PWA, and Ickes was moving slowly. One problem was the very size and nature of the projects the PWA was undertaking. Some of the blueprints anticipated structures that were clearly grand in scope and execution, such as the Triborough Bridge linking Manhattan, Queens, and the Bronx in New York City, or the bridge spanning San Francisco Bay that would connect Oakland and San Francisco. But others were multipurpose works whose combination of ambition and good intentions was meant to effect change on a much wider scale. The PWA was now responsible for the construction called for in the region-wide hydroelectric, flood control, and irrigation projects of the Interior Department's Bureau of Reclamation. One of these was the Colorado River Project. Its centerpiece, the huge Boulder Dam in a deep chasm of the Colorado in Nevada, had been started in 1931, but the plans called for more dams up and down the Colorado that would supply water and electricity to parched urban outposts such as Salt Lake City and Las Vegas, and also pipe irrigation water to farmers in California's Imperial Valley. The Grand Coulee Dam on the Columbia River at Spokane, Washington, would absorb $63 million in PWA funds; more than 500 feet high and 4,173 feet across the top, at the time the largest structure in the world, it would back up water 150 miles all the way to Canada. At almost four miles in length, Montana's Fort Peck Dam, costing $50 million, would be four times longer than any other earth dam in the world, and would back up the Missouri River into a 175-mile recreational lake while providing similar benefits of electricity, flood control, and water. By their nature, projects such as these, requiring elaborate and time-consuming preparations ranging from land purchases and site surveys to engineering, topographic studies, and sheafs of blueprints, took a long time to reach the construction stage, when at last they would put needed paychecks in the hands of workers.

But another problem was Ickes himself. Sixty years old, rotund, bespectacled, and affable-looking, he concealed within this avuncular exterior a vein of fretfulness and a host of prickly sensitivities that he recorded in a daily diary. He was intensely mindful of his role in the administration and his perception of how the president treated him. He was equally mindful of his stewardship of the $3.3 billion with which he had been entrusted. He was determined that the money be spent on substantial projects that would enhance the national wealth, and that corruption and graft would not intrude. This attention to the public trust had marked his career as a politically active lawyer dedicated to progressivism. It had earned him the nickname "Honest Harold," though this was a tag he didn't like nearly as much as another nickname, the "Old Curmudgeon," which did indeed suggest his personality. He signaled early on that he was likely to vet each project application personally to make sure it fit his standards for planning, engineering, and legal and financial soundness. This meant that applications backed up while Ickes went over the fine print.

A further complication lay in the fact that contractors would do the hiring for PWA projects and there was no requirement that they give preference to or even take workers on relief. And while simple labor certainly would be a component of each project, the skills inherent in these elaborate jobs meant that many of the first people hired for them were less likely to be on relief.

Yet another hope for reversing unemployment, albeit indirectly, lay in Title I, the other half of the National Industrial Recovery Act. This was the component that meant to bring work standards and production limits to industry, and within weeks of passage the act's governing arm, the National Recovery Administration (NRA), had become synonymous with the New Deal. Its head, General Hugh S. Johnson, was profane, hard-drinking, and inexhaustible, a retired army general who had run the purchasing arm of the War Industries Board during the world war. Also known as "Old Ironpants," Johnson had written the act and seen its two components as working hand in hand. He was furious when Roosevelt put Ickes in charge of public works, but he swallowed his anger and stayed on to run the NRA. Even without the PWA as part of his arsenal, he managed to command public opinion in favor of the NRA and to persuade associations representing 2 million employers to adopt the codes. Those who signed on displayed a logo symbolizing their participation. The blue eagle, topping a message of solidarity against the depression—"We Do Our Part"—vaulted into prominence during the summer of 1933.

As far as new jobs were concerned, however, the NRA ultimately proved to be a force for stabilization rather than expansion; it was designed to increase purchasing power among those already working. The idea was that the money they returned to the economy would lead to increased production and thus more jobs. At best, this would be a gradual process. Therefore, with neither private industry nor the PWA adding jobs fast enough, and winter on the way, some new job-creating engine had to be found if the millions on relief—and those who soon would be—were to make it through the winter.

8. THE BIRTH OF THE CIVIL WORKS
ADMINISTRATION

FERA continued to compile data revealing the sweep of unemployment idling laborers, skilled-trades workers, and professionals. Harry Hopkins, looking at their full range of talents, could imagine "a stupendous and varied work program." And as he looked at the approaching winter, the more he believed such a program had to be put together quickly.

Roosevelt shared his dismay at the slow pace of jobs growth, but unlike Hopkins, the president had politics to think about. He wanted to keep peace with organized labor, and he needed a sign that the unions would support a new federal jobs program. So Hopkins bided his time while he looked for a means of persuasion. Late in October, he boarded a train for a football weekend in Chicago and lunch with University of Chicago president Robert Hutchins. Frank Bane and Louis Brownlow, director of the Public Administration Clearing House, who like Bane was serving Hopkins as an unofficial and unpaid advisor, met him on arrival. As they drove him to his appointment, they laid out statistics that argued for a jobs program aimed strictly at unemployed workers on relief. The figures were persuasive and gave Hopkins new selling points, but they did not give him the labor endorsement that the president required.

His next destination was Kansas City, Missouri, where he was booked to speak at a conference. His contacts there included Judge Harry S Truman, the federal reemployment director for Missouri, who also told Hopkins more job projects were needed. It was when he was in Kansas City that he received an excited call from Aubrey Williams, who was overseeing FERA's relations with the states. Williams said he had spoken with labor expert John R. Commons in Madison, Wisconsin, and Commons had told him that back in 1898, American Federation of Labor founder Samuel Gompers had recommended a government work program for the unemployed. Commons had reported this in the union magazine, the *Federationist*, and it was just what Hopkins needed to sell his plan to Roosevelt.

Hopkins saw the president over lunch the day he returned to Washington, and pressed his case. He said he could create 4 million jobs if he had the money to do it. Roosevelt mused that with Ickes moving so slowly, the PWA's $3.3 billion remained largely unspent. Maybe Hopkins could use some of that money to help the unemployed through one more winter.

Five years earlier, during a visit to England, Hopkins had found himself at the house where poet John Keats had written "Ode to a Nightingale." A Keats enthusiast, he wrote home that in recalling the experience, "I fairly walk on air." Now, leaving the White House, he had the same exhilarated feeling. Roosevelt had promised to take $400 million from Ickes's PWA to allow him to build a short-term jobs program, and the president hinted at the new program in a press conference the next day, November 3. "There is a great deal to be said for it.... It adds to the self-respect of the country," he said. He stopped short of committing himself publicly, but Hopkins read between the lines. When an aide asked if Roosevelt had approved his proposal, he replied, "Approved it, hell—he has just announced it at his press conference."

Hopkins hurriedly brought his staff together to begin mapping out the details. Working through the night in sessions at downtown Washington's Hotel Powhatan, Hopkins, Williams, Baker, Bane, and others sketched out their thoughts and refined them, and in two days' time sent a plan to Roosevelt for a temporary jobs agency that would last through the deepest part of winter.

Ickes learned about the raid on his budget on November 6, when the president sent Hopkins and others to meet with him to work out the $400 million transfer. The normally fretful Ickes raised no objections. He, too, thought the need for jobs was critical, and he saw Hopkins's plans as a pale and puny imitation of what real public works were all about. "It will put up no buildings. It won't build any sewers or water works or incinerators or bridges," he wrote in his diary, so the new agency's projects would be "of a minor character." Nevertheless, he attempted to rope off big projects for himself, sending out a decree that no project sponsor could withdraw its application for Public Works Administration funds in the hope of getting the same work done by the new agency without having to put up matching money. If it did so and failed to win approval, that sponsor could not resubmit its plans to the PWA.

On November 9, 1933, less than two weeks after Hopkins's Chicago visit and exactly a week after the lunch at which Hopkins had presented him with the idea, Roosevelt signed an executive order using Title II of the National Industrial Recovery Act to create the Civil Works Administration (CWA). He announced the program the same day, and jobless workers saw their prospects brighten beyond what FERA had been able to provide—if only for a time.

9. FOUR MILLION JOBS

Hopkins had high ambitions for the CWA, which he signaled right away. The United States had mobilized 4.7 million soldiers, sailors, and marines to fight in the world war. Summoning governors and mayors to a November 15 conference in Washington, he told them he intended to employ almost that many—4 million—within one month. Immediately, they started jostling for a share of the goodies. From coast to coast, in towns and cities crumbling from neglect, with thousands upon thousands of jobless families on relief, officials looked at their public buildings, playgrounds, streets, and—Ickes's expectations notwithstanding—sewers and called back engineers they had laid off for lack of funds to start drawing up improvement plans. In farm states, officials mapped rural road improvements as a source of jobs for idle farmers. The planners moved quickly. In Massachusetts, when the state's CWA coordinator called a meeting to explain what projects would be eligible, the mayors of Worcester and Lowell walked in carrying already completed applications, and left the same day with approvals.

By now Hopkins and Ickes had developed a clear rivalry, although it was still in its mild stages. Hopkins was impatient with Ickes's careful style, while Ickes took Hopkins to be impetuous. Hopkins knew that Ickes dismissed the projects under his control as insubstantial and was determined to change that, to make them more than the works "of minor character" that Ickes had forecast in his diary. To ensure that they would have lasting value, he created an engineering division charged with helping develop project applications and shepherding through to completion the projects that were funded. Its head was John Michael Carmody, a former president of the Society of American Engineers, who had his pick of experienced supervisors to oversee state and local projects since it was estimated that half the country's engineers were out of work.

CWA reviewers processed applications with astonishing speed. Indiana, for example, had 122 projects approved on November 20 and 109 more the next day. Less than a week later, on November 26, 920 projects had been approved for Indiana and 48,500 men were already at work there.

Half the workers came from FERA's work relief rolls, which at the time numbered about 1.9 million. The remainder were new hires, who clamored for CWA jobs in part because they needed them, but also because Hopkins had rejected means tests, so people applying did not have to prove how poor they were in order to be eligible. From the beginning there were more applicants than jobs. CWA offices in North Carolina took 150,000 applications during the first week. In Chicago, 70,000 appeared on a single day. Within two weeks of the program's beginning, about 1 million workers were on the payroll, and the Bureau of Printing and Engraving had to work three shifts just to print their checks. To distribute them, Hopkins commandeered the disbursement system of the Veterans Administration, which was the largest such system in the nation. More than 800,000 workers received checks on the CWA's first payday, November 23.

Still, despite the rapid pace of hiring, Hopkins missed his initial target; CWA workers in mid-December numbered just over 2.6 million. Nonetheless, with Christmas approaching in a winter that would prove to be one of the worst in memory, hundreds of thousands of families suddenly had the means to fill their larders and put something under the tree. Moreover, field reports testified to the program's popularity. Lorena Hickok, a former Associated Press reporter and a close friend of Eleanor Roosevelt, was one of sixteen field investigators dispatched by Hopkins under FERA to file no-holds-barred reports on conditions around the country. "Go out around the country and look this thing over," he told her. "Tell me what you see and hear. All of it. Don't ever pull your punches." Among those reporting were the young Martha Gellhorn, who would go on to cover the Spanish Civil War and briefly marry Ernest Hemingway, and Lincoln Colcord, who had been born on his father's schooner rounding Cape Horn and, with his sister, spent most of his youth at sea before becoming a poet, journalist, and maritime historian. Their reports supplemented the hard data that FERA's research division was providing. They put faces on the numbers, providing vivid anecdotal evidence of the human devastation wrought by the depression. Hickok's October 30, 1933, dispatch from Dickinson, North Dakota, was an example. She had met some farm families in a church there: "Of the men I saw this afternoon none had any income except a little here and there from cream checks. And this will soon be stopped, for their cows are going dry for lack of food. For themselves and their families they need everything. Especially clothing."

One man told her everything he owned was on his back. "His shoes were so far gone that I wondered how he kept them on his feet. With one or two exceptions none of the men hanging about the church had overcoats. Most of them were in denim—faded, shabby denim. Cotton denim doesn't keep out the wind very well. When we came out to get into the car, we found it full of farmers, with all the windows closed. They apologized and said they had crawled in there to keep warm. The women and children are even worse off than the men. Where there has been any money at all, it has gone for shoes for the children and work clothes for the men. The women can stay inside and keep warm, and the children can stay home from school."

The field reports brightened once the CWA was under way. Hickok wrote from Sioux City, Iowa, to report on the city engineer's astonishment at the changed attitudes of relief recipients: "You just can't believe that these are the same men who were listlessly and unwillingly doing their time a week ago on work relief projects to get their grocery orders." Moving north, she relayed the comment of the *Wisconsin State Journal* that the "click of pick and clink of shovel are Christmas bells to many at this time."

There were stories of rejuvenated buying power, of workers thrusting cash and not chits across store counters to buy what they required, of shoes disappearing from store shelves so fast that factories re-opened in order to replace them. Louise Armstrong, who headed her county CWA office in the Upper Peninsula of Michigan, later wrote, "We saw a little less of sorrow and discontent and a little more of happiness in the faces in the office. Christmas during CWA was a cheerful episode."

But not everybody was convinced. Al Smith, for whom opposing Roosevelt had become a full-time job, called the CWA a smokescreen for the Public Works Administration's ponderously slow start. He charged that it would do no useful work, encourage idleness, and disrupt local wage scales. "Half way between a lemon and an orange is a grapefruit, and half way between a public work and a relief work is a civil work," Smith said cryptically.

Hopkins popped off the kind of reply that was beginning to ruffle feathers in the anti–New Deal camp. If putting 4 million people to work meant he was in the grapefruit business, he was delighted to be in it. "Al Smith taught me the word 'baloney,' " he added, "and now he has taught me sour 'grapefruit juice.' "

Finally, around mid-January, Hopkins was able to achieve the employment numbers that he sought. He reached his goal by focusing on small, quick-starting projects such as road and street repair, repair of public buildings, playground development, and rural road improvements. At its peak that winter, the CWA employed 4,264,000 men and women.

10. EMPLOYMENT POLITICS

Naturally, the bulk of the CWA money flowed to the largest states. Eleven of them—much of the industrial Northeast and Midwest, and Texas and California—got 57 percent of the total. This produced accusations that contradicted one another. Republicans charged the administration with buying votes with patronage, while Democratic senators in the job-heavy states complained that they were given no input in choosing CWA supervisors. Colorado senator Edward Costigan, a Democrat and a Roosevelt ally, said plaintively, "Is it too much to ask that names considered for important official administrative posts here be referred to me in advance for advice?"

In California, where administrator Ray Branion was running both the CWA and FERA, Senator William McAdoo went to war because Branion was a Republican and accused him of political corruption and incompetence. Although McAdoo was just entering his first term, he was seventy years old and others were already vying to succeed him, so political maneuvering complicated the scenario. The United States attorney in San Francisco, who had applied for Branion's job, followed McAdoo's lead and indicted Branion and Pierce Williams, Hopkins's CWA field representative for California, on charges of conspiracy to defraud the government. Hopkins countered by dispatching a Justice Department attorney from Washington to investigate the charges, with Roosevelt's consent to quashing the indictment if the department approved. The investigation proved them innocent and the charges were dropped, although Hopkins had to move both Branion and Williams out of California.

Everybody wanted a piece of the CWA money. The Chicago Democratic machine tried to steer it to projects that were not approved, forcing Hopkins to interpose engineers to enforce high project standards. Labor unions in some locales claimed that workers had to join their ranks before the CWA would hire them, and the American Legion tried a similar tactic aimed at enlarging its membership before the CWA halted these practices.

The Republican National Committee attacked the CWA from the outset, charging it with "gross waste" and "downright corruption" without ever mustering specifics. Almost all such accusations were politically inspired, and Hopkins, knowing that even the hint of graft or favoritism could undermine public support, did a good job of staying out in front of them. Following the advice he'd received from the president on his first day on the job at FERA, he continued to run the relief apparatus without favoring Democrats. He rejected political hacks in favor of professional administrators who knew how to identify the needy and get them what they needed, be it food, clothing, or jobs. It was inevitable that political interference would take place, but he had stopped getting mad about it, he told a congressional committee in January when CWA jobs were at their peak. He was "amazed at the number of people who are trying to horn in on making a little money," he said, and was dedicated to exposing this himself. "I may have made a mistake in kicking a lot of this stuff outdoors," he said. "But I don't like it when people . . . finagle around the back door."

Hopkins's quote, and his picture, made the cover of *Time* magazine on February 19, 1934, confirming his growing national prominence. The story described his efforts to run the jobs program and keep politics and fraud at bay. It credited him with "a thoroughly professional job." On his orders, CWA payroll and purchase records were open to the public. He had a staff of 130 investigators checking reported cases of fraud. Accountants pored over the agency's books. Accusations of graft and corruption far outweighed the reality. What cases there were mostly involved violations and irregularities that fell short of criminal magnitude. They were handled with dismissals and restitution, although seventy-seven cases eventually were referred for prosecution and resulted in seventeen convictions.

Roosevelt, aware of the potential political dynamite in the accusations, did some intelligence gathering of his own. He sent his old friend Frank C. Walker to test reactions to the jobs program and to look for signs of corruption, incompetence, and waste. Walker was a Butte, Montana, copper miner turned lawyer and New York businessman—he owned a chain of movie theaters—who had known Roosevelt since 1920 and been one of his earliest presidential backers. Now he directed the president's Executive Council and also the National Emergency Council, both bodies consisting of department and agency heads and cabinet secretaries. The councils were supposed to coordinate the government's multifarious initiatives but were just as likely to break down in bureaucratic squabbles, and Walker, a staunch supporter without ambitions of his own who was good at soothing tender egos, served as a peacemaker. To assess the CWA, he left Washington and roamed the country. Back home in Butte, where he had practiced law, he found men he knew digging ditches and laying sewer pipe in their business suits and shoes because they couldn't afford work clothes. He was surprised, when he talked with them, to find that they weren't bitter. One man pulled out some coins and told Walker, "Do you know, Frank, this is the first money I've had in my pockets in a year and a half. Up to now I've had nothing but tickets that you exchange for groceries." Another said the CWA job had been all that prevented him from heaving a rock through the window of the local bakery and stealing bread to feed his children.

Returning to Washington, Walker told Roosevelt to ignore criticism of the CWA and the way Hopkins was running it. The jobs it provided had "averted one of the most serious crises in our history" and the threat, if not the reality, of revolution.

Obviously, not all of the CWA hires embraced their jobs enthusiastically, and many worked under poor conditions. CWA rules dictated that most project dollars be spent for labor, while local officials argued that leaving out equipment, material, and administration costs would make projects harder to complete successfully. Hopkins was able to ignore most of these protests, but not all. In late 1933, Fiorello La

Guardia had just been elected mayor of New York City and had asked Long Island parks commissioner Robert Moses to take over the city's parks as well. Moses, whose lust to build would prove to be equaled only by his love of power, had one single focus when it came to the growing number of projects under his iron control: they would be done his way or not at all. Anticipating the city parks job before the state legislature gave him permission to accept it, Moses and his top aides spied on some of the 68,000 CWA workers assigned to park cleanup and other projects in the city. They found a ragtag workforce that was ill-equipped and badly supervised. Workers laid asphalt roads and paths without adequate foundations, so these broke up from frost action within days. Other workers shoveled sand from truck beds to build up a reef off Staten Island, and as they waited for the next truckload they watched waves already washing away the sand they had just shoveled. Moses and his men saw thousands of laborers at Brooklyn's Marine Park, 2,000 acres of undeveloped salt marsh at the entrance to Jamaica Bay, warding off the cold wind from the water by passing around wine bottles concealed in paper bags and huddling over fires made from the chopped-up handles of their shovels. The few men whose consciences prompted them to work had little to do but rake the sand or rearrange the landscape's scattered stones.

Moses was sworn in as New York City's consolidated parks commissioner in January 1934, and within days he strong-armed the city's CWA administration into freeing money for plans, materials, and supervision. He used a favorite tactic: he threatened to quit if his demands weren't granted. And once he forced the CWA to change its rules and put real oversight in place, he hired hundreds of architects and engineers from the ravaged ranks of those professions. He put them to work in the red-brick Arsenal in Central Park, kept them at their desks for fourteen-hour days, and told those who didn't last not to bother coming back. The plans they turned out went into the field practically before the ink was dry. There, construction "ramrods" whom Moses had hired on loan from contractors as far away as Pennsylvania and New England ordered the CWA laborers to leave their wine and bonfires and get to work. Those who didn't were fired on the spot.

In fact, most workers were conscientious, like those Frank Walker had encountered in Montana. Diligence was the norm, not the exception, in almost every city and town around the country. CWA crews worked into a winter that in much of the nation was one of the worst ever. Temperatures fell to 56 below zero in the higher elevations of New England, 14 below in New York City, and 6 below in Washington, D.C. Few of the men sent out to work in those conditions were equipped for it, as Walker too had observed. Former white-collar workers had never owned the right clothes and shoes for work as laborers, and the onetime factory workers and mill hands who might have had decent work clothes in the past had been unable to replace them. Working for the CWA, the $13.44 a week they made on average disappeared into hungry mouths at home, which took priority over any other needs. To stretch their budgets for necessities, some men walked long distances to their jobsites rather than pay carfare.

Laborers held most, but not all, of the CWA jobs. Hopkins and his staff saw no sense in forcing artists, writers, and musicians to become third-rate laborers when they had skills that could be used in other ways. About 190,000 CWA-paid workers were classified as "nonmanual and professional." Three thousand of these were artists, including painters, etchers, sculptors, and mural painters. Gutzon Borglum, the monumental sculptor who had been carving the profiles of four presidents out of the granite of Mount Rushmore in South Dakota since 1927, applauded the hiring of artists. He wrote Aubrey Williams in 1933 to say that Hopkins and the CWA had "almost immediately shifted public aid from cold business to human helpfulness" and created "an army of workers whose goal must be to better, to make more livable our towns and cities, our schools more cheerful, our playgrounds and our parks a pride and a delight." As for the artists who were part of that army, Borglum wrote that they were hungry not just for food but with "unexpressed, creative longing" and were "anxious to be a part of the great comeback."

Most of the white-collar jobs were held by teachers, as they had been under FERA. Around 50,000 of them taught at all levels of the primary and secondary public education system, and in adult education. For others, innovative job creation was employed. Window dressers and clerks were sent to museums to help build displays and put old records in order; statisticians reported to hospitals to track disease patterns; bookbinders went to libraries to repair tattered books; and historians and architects were dispatched to far-flung spots around the country to compile the beginnings of a list of historic American buildings.

Republicans and the anti-Roosevelt press were quick to criticize jobs such as these, but Hopkins had little patience for their views. Of the white-collar jobholders he said with his usual terseness, "Hell! They've got to eat just like other people."

11. THE JOBS THAT PAID TOO MUCH

Hopkins's success at job making had two consequences. The first was budgetary. Having already demonstrated that he could spend $5 million in two hours, he had no trouble burning through the CWA's $400 million in three months. In mid-January, with the coffers running low, Roosevelt at Hopkins's request asked the Congress for $950 million more, $450 million to keep the program going through the winter and then wind it down, and $500 million for the direct relief that would be needed when the jobs disappeared.

The second consequence was psychological. Among the workers, the euphoria of finally having paychecks faded with the falling needles of the Christmas trees, and in its place rose concerns about pay and job conditions. And the 4 million jobs still left some 9 million unemployed, spurring protests among those who had failed to land on the CWA rosters. The mayor of Chelsea, Massachusetts, Lawrence F. Quigley, wrote Hopkins in January to report that the unemployed in his town continued to be the lopsided majority. While 155 Chelseans worked at CWA jobs, 2,000 remained out of work and had taken their anger to city hall, where they were apparently milling inside the building as Quigley composed his letter. It would take only a spark, he wrote, to "change them into a mob." He also suggested that the government, having acknowledged its responsibility by creating a jobs program, now was obliged to "put every unemployed man to work."

Lorena Hickok, writing from Georgia on her first trip into the Deep South, reported a conversation with Lincoln McConnell, the state reemployment director. A day or two before he talked to Hickok, McConnell had been in the north Georgia town of Carnesville, where 1,800 men had registered for jobs. Told that the quota was filled and no jobs were available, the men threatened to riot, burn trucks, and sack the CWA offices.

At the same time that the CWA was facing the anger of men it hadn't been able to employ, Hopkins had to cut the pay of those it had. With money running low and Roosevelt's request for additional funds still pending, he wanted to stretch what was left of the $400 million as far as he could. When it began, the CWA had adopted the Public Works Administration pay scale, which for unskilled labor was 40 cents an hour in the Southern Zone, 45 cents an hour in the Central Zone, which included most of the Midwest and West, and 50 cents an hour in the industrial Northern Zone. Skilled workers made from $1 to $1.20. Unskilled and skilled laborers could work only thirty hours a week, clerical workers and professionals thirty-nine.

The pay rates were based on prevailing wages in the different regions of the country but were supposed to be low enough not to compete with private jobs. Farmers in the South, however, were used to paying black and poor white farm hands as little as 5 cents an hour. Southern politicians protested that the CWA wages would lure workers from the fields and leave farmers unable to plow their fields or plant their crops. These protests also had a racial component: as little as a white farm owner might pay white laborers for hoeing corn and picking cotton, it was an unspoken rule in the old plantation belt that he would pay his black workers even less.

The loudest protester of all was the governor of Georgia, Eugene Talmadge. Talmadge was a flamboyant, suspender-snapping country lawyer who had ridden into office on the farm vote. He opposed relief in general and federal relief in particular, and considered all the people on relief as "bums and loafers." This judgment fell heavily on his constituents, since 28 percent of Georgians received some form of assistance. City dwellers on relief were a cut below the average; he viewed them as chiselers trying to "outsmart you," while outside the cities reliefers were merely victims of temptation, being lured by fancy wages to abandon the moral virtues of a day's work in the hot sun. Even the lowest payments were too much, since farmers typically paid black tenants $3 a week for an entire family's labor during the planting and harvest seasons. Talmadge even opposed the CCC, deriding the goverment for letting "a lot of young fellows run around in the woods" and paying them for it; they were bums and loafers too.

Talmadge had set out from the beginning to frustrate FERA and the system of federal relief, installing patronage hacks to do his bidding. Field representative Alan Johnstone had reported to Hopkins in September 1933 that "days and weeks of delay interrupt the organization. Appointments are held up. The Governor insists on signing every check. Wants to know the name and address of every person on staff and almost the name and address of every person on relief. Harasses the administration by continued criticism.

"In order to do in Georgia what ought to be done," Johnstone recommended, "it is literally necessary to take the State of Georgia away from Talmadge on the question of relief and the whole relief program."

With the advent of CWA, Talmadge had renewed his complaints and continued to undermine the program. He fired the director of the women's division, nurse Jane Van de Vrede, on the grounds that she was not a Georgia native and therefore could not understand Georgians' problems. And he forwarded to the White House a note that a constituent had sent him protesting the wage scale: "I wouldn't plow nobody's mule from sunrise to sunset for 50 cents a day when I could get $1.30 for pretending to work on a DITCH."

Roosevelt, no fan of Talmadge, dictated a withering reply that eventually went to Talmadge over Hopkins's signature. "I take it...that you approve of paying farm labor 40 to 50 cents per day." Calculating that this amounted to $60 to $75 a year for seasonal farm work, he added, "I cannot get it into my head that wages on such a scale make possible a reasonable American standard of living."

Speaking for himself, Hopkins was more direct: "All that guy is after is headlines," he said of Talmadge. "He never contributes a dime, yet he's always yapping. Some people can't stand to see others making a living wage."

Hopkins said that since Talmadge didn't want CWA jobs in Georgia, he would shut down the state program and use the money elsewhere. This triggered a flood of telegrams and letters from Georgia congressmen, local officials, and citizens urging him to keep the works program intact. With that ammunition, Hopkins used his power to federalize the program, dissolving the Talmadge-appointed relief board and naming a professional social work administrator, Gay Shepperson, to run the state program, reporting to him and not to Talmadge. At the same time he reinstated Van de Vrede as head of the women's division. It was the first time, but not the last, that Hopkins would take a state work program from its politicians and run it through his own appointees.

The southern protests over CWA wages died down when, for budgetary reasons, the CWA cut workers' hours to twenty-four a week in cities over 2,500 and to fifteen in rural areas. That cut the average weekly pay nationally from around $15 to $11.52, and below $10 in most places in the South.

Hickok wrote Hopkins from the southern Georgia town of Moultrie on January 23, 1934: "It meant cutting most of them from $9 to $7.20 and $4.50 a week and from $12 to $9.60 or $6, depending on whether they lived in Moultrie or out in the country and what kind of work they were doing." But the consensus, she said, was that even the reduced pay was "better than being laid off."

12. THE BRIEF SHINING LIFE OF THE CWA

Before long, however, they would be. Almost as soon as it began, the CWA began to wind to a conclusion. Roosevelt got from Congress the $950 million Hopkins had sought to complete the program and resume direct relief, but refused appeals from some senators and governors to ask for more. New York's Governor Lehman said he feared "grave social and economic consequences" when the program was shut down. The American Association of Social Workers, citing a "serious feeling of insecurity," urged that it continue. And after the announcement that it actually would end, the White House received more than 50,000 protesting letters and 7,000 telegrams in a single week.

CWA field workers reported that the program had raised expectations that might be difficult to bring back down to earth. "I'm a little afraid," Hickok wrote from Georgia, "that some of these people down here do not realize that the CWA business can't go on forever."

But Roosevelt refused to relent. The program had cost more than he anticipated, and despite Hopkins's largely successful efforts to find and expose corruption before it could fester, he worried that accusations alone, coming from Republicans and the anti–New Deal press, would become a liability in a midterm election year. Conservative

Democrats had voiced fears, shared by some of Roosevelt's advisors, that the government would never be able to wean people from their jobs if they got too used to them, and Hickok's letter to Hopkins suggested the same thing. The Public Works Administration had at last broken ground on several multimillion-dollar projects, including the Boulder Dam across the Colorado River in Nevada and the Triborough Bridge in New York City, and Roosevelt hoped these would finally give the economy the boost he had anticipated when the agency was launched. He didn't want citizens to think the depression was permanent, or that the jobs the CWA provided would "become a habit with the country." And while the winter was hurling record cold and snowfalls at the East, he took it for granted that nobody was going to starve once the weather moderated.

The *Time* magazine issue that featured Hopkins on its cover reported that he agreed wholeheartedly with Roosevelt that the CWA had been intended as a temporary emergency measure and "should be gradually demobilized." But in his heart of hearts, wrote historian Robert Sherwood, Hopkins was reluctantly "obeying orders." As in the *Time* report, his public comments masked his disappointment. He had announced rules and regulations for the phaseout at a news conference three days earlier, which he opened with an anecdote. "You know, this is a great job," he said. "Here is a letter from a man who had a faithful wife, but he was unfaithful to her. He wants me to write her to take him back."

"Well, you are the relief administrator and he needs relief," said one of the reporters.

After some more banter, Hopkins went on to say that the CWA would drop workers in families where more than one person was employed, as well as all people "with other resources," in an effort to keep the program at full strength in all industrial cities through the winter. And again he repeated his support of Roosevelt's position: "We have tried here to do an emergency job and we believe that it has been done, and these appropriations from Congress are for the purpose of meeting the emergency needs, and do not represent an indication of permanent government policy."

Once it began in the third week of February, the phaseout first hit rural areas and the warming South. The pink slips that signaled the program's end, advancing north with the weather, left remarkable changes in their wake. At the literal end of the United States in Key West, Florida, CWA workers had swarmed over the rundown buildings of the flat-broke town, hammering, plastering, painting, and even building an aquarium to encourage tourism that would be brought by a new road. In Palatka, Florida, azaleas and palm trees planted by the CWA had transformed a fifty-nine-acre ravine carved by the St. Johns River into a magnificent garden. Dozens of public buildings in Texas and Oklahoma displayed new western-themed murals. CWA workers in Pittsburgh had helped move the forty-two-story Cathedral of Learning at the heart of the University of Pittsburgh closer to completion. In Helena, Montana, they renovated parts of the state capitol and refaced the building's copper dome. Atop Telegraph Hill in San Francisco, the walls and stairwells of the new Coit Tower were being filled with vibrant scenes of street life in the city by the bay. In Mississippi, sagging rural schools were shored up and plumb and sparkling with new paint; more money had been spent on them in the CWA's brief life than in the previous twenty years.

New sanitary privies had appeared in great numbers, 150,000 or more. Hopkins joked that some of them might be named for him, since contractors had been told to put up CWA signs at each jobsite and one had cabled to ask if he wanted a sign on each privy or one for the whole site.

By February 23, 720,000 CWA workers had been demobilized, and some 3 million remained at work. CWA workers were still on the job in Salt Lake City on the morning of March 12, painting the inside of the capitol dome, when an earthquake struck; it wrenched their scaffold into a dizzying spin that then subsided so they were able to climb down, shaken but unhurt. In New York City, parks commissioner Moses kept men at work in three shifts around the clock, digging, paving, painting, and planting through snow, sleet, rain, and cold. Then, despite the appeals of Norman Thomas and others in a march on Washington, on March 31 the CWA's construction program ended. Artists and researchers kept working under other programs, and half the remaining workers shifted onto FERA's payroll to mop up unfinished jobs. The rest went back on direct relief.

In its brief life the CWA had spent almost a billion dollars. Earning an average salary of $13 a week, its workers had built or improved some half a million miles of road, not just in the United States but in every U.S. territory. They had built or renovated 40,000 schools and 3,700 playgrounds and athletic fields. Under the whip hand of Moses and his "ramrods," they had restored every park in New York City. They had built 469 airports and improved 529 more. They had dug ditches into which they had laid 12 million feet of sewer pipe, and built 250,000 outdoor privies. CWA-paid masons, carpenters, painters, and cleaners had improved thousands of public buildings including state capitols, city halls, county courthouses, libraries, police stations, hospitals, and jails. Hundreds of other buildings that were beyond rehabilitation had been torn down. Workers had refurbished irrigation ditches in the drought-parched West. In the South, they had drained thousands of acres of swampland and in the process advanced malaria control. They had restocked countless lakes and streams with fish. Ninety-four Eskimos working in the Kodiak Islands of what was then the Territory of Alaska replenished the snowshoe rabbit population. CWA sewing rooms, using surplus cotton, made tens of thousands of mattresses that went to relief families. The agency took over a bankrupt underwear maker, rehired its workers at CWA wages, and produced sets of underwear for families who could not afford to buy their own. About 300,000 women worked at CWA jobs, in the sewing rooms, as teachers, and in professional roles such as nurses and home economists within the growing relief system.

Hopkins summarized the program this way: "I think it was a grand thing and that it was altogether successful . . . these millions of men and women did excellent work, worked hard and earned their money. As an effort on the part of the government to meet a critical situation, it seems to me that it did the trick and that the stories about graft and politics and inefficiencies were relatively unimportant, and that it has resulted in works of social usefulness that will be beneficial for years to come. When you realize that not a single county in America was omitted from this enterprise, it seems to me that it speaks well for the kind of cooperative endeavor that can be done by the American people in a crisis."

But by the time he said this, at a March 30 news conference as the clock was ticking to its zero hour, he was already backing away from his earlier statements supporting its demise. The CWA may have been a temporary program to meet an emergency need, but he hoped the government would stay in the business of providing jobs to the unemployed: "I would hate to see a decline in the work program and a return to direct relief. Of course, we have some serious financial problems to work out."

He was working on these problems, Hopkins said. But for the moment, in the spring of 1934, the great surge of public works and jobs was in retreat as the hopeful administration awaited signs that the economy might finally be improving on its own.

PART III

THE DAWN OF THE WPA

$3,187,000 Relief Is Spent Teaching Jobless to Play:
"Boon Doggles" Made

—HEADLINE, <u>NEW YORK TIMES</u>, APRIL 4, 1935

They are damn good projects—excellent projects...dumb people
criticize something they do not understand, and that is what is going
on up there—God damn it!

—HARRY HOPKINS, APRIL 4, 1935

1. TOWARD A PERMANENT JOBS PROGRAM

The Civil Works Administration was over, but its vast spending and its swarms of workers, its variety of jobs and range of projects, were a vivid prelude to what lay ahead. The patronage grabs that it inspired, the bureaucratic jockeying and political warfare, were also a foretaste. And when this prelude was gone, the first to miss it—other than the workers it helped sustain through the harsh winter—were governors and mayors who saw the dust settle on open ditches, partly surfaced roads, and public buildings hung with scaffolding as the workers who had manned them headed back to the relief lines.

With the demise of the CWA, FERA resumed its role as the lead work relief agency. In addition to picking up as many of the unfinished CWA projects as he could, Hopkins also sent word through his state offices that FERA was accepting a limited number of new applications. Many FERA reliefers worked on construction or sewing jobs; others taught, immunized children, or performed research. But compared to the flurry of jobs created by the CWA, the number of workers under FERA continued to be a small percentage of the total unemployed. There were never more than 2.5 million workers employed on FERA projects, 2 million fewer than those who worked for the CWA. The hated means test was back in force, and the private economy was still not picking up the slack. In the spring of 1934, therefore, unemployment remained stubbornly above 10 million, and more than 18 million were receiving some form of relief.

Within the inner councils of the White House, Hopkins continued to argue for a much expanded jobs program. This went against the counsel of other of Roosevelt's advisors, including postmaster general and politico Jim Farley, who was looking ahead to the fall elections and trying to win business support by holding down relief spending. By April, Hopkins believed that he had won the day. In an April 18 telephone conversation with Colonel Henry M. Waite, the deputy administrator of the Public Works Administration and the author of the PWA's project criteria, Hopkins hinted that Roosevelt was ready to launch a three-to-five-year program that would spend as much as $6 billion on "projects we will get the dollars back on." Such projects included building housing, highways, and traffic-easing grade eliminations at congested road and rail crossings, and carrying electricity deeper into rural areas. "The big boss is getting ready to go places in a big way," Hopkins told Waite.

His reading of the president was premature. Roosevelt continued to believe that families on relief would fare better during the summer months, and he still held out hope that the economy would rebound before the next winter arrived, foreclosing the need for massive work relief. In the meantime he, like Farley, had the upcoming elections to consider.

But Hopkins pushed forward undeterred. He and his top aides had recognized that the CWA had had a limited effect. It had boosted sales and production levels for a short time, but it had not pushed the economy past the tipping point into strong growth. Once the stimulus provided by the jobs was removed, sales and production lapsed back into stagnation. Assessing these results, they believed that only a big and ongoing works program could pump enough money into the economy to bring it around. They also believed this kind of program was necessary to prepare jobless workers physically, psychologically, and spiritually for the moment when the private economy finally did take off. It would "prevent deterioration of moral fibre, not only in the persons engaged on the projects, but in their families, by maintaining the heads in the normal relationship of breadwinners for their dependents." It would also forestall "the lapsing of skilled workers and highly trained and professional people into a vast pool of unqualified inepts" by keeping them "in practice and in physical condition." A massive public jobs program would thus serve a dual purpose: it would help bring the economy to life and at the same time ready workers to face the requirements that new and longed-for day would thrust upon them.

Before that happened, however, there were still many hungry mouths to feed. Farm surpluses provided one potential source of food, but attempts to use these surpluses got off to a macabre and troubled start. The year before, Roosevelt's push to control farm production through the Agricultural Adjustment Administration had come too late to affect the planting season; wheat and corn were already in the ground. At the same time, hog producers were seeing their stock grow healthy and fertile on the previous year's feed corn. Drought forestalled a wheat surplus in 1933, but in the South the cotton grew profusely and in the corn belt farrowing hogs produced a bumper crop of piglets. With warehouses already groaning with baled cotton, and hogs selling for less than they cost to raise, the administration asked farm experts for advice. The answer was unanimous: pay the farmers, kill the piglets, and plow the cotton under.

This went deeply against the grain. It offended the act of farming itself. Milo Reno of the Farmers' Holiday Association said that "for the government to destroy food and reduce crops...is wicked." Nevertheless, the plan went forward and that August, across the cotton belt, farmers beat their mules to make them do the very thing they had taught them not to do—trample the cotton stalks as they walked down the plant rows. Together mules and machines plowed up 10 million acres of new cotton, for which farmers collected $100 million. And the following month, the AAA bought 6 million piglets and 200,000 pregnant sows and had them slaughtered, producing shocked news headlines and a public outcry, aimed not at the slaughter itself but at the fact that the slaughtered pigs were young or gravid.

In a much-quoted statement, agriculture secretary Henry Wallace, forced to defend the program, wondered why people thought that "every little pig has the right to attain before slaughter the full pigginess of his pigness. To hear them talk, you would have thought that pigs were raised for pets."

But the protests against the slaughter, and the problem of farm surpluses in general, pushed the administration to create a way to turn waste into relief stores. As Hopkins put it later, "If there were great food surpluses while people went hungry, the public could rightly be revolted." The result was the Federal Surplus Relief Corporation, chartered on October 4, 1933, with Hopkins as its president and Wallace and Harold Ickes of the PWA its other officers. This was an arm of FERA, which would distribute the supplies through its nationwide network of relief offices. Authorized to spend $75 million, the corporation negotiated prices and processed the surplus products into food, clothing, and other necessities. More than 100 million pounds of baby pork immediately went into the relief food chain. In 1934, as the operation grew more sophisticated, it expanded to include beef and veal, butter and cheese, wheat and flour, potatoes and rice, cereal, apples, cabbage, sweet potatoes, sugar, and cane syrup. It distributed heating fuel, mostly in the form of coal. It bought raw wool and had it processed into blankets that went to relief families, and almost 120,000 bales of surplus cotton were made into clothing or bedclothes at FERA sewing operations. The corporation also purchased feed and seed that allowed drought-stricken farmers to maintain their stock and to plant again.

But now the drought that had stunted the 1933 wheat crop continued into 1934. Drought had been a fact of life in the Great Plains and the West for at least three years. Grass cropped close by grazing sheep and cattle had withered and died, and with nothing to tie the topsoil to the earth beneath, the prairie winds had sucked it up into the sky. Fourteen dust storms hit the five-state region of Colorado, Kansas, New Mexico, Oklahoma, and Texas in 1932, thirty-eight in 1933. These storms, airborne avalanches of dirt, blocked the sun, turned day to night, buried buildings and vehicles, and choked humans and animals caught out of doors when they descended. The dust invaded everything. It blew through keyholes, under doors, and around window frames. Families wore dust masks and sealed the sills with towels or tape at night, and still woke up to find bucketsful of dust drifting on their floors. It found its way inside sleeves, up pants cuffs, and down collars; it got into food, so every bite was gritty. Despite the masks, it caused dust pneumonia in the lungs and made people who gulped for air vomit dirt. And the drought zone kept widening, affecting the Dakotas, Texas, Arizona, Utah, and ultimately twenty-seven states in all. Dust clouds could be seen as far east as Albany, New York.

The worst storm of all came in May 1934. Starting on May 9, strong winds vacuumed some 350 million tons of dirt into the sky and carried it eastward on the jet stream. It fell like black snow across Chicago, darkened Washington, D.C., turned street lamps on at noon in New York and Boston, and dusted the decks of ships at sea in the Atlantic. In its aftermath came summer heat so intense that on top of the drought and loss of grazing land, it brought millions of sheep and cattle to the brink of starvation. In Navajo County, Arizona, hungry cattle roamed into Holbrook, the county seat, and cropped at shrubs and flowers. In Utah, the Mormons prayed, the Coyote Clan of Hopi Indians performed snake dances, and according to historian Leonard J. Arrington, "even the grasshoppers were starving" from the lack of rain.

The government intervened to try to ease the drought and the tragedy of starving livestock. FERA workers used $1 million in emergency funds to build wells and irrigation projects in Utah. Four million sheep and cattle were killed and buried in the dusty earth that could not sustain them, but millions more, purchased by the AAA, were rounded up and shipped to slaughterhouses for processing into food, leather, and wool by the Federal Surplus Relief Corporation. More than 650 million pounds of dressed canned beef went to relief families, along with countless blankets and pairs of shoes.

But these were stopgap efforts, not a substitute for work, and FERA's work programs were still providing only a fraction of the jobs required. So as the year progressed, Hopkins and his aides drafted several plans for large jobs programs with costs ranging from $4 billion to $9 billion, and then waited for the right time to try to sell them to the president.

2. PROTESTS LEFT AND RIGHT

Thus far, the New Deal's efforts to combat the depression had dominated economic and political debate and overwhelmed all opposition. But by the middle of 1934, with the midterm elections looming, opponents on the left and the right began to find new voice. Most threatening to the administration was a chorus of populists who in their various ways were protesting the country's widespread and apparently intractable poverty.

Dr. Francis E. Townsend was among them. A native of Illinois who had practiced medicine in South Dakota before moving to California for his health, Townsend had leapt to national prominence by proposing a scheme of old-age pensions. As he told the story later, he glanced up from shaving one morning to observe three old women scavenging for food in the garbage cans behind his house. His howls of outrage brought his wife running, protesting that the neighbors would hear.

"I want all the neighbors to hear me!" raged Townsend, who was sixty-six at the time. "I want God Almighty to hear me! I'm going to shout until the whole country hears!"

His campaign for national attention began with a letter to the Long Beach *Press-Telegram* in September 1933. In it, Townsend proposed that the federal government pay monthly pensions of $150 to everyone over sixty, provided that they spent it all within a month. A nationwide sales tax on all transactions would provide the funding. Townsend's plan—others had floated similar ideas—had the appearance of perfection; it would remove the elderly from the job market, open up jobs for younger people, pump money into the economy, and essentially fund itself with the sales tax. If there was a drawback, as one editorial cartoonist saw it, it was the strain the old people would undergo from burning the candle at both ends to spend their money every month. Townsend brought in a Texas real estate salesman he had dealt with in the past, Robert Earl Clements, and on January 1, 1934, they announced the formation of Old Age Revolving Pensions, Ltd. By then they were talking pensions of about $200 a month. Soon, Townsend Clubs were springing up throughout California, peopled by elderly members who paid a dime a month to beat the drums for the Townsend plan with telegrams, letters, and petitions to the Congress.

This nationwide yearning for security in old age was born of deprivation; twenty-eight states had programs for old-age assistance, but these were based on need and in the depression they depended on erratic appropriations that totaled just $32 million in all of 1934. Elsewhere, before FERA, all that the elderly without resources or family had to fall back on was a patchwork of private and local charities, leaving them to spend their final years in a twilight of penury. Nettie Burk, once a famed bareback rider for P. T. Barnum's Greatest Show on Earth, provided an example: she had been evicted from her apartment in New York at age eighty-six and, as the *New York Times* oddly stated it in her obituary, "fought a stubborn, cheerful battle against starvation" while depending on the care of neighbors before she died in 1932. Add to their plight the dearth of jobs, the Hoovervilles, the hungry children, and the wandering homeless, and the vicious economic disparities brought to light by the depression were a tinderbox waiting to be ignited into a firestorm by demagogues.

In the Detroit suburb of Royal Oak, where a mellow-voiced priest at a church named for St. Thérèse, the "Little Flower of Jesus," had been giving weekly radio broadcasts since 1926, Father Charles E. Coughlin was now achieving national popularity. At first these broadcasts had focused on bringing in new parishioners and fighting the anti-Catholic Ku Klux Klan after a cross was burned in his churchyard. But with the onset of the depression, the predominantly religious message had changed: Coughlin, at age thirty-eight, now started to talk about politics and money.

Detroit was as hard hit by the depression as any city in the land. Lincoln Colcord, one of Hopkins's field reporters, wrote that it was not so much disturbed as "prostrated," and called the auto capital "the spear point of the depression." As its laid-off autoworkers left the hiring halls and factory gates for breadlines and meetings of the Unemployed Councils, and the city pitched tent villages to house its homeless, there was ample evidence to provoke a good Catholic's social conscience. Coughlin was no Hooverville priest like Pittsburgh's Father Cox, but he preached a social gospel as described in Pope Leo XIII's 1891 encyclical *Rerum Novarum,* or *On the Condition of the Working Class.* In it, Leo had warned that widespread poverty was a breeding ground for Socialism and that societies should "save unfortunate working people from the cruelty of men of greed, who use human beings as mere instruments for money-making." Coughlin's message echoed this: "Let not the workingman be able to say that he is driven into the ranks of socialism by the inordinate and grasping greed of the manufacturer."

As he inveighed against greed, corruption, and the concentration of wealth, the *Golden Hour of the Little Flower* grew ever more popular. He traded on this popularity to acquire friends in politics, and as his influence grew, his messages became nakedly political. Coughlin denounced Hoover's policies during the campaign of 1932, and after the election lavished praise on Roosevelt, telling his listeners that it was "Roosevelt or ruin." Religion went into the mix without reserve: "The New Deal is Christ's Deal," he preached, peppering his broadcasts with economic opinions that favored the Roosevelt policies. But before long Coughlin not only began acting like an administration spokesman but assumed that in return he ought to be entitled to a key to the White House and the president's ear on monetary policy. All the while his popularity kept growing. By 1934, the network of stations carrying his broadcasts in the cities of the East and Midwest had ballooned. Listeners deluged him with money; he received 10,000 letters a day. The attention, the access, and the power were addictive, although Roosevelt, and those around him, now began to consider him a pest—a useful one, but still a pest.

And also by the spring of 1934, around the time the CWA ended,

Coughlin realized the administration was ignoring his advice, and he gradually drifted out of its orbit. In November, he formed the National Union for Social Justice, conceived as a non-partisan lobby to exert pressure for his economic agenda. But now he started to attack the New Deal for failing to drive the moneychangers from the temple; Roosevelt's political advisors looked ahead to the 1936 election and saw him as a potential threat. In fact, he looked even more ominous when the president's men contemplated the nightmare possibility of an alliance between Coughlin and another dangerous populist orator, Senator Huey P. Long of Lousiana.

Long was fiercely smart, persuasively eloquent, and brazenly unscrupulous, and his towering ambition was unfettered by self-doubt. Born in 1893 in the red-clay piney woods of Winn Parish, he had cut his eyeteeth on populism. This region in north-central Louisiana had a contrarian streak that ran long and deep. Local farmers had preferred the Union army to Confederate taxes during the Civil War. Later, the same rebellious urges spurred progressive and radical farm movements. In fact, in 1912, more than 35 percent of parish voters had marked their presidential ballots for Socialist Eugene V. Debs, and the Socialist slate took over city hall in the county seat of Winnville.

Long was still in his teens when he made a prediction to his future wife. He would run for president someday and win, he told her, after he first worked his way up the ladder as governor and U.S. senator. He dropped out of high school, sold cottonseed cooking oil door-to-door, became a lawyer, and in 1918, discovering that the Louisiana constitution had not set a minimum age for the state's railroad commission as it did for other statewide offices, he ran for a commission seat and won. The commission regulated more than railroads; telephone and telegraph services, pipelines, and utilities also fell within its domain. Long single-handedly transformed the three-member commission from a retirement home for fading politicians and a rubber stamp for the utilities to an advocate for better, cheaper, and more inclusive services. Railing against concentrated wealth and power, he made himself the bane of New Orleans's bankers, aristocrats, and oilmen. But his ambitions were far grander.

As soon as he turned thirty, the minimum age, Long ran for governor. The thrust of his campaign was simple: he attacked money and all forms of power. He finished a close third in the January 1924

Democratic primary and immediately started laying plans for 1928. He mended the mistakes of his first campaign by courting interests downstate, where he had done poorly, but he didn't change his style. He told the people they had been neglected and shortchanged by the powerful interests. In southern Louisiana's Cajun country, speaking in the shade of the oak tree made famous by Longfellow's poem, he evoked the legend of lovelorn Evangeline to whet the people's appetite about their future.

"Evangeline is not the only one who waited here in disappointment," Long said. "Where are the schools that you have waited for your children to have, but have never come? Where are the roads and the highways that you sent your money to build, that are no nearer now than ever before? Where are the institutions for the sick and disabled?"

He adapted his campaign slogan from the populist rhetoric of William Jennings Bryan: "Every Man a King, but No One Wears a Crown." He picked up—and reveled in—a nickname from the popular *Amos 'n Andy* radio program: the "Kingfish." He campaigned tirelessly, red-faced and drenched with sweat, his red-brown hair flopping every which way above his pug-nosed, puffy face, firing up crowds in courthouse squares, churchyards, and school auditoriums, displaying a folksy grin when they shouted, "Pour it on 'em, Huey!" When the votes came in they showed the pattern that Roosevelt and his advisors would view with concern six years later. Long had divided voters by wealth and class, and it was workers and the poor who had given him their votes. He satisfied them from the day he took office, from a foot-stomping inaugural celebration at the capitol in Baton Rouge to free books in the schools, a ten-fold increase in paved roads, better health care and mental health facilities, and higher corporate taxes to pay for it all. He created a patronage machine to ensure his control, survived an impeachment attempt mounted by Standard Oil and other oil interests, and, halfway through his constitutionally limited four-year term, ran for and won election to the U.S. Senate. By then he was being noticed outside Louisiana and was acquiring the beginnings of a national base.

Long displayed a level of flamboyance that was remarkable even by the standards of southern politicians. He received diplomatic guests in silk pajamas, paraded at the head of the Louisiana State University marching band, engaged an Atlanta editor in a letter-writing debate about the proper method for eating cornbread—dunked or crumbled into the "potlikker" at the bottom of a pot of collard greens; Long said dunked—and traveled like a potentate, surrounded by the trappings of the very power he inveighed against. All this got him front-page coverage. And then he started spreading his political message to a wider audience. In the summer of 1931, with frustration building over the worsening depression and Hoover's inadequate response, Long proposed a radical new tactic to reduce the cotton surplus and thereby revive prices. He called for a "cotton holiday," a moratorium on planting cotton in 1932 to be imposed by legislatures in the cotton states. When, unsurprisingly, the plan failed, he had achieved his goal. Long walked away with a bumper crop of exposure and the adoration of 2 million southern cotton farmers.

At that point, two years into his Senate term, he had hardly set foot in Washington. But even from afar, he kept his hand in national politics. He supported Roosevelt's bid for the Democratic nomination, campaigned for him in the Midwest, and engineered the surprising upset victory of Hattie W. Caraway of Arkansas in her bid to return to the Senate, where she had filled her husband's seat after his death the year before. As always, the speeches he made revolved around the theme of disenfranchisement of the many and the concentration of too much money in too few hands. He proposed limiting large fortunes and spreading the wealth among the people. When he finally did start speaking in the Senate, he gave voice to what others were thinking and saying more discreetly. If, Long said, "I should see my children starving and my wife starving... laws against robbing and against stealing and against bootlegging would not amount to any more to me than they would to any other man when it came to a matter of facing the time of starvation." The Senate quickly learned that he was a one-man wrecking crew who disregarded the decorum of the august body and filibustered against any piece of legislation he opposed. And when the Congress adjourned at the end of the Hundred Days, he announced that the New Deal initiatives had not relieved the troubles of "the poor and the downtrodden, the blind, the helpless, the orphaned, the bleeding, the wounded, the hungry and the distressed," and refused to join the Democratic victory party.

Long had originally claimed that Roosevelt's campaign mirrored his own proposals to redistribute wealth. Now, he said, the president had broken his promise to break up fortunes and spread the wealth around. His plans were radical and confiscatory; he wanted to set a $1 million cap on yearly income, and he sent his audiences into populist ecstasies by sarcastically imitating whining millionaires complaining that they would have to live on less. Roosevelt's first step was to stop consulting Long about federal jobs in Louisiana. After that, and publicity about a humiliating fight in a nightclub bathroom from which he emerged black-eyed and bloody, Long seemed to be sliding toward irrelevance.

But the Kingfish was far from finished. At the end of 1933, when he was only forty, he had published his flattering autobiography, *Every Man a King*. He resurrected *Louisiana Progress*, a campaign newspaper he had started during his Senate campaign, renamed it *American Progress*, and used its weekly editions to introduce himself and his ideas to a national readership. He touted those same ideas in radio broadcasts that, when they aired, rivaled Coughlin's *Golden Hour of the Little Flower* in popularity.

These populist promises—of Long to make every man a king, of Coughlin to bring down men of greed, of Townsend to give every old person a comfortable pension—shimmered in the dreams of those hit hard by the depression. They were a mirage of salvation against the gray wastes of impoverishment, seeming to offer what Roosevelt, despite his efforts, had not been able to deliver.

And as the populists clamored for a leftward swing to spread the wealth, a recharged and newly vocal right campaigned to renew its old privileges and status. For some time, conservatives in business and politics had been itching to take up arms again. They hated the fact that they had been forced to tailor their business agendas to meet social needs, specifically through the National Recovery Administration codes that set working conditions, wages, and hours within industries and imposed production limits. Just as odious to them was the Agricultural Adjustment Administration's version of economic planning, in which food distributors were taxed in order to pay farmers to limit their crop and livestock production. This was unacceptable meddling. The government had no right to control their property and income. It was the beginning of the end, the start of a long slide from centralized government and the dilution of states' rights straight downhill to socialism. The more strident among them mixed their metaphors and compared Roosevelt to the most odious dictators in their roster, Hitler on the one hand and the Soviet Union's Josef Stalin on the other. In 1934 these feelings coalesced in an organization formed to defend what it called the constitutional "rights of persons and property."

The group called itself the American Liberty League. Its roots had formed during Prohibition, in a business coalition that lobbied for the return of alcohol with the thought that if the government taxed beer and whiskey, it might then cut business taxes. When the states ratified the Twenty-first Amendment and ended Prohibition in December 1933, the group found a new cause—and a name—in anti–New Deal issues. Its chief movers were Alfred E. Sloan and William Knudsen of General Motors, the du Pont family and du Pont executives, conservative Democrats in Congress, Al Smith's patron John Raskob, and, most loudly, Smith himself. For its president, the league tapped Jouett Shouse of Kentucky, who had resigned as head of the Democratic National Committee after the party nominated Roosevelt.

The Liberty League—the group was commonly referred to by this shorthand version of its name—announced its formation on August 22, 1934, and promised an "unremitting" fight against "government encroachments upon the rights of citizens." Roosevelt and the New Deal now faced a well-financed and assertive voice joining the Republican National Committee on the right, while the populists harangued the administration from the other end of the spectrum. But for all of the sound and heat generated by both sides, neither addressed the ongoing toll of unemployment and the need for jobs to bring stability to the economy.

3. "THIS IS OUR HOUR"

The *New York Times* carried news of the Liberty League's formation on its front page the next day, when a transatlantic liner nosed into a pier on the Hudson River and discharged its passengers. Among them were Harry Hopkins and his wife, Barbara, back from a fact-finding trip. Roosevelt had sent Hopkins off to gather information about public housing and social insurance schemes in England, Germany, Austria, and Italy, but the president had an ulterior motive. Hopkins had exhausted himself putting together the CWA and then dismantling it within five months. He had always worked without regard to his health, having twice contracted pneumonia in his days as a social worker, and the rich diet and cocktails of high living, together with his chain smoking and caffeine intake, did nothing to improve it.

"Incidentally," Roosevelt had told him in a note in making the assignment, "in view of the steady grind you have had, I think that the sea trip will do you a lot of good."

Hopkins and Barbara had sailed aboard the SS *Washington* on July 4, leaving their baby daughter, Diana, in the care of friends in Washington. By the time they returned on August 23, Hopkins had seen impressive low-income housing programs. He also had met

Benito Mussolini, the Italian dictator, although Mussolini did not follow the agenda. "I had come to see him about public works and housing but when he learned I had just been to Berlin it was perfectly clear that he wished to talk of Germany. This quite suited me because it is the subject of all others that everyone in Europe is discussing," Hopkins wrote on stationery of the American embassy in Rome. "I was not prepared for the contempt which he expressed of Hitler's murders and his stupidity." The murders to which he referred occurred in the blood purge that became known as the "Night of the Long Knives," in which Hitler wiped out his enemies and consolidated his power. He had announced the purge—he said seventy-seven had died, most shot for treason, but the number was undoubtedly far higher—to the Reichstag on July 13, before Hopkins reached Rome. Hopkins also recorded, in vivid terms, his impressions of Mussolini: "[He] talks with his eyes and his hands—his eyes grow enormously big—they flash—roll in the most amazing fashion. His hands and arms move constantly.... He is an actor—and controls his emotions like stops on an organ. I fancy he could pretend great anger or pleasure with great effect."

When he and Barbara returned to Washington after disembarking in New York, Hopkins reported to Roosevelt that he had been impressed with England's public housing and income security schemes but believed such efforts in the United States would have to be done "in an American way." That was in fact what the president intended. Ten weeks earlier, in June, he had formed the Committee on Economic Security and charged it with developing a plan for unemployment and old-age insurance. This was not, as might have been expected, a response to Dr. Townsend; he and his $200-a-month pension scheme were still largely unknown outside of California, and besides, Roosevelt had had a plan like this in mind from the beginning. Indeed, labor secretary Frances Perkins, who chaired the cabinet-level committee, had insisted that she be allowed to explore possibilities for creating an economic safety net before she agreed to come to Washington. More recently, unemployment compensation and old-age security bills had been introduced in Congress. But Roosevelt wanted to tackle these issues in a single piece of legislation, so he asked that action be put off until the committee had a chance to produce recommendations of its own. He set a deadline of December, which meant that the administration approached the midterm elections in November, now barely three months away, with no proposals of its own to counter the clamor on the left and right.

The populist crusaders, the angry business lords, the office seekers vying for seats in the next Congress were all scrambling for attention from voters and the press that fall, but crime, that old standby, stole the biggest headlines. After agents of the U.S. Bureau of Investigation gunned down bank robber John Dillinger outside the Biograph Theater in Chicago in July, the agency elevated Charles "Pretty Boy" Floyd to iconic stature, naming him public enemy number one. By then Floyd had reputedly robbed thirty banks and killed at least ten men, including one law officer. But like the notorious Al Capone, now serving his federal tax evasion sentence at Alcatraz, he had become an anti-hero; Capone had his soup kitchen, and Floyd, who had grown up on a small farm in Oklahoma, was now called the "Sagebrush Robin Hood" for giving part of his robbery proceeds to the poor. Agents tracked Floyd to a farm outside East Liverpool, Ohio, where they shot him to death on October 22, barely two weeks before the election. Twenty thousand people, mourners and curiosity seekers, attended his funeral, but his reputation lived on in Woody Guthrie's "Pretty Boy Floyd the Gambler," with lines such as:

> Well, you say that I'm an outlaw, and you say that I'm a thief
> Here's a Christmas dinner for the families on relief.

On November 6, the administration took the headlines back, and with a vengeance. Conventional political wisdom says the party in power loses seats in midterm elections, but 1934 defied that wisdom. Democrats gained seats in both houses, and when the new Congress convened in January 1935, they would outnumber Republicans 69 to 25 in the Senate, and an astounding 322 to 103 in the House.

"He has been all but crowned by the people," wrote William Allen White, a public sage whose widely respected Emporia, Kansas, *Gazette* was a reliable gauge of grassroots opinion. Arthur Krock of the *New York Times* called the voters' endorsement of New Deal policies "the most overwhelming victory in the history of American politics." William Randolph Hearst joined in, comparing Roosevelt's popularity to past presidents Thomas Jefferson and Andrew Jackson.

For Hopkins and the others who wanted to see a new and expanded jobs program, it meant a chance to regain the momentum lost when the CWA was dismantled.

Hopkins was exultant. "Boys, this is our hour," he told Aubrey Williams and other FERA colleagues one warm post-election November afternoon as they were driving to the racetrack at Laurel, Maryland. "We've got to get everything we want—a works program, social security, wages and hours, everything—now or never. Get your minds to work on developing a complete ticket to provide security for all the folks of this country up and down across the board."

Back from the races, they went right to work. Laboring in the FERA offices in the Walker-Johnson Building and in the St. Regis Hotel three blocks north of the White House, Hopkins and his staff laid out a plan modeled on the CWA and drawn up with input from Harold Ickes, who wanted to be sure his Public Works Administration was not encroached upon. When it was ready, before Thanksgiving, Hopkins got on a train and headed for Georgia to show it to the president.

Roosevelt had been in Warm Springs for over a week; in the two years following his election, his visits to the spa's therapeutic waters had given his cottage there the nickname the "Little White House." The tile-lined baths and rehabilitation pools, rooms for physical therapy and treatment, and cottages and dining halls that constituted the Warm Springs complex were set amid low hills, and some of the goings-on there could be observed from the crest of a hill outside the property, so it was here that reporters stationed themselves to pick up hints of the president's activities. Conservative Democrats, including Eugene Talmadge, had come calling during the first part of the week. The Georgia governor wanted his patronage back; he remained set against federal relief but wished to regain the control of relief appointments that he had lost when Hopkins federalized the Georgia program. With Hopkins's arrival, reporters saw scenes of play and relaxation as the president and his advisors tossed a ball back and forth in one of the pools. The hard work going on elsewhere was less visible; the team worked in private discussing the organization and costs of the envisioned work relief program and refining Hopkins's plan for its public debut.

Still, reports leaked out. A Thanksgiving Day story in the *New York Times* by Louis Stark put the program's cost at $8 billion to $9 billion, a virtually unheard-of amount of money at the time. Delbert Clark of the *Times* called it Hopkins's "End Poverty in America" plan. This was a reference to the failed gubernatorial campaign of novelist Upton Sinclair, whose 1934 End Poverty in California (EPIC) platform had shared a vision of utopia with Townsend. It had called for collectivizing land and factories so that jobless workers could grow their own food and make their own clothes. Hopkins's plan, unlike Sinclair's, was politically realistic, but its dimensions were vast enough to shock already roiled conservatives in advance of its formal announcement.

4. "WORK MUST BE FOUND . . ."

January 4, 1935, a Friday, was a cool, bright day in Washington, D.C. Elsewhere, the news absorbing readers and radio listeners included the trial in New Jersey of Bruno Hauptmann for the 1932 Lindbergh baby kidnapping, the French foreign minister's appeasement of Mussolini's Italian adventures in North Africa, the messy society divorce case of Snowden and Helen Fahnestock, and the third marriage of Cornelius Vanderbilt Jr. A tennis promoter was dangling big checks in front of U.S. Open champions Fred Perry and Helen Jacobs to persuade them to turn pro, and in New York, a battle of basketball unbeatens loomed between Kentucky and New York University. But in Washington, as always, the first sport was politics, so all eyes were on the Capitol for Roosevelt's annual message to the Congress.

A protester leaped from the crowd and screamed at the president as he was helped from his car outside the Capitol a little after noon: "Pass the bonus! We want prosperity!" It was a reminder of the depression's unnerving persistence. Like prosperity, the bonus was an elusive goal, and the veterans had continued to press for it with each new Congress despite rebuffs from the White House.

Inside the Capitol, the galleries of the chamber of the House of

Representatives were full, and lines had backed up outside the entrance doors. The president's mother sat in the front row knitting something blue. The Senate marched in from its side of the Capitol, followed by the members of the Cabinet. Police stopped a man who looked suspiciously rustic amid the formal surroundings; he proved to be agriculture secretary Henry Wallace, and after producing identification he took his seat with the nine other secretaries. In the galleries and on the floor, the murmur of conversation filled the chamber as the packed house waited for the president.

The murmur rose to wild applause when Roosevelt was announced. He wore a frock coat and leaned on the arm of his son James as he made his slow way to the podium, illuminated by a massive bank of spotlights set up in the corners of the chamber to assist photographers and the giant movie newsreel cameras. He greeted Vice President Garner and the new House Speaker, Joseph W. Byrns of Tennessee, by their first names and then turned to the crowd and the microphones in front of him. His opening line contained, for the first time, the language by which the speech would be known from then on: "The Constitution wisely provides that the chief executive shall report to the Congress on the state of the union."

Halfway into the six-page address, he began to talk about the need to put the nation back to work. He spoke of the effects that government handouts had on their recipients. Continued dependence on relief, he said, "induces a spiritual and moral disintegration fundamentally destructive to the national fibre. To dole out relief in this way is to administer a narcotic, a subtle destroyer of the human spirit. It is inimical to the dictates of sound policy. It is in violation of the traditions of America. Work must be found for able-bodied but destitute workers."

The speech had both energy and moral urgency, and the crowd in the chamber belonged to Roosevelt. Three-quarters of the seats were taken up by Democrats. They spilled across the aisle and pushed the Republicans into an island of glum silence while they interrupted him repeatedly with applause and shouts of support. Even conservative Democrats, no fans of the New Deal, could count votes, and they had absorbed the lesson the CWA had taught them: jobs were popular.

"The federal government must and shall quit this business of relief," Roosevelt declared, drawing an explosion of applause. The president waited until it ebbed, then took up his speech again: "I am not willing that the vitality of our people be further sapped by the giving of cash, of market baskets, of a few hours of weekly work cutting grass, raking leaves or picking up papers in the public parks. We must preserve not only the bodies of the unemployed from destitution but also their self-respect, their self-reliance and courage and determination."

Five million jobless men and women occupied relief rolls, the president said. Of these, 1.5 million could not work, and responsibility for them would be thrown back onto state and local governments and private charities for a continuation of direct relief.

For the rest, he said, "it is a duty dictated by every intelligent consideration of national policy to ask you to make it possible for the United States to give employment to all of these three and one-half million employable people now on relief, pending their absorption in a rising tide of private employment.

"It is my thought that with the exception of certain of the normal public building operations of the Government, all emergency public works shall be united in a single new and greatly enlarged plan."

The overriding criterion of the new and so far unnamed program, said the president, was that "all work undertaken should be useful—not just for a day, or a year, but useful in the sense that it affords permanent improvement in living conditions or that it creates future new wealth for the nation."

He went on to say that payments for work should be larger than the dole, but small enough to make private employment preferable. Projects should not compete with private enterprise, and they should spend a high proportion of their cost in labor. They should be placed where the most workers on relief were located, and they should be capable of being wound down quickly in the event that private jobs became available. He listed among the types of jobs he had in mind slum clearance, rural housing and electrification, reforestation and erosion control, road improvement and construction, expansion of the work of the Civilian Conservation Corps, non-federal projects that would pay for themselves, "and many other projects which the nation needs and cannot afford to neglect."

The president set no price tag on the program except to say the costs "will be within the sound credit of the government." He ended the

speech with an appeal to divine providence "for guidance and foster-
ing care," and made his way from the chamber through cascades of
applause. That night, twelve House and Senate leaders attended one of
Roosevelt's indifferent suppers at the White House—neither the president nor Mrs. Roosevelt cared much about food, an attitude in keeping with the unremarkable cooking skills of the White House
housekeeper, Henrietta Nesbitt—where after dining he told them he
intended to ask for $4 billion for the works program. He soothed the
impact by saying he did not actually expect to use that much since increasing private employment would allow the program to taper off.

Reaction the next day was generally positive, and even a bit surprised, given the exaggerated dreams churned up by the populist trum-
peting of Townsend, Coughlin, and Long. Townsend's appeal had
spread beyond California by now; 3 million Americans were giving
their monthly dimes to Townsend Clubs to lobby for his scheme of
old-age pensions. Coughlin's radio audience was larger than ever,
drawn by his denunciations of wealth, excess profits, and "the exploitation of the laboring class"; he was now calling for nationaliza-
tion of utilities, banks, and natural resources such as oil and minerals.
Long's Share Our Wealth Society, announced the year before, had now
grown to 27,000 chapters and claimed millions of members drawn to
his proposals to "soak the rich" by breaking up "the swollen fortunes
of America and to spread the wealth among the people." He called
for giving every family a $5,000 homestead and $2,500 a year.
The popularity of these appeals led many to expect something more
radical from Roosevelt, such as an extreme wealth redistribution
program. They were surprised when he stayed close to the middle of
the road.

The National Association of Manufacturers, the powerful business
lobby that was usually suspicious of Roosevelt when not openly hostile to him, now focused favorably on his determination not to create
jobs that would compete with private industry. The *Boston Herald*
agreed, calling the plan "a little more rightish than leftish." The *Los
Angeles Times* said the same of the president's determination to end
the federal role in direct relief. Typically, the U.S. Chamber of
Commerce issued a statement favoring direct relief as less costly, and
the Baltimore *Sun* thought that Roosevelt "would have done better to
have provided for direct relief in conjunction with the States. The cost

would have been less." But even the Liberty League reserved judgment pending budget figures.

Only the *Washington Post* seemed to have a sense of the vastness of the program that the president had sketched. As the paper's editorial page wrote, "There is no parallel in history for a successful effort by any government, perhaps excepting that of Soviet Russia, to create direct employment for an army of 3,500,000 people, as Mr. Roosevelt asks the Congress to make it possible to do."

5. A WORD IS BORN

Harry Hopkins had greeted the new year with fever and a bad case of the grippe. Both he and Barbara were sick. They gulped orange juice between visits from doctors and nurses, and tried to prevent their illness from spreading to two-year-old Diana. But both were well enough to listen to Roosevelt's address on the radio, and Hopkins congratulated himself when he heard it. "I thot it was a grand speech," he wrote in his diary in his strong, forward-slanting hand, employing his usual shorthand for *thought*—"and particularly because I had worked on it with him."

Hopkins was one of two obvious choices to command the forthcoming army of workers. Ickes was the other. Their stylistic differences—Hopkins's brash, freewheeling ways and Ickes's brooding attention to detail—already coexisted uneasily under the administration's big top. It was part of Roosevelt's style of governance to generate creativity from the dynamic tension between rivals, and with the announcement of the jobs program those differences became both more public and more pronounced.

The morning after the State of the Union speech, the *Post* reported that Hopkins was most frequently mentioned as the likely appointee. Ickes, however, thrust himself into the picture by reminding reporters that he had handled the existing public works program. He was sure that Hopkins would "have a very important part" in the new program, he said, thereby promoting the inference that Hopkins would work for him.

Roosevelt, of course, gave no sign of his preference one way or the other. On the Sunday following the Friday speech, he had his secretary, Marguerite "Missy" LeHand, call Hopkins to thank him for his congratulatory telegram. The subject of the job didn't come up; Roosevelt too was bedridden with a cold, and he confined himself to flirting with Hopkins's wife by calling out in the background, "Tell Barbara to come down and be sick with me—there is lots of room in my bed." When asked about it directly, the president declined to say. "I am going to get my program first and I will not settle as to who is going to run it until I get my program," he told treasury secretary Henry Morgenthau Jr. Morgenthau, however, showed up at Hopkins's apartment on the same day as the call from Missy LeHand, and told him he thought Roosevelt was going to give him the job.

Ickes was the next to turn up there. He arrived at two o'clock on Monday, January 7. It was a rainy day and Hopkins, still ailing, had deemed it too miserable to go into the office. (It was also the day that Roosevelt made the cover of *Time* magazine as its Man of the Year for the second time.) Ickes told Hopkins he had heard all kinds of rumors and was worried about who was going to run the works program. He proposed that a new cabinet position be created to oversee social services, which Hopkins would run, while Ickes would remain in charge of public works. If the new department didn't fly, he said, Hopkins could be his deputy, but he would resign if Roosevelt asked anyone else to do the job. "He thinks Pres. has treated him badly on one or two things," Hopkins wrote in his diary, describing Ickes's dark suspicions. "Feels sure Mrs. Roosevelt is after him—I told him that administration was up to Pres. and I was making no suggestions."

But if Hopkins knew anything, it was that he wasn't going to work for Harold Ickes. And thus the rivalry between the two men escalated as Congress began to debate the new program and its costs.

The House acted quickly. It passed the emergency relief appropriations bill that contained the jobs program on January 24, less than three weeks after Roosevelt made his case in the State of the Union address. There were only seventy-eight dissenting votes. The bill promised $4 billion for work relief, and another $880 million in funds already appropriated but unspent, to wind down current relief activities.

But the Senate moved more deliberately. Senators were being asked to approve a huge spending plan with virtually no strings attached, and relinquishing the power of the purse offended them, just as it offended them not to be consulted on high-level relief appointments in their home states. Hopkins and Ickes, called to testify about the administration's plans, were vague. They weren't dissembling; details would emerge only under the program's administrator, whoever that would be, and all they had in the meantime were the broad outlines. Two months were to elapse while the upper chamber quarreled over patronage and other aspects of the program, such as wage rates and total spending. It was during that time that aldermanic hearings in New York City gave Roosevelt's opponents something they had sorely lacked—an instantly recognizable shorthand for mocking the New Deal.

On April 3, 1935, as the Senate was nearing a vote on its version of the work relief bill, a committee of the Board of Aldermen was holding the last of three hearings on the spending of FERA relief funds in the city. Outside the French Renaissance–style city hall in lower Manhattan, the day was fair and cool, typical of early spring. Inside, the heat and pressure were intense.

Criminal trial attorney Lloyd Paul Stryker was the committee counsel. Stryker was a colorful courtroom performer, and he had brought his full arsenal of theatrics to the hearings to wield against a string of witnesses. On this day they were white-collar relief recipients who had been hired to teach in various recreational projects in the city. Stryker—and some of the committee members—treated the witnesses to a barrage of disbelief and scorn when they described the subjects they were teaching.

A supervisor of dance programs testified that she oversaw classes in social, tap, folk, and eurythmic dancing. "What is eurythmic dancing?" Stryker asked.

"A natural type, simple form of dancing," Myra Wilcoxon answered. "Any kind of dancing is eurythmic dancing." Stryker invited her to demonstrate, but she had the sense to keep her seat and her hands demurely folded in her lap.

When a recreational training specialist testified that he was in charge of a craft school for men and women, one of the aldermen pretended that he didn't hear and asked, "Was that a 'craft' or a 'graft' school?"

"Craft. We do not have the other," the witness said blandly.

But for sheer historical moment, the star witness was another training specialist and craft teacher, Robert Marshall of Brooklyn. Marshall told the committee that he taught "boon doggles."

Asked to clarify, Marshall replied—"somewhat sadly," according to the *New York Times*—"I spend a good deal of time explaining it. Boon doggles is simply a term applied back in the pioneer days to what we call gadgets today—to things men and boys do that are useful in their everyday operations or recreations or about their home.

"They may be making belts in leather, or maybe belts by weaving ropes, or it might be belts by working with canvas, maybe a tent or a sleeping bag. In other words, it is a chamber of horrors where boys perform crafts that are not designed for finesse and fine work, but simply for a utility purpose."

At the time, other aspects of the hearings drew more attention. The white-collar jobs FERA was funding included work on various arcane research projects at New York City universities. These included the compilation of a standard Jewish encyclopedia, a study of the making of safety pins, and sociological investigations into matters such as the non-professional interests of nursery school, kindergarten, and first-grade teachers, and "The Task of Educating Public Opinion Relating to Socio-Economic Problems."

"High-spun theoretical bunk," snorted Stryker.

Critics first focused on these research projects. Hopkins bristled on cue when reporters in Washington asked him if he was going to investigate relief spending in New York as a result of the aldermanic hearings.

"Why should I?" Hopkins retorted. "There is nothing the matter with that. They are damn good projects—excellent projects. That goes for all the projects up there. You know some people make fun of people who speak a foreign language, and dumb people criticize something they do not understand, and that is what is going on up there—God damn it!"

He went on, "They can make fun of these white collar and professional people if they want to. I am not going to do it. They can say, let them use a pick and shovel to repair streets, when the city ought to be doing that. I believe every one of these research projects are good projects. We don't need any apologies!" Mayor Fiorello La Guardia also defended the program, saying, "Educated persons and college graduates must eat."

But nuances like these were ultimately lost in light of the *New York Times*'s indignant front-page headline over the story on the hearings. "$3,187,000 Relief Is Spent Teaching Jobless to Play," it read, and below it at the top of a stack of subheads, " 'Boon Doggles' Made."

Marshall had testified that the classes weren't that popular, but the term was. With the *Times* headline *boondoggle* leaped from the obscurity of the campfire to political prominence as a way of describing work of thin value. Indeed, it would outlive work relief itself, becoming a permanent addition to the language.

6. THE MACHINERY TAKES SHAPE

The Senate passed its version of the works bill on April 5. It contained restrictions against military spending, required Senate approval of all appointments to jobs paying more than $5,000, and said hirees would be paid a "security wage" below the local prevailing wage rate. By April 8, the two houses had agreed on all the details and passed the Emergency Relief Appropriations Act authorizing $4.8 billion to be spent on work relief. The measure reached Roosevelt aboard a train as he returned from a Florida fishing vacation, and he signed it the same day. His choice to head the program remained unknown.

But the deck was stacked in Hopkins's favor. He already had Roosevelt's ear on the work plans he had been outlining in sessions at the White House. After one such session Hopkins made an entry in his diary: "We went over the organization of the work program—more charts in pencil—he loves charts—no two of them are ever the same, which is a bit baffling at times."

The goals of the work program also favored him. The "light" public works he had overseen at the CWA and FERA spent a far higher percentage of their budgets on labor—75 percent versus 30 percent—than Ickes's "heavy" ones, which spent more on materials. This meant the government would pay less to reduce unemployment under Hopkins's way of doing things, and also reduce the costs of direct relief since workers would be taken from the relief rolls. Moreover, these workers would spend their money right away, pumping their paychecks right back into the economy.

Finally, Hopkins had already demonstrated he could put people to work quickly. In the end, this tipped the balance. Roosevelt wanted speed. "Harry gets things done. I am going to give this job to Harry," he told Donald Richberg, who had replaced Frank Walker as chair of the Executive and National Emergency Councils when Walker resigned from the two coordinating agencies in 1934 to attend to his private affairs.

So as not to upset Ickes, and if only to keep him from threatening to resign, the president assembled a structure for running the new program that gave him an illusion of control. It was a three-headed beast, one head each for receiving and screening applications, funding projects, and monitoring the work once it was started. The Division of Applications and Information was the funnel into which state and local governments, federal agencies, and any other sponsors poured their work proposals. It was headed by Walker, who had returned from his personal sabbatical. The proposals that passed the initial screening went to the next body, the Advisory Committee on Allotments. Ickes chaired this sprawling group, which included the secretaries of agriculture and labor as well as the interior; agency directors with responsibilities for soil erosion, emergency conservation work, rural resettlement, and rural electrification; the chiefs of the U.S. Army Corps of Engineers, Forest Service, Bureau of Public Roads, Urban Housing Division, and various other governmental units charged with the country's natural resources and its infrastructure. The Advisory Committee also included representatives of the Business Advisory Council, farm groups and organized labor, the American Bankers Association, and the U.S. Conference of Mayors. The committee was commanded "to meet in round table conference at least once a week," and as Robert Sherwood has pointed out (though putting it mildly), the meetings "must have required quite a large round table." Its recommendations went to the president for final approval.

The third unit was the Works Progress Division. This was the unit responsible for tracking the work projects and keeping them moving on schedule, and it was in charge of this that Roosevelt placed Hopkins.

Having decided on this structure, Roosevelt called Hopkins, Ickes, and a few others to the White House on the evening of April 26 and told them that he was committed to the program. He said he expected "everything to go like clockwork" and would "accept no excuses."

Two nights later, on Sunday, April 28, he sat before microphones in the White House and delivered the seventh fireside chat of his presidency. It was his first address to the nation since the State of the Union address on January 4, and he used it to introduce the works program and ask the people to help keep it honest and free of politics.

"I well realize that the country is expecting before this year is out to see the 'dirt fly,' " the president said. "Our responsibility is to all of the people in this country. This is a great national crusade to destroy enforced idleness, which is an enemy of the human spirit generated by this depression. Our attack upon these enemies must be without stint and without discrimination. No sectional, no political distinctions can be permitted."

Anticipating attacks before they occurred, he forewarned his listeners, "There are chiselers in every walk of life. Every profession has its black sheep.... The most effective means of preventing such evils in this work relief program will be the eternal vigilance of the American people themselves. I call upon my fellow citizens everywhere to cooperate with me in making this the most efficient and the cleanest example of public enterprise the world has ever seen.

"It is time to provide a smashing answer for those cynical men who say that a democracy cannot be honest and efficient. If you will help, this can be done. I therefore hope you will watch the work in every corner of this nation. Feel free to criticize. Tell me of instances where work can be done better, or where improper practices prevail. Neither you nor I want criticism conceived in a purely fault-finding or partisan spirit, but I am jealous of the right of every citizen to call to the attention of his or her government examples of how the public money can be more effectively spent for the benefit of the American people."

Roosevelt called the effort that was about to start "the most comprehensive work plan in the history of the nation," and gave an additional hint of its scope when he referred to the "two hundred and fifty or three hundred kinds of work that will be undertaken."

Applications for funding began pouring in.

At the same time, the machinery of the works program evolved. The Works Progress Division did not remain one of an equal trinity for long. When Roosevelt sat down at his desk on May 6 to sign the executive order creating the new organization, the Works Progress Division had become the Works Progress Administration. The order said it "shall be responsible to the president for the honest, efficient, speedy and coordinated execution of the work-relief program as a whole, and for the execution of that program in such manner as to move from the relief rolls to work on such projects or in private employment the maximum number of persons in the shortest time possible."

The tone of the president's order and the extent to which Hopkins commanded the new program was captured the next day in the *New York Times*. "Only a brief paragraph in the order is devoted to Mr. Walker's and Mr. Ickes's divisions, but two full pages refer to Mr. Hopkins's Works Progress Administration," the newspaper reported.

The name, inevitably shortened to the initials WPA, caused some contention. Ickes, used to seeing the initials of his Public Works Administration used as a shorthand for work relief, thought Hopkins had chosen it deliberately to create confusion. But Hopkins apparently didn't like the name, either, and the choice is usually attributed to Roosevelt. No matter its origin, it captured two things the president wanted to convey—works were under way, and that meant progress.

The first meeting of the Committee on Allotments, held on May 7, found Ickes presiding in the White House Cabinet Room, self-consciously occupying the president's chair. Roosevelt sat to one side. La Guardia had come from New York to represent the Conference of Mayors, as well as New York's large sheaf of applications. (Roosevelt recognized him, saying, "Of course, the mayor will try to get as much as he can in the way of a grant and possibly as little as he can in the way of a loan.") Projects totaling $100 million were on the table, having passed through the Division of Applications and Information. Roosevelt reminded the members that the jobs approved should stress employment, and Hopkins presented maps and charts he said showed how to spread the work around.

But while Ickes may have presided, Hopkins dominated that first meeting, and he would swing the allotment process to his advantage from then on. The executive order gave him the power to maneuver projects from the PWA if he could demonstrate that they would lighten the relief rolls, and he used it with impunity. He had agreed that the WPA should handle all projects costing less than $25,000, which seemed to give Ickes the pick of larger jobs, but in fact Hopkins also kept the option of taking on substantial projects if he chose. "For instance," he said at a press conference in July when the agency was two months old, "the City of New York may want to build a new park...which may cost three and one-half million dollars. That is a proper project to bring to us in the first instance, which we would approve. They may want to build in New York fifty swimming pools. That would be a proper project to bring to us irrespective of the cost. The same thing is true of playgrounds, also extensions, sewer systems, water systems or extensions to buildings. Many of those projects will be in excess of twenty-five thousand dollars. We might have one which would read, 'repairing and repaving of twenty-seven miles of city streets in Los Angeles. The cost is four million, six hundred thousand dollars, of which the City of Los Angeles is prepared to put up eight hundred thousand.' That would go directly to us in the first instance."

Hopkins held the trump card whenever a project would reduce the numbers on relief. But his final and ultimately greatest advantage over Ickes lay in the fact that PWA projects required a 55 percent contribution of the cost from their state or local sponsors. WPA project sponsors were expected only "to contribute equipment, materials and services to the maximum amount possible." Given the option of paying more than half a project's cost or as little as nothing, city and state governments turned overwhelmingly to the WPA, while Ickes's project reviewers looked at their empty in-boxes and fumed.

Ickes asked the president to draw a sharper line between the two agencies. "The demarcation...should be clearly defined at once by you as the only one who can speak with authority," he wrote in a memo that lobbied for a larger role for the PWA. "We have the personnel, we have the experience, and we have built up a reputation for integrity and efficiency that will stand the administration in good stead in the stormy political days that lie just ahead," he wrote. "I do not even intimate that Harry Hopkins cannot do the work as efficiently as PWA, but he cannot do it short of building up what would amount to a duplicate organization."

By then, however, the allotments committee had already relegated the PWA to a narrow range of activities. The first billion-dollar allocation announced by the committee, subject to the president's approval, gave the PWA $250 million for clearing slums and building low-cost housing. The Rivers and Harbors section of the U.S. Army Corps of Engineers got $147 million for a variety of projects on navigable waterways. The remainder was designated for projects that would use WPA labor: to the Bureau of Roads in the Department of Agriculture for building roads and eliminating grade crossings, and to states and cities for more street and road work, public buildings, water and sewer lines, and a variety of other projects. These were the jobs the WPA was created to fill, and soon the sight of men wielding shovels and pushing wheelbarrows would be ubiquitous throughout America.

7. FULL SPEED AHEAD

Roosevelt had planned to ask for renewal of the National Industrial Recovery Act when it expired in June at the end of its two-year authorization period. Its many codes—there were more than 500, governing industries from steelmaking to pickle packing—were becoming increasingly harder to enforce, and the administration saw a chance to fix its shortcomings and preserve its gains with a new bill. He had said as much in his April 28 fireside chat on the works program: "We must continue to protect children, to enforce minimum wages, to prevent excessive hours, to safeguard, define and enforce collective bargaining, and...to eliminate, so far as humanly possible, the kinds of unfair practices by selfish minorities which unfortunately did more than anything else to bring about the recent collapse of industries."

Meanwhile, a number of cases challenging the National Recovery Administration, the enforcer of the current act, had been making their way up the judicial ladder. The codes were a patchwork that varied from industry to industry, but thus far they had withstood scrutiny in all but a few lower court cases. Their underpinnings lay in the commerce clause of the Constitution, which gave Congress the power to regulate interstate commerce. Yet the various permutations of the codes, and the industries they covered, offered different points of attack on their constitutionality.

One case involved a supplier of kosher chickens to New York retail butchers. The A. L. A. Schechter Poultry Corporation, located in Brooklyn, had been convicted of violating the code governing the live poultry industry. The Second Circuit Court of Appeals in New York, while upholding key aspects of the code, struck down the wage and hour provisions on grounds that the employees covered, who slaughtered chickens according to kosher law, were not themselves involved in interstate commerce. The administration appealed to the Supreme Court, and the case was argued early in May.

The court returned its unanimous ruling on Monday, May 27, 1935, and, as Arthur M. Schlesinger Jr. has written, "knocked down with a series of blunt strokes the entire edifice of NRA."

The court cited the issue of delegation as the reason for its ruling—that the Congress, even in the economic emergency of the depression, lacked the constitutional right to delegate rule-making powers to the executive branch. The ruling gutted NRA's codes whether or not the companies were involved in interstate commerce. "Extraordinary conditions do not create or enlarge constitutional power," said the court. The subtext was the court's opposition to the extension of federal powers that were a key to the New Deal. As Justice Louis Brandeis expressed it as he changed out of his robes in the court cloakroom, "This is an end to this business of centralization." Schlesinger called it, in a comparison to the Black Tuesday stock market crash that brought on the depression, "the Black Monday of the New Deal."

NRA codes had set minimum wages and maximum hours, established safe working conditions, and put an end to child labor. Two million businesses across the country displayed the blue eagle that signified voluntary compliance with the codes. Business leaders rejoiced in the court's ruling, while labor leaders feared the return of sweatshops and child labor. As the administration pondered new laws to protect workers, the New Deal now seemed divisible into two parts. The First New Deal referred to the laws passed during the Hundred Days that struck at the depression by imposing controls on industrial practices and production and on farm output. That New Deal, under attack, was coming to an end, and in its place were rising the initiatives of the Second New Deal. These included the recommendations of the Committee on Economic Security for payroll taxes to fund a system of old-age pensions and unemployment insurance. This plan now had a name—Social Security—and was being debated in the Senate after passing the House. Its companion centerpiece was the WPA.

Ickes and Hopkins continued to feud. Each held to the conviction that his way of running a works program was best. Ickes fretted to his diary that his rival's domination would mean "thousands of inconsequential make-believe projects in all parts of the country." Meanwhile Hopkins, in one of his rare diary entries, expressed his impatience with Ickes in language that was typically direct. On May 13, he noted a morning visit to the White House at which he discussed wage rates in the work program with Roosevelt and heard from the president about his weekend poker losses. "He really shouldn't play poker," Hopkins wrote. "His game is terrible but he likes it." Then he wrote, "All day planning the work program, which would be a great deal easier if Ickes would play ball—but he is stubborn and righteous which is a hard combination. He is also the 'great resigner'—anything doesn't go his way, threatens to quit. He bores me."

Hopkins, concerned with speed, pushed to assemble his organization. His top administrators—Aubrey Williams, Corrington Gill, and Jacob Baker—moved with him from FERA, which would now start winding down. Ellen S. Woodward, his choice to head the women's division, also came from FERA, where she had the same responsibilities and had assembled work programs for teachers, nurses, librarians, and other professional women. Alan Johnstone, Pierce Williams, Howard O. Hunter, and the other FERA regional field representatives also came to the WPA. All of them had done duty with the CWA as well. They "have been with me from the beginning, and they suit me," said Hopkins. "I cannot hire any better and if they cannot do it, I cannot get any better to do it." The core staff, though still small by bureaucratic standards, now sprawled well beyond the Walker-Johnson Building and occupied all or parts of nine buildings.

These buzzed with extraordinary levels of activity as the framework of the new agency took shape. Men and women, working in shirt-sleeves, sat where they could, at desks doubled up in offices and jammed into hallways amid boxes and filing cabinets. They whipped out memos and reports at such a rate that the papers piled up faster than the messengers scurrying between offices and buildings could move them to the next recipient. Workdays started at eight in the morning and scarcely paused for lunch, whether it was a sandwich and a cup of coffee at the desk or a working session in which some administrative question was discussed, and ran on into the evening. Between eight and ten at night, staffers and administrators would decamp in groups for supper, frequently returning afterward to work some more. Lights blazed at the windows until midnight and beyond. The creak of the elevators was constant; the phones were busy seven days a week. Woodward wrote a friend of the tremendous pressure, which she said seemed "almost as bad as war times." Everyone took their cues from Hopkins; if he was willing to work such exhausting hours, so were they.

Nor, when he was home, did he get much rest. A friend had given the Hopkinses a cocker spaniel puppy for Diana, but it wasn't going well: "We have done everything possible to make this new dog of ours a member of the family," Hopkins wrote the donor, Harold B. Johnson of the National Surety Corporation, "but the veterinarian tells us it cannot be done for a variety of reasons, the principal one of which is we haven't a house with a yard. He tells me the dog is what is known as a 'Howler' and is afraid of the dark, and that it will be impossible to get him adjusted in an apartment.

"I cannot tell you how much I regret this because the dog is a real beauty and Barbara and the baby were much attached to it. Under the circumstances, I think there is nothing to do but send him back."

Early in June, he summoned his newly appointed state administrators to Washington to let them know what he expected of them. Fourteen were FERA carryovers, whose appointments bypassed the requirement for Senate confirmation since they were already on the government's payroll. Two others had agreed to take less than $5,000 a year, also to avoid running the gamut of Senate confirmation. But the rest had needed Senate approval, and some of these were political appointees with no relief experience. In such cases, where he could Hopkins had slotted his FERA administrators as WPA state deputies and told them in private that he expected them to run things. And he warned them all, political appointees and professionals, to resist politics in running the state programs. "I have been in this game now for two years," he said, "and if there is one way not to do it [buy an election], it is by giving relief, because none of the clients like you. They all think you're terrible, and you are not going to buy any elections that way."

He instructed them to hire competent people who could do the job and to weed out those who couldn't. He told them he wanted honesty and the ability to resist political pressure. The program's main goal, he said, was to put people to work.

Even the politicos had cause to pay attention. McAdoo in California had fought Hopkins to a standstill, but in March Hopkins had faced down Ohio governor Martin Davey over relief patronage. As he had with the recalcitrant Georgian Eugene Talmadge, and in North Dakota when governor William Langer had pressed relief workers for contributions, Hopkins federalized Ohio's relief operations and appointed his own people, who reported to Washington. And he got a long last laugh in May when Davey, who had sworn out a libel warrant after Hopkins had criticized him at a news conference, dropped the warrant two days before Hopkins visited Cleveland to speak to the Citizens League there.

Components of the new agency continued to fall into place. In late June, Roosevelt created the National Youth Administration as a division of the WPA, placing it in charge of Aubrey Williams. The NYA grew out of concern that, depending on one's politics, too many unemployed young people were drifting either toward apathy or toward revolution. Williams's charge was to create part-time jobs for high school and college students, so they could earn money while continuing to study. He took this new job while also continuing in the role of Hopkins's deputy.

In July, Hopkins turned his attention to white-collar unemployment, with special emphasis upon the arts. But first he faced a personnel decision. Jacob Baker had headed the Division of Professional and Service Projects that employed white-collar workers on relief under CWA and FERA. But as many as 25 percent of working women were the kinds of professionals for whom Ellen Woodward had developed programs under her division. She had been frustrated at finding enough jobs for them, so she lobbied Hopkins to place professional projects under her control. By July, she had convinced him. He gave her the responsibility for creating jobs for clerks, stenographers, researchers, and other white-collar types, and signaled the change by renaming her section the Division of Women's and Professional Projects. She also controlled arts projects at the state and local level.

The more ambitious of the arts projects, however, would stay under federal control. Baker, though pushed out of professional programs oversight by Woodward, remained in charge of the federal arts initiative, which had not yet been announced but would include programs in art, music, theater, and writing that would be directed out of Washington.

Finally, owing to the large construction component of the program, Hopkins agreed to take on a chief engineer from the Army Corps of Engineers. This was the suggestion of Colonel Lawrence Westbrook, an army reserve officer who advised Hopkins on rural relief and other special problems. Hopkins accepted the notion with reluctance, because he was not sure the army shared the goals of the relief program. But he did recognize that the WPA's top ranks were filled with people who knew more about human needs than the technical demands of a wide range of heavy and light construction, from road, bridges, and buildings to water and sewer systems, so he allowed Westbrook to recruit Colonel F. C. Harrington to oversee engineering for the agency.

8. "CAN YOU SPEND MONEY?"

Hopkins did not often wax eloquent about his vision for the WPA or for America under the New Deal. He was too busy. Sharp retorts and easy bantering were more his style, and while these left enemies and friends alike with no doubt where he stood, he rarely gave voice to the full flights of his idealism. But that July, he revealed his dreams for the arts and more on a cross-country rail trip with Hallie Flanagan, his choice to head the theater program.

The two had been classmates at Grinnell. Flanagan had gone on to head the well-regarded experimental theater program at Vassar College. On leave in 1934, she had traveled in Europe and Africa studying what theaters were offering; previously, she had investigated theatrical fare in Scandinavia and Russia. But she was back at Vassar when Hopkins invited her to Washington to talk about unemployment in her branch of the arts. "I don't know why I still hang on to the idea that unemployed actors get just as hungry as anybody else," he told her when she reached his spartan office.

The two of them left Washington on July 25 on the Capitol Limited, bound for Iowa City and the National Theater Conference at the University of Iowa. The train rolled through small towns, the slums on the outskirts of Chicago, and sprawling midwestern plains and

farmlands, and the America revealed through the train's windows
must have inspired Hopkins. As Flanagan related later in her memoir,
Arena, he talked "about engineering, about the building of airports,
about the cities and the countryside through which we were passing; but no matter what we started to talk about, it ended up with
what was at that time the core and center of his thinking—the relationship of government to the individual. Hadn't our government
always acknowledged direct responsibility to the people? Hadn't it
given away the national domain in free land to veterans and other
settlers? Hadn't it given away vast lands to railroad companies to help
them build their systems? Hadn't the government spent fortunes on
internal improvements, subsidizing the building of roads and canals,
waterways, and harbors? Hadn't the government subsidized infant industries by a protective tariff? Hadn't the government also given away
other intangible parts of the public domain, such as franchises to public utilities, the power to issue currency and create credit to banks,
patent rights to inventors? In all of these ways, government enlarged
industries, put men to work and increased buying power."

Hopkins argued that the new work program "would accomplish
these same ends by giving of the nation's resources in wages to the unemployed, in return for which they would help build and improve
America," Flanagan wrote.

When they were passing gray Chicago tenements that seemed to
wither in the blinding sunlight, Hopkins asked Flanagan a question he
had answered satisfactorily for himself. "Can you spend money?" he
demanded.

She said she could. "It's not easy," he warned her. "You can't care
very much what people are going to say because when you're handling
other people's money whatever you do is always wrong. If you try to
hold down wages, you'll be accused of union-busting and grinding
down the poor; if you pay a decent wage, you'll be competing with private industry and pampering a lot of no-accounts; if you scrimp on
production costs, they'll say your shows are lousy; and if you spend
enough to get a good show on, they'll say you're wasting the taxpayers' money. Don't forget that whatever happens, you'll be wrong."

He continued to hold forth as the train moved west. His words to
Flanagan were a New Dealer's reverie of possibilities. "What's a
government for," he asked, if not for providing jobs when the private

President Franklin Delano Roosevelt took office at the depth of the depression. He used modern techniques, including "fireside chats" on the radio, to communicate new hope to the American people. *(Courtesy of the Franklin D. Roosevelt Presidential Library.)*

Millions were jobless, with no way to eat but breadlines like this one in New York City. *(Courtesy of the Franklin D. Roosevelt Presidential Library.)*

A Volunteers of America soup kitchen in Washington, D.C.
(Courtesy of the Franklin D. Roosevelt Presidential Library.)

Many of the homeless lived in shantytowns derisively called "Hoovervilles." This one was in Sacramento, California. *(Courtesy of the National Archives.)*

Drought and dust storms were another mark of the depression. This wall of dust bore down on Rolla, Kansas, in May 1935.
(Courtesy of the Franklin D. Roosevelt Presidential Library.)

Roads and other segments of the nation's infrastructure dated to the horse-and-buggy era. The entire country needed work. *(Courtesy of the National Archives.)*

The Civil Works Administration (CWA) was the Roosevelt administration's first major work program. These men are working on a road in San Francisco. *(Courtesy of the Franklin D. Roosevelt Presidential Library.)*

Harry Lloyd Hopkins headed the Works Progress Administration (WPA) and its predecessor, the CWA.
(Courtesy of the National Archives.)

From its advent in 1935, the WPA employed the majority of its workers in construction.
(Courtesy of the Franklin D. Roosevelt Presidential Library.)

WPA laborer Joseph Vollger displays his
paycheck, dated October 9, 1935.
(Courtesy of the National Archives.)

WPA workers building a connecting road between two highways in Lawrence County,
Tennessee. *(Courtesy of the National Archives.)*

Children had to walk to school along this road in Frederick County, Maryland, before WPA repairs allowed it to be used by vehicles.
(Courtesy of the National Archives.)

The WPA employed women in sewing rooms in almost every city and small town. This one was in Louisville, Kentucky.
(Courtesy of the National Archives.)

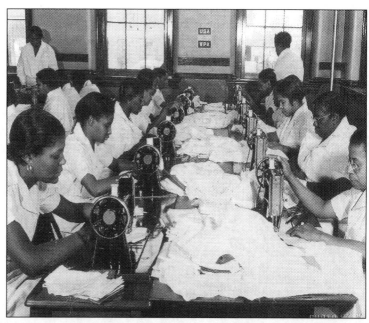

Outlets like this one in St. Louis, Missouri, distributed the products of WPA sewing rooms to clients on relief. *(Courtesy of the National Archives.)*

WPA "packhorse librarians" delivered books and magazines by horse, car, and boat to isolated rural areas. This rider is working in Knott County, Kentucky. *(Courtesy of the National Archives.)*

A WPA traffic safety worker guards children at a dangerous intersection in Connersville, Indiana. *(Courtesy of the National Archives.)*

The WPA worked at malaria prevention, as in this swampy mosquito-breeding area near the center of Southington, Connecticut. *(Courtesy of the National Archives.)*

The same area after it was converted to a free-flowing canal by the WPA. *(Courtesy of the National Archives.)*

The Beaver Dam School in Bleckley County, Georgia, served African-American children. This is the school in 1935.
(Courtesy of Hargrett Rare Book & Manuscript Library / University of Georgia Libraries.)

The Beaver Dam School in 1936 after renovation by the WPA.
(Courtesy of Hargrett Rare Book & Manuscript Library / University of Georgia Libraries.)

When the Ohio River flooded in January 1937, the WPA mustered nearly 200,000 workers to save lives and property and clean up afterward. A WPA official takes flood workers' applications in Louisville, Kentucky. *(Courtesy of the National Archives.)*

This worker, photographed near Louisville, Kentucky, has saved a flood victim's radio. *(Courtesy of the National Archives.)*

The Ohio River flood left a million people homeless. Refugees holding WPA blankets wait to be assigned to temporary camps. *(Courtesy of the National Archives.)*

The flood also created refugees along the Mississippi. This WPA school, in Memphis, Tennessee, is set up with cots to serve young children. *(Courtesy of the National Archives.)*

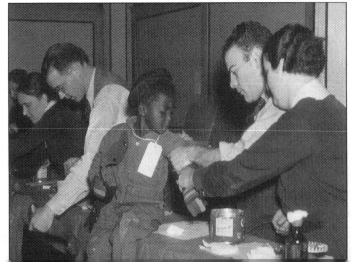

Flood victims being inoculated by WPA health teams in Memphis, Tennessee. *(Courtesy of the National Archives.)*

he said, would not be a problem: "What we want is a free, adult, uncensored theater."

Federal Project Number One, the entity overseeing the four arts projects, was announced in Washington on August 2. The name was grandiose-sounding but accurate; it was the first federally sponsored project under the WPA. Informally shortened to Federal One, before long it had painters and sculptors, musicians and composers, actors and stagehands, and playwrights and writers all around the country applauding their good fortune and, for those who were politically inclined, the opportunity to speak their minds.

sector failed? "These people can be useful; they can do jobs no one else can afford to do. Why, we've got enough work to do right here in America...to lay out a program for twenty years and to employ every unemployed person in this country to carry it out." He talked of building houses, parks, playgrounds, and recreation centers, of providing medical care, supplying children with fresh milk, and undertaking a host of other actions that would improve both people's lives and the nation's stock of airports, roads, and buildings. As for the arts, they could educate and delight vast new audiences, and "were not happy people at work the greatest bulwark of democracy?"

When they reached Iowa City, Hopkins laid out his vision anew, this time before an audience of farmers in a huge, sweltering auditorium on the campus of the University of Iowa. They had come together in the July heat from all across the state, and they brought with them sizable doses of healthy midwestern skepticism. Hopkins took the stage wearing a suit that was rumpled from travel and the weather, and introduced himself as a harness-maker's son back in his home state. He recounted the social devastation in the first years of the depression, when private charities and local governments were dribbling out pittances and grocery chits to families without work. Then he spoke of the benefits of work, spinning glittering pictures of what the WPA could build. He had just topped off his speech triumphantly when a voice from the audience called, "Who's going to pay for all that?"

It was an invitation to waffle, but for Hopkins, waffling was never an option. He surveyed the audience, tossed his jacket on a chair, took off his tie, and rolled up his sleeves. Then he leaned on the podium, gripped its sides, and said, "You are." He paused to let this sink in. "And who better?" he continued. "Who can better afford to pay for it? Look at this great university. Look at these fields, these forests and rivers. This is America, the richest country in the world. We can afford to pay for anything we want. And we want a decent life for all the people in this country. And we are going to pay for it."

Flanagan didn't record how the audience reacted. But the National Theater Conference gave him an overwhelming reception shortly afterward, when he announced the government would sponsor a national theater and other arts projects under the WPA. Hopkins's hopes for the theater were as pure as his hopes for work relief. Censorship,

"I see one-third of a nation ill-housed, ill-clad, ill-nourished," said Roosevelt in his second inaugural address. Students in this Washington, D.C., school lunchroom are eating hot lunches prepared and served by the WPA.
(Courtesy of the National Archives.)

Harry Hopkins spoke to leaders of the WPA's Division of Women's and Professional Projects at a luncheon in Washington, D.C. Seated left to right are deputy administrator Florence Kerr, first lady Eleanor Roosevelt, and Ellen Woodward, who headed the division.
(Courtesy of the National Archives.)

WPA craft workers built and repaired toys, which were then borrowed from toy "libraries" like this one in Atlanta, Georgia. *(Courtesy of the National Archives.)*

These boys are turning in shoes to be repaired by a WPA shoemaker at their school in Asbury Park, New Jersey.
(Courtesy of the National Archives.)

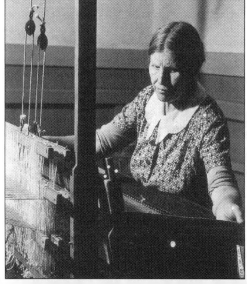

The WPA not only built Oregon's Timberline Lodge, but WPA craft workers made all its furnishings and decorations.
(Courtesy of the National Archives.)

The WPA used native materials whenever possible. These women made mattresses out of Spanish moss in a Savannah, Georgia, program.
(Courtesy of the National Archives.)

A coal fire had burned under New Straitsville, Ohio, for more than fifty years when the WPA began firefighting efforts. These workers are removing flammable material from a mine shaft.
(Courtesy of the National Archives.)

Harry Hopkins joins Hallie Flanagan, head of the WPA's Federal Theatre Project (wearing wide-brimmed black hat), in a meeting with actors. *(Courtesy of the National Archives.)*

Hopkins talks with a worker on his lunch break during a visit to the Timberline Lodge construction site on Mount Hood, Oregon.
(Courtesy of the National Archives.)

9. THE DIRT FLIES: PRELIMINARIES

The Ickes-chaired Committee on Allotments had approved $3.5 billion worth of projects by the end of August (and Hopkins had blocked nearly 2,000 PWA projects worth $375 million for their failure to reduce relief rolls), but much of the money remained tied up in bureaucratic bottlenecks that postponed hiring and job starts. Hopkins had become frustrated with the pace of matters as early as June, when he told a caller, "I have no money down here. I have no appropriations. We can't make any commitment about what we can do."

Manning the chief roadblock against faster WPA spending was the U.S. comptroller general, John R. McCarl. McCarl had been the comptroller general ever since the position was created by the Budget and Accounting Act of 1921, and his job as head of the government's General Accounting Office was to approve government spending before the fact and audit it afterward. To lessen political pressures, the act gave him a fifteen-year term. McCarl was a string-tie–wearing Nebraska Republican who had been appointed by President Harding, and he was ill-disposed toward the New Deal generally and work relief specifically. He took the greatest pleasure in his nickname, the "Watchdog of the Treasury," looking askance at Roosevelt's spending programs. As such, he represented a final hurdle beyond the tripartite work project approval process represented by the Division of Application and Information, the Advisory Committee on Allotments, and the president. He refused to enlarge his staff of twenty-two, so project applications stacked up in his office waiting for review. Florida officials, for example, estimated that 30,000 relief recipients would have received WPA jobs in August instead of 10,000 if McCarl had processed applications more swiftly.

While McCarl kept money from flowing freely into WPA work, all state and local officials who came to Washington to lobby for their projects heard about the Hopkins-Ickes feud. When Oakland, California, city manager John F. Hassler returned to the West Coast on September 14, he announced that "strife between Harry L. Hopkins and Harold L. Ickes concerning the best plan to disburse federal funds" had delayed many projects. Hopkins, he said, "is trying to push things along. I had a long talk with him, and he said that Ickes was blaming him for the delay in getting projects started. He said he would pass everything back to Ickes and make the latter explain why projects are being held up."

Still, despite the infighting Hassler had received WPA approval for $500,000 worth of Oakland projects, with $1.25 million more awaiting action. Many of them had been started under the California Emergency Relief Administration and suspended when money ran short. Hopkins didn't offer hope for any grand public monuments. He had told Hassler that with 3.5 million people to put to work, he "contemplated a purely relief program with very little going to public buildings or permanent construction programs." For the moment, those would be left to the Public Works Administration, which was putting money into the Bay Bridge from Oakland to San Francisco, an island of dredged land in the middle of the bay that was planned as the site of a future world's fair, and a new Alameda County courthouse, for which ground was about to be broken in Oakland.

The projects approved by the WPA for Oakland were the kind that Harold Ickes had predicted, small and at first glance relatively insignificant. They included rat control, book repairs at public libraries, park and playground improvements, painting and repairs to schools and other public buildings, the construction of fire trails, concrete curbing installations, clearing mud slides and loose topsoil from city streets, underground conduits for police and fire alarms, and the like. Applications for projects like these had come from virtually every local government around the country. They had the virtue of being labor-intensive and quick to start, and they did improve the infrastructure in small ways, as well as improve people's lives. By and large, they were not the kind of effort that would return value to the national balance sheet in the way that Roosevelt and Hopkins had imagined, but it was early days.

In New York City, Robert Moses's cadres of engineers and architects continued beavering away in the Arsenal in Central Park, producing detailed proposals that virtually guaranteed instant approval from WPA administrators, who were eager to get the money flowing. Although the army engineers in Washington who scrutinized applications found many that had to be returned, New York's were consistently in order. Between Moses and Mayor La Guardia, who had firehouses, police stations, and public housing in mind among the many projects to be built with WPA labor, New York accounted for more than a tenth of applications that were working their way through the system. The two men didn't always see eye to eye, but both regarded public works as an opportunity to repair the corrupt neglect of the Tammany Hall decades, and both chased the federal dollars with a vengeance. The city had rented an apartment in Washington for La Guardia to use, and he did so frequently. He flew to the capital as often as twice a week, and he had a particularly strong relationship with Roosevelt that gave him the president's ear almost anytime he wanted it to promote his projects. "He comes to Washington and tells me a sad story," Roosevelt said. "The tears run down my cheeks and the tears run down his cheeks and the first thing I know, he has wangled another fifty million dollars."

Indeed, New York's proposals were being approved at such a rate that within six months the city would be receiving one-seventh of the WPA funds for the entire country. Its work relief apparatus was so vast that in June, Hopkins had decided to give it status as the "forty-ninth state," with its own WPA administration. General Hugh Johnson, the fiery former head of the NRA, had reluctantly agreed to head the New York City operation during its first months. "I didn't want to do it, but the president said I had to," he told reporters.

La Guardia was not the only urban wangler. Dallas, Texas, was laying big plans for an exposition to celebrate the state's centennial in 1936. The city wanted visitors to roll in on smooth new roads, and its engineers were readying a $4 million road improvement proposal to submit for WPA approval. One facet of the plan was to create a new western gateway to the city by bringing together three existing streets under a railroad bridge surrounded by a park. Plans for the "triple underpass" called for a commanding concrete structure in the art deco style, under which the streets would merge like the waist of an hourglass. Then they would diverge again on either side of the underpass as they rose through grassy knolls and parklands. Standing nearby overlooking the planned construction was the Texas School Book Depository. The site was designated Dealey Plaza Park after *Dallas Morning News* publisher George Dealey, but Dallasites came to call it simply Dealey Plaza.

Farther west in El Paso, planners were drawing up a proposal that would improve more than 1,000 county roads, with accompanying bridges, culverts, and sidewalks. Among many other projects, the Texas Highway Department had in the works a proposal to use WPA labor to finally pave the remaining gravel sections of the main highway between El Paso and San Antonio. And Texas, as well as every other farm state, had its road department working on plans for farm-to-market roads that would end the seasonal mudbath farmers frequently encountered as they tried to move their stock and produce into the hands of buyers. Not only farmers, but truckers, salesmen, and ordinary travelers confronted long, tortuous, and sometimes dangerous routes that were descendants of native paths and wagon trails. In every section of the country there was road work to be done.

Roads were standard WPA application fare, having been encouraged under its CWA and FERA predecessors. Not so projects aimed at the well-to-do that could sometimes seem odd when viewed against the backdrop of the depression. Skiers around Portland, Oregon, had long wished for a shelter on nearby Mount Hood where they could warm themselves overnight. The mayor of Fort Myers, Florida, Dave Shapard, looked at the dredges digging the cross-Florida waterway from Lake Okeechobee to the Caloosahatchee River and realized his city needed a marina for yachts stopping there overnight. Smack in the middle of Kansas, outside of Hutchinson, golfers William and June Carey decided they wanted to build a golf course in the prairie dunes two miles beyond the last paved road. Idaho Falls, Idaho, across the Wyoming state line from Yellowstone National Park, wanted to attract tourists who could afford to arrive by plane or take sightseeing flights by improving its gravel landing strip.

Scholars, too, could hardly contain their delight with the WPA. Archaeologists of the Smithsonian Institution who had used FERA funds to dig at Marksville, Louisiana, two years earlier saw an opportunity to begin a vastly expanded program of digs at native American sites. Major William S. Webb at the University of Kentucky—a physicist by training who headed the university's Department of Anthropology and Archaeology and had become one of the moving forces of American archaeology—was mapping out ambitious plans to dig at nearly every known Indian site in Kentucky's Ohio River Valley.

Indeed, the "usefulness" that Roosevelt had pegged as a key to work-project approval meant many things to many people. Black children in the Beaver Dam section of Bleckley County, Georgia, might have understood usefulness in terms of paint on the walls of their tumbledown school, resting the building on columns of bricks rather than stacked fieldstones, a coal stove that actually provided heat, and glass windows to keep it in and the bugs out instead of the warped shutters of raw board that were there now. The citizens of New Straitsville, Ohio, would have thought useful meant putting out the fire that had been burning in the coal shafts under their homes for more than fifty years. City manager Hassler, in Oakland, saw a definition of usefulness not just in rat control but in a long list of other projects as well, including new sewer lines to serve his constantly expanding city and keep waste from dumping into San Francisco Bay. Where sewer systems did not yet exist around the country, new privies met the definition. Airline passengers bound for New York City and Washington, D.C., would have found modern airports useful. New York's only commercial airport was not even in New York, but across the Hudson River in Newark, New Jersey, a festering wound to civic pride, while the nation's capital was served by a consolidation of two small fields split by a major road, so when a plane approached or was ready to take off, flagmen had to scramble out and wave down traffic. Teachers in remote rural schools needed more books in their classrooms, and librarians thought it would be useful for someone to repair the books they had. Civic boosters in San Antonio, Texas, thought sprucing up the banks of the San Antonio River where it meandered through their city would be a worthwhile job. In Columbus, Ohio, and Baton Rouge, Louisiana, planners at the two great state universities saw that additional stadium seating could also incorporate dormitory space. Zoo directors thought a new concept in zookeeping, monkey islands, would make their monkeys happier and bring in new patrons to watch them romp in cage-free habitats. Social workers in Milwaukee and many other cities dreamed of brightening the lives of poor children by refurbishing discarded toys. Therapists at hospitals believed murals on the walls would help patients to recover. Conservationists within the government believed it would be useful to convert exhausted and eroded land into parks for family recreation and environmental education. And the National Park Service, concerned about the deterioration of America's most revered monument, the Statue of Liberty in New York Harbor, thought it would be useful to repair it.

The list went on. There were at least as many kinds of work as Roosevelt had enumerated in his address of the past spring. The earlier work programs, as extensive as they were, had only begun to explore the possibilities, and those first steps had whetted appetites. Now, with a full year's funding rather than only a few months of money committed to creating jobs, and with the focus wholly on those jobs rather than relief, states and cities dared to dream of new and more elaborate projects. A great explosion of construction, new (and sometimes previously unheard-of) services, and art creation was primed and ready to occur. The country, as the president had put it, was about to "see the dirt fly."

PART IV

FOLLY AND TRIUMPH

... all of these projects, all of this work that we are doing, spring from a necessity, a definite human need, a need of this generation, a need of the year in which we live and of last year, and the year before.

—FDR TO THE STATE EMERGENCY COUNCIL OF NEW JERSEY, JANUARY 18, 1936

You can start out from Baton Rouge in any direction and pass through town after town which has water facilities or sewer facilities or roads or streets or sidewalks or better public buildings, which it would not have had but for the Works Progress Administration.

—HARRY HOPKINS AT LOUISIANA STATE UNIVERSITY, NOVEMBER 28, 1936

1. DEATH OF A POPULIST

Senator Huey Long was dead. His clamorous romp across the American political scene ended on September 10, 1935, two days after an assassin shot him in the Louisiana state capitol in Baton Rouge. The Kingfish had just finished muscling through the compliant legislature a package of bills that would keep his kingdom and political base intact and unassailable. One bill allowed state authorities to throw pesky New Dealers in jail for interfering with Louisiana's constitutional powers. Another gerrymandered the district of an opposition judge. Long was crossing the marble rotunda of the capitol a little after nine on the night of September 8 when a young man dressed in a white summer suit stepped from behind a column and fired a small pistol point-blank into his body. What they had lacked in vigilance Long's bodyguards made up in belated firepower, shooting the man more than sixty times with pistols and submachine guns. When the bullet-riddled body was identified, the assassin proved to be twenty-nine-year-old Carl A. Weiss, a Baton Rouge physician and the son-in-law of the judge whose district Long had just erased, and about whom he was allegedly spreading rumors of black ancestry.

Roosevelt, ironically, was lunching with Father Coughlin at Hyde

Park when news broke of Long's death. Despite his attacks on the New Deal, Coughlin still craved influence as a policy advisor, and he had used his fellow Irish Catholic Joseph P. Kennedy, the Massachusetts financier and chairman of the new Securities and Exchange Commission, to reach out to the president. At the luncheon, which included Kennedy, Roosevelt as usual was cordial and noncommittal to Coughlin's policy suggestions. Nobody recorded how the two men reacted at learning Long had died—Coughlin said he brought the news to Roosevelt, but the president said his secretary Missy LeHand had told him earlier—but Coughlin would say later that the assassination was "the most regrettable thing in modern history."

Aside from condemnation of the murder, which Roosevelt dutifully conveyed to the nation and Long's widow, regret would not have been the president's reaction; with Long died not only his excoriating brand of demagoguery but also his ability to take votes from Roosevelt in the next year's reelection campaign. Without its charismatic figurehead, the Share Our Wealth Society soon withered. Millions still listened to Coughlin on the radio—in December he would declare his final break with the administration—and the Townsend Clubs still peddled their dream of golden-age prosperity. But only Long had possessed the actual potential to threaten the president's bid for a second term.

And with his death the New Deal's programs regained some of their appeal among the old and unemployed, who saw them once again as a main source of hope. Just the month before, Roosevelt had signed the Social Security Act into law, culminating a fourteen-month process that had begun with his appointment of the Committee on Economic Security in June 1934. The committee had made its recommendations on schedule, the president had mentioned their broad outlines in the State of the Union address in which he announced the jobs program, and he had sent legislation to the Congress on January 17, 1935. It called for a program of federal old-age insurance and federal-state partnerships in providing unemployment insurance. Less prominent parts of the proposal—at the time—were provisions for federal grants to the states for aid to the blind and disabled, the poor elderly, and dependent children and their mothers, and for maternal and child health. The unemployment and old-age payments would be funded by payroll taxes on employers and employees. Employee contributions,

Roosevelt said later, would give workers a "legal, moral, and political right to collect their pensions and their unemployment benefits. With those taxes in there, no damn politician can ever scrap my social security program."

Weeks of hearings and months of debate ensued. Conservatives, predictably, forecast the end of the republic; Americans would lose their initiative and sense of individual responsibility and fall to the level of the state-dependent European. The National Association of Manufacturers, in a comment typical of organized business, said it would open the door to "ultimate socialistic control of life and industry." The American Medical Association convened an emergency meeting of its Board of Delegates, which voted to oppose any attempt to add health insurance to the bill's provisions.

But the growing popularity of the Townsend Clubs dictated that the bill would pass. By the spring of 1935, when the congressional debate was taking place, there were 5,000 of the clubs with over 2 million members nationwide. Many of them were busy exhorting politicians with torrents of mail, and if Congress didn't read the letters they could certainly read the numbers. The House passed the bill overwhelmingly in April, the Senate followed suit exactly two months later, on June 19, and House and Senate conferees agreed on a final version of the bill on August 9. Roosevelt signed it in the White House Cabinet Room on August 14 surrounded by its backers in and out of Congress and declared, "Today, a hope of many years standing is in large part fulfilled." Huey Long, scant weeks from assassination, filibustered to prevent the apparatus of the new system from receiving funding, but Roosevelt took money from the NRA and the WPA administrative budgets to allow the three-member Social Security Board to set up shop.

The Social Security Act was a huge step toward guaranteeing Americans a level of economic security they had never had before. They would not see any money for quite some time, however. The payroll taxes that would fund unemployment compensation would not begin to be deducted until January 1936, and the first benefits would be paid that April. Old-age pensions were even further in the future. January 1937 was the starting date for the collection of the payroll taxes—1 percent on employers and employees up to $3,000 of earnings a year—that would establish the Social Security trust fund from which the pensions would be paid, and the first regular checks would not arrive in retiree mailboxes until January 1940.

All of this meant that for the near future, the first hope of the unemployed remained the jobs promised by the WPA.

2. HOPKINS ASCENDANT

Those jobs were not embraced enthusiastically in every case. For the 2 million workers employed on FERA projects, the WPA's security wage scale meant a big change, especially for those in the skilled trades. They had been receiving the local prevailing hourly wage rate for their jobs and skill levels. That meant their hours were limited according to their pay; skilled workers in New York had worked anywhere from four to eight 8-hour days a month to earn a $60 paycheck. But under the WPA's new rules, these workers were lumped into a single category that required them to work 120 hours in a month for $93.50; they made more but they worked more, too, with fewer opportunities for moonlighting. Non-professional white-collar workers such as clerks and typists took a smaller pay cut from their FERA pay rates of $55 to $60 a month, but with the new rules limiting WPA jobs to one per family, and paying workers every two weeks instead of weekly, they, too, saw reason to protest.

In August, George Meany of the Central Trades and Labor Council had called a city-wide strike of skilled WPA labor in New York. A number of jobs were under way in the city, most of them FERA carry-overs, and the labor boss meant to test the administration's will. Walkouts had already shut down several jobs, including a Lower East

Side low-income housing project and an Olympic-size swimming pool at Highbridge Park in upper Manhattan—one of eleven large pools that parks commissioner Robert Moses was building throughout the city using WPA labor. And the discontent was not confined to New York: both spontaneous and planned strikes were occurring all over the country. Strike sentiment was strengthening as well among white-collar and professional workers, especially young men who were liable to be assigned to "light manual labor" such as sewer cleaning and snow removal under WPA rules.

Hopkins responded by ordering that any worker who refused a WPA job could not receive federal home relief funds. "No one has to work who does not want to," he said. "Those declining to work will go off our rolls and what happens to them after that is not our business." Roosevelt backed him up. This left mayors and governors facing the question of whether they should pay relief from their own treasuries to support the families of workers who refused to work.

Meany had called the New York strike for August 12, a Monday. He predicted that more than 10,000 tradesmen would pack their tools and shut down jobs across the city, but at the end of the day it appeared that Hopkins's and Roosevelt's "work or starve" order had broken the strike before it started. General Hugh Johnson, the city's WPA administrator, reported that 656 workers had stayed off the job, fewer than during the spontaneous walkouts of the week before.

But as time went on, the unions persisted in pulling workers off the job and disrupting the WPA's construction schedules. Strikers threw stones at men who kept working on the Lower East Side housing project in New York, and in Jasper, Alabama, a WPA truck driver was peppered with birdshot as he prepared to drive a truckload of workers to a job that strikers had shut down.

The widespread shutdowns slowed both work schedules and the WPA's efforts to pull more people off the relief rolls into jobs. Hopkins first tried to rub out individual trouble spots. The WPA had three tiers of wages, ranging from Classification 1, in the industrial Northeast and Midwest and California, to Classification 3, in the South and other rural areas. Iowa was one of the in-between states that fell into Classification 2, but in mid-August Hopkins bumped Iowa up to Classification 1 on the grounds that its living expenses were just as high as its neighbors. The change, he said, was "in the normal course of events" and not a response to strikes and protests. As a result, unskilled laborers made $8 more a month and professional workers got a $15-a-month raise. By the end of August, New York workers at the low end of the scale saw their pay raised from $55 to $60.50 a month.

In September, with the pace of work still lagging and the unions still able to keep their workers off the job, the WPA compromised. It took a step back toward prevailing wages, creating an exception to the security wage in "exceptional and unusual circumstances." In New York, this allowed skilled laborers to work 80 hours a month for their $93.50, an effective hourly rate of $1.17. It was less than the $1.50 the unions wanted, but far better than the 78 cents they would have made working for 120 hours. This, combined with the fact that the WPA was in the process of abandoning biweekly paychecks and going back to paying every week, caused Meany to call off the strike. Union locals across the country followed Meany's lead, and the WPA was back in business.

Just as the wage issues were being resolved, the outsized personalities at the center of WPA activities in New York produced a round of political name-calling. Inevitably, the imperious Robert Moses was involved. Acting in his usual bullying style, Moses complained that while he now had 11,000 WPA workers to labor on improving city parks, Johnson had provided him no supervisors to oversee them. "As a result," he said, "hundreds of men have been lying around in the parks, doing absolutely nothing except jeering at workers, shooting craps, drinking and generally creating a nuisance and a menace to the public." They were "bums," he charged, and he threatened to "clean them out." The WPA itself was "arrogant" and "stupid."

Many of these men were homeless boardinghouse residents. Others lacked work clothes, which prompted the city's Emergency Relief Bureau, in charge of moving workers from home to work relief, to request a clothing appropriation from the city. The bureau had in mind workers such as Mick Frank, an unemployed garment center pleater who had a wife and six children—including triplets who made the front page of the *Daily News* when they were born on July 15, 1927—and who had only a threadbare suit to wear to his WPA job at Jacob Riis Park on Jamaica Bay. Such inadequate work garb and his own rancorous behavior gave Moses's complaints a tinge of high-handedness. Johnson would have none of it. "We don't call them riffraff. We call them unemployed," he retorted, and Mayor La Guardia said he resented "any slander or slur on hundreds of thousands of men who, through no fault of their own, can't wear a tuxedo when they go to work for Mr. Moses."

But Moses, as usual, got the best of the exchange. Johnson agreed to supply almost 700 foremen, taking some from other WPA projects, in order to keep the park work going. He had previously announced that he would step down on October 15, and he said that with his self-imposed deadline only a month away, he did not want to keep debating Moses in the newspapers. By the middle of September, some 36,000 WPA workers were laboring in city parks.

But Johnson, Moses, and La Guardia were merely a sideshow to the main event in Washington. The Hopkins-Ickes feud had reached the point in mid-September where Roosevelt needed to step in. During the summer, after Ickes pleaded for a "demarcation" between the contending agencies, the president had written a short memo to Hopkins expressing the hope that the two would "work out some plan" to curtail their competition, but unsurprisingly, this had had no effect. So far, Ickes had not received a single penny from the $4.8 billion work relief fund beyond the original $250 million given to the PWA for slum clearance and housing. Applications still flowed overwhelmingly to the WPA, and when they did not, Hopkins continued to exercise his de facto veto power over the PWA applications, arguing that the program did not employ enough labor from the relief rolls. The battle between the two men was an open secret, the subject of news coverage, vigorous opinion columns, and sardonic cartoons. In the *Columbus Evening Dispatch,* cartoonist Raymond Oscar Evans drew Hopkins and Ickes in a kitchen, apron-clad, fighting over a mound of "PWA dough." Hopkins is filling pie tins labeled "Jobs," while Ickes complains, "T'ain't fair—you come into MY kitchen and use MY DOUGH for YOUR PIES." Ickes had indeed been complaining, issuing statements to the press that the projects Hopkins was blocking were "all good projects," and that in the original approval process, "no individual member was given the right to veto a project." For his part, Hopkins insisted he was far too busy to be waging turf wars. "Mr. Ickes and I have no quarrel," he said. "I have a job to do and am going to do it."

The president summoned the two of them, as well as Frank Walker, the third member of the so-called relief cabinet, and a few others, to Hyde Park to settle matters. Hopkins emerged from the meeting a clear winner. Ickes already had substantial projects under way from the first two years of relief appropriations, but of the $4.8 billion voted that spring he ended up with less than $500 million. Hopkins got the rest. He won on the numbers, as he had from the beginning. Even with the wage increases gained by the trade unions, it cost the Treasury an average of $82 a month to provide a WPA job versus $330 a month for a PWA job, and the WPA jobs cut the relief rolls. Roosevelt wanted men—and women—working. He had given up any immediate plans for balancing the budget, but he wanted to avoid falling deeper into the red than necessary.

Later in the month, Roosevelt offered the two hard-driving men a rest cure that both needed and had earned. Hopkins had learned in July that he had a duodenal ulcer, for which the prescription was "nothing to drink and a strict diet." Ickes had lost his wife, Anna, in an automobile crash in New Mexico in August, and though the couple had long been estranged, the funeral and family details had been difficult and draining. The president's plan was a cross-country trip culminating in a sea cruise. The party left Washington late on September 26, arrived in Los Angeles on October 1, and sailed aboard the USS *Houston* out of San Diego the next day.

The *Houston* was a heavy cruiser of the *Northampton* class, 600 feet long, sheathed in armor and bristling with guns, with a crew of more than 600. She was Roosevelt's favorite ship. She was destined to be sunk by an overwhelming Japanese force off the island of Java early in 1942, but now she gleamed with new paint and her crew's pride at the president's attentions. As the commander in chief and his guests fished and played poker and blackjack, the ship took in Cocos Island, halfway between Costa Rica and the Galapagos Islands, then passed through the Panama Canal on its way to the journey's end in Charleston, South Carolina. Neither Hopkins nor Ickes was known for outdoor pursuits, and the sight of them at sea produced some amused coverage in a tongue-in-cheek special edition of the onboard newspaper, to which Hopkins was probably the main contributor: "Hopkins, as usual, was dressed in his immaculate blues, browns and whites, his fine figure making a pretty sight with the moon-drifted sea in the foreground.

"Ickes wore his conventional faded grays, Mona Lisa smile and carried his stamp collection."

Their feud was pronounced buried at sea, with the president officiating "at the solemn ceremony which we trust will take these two babies off the front pages for all time."

While Hopkins was away on the month-long cruise, Aubrey Williams acted as WPA adminstrator and announced, on October 22, that the logjam in the comptroller general's office had been broken at last. McCarl approved projects valued at $1.5 billion, and Williams sent word to state WPA administrators that they had $700 million in cash to work with, putting men on the job on projects that had been bottled up. The agency's strategy had been to get two projects approved for every one it expected to undertake, thereby providing state administrators with a choice. With the money now starting to flow freely, Williams said the WPA headquarters staff would work double shifts to reach Hopkins's goal of putting 3.5 million of the unemployed into jobs by November.

3. HURRICANES AND PIPE DREAMS

L urching out of the gate, the agency committed some costly missteps in its early days. Two of them occurred in Florida.

In the Florida Keys, some 700 world war veterans, among the remnants of the Bonus Army, were building a road that paralleled Henry Flagler's rail line to Key West. It was part of the push to increase Key West tourism that had seen Civil Works Administration workers cleaning up the town itself. The road job, sponsored by the Florida Highway Department, had started under FERA and was to be transferred to the WPA.

As Labor Day weekend approached, hurricane warnings went up over the Keys. As the storm bore down, a train was assembled in Miami to evacuate the workers from the camps where they were living, many with their families. One was on Windley Key and two on Lower Matecumbe Key, about eighty miles south of Miami. The train left Miami a little after 4:00 P.M. on Labor Day, September 2. It steamed south to Homestead under darkening skies. In Homestead, near where the mainland gave way to the curving string of islands, the engineer reversed the train and backed a string of empty coaches down the rails across islands where the trees were flattened by the wind and over bridges lashed by crashing waves. Night fell and the winds grew even stronger as the train chugged deep into the danger zone. It had reached Islamorada on Upper Matecumbe Key when a wall of water seventeen feet high surged over the island and swept the coaches off the rails. Only the engine, Number 447, survived the tidal wave. The wave and winds as high as 200 miles an hour ripped the flimsy workers' camps apart. Some of the veterans had tied themselves to trees or to boats at anchor as the winds rose. Most of them didn't make it. The hurricane's narrow path spared Miami to the north and Key West to the south, but it killed more than 420 people in the Upper Keys—most of them veterans and their wives and children.

Hopkins immediately sent $200,000 for cleanup and relief to Florida. WPA and CCC workers and volunteers plunged into shredded mangrove thickets to look for bodies and found them bloated and deteriorating in the late summer heat, lying in the shallow water or in the trees they had tried to cling to for safety. Governor David Sholtz hinted that the rescue train had not been sent soon enough. "Grand carelessness somewhere was responsible for the tragedy," he said.

Hopkins's first response was to blame the weather forecasts: "I don't think, from reading those weather reports, that anybody would necessarily have evacuated those people," he said. But the weather reports had been accurate enough to persuade a Florida State Highway Department supervisor to move his equipment to high ground and tie it down, and an outcry rose from veterans groups, including the American Legion. Hopkins sent Aubrey Williams to conduct an investigation. When Williams concluded that the disaster was an "act of God" beyond any "human factors," the veterans groups and others, including Key West resident Ernest Hemingway, dismissed his report as a whitewash. The novelist's indignation produced a scathing piece that he wrote for the Communist Party USA journal *New Masses*, implying that Roosevelt and the New Deal were guilty of manslaughter for sending the veterans to the Keys and keeping them there during hurricane season.

The WPA's credibility was not much harmed by Hemingway's fulminating in a Communist house organ; if anything, criticism from the left counterbalanced the generally harsher attacks coming from the right. But the start-and-stop history of another project in the state had the potential to do much greater damage. This project was the Florida Ship Canal, an overreaching effort to dig a route for deepwater shipping across the peninsula of Florida from the Atlantic Ocean to the Gulf of Mexico. It was a lobbyist's creation, promoted by business and banking interests in Jacksonville, which would be the canal's Atlantic entry point, and it had some military backing, since a canal would allow tankers carrying Texas oil to reach East Coast refineries without going around Florida's "hurricane-blistered thumb." It would also protect them from submarine attacks, a form of naval warfare that had emerged during the world war. Such a project normally would have fallen under the War Department budget as approved by Congress, but the day after the Labor Day hurricane struck the Keys, the White House announced a $5 million grant of work-relief funds to jump-start work on the canal.

This was a pittance compared to its eventual cost, projected at nearly $143 million, with construction estimated to take several years under the supervision of the U.S. Army Corps of Engineers, which was responsible for projects on navigable waterways. WPA projects generally were expected to start and end within a single fiscal year, but Roosevelt was eager to push it forward. Moreover, it would employ 6,000 or more men, a high percentage of them from relief rolls, when the job was fully under way.

The canal work attracted laborers from as far away as New York and California to Ocala, the small farm town in north-central Florida where the work was centered. Their first paychecks, distributed on September 17, were a bonanza for Ocala merchants. The J. C. Penney store downtown cashed 700 checks in ninety minutes. Work clothes and boots flew out the door. The butchers at the A&P and Piggly Wiggly couldn't cut steaks and pork chops fast enough, and quick-stepping stock boys wore themselves out keeping potatoes in the produce bins and filling the shelves with cans of pork and beans. Fred Malaver waited on a customer at his clothing store who told him, weeping, that it was the first paycheck he had seen in six months.

Two days later, on September 19, the canal got its official kickoff with a ceremonial dynamite blast triggered by Roosevelt himself from his home in Hyde Park, using a special telegraph keyboard covered with nuggets from Alaska's Klondike gold rush; it had been used by presidents since William Howard Taft to launch significant events. By the following Tuesday, September 24, 3,000 men were on the job and the project faced a labor shortage. WPA officials in Jacksonville issued an ultimatum: men who refused to leave their homes in other counties to live in the tent camps along the route and work on the canal would be ineligible for any jobs with the WPA. Yet even as merchants restocked for the second WPA payday, the future of the canal appeared to be in trouble.

Lieutenant Colonel Brehon Somervell, supervising the project for the Corps of Engineers, went to Washington on October 1 to say he was going to be out of money. The work was going so fast, he told the chief of engineers, that his initial $5 million would run out by the end of the year, and he needed another $20 million. Meanwhile, farmers around Ocala claimed the canal would admit seawater to the Florida aquifer, the state's source of fresh water, and harm both crops and drinking water.

At the same time, a new source of opposition was developing. The Rivers and Harbors Act of 1899 affirmed one of Congress's most jealously guarded prerogatives, the power of the purse. It prohibited the construction of any bridge, dam, dike, or causeway over or in navigable waterways of the United States without the approval of the Congress. Roosevelt's allotment of relief funds to begin construction of the ship canal did not alter that prerogative; it merely bypassed it temporarily. And on February 10, 1936, the House Appropriations Committee carved $12 million Roosevelt had requested for the ship canal out of the War Department's appropriations bill.

In the short term, work continued under previously signed contracts; almost 7,000 men worked alongside big draglines and earthmovers to excavate and groom the canal route. But more bad news followed swiftly. On March 17, the Senate voted with the House against the ship canal. A second vote, set up by a call for reconsideration, also failed. Roosevelt could smell defeat. On March 19, he sent Hopkins a memorandum saying, "I am inclined to think that we should take immediate steps to stop the relief workers now on the canal, or at least have them try to do permanent, useful work, such as clearing the lands" along the right-of-way.

On April 10, with a new relief request of $1.5 billion before the House Appropriations Committee, Hopkins promised committee members that none of the money would fund further work on the canal. Roosevelt, five days later, affirmed that he would give it no more money without specific approval from the Congress.

There was one final effort at revival, a proposal to place the canal's fate in the hands of an independent study group of engineers, but it too failed. Republican senator Arthur H. Vandenberg of Michigan, the chief opponent of the project, scoffed at the "pipe dreaming on the phantom Florida canal" and said there was never any justification for it.

Almost as quickly as it had become a boomtown, Ocala became a backwater again. Employment on the ship canal stood at 2,750 at the end of May, but the *Ocala Star* reported that by August, the only workers left would be caretakers and watchmen.

In Washington, Hopkins and his aides salvaged what they could from the abandoned project. More than $5 million had been spent with no discernible return, but the administration wanted to report something positive, since the country would soon be waking up to the fact that it was an election year. Eventually Hopkins was able to turn the buildings constructed in Ocala to serve as a headquarters for the canal into a WPA-sponsored vocational school, and the political fallout was kept to a minimum.

The huge earthmoving machines that worked on the canal were either dismantled and moved or left to rust. A big steam-powered dragline abandoned near Dunnellon became a boys' plaything. When it was operating, men had fed six-foot logs into its firebox to keep its big bucket clawing out the earth. Now the bucket was drawn up and locked at the end of its ninety-foot boom, but the machine's pivot point was unsecured. A few boys pushing could make the cab and boom spin over its earthbound treads, so some would climb up the boom and ride the bucket while their friends pushed them in a circle over the sandy landscape that was once again sprouting with weeds and oak and pine saplings. And with the moldering equipment and revegetating landscape came a political reminder that the president would disregard at his peril in the future—that to ignore the Congress was to invite its opposition.

4. A LODGE AT THE TIMBERLINE

Far to the west, in Portland, Oregon, skiers attracted to the snowy escarpments of 11,239-foot Mount Hood had been kicking around the idea of building a ski facility on the mountain since at least the 1920s. At first it was just a shelter where they could take overnight respite. But in 1926 the U.S. Forest Service decided it wanted to attract more visitors to the million-acre Mount Hood National Forest, which stretched south from the Columbia River through sixty miles of mountains, streams, and woodlands, and started sketching drawings for a lodge for skiers and mountain climbers and trying to find funds to build it. In 1934, a group of well-to-do local skiers formed the Mount Hood Development Association to support construction of a lodge. With that, two of the elements needed to push the idea forward were in place.

And the creation of the WPA produced the third component.

Emerson J. Griffith was Oregon's WPA administrator. Griffith, who was fifty in 1935, was a California native with a dapper thin mustache. He had married well, and spent the early part of his career as a newspaper reporter before setting up a steamship brokerage and shipping agency, the profits from which allowed him and his wife to travel and improve their bridge games. They also allowed Griffith to become active in Democratic politics; he headed Al Smith's Oregon campaign in 1928, and Roosevelt's in 1932, and was the state Democratic treasurer both years. After taking the WPA job, Griffith fit into the Hopkins mold, laboring to keep Oregon's WPA administration free of party hacks. He was also probably the only WPA administrator to have authored a mystery novel, 1933's *The Monkey Wrench*, which he wrote with his wife during a trip around the world.

Griffith, a skier himself, knew of the efforts to locate a ski lodge on the south face of Mount Hood. When the Forest Service stepped up as the sponsoring agency and the Mount Hood Development Association sold $12,290 worth of bonds to finance the purchase of plumbing and electrical supplies and other materials, thereby allowing the WPA budget to be spent on labor, the proposal advanced quickly.

The Advisory Committee on Allotments approved funding for the lodge in December 1935. It was WPA project number 1101. The budget of $275,513 included a grant of $246,893 from the WPA, a "public donation" of $20,000 from the Mount Hood Development Association, and $8,620 from the Forest Service for truck and machinery rentals.

Linn Forrest was among the many architects hit hard by the depression. He had earned only $120 in 1932, and with a wife and young child to support, he had taken a job with the Forest Service designing fire watch towers and ranger stations. It was late in 1935, as he later recalled, that the Forest Service's regional engineer, Jim Franklin, came into the office Forrest shared with two other architects and asked them all a question: how much would they spend to build a lodge at the timberline?

Forrest answered, "Nothing." He had been to the timberline, more than two-thirds of the way up the mountain at 8,540 feet. Above it, bare rocky crags rose to a spectacular peak, while below, the pine forest softened the steep landscape. It was beautiful but barely accessible, and he thought the lack of access would keep visitors away.

But with the WPA's approval in hand, the Forest Service architects began a series of drawings that shuttled back and forth between them and Griffith at the state WPA headquarters in Portland. Gilbert Stanley Underwood, an architect with a long history of designing lodges and hotels in the national parks and an expert at blending them into the natural terrain, was brought in as a consultant. At Griffith's urging, the lodge kept getting larger. As it took shape, two wings branched off from a central axis. Cedar shake and clapboard walls rose above a first floor faced with stone. It had steep rooflines that rose sixteen inches for every twelve inches they covered horizontally, so as to shed winter snows that averaged a formidable 250 inches. Dormer windows were set into the roof, and chimneys rose from the roof peak.

Far below the timberline at a spot called Summit Meadows lay the site of an abandoned CCC camp, used by the young corpsmen as a base for planting trees and building hiking trails in Mount Hood National Forest. Here in March 1936, with the calendar if not the weather promising the approach of spring, WPA crews started clearing snow as a prelude to refurbishing the camp to house workers on the lodge. It would also provide a starting point for crews to improve the switchback roads that would carry men and materials up the mountain to the building site, and eventually tourists to the lodge. Plans called for cold-weather tents raised off the ground on wooden platforms, as well as mess tents, cookhouses, a machine shop, a sawmill, and sanitary facilities. Summit Meadows lay near the path of the old Oregon Trail; below it at the base of the mountain was a village called Government Camp, on the highway between Portland and points south and east. It was here that the climb to the timberline, several miles by road and trail, began.

The cold and snow on Mount Hood were apparently more daunting than joblessness as supervisors tried to get construction under way. It was the WPA's practice to use, wherever possible, native materials so as to save money for labor costs. For the Timberline project, this meant cutting native cedars and hewing cedar shakes for the lodge's roof and walls, a subproject requiring twenty-seven men to live and work in a remote mountainside camp for sixty days. But by March 12, only two men had appeared, and before the month was out the shake camp was scrubbed and bids for cedar shakes put out on the open market.

On April 23, the snow at Summit Meadow now cleared, twenty WPA hires arrived to begin the camp's refurbishment but found something missing. This oversight started a chain of telephone calls that went all the way to Harry Hopkins in Washington, and from Hopkins back to the Forest Service at Mount Hood. His request: to borrow some camp stoves to heat the workers' tents, since WPA procurement had failed to requisition any.

While a shipment of camp stoves was being assembled, a classically trained chef named Albert Altorfer roamed a government warehouse in downtown Portland, checking off chairs, tables, stoves, pots and pans, and dishes and utensils from a list of things he needed. It was a long list. Altorfer had been hired as the head chef for the Timberline work camp, and he would be cooking for 200 or more men at a sitting. These were numbers he was used to; a native of Switzerland who had trained at the Hôtel du Lac in the resort town of Neuchâtel, he had landed in Portland in 1923 and cooked at some of the city's best restaurants, hotels, and private clubs. He was working as a private chef to Aaron Frank, who owned Meier and Frank, a leading department store, when the stock market crashed in 1929. Even people such as Frank had to tighten their belts, and by 1935, with his resources exhausted, a wife and two daughters to support, and no private jobs available, Altorfer turned to the WPA. The day he applied, he found himself mingling with doctors and lawyers he had seen in his restaurants and dining rooms.

Altorfer followed his pots and pans to Summit Meadow. The stoves from the Forest Service had arrived, and the camp soon took shape. By May it was ready for full-time occupation.

Up the mountain at the timberline, the snow was still eighteen feet deep, but drivers had managed to reach the construction site with snow shovels and tractors and clear the working areas so that the architects and a team of surveyors could map out the final location of the lodge. Each day's work began with the men riding up the mountain on a sled towed behind a tractor on alligator treads. Where deep snow still remained, the team used probes to detail the site's topography. They deemed snow cornices jutting over the Salmon River canyon near the original site too dangerous to build near, so they moved 300 yards west to solid ground, where the shape of the land was roughly the same. At the end of their workdays, they skied back down the mountain.

Construction began at last on June 13. Snow still clogged the road up the mountainside, and it fell to Captain C. G. Jones, a Forest Service engineer, to see that it was cleared each day for the transportation of materials and a growing complement of men. He oversaw the job with such a sense of urgency that he quickly acquired a nickname: "Hurry-Up" Jones. The official groundbreaking came a month later. The site was finally clear of snow by then, and officials gathered as Griffith of the WPA and Major James Frankland of the Forest Service wielded ceremonial shovels, cameras snapped, and work on the Timberline Lodge was declared properly begun.

5. A NATION AT WORK

The WPA was just over a year old at the time of the Timberline groundbreaking. The money squandered on the ship canal—and another $7 million in work-relief funds spent on a system of dams designed to generate electricity from the tides on the northern coast of Maine before it, too, was halted by the Congress—had produced less of an outcry than might have been expected. Other New Deal developments, the stirrings of the presidential campaign, and the march of fascism in Europe were getting more attention from the press. And for the most part, the agency was working as intended. Midway through 1936, it had met its employment goals: men—and a great many women—were at work in every single county of the nation. Most of the work was unskilled labor, which was what most of the jobless had to offer. Men with shovels and pickaxes cleared land, dug trenches, scattered gravel. Others laid asphalt, pushed wheelbarrows, and mortared bricks as they built new and improved roads and airports, schools, hospitals, courthouses and city halls, sidewalks and sewer systems, playgrounds, parks, and zoos. From the Mendocino Woodlands of northern California to the Catoctin Mountains of Maryland, more workers still were building campgrounds—forty-six of them—where families could rent cabins and enjoy the wonders of nature.

Eye-catching signs marking these projects told the public how its tax money was being spent. They mixed patriotism in red, white, and blue with graphic impact—"USA" at the top in big letters flanked by stars, "WORK PROGRAM" on a white stripe across the middle, and "WPA" at the bottom. Hopkins had instituted the sign program back in March, and they quickly became as familiar as the NRA's blue eagle logo had been in its heyday. Republicans and the anti–New Deal press predictably complained that they were propaganda. In New York, parks chief Robert Moses banned them despite the fact that 71,500 WPA employees were working at parks jobs, setting off a weeklong spat with Victor Ridder, who had followed Hugh Johnson as the city's WPA administrator. Ridder had to threaten to pull all WPA employees from the parks before Moses agreed to allow smaller signs to be displayed.

The WPA was also gaining a reputation for disaster response, working with the Red Cross, National Guard, and other military and law enforcement agencies. In March, a swift spring thaw had caused flooding from New England to the Ohio River that left 171 dead and 430,000 homeless, and the WPA had thrown almost 100,000 workers, from laborers to clerks to nurses, into rescue, recovery, and cleanup efforts. Residents of Washington, D.C., had seen men of the WPA filling sandbags and building levees along the Potomac River in view of the Washington Monument and Lincoln Memorial. In April, thousands of WPA rescue and cleanup workers moved in after two of the worst tornadoes in the country's history struck twelve hours apart in Tupelo, Mississippi, and Gainesville, Georgia, killing more than 200 people in each city and destroying Gainesville's downtown and courthouse square. And in the tinder-dry summer that was now affecting the upper Midwest, at least 20,000 WPA workers would join the fight against forest fires that ravaged timberland and threatened towns in Michigan, Minnesota, and Wisconsin.

Building work and disaster response were obvious jobs for the WPA. Some other jobs were not. But Hopkins needed to put men who were not laborers, and women other than teachers, nurses, and seamstresses, to work, and so across America the WPA paid people to copy old records that were moldering to dust, repair toys for poor children's

Christmas stockings, rebind books for libraries, index newspapers, compile lists of historic buildings, and record folk songs. Much of this work never would have been done had the WPA not needed to create jobs for these segments of the population; with it, the WPA was helping to preserve the country's past even as it was helping to build for the future.

Hopkins being Hopkins, he continued to enrage the New Deal's enemies. He remained impatient with politicians who questioned the need for relief or who wanted to postpone it to see how other programs would "work out," and his responses were scathing and quotable. "Hunger is not debatable," he said once, and "People don't eat in the long run, they eat every day." His blunt-spoken ways endeared him to working reporters who covered the WPA. The columnist Ernie Pyle, just beginning his climb to fame, described his grassroots appeal on October 26, 1935, in his column syndicated by Scripps-Howard to about 200 newspapers:

And you Mr. Hopkins, I like you because you look like common people. I don't mean any slur by that either, because they don't come any commoner than I am, but you sit there so easy swinging back and forth in your swivel chair, in your blue suit and blue shirt, and your neck is sort of skinny, like poor people's necks, and you act honest, too.

And you answer the reporters' questions as tho you were talking to them personally, instead of being a big official. It tickled me the way you would say, "I can't answer that," in a tone that almost says out loud, "Now you knew damn well when you asked me that I couldn't answer that...."

And that old office of yours, Mr. Hopkins, good Lord, it's terrible. It's so little in the first place, and the walls are faded and water pipes run up the walls and your desk doesn't even shine. But I guess you don't care. Maybe it wouldn't look right for you to have a nice office anyway, when you're dealing in misery all the time.

One nice thing about your office being so little, tho, the reporters all have to pack close up around your desk, and they can see and hear you and it's sort of like talking to you in your home, except there they'd be sitting down, I hope.

The reporters tell me, Mr. Hopkins, that you're about the fastest thinker of any of the big men who hold press conferences. Ickes is fast too, and so is Farley they say, but you always come back right now with something pretty good. And you've got a pleasant, clean cut face, too, and they say you never try to lie out of anything.

At the other extreme was the *Chicago Tribune,* owned by the rabidly anti-Roosevelt Robert Rutherford McCormick. A large and blustery man, McCormick had served as an artillery officer in France during the world war, and people had addressed him as "Colonel" ever since. He championed Republican orthodoxy and American isolationism and ran an American flag on the front page of the *Tribune* along with the legend "World's Greatest Newspaper," the first letters of which he unapologetically applied to the radio station he had bought in 1924 when he changed its call letters to WGN.

"Turn the rascals out," a *Tribune* editorial exhorted on April 17, 1936. "Only 201 days remain in which to save your country." The editorial attacked the New Deal in general and Hopkins in particular: "Mr. Hopkins is a bullheaded man whose high place in the New Deal was won by his ability to waste more money in quicker time on more absurd undertakings than any other mischievous wit in Washington could think of. The scandal of the political manipulation of funds under his control is growing and to it may be added the scandal of the uncared-for destitute."

Hopkins, who was happy to be known by his enemies, enlarged the editorial, framed it, and hung it on his office wall.

In the year since the New York aldermanic hearings, *boondoggle* and its verb form had become favorite words in the anti–New Deal vocabulary, used to mock WPA projects as frivolous abuses of public spending power. One of these was a dog shelter in Memphis, Tennessee, built at a cost of $25,000. Republican senator Daniel O. Hastings of Delaware charged in the Senate that its art deco facade, shower baths, outdoor exercise runways, and daily changes of straw bedding were examples of high boondoggling. His colleague from Tennessee, Democrat Kenneth McKellar, responded that the pound was needed because Memphis had a high incidence of rabies. "As vitriolic as the senator from Delaware is, I wouldn't have him bitten by a mad dog," said McKellar.

The conservative New York *Sun* started a daily feature called

"Today's Boon-Doggle." In early 1936, it derided an animal shelter in New York, a veterinary hospital in Auburn, Alabama, a flood control dike in Boulder, Colorado, a road-straightening plan in Cerro Gordo County, Iowa, and a livestock trail from the city limits to the stock-yards in Caldwell, Idaho. Other boondoggle targets included the WPA arts programs, a plan to clean and varnish desks in the Gadsden, Alabama, schools, road landscaping in Tucson, Arizona, a $65,000 monkey house at the zoo in Little Rock, Arkansas, and a city-wide program of park improvements in Chicago.

In the *Sun*'s view, WPA employees were a sorry lot. They were sloth-ful and not to be trusted—unless, that is, they had something critical to say about the WPA. This was the case after a big push in the sum-mer of 1936 to complete an athletic field and stadium at Randall's Island in New York City's East River in time for the president to open the Triborough Bridge, which arched over the island, connected Manhattan with the Bronx and Queens, and gave the island itself its first road access. The $1.2 million stadium was a WPA project, the bridge a $44.2 million project of the Public Works Administration. It was dedicated by Roosevelt on July 11 among a party that included Hopkins and Ickes, Mayor La Guardia, and parks commissioner Moses, who made his headquarters on Randall's Island and for whom the bridge represented a vast expansion of his empire since he had added control of the Triborough Bridge Authority to his parks duties in 1934. Afterward, the *Sun* reported that the stadium had been fin-ished in such haste that the concrete was honeycombed with air pock-ets and contained pieces of wood and even tools dropped by workers who were given no time to retrieve them, and would require extensive repairs. The paper's source was inspection reports by "WPA engineers, selected for supervisory positions because of their long experience." Moses, who was normally critical of the WPA, now managed to attack it and defend it all at once, calling the inspectors "irresponsible" and contending that the stadium was "in good condition."

The Republican National Committee and the Liberty League also took their turns at bat. Their criticisms usually revealed nothing but their bias against government, as when the Liberty League singled out a shoe repair program on Long Island as an example of boondoggling. Majority leader Joe Robinson responded with sarcasm on the Senate floor: "Think how demoralizing it must have been, with the thermometer ten degrees below zero, to have Uncle Sam supplying funds to repair the damaged shoes of children who were forced to trudge back and forth to school. The du Pont brothers must have been shocked when [Liberty League president Jouett] Shouse showed them that classic example of undermining the moral fiber of children on relief."

The Republicans and the Liberty League, said Robinson, were "playing politics with human misery." But Roosevelt took a lighter tone. "If we can boondoggle ourselves out of this depression," he said, "that word is going to be enshrined in the hearts of the people for many years to come." Nonetheless, the WPA's Information Division kept a state-by-state file of boondoggling charges and issued detailed refutations that went out under the heading "The Facts Are."

There was no defense for some miscues, however. The WPA gave its enemies more ammunition than they needed in tiny Mount Airy, North Carolina, when workers there built a lake that proved not to have a water source. Sardonic stories in the press described the 200-yard-long, 40-foot-thick dam of native rock and concrete holding back a six-inch puddle, the order placed for 30,000 fish to stock the lake, and the town residents who had built boats in anticipation of going fishing. Something similar happened in Butte, Montana, where a WPA ice rink was built too far from a hydrant to be flooded. WPA recreation workers finally solved the problem just in time for the spring thaw, and then turned the rink into a softball field.

Yet despite the wild charges and the occasional blunder, for the most part the WPA was being run efficiently and free of scandal. Hopkins had followed Roosevelt's call for citizen oversight with vigorous self-policing through an investigations unit. The "W-men," announced in October 1935, were a squad of fifty investigators working out of Washington and thirteen regional offices under the authority of WPA Division of Investigation chief Dallas Dort. The squad was assigned to look at fraud, corruption, and practices such as payroll padding, the use of relief workers to improve private property, and the extortion of money from workers in exchange for jobs; it had the option of calling on other federal investigative agencies, including the Secret Service, if necessary. "Our job is to keep graft out of the program and we are going to do it," Dort said. Hopkins was swift to axe offenders and issue news releases before scandals had a chance to build. Moreover, as he had from the start, he kept the agency's administrative costs low, running around 4 percent of total spending. As a result, partisan attacks failed to gain traction and public and legislative backing remained high.

And the president continued to encourage support for work relief as an obligation of the government, making the case against conservatives who wanted it to retreat to its pre–New Deal inaction. He had challenged them anew in his third State of the Union address, asking, "Shall we say to the several millions of unemployed citizens who face the very problem of existence, of getting enough to eat, 'We will withdraw from giving you work. We will turn you back to the charity of your communities and those men of selfish power who tell you that perhaps they will employ you if the Government leaves them strictly alone'?"

That State of the Union address, on January 3, 1936, had come at a crucial time. Roosevelt had seen the National Recovery Administration undone by a unanimous Supreme Court the year before. Now, a challenge to the Agricultural Adjustment Act also awaited a court ruling. The justices had heard arguments in the fall term, and there was no reason to suspect that they were any less hostile to what Justice Brandeis had called "this business of centralization," by which he meant the government's effort to control business practices and the economy. And indeed, the president's State of the Union appeal to Congress to keep passing laws that protected farmers—as well as homeowners, child laborers, the elderly, investors, unions, the poor, and the unemployed—preceded the court's ruling on the AAA by just three days. On Monday, January 6, Justice Owen Roberts read a six-to-three opinion that it, too, ran afoul of the Constitution. The ruling attacked the government's system for moderating farm production, which taxed food processors and textile manufacturers and used the proceeds to pay farmers for planting less acreage and raising fewer animals for food. It said the processing tax violated the government's constitutional authority to tax and spend because it required production cutbacks in return, and this was a coercive contract that trampled on states' rights, which applied because agriculture was a local business and not a national one.

This time, however, Brandeis had sided with the administration. He and Justices Benjamin Cardozo and Harlan Stone objected to the majority's invocation of states' rights because, said Stone in his dissent, the constitution allowed taxation that "provide[d] for the...general welfare" and the agricultural depression was clearly general, meaning national, in scope. But the three votes were of little consolation. The ruling left Roosevelt virtually helpless in regard to the government's ability to impose its goals on the economy and to moderate the harshest industrial practices.

As for the economy's still staggering rate of unemployment, here at least the administration was still allowed a relatively free hand. Three and a half million people were on the government's work-relief rolls that January. Of those the vast majority, 2.8 million, were WPA workers, with the rest divided between the Public Works Administration and the Civilian Conservation Corps. They remained the cross section of the American workforce that Hopkins had referred to the year before: workers from building, manufacturing, transportation, communication, and service fields, skilled and unskilled, men and women, urban and rural. Because of the work program, they received more money and were better cared for than they had been a year earlier, Hopkins said, though he contradicted a reporter who asked if relief was "sitting pretty."

"I would not use the term 'sitting pretty' on any relief business," he said.

However, the fog of numbers and broad categories such as these obscured the individual human beings who were, after all, the objects of the program. Statistics blurred them into nothingness. As Hopkins would write in *Spending to Save*, his account of the depression and the relief programs he ran, "You can pity six men, but you can't keep stirred up over six million." But at the root of the statistics were real people doing real jobs, providing for their families, and touching other people as they worked. Almost every project, large or small, had its story, and many were impossible to imagine outside the context of the WPA and its inventiveness in job creation.

6. KENTUCKY'S PACKHORSE LIBRARY
(LIBRARIAN GRACE OVERBEE)

The bulk of WPA jobs were concentrated in its vast array of building projects that employed men of varying skill levels. But women, too, headed families or needed to support themselves. In fact, they had constituted 22 percent of the workforce in 1930, a percentage so far not attained under any of the New Deal work-relief programs, so the Division of Women's and Professional Projects under Ellen Woodward was constantly struggling to create new opportunities. Library services fell within this division, and librarians saw that WPA job slots could help them reach out to readers.

Getting books to people in the countryside had always been a challenge. Most of the nation's rural counties had no libraries. A few had lending agreements with city libraries, but these provided mostly hand-me-downs, tattered books and dog-eared magazines that were severely out of date by the time they finished circulating among their primary customers. State and local governments that had never had much incentive to spend money on libraries in the first place had even less with the depression sapping their ability to pay teachers, provide relief, or on occasion even keep their citizens from starving.

Kentucky was among the states that had scrimped on library services. Sixty of its 120 counties had no public libraries, and the state spent an average of 10 cents per capita on library-related activities, versus 30 cents nationally. When the depression hit, librarians struggled in vain to supply books to schools, but elementary schools on average had only one book for every two children. In 1931 and 1932, counties statewide spent a mere 2 cents per pupil for books on average, and twenty-four poorer counties spent no money at all. Most of these counties were in eastern Kentucky, a region of few roads, inaccessible terrain, scattered pockets of isolated people, and the occasional school that could not be reached except on foot or horseback.

These conditions were mirrored in other rural areas around the country. Creative librarians soon saw that with the WPA, they could hire a new breed of outreach workers—women and men who would carry books into the rural outbacks using horses, mules, and rowboats. These came to be called packhorse libraries, rough-rider cousins of the recently invented bookmobile.

The idea of sending book-toting librarians into remote areas on horseback preceded the depression in Kentucky. Eastern Kentucky coal baron John C. C. Mayo, who made a fortune selling mineral rights in the Big Sandy coal fields at the turn of the century, had funded a mounted library in his adopted hometown of Paintsville, in Johnson County, in 1913. But when he died of kidney failure a year later, the librarian who had conceived the plan was left without a sponsor. Elizabeth Fullerton, the state administrator for women's projects under FERA, knew the history of the Paintsville library. In 1934, when a clergyman in Leslie County offered to share the books at his community center if they could be carried into rural areas, Fullerton found room in her budget to hire carriers, and the packhorse library was back in business. The word spread to nearby counties, and when the WPA took over work relief the following year, county school boards and parent-teacher associations pressed their local WPA administrators to expand the program. At the heart of the effort was the Kentucky Congress of Parents and Teachers, and its chair of library service, Lena Nofcier.

A notice that jobs were available for book carriers went up in the WPA office in the Lee County seat, Beattyville, early in 1936, about the time that a tall, black-haired mother of two, Grace Overbee, was considering how to subsist.

Grace wasn't slowly starving on a diet of soup made from wild this-
tles, as some desperate rural families were, but she was beginning to
run out of options for her family. She had married her husband, Taylor
Overbee, when she was just sixteen; their son, Richard, had come
along on schedule nine months later, his birth coinciding more or less
with the start of the depression. Now the boy was six, his sister,
Elizabeth, three, and Taylor Overbee was gone, kicked out by Grace
after he sold her frying chickens to buy whiskey.

When that happened, Grace and the children moved back to her
parents' house. Martin and Drusha Caudill's farm, near the spectacular plunge in Brush Creek called Canyon Falls, had a bumper crop of
gorgeous views, but its twenty-five acres were almost too steep to
plow. The farm put food on the table but no money in the till for flour,
kerosene to light the lamps, and other necessities. Grace kept a garden
and worked where she could. The oldest of nine children, she had
helped raise her younger siblings from the time she was seven, so work
was nothing new. Lee County was home to a few productive and relatively prosperous bottom farmers and other folks with steady incomes:
teachers, Spanish-American War pensioners, and wounded world war
veterans who received disability payments. She would weed their gardens and clean for them and come home with a few coins and a bundle
of old clothes. Sometimes she would pick corn all day long in exchange for a bushel of her own to feed the milk cow. Still, there were
things the children needed that barter, hard labor, and gardening were
unable to provide, but she resisted applying for relief until she heard
the news that the WPA had jobs to offer.

Grace borrowed the mule her father used for plowing to make the
ten-mile trek to town. Beattyville nestled on the north bank of a river
bend where the North and South Forks of the Kentucky River came
together. When she found the WPA's downtown storefront, she was
disappointed to see that most of the job postings were for men. The
WPA was paving and graveling and building in the county, turning
rutted tracks and stream fords into roads and bridges that a car or
truck could use year-round. Then she saw a notice for a position that
wasn't just for men. The job was delivering books to remote schools
and individual families scattered about the mountain coves and hollows beyond the reach of roads. It paid about $7.50 a week. She
snatched the notice off the wall and went to a desk inside the office.

The clerk at the desk was not someone she knew, but it still killed her to sign the paper admitting that she was a pauper eligible for relief. But once she swore to that and the fact that she was the head of her household, the job was hers.

On her first day, she hitchhiked to town to collect her supply of books and magazines from the Beattyville storefront the county school board was using as a library. She took about a dozen books and several magazines, enough to fill a saddlebag. Since her father was unable to spare the mule from its daily farm work, she walked her route, carrying her saddlebag of books slung over a shoulder. She had been assigned to service three schools, plus a few families along the way. Monica, the closest school, was just two miles from home. Primrose and Oliver were farther. Sometimes she hitchhiked and caught rides, but even then the road didn't go as far as she was going, so she still walked most of the distance.

Once she received her first paycheck, life got easier. She and the children moved back to the two-room cabin, half a mile from her parents, where they had lived before she booted Taylor out. A neighbor owned a big black horse he was willing to rent for 50 cents a week plus feed. The horse's name was Bill, and he doubled her book-carrying capacity. In addition to the schools, her circuit took in the tiny communities of Bear Creek, Brush Creek, Wide Creek, Burton Bend, and Tallega, each consisting of just a few families, and several isolated farmsteads.

The days she rode out started with her dressing in her side of the cabin by the light of the kerosene lamp. What she wore depended on the weather, but she always wore pants and riding boots. It was still dark when she roused the children, and while they got dressed she saddled Bill in the barn and slung the saddlebags over his flanks, then led him to the cabin and mounted before she pulled Richard and Elizabeth aboard, one in front of her, one in back, so she could drop them at her mother's before starting on her rounds.

Her route was too long to cover in one day, so she split it into several sections. The only requirement she gave herself was to hit every house and school at least once every two weeks to trade fresh books and magazines for old ones. Once a month, she rode to Beattyville to meet the other traveling librarians and swap materials; what was old to her readers would be new to those on other routes. These trips often intersected with WPA road crews clearing ditches or crushing gravel to spread across the muddy tracks. The men welcomed distractions from their work, especially a young and pretty woman, and they always paused to wave and shout greetings. She took these as the compliments they were, and also as a form of camaraderie: *We're all in this together, working for the WPA.* Sometimes her father, Martin, was one of the men waving, since he had qualified for the WPA in order to raise cash by working with the road crews.

The terrain she traveled was tough and her rides harrowing. One stretch followed cliffside trails so narrow she had to lead the horse rather than ride him, where one misstep would take them off the edge. They forded creeks that swelled up with rain until the water reached the bottom of her saddlebags. Winter was the worst; snow obscured the trails, ice made footing treacherous, and more than once, trying to dismount at her destination, she found she couldn't move because her boots were frozen to the stirrups. There was a human factor, too. Moonshiners who plied their trade in the Kentucky hills were jealous of their territory and wary of intruders, and when she encountered signs that warned travelers in no uncertain terms to stay away, she obeyed them.

Grace was not much of a reader herself. She had gone through the fifth grade before dropping out to help her parents, and after that she had never had the time. Being honest, she would say she did not feel the call of books and words, although on the days between her travels she often browsed through the materials she had ready for delivery. Being a packhorse librarian was a job in her eyes, not a mission, but what amused and touched her most, as she recalled it years later, was that she was welcomed like a queen practically everywhere she went. Her job had status, which she had not anticipated at the start. She felt necessary, like a person delivering the mail.

So eagerly was she received that she came to feel that the people all along her route were starved for experiences outside their own. Books gave them this, apparently, and almost any book would do. The children loved adventure stories. They doted on the tale of the shipwrecked Robinson Crusoe and the strange predicament of Lemuel Gulliver, as generations of children had before them. Her own son, Richard, was held in thrall by a book called *Bears of Blue River*, especially the section where its boy heroes were fishing on a log when they found themselves trapped by a bear, and cleverly decided to throw their fish at it so they could scramble off the log to safety. They also liked reading and reciting poetry. She noted that the adults tended to like history, especially accounts of the Civil War and the world war. Farmers wanted books and magazines on crop improvement, their wives information on their health and their children's. Some—not many—would read penny dreadfuls or romantic novels, but as an anonymous report covering all the Kentucky packhorse programs lamented, "It has been discovered that novels in general will not be read." Nonetheless, Grace found that all her clients eagerly took whatever books she had on hand, and were just as eager to exchange them for new ones on her next visit. Those who could not read looked forward to her visits, too; instead of books they took magazines and catalogues for the pictures of places they had never been, things they'd never seen, goods they might have seen but never owned. And some who lived all alone in the remote hills wanted nothing more than the sight and sound of another human being.

She saw the worst effects of the depression on her routes: gaunt children, men lost inside their overalls, women whose threadbare dresses could not possibly keep out the cold. There were rumors of starvation; a member of the Tolson family died, and people said he hadn't gotten enough to eat. The Deaton family, too. Neither family was on her route, but at one farm she visited, where it was clear the children barely had sufficient food, the woman of the house always insisted that she stay for dinner. She felt as though she was taking food from the children's mouths; before the WPA put her to work there were many nights when her own children had eaten nothing but cornbread and milk. But the proud family insisted on its hospitality.

The best days brought her to the schools on her circuit. Grace's friend Carlie Lynch taught forty-five children at the one-room school at Monica, where Richard started in the fall of 1936. Grace knew that when she and Bill approached the school, the children would hear the horse's hooves and rush outside to greet her. Sunshine, rain, or snow, when she came around the last bend in the trail they would be gathered in the yard, calling out: "Book lady's comin'! Book lady's comin'!"

The WPA's Division of Women's and Professional Projects eventually deployed 107 packhorse librarians across eastern Kentucky—96 women and 11 men—reaching into more than fifty counties. But even in 1936, when the program was still limited to Lee and nine other counties, they delivered 33,000 books and magazines to 57,000 families. Over time, their collections of books and magazines improved as news of the roving librarians reached cities such as Boston and Chicago, accelerating donations, and the Kentucky Congress of Parents and Teachers campaigned for pennies to buy books. Meanwhile, volunteers mustered by local parent-teacher associations attracted more gifts of reading matter, from books and magazines to catalogues and recipes.

WPA traveling libraries, using horses, mules, cars, and boats, were also deployed in rural Ohio, in rural counties of Georgia, South Carolina, and most other southern states, and in each of the eighty-two counties of Mississippi, where 1,240 WPA workers distributed 168,000 books. And everywhere there was a library struggling to reach readers, there were WPA book repairers working with old cloth, razor blades, cardboard, glue, and sewing awls to bring worn and damaged books back to useful life, allowing meager budgets for new books to stretch further. As the concept spread, WPA library services set up distribution points in schools and remote stations in Kansas, Iowa, Rhode Island, South Dakota, Michigan, Missouri, Nebraska, Ohio, Oklahoma, Montana, Vermont, Maine, and Pennsylvania. These were welcome additions, of course, but they lacked the personal touch the packhorse libraries provided; they used the U.S. mail to deliver books to individuals.

7. THE 1936 CAMPAIGN

The year had started out badly for Roosevelt and the New Deal. Not only had the Supreme Court overturned the Agricultural Adjustment Act, but before January was over the Congress had resoundingly rejected his second veto of legislation granting world war veterans immediate payment of their bonuses. By the summer, however, $1.1 billion had reached the hands of veterans and Roosevelt had won by losing, the idea being that he had not worked hard to see the veto sustained and therefore had acquiesced to Congress and the veterans. The president and the American Legion both contrasted his behavior with Hoover's in 1932, when MacArthur expelled the veterans and torched their camp, and that contrast became an early theme of Roosevelt's campaign for reelection.

Hoover was styling himself as the anti-Roosevelt in any case. He had used the Republican convention, held in June in Cleveland, to call for a "holy crusade" against Roosevelt's programs, but the party's nominee, Kansas governor Alfred M. Landon, initially resisted this call to arms. Instead of condemning the New Deal's initiatives, Landon, who was an oil millionaire and a progressive who had supported Teddy Roosevelt, simply implied that he could manage them better. He tried to appeal to the grassroots by calling himself "the everyday American."

The Democrats had convened in Philadelphia to renominate Roosevelt. He responded with one of his classic speeches to an outdoor crowd at Franklin Field on the University of Pennsylvania campus. The Penn Quaker football stadium held 52,000 fans, but floor seating doubled its capacity, and an audience of 100,000 greeted Roosevelt on a moonlit night following a rain. They heard the president call his opponents "economic royalists" who "complain that we seek to overthrow the institutions of America. What they really complain of is that we seek to take away their power." He went on to assert eloquently that the government bore basic obligations to its citizens: "Governments can err, presidents do make mistakes, but the immortal Dante tells us that divine justice weighs the sins of the cold-blooded and the sins of the warm-hearted in different scales.

"Better the occasional faults of a government that lives in a spirit of charity than the consistent omissions of a government frozen in the ice of its own indifference.

"There is a mysterious cycle in human events. To some generations much is given. Of other generations much is expected. This generation of Americans has a rendezvous with destiny."

It was a stirring and memorable phrase: "a rendezvous with destiny." The election loomed as a crossroads that would show whether America could sustain an industrial society that supported private enterprise and at the same time protected the rights and opportunities of working men and women. "We are fighting to save a great and precious form of government for ourselves and for the world," the president proclaimed. Cheers rose from the audience to drown out his final words and continued for ten minutes until the band played "Auld Lang Syne." Roosevelt sang together with the crowd, then circled the floor of the stadium in his car, waving as applause cascaded from all sides.

As the campaign moved into the fall, Landon toughened his talk and became the firebreathing anti–New Dealer that conservative Republicans were hoping for. The WPA was one of their favorite targets. Given those dry lakes and monkey islands, it could be an easy one. The fact that it favored inefficient hand labor over machinery in order to maximize jobs meant that workers were often standing around waiting. A man digging a ditch had to wait for the wheelbarrow he had filled to be dumped and returned. The man pushing the wheelbarrow had to wait for it to be filled again. Observers could easily conclude that WPA workers were idle much of the time, and there were jokes galore: that the initials stood for "We Piddle Around" or "We Poke Along." Wisecrackers said they liked to advise WPA workers leaning on their shovels to shift sides from time to time to avoid curvature of the spine. An anti-Roosevelt "inventor" announced the WPA "comfort shovel," featuring an armrest and a seat.

Nor did the workers themselves always protest these dim assessments. Some found humor in their job avoidance skills. One joke, which probably had several versions according to the teller's national origins, had a worker at a WPA job site urgently needing a bathroom break. Approaching the privy, he saw a long line. A friend and countryman was at the head of the line, though, so the worker approached him and asked, according to the Irish version, "D'you think I might go ahead of you, Mike? I'm in an awful hurry."

"Go ahead, then, Pat," his friend replied. "Y'see, there's no one in there."

Roosevelt and the Democrats worked as hard to keep the WPA out of the campaign as the Republicans worked to attack it. Hopkins remained sensitive to the president's original instruction not to play politics with the relief rolls. Every regional, state, and local administrator had been told repeatedly that workers were not to be pressured to join, contribute to, or vote for a particular party. Johnny Mills, a laborer scrambling to make a living in the mountains of Jackson County, North Carolina, said that as a Republican he had never been able to get a state job, but that the WPA, which employed him at road and other work for several years, "was always fair." Indeed, the agency was so determinedly non-partisan that Democratic politicians in at least four states—California, Kentucky, Massachusetts, and Washington—complained that Republicans ran the show at the expense of the Democrats.

Nonetheless, as a leading administration figure, Hopkins was no stranger to the campaign trail, making speeches defending the New Deal. But when he snapped that Landon's state of Kansas "has never put up a dime for unemployment," he was quickly pushed to a backseat. James Farley, who had resigned as postmaster general to manage the campaign, thought him too outspoken and the WPA too vulnerable to conservative attack, justified or not. Meanwhile, WPA jobs were to be non-partisan but numerous. Under orders to curb spending, Hopkins had been reducing the rolls gradually since the spring, but with the election just a month away, Roosevelt himself forbade a cut that would have dropped additional workers. "Not one person is to be laid off on the first of October," he told treasury secretary Henry Morgenthau Jr.

As the campaign continued, Landon moved ever further to the right, adopting Hoover's slashing rhetoric. No longer did he say that New Deal programs merely needed better management; now they had to be done away with altogether. There was no middle ground if the American system was going to survive. He denounced the Social Security system, which had begun distributing public assistance and unemployment benefits, as "a cruel hoax." He charged that Roosevelt had put the country on the path to a dictatorship. By abandoning the middle of the road and dishing up political red meat, Landon pleased Republican reactionaries and most of the big-city dailies, 75 percent of which supported him. The *Chicago Tribune* banished news of Roosevelt from the front page and headlined Landon's every move. In September, William Randolph Hearst had his papers run a front-page editorial that said Moscow had ordered Communists to work on Roosevelt's behalf.

And Al Smith, just eight years earlier the Democratic presidential candidate, took the final step away from his lifelong party by endorsing Landon. He railed against New Deal attempts at economic planning as Communist-inspired. Another chorus, just as shrill, rose on the left, where the remnants of Huey Long's supporters had joined with Father Coughlin and Dr. Townsend in endorsing Union Party candidate William Lemke, a congressman from North Dakota. The Union Party grew out of Coughlin's National Union for Social Justice and it attacked Roosevelt for being too conservative. Coughlin, who had said the drought in the Midwest was God's punishment on the country for electing FDR, now used his radio program to hurl a series of increasingly wild accusations, calling him anti-God and a liar and his cabinet members Communists.

But the American people felt otherwise. They mobbed Roosevelt, calling out thanks and blessings when he appeared on the campaign trail. And they talked back to his attackers, booing the press cars of the *Tribune* during the president's October 14 appearance in Chicago.

There, he told a roaring crowd of nearly a hundred thousand that he believed in individualism "up to the point where the individualist starts to operate at the expense of society." He reminded cheering audiences everywhere that conditions had improved dramatically in his four years in office. Farmers, workers, merchants, investors, business owners—all were better off. He had not killed the system of free enterprise; he had saved it through reform. Finally, as the campaign reached its climax on October 31 in New York's Madison Square Garden, he challenged anew the forces of "business and financial monopoly, speculation, reckless banking, class antagonism" that wanted to reclaim their power.

"Never before in all our history have these forces been so united against one candidate as they stand today. They are unanimous in their hate for me—and I welcome their hatred," he said to wild applause. "I should like to have it said of my first administration that in it the forces of selfishness and of lust for power met their match. I should like to have it said of my second administration that in it these forces met their master."

The *Literary Digest*, a monthly opinion magazine known for its accurate political straw polls, had correctly forecast the outcomes of the previous four elections and now predicted an easy victory for Landon. On election day, November 3, its prediction was crushed by the outcome. Roosevelt carried forty-six states, Landon only Maine and Vermont, prompting Farley to restate the old saw casting Maine as a political bellwether for the nation: "As Maine goes, so goes Vermont," he cracked. Roosevelt polled 27,747,636 votes to Landon's 16,679,543. He won 523 electoral votes to Landon's 8. It was the most thorough presidential victory since George Washington and James Monroe ran unopposed. The Union Party candidate, William Lemke, polled fewer than 900,000 votes, Father Coughlin retired from the radio, and the *Literary Digest* ceased publication the next year. Roosevelt's second term was soon to begin.

8. HOPKINS IN LOUISIANA

Harry Hopkins resurfaced after the election. On November 28, he traveled to the Louisiana capital of Baton Rouge, where he encountered a reception that was markedly different from the one he would have gotten fourteen months earlier, when Huey Long was still alive. The Kingfish's death had brought a change in the state's attitude toward federal officials. Once viewed with suspicion, now they—and the relief dollars they had the power to distribute—were welcomed unreservedly. And this new hospitality had been rewarded. Tens of thousands of Louisianans had WPA jobs, many of them working on the very structure that Hopkins had come to Baton Rouge to dedicate.

The administration could not have chosen a better project for winning the hearts of Louisianans, whose allegiance to the Louisiana State University Tigers football team verged on the fanatical. Since the first of the year, at a cost of $700,000, WPA workers had been building a horseshoe around one end of the LSU football stadium, linking two existing grandstands and doubling its seating capacity to 48,000. Under the new grandstand were dormitory rooms for 1,000 male students. The WPA was spending $1.5 million in improvements on the LSU campus, but the stadium was the largest single project and by working at a furious pace the construction team had finished it six weeks early, in time for the undefeated Tigers' season-ending game against Tulane, its traditional downstate rival from New Orleans. With temporary seats added, a crowd of 52,000 was expected, the largest sports crowd ever gathered in the South. They were still filing into the stands when Hopkins joined university, state, and WPA officials on a speakers' platform on the field.

The pregame speeches were effusive. Senator John H. Overton compared the fight against the depression to a football game between the "WPA Invincibles and the Unemployment Wave." Governor Richard W. Leche—credited with the winning touchdown in Overton's speech—offered "our most heartfelt appreciation to Franklin D. Roosevelt, who made the WPA possible." Across town, beneath the state capitol grounds where he was buried, Huey Long was spinning in his grave.

Hopkins keynoted the dedication. In vintage style, he took on the critics who disparaged WPA workers as shovel-leaning idlers and defended the unemployed, their right to work, and the program that was giving them the opportunity. "A whole army of Americans got penalized nearly all the way to the goal line through no fault of their own," he said. "I think we ought to dedicate this stadium to the workers of the WPA, not only those who worked on it directly, but also the millions who are creating a hundred thousand other public improvements all over America.

"I want to ask every one of you here today, whenever you hear anybody making an unkind remark about the workers of the WPA, to tell him about this stadium. The reason you are here in such numbers is because it was finished forty-five days ahead of schedule. The reason we can be so comfortable and so safe in this tremendous tier of seats...is because the quality of this workmanship compares favorably with any structure on the campus....

"You can start out from Baton Rouge in any direction and pass through town after town which has water facilities or sewer facilities or roads or streets or sidewalks or better public buildings, which it would not have had but for the Works Progress Administration," Hopkins continued. He pointed out that the improvements were based on local needs. "We didn't go into a bureaucratic huddle in Washington and just imagine them," he said. "They were originated and asked for by local officials."

Not to have done such work would have been bad enough, said Hopkins. "But far worse than that would have been the destruction by their long idleness of [workers'] spirit and their very ability to work. The things they have actually accomplished all over America should be an inspiration to every reasonable person and an everlasting answer to all the grievous insults that have been heaped on the heads of the unemployed."

As he spoke, an outsized version of the familiar WPA billboard loomed above the highest tier of new seats where everybody in the stadium could see it. And just in case they missed it, the LSU Cadets marching band took the field before the kickoff and arranged itself into a formation that spelled out "WPA" from one goal line to the other.

Stadiums were a staple of WPA construction, though not everybody liked them. The *Charleston* (South Carolina) *News and Courier* said that building stadiums to feed the hungry was reminiscent of the Roman circus, since only the rich could afford stadium events. But the *Leader Call* in Laurel, Mississippi, shared Hopkins's view of both the physical improvements and the benefits of work.

"The high school stadium is nearly finished," the paper wrote. "The bricks for it were made by WPA employees. The wood to burn those bricks was cut by other WPA employees. At first this cost the government nine dollars a cord. Before the project was finished, it cost the government one dollar a cord.

"Where lay the difference of eight dollars? In the skill of hands that had to feel their way at first, and minds that were indifferent to begin with; but the hands learned to work swiftly and gladly in a task that gave a living.

"In the same stadium, the first row of seats was built by nine masons in two and a half days. The last row, exactly like the first, was constructed by four masons in one and a half days.

"Magnificent things have been accomplished in Laurel by WPA workmen. The stadium is one example; others are found in schools repainted, sidewalks built, parks and school grounds improved. But there have been changes not so apparent: changes in the hearts of men who were discouraged and unhappy, and are that no longer; in whom hope is revived and life once more holds a promise."

At Baton Rouge, when the speeches were finished and the game began, fans of the Tigers had rhapsodic moments of their own. LSU won the game, 33–0, to complete its undefeated season and went on to the 1937 Sugar Bowl in New Orleans, where it lost to California's Santa Clara Broncos, 21–14.

9. AT WORK ON THE TIMBERLINE
(LABORER AND HELPER HENRY MOAR)

On Oregon's Mount Hood, the ski shelter originally envisioned at the timberline had become a far grander project. Now it embodied almost every aspect of the WPA's sweeping approach to job creation. This new vision had emerged back in September, when Hopkins had visited the lodge as part of an inspection tour of WPA activities. By then the design had evolved into a wide V, with a long west wing and a shorter east wing joined by a six-sided "head house" that would rise above the wings as a visual hub and incorporate the building's entrance and main lounge. Stonemasons, carpenters, plumbers, electricians, and laborers were all hard at work as Max Lorenz, the Portland contractor overseeing the construction, pushed to get the lodge enclosed before the first snows of winter.

When he reached the lodge on September 14, arriving in a party of thirty-five that included Oregon WPA chief E. J. Griffith, Hopkins circulated among the workers, clambering on piles of lumber and mounting ladders as he surveyed the project and the sights. The weather alternated between sunshine and snow flurries. "He was a nice guy; he talked to most everybody, and everybody took to him," recalled William Wechner, the project supervisor, in an interview much later. William L. Turner, one of the Forest Service architects, recorded the event in stilted language: "The plans were explained briefly to Mr. Hopkins and he in turn expressed himself as being enthusiastic relative to the development."

The plans now included a vision for the lodge's interior, and it was here that the Timberline Lodge would depart from a building that was merely architecturally impressive to a living example of all that workers for the WPA could do. The vision was Margery Hoffman Smith's, a Portland interior designer who was being paid as a consultant on the project, and she shared it with Hopkins during his inspection trip. Such a majestic building should have an interior to match, she said. Already, plans had been laid to include pioneer and Indian motifs, murals and framed pictures, wood carvings and wrought iron work, but Smith wanted to go further. She wanted to commission rugs, draperies, bedspreads, and furniture. All this could be done with the skills at the WPA's disposal; she wanted to have weavers make the drapery and furniture upholstery fabrics out of Oregon linen and Oregon wool and Oregon rawhide. She wanted hooked rugs made from the upholstery scraps. She wanted hand-crafted chandeliers and lamps of wrought iron, and lampshades of animal hides. All this, she told Hopkins, not only would employ countless WPA art and craft workers but would make paying guests want to visit Timberline.

Hopkins was impressed with Hoffman Smith's ideas, and he agreed to fund them. In October, when he was back in Washington, the WPA sent word that it had expanded the Timberline budget by $39,000 for furnishings, accessories, and additional decorations. Hoffman Smith, who was soon to be named assistant director of Oregon's WPA art program, started setting up weaving and other craft workshops in Portland, and contacted blacksmiths to discuss metalwork designs.

Now, in late November, the push to enclose the lodge before the snows was picking up pace. Among the workers toiling to get the job done was a small, unassuming laborer named Henry Moar. He had been assigned to the project on Mount Hood five months earlier, and by then he was already a veteran of the WPA.

He had been a single man living with his mother and trying to support them both without much luck when the agency first started hiring in Portland. Once he qualified, he shuttled among various WPA projects around the city, working on one until it closed and then being directed to the next. By late 1935, more than 7,000 workers were spread out among sites marked by the now familiar WPA signs. Most, like Moar, were doing road or street work, landscaping in the city parks, or making improvements at the commercial harbor along the Willamette River north of downtown. Hundreds more were working out of camps west of the city on the Wilson and Wolf Creek highways, clearing timber and blasting rock for two new roads mapped through the Tillamook Burn, a 240,000-acre swath of Douglas fir, spruce, cedar, and hemlock forest that had been burned by wildfire three years earlier. The roads would take Portlanders to Tillamook on the Pacific coast and save them hours of travel. There were even twenty women learning to make furniture in a WPA adult education class that Moar read about one Sunday in the *Oregonian*. Given all this work going on all over the Portland area, he was surprised to be assigned to Mount Hood.

Moar was twenty-seven years old at the time, and he had just gotten married. Unlike the day jobs in and around Portland, working on the mountain meant that he'd be gone at least a week at a time. This pained him as a newlywed, but one of the conditions of working for the WPA was that you took the job you were assigned. So when the time came, he reported to a pickup point, a cardboard suitcase stuffed with work clothes in hand, and boarded a bus headed to the camp at Summit Meadow.

The camp was fully functioning by the time of Moar's arrival. It was a civilian version of an army camp, with sleeping tents laid out in a grid, a central mustering area, a large mess tent, latrines, and showers. Each of the sleeping tents, set off the ground on timber pallets, had cots for eight men, a woodstove for warmth, and a barrel filled with firewood to feed the stove. A flagpole rose over the mustering area where the men assembled for their work assignments, and the flag was raised each morning and lowered every night. Doctors and male nurses formed a medical staff, guards and watchmen acted as a police force, engineers kept the heating, water, and cooking systems running, and a full kitchen was staffed with cooks, dishwashers, waiters, butchers, and a produce man. Forest Service and construction supervisors lived at the camp along with the workers.

There were several potential work assignments. Not every person on the mountain was working on the lodge. There was an all-weather road to be built from Government Camp to the lodge site, so men were grading, piling rock abutments into place, and building stone retaining walls. Others were dispatched to cut firewood and timber, which was loaded aboard trucks and hauled to lots for storage or to an on-site sawmill for ripping into boards and beams and finishing. Some cleared trails, worked in nearby gravel pits, or assembled machinery. Still others hewed great stones for the lodge exterior from a quarry above Government Camp. Moar, however, was sent up the mountain to work as a helper on the lodge.

Being a helper meant doing whatever he was told. Sometimes it meant pouring concrete. Sometimes it meant packing lumber, carrying two-by-fours from a storage lot to the carpenters framing the lodge. Moar was barely five feet tall, but if he tried to get by carrying one bundle, the construction boss told him to carry two. He and the other workers quickly learned that the building would have to be roofed and enclosed before the snow fell.

The first weekend came, and with it, a break in the work schedule. Some of the men stayed in camp, using the break for hunting and fishing, or hiking on the mountain. Moar had always wanted to climb Mount Hood, but instead he went home to his young wife. At the end of the second week, Moar and his crew of laborers and tradesmen boarded buses for home while a new group of workers arrived. They would put in two weeks; then the first crew, with Moar, would return for another two-week shift. Rotating the crews was a way of limiting the men to eighty-hour months, the WPA's practice since the union strikes of the year before. It increased the number of jobs provided and took a bigger bite out of the relief rolls.

Albert Altorfer, the chef, saw to it that the men ate well when they were on the mountain. "Three times a day the men were fed, and they were fed real good," he recalled later. The menu was typical of WPA construction camps, chosen to fuel a hard day's work: for breakfast, hot or cold cereal, fried ham, bacon or sausage, potatoes, eggs or omelets, and hotcakes or French toast, plus a selection of fresh or canned fruit; for supper, a salad, a main course of beef or fish, with mashed or fried potatoes and two vegetables, usually beans or peas or corn, and for dessert bread pudding or Jell-O plus cake and cookies. They had their choice of milk, coffee, or tea, and there were always jelly and peanut butter and garnishes such as pickles and radishes on the tables. The food was served homestyle, and it kept coming as long as the men called for it. "There was no such thing as, 'There ain't no more,' " said Altorfer. When the evening meal was over, the kitchen crew formed a production line to make sandwiches for the next day. One man laid out slices of bread, the next brushed them with butter, the next put on a piece of lettuce, the next added cheese or ham. A fifth man added another piece of lettuce and the top piece of bread, then wrapped the completed sandwich and stuffed it in a lunch sack. Each sack contained two sandwiches, plus an apple or a pear. Crews in the field also carried the day's soup in farmers' milk cans. All this cost the workers 21 cents a meal. The money was deducted from their pay.

As fall deepened, the temperature kept dropping but the snow held off. By the end of November, the two wings had been roofed but the headhouse roof was incomplete. It had to incorporate the huge stone chimney rising from the central fireplace below, and the stonemasons were behind schedule. A huge gin pole—so tall that a man on the floor had to use a megaphone to talk to a man working on the top—held up the roof until massive ponderosa pine logs were lodged into notches at the support points. Finally, carpenters built a wood shelter over the apex of the roof so the chimney could be completed after the snow fell.

Henry Moar had moved inside and shifted jobs. From a wood hauler, he now became a helper in the team working under chief blacksmith Orion B. Dawson. The man he worked for handed him a ten-pound hammer. It wasn't the easy job he had hoped for, but it was inside and out of the cold, and soon he was shaping white-hot iron train rails into andirons for the headhouse fireplaces. The andirons matched the heroic scale of the rest of the lodge's furnishings, so as not to be dwarfed by their oversized surroundings. The fireplace openings yawned five feet wide and six feet high at their peak. The andirons— rails stripped of their flanges and hammered into spirals for the upright portions, with the intact rails forming the firelog supports— measured twenty inches high by five and a half and six feet deep. Moving them was just about impossible, since the rails weighed ninety pounds for every foot of length.

The same visual trick had been applied by the architects when they designed the lodge's exterior: to reduce the appearance of mass amid the small, slow-growing firs and rock outcroppings at the timberline, they had made the building's components larger, calling for massive foundation stones and doubling the distance between the vertical battens above. The style was known as "Cascadian," denoting an American version of European alpine architecture that blended with the natural beauty of the site without overwhelming it.

By December, every day was a race against the deteriorating weather. Two concrete reservoirs fed by the Salmon River formed the lodge's water supply system. Concrete for the second reservoir was poured in subfreezing weather, and Ward Gano, a Forest Service structural engineer, manned a fire all night long to keep it from freezing and cracking before it could set. Seventy-mile-per-hour winds drove grainy "tapioca" snow into a worker's face until he choked and almost died before William Wechner, the project supervisor, dragged him into a shed and covered his face with a sweater so he could draw a breath. Diesel generators supplied heat to keep the pipes between the reservoirs and lodge from freezing and bursting. Two diesel engines fired steam boilers to heat the lodge itself. The stonemasons got the worst of the increasing cold as they fit stones into the outside walls and the snow-protected arch leading to the main entrance, a job that required the constant adjustment of a jigsaw puzzle whose pieces weighed hundreds of pounds each. Eventually the masons set up around small stoves to keep their hands from freezing while they worked.

Down at Summit Meadow, Chef Altorfer began to plan his Christmas meal. The men raised wood roofs over the tents against the weight of the coming snow. The cookhouse crew created decorations, toilet paper streamers and puffs made out of colored-tissue fruit wrappings, all glued together with flour paste. They assembled a cardboard fireplace and placed real wood inside. They set up a Christmas tree, strung with garlands of popcorn and cranberries and ornamented with knives and forks and spoons. A group of children arrived from Portland to sing Christmas carols. A young woman accompanied them on the violin. She played wonderfully, and in her skill revealed yet another of those twists of the depression—lessons paid for by a wealthy father who lost everything after the crash and who now was one of the WPA laborers working on the lodge, living at the camp and, at that moment, listening to his daughter play. Altorfer watched him and saw tears coursing down his face. "Mine, too," he would recall much later. "It was really beautiful."

By then the snow was falling steadily, but the lodge was safely roofed. The workers moved into its shelter as the drifts rose against the outside walls, and attention turned to the interior art and craftsmanship that would make Timberline a virtual catalogue of the WPA's own wide-ranging virtuosity.

PART V

T H E   A R T S   P R O G R A M S

*We don't think a good musician should be asked
to turn second-rate laborer.*
—AUBREY WILLIAMS, WPA DEPUTY ADMINISTRATOR

*No one who has seen these thousands of theatre workers
rehearsing . . . spending far more than the required hours, working
with energy and devotion . . . can believe that the Federal Theatre
as it gathers momentum will be any less potent because it
has the remembrance of hunger in its stomach.*
—HALLIE FLANAGAN, FEDERAL THEATRE PROJECT ADMINISTRATOR

1. THE DILEMMA OF ART AND POLITICS

The potential for artistic outreach and creativity that Harry Hopkins had described so enthusiastically to Hallie Flanagan on their rail trip to Iowa had been largely realized by the end of 1936. The WPA's Federal One had freed the arts from their need to please commercial tastes and elite patrons. With the government funding artists and actors, playwrights and musicians, their work had spilled out of haute temples in big-city theater districts and gallery rows into parks, schools, churches, and community centers. Millions of Americans, many for the first time in their lives, thronged to concerts and plays and studied paintings and drawings, much of the time without having to take a penny from their pockets. They were sending their children to free art and music classes, and attending these classes on their own. After a year and a half, the WPA's mission to take the arts to the people and keep arts workers out of breadlines was by most measures a complete success.

Federal One had by now spent approximately $40 million and employed a total of some 40,000 workers. Both figures were minuscule portions of the WPA's total funding and jobs, but the arts projects had already received an outsized share of attention and publicity—and notoriety. Some critics, among them the *New York Times,* objected on principle to the idea of paying artists to create art rather than build roads. "Their usefulness has been widely doubted," the newspaper wrote in a September 1, 1936, editorial decrying the 25 percent of the WPA budget spent on the arts and other white-collar projects in New York. Such "boondoggling," it went on, "tends to bring the engineering projects into discredit with it," and ought to be abandoned. The maverick nature of the arts in general and of artists in particular— their "bohemian" lifestyles, often leftist politics, and insistence on "artistic freedom"—had generated a stream of corrosive coverage that placed the projects on the defensive.

It was certainly true that firebrand arts workers, particularly in New York and San Francisco, had spent as much time in protests and radical activities as they had in making art. The latest of these actions was a round of sit-ins and marches that greeted the layoffs made in the wake of the 1936 elections. Protests such as these, and the news stories they generated, reinforced the anti–New Deal right's conviction that it was correct to view the arts as dangerous, anti-American, and not worthy of support. As time went on these views were to intensify.

Artists had had high expectations when the projects started. Douglas Lynch, in Portland, Oregon, had been eking out a living painting scenic backdrops for department store window displays. When he heard the news it was as if "we artists had received a commission from the Medicis." Printmaker and lithographer Will Barnet was brought into the New York project to improve the quality of the print division's work. He viewed Federal One as overdue recognition by the government that the arts deserved public support. "It was one of the greatest efforts in history to make a democracy a democracy," he said years later. Artists took it as a natural evolutionary stage in the nation's development; it was finally following the lead of European countries in providing the arts with public subsidies.

The directors of the four programs held this view as well. They were a mix of styles, personalities, and backgrounds. Flanagan, Hopkins's Grinnell College classmate who headed the Theatre Project, was, according to director John Houseman, "a wild little woman who believed and publicly stated her conviction that 'the theatre is more than a private enterprise; it is also a public interest which, properly fostered, might come to be a social and an educative force.' " Holger Cahill, the Icelandic immigrant appointed to lead the Art Project, was fiercely defensive of his vision for the project, which was to extend the educational reach of art through local galleries and art centers and magnificent murals adorning public spaces. The director of the Music Project, Russian-born Nikolai Sokoloff, was less fiery but more vain than either Flanagan or Cahill, and adamant about his goal of "enlightening" musical audiences through a steady diet of classical music. Henry Alsberg, the New Yorker at the head of the Writers' Project, commanded allegiance through the rumpled authority and deep respect he brought to the writers under his command, and like Cahill he had an instinct for political survival.

Jacob Baker, after losing control of professional projects to Ellen Woodward, had remained in charge of Federal One for its first year. But he believed the arts programs, and their budgets, should be turned over to the state WPA operations instead of run out of Washington. While this may, as Baker thought, have been a better arrangement for political and administrative reasons, the project directors were convinced it would dilute artistic standards. They also were certain that because artists, writers, and performers were clustered in a handful of cities, only federal control could direct them as needed to areas that lacked strong arts communities, both to perform and to teach. Baker had pressed his plan with Harry Hopkins, complaining that the arts people were "haughty" and "uppish" and "won't listen to anything," but in July 1936, Flanagan and Cahill, with tacit support from Alsberg and Sokoloff, revolted. They had Eleanor Roosevelt's ear, and it was she who in turn suggested to Hopkins that "the problem might be Mr. Baker." Hopkins resolved the conflict by sending Baker off to study cooperatives in Europe, and Federal One and its directors, with Woodward's loose hand on the reins, continued to run their programs out of Washington.

It had been a rough time; long afterward, Cahill remembered the contest over control of the arts projects as both bitter and personal. He had been in Atlanta, "taped up from shoulders to navel" after an automobile accident, when his assistant summoned him back to Washington in a desperate bid to fight off Baker's plan. Meeting Baker later, after he had left the administration, a still very angry Cahill told him, "Damn your heart. You stabbed a knife right between my shoulder blades and you said, 'That's the end of you and Hallie Flanagan.' But we destroyed you, you bastard."

Of the four projects under Federal One, Flanagan's Federal Theatre Project was the most insistently politically outspoken. It was this insistence that would bring down the wrath of conservatives upon it. But it also recognized that its first duty was to entertain, and long before the New Deal's enemies saw red in a few selected play scripts, the project launched its debut performance not on a stage but in a sawdust ring, its only purpose to send an audience of children into shivers of delight.

2. THE FEDERAL THEATRE PROJECT: PRELUDE

Aclown in a red wig and a bum's droopy pants burst into the arena at the Second Naval Battalion Armory in Brooklyn, New York, chased by a caricature cop in hot pursuit. The pair scampered around and disappeared, and when the bum reappeared he had left his pursuer in the wings. He preened in pantomime. Then the dastardly cop slipped back into sight. The clown didn't see him. A thousand children screamed a warning, but the clown didn't understand. He cupped a hand to one ear and looked bewildered until the cop, one exaggerated footstep at a time, crept up behind him and bopped him on the head with a floppy rubber nightstick.

As the kids shrilled their approval, a fanfare of trumpets drowned them out. A scarlet-suited band, sixty members strong, stepped onto the floor, followed by a procession of performers—first a ringmaster wearing high black boots and a top hat and cracking a long whip, then unicyclists, acrobats, trapeze artists, tightrope walkers, a strongman, more clowns, trained dogs and ponies, and two monkeys. The WPA Circus was making its debut.

For two and a half hours, spellbound children from orphanages and families on relief laughed at the miming clowns, held their breath as the tightrope walkers teetered from pole to pole under the rafters, and gasped at the dizzying feats of the aerialists on the flying trapeze. They cheered when one of the trained dogs took a fifteen-foot leap into a fireman's net. They stood up for "The Star-Spangled Banner" and sang along with the band between bites of free peanuts and popcorn handed out in paper bags by WPA concessionaires. Admission was free, and the kids got more than their money's worth: some of the performers entertaining them had raked in $1,000 a week during vaudeville's heyday.

This circus performance on October 17, 1935, launched the Federal Theatre Project in New York. If there was anything missing, it was the exotic animals that were a staple of established circuses. Hallie Flanagan, interviewed for the project's magazine, said that the show would have featured elephants except that "none were on relief." But animal trainers were, and in time the WPA Circus in New York would add the elephant Japino for the cost of trainer Honest Bill Newton's relief check. The aging Japino was such a popular addition that in 1937, schoolchildren successfully petitioned Roosevelt to save him from a death sentence imposed on grounds of "senility."

Flanagan would soon have tougher crowds to please. Rolling out the circus had been easy, since it was one of the units she had inherited from the FERA jobs program. Circuses of varying compositions were performing all over the country during the WPA's first summer. So were variety and vaudeville troupes and puppet and minstrel shows. A company whose repertoire consisted of seven of Gilbert and Sullivan's light operas was among the most popular of these preexisting units, which took their acts into schools, hospitals, settlement houses, and even prisons.

But Flanagan had more than puppeteers, coloraturas, and former vaudevillians on her hands, and more ambition for her project than circuses and conventional repertory. New York was the center of the theater world, with a large population of actors, stagehands, dressers, set and lighting designers, playwrights, and producers who were out of work, desperate, and available. From this mix could come bold new works that fulfilled her vision of theater's role in society. One of her first decisions was to centralize the project's service functions—research, publicity, production schedules, and a magazine chronicling its activities from coast to coast—in the city.

Elmer Rice, a successful producer and playwright in New York, had agreed to head the project there. Consulting with Flanagan, he had set up five main units—the Negro Theatre, the Tryout Theatre that would audition scripts for commercial producers, the Experimental Theatre that would present "new plays in new manners," a unit that would produce original plays by new playwrights that was inexplicably called the Popular Price Theatre, and the Living Newspaper, a new and unusual play format that would dramatize current news events.

Other than the circus and other carryover units from the previous relief programs, the New York operation—like those in the rest of the country—was slow getting started. One of its problems was shared by all the arts programs. Federal paymasters knew how to operate "when you want to build a road, or build an airport, but how do you put an artist on a payroll?" asked Robert Asure, a finance officer in Federal One. "Should he be paid by the hour, or by the yard, who should supervise him, what constitutes production?—it was just endless." Flanagan also had trouble getting money out of Washington for theater rentals, causing her to rail at the "stupidity, inefficiency, and delay" of the WPA bureaucracy. And then, when the $20,000 authorized for rentals was finally released, the theater owners resisted renting their houses to the project because they saw it as low-priced competition.

Broadway tickets cost $2 to around $5 in 1935. Hopkins had decided that WPA theater ticket prices should start at a dime and go no higher than a dollar, and some offerings would be free. The New York units planned to charge 25 or 50 cents for most seats. It was not Flanagan's intention to produce bad plays, but while it was conceivable that some of them might catch on and find an audience, realistically none of the project's offerings was going to be a threat to Broadway. Nevertheless, owners and commercial producers tried to keep the WPA out of the ten-block heart of Broadway between 40th and 50th Streets. Finally they relented and allowed the project to rent the Biltmore, on 47th Street near Eighth Avenue.

The Living Newspapers would be offered at the Biltmore. The Popular Price Theatre got the Manhattan, at 53rd and Broadway. Daly's, on West 67th Street near Central Park, would house the Experimental Theatre. The Tryout Theatre would stage its hopeful offerings at the Willis in the Bronx and the Shubert-Teller in Brooklyn, and the Negro Theatre would present its plays at the Lafayette, on

Seventh Avenue between 132nd and 133rd Streets. The various units started moving to their respective venues in late October 1935.

Together with black actress Rose McClendon, John Houseman, then a rising theatrical director, had agreed to head the New York Negro Theatre unit. (There were also units in Birmingham, Boston, Chicago, Hartford, Los Angeles, Newark, Philadelphia, Raleigh, San Francisco, and Seattle.) Its first task was renovating the severely deteriorated Lafayette, built before the turn of the century; its windows and doors were boarded over, and rats and other vermin lurked amid the broken seats and rotting carpet in the dank auditorium. But WPA work crews assembled from lists of unemployed black stagehands ripped the old theater down to its healthy bones and had it ready for audiences by the beginning of December.

Once he was sure the theater was going to be ready, Houseman faced creative choices. McClendon was fighting what would ultimately be a losing battle with cancer, and her frequent absences left him to decide what plays the 750-member troupe should mount. It ranged from a core of non-relief professionals—actors, technicians, and administrators—to people who had never set foot on a stage but had managed to win assignments to the project before its quota was filled. It was a ticklish time in Harlem. Riots the previous March had left heightened racial tensions, and white motives were suspect in anything that had to do with black people. But Houseman was equipped to deal with these suspicions. Harlem was not new to him. The year before, he had directed the Virgil Thomson–Gertrude Stein experimental opera, *Four Saints in Three Acts,* with an all-black cast on Broadway. The successful show had been preceded by months of rehearsals during which he had learned to balance the neighborhood's competing forces—the local Communist Party on one hand and the decorous Urban League on the other. The one thing he wanted to avoid was mounting recent Broadway hits with all-black casts, or reviving popular black vehicles such as *The Emperor Jones, All God's Chillun Got Wings,* or *Porgy and Bess.* He knew that to do this would be interpreted as patronizing, as would the revues and musicals that traditionally featured black entertainers.

Houseman decided to divide the company into two. One troupe would present plays on black subjects, focusing on contemporary issues. The other would be a classical repertory company performing

Shakespeare and other great playwrights. To direct the classical arm, Houseman turned to young Orson Welles, who was only twenty but already famous for his theatrical ambitions and his flamboyance.

Welles accepted. Soon afterward, he called Houseman at two in the morning to say that his wife, Virginia, had had an inspiration: they should do *Macbeth*. But instead of the bleak setting of the Scottish heath, Shakespeare's tragedy of mad ambition would take place in the dripping lushness of the Haitian jungle. There would be voodoo priestesses instead of witches around a boiling cauldron, and Napoleonic military costuming to replace Elizabethan gowns and tunics. The concept was loosely based on fact; it sprang from the wars and intrigues surrounding the struggle of Haitian slaves for independence. Henri Christophe, who had declared himself King Henri I in 1811 after conspiring in the assassination of his predecessor, was the parallel for Macbeth's dark strivings. The plan's boldness excited Houseman. It made him believe he could actually create art in addition to providing jobs, and he green-lighted the production. Before long he and Welles were conducting auditions in a Harlem Elks Club recreation hall. Among those winning roles were an African witch doctor and his drummers, who had been stranded in New York during a failed tour.

At the same time, Elmer Rice was moving ahead with the production of the first Living Newspaper. This was Flanagan's concept, growing from the Russian leg of her 1926 European theater tour. She recognized that what she had seen was Soviet propaganda, the glories of the revolution dramatized for illiterate audiences, but the simplicity of the productions had appealed to her. Their basic sets and staging fit with the WPA rule directing that most of a project's budget be spent on labor. Flanagan's idea was to use music and lighting sparingly, and for the most part simply to put actors onstage to bring the news to life.

Among the most dramatic stories in that fall of 1935 was Mussolini's invasion of Ethiopia, accompanied by biplanes and bombers of the Regia Aeronautica that rained explosives and mustard gas down on civilian villages in what had once been an Italian colony. Ethiopia had been independent for forty years, but the Italian dictator, known as Il Duce, was bent on regaining Italy's foothold in North Africa and avenging a series of embarrassments dating back to 1896 and the Ethiopian—then Abyssinian—defeat of an invading Italian force. The

League of Nations protested the invasion and bombing, to no effect. In the United States, a strong bloc of isolationists in Congress, with widespread support from the public, who remembered that 116,000 American soldiers had died in the world war and wanted to stay away from any foreign conflicts, defeated Roosevelt's request for a ban on arms exports to Italy. The Living Newspaper decided to feature this example of fascist militarism in its first "edition" and wrote a script that included a goosestepping Mussolini.

Flanagan approved the script. Hopkins, after all, had promised a "free, adult, uncensored" theater, and she, taking him at his word, thought it unreasonable for anyone, politicians included, to second-guess the content of a play. But when word of the impending production reached the White House, warning flags went up. Roosevelt sent word that depicting foreign dignitaries was "skating on thin ice" and dangerous to foreign relations.

Flanagan protested and called on Eleanor Roosevelt for help, but even her intervention failed to move the president. Jacob Baker, as yet undeposed by the coup that was to send him packing off to Europe halfway through 1936, decreed that Living Newspaper producers had to secure approval from the State Department before presenting characters that represented foreign heads of state. Flanagan weighed resigning but decided against it. Elmer Rice, however, quit with a flourish. On January 24, 1936, he invited the press to a dress rehearsal of *Ethiopia,* and after the curtain fell he announced his resignation with a speech comparing censorship with fascism.

Ethiopia was never seen again, nor was it the only Federal Theatre Project production to be abandoned on grounds of political sensitivity, real or imagined. While its writers were preparing their script in New York, the Chicago unit was readying a play called *Model Tenement,* by Meyer Levin. Rehearsals had started when word came from the Chicago office of the WPA to halt the production. Complaints that its rent strike theme was anti-landlord propaganda had gone all the way to Washington. Chicago's mayor, Edward Joseph Kelly, was the prime suspect. He denied any role in having *Model Tenement* shelved; in fact, he said, he had never heard of it. But events were clearly proving that Hopkins's promise to Flanagan that she could operate free of censorship would be impossible to keep.

3. THE CURTAIN RISES

*E*thiopia was to have been the New York project's first original production. The Negro Theatre filled the void with *Walk Together Chillun!* by Frank Wilson, a well-known black actor. Houseman didn't like the play, but it was politically inoffensive; it opened to lukewarm reviews on February 5, 1936, and ran a month before modest audiences. Another New York unit mounted a poor production of *The Comedy of Errors*—so inept that Flanagan thought Shakespeare's title could be applied across the board to all of the early New York productions. The worst of these laughable embarrassments, in her view, was *Jefferson Davis*, a biographical play forced on her by the Daughters of the Confederacy, who were sponsoring its southern tour.

But March saw quick improvement. That month, eight productions opened at the various New York project theaters and in community spot bookings, and they brought both crowds and reviews that ranged from decent to enthusiastic. *Everyman*, a noted fifteenth-century morality play, started traveling to schools and churches. The Tryout Theatre opened *Woman of Destiny,* and one of the Hollywood studios paid $25,000 for an option on the script. *Chalk Dust,* the first of the Experimental Theatre offerings, depicted bumbling teachers and high-handed administrators as a way of calling for reforms in public education. The Yiddish Theatre, another of the New York project's units, opened *The Idle Man* to community spot bookings. *Conjur' Man Dies,* a comedy mystery filled with inside jokes that black audiences appreciated, drew huge crowds at the Lafayette and rocked the house with laughter. *In Heaven and Earth* followed *A Woman of Destiny* at the Tryout Theatre and won critical applause. The poetry of T. S. Eliot's *Murder in the Cathedral* at the Manhattan revived the 300-year-old story of Archbishop Thomas à Becket's assassination at Canterbury Cathedral.

The Theatre Project was allowed only limited advertising, another of the rules designed to ease the commercial houses' fear of competition. It could list its offerings only in the theater classifieds—no display ads—and only on Mondays, when theaters traditionally were dark. But Halsted Welles's direction of *Murder* as "a kind of religious ritual" and Harry Irvine's performance as Becket won rave reviews and word of mouth. The buzz, plus the fact that it was a limited run, made it the hottest ticket in town. Well-heeled Broadway crowds snapped up the 50-cent and $1 tickets. So did scalpers, who resold them for going Broadway prices.

March also saw the first opening of a Living Newspaper. This time, the writers turned their attention homeward. Its title, *Triple-A Plowed Under,* referred to the Supreme Court decision invalidating the 1933 Agricultural Adjustment Act, placed against the backdrop of recent farm history—the overproduction that had killed prices, land and equipment mortgaged to produce still more, drought and dust storms that had destroyed 50 million acres of farmland, the mortgage sales that evicted families from their farms and homes, and the middlemen who squeezed the farmers and jacked up prices to consumers that the AAA had tried to regulate. And with all this material to work with, the writers still took dramatic license, raising the stakes with a real-life tabloid tragedy.

A young mother, Dorothy Sherwood, was the centerpiece of this depression parable. Born in a small town in the West, she lost her mother at nine and spent the next seven years between orphanages, her itinerant father and his succession of wives, and Salvation Army foster homes, working as a household drudge and receiving "scattered and interrupted schooling." At sixteen, she became a chorus girl in traveling shows in the Midwest. At nineteen, she met and married a stage electrician named Fred Sherwood, and at twenty bore a daughter. The family settled in Newburgh, New York, a small city on the Hudson River. Her husband worked in a movie theater, and they had a second child, a son who they named James. Then Fred Sherwood contracted tuberculosis. He was sent to a sanitarium, and his mother took their daughter, while Dorothy moved to a rooming house with her young son, leaving him in the landlady's care while she waited tables in a restaurant. Fred Sherwood died in April 1935. Soon another man appeared who promised to take care of her and raise her son. He fixed a date that he would take her away, back to the West, and she packed, quit her job, gave notice to her landlady—but her savior never came. Weeks passed as she tried to find another job. She and the boy grew hungrier, and she could not pay the rent. On the morning of August 20, 1935, the landlady gave her notice of eviction. At around noon, she put two-year-old James into a stroller and walked three miles to nearby New Windsor, to a spot where a brook ran near the road.

Later that day, a Newburgh lieutenant looked up to see the twenty-seven-year-old woman standing at his desk, holding a toddler dressed in a clean suit. She held him out to the officer and said dully, "Here he is."

"You killed him?" said the shocked lieutenant when he realized the boy was dead.

"Yes, I drowned him."

"What did you do that for?"

"I couldn't take care of him any longer and I thought he would be better off dead."

The Living Newspaper played this moment for more drama still. *Triple-A Plowed Under* gave its audience short scenes in quick succession, using pantomime, skits, and radio broadcasts, among other techniques, to recount the devastation of the farms. Drought was conveyed by a farmer repeating a forecast of dry, hot days and then letting soil trickle through his fingers to his defeated exclamation, "Dust!" Dorothy Sherwood, played by a relief actress named Jane Johnson, handed her dead son to a policeman, but she was angry, not defeated, when she said, "He was hungry, I tell you. Hungry, hungry, hungry!" The real Dorothy Sherwood may never have heard of the Agricultural Adjustment Act, but conflating her son's suffering and his mercy killing with the ruling striking down the AAA amounted to accusing the Supreme Court of murder.

Upping the ante proved effective. The cast had wondered whether New York audiences would care about problems in the faraway farm belt, but when *Triple-A Plowed Under* opened at the Biltmore on March 14, it attracted an audience that was not only younger and more aware of social issues than was typical for Broadway but also less reserved. By the time the black-robed actors playing the Supreme Court took the stage, the house was primed, and greeted them with waves of boos and hissing.

Brooks Atkinson, the theater critic for the *New York Times*, applauded the show's conviction, contrasting it to Broadway's usual reluctance to take stands on social issues. He called it "hard-hitting" and "frequently brilliant." The Hearst newspapers, predictably, decried it as Socialist propaganda. But it was a hit, proving to Flanagan that the Federal Theatre could make drama from complex events. Her conviction would produce more plays that dramatized, as she put it, the "struggle of many different kinds of people to understand the natural, social, and economic forces around them and to achieve through these forces a better life." It was inevitable that they would draw political reaction.

4. THE VOODOO MACBETH

As the winter of 1936 turned into spring, the Negro Theatre's *Macbeth* was in final rehearsals. Welles had finally honed the production sufficiently to let Houseman attend. Other rising stars in the theatrical arts also had been hard at work: Virgil Thomson writing and rehearsing a musical score, Abe Feder setting up the stage lighting, and Nat Karson designing and supervising the construction of the set. As the set took shape backstage at the Lafayette, it edged the actors in the still-running *Conjur' Man Dies* ever closer to the footlights. Meanwhile, the *Macbeth* cast rehearsed in the hall of the Monarch Lodge of the Elks Club on 137th Street. Finally, its 137 actors, understudies, and support staff shifted to the Lafayette and rehearsed between midnight and dawn. Jack Carter, cast in the title role, joined Orson Welles in whipping the cast and crew through the killing schedule. The opening was set for April 14.

Rumors raced through Harlem as the day approached. One claimed the play was a white man's trick to embarrass the black community, another that the set and costumes would bankrupt the Negro Theatre and force it to close. Curiosity spread. Anthony Buttitta, a writer for the theater project magazine, caught the subway uptown a few days before the opening to take notes for a story and walked into a buzz of expectation. He realized that painters had been at work on the sidewalks, stenciling "Macbeth" in glowing letters at the corners of each block. A sign in the box office window announced that opening-night tickets were sold out. Bystanders had clustered around the stage door to watch the delivery of vividly colored costumes. And he learned that Karson had sent assistants to forage in Central Park and suburban woodlands for foliage to forest the Haitian Birnam Wood.

Two days before the opening, Houseman staged a free dress rehearsal. The theater filled so quickly that 3,000 people crowded outside, jostling and protesting, until a squad of riot police arrived to disperse them.

Early on opening night, eighty-five members of the Monarch Lodge Elks band assembled in formation outside their recreation hall in their light blue, gold, and scarlet uniforms. At a signal, they set forth in two groups for the Lafayette, four blocks away. The lead marchers carried crimson banners that stretched across the width of the street: "Macbeth, by Wm. Shakespeare." The bands reached the Lafayette about six-thirty. By then there were 10,000 people milling around the vicinity of the theater, and the police struggled to keep the entrance clear. Every major drama critic in the city was attending—although one of them had asked that he and his wife be seated "not next to Negroes"—and the audience wore jewels and furs. Hallie Flanagan, no stranger to the pomp of opening nights, appeared with her customary corsage pinned to the cape draped across her shoulders. Truck-mounted floodlights beamed a path into the lobby, and popping flashbulbs and grinding newsreel cameras marked the passage of dignitaries and celebrities as they made their way inside.

The curtain rose to the thunder of drums and an orgy of voodoo incantations. From the opening moment, the production's furious action, lush set, lavish costumes, and compelling performances mesmerized its audience. When the final curtain fell it erupted into tumultuous cheers and applause.

The reviews, as Houseman later wrote, "were a joy to read." With one exception, they praised the performances and the concept of what was being called the voodoo *Macbeth*. Reporter Martha Gellhorn, previously one of Harry Hopkins's field investigators dispatching their views of the depression from around the country, described "a hot richness that I have almost never seen in the theatre or anywhere else";

the audience watched and listened "as if this were a murder mystery by Edgar Wallace, only much more exciting."

The exception was Percy Hammond's review in the politically conservative *Herald Tribune*. Hammond echoed the paper's anti–New Deal stance with an article in the next day's paper that was basically a political screed: "The Negro Theatre, an offshoot of the Federal Government and one of Uncle Sam's experimental philanthropies, gave us last night, an exhibit of deluxe boondoggling."

That afternoon, Houseman came upon the witch doctor and drummers studying the notices. They had singled out Hammond's and wanted to know if it was "evil." Houseman agreed that it was. Was it the work of an enemy? they asked. Was he a bad man? Houseman agreed on both counts, then left to celebrate the block-long line outside the box office.

The house manager reported to Houseman the next day that he had heard angry drumming and "weird and horrible" chants issuing from the theater basement deep into the night. Houseman knew the Africans took their voodoo seriously. After he and Welles had cast them, they had requisitioned five live black goats, which they ritually sacrificed, then turned the hides into drumskins. And when Houseman and Thomson had asked during rehearsals if the voodoo numbers could sound more wicked, the witch doctor warned the spell might become too strong, darkening the incantations only after Houseman insisted. But he was stunned to read the news on the afternoon of the sixteenth that the critic Percy Hammond had suddenly fallen ill. He died several days later, reportedly of pneumonia.

By the time *Macbeth* opened in Harlem in April 1936, the Federal Theatre had put 10,700 theatrical workers back to work across the United States, 5,000 in New York alone. Actors, including vaudeville and circus performers—one was a young acrobat and gymnast named Burt Lancaster—accounted for nearly half the total, along with directors, costume and scene designers, playwrights and researchers, costumers, ushers, theater and box office managers, ticket takers, stagehands, clerks and office workers, watchmen and janitors, and teachers. Like Lancaster, Joseph Cotten, and Sidney Lumet, some of the performers would become household names.

Theater project units operated in thirty-one states. Eleven cities had black companies. Like New York, California had its own Yiddish group. In heavily Cuban Tampa, Florida, Cuban performers formed a Federal Theatre unit and served up a song and dance revue and plays in Spanish. Units in Chicago and California revived theatrical milestones such as *Under Two Flags* and *Shenandoah,* produced by older actors who gave the productions the look of the originals. In half a dozen units, playwrights labored to build dramas around local historical events. Classics such as Euripides and popular repertory from Shakespeare to Ibsen, Gilbert and Sullivan, Shaw, and Oscar Wilde were being mounted. Circus, marionette, and dance troupes toured in every section of the country.

In the March 1936 issue of the *Federal Theatre Bulletin,* Hallie Flanagan wrote, "No one who has seen these thousands of theatre workers rehearsing in barns, lofts, and studios, spending far more than the required hours, working with energy and devotion to re-learn the exacting techniques of the stage, can believe that the Federal Theatre as it gathers momentum will be any the less potent because it has the remembrance of hunger in its stomach."

5. SELLING THE THEATER (YOUTH PUBLICIST FRANK GOODMAN)

When Flanagan was working in New York as opposed to traveling or attending to administrative chores in Washington, she used an office on the mezzanine of a bank building in the theater district that the Federal Theatre Project had taken over as its headquarters. It was yet another of the ironies of the depression that government employees, many of them dedicated to dramatizing capitalist shortcomings, should now occupy a former branch of the Bank of the United States. Its four-story building at Eighth Avenue and 44th Street, fronted with columns in the style of a Greek temple, had closed, along with fifty-nine other branches, in December 1930. The bank had some 400,000 depositors, many of them immigrants in the New York garment trades; its failure was the largest in the country to that date, and it underscored the absence of systems to protect depositors. Two of the bank owners eventually went to the New York state prison at Ossining for questionable stock dealings, but that was no consolation for the customers who lost their life's savings.

The project's operations had overflowed into other locations. One, another former bank two blocks away, housed the operation that researched plays for rights clearances. An ordinary office building at Sixth Avenue and 23rd Street was home to the information and promotion department, which included press, photography, and radio. It was here that a child of immigrants sat at a desk hammering away with two fingers on the keyboard of a battered Royal Number 10 typewriter. The jacket of his three-piece suit hung on a coat hook, his shirtsleeves were rolled up to his elbows, and he clenched a pipe between his teeth, the B-movie model of a theatrical press agent. His name was Frank Goodman and he was just nineteen, but he had half a dozen people working under him in his domain, which peddled stories to high school and college newspapers. The job required skills that matched his wardrobe: he was a fast-talking, irrepressible salesman.

Goodman had been born in 1916. His father, a waiter in a restaurant, died in the influenza epidemic two years later, leaving his mother to care for Frank and his infant brother, Larry. Rebeccah Goodman had few skills: English had failed to supplant the Yiddish she had spoken in her native Poland, and she struggled to support her young family with housecleaning jobs, moving them from a Lower East Side tenement to East Harlem in 1928.

Their marginal existence became harder still after 1929. Goodman, barely in his teens, hustled odd jobs before and after school to earn money: he shined shoes, pushed rolling clothes racks through the garment district, hawked newspapers. Every morning, he loaded a twine-bound hundred-copy stack of the *Daily News* and a stack of *Daily Mirror*s into a child's wagon and pulled it to a stop under the Third Avenue el, where he cried out the morning's headlines to work-bound riders and made change from a canvas apron tied around his waist. At the end of the day he caught the same riders coming home and sold them copies of the lurid *Evening Graphic*. But he and his mother could not earn enough between them to keep the family together. She finally took a live-in housekeeping job, and Frank and Larry were sent to foster homes. She was given one free afternoon a week, on Saturday, when the two boys would journey from their separate foster homes to meet her in a park or a diner, where she would nurse a nickel cup of coffee for hours while they talked.

At some point Rebeccah left her live-in job and retrieved her sons from foster care. She rented a rundown apartment in the Morrisania section of the Bronx, south of Crotona Park. They lived on meager meals of potatoes or macaroni boiled with spinach, and Frank and his brother coached her to improve her English. They all wore discarded clothes given them in twice-a-year visits to the Hebrew Sheltering Guardian Society. Larry's clothes were twice passed along: he wore Frank's hand-me-downs.

When Frank was about sixteen, the child welfare system placed him in the Murray Hill Vocational High School, on the East Side of Manhattan in the thirties. When the other kids hazed him unmercifully, he ran away, then enrolled in Haaren High School, a cooperative school that mixed academics and job training. Frank attended its aviation annex, which offered courses in avionics and aircraft mechanics, and got himself assigned to work as a mechanic's assistant, spending alternating weeks at Floyd Bennett Field in Brooklyn and North Beach Airport in Queens. Sometimes he actually flew from one site to the other in the small planes whose pilots flew *Daily News* photographers on assignment, or with one of the pilots who worked for Rudy Arnold, a commercial aviation photographer. He always carried a notebook, in which he scribbled notes for the school newspaper he'd started, *Sky Scandal*. He enjoyed flying, but his real gift was for gathering and dispensing information.

Frank Goodman also had an instinct for what today would be called networking. He asked magazines such as *Aero Digest* and *Aviation* to give him their used engraving plates so he could improve *Sky Scandal*'s graphics. Before long he started to look around at other high school papers in the city. Columbia University had started the Columbia Scholastic Press Association about ten years earlier to encourage excellence in the nation's high school papers, and Goodman thought he would do the same thing in New York. He approached the *Post* and the *Herald Tribune* for a meeting room, and in a matter of weeks the New York Scholastic Press Association, comprising both college and high school editors, was holding monthly meetings.

Next, he cast his sights on the theater. He was confident that theatrical publicists would welcome the attention of a high school newspaper, and badgered them for tickets to plays he wanted to review. This brought him in touch with Broadway press agents, including Phyllis Pearlman, who worked for playwright Elmer Rice and had gone with Rice when he accepted Flanagan's offer to head the WPA theater project in New York. As soon as Goodman graduated from high school in 1935, he approached Pearlman for a job. When she told him he had to be on relief in order to qualify, he promptly went downtown to the former Siegel-Cooper department store building to fill out an application.

New York was full of symbolic contrasts between boom and bust, and one of them was the beaux arts Siegel-Cooper building. The six-story, block-long store, built before the turn of the century on Sixth Avenue's "Ladies' Mile" of posh emporiums, featured marble facing, high arched entrance doors, and columns reminiscent of the Roman Forum. Its elegant shoppers had long been history, and the once-magnificent surroundings were now crowded with the poor applying for relief and the clerks who processed them. On the echoing first floor, Goodman, his mother, and his brother joined the line of threadbare men and women with children in tow, all waiting their turn under the light of bare bulbs suspended from the ceiling.

When they reached the clerk, Goodman introduced his Yiddish-speaking mother and his younger brother and said he was their sole support. That was true, except for the few unpredictable dollars his mother earned cleaning houses. The processor approved him for relief, and he returned to Phyllis Pearlman with his papers the same day. She sent him to the press department, where he was assigned a clerk's job that paid $16.50 a week. But unsurprisingly, Goodman saw this only as a start. Before long he proposed to Ted Mauntz, a former newspaper reporter who headed information and promotion for the project in New York, that he could spread the word by getting WPA theater news into college and high school newspapers.

Mauntz was impressed. "Write it up, kid," he said. "I'll kick it up to Washington."

Goodman put his plan on paper and gave it to Mauntz. The next thing he knew, he had an appointment to see Hallie Flanagan in Washington. In February 1936, he turned in a travel voucher, took a train at Penn Station, and met Flanagan at the Federal One offices in a cavernous D.C. auditorium. She liked the plan he spelled out, but sent him for a second opinion to her new deputy, William P. Farnsworth, an attorney who had helped administer codes governing the amusement industry, one of the myriad business sectors regulated under the short-lived National Recovery Administration. Goodman repeated his spiel. "Why should we do it?" Farnsworth asked bluntly.

"Politically or economically?" asked Goodman.

"Politically."

"Because the kids I want to reach in this plan are tomorrow's voters."

Farnsworth responded just as Goodman hoped he would. When the nineteen-year-old boarded the train back to New York, he had a job running a national press operation for high school and college papers out of the Federal Theatre Project's New York office. He would earn a supervisor's pay of $32.50 a week and have a staff of six. Using his scholastic press contacts, he quickly developed an extensive list of target papers in New York and the other cities that had active theater project production units, notably Boston, Chicago, Los Angeles, and San Francisco, and started bombarding them with weekly listings. And within a month, flush with his new riches, Goodman could afford to discard his secondhand clothes and purchase a wardrobe befitting a press agent, complete with a fedora.

6. THE ART PROJECT:
MURALS AND INTRIGUE

By the middle of 1936, the Federal Art Project was employing some 5,000 mural and easel artists, printmakers, sculptors, poster artists, and art teachers. The conservative press and politicians sneered that this was a gigantic boondoggle, but were not yet hurling accusations of Communist influence and infiltration.

This was not the only federal artwork program. Acting on a suggestion by Roosevelt's old friend George Biddle, the Treasury Department had started its Public Works of Art Project in 1933 under the Civil Works Administration to decorate new and existing federal buildings. This had evolved into the Treasury's Section of Painting and Sculpture, still with the adornment of federal buildings as its goal. But the Treasury program awarded contracts based on competition among artists. This meant it hired artists who were already likely to have work. The WPA, however, was commanded to take its artists, excluding supervisors, from the relief rolls. Their talents varied widely, requiring Holger Cahill and his staff to create opportunities for every level of ability as well as for emerging styles, such as expressionism and other abstract forms, that had not gained wide acceptance.

The Federal Art Project, like the other arts projects, was confusing to accountants who tried to apply standard guidelines to purchases and productivity. Robert Asure, the Federal One finance officer, remembered hours of negotiations "about the purchase of paints, because they thought you write specifications like you do for tons and shiploads and trainloads, carloads of other things, and [they could not fathom] the notion that one artist wouldn't like the kind of paint that some other artist wants, or that they might have to import these from abroad, or something."

These same accountants also wanted to be sure the government got its money's worth from the WPA artists. But they didn't have a clue about the way artists worked. Cahill resisted having them punch a time clock, since most worked in their own studios at their own pace. They might go for days without painting a stroke, and then work for days and nights without stopping. He tried to set production quotas instead, giving watercolorists three weeks to produce a painting and oil painters four to six, depending on the size of the canvas; printmakers had a month to produce an etching, lithograph, or block print. Cahill thought this was sufficient to prove they were actually working.

But WPA administrators in the states and in New York City, which was treated as a state, still retained some measure of control since they issued the paychecks, and they echoed Washington's demands and shared the inability—or unwillingness—of officials there to understand the world of artists. This was especially true in New York City, where Hopkins had installed Lieutenant Colonel Brehon Somervell as the administrator after work shut down on the Florida Ship Canal. Somervell insisted on time cards, with the resultant petty inconveniences. Mabel Dwight was a Staten Island printmaker with a wry touch to her work. In 1926, she was sixty years old and too deaf to trust herself to wake to her alarm clock, so she forced herself to stay up all night in order to take the ferry to Manhattan at first light, board the subway, and sign in at the project offices. Then she went home again.

"What good did the signing in do her?" Cahill asked rhetorically in an interview long after the project's close. "Nothing. It just meant that she was reporting. . . . This was the phoniness of this sort of thing."

In fact, recalled Audrey McMahon, the Federal Art Project director for the New York region, "to say that Colonel Somervell did not like and did not understand the project or the artists is a vast understatement. He was not only of the school of critics who felt that 'his little Mary could do as well' as, shall we say, a distinguished painter like

Ben Shahn or Stuart Davis, but in addition, he had a profound conviction that to create 'pictures' was not 'work.' "

The artists, of course, developed ways of coping, not all of which
were legal. Twenty-three-year-old Jackson Pollock started on the project in 1935 as an assistant to a muralist because the work rules for
murals were easier. Later, when Cahill relaxed the rules for easel
artists, he switched. At the time Pollock was living in a downtown
New York loft with his brother Sanford, called Sande, who was also
on the project. When they learned that only one member of each
household with the same last name could collect a WPA paycheck,
Sande changed his name to McCoy, an ancestral name, so they could
both stay on the rolls. The deceptions artists were willing to employ
highlighted the fact that for most of them, the WPA was allowing them
to work full-time at art for the first time in their lives, and not have to
supplement their usually meager income from art with teaching or
other jobs.

Cahill was a perfect leader for the mix of talents and temperaments
at his command. He had no interest in conforming to artificial academic standards, preferring a range of experience and experimentation
to the rigidity often associated with art "movements." This was how
he had lived his own life. His family had left Iceland when he was an
infant, first for western Canada, then to North Dakota. When he was
eleven, in 1898, his father abandoned the family, and so Cahill spent
his youth in orphanages or working on farms in Canada and the
Midwest, occasionally taking to the road in search of his mother and
his sister. Eventually he found them working on a farm in North
Dakota, but after a brief reunion, he struck out on his own again. He
worked as a cattle driver, a railroad clerk, and a coal shoveler on a
boat to Japan and China, where he jumped ship in Shanghai. When he
finally returned to the United States, he landed in New York, attending
college classes at night while working as a dishwasher and a short-
order cook. It was about that time, near the end of the world war, that
he changed his birth name, Sveinn Kristjan Bjarnarsson, to Edgar Holger
Cahill—Eddie to his friends—and took up journalism. In the 1920s,
he plunged deep into the art world and began to write about art.
Painters were his friends, among them John Sloan, Max Weber, and
Joseph Stella. He joined the staff of the Newark Museum in 1922, where
he curated important shows on American folk art. In 1932, when he

was the acting director of the Museum of Modern Art in New York, he brought together the work of early American folk artists in a show that proposed that their art and popular culture fertilized fine art and high culture. Other shows he curated also linked primitive art with the work of modern masters. Along the way, he also found time to write books and essays about art, as well as novels and short stories, and his reputation in the art world grew. He was thus a natural choice for the short list to head the Federal Art Project. He accepted the job, intending to stay for just six months, after hearing that the other leading candidate was the head of the American Academy, a prescription for buttoned-down academic standards.

It was inevitable that most project art would fall into the representational school known as American scene painting. While European artists had embraced modernism as a departure from the past, at this time American artists believed that depictions of real people in real settings would help them reveal American democracy and create a uniquely American art form. Still, they fell into two camps; both were shaped by the depression, but one tended to highlight the country's virtues, the other its flaws. Grant Wood and Thomas Hart Benton practiced American regionalism, evoking in their paintings the simplicity of the heartland—farms and small towns where life was orderly and crops grew from land curiously untouched by drought. The social realists had a different take. Artists such as Joseph Hirsch, Ben Shahn, and Jack Levine looked at urban and industrial America; found corruption, slums, and blighted lives; and created paintings and prints filled with outrage and a sarcasm that often featured scathing caricatures.

Benton taught WPA artists, including Jackson Pollock, and Hirsch, Shahn, and Levine all worked for the WPA. Many project artists, however, had more earnestness than verve; their depictions of poverty and poor working conditions strove to deliver a political message. Critics were inclined to find such works "depressing." "Gloom pervades practically all" the paintings, reported the *New York Times* about one WPA easel show.

But then there were the murals. In an America that was striving to make sense of itself, to review its origins and trials and mark its progress, these WPA creations would evolve into a form all their own. Their muscular men at work in fields and factories, women tending hearth and home, historical figures and events, street scenes, and magnificent machines would become what people thought of when the phrase "New Deal art" was spoken. The works of easel painters were parceled out to government offices and buildings whose occupants may or may not have appreciated them. But muralists were sure of prominent display. They had entire walls at their disposal—and there were walls everywhere. Although the Treasury Department held the franchise on post offices and most other federal buildings, WPA muralists had schools, libraries, city halls and county offices, hospitals, airports, and colleges to work with; the chief requirement was that the institutions pay for the materials the artists used. Hospitals and public schools were especially eager for the murals, the hospitals seeing them as therapeutic and the schools as educational.

And these spaces could be utterly magnificent. Edward Laning, who won the design competition to decorate the dining room at the Ellis Island immigration center, had the entire circumference of the room to work with—a space 110 feet long by 8 feet high. In this area, almost half as long as the famous Bayeux Tapestry in France, he painted a story he titled "The Role of the Immigrant in the Industrial Development of America." Later, still as a WPA artist, he illustrated the history of writing and printing, a span that began with Moses' stone tablets chiseled with the Ten Commandments and ended with Ottmar Mergenthaler's Linotype machine on four panels in the New York Public Library. He called it "The Story of the Recorded Word."

At New York's Harlem Hospital, Charles Alston headed the first group of African American artists to win a major WPA mural commission. Their sketches were originally rejected by hospital superintendent Lawrence T. Dermody as having "too much Negro subject matter," but protests from the community and the artists got the decision reversed and the work went forward. There were five murals, two by Alston contrasting traditional healing with modern medical procedures, a panel on surgery and anesthesia by Alfred Crimi (the only white artist in the group), Vertis Hayes's *Pursuit of Happiness* depicting African American progress from slavery to a foothold in the professions, and Georgette Seabrooke's *Recreation in Harlem*.

In Newark, New Jersey, a Russian immigrant named Michael Lenson had long since spent the $10,000 grant he won in 1928 that had staked him to four years of art study in Europe. By 1935 he was relying on his father and his brother for handouts, but when their gifts grew more grudging, he went to the WPA office on Halsey Street in Newark and lied his way onto the relief rolls. Soon afterward, he was competing with other artists for the job of installing a mural at the Essex Mountain Sanitorium in Verona, New Jersey. This was a tuberculosis hospital that had originally been a home for orphaned and delinquent girls, and the mural site in its large dining hall was a wall sixteen feet high and seventy-five long. Lenson won the competition with a design titled "The History of New Jersey," which traced the state's roots from precolonial Indians through the bloody Battle of Trenton in the Revolutionary War to modern scenes of industry, agriculture, and transportation. Rather than working directly on the wall in gesso, he and four assistants stretched large canvases which they painted and mounted in the enormous space.

As Lenson worked on the mural into 1936, WPA administrators noticed that he possessed other talents as well: he spoke in public, he belonged to artists' groups, he held offices in these groups. Before long Audrey McMahon recruited him to give talks about the art project and the WPA. Soon afterward he was promoted to assistant state supervisor of the mural and easel division. On Newark's Halsey Street, where the WPA had space in two adjacent buildings, Lenson installed a large workshop. In one corner, he set up cabinetmakers to build artist-designed furniture. Another space was given over to lithography, where artists worked on stones and printed images from them on a press. Muralists worked on their designs in yet another area, and a room at the front of the building became a gallery for walk-in visitors to view paintings and prints by project artists. And when a show came down in Newark, it went on the road, appearing in galleries and public exhibition space around the state.

Lenson proved to be as adept as Margery Hoffman Smith in Oregon at finding roles for artists that ranged beyond the standard formats of murals, prints, easel art, and sculpture. Scouting for projects in Atlantic City, he learned of women on the relief rolls there who weren't artists but were good with their hands. If the Art Project could produce artist-designed furniture for government offices, Lenson thought, artists could design other kinds of furnishings as well. He decided that the Atlantic City women, following artists' patterns, could make rugs and wall decorations from scrap materials. The word went out to WPA sewing rooms across the state to save their cuttings, and before long these new Art Project employees were at work hooking large, colorful rugs and hangings.

Then Lenson got wind of an old glassworks in Vineland, New Jersey. Vineland and Millville to the south had once formed the nexus of a glassblowing area in south-central New Jersey. The sand there was fine and free of impurities, perfect for glassmaking, but the glass factories, overtaken by modern manufacturing methods, had now closed, leaving dozens of glassblowers jobless. Lenson sought them out and told them he had a plan to put them back to work.

"They thought it was too good to be true. They loved it," he said later. The WPA funded a partial restoration of the moldering art glass works in Vineland, breathed a kiln to life, and brought in some sand. Some of the craftsmen had not blown glass in years and so had lost the calluses built up from handling the metal rods called punties that were used for shaping hot glass. But they regained them quickly, and also reestablished the unique traditions of their workplace. When one of them breathed into his blowpipe to form the cavity he wanted in a piece of molten glass, the others joined in a collective pause. The process required a steady breath and concentration, but sometimes the glass cracked with a loud pop, and then all the blowers joined in a shout of "Hallelujah!"

The Art Project's glassblowers shaped vases, perfume bottles, bowls, pitchers, and candle holders, replicating early American pieces and producing new designs. The New Jersey project also worked with the Armstrong Cork Company in Millville, launching a similar program there that made vases, other freeblown vessels, and paperweights. Because it was prohibited from competing with private glassworks, the project all but gave its work away to hospitals and libraries, charging only the cost of the materials. "There were fabulous vases on tables all over the state," said Lenson. Eleanor Roosevelt bought a set of them for the White House. But New York State's large Corning Glass company believed that if public buildings in New Jersey had beautiful vases on their tables, those vases should come from its Steuben art glass subsidiary, so when Millville's reputation spread, Corning complained. Eventually, it succeeded in shutting the project down and sending the glassblowers back on relief.

In most areas of the country, however, artists worked unimpeded by complaints of competition, and they kept expanding project boundaries. In Portland workshops and on Mount Hood, Hoffman Smith's vision for furnishing and decorating the Timberline Lodge had brought together cabinet and furniture makers, weavers, rug hookers, blacksmiths, and wood carvers as well as traditional artists. Handicraft programs were under way in Milwaukee, New Orleans, and other places around the country. In San Francisco late in 1936, the Art Project discovered Armenians and Turks on relief who possessed ancient skills in tapestry making, and set up a unit to employ them. At the same time, muralists were continuing to enhance public buildings with art that would last for decades. One of them was Lucien Labaudt, a former dress designer, who executed in fresco a series of vibrant San Francisco city scenes for the walls of a restaurant and changing house called the Beach Chalet at the west end of Golden Gate Park, across from Ocean Beach on the Pacific. Labaudt had also sketched mosaics and wood carvings for the Beach Chalet, which were completed by two other WPA artists, mosaicist Primo Caredio and sculptor Michael Von Meyer.

Graphic artists were at work as well. Printmakers were producing fine art prints using wood block, silkscreen, and lithographic processes, but the far larger output came from Art Project poster makers using the same techniques. Their work was more directly functional than decorative, but it was equally striking. Their posters advertised WPA art exhibits and theater and musical performances, urged workers to protect their eyes and hands, encouraged caution against syphilis, gonorrhea, and pneumonia, and suggested that Americans visit the zoo, travel, exercise, attend educational programs and community events, write letters, and save trees. Graphic arts programs operated in seventeen states and the District of Columbia. Most who saw their bold and colorful designs probably did not equate what they saw with "art"—but art it was, and it informed an audience of millions.

7. THE INDEX OF AMERICAN DESIGN (AND COMMUNITY ART CENTERS)

For all of the Federal Art Project's visible output, much of its work remained unseen. One such effort was a huge and valuable undertaking that aimed to preserve a record of America's disappearing past. Project researchers, artists, and photographers were at work unearthing art and artifacts in order to compile an exact pictorial record of the stuff Americans had lived, worked, and played with from the eighteenth century on.

The path to this vast project began with Romana Javitz's problem. Javitz was the curator of the New York Public Library's picture collection. In the 1920s, she had visited libraries and museums in Europe and been struck by the attention they paid to keeping native arts and crafts alive through pictures. Records of folk arts such as these—depictions of the houses in which people lived, their furnishings, their kitchen and work tools, what they wore, their children's clothes and toys—had never been systematically collected in America. When Javitz joined the library some years later and began to take requests from artists and decorators for research that would let them duplicate these old materials, all she had to show them were scattered pictures—and those few were fragile and crumbling from heavy use.

One of these artists was Ruth Reeves, a painter and textile designer.

Together, she and Javitz promoted the idea that the WPA could put commercial artists to work locating examples of American design and recording them in accurate detail. They foresaw the result as an invaluable research tool.

Holger Cahill liked the idea. Its concept fit with his appreciation of grassroots art. He could see that it was a massive task and he doubted that it would ever be finished, given that the arts projects, like the rest of the WPA, were funded from year to year, but he approved it nonetheless. Not all the artists assigned to the index—ultimately there would be 500 in all, including photographers—welcomed their assignment. They were artists, after all, not copyists. But it did not take them long to appreciate the quality that Cahill was demanding. He likened it to the vividly realistic paintings of the nineteenth-century American trompe l'oeil master William Harnett, who rendered objects so faithfully that they almost begged to be lifted from the canvas and used. Index artists were trained in a distinctive technique of watercolor painting developed by Egyptologist Joseph Lindon Smith in the early twentieth century to record archaeological objects he was unable to bring home. "It required exact precision, and our copy was a little better than a photograph," said one of the artists, Joseph Delaney.

First, of course, the objects themselves had to be found. Frances Pollack, director of educational projects for the WPA in New York, worked with Javitz and Reeves, directing the research as well as administering the growing collection of picture plates. Field researchers and artists fanned out to thirty-five states, finding and recording in minute detail costumes, dolls, ballet slippers, pottery and glass, furniture, Southwestern Indian and Pennsylvania German folk art, andirons, door knockers, tin boxes, and other metalwork. They photographed and painted Shaker crafts and clothing, quilts and weavings, weather vanes, toys, and wood carvings that ranged from shop signs to the figureheads of sailing ships. The index survived through one funding cycle after another and the picture plates piled up, building to a total of 22,000 images. What began as Romana Javitz's problem became the Index of American Design, one of the Federal Art Project's most enduring works.

While the design index researchers and artists were making a permanent record that would inform future artists and designers, fully a quarter of Art Project workers were extending the reach of art still further. Cahill had envisioned the project not just as an artists' employment service but as a way to take art to people who lived in areas where painting and sculpture were hardly ever seen. This idea had struck him prior to joining the project, when he accompanied a father and son to a performance by a group of southern gospel harmony singers in Chattanooga, Tennessee. Afterward, the conversation turned to art, and the son, who was painting ads for movies showing at the local theater, told Cahill he wished he could learn more. "But I can't," he said. "There are no pictures here that can help me in any way." Later, when Jacob Baker was screening Cahill for the Art Project job and the two were still on cordial terms, he recounted the story. "I would like to put up centers where you could help people like that," Cahill told Baker.

As the story circulated among Cahill's staff, the movie ad painter became a barefoot hillbilly walking for miles across rugged mountains to look at an oil painting because he'd never seen one. But Cahill's vision was more practical than sentimental, and he pushed on with the plan to place art centers in communities that had little access to art and art education. These centers would not only display artworks but also offer classes in drawing and painting for aspiring artists and classes in art appreciation for people who simply wanted to know what to look for in a painting or a piece of sculpture.

By the fall of 1935, North Carolina state director Daniel Defenbacher had opened the first of the Federal Art Project's community centers in Winston-Salem. There were two more in North Carolina by the end of the year. A year later, the Art Project had opened a total of twenty-five centers across the South and West, and the response to them fully justified Cahill's initiative. Parents were enrolling their children in classes for a level of knowledge about art history and techniques that the impoverished public schools could not provide, and they themselves were attending evening classes and public lectures. By the end of 1936, more than 1 million people had participated in free programs at these WPA art centers.

The community centers were slower to arrive in major cities, but when they did they were especially welcome. A hunger for art classes was first filled in New York City's Harlem by WPA muralist Charles Alston, who turned an old stable on 141st Street into a teaching studio that became an arts salon. The WPA later funded the Harlem Art Workshop at the 135th Street branch of the New York Public Library, and in 1937 it established the Harlem Community Art Center in a loft at 125th Street and Lenox Avenue. Among the many artists to gather and receive instruction at these centers were the collagist Romare Bearden and the young Jacob Lawrence, who later worked for the WPA easel division and would become famous for his series of works depicting the black migration to the North. In Chicago, the WPA's South Side arts center would not open until 1940, but would produce alumni that included photographer Gordon Parks and artist and poet Margaret Burroughs.

The Index of American Design was one of several WPA programs to preserve records of America's past. The Historic American Buildings Survey was established in 1933 under the Civil Works Administration in conjunction with the National Park Service, and later continued under the WPA, to employ architects, draftsmen, and photographers. Its aim was to create pictorial records and measured drawings that could be used to duplicate significant buildings and structures if they were destroyed, or to restore or reproduce them. The buildings measured, photographed, and drawn ranged from covered bridges to churches, courthouses, private homes, and commercial and industrial buildings.

The Historical Records Survey first fell under the Federal Writers Project and later became independent within the Women's and Professional Projects Division of the WPA. It employed writers and copyists to inventory and duplicate moldering and scattered records, including census documents, cemetery interments, school and military records, birth and death records, land transaction records, maps, and newspapers.

8. THE MUSIC PROJECT: "REAL MUSIC" FOR AMERICA

American music had never been more energetic and alive than the time when the depression struck. Jazz was still a recent word, and musicians such as Count Basie, Duke Ellington, Louis Armstrong, and King Oliver were redefining and advancing the form. Swing had evolved from ragtime's stride and syncopation. Benny Goodman's band had turned up the temperature and made "hot swing" popular when it wowed an audience at the Palomar Ballroom in Los Angeles in August 1935, playing tunes by the black arranger and bandleader Fletcher Henderson. The big band era was under way, bringing wildly popular dance tunes arranged by innovators such as Ellington and Artie Shaw to listeners everywhere through the relatively new medium of radio. Far from the sophistication of the New York and Chicago dance clubs as personified by Ellington's white tie and rakishly tilted top hat, self-taught musicians in the hidden reaches of the Appalachian mountains were translating the bagpipe and fiddle laments of their Irish and Scottish forebears into bluegrass and the roots of country music. And in black churches in the South and North alike, harmonizing gospel choirs were bringing the passion of religion into what became the underpinnings of the blues.

Yet even as this fresh new music bubbled up, in the United States musicians themselves were reeling. Performers had suffered multiple blows even before the depression. First came talking pictures, which eliminated the live orchestras that played in movie house orchestra pits to accompany silent films. Then radio and phonograph recordings became available and the demand for live music declined still further. But the depression was by far the hardest shot. By 1933 in New York, where the largest concentration of musicians lived and worked, 12,000 of the 15,000 local members of the American Federation of Musicians were out of work. The situation was no better in the nation's other music centers; in Boston, Chicago, Philadelphia, Los Angeles, and San Francisco, as many as 70 percent of professional musicians had no jobs. Across the entire country, only eleven privately funded symphony orchestras had managed to continue operating.

Harry Hopkins had assembled a few bands and orchestras and offered music classes under both the CWA and FERA, but these were stopgaps that benefited musicians and educators in only a scattering of states. It was not until the WPA that the government undertook a comprehensive program. But Hopkins's choice of Nikolai Sokoloff, the founding conductor of the Cleveland Symphony, to head the Federal Music Project was not universally applauded.

Sokoloff's path to musical prominence in America had begun in 1898 on a train platform in Kiev, Russia. Only twelve years old, he was already an accomplished classical musician, playing violin in the Kiev Orchestra, conducted by his father. Now he and his family were beginning the long journey to America, and the departure must have been bittersweet for the young violinist because part of the price of passage had been gained by the sale of his violin.

Once in America, however, the gifted youth quickly made his mark. At thirteen, he won a special scholarship to the Yale University School of Music, where he studied for three years. By the age of sixteen, he held the first violinist's chair in the Boston Symphony Orchestra. Three years later he left for France to begin several years' more study, which culminated in 1911 with successful tours in France and England. Back in the United States, he joined Modest Altschuler's Russian Symphony Orchestra of New York as concertmaster, and then was named conductor of the San Francisco Philharmonic. After America entered the world war, he went to France to organize and conduct concerts for American soldiers. A concert series he conducted in Cincinnati at the war's end drew the attention of the new Cleveland Symphony, which hired him as its first conductor in 1918. In 1933, he retired to Connecticut, where he organized local concerts until Federal One was created in 1935 and Hopkins asked him to come to Washington.

As with each of the directors of the Federal One projects, Sokoloff's background would shape the goals of the project he headed. The music that he knew and understood, the music that he had been playing since he was five years old, was that of the European masters: Mozart and Bach, Beethoven and Brahms. In his view, this music was far more than entertainment; it elevated its listeners from mere existence to meaningful life. While the other arts projects sought and celebrated an American vernacular—Cahill's embrace of grassroots arts forms was just one example—Sokoloff had decided from the start that he would give Americans a diet of classics in order to improve their taste. He was willing to include American composers as long as their music was "refined," but despite its popularity he did not consider the music of dance halls, black churches, cowboy campfires, jazz clubs, and brass bands to be sufficiently enlightening. What the people needed if they were to become part of an "accepted civic and cultural system" was the music of conservatories and concert halls—and this was what the Federal Music Project would bring to them.

Sokoloff enjoyed great prestige in classical music circles, but not surprisingly, many supporters of American music considered him a musical snob and opposed his appointment. Treasury Secretary Morgenthau's wife, Elinor, wrote Hopkins to say that in her opinion Sokoloff lacked the "temperament and character" to head the Music Project, and that he would do harm to American music if left on his own. Project directors in California wanted "a native-born American musician" to run things. Indeed, Sokoloff's public statements often confirmed the views of those who opposed him. Swing music, he said, "is like comparing the funny papers to the work of a painter." (Roy Lichtenstein, who would famously conflate cartoons with art, was only eleven years old in 1935.) He told the project's state directors that American musicians and composers "will get no place playing stupid things," nor would a composer's work be played just because he was American. And for the most part, he managed to appoint administrators who supported his musical paternalism. The pianist and composer Lee Pattison was his regional director in New York. Echoing Sokoloff, Pattison emphasized the goal of creating an audience to support "really good music in this country," and the importance of "educating the public musically, and supplying them with the correct musical outlets."

Providing jobs to out-of-work musicians was obviously the project's first priority. But they were as proud as other people and, like many of the depression jobless, had been reluctant to acknowledge their poverty and apply for relief. The key to a WPA job from the beginning had been eligibility for the relief rolls, but only 5,000 musicians were listed, so the first task of Joseph Weber, who headed the 105,000-member American Federation of Musicians, was to persuade the WPA to extend the application deadline for musicians from the original cutoff date of May 30, 1935, to November 1.

But then Sokoloff tried to tilt the playing field toward the music he preferred and the musicians who played it. The project was no place for "every Tom, Dick, or Harry who has no musical ability," he pronounced. To that end he established a classification system that would rate musicians according to their skills, which were skills that reflected his own background and musical education. Thus those who read music would be hired more quickly than those who played by ear, and those with classical training had a considerable advantage over dance hall drummers and marching-band tuba players. They were also paid more. Weber, complaining that this was patently unfair, lobbied for a larger share of project resources for "popular" musicians. Since outside major cities these constituted the vast majority, eventually Sokoloff capitulated and put all performing musicians who had come from the relief rolls on the same $23.86 weekly wage.

Joseph Weber was one of the twenty-five members of an advisory committee that Sokoloff, together with Hopkins, chose from among the leading lights of American music. George Gershwin, *New York Times* music critic Olin Downes, conductor Leopold Stokowski, and Mrs. John Jardine, head of the National Federation of Music Clubs, were among the others. The committee's underlying purpose, advice aside, was to encourage support for the project by showing that Sokoloff was aligned with the music establishment and that it agreed with his musical judgment. In fact, despite the arguments about his musical choices and emphases, the Federal Music Project worked as hard as any of the other projects to reach a large and varied audience. Hopkins had let it be known that his goal was to provide music to people "who have been kept away by price"; it was to be offered "not alone in symphony halls, parks and schools but even in railway stations." Sokoloff in turn told his project administrators to honor all requests for performances and to solicit more, as a way both of lifting the country's musical IQ and of attracting large audiences in numbers that would show off the project's popularity. Ensembles, bands, chamber groups, and orchestras were to play in any setting that could provide countable warm bodies.

Because the classical units took time to assemble and rehearse, the first groups to debut under the WPA banner were precisely the kind that Sokoloff tended to dismiss; among them was the brass-blaring, cymbal-crashing band of red-suited strutters that had led the WPA Circus into the Second Naval Battalion Armory in Brooklyn two months into the project. By November 1935, the Music Project still had fewer than a thousand musicians on the payroll.

The pace quickened dramatically in 1936. Project units jelled and began to offer concerts of all kinds, high and low, across the country. The musicians performed symphonies in concert halls, but they also marched in parades, played at baseball parks, and strummed cowboy songs for schoolchildren. No audience was too small or event too unlikely. On April 25, 1936, a WPA brass band consisting of nine musicians from the Lay Missionary School on East 14th Street in New York stood on the decks of a steamship at Pier 58 on the Hudson River and tootled a farewell to twenty-two-year-old Sister Frances Jolly of Anoka, Minnesota, who was sailing off to missionary work in Africa. That same month, the WPA Federal Civic Opera company of San Diego scheduled two free performances of Mascagni's *Cavalleria Rusticana* at the Russ Auditorium. The two stretched to seven, one of them lighted more brightly than usual for the benefit of an elderly audience with presumably dimming eyesight. The lead singer was a non-reliefer, José de Arratia from the Royal Opera Company of Mexico, but there were enough principal singers from the relief rolls to form two casts. The Federal Philharmonic Orchestra and a fifty-member chorus, both of them San Diego project units, accompanied the singers, who wore costumes made by WPA sewing workers. More than 15,000 San Diegans saw the opera. They were among 32 million

Americans who, according to a project count, attended Federal Music Project performances between January 1 and September 15, 1936.

These audiences paid bargain prices. Tickets cost 25 or 50 cents, and 10 cents for children, when they cost anything at all. Many performances, such as the regular Friday night and Sunday afternoon band concerts at the Bronx County Building in New York, were free. To some reviewers, this presented a dilemma. The *New York Post*'s Samuel Chotzinoff wondered in print if he should "modify the standards of judgment where the entertainment is free or the admission fee is a fifty-five-cent top." He went on to answer his own question, describing "outworn or young or crude voices" in an opera in arguing that listeners—and reviewers—should not have to make allowances.

The WPA advertised the Music Project as vigorously as it did its construction jobs. The lettering on the signs may have been adorned with curlicues and serifs, but the WPA name was featured everywhere, from advance posters—done by the Art Project—to the program notes to the WPA logos scrolled elaborately on the conductor's podium and the stands that held the sheet music or scores. Harry Hewes, chief of the project's Office of Information, headed this high-powered publicity machine and maintained a pipeline to the country's major music publications as well as its general magazines and newspapers. Even more effective was the project's use of radio. The project recorded its symphony performances, picked out the best, and made them available without charge to any station that asked. Sokoloff himself oversaw the recording of fifteen-minute snippets of concert, symphony, and black choral music that aired on local stations in donated time.

More than his Federal One counterparts, Sokoloff did endeavor to avoid suggestions of left-wing sentiment within the Federal Music Project. He did not have the aggressively political playwrights of the Living Newspaper to contend with, or the flaming radicals who would emerge in the Writers' Project, or even the artists in whose murals critics would find goateed men they thought resembled V. I. Lenin; few of the project's musicians were outspokenly radical in any event. What complaints they did express were likely to be over work issues: job cuts, wage reductions, or the conditions in which they had to play. When the forty-member New York City Parks Department Band was ordered to perform for ice skaters in Central Park on a January day when the temperature was in the twenties, the band members said they feared frostbite and refused. The taskmasters of Robert Moses's Parks Department fired them summarily, though they were reinstated the next day.

Sokoloff's awareness of political realities also led him to perform works he might not have chosen under other circumstances. WPA concerts regularly featured the works of the most popular American classicists, composers such as Gershwin, Victor Herbert, and John Philip Sousa. Music project units also performed the heavily Eurocentric works of Americans George Chadwick and Edward MacDowell, as well as the Broadway-style music of Jerome Kern, Oscar Hammerstein, and Irving Berlin, sometimes to such an extent that audiences complained of missing the familiar European classics.

Although the project did seek new works by American composers, the composers had to write on speculation; if their works failed to meet Sokoloff's standards, they weren't paid. Moreover, those works that passed muster endured an additional gauntlet of auditions before they were publicly performed. Nevertheless, a good number made the cut: sixteen operas, seventeen choral works, five liturgies, thirty-seven symphonies, thirty concertos, and forty-one symphonic and tone poems were performed in the first ten months of 1936. They revealed, said Sokoloff, "an amazing wealth of creative talent."

However, he did fail to find similar riches in idiomatic and ethnic forms of music. Early in 1936, the Federal Music Project's Kentucky unit organized the Kentucky Mountain Minstrels, a folk music group that played a repertoire of folk songs and fiddle tunes for local audiences. The regional director for Kentucky, pianist Guy Maier, saw publicity value in the group and sent pictures to Harry Hewes in the project's information office, but under Sokoloff, the fate of the Kentucky Mountain Minstrels was ordained. Hewes never distributed the photos, and the unit disbanded in July when its funding was cut. Similar groups that played regional or ethnic genre music, such as three Mexican *tipica* orchestras in Texas, were lumped under the heading of "novelty" bands for project purposes.

Nonetheless, the project did recognize the need to preserve some indigenous music forms, and in New Mexico it funded an effort to collect songs and music of the Spanish Southwest. And in its third year, Federal One would establish a joint committee on the folk arts that brought the theater, music, and art projects together to seek out and preserve, if not perform, distinctive regional music.

The music project branched out in other ways as well, driven by the need to employ men and women who were not performers or composers but filled supporting roles in the music world. One of its programs was a music copying service. Reproducing different arrangements of orchestral and operatic scores was a painstaking and time-consuming specialty in the days before photocopying; it involved copiers who worked by hand applying sharps and clefs to score sheets in India ink. Once the Federal Music Project proved it could provide accurate scores, the service found eager subscribers among privately funded orchestras, as well as university and public libraries, which enriched their collections by tens of thousands of scores.

The project also greatly expanded music education, through both concerts in the schools and classes that were offered directly in WPA facilities. This proved to be one of its most successful ventures. Across the country, the combination of concerts and classes in music history, theory, appreciation, composition, and choral and instrumental conducting, as well as folk music and dancing, brought a new knowledge of music to millions who had never had a music class of any kind. The classes were extremely popular; South Carolina begged for a fifty-fold increase in teachers, and it was said that classes taught by 100 WPA music teachers in Mississippi, and attended by 69,000 people, prompted a sharp rise in the demand for used pianos.

Counting the musicians themselves, the score copiers, and the many music educators—more than 6,000 teachers worked for the project at its peak—the music project became the largest of the arts project employers, with 15,842 workers on the rolls.

And as always, there were heartwarming tales of talent employed by the WPA that transcended, as Flanagan had put it, "the remembrance of hunger in its stomach." Frank Gullino was a twenty-year-old violinist who had played since he was eight and took lessons at a settlement house music school in New York's Greenwich Village, where he lived in a sixth-floor tenement with his father, an out-of-work tailor, and two sisters. A neighbor heard him playing and steered him to the music project. He soon landed a place in the New York Civic Orchestra, which skimmed the cream of the city's WPA classical units, and he also played as a soloist in the WPA New York Festival Orchestra, which toured statewide. In May 1936, after months as a relief violinist, he answered a call to audition for the Metropolitan Opera's orchestra. Some 350 musicians showed up, and Gullino was one of the few hired, trading his $1,150 a year in relief earnings for a contract for $2,400 for the upcoming sixteen-week-long winter season.

9. THE WRITERS' PROJECT

The writers of America were jealous. The starving artists had been taken care of, but to their minds the starving writers had been left out in the cold. Indeed, prior to 1935, the New Deal had responded only fitfully to demands to put writers back to work, and writers' groups, looking at jobs programs for artists, called for similar treatment.

Writers "do not intend to continue under the semi-starvation conditions meted out to them, particularly while painters of pictures... receive adequate treatment from the government," wrote the New York chapter secretary of the left-wing Unemployed Writers' Association to the Civil Works Administration. Without some kind of program, he went on, writers would be forced to organize and fight. The newly formed Newspaper Guild demanded a national program for unemployed writers and reporters. The Authors Guild, the oldest professional writers' organization in the country, proposed in February 1934 that writers be hired to compose detailed chronicles of people's daily lives around the country. A year later, the Writers' Union, another left-wing group, marched in New York City; one member carried a placard that read, "Children Need Books, Writers Need Jobs, We Demand Projects." The union sent a three-man delegation to Washington early in 1935 to meet with relief officials, and to the delegates' surprise they got a warm reception; Aubrey Williams helped them improve their proposal for a writers' project, and Hopkins himself dropped in to wish them luck.

A few programs for writers did exist prior to the WPA. CWA and FERA had hired some writers and reporters, along with photographers, clerks, researchers, and typists. Some were assigned to explore pieces of America's disappearing past, setting down folktales and interviewing former slaves. Most, however, had wound up in the agencies' public information offices, where they compiled reports and statistics on relief activities to distribute to the media. When the WPA was formed, these workers were absorbed into what at first was called the Reporters' Project and eventually became the WPA's Information Division; the slave interviews and folklore research were continued and over time expanded, with the manuscripts to be placed in the Library of Congress. Still, all these fell far short of providing enough jobs.

There were also a handful of state programs. Although most of them involved academic research studies, Connecticut had had a better idea. There, eleven relief workers paid by the CWA and later FERA, and assisted by volunteers, had assembled the material for a state guidebook. Author and retired minister Edgar L. Heermance, who had roamed the state promoting conservation of its parks and forests, wrote the guide, and the Connecticut State Planning Board sponsored its publication. *The Connecticut Guide: What to See and Where to Find It* was coming off the press in Hartford late in 1935, just as the Federal Writers' Project was beginning to focus on a similar but far larger mission.

The idea that the Writers' Project should undertake a national series of guidebooks was a child with many parents. One of them appears to have been the poet Marianne Moore, who had urged the CWA to hire out-of-work writers to prepare guidebooks and state histories. Moore, already something of a literary celebrity, had noticed that more people were traveling by car, and she knew the value of a guidebook because she herself had traveled throughout Europe before the world war. Another parent was a FERA supervisor in Michigan, Henry S. Curtis. But the prime mover was a writer and traveler named Katherine

Kellock. Kellock, like Moore, had traveled widely in Europe and had become a fan of the Baedeker country guides, which provided historical and contemporary insights as well as the directions travelers needed to get from place to place. The Baedekers, named after their German publisher, were so popular among dedicated travelers that the name had become synonymous with *guidebook*. If you were going on a trip, it was enough to say that along the way you would consult a Baedeker.

Kellock had written for magazines and newspapers, and contributed many biographies of prominent Americans to the *Dictionary of American Biography*. Her first New Deal job had been in the Resettlement Administration, an experiment in collective farming that sought—ultimately unsuccessfully—to move farmers from land gone bad from drought or overplanting and reestablish them in new communities with access to good land. When Henry Alsberg asked her to join the Writers' Project as a field supervisor, she jumped at the chance. The pay was less, but she would have the chance to push the creation of the guides.

There was a Baedeker *United States,* which despite its advanced age—it was first published in 1893 and last revised back in 1909—was the model for what the project wanted to do. Jacob Baker and his aides at Federal One envisioned five regional guides that would eventually be combined into a single all-encompassing guide. (In the original conception of the project, writers would also be put to work compiling an encyclopedia of government functions in Washington and performing special studies in various professional disciplines such as economics, sociology, history, and the arts. The encyclopedia of government functions promised to be a huge collection of deadly prose on deadly subjects, and fortunately was never started, nor were the special studies, which were never precisely defined.) The concept of five regional guides and a single master guide died in favor of state guides, in part because state and local politicians were more likely to support them.

Alsberg, at the head of the new Writers' Project, understood the necessity of political support. At the same time he commanded the respect of professional writers because of his personal history of work for social justice, inventive mind, vast fund of knowledge about a variety of subjects, and excellent literary taste. He had a deep belief in those who pursued the writing life, and understood that they could be fractious, self-interested, and frequently radical. His friends found him lacking in administrative skills, and he did tend to prefer amusing dilettantes to people who worked hard but were boring, but he managed to exude authority, thanks in part to a deep-toned voice that a colleague likened to that of an Old Testament prophet.

Now fifty-seven, Alsberg had been raised in a prosperous family, graduated from Columbia's law school at twenty, and practiced law for three years before entering Harvard to study literature. He found this dull and took up journalism. He wrote editorials for the New York *Evening Post,* spent five years as secretary to America's ambassador to Turkey, and then became a roving foreign correspondent for the *Nation,* the New York *World,* and the London *Daily Herald.* He had traveled to Russia several times in the wake of the revolution. Famine and violence were widespread there, and these conditions prompted Alsberg to join the American Jewish Joint Distribution Committee, dedicated to funneling aid to Jews and Jewish communities overseas, as a director.

Returning to Russia in his new role, but now traveling incognito and carrying $10,000 in cash to give to Jews in need, Alsberg lived in the underbelly of the ferment, shuttling from one contact to the next, sleeping in haystacks and riding in boxcars. He spent seven months traveling before the police in Moscow decided to bring him back there for questioning. The policeman who tracked him down so enjoyed the liquor Alsberg offered him on their long and frequently interrupted train journey that Alsberg had to carry him into the man's Moscow police station on his return. He heaved the sodden agent onto a desk and said, "Here is the man you sent out to find me." By then his sympathy for the aims of the revolution had faded, replaced by opposition to Lenin's Bolshevik government and its brutal persecution of opponents and stifling of civil liberties. But he kept these feelings to himself until he was back in the United States; then, starting in 1923, he worked to expose the regime's excesses.

During the rest of the decade Alsberg distanced himself from former friends and classmates who were enjoying the fruits of the financial boom, and plunged into the arts. He showed his literary versatility by adapting S. Ansky's famous Yiddish play *The Dybbuk* for off-Broadway, where it ran for two years and went on to Broadway, Chicago, and London. Drawn deeper into the theatrical world, he became a director of the Provincetown Playhouse in Greenwich Village, adapting other plays until the small experimental theater went dark in the depression. He joined Jacob Baker's staff at FERA in 1934 and edited two agency magazines before being chosen to head the Writers' Project when it was created.

During the first months, disorder reigned. Alsberg's limitations as an executive contributed, but were less to blame than an array of other factors. Strong state directors were vital to organizing the flow of information that would go into the guides, but these were hard and in some cases impossible to find. Even the good ones faced a deluge of bureaucratic regulations from Washington that overwhelmed their real work, as did a thick set of production guidelines that, like the artists' time clock, proved unworkable. One early rule demanded that project writers produce 1,500 words a week to earn their paychecks, although few writers other than experienced journalists were competent to produce on demand.

Furthermore, ideological arguments raged in most of the big-city project offices where writers tended to be concentrated. Many of them were love-struck by various forms of left-wing thinking, from anti-fascism and socialism to the Communist Party and beyond. "The Communists moved in on the projects very quickly," Jacob Baker said later of the early days of Federal One. They were quick to organize and prone to strike—and most of all, they were dizzily attached to their pet interpretations of radical ideology.

At the California project headquarters in San Francisco, a noisy minority of Communists styled themselves as followers of Josef Stalin. The devotees of Leon Trotsky were fewer in number, but more vocal. The Trotskyites disdained the Stalinists and claimed they were purer disciples of the Marxist-Leninist ideal that the Soviet Union under Stalin had perverted since Lenin's death in 1924. These differences were too subtle for outsiders to decipher, but the two factions managed to harangue each other—and their fellow workers—into states of fury and frustration. The same factions battled in New York, where in the fall of 1935 this war of ideological epithets and dueling pamphlets virtually paralyzed the project. The poet Harry Roskolenko, a Trotskyite, called the New York project "more of a Leftist five-ring circus than a fertile field for thought about research and writing." In Chicago, on the other hand, although the Illinois project had its share of leftists, most of them needed their jobs too badly to disrupt the flow of work. In Boston, the novelist and poet Conrad Aiken, who took a relief job on the Massachusetts project, quit after five months of coping with Marxist editors who objected that his work stressed American individualism rather than collective achievement.

WPA rules barred firing workers for their political affiliations. But they could be and were fired for not working, in which case those discharged were always quick to charge that it was their politics, not their idleness, that was to blame. All supervisors could do was to try to stay above the fray, though in some cases they joined in willingly. The left-wing poet and newspaperman Orrick Johns got his job as the second director of the New York project by convincing administrators that it took a radical to oversee radicals, but even he couldn't bring about a productive peace between the factions.

Politics was only one of the problems. Alcohol was another favorite indulgence of professional writers. Eleanor Roosevelt, lobbying for a project job for a family friend with a drinking problem, suggested to Alsberg in a phone call that he not be given too much responsibility since he liked to "go off on a spree every now and then." Alsberg told the first lady that if the project rejected "writers given to drink, we would probably not have a Writers' Project."

By the time he had them all in place, Alsberg's state directors were a decidedly mixed group. More than half were journalists or novelists, then—in order—came academics teaching college history and English, amateur poets and writers, and people who had worked in education, medicine, and publishing. Fourteen were women. The administrative structure made their jobs no easier. Like all of the Federal One state directors, the state chiefs of the Writers' Project answered to Washington and were supposed to be able to hire and set priorities free of local interference. But some state WPA administrators, who controlled every other aspect of the WPA's work in their states, resented this parallel structure. And because they had the power to influence job quotas or to demand extra workers for other non-arts projects, they could strip the arts projects of employees or force them to take bad ones. And inevitably, politicians interfered; in Missouri the Kansas City political machine of Tom Pendergast—Harry Truman's early patron—insisted on placing in the director's post a society woman who so enraged the other workers that Alsberg had to shut the project down for several months. And in Nebraska, Senator George Norris dictated the hiring of a wildly incompetent director whose paranoid accusations were so disruptive that Alsberg finally had to move her, complete with secretary and salary, out of the Omaha office into her own home so that the project could proceed.

The competent state directors faced the same question Alsberg did: who was a writer and who wasn't? Most of the 6,500 people hired by the project did not write professionally. Many were college students or graduates, meaning they had at least basic research and composition skills, but others were people who at best could be said to have the ability to read and write and who were shunted into the project because there was no other place for them. Moreover, those who *could* write—and the project boasted some excellent writers, from Aiken in Massachusetts to John Cheever and Ralph Ellison in New York, poet Kenneth Rexroth in California, and Nelson Algren, Saul Bellow, Richard Wright, and Frank Yerby in Chicago—didn't always think that guidebooks were worthy of their time, and agitated to work on their own writing.

Alsberg had originally set a deadline of May 1, 1936, for state directors to have their guide copy cleared by Washington. The date came and went. Though the guides were not the project's only task—writers were also assembling local histories and folktale compilations, and some were even working on fiction—they were far and away its most visible product, and not a single guide was even close to publication.

From the outside, the Writers' Project appeared to be dawdling. The Federal Theatre Project was producing plays in cities, taking road shows into remote areas, and winning raves from some of the same papers whose editorial pages dripped with scorn for the New Deal; the Music Project was jazzing up listeners with dance bands and enlightening them with symphony and chamber concerts; and the Art Project's glowing murals were attracting attention in schools, hospitals, and other public places. Of the four arts under Federal One, these three did have much shorter production cycles. But even allowing for the glacial pace of book publishing, to which the tasks of research, writing, copyediting, and printing all contributed, the fact was that in many offices no real work was being done. Even when it was, the anti–New Deal press cared little for the nuances. That the Writers' Project had nothing to show for its first months, for whatever reasons, was enough to prompt attacks.

10. AT WORK FOR THE WRITERS' PROJECT (RESEARCHER THOMAS C. FLEMING)

Thomas C. Fleming was proud, like so many others. When his money ran out around the beginning of 1936 and he first confronted the need to apply for relief and get a WPA job, he disdained the idea as just another form of welfare. Then he didn't have a choice.

Fleming was a college student in Berkeley, California, at the time. He was stocky, bright, talkative, and black. The depression had crept up on him gradually, as it did many. He was working on the Southern Pacific Railroad as a third cook, making $72 a month, when the market crashed in 1929. He was twenty-two at the time, and his personal odyssey already had carried him from Jacksonville, Florida, where he was born, to New York City as a stowaway on a White Lines steamship, back to Jacksonville, and then west by train to Chico, California, where his mother lived after she and his father were divorced. He graduated from high school in Chico in 1926, went to San Francisco, and worked as a steward on the train ferries across San Francisco Bay. Then he got hired by the railroad.

The effects of the crash took some time to ripple down to the Southern Pacific and its business travelers, so at first life went on as if nothing had happened. In January 1930, Fleming signed up for a trip to Chicago, where on his layover, on a snowy night, he saw Duke Ellington perform. But after that, trips got harder to come by. The younger men kept getting bumped by those with more seniority. "That's the way it was," he said in an interview years later. He shifted from the Chicago run to the Cascade, which ran between San Francisco and Portland, but by 1931, there were no runs left for a man with only four years on the job. Fleming left the railroad.

People he knew told him to go back to school. The two-year college in Chico had converted to a four-year school in the California university system since he'd been away. His grandmother still lived there, so he knew he'd have a place to sleep. He enrolled, earned money doing odd jobs, and lasted three semesters before the city lights drew him back to San Francisco, where he attended San Francisco State. Then he moved across the bay and entered the University of California at Berkeley.

But with each move, Fleming found it harder and harder to find the part-time jobs he needed to pay tuition and his bills. In the fall of 1935, he was living with other black male students in a rooming house at the corner of Harper and Russell Streets in Berkeley, halfway between the bay and the hills that rose behind the campus. Mama Williams, the landlady, was famously tolerant about late rent payments, but she, too, had bills to pay.

The men in the house followed politics. They talked a lot about the Problem, by which they meant the problem of race in the United States, and how blacks were the group hardest hit by the depression. They talked about the riots that had torn apart Harlem in New York that spring: two days of looting, triggered by a minor incident at a white-owned department store, that focused national attention on job discrimination, wretched housing, intolerable disease and infant death rates, and mistreatment and neglect by New York's almost all-white police force. They liked Eleanor Roosevelt for her progressive racial views and for inviting blacks regularly to the White House. They listened to the president's fireside chats. Fleming recalled that he sounded "so cozy, like he was in your own home"; he felt he was being talked to by a friend. After Roosevelt announced the works program, he and his housemates debated it. Fleming argued that it was make-work, no different from welfare. His friend George Townes, an economics major, disagreed; it was real work, and there was no shame in working for the government. When Fleming reached the point where he had to drop out of school, was eating surplus beans and bread and butter from the relief food banks, and literally did not have two dimes to rub together, he decided Townes was right.

On a winter morning, he caught a Key System trolley car to Oakland. The ride cost 7 cents. He got off in downtown Oakland and went to the main WPA office for Alameda County. There, he found a room full of men—black, white, and a smattering of Asians—milling about in line in a large room with scattered desks. He was shocked to realize that his sweater and corduroy trousers set him apart as better dressed than most. Some were in coveralls and scuffed work boots; others wore threadbare business suits under their sagging overcoats. Fleming joined a line that was inching toward an interviewer's desk.

When it was his turn, Fleming told the interviewer he had been a railroad cook. There were no jobs for cooks, the man said, but he could put Fleming to work the next day if he'd do labor. Fleming said he'd do anything to put some money in his pocket.

He returned to Oakland again the next morning, using money he had borrowed against his first paycheck, and got off where the streets sloped down from the business district toward Lake Merritt. A block or so above the lake, men and machines were erecting steel framing for a building. Signs said it was a new Alameda County courthouse funded by grants from the Public Works Administration. Nearby, more men swarmed around an open trench. Somebody handed him a shovel. The WPA was installing new sewer lines in downtown Oakland. Fleming's job, like that of scores of other men who were collecting shovels and climbing down into the trench, was to dig the routes the mains would follow.

Fleming dug for two days, deep in a wide trench braced with heavy timbers to keep the sides from caving in. On the third day, talking to the job foreman during a lunch break that Fleming passed without eating—he was under the impression that he wouldn't get his $15 a week laborer's pay until he had worked a month—Fleming mentioned that he'd had two years of college. The foreman told Fleming he didn't need to be there in that case; he should go back and get himself a white-collar job.

Fleming stacked his shovel and returned to the WPA office. An interviewer found his file, asked him some questions about his college work, and reclassified him to work in the WPA's professional division. His wage jumped to the $23.86 a week accorded "senior research workers," and his new duties could not have been more different. He was told to report to the Bancroft Library on the Berkeley campus, within walking distance of his rooming house. There, a supervisor handed him an assignment to research an episode of California history. He was to boil down what he'd learned into a few paragraphs and hand it in at the end of the day. Fleming found the books he needed, sat down, and started taking notes.

He had not been working long when he saw the flare-ups that frustrated some administrators in the Writers' Project. "There was one guy with a Ph.D. in chemistry from Michigan. I don't know what the hell he was doing there," Fleming said. "Another had graduated from Yale. There was one guy who had worked on a daily paper. Some of the guys had worked on the *People's World* [the San Francisco Communist paper], which I read. You could see the attitude. The first thing they did was form a union. The first thing the union did was demand a wage increase. They raised more hell over that than anything else. They were always arguing with somebody about something."

Nonetheless, Fleming admitted that his work was the closest thing to heaven that a broke young college dropout was likely to find during the depression, especially when the alternative was digging a sewer ditch in Oakland. Each morning, he rose at Mama Williams's house in Berkeley, ate a bowl of cereal in the common kitchen, and walked to campus. At that time, the Bancroft was a library within a library, the larger Doe Library, where Fleming signed in and picked up his day's assignment. Then he went to the fourth floor, which housed the rich holdings of California history donated by Hubert Howe Bancroft. In the stacks under the eaves, Fleming was learning the details of California's past. At the end of each day, he turned in his handwritten paragraphs at the desk he had checked in at in the morning. Even years later, Fleming said he did not know what had been done with the material he handed in, but it seems clear that his paragraphs, and thousands like them, were being fed into the editorial process that would create the California guide.

11. ONE NATION, ONE PLAY

That summer, Hallie Flanagan steered the Federal Theatre Project on its most ambitious project, one about which she was later to grumble, "Who thought up this idea, anyway?" The idea was that in eighteen cities nationwide, the Theatre Project would launch simultaneous productions of a play based on Sinclair Lewis's best-selling novel *It Can't Happen Here*. The October 1936 openings would be a kind of anniversary celebration for the project. The book, published in 1935 and mirroring ongoing events in Germany and Italy, told the story of Senator Buzz Windrip, who establishes a fascist dictatorship in the United States after he is elected president, and uses a brutal private army called the Minute Men to erase liberties and crush dissent. MGM had paid $200,000 for the film rights, then shelved the project as too controversial. Lewis, who had won the Nobel Prize for literature in 1930 for works such as *Main Street, Babbitt,* and *Elmer Gantry,* gave the theatrical rights to the Federal Theatre Project because he admired its work and expected it to treat the material evenhandedly.

He adapted the novel himself with the help of a Paramount Pictures writer, John C. Moffitt, but their collaboration was difficult. The two writers, working first in Vermont and then in separate suites at the

Essex House in New York City overlooking Central Park, kept producing differing versions of characters and scenes while Flanagan shuttled from one to the other trying to persuade them to agreement. Cascades of changes rained down on the directors and actors, who tried to fight off panic as opening night—set for October 27—neared. Telegrams poured into Flanagan's office from the various production units around the country. A message from the project in Los Angeles spoke for them all: "MAKING SUPERHUMAN EFFORTS TO MEET OCTOBER 27 LEWIS PLAY STOP IMPERATIVE HAVE NO MORE REVISION STOP STOP."

Convinced that there had to be an ulterior motive in the plan for simultaneous productions but not sure what it was, the press swirled around the project, speculating as to whether it was meant to be pro-fascist, anti-fascist, or some propaganda-based variation in between. The Louisiana project canceled the opening scheduled for New Orleans, where the memories of Huey Long's near-dictatorship burned bright, and Flanagan called off the St. Louis production rather than tone down the script as requested. Since the opening was just a week before the presidential election in November, the multiple presentations also were suspected of trying to exert some kind of pressure at the ballot box, presumably in Roosevelt's direction, though again, just how the play was to accomplish this, nobody knew.

Rewriting went on virtually to the rise of the opening curtain. Somehow, Flanagan managed to keep the scheduled date intact despite Lewis's fits of pique that held up the writing, problems with the set construction, and the requirements not only of typing, copying, and mailing each new version of the script but also of translating it into a Yiddish version to be shown in New York and a Spanish one in Tampa. On the night of October 27, the show went on as planned in Birmingham, Alabama; Boston; Bridgeport, Connecticut; Chicago; Cleveland; Detroit; Indianapolis; Los Angeles; Miami; Newark; New York City; Omaha; San Francisco; Tacoma, Washington; Tampa; and Yonkers. The Los Angeles project mounted two productions, New York four. New York's main production took place at the Adelphi Theatre on 54th Street, and included in its cast a child actor named Sidney Lumet. After the curtain fell, the audience clapped for a dozen curtain calls, until Lewis finally took the stage to calls of "Author! Author!" When the calls changed to "Speech! Speech!" the tall, slumped Lewis took out his watch and answered, referring to the play, "I've been making a speech since eight-forty-five."

The concept of the play, if not its quality, won the Theatre Project another round of critical applause. Audiences and most reviewers responded to the central theme that fascism need not be imposed through an outside military takeover; it could arrive when well-meaning citizens fail to defend essential freedoms. To Flanagan, it meant that the "first government-sponsored theatre in the United States was doing what it could to keep alive 'the free, inquiring, critical spirit' which is at the center and core of a democracy."

It Can't Happen Here continued in its original venues, added new ones, and would go on to play for a total of five years' worth of theater nights and reach an audience of half a million. And as the play was beginning this long run, Americans went to the polls on November 3 and voted for a second term for their president, once more asserting their preference for democracy.

12. AT WORK OFFSTAGE (ANTHONY BUTTITTA AND MILTON MELTZER)

A young writer stood at the back of the sold-out Adelphi on opening night and took in the excitement surrounding *It Can't Happen Here*. Six months earlier, he had come to New York on a gamble to join the fun, to be a part of "Uncle Sam's pioneering adventure in a nationwide theatre." He was barely five feet tall, with a shock of black hair, a prominent nose, and large black-rimmed glasses that made him look like a cartoonist's caricature of an anarchist. He was twenty-eight years old. His name was Anthony Buttitta.

Buttitta had been born in Chicago. His father was a grocer, but every time he tried to turn his offspring into one—in stores in New York; Monroe, Louisiana; and back in New York—the youth ran away to find the local version of bohemia. He studied government and history at the University of Texas. At some point he lived in Tunisia and Morocco. At the University of North Carolina, where he was studying creative literature around 1931, he and some friends started a literary magazine they called *Contempo*. They conceived it as a forum for new ideas and "an asylum for aggrieved authors." The business plan was simple: pay nothing for articles, and sell enough ads for each issue to cover the $24 printing cost. Soon the greatest authors and poets of the day—Sherwood Anderson, William Faulkner,

Langston Hughes, James Joyce, George Bernard Shaw—began receiving letters signed by Buttitta saying, in effect, "Send us something that nobody else wants. We can't pay you anything, but we'll print it."

Surprisingly, the famous authors responded. *Contempo* began a controversial three-year run. The Langston Hughes issue almost got them ejected from the university. In it, the black poet and essayist took aim at southern justice in the notorious case of the Scottsboro Boys, nine black men accused of raping two white prostitutes riding in a railroad coal car in 1931, and imagined how the second coming of Jesus would be received if he appeared as a black man in the South. The magazine and an experimental play Buttitta had written as a student, produced by the Carolina Playmakers, had brought him to Hallie Flanagan's attention. She had wired him the previous October to ask if he'd help edit a Federal Theatre magazine.

At the time Buttitta was living in Asheville, in the North Carolina mountains, where he had been surviving the depression reasonably well. He owned a small bookstore that F. Scott Fitzgerald, who was in Asheville recovering from tuberculosis and depression, frequented when he wasn't drinking. Buttitta also was writing press releases for the WPA-sponsored North Carolina Symphony Orchestra, whose director persuaded him to stay on. But he kept up with the Federal Theatre Project from afar, and in February 1936, when the orchestra cut all non-musicians from its payroll, he sent Flanagan a telegram to say he had reconsidered. She wired back to say she still wanted him but would have to get approval since WPA rules prevented projects in one state from hiring workers from another. Buttitta was too eager to wait. He closed a deal to sell his bookstore, then boarded a train to New York.

As soon as he arrived he headed to Flanagan's office, passing (as he was to write years later) "empty stores and dark theatres, their fronts plastered with 'For Rent' signs, posters of new films, and faded three-sheets peeling off the houseboards...gaudy movie houses, smelling of unwashed bums who used them for sleeping...souvenir and novelty shops, nickel hotdog, hamburger, and juice joints, catering to sharpies, people looking for jobs, professional beggars rattling tin cups, and visitors from the hinterlands looking for the fabled street of song and dance."

Flanagan was out of town. Someone told him he needed to fill out a job application, and directed him to the Siegel-Cooper Building. After rattling downtown on the Sixth Avenue el and joining the crowds in the cavernous space under the suspended bulbs that he thought looked "like fuzzy giant spiders," he learned that a WPA job meant declaring poverty and applying for relief. And a clerk confirmed Flanagan's warning: he needed two years of residency to be eligible in New York. He wondered if his long train ride into the dismal New York winter had been a big mistake.

But his spirits lifted the next day, when Flanagan returned from Washington. She squeezed him in between competing grievance committees, explaining that the group waiting in her outer office was threatening to picket the Lafayette if Houseman allowed black stagehands to work there. Grievances came in all varieties. The stage unions seethed with old-fashioned racism on one hand and radicalism on the other. A Jewish vaudeville unit wanted independence from the Yiddish theater. Veterans protested the presence of Communists in some project units, while the Communists complained that reactionaries were feeding play scripts to the Hearst press in order to draw negative coverage. A committee of older actors, clad in darned tweeds and patchy furs and keeping haughtily apart from the others, petitioned to have their names kept out of the programs so as not to have it known they were on relief.

When she had finished tallying the day's assortment of complaints for Buttitta, Flanagan said she had just had an editor thrust upon her by John Nance Garner, the vice president. Pierre de Rohan was his name, and if Buttitta could work with him she'd put him on the payroll as a non-relief supervisor to get around the residency requirement. The Rockefeller Foundation had just donated a press, so the Federal Theatre magazine could now at least be printed; its first three issues, starting in November 1935, had been run off on a mimeograph machine. Buttitta told her he wanted the job, and Flanagan sent him off to meet de Rohan, who worked out of an office two blocks away on 42nd Street.

De Rohan walked in after Buttitta arrived. He was resplendent in a velvet-collared coat, spats, and a homburg, and carried a Malacca cane. Buttitta had already talked with Mark Marvin, one of the other writers on the magazine, and been told that de Rohan had written for one of the Hearst papers but was "no editor." His main contribution to the magazine would be an amusing "Box Score" that did not shrink from criticizing project productions. He was preparing the first of these for April, the fifth edition of the magazine and the second to come off the new press, and would give the New York billings "three runs, four hits, and two errors." He initially told Buttitta he didn't need him on the magazine, then relented and sent the newcomer out to gather stories.

As Buttitta fanned out through the five boroughs to take notes on musicals and puppet plays, Shakespeare and Molière, Yiddish theater, children's plays, vaudeville, and the circus, another new arrival was making his appearance.

Milton Meltzer was older than Frank Goodman, but then so was everybody working under the precocious Goodman. Meltzer hailed from Worcester, Massachusetts, the son of eastern European immigrants. His father washed windows in factories, stores, and offices to make a living. Clean windows were among the first things a business could do without in hard times, and as the times got harder, more windows were boarded over than washed, and the depression hit the Meltzers. Nevertheless, Milton started college in 1932, entering an experimental teacher-training program at Columbia University in New York City with a scholarship paying part of his way. The program combined classroom study with a year of farm or factory work. To subsist, he worked part-time in an uncle's garment factory, found odd jobs, and took a loan to supplement his scholarship. He spent his year of factory work back in Worcester spray-painting women's shoes, and then returned to New York in 1934. He started his senior year at Columbia in the fall of 1935.

But that fall his father died of cancer, and the economic news he read in the papers convinced Meltzer that his prospects were bleak: one-third of last spring's college graduates had been unable to find work. He remained in school through the winter, but dropped out in March 1936, less than three months from graduation. Then, instead of returning home to Massachusetts, he rented a fifth-floor walkup in the shabby west twenties of Manhattan and applied for home relief, claiming he was an unemployed writer. He had a few clippings to his credit and was approved; thereafter, the city paid his $3 weekly rent and gave him $5.50 every two weeks for food. He lived on cheese sandwiches and coffee, and put the cardboard from discarded egg cartons inside his shoes to keep out the rain.

Meltzer's older brother Allan was working in the Federal Theatre's publicity department, press-agenting shows including the voodoo *Macbeth*. Observing that one of Frank Goodman's staff was spending more time trying to recruit his coworkers into the Communist Party than he was preparing materials for the youth press, he urged Goodman to hire his brother.

Bossing a Columbia dropout appealed to the high-school–educated Goodman. The workers Ted Mauntz had given him all had had some college, except for the deaf and speechless man who served as his chief clerk. (They communicated by writing notes back and forth, and Goodman considered the clerk "the best thing that ever happened.") They could write well enough but were snobbish and a little lazy, while they in turn thought Goodman was the B-movie press agent he resembled, a shameless hustler who didn't appreciate the cultural worth of what he was promoting and was overbearing to make up for his youth and lack of education. Still, no one could deny that he got the information out.

Goodman looked at Meltzer's clips and took him on, assigning him to prepare the special mailings that went out to English, speech, and drama teachers before project performers visited their schools. Meltzer came to agree with his colleagues about Goodman, but the standard white-collar pay of $23.86 a week was a vast improvement over home relief, so he kept his opinions to himself. He, like Tony Buttitta, would remain with the Federal Theatre Project until 1939, when a rising tide of anti-Communist hysteria produced by congressional hearings engulfed the project and threatened not only the remaining arts projects but the entire WPA.

13. THE AMERICAN GUIDES: IDAHO VERSUS WASHINGTON, D.C.

The American Guides were slowly beginning to take shape. Even the dueling radicals came to understand that they had to show some progress if the project was to continue and they were to keep their jobs. The field supervisors were in charge of whipping various state operations into shape, and the prodding by hard-nosed supervisors such as Katherine Kellock, who was determined to see the guides fulfill her original vision, began to produce results. The territory Kellock oversaw was the Southeast, from which she wrote fiery memos describing inaction and incompetence. One of her first actions was to jettison the American Guide manual as impractical. She told the state director in South Carolina to ignore the 1,500-word weekly writing requirement in favor of producing hard information. And the information, she emphasized as she moved from state to state, was to be lively and engaging. Her biggest challenge was to convince some state directors they weren't producing dry government manuals that would gather dust but books, *real* books, books meant to be used, to be read for pleasure as well as information, and to be talked about.

The Federal One headquarters were now located in mining heiress Evalyn Walsh McLean's former mansion in northwest Washington. Crystal chandeliers hung over the desks occupied by the Writers'

Project editors, who at last were starting to receive, in scuffed manila envelopes bearing postmarks from across the country, the troves of information they had anticipated at the outset. Alsberg and his staff saw just how rich the guides could be and felt vindicated. Tom Fleming at the Bancroft Library, writing his sketches of California history, was one small cog in what was now a functioning machine, and other writers and researchers—at Bancroft, across the bay in San Francisco, in Los Angeles, moving throughout the state—were adding more and more material. They were looking at California's past and its present; at its geology and conservation programs; its climate, flora, and fauna; its Indian tribes and archaeology; transportation; agriculture; industry, commerce, and finance; labor; education; public health and social welfare; sports and recreation; newspapers and radio; folklore; literature; music and theater; art; architecture; and, uniquely in the case of California, movies.

Other writers were compiling pictures of the state's major cities, with descriptions of their landmarks and points of interest. Still others drove between cities and small towns, watching the car's odometer as they made notes and measured driving distances for a series of tours that ranged the 780-mile length of California and touched the borders of Oregon and Mexico. Photographers were recording contemporary scenes; archivists searched files for historical photographs and prints; draftsmen drew the kinds of maps that would allow urban explorers to make the correct turn at the right corner.

Work like this was going on all around the country. Until the Federal Writers' Project, America had been defined largely from abroad by writers such as Frenchman Alexis de Tocqueville in *Democracy in America* and Englishman Findlay Muirhead in the Baedeker *United States*. But the depression had brought a new level of introspection. The nation seemed determined to take a new look at itself, and just as Federal One painters were seeking out America in bucolic farms and troubled cities, playwrights were exploring it through Living Newspapers, and composers were making new American music, the Writers' Project was finding and revealing new evidence of its multilayered richness. This was the project's unstated genius, not only in the guides but in other writings from slave narratives to folkloric studies. When all this was compiled and printed, Americans would be able to see America anew.

And now, deep into 1936, a race began. Alsberg and his staff determined that for political reasons, the Writers' Project guide to Washington, D.C., would be their debut volume. *Washington: City and Capital* would quiet the project's congressional critics and prove to the doubters that serious work had been proceeding after all. Then came word from Idaho, where western novelist Vardis Fisher was the state director, that his own manuscript was almost finished and a publisher, the Caxton Press of Caldwell, Idaho, lined up.

Fisher had worked against overwhelming odds to put the Idaho guide together. He had a tiny staff, no office space or furniture, and a state WPA administration who had tried to sabotage him by assigning him former mental patients and spies looking for dirt. As a result, he had done most of the work on the guide himself, including driving the state's roads for the tour section.

Anybody who had read Fisher's early works might have known he would be difficult to manage. The heroes of his books were rugged individuals, both men and women, who had carved lives out of the Idaho frontier. In fact, he was one of them—albeit one with a Ph.D. from the University of Chicago—and he had displayed his individualism throughout most of his work on the project. The guide formats were supposed to be uniform—for example, following north-to-south and east-to-west directions to describe the tours. But Fisher said most of the traffic in Idaho moved south to north, and wrote his tours up that way. There were other editorial squabbles as well, but Washington was sufficiently impressed with the quality of Fisher's writing to let them be. George W. Cronyn, who was Alsberg's associate director and oversaw the project's editing, even told him he was "raising Guide writing to the plane of permanent literature."

However, when Fisher announced that the Idaho guide was ready to go to press, Alsberg suddenly tried to delay its publication. He threw revisions at its author by the thousands, and Fisher reacted with the obstinacy of a dug-in homesteader. He enlisted Idaho senator James P. Pope, who told Alsberg the guide's publisher would back out if there was a delay. Next Alsberg tried persuasion. He called Fisher to impress on him the need to bring out the Washington guide first, then some other large-state guides; Idaho would come eventually. Fisher cursed into the telephone and refused to budge. Alsberg's final step was to send an editor to Idado with still more revisions and corrections and a demand to review the photos Fisher had selected. Fisher would later describe the confrontation in a thinly veiled scene in his autobiographical novel *Orphans in Gethsemane.* In it, the editor rejected all of Fisher's photo choices, even shots of Idaho potatoes, but was then plied with liquor by Fisher and his publisher until they got him drunk enough to haul him to the railroad station and pour him on a train back to Washington.

Fisher won in the end. *Idaho: A Guide in Word and Picture,* was published in January 1937. It contained 431 pages, of which Fisher himself had written 374, all of the photographs that Fisher had selected, and fifteen maps. It covered everything about Idaho: its Indians, plants, animals, hunting and fishing, natural resources, agriculture, businesses, and industries. It included chapters of ghost stories and folktales. And it served notice in Fisher's vivid opening paragraph that it intended to debunk western myths found in "these villains with the Wild Bill moustaches, these apple-cheeked heroines agog with virtue, and these broad adolescent heroes who say 'gosh ding it' and shoot with deadly accuracy from either hand." They were "remote in both temper and character from the persons who built the West," he wrote. "They are shoddy sawdust counterfeits." Fisher's eloquently vigorous style resonated from the first page to the last—and by virtue of WPA rules against naming individual authors, his name appeared nowhere in the book.

This very first WPA guide attracted a great deal of attention; Alsberg and his staff in Washington had to have been relieved, if not elated, at the notices. There were rave reviews in papers from the *New York Times* to the *Salt Lake Tribune,* and most of the reviewers praised it for bursting the limitations of its form. A very perceptive article in the weekly *Saturday Review* noted just how much it had achieved. If the rest of the guides equaled Idaho's, wrote editor Bernard De Voto, they would "heighten our national self-consciousness, preserve valuable antiquarian material that might have perished, and facilitate our knowledge of ourselves."

14. LAYOFFS AND PROTESTS

The arts projects, along with the rest of the WPA, now faced a dilemma. By most objective measures, the jobs program had been a success. Both the women's and professional projects division that included the arts and other white-collar programs, and the much larger construction division, had met the twin goals of providing jobs and adding significant improvements to the national landscape, physically, aesthetically, and socially. But for an agency like the WPA, created to cope with an emergency, the price of success was retrenchment.

By 1936, the massive spending that had characterized the New Deal since its launch in 1933 had eased the economic crisis but not erased it. Unemployment had fallen from its March 1933 high of 24.9 percent to below 17 percent as manufacturers cautiously took on new workers, and farm income had climbed back almost to its 1930 levels. But the cost of even this limited comeback was growing pressure to halt the deficit spending that had fueled it.

Roosevelt had made the first cuts in July, well ahead of the November election, when he slashed the WPA budget by 25 percent and Federal One by a third. In September, Hopkins rescinded the exemption he had given the arts projects at their outset that allowed them to employ 25 percent non-relief workers instead of the standard 10 percent in order to get the projects off the ground. Many of the laid-off workers were recalled in the weeks leading up to the election, but once the November landslide was in the books, the WPA was cut again. Almost 2,000 arts workers received pink slips in New York, and twice that many across the country.

The New York workers responded to the layoffs with a series of disruptive "stay-in" strikes. On December 1, more than 200 arts project workers took over the project's headquarters in the College Art Association Building on East 39th Street. They pushed desks and chairs against the doors of the eighth-floor offices to keep the police from entering, and cut the telephone wires. When seventy-five policemen arrived, crashed through the barricades, and ordered the strikers off the premises, the workers formed a ring around them and locked arms. At that, the police pulled their nightsticks, began to club the workers on the wrists and arms, and dragged them out into the elevator lobby. Some went quietly, but others fought. When the melee ended, seven men and five women, along with one policeman, had been injured, and 219 arts workers were in the Tombs, New York's holding jail, charged with disorderly conduct. One of them was poster artist Theodore Egri, who said the workers gave the police names such as Picasso and Cézanne and laughed away the night in their cells.

Writers' Project protesters were more successful at their own office takeover two doors away. They used a clothesline, telephone wires, neckties, and yarn from an unraveled sweater to haul boxes of sandwiches from the sidewalk all the way up to their redoubt on the seventh floor, defying the efforts of the police to starve them out.

The protests spread to a shutdown of the Theatre Project offices, and on December 7, a hundred men and women occupied the space in the old bank building that served as the New York headquarters. They vowed to stay for two days, and no police showed this time. More ominously, however, seventy-five agents of J. Edgar Hoover's FBI moved onto the premises and watched them. No one would say who had called the FBI, and the agents would say only that they were there to protect government property. Still, despite the layoffs and the government surveillance, the project's plays went on, and so did the seasonal concerts of the music project.

Mayor La Guardia sped off to Washington to try to get the layoffs reduced or rescinded altogether. Somervell headed to Washington at the same time, less to lobby for the arts workers than to assess cuts in his entire New York City program. Confirming Audrey McMahon's view that he was no friend of the arts, he sent an abrupt memorandum to employees participating in the sit-ins on December 4: leave or be fired. Strikers marching in picket lines responded caustically; their signs read, "Merry Christmas—Wish You Well; Here's Your Pink Slip—Somervell."

Even the usually equable musicians protested the job cuts. On Christmas Eve several hundred New York schoolchildren came to City Hall for a round of caroling next to the lighted outdoor tree. They had been trained by WPA music teachers and were accompanied by a WPA band, but as they sang, demonstrators from the music project drowned them out with shouts of "We want jobs!"

Hopkins, in Washington, eventually eased the New York layoffs, relying on his usual tactic of dipping into unused PWA funds and persuading Roosevelt to go along. As Somervell observed on January 15, his roster of arts workers before the cuts was 10,560, and "after all the trouble, the strikes, the walkouts, the picketing and name calling, we have 10,566."

Roosevelt was sworn in for his second term on January 20, 1937. It was another cold and rain-drenched inaugural day in Washington, so foul that Senator George Norris of Nebraska was forced to defend his authorship of the Twentieth Amendment to the Constitution, which had shifted the inauguration from March to January. Almost two inches of rain fell before the day was over, but Roosevelt refused to move the ceremony inside to the Capitol rotunda; if the crowds outside could take it, so could he. The ancient Roosevelt Bible was another story; someone wrapped it in protective cellophane before the president placed his hand upon it and took the oath of office.

The rain did not diminish the president's customary eloquence as he addressed the nation, and his words gave heart to those for whom the government represented the only prospect of a job; despite the WPA layoffs, he made clear his intention to keep fighting on behalf of workers. He spoke of the distance traveled "from the days of stagnation and despair," and of the journey still ahead. Here, he said, "is the challenge to our democracy: In this nation I see tens of millions of its citizens...who at this very moment are denied the greater part of what the very lowest standards of today call the necessities of life. I see millions of families trying to live on incomes so meager that the pall of family disaster hangs over them day by day. I see millions whose daily lives in city and on farm continue under conditions labeled indecent by a so-called polite society half a century ago. I see millions denied education, recreation, and the opportunity to better their lot and the lot of their children. I see millions lacking the means to buy the products of farm and factory and by their poverty denying work and productiveness to many other millions. I see one-third of a nation ill-housed, ill-clad, ill-nourished."

"One-third of a nation" quickly joined the short list of Roosevelt's iconic phrases. But in his second term, he would not enjoy the consensus on fighting the depression that had come so easily to him in the first. The economic weakness would continue, the result in part of his own policies as his advisors, led by Treasury Secretary Morgenthau, argued for spending cuts and deficit reduction; while at the same time the conservative opposition would regain its voice and frustrate continued efforts at reform. These developments were to reverberate throughout the WPA and ultimately the entire country.

First, however, an urgent new task loomed for the WPA. The storm clouds that blanketed Washington on inauguration day stretched back across the midsection of the country. They had been hovering there for weeks, and they were bringing the WPA a new chance to demonstrate its prowess. The agency had many services on offer to the nation—roadwork, building, sewing, professional services, the arts. All of these brought organizational talent and administrative will to bear in directing a mass of available workers. But now the stakes were raised. A major natural disaster loomed, and the WPA would slash red tape and hurdle bureaucratic roadblocks in its all-out fight to save lives and property.

PART VI

The WPA is proud that from the ranks of those who can't find jobs it can provide "the shock troops of disaster."

—FROM THE WPA NEWSREEL

MAN AGAINST THE RIVER

When people talked about, you know, leaning on the shovel, well, we did a lot of work. And a whole lot of hard work. It wasn't no different than no other job. You earned the money.

—JOHNNY MILLS, WPA LABORER

1. FLOOD ON THE OHIO

Much of the country was locked in the grip of wretched weather. The rain-soaked inaugural in Washington was an abbreviated version of the misery residents of the Ohio River Valley had been experiencing since December. The precipitation came down first as snow, then rain that melted the snow and softened the ground underfoot to mud. It was the kind of rain Ohioans as well as the residents of Kentucky, Indiana, and southern Illinois were used to in the winter, cold and unrelenting, and they went about their business in heavy shoes and clammy coats and attitudes of resignation. Then, on January 13, skies that had been merely gray darkened to the color of slate, and the deluge—now alternating rain, sleet, and snow— took on an almost biblical intensity. Indeed, the previous fall, a preacher in Jeffersonville, Indiana, had told his flock he had seen an angel with a measuring rod who showed him twenty-two feet of water covering the town's main street. People had laughed at the Reverend Billy Branham at the time.

Rain drummed down for fourteen hours straight across the middle of the river valley, reaching a total of three inches. The Scioto and Great Miami rivers, the Kentucky and the Licking, the Wabash, and dozens of smaller tributaries spilled their swollen burdens into the

Ohio itself. Along the river from the Ohio–West Virginia border to Cairo, Illinois, where it joined the Mississippi, worried residents watched the coffee-colored, ice-skimmed waters creep higher and higher up the muddy banks. In Cincinnati, the Ohio rose two feet in the space of five hours.

By the third week of January, meteorologists and flood experts predicted that a combination of slowing rain and colder temperatures would stem the rising waters. Their forecasts were wrong. The Ohio and its tributaries kept rising. The waters lapped above the levels reached in the previous spring's floods and took aim at levels reached in 1913 and 1884. The flood of 1884 on the Ohio had been the worst in history.

With only months since the last floods and their large toll of dead and homeless, officials did not need to be reminded of the river's power. Disaster planners started to marshal their forces from among the Army Corps of Engineers, Coast Guard, National Guard, Red Cross, and WPA, whose Information Division had begun calling mustered workers the "shock troops of disaster." WPA administrators in the river states halted construction projects and began to move workers to the river.

John K. Jennings, who had ten southern Indiana counties in his charge, was among the first to act, and other Indiana WPA chiefs followed suit. Residents fleeing north away from the rising waters passed convoys of National Guard trucks lumbering south carrying men from Indianapolis and Terre Haute, Kokomo and Marion. Three hundred WPA men arrived in Lawrenceburg, near the Ohio state border; a thousand reached Jeffersonville, where Reverend Branham had been shown the specter of the waters; thousands more were dispatched to other flood-torn areas along the river. In Evansville, WPA men worked alongside soldiers and guardsmen in wind, rain, snow, and sleet. The surrounding Vanderburgh County had some 4,000 WPA workers, who evacuated residents, filled sandbags, and stacked them on levees threatened by the rising tide. They worked exhausting twelve-hour shifts in freezing water as much as three feet deep, then rotated off to hastily assembled shelters in schools, churches, and community halls, where they huddled around stoves, ate, slept, and dried their clothes as best they could, and went out again.

It was the same in Ohio, Kentucky, and Illinois: agency administrators consulted with mayors and county heads and threw WPA workers into the fight alongside volunteers and local police and firemen. In Illinois, as in Indiana, the army and National Guard provided trucks to carry thousands of WPA and CCC men into the storm to toil "through the freezing weather, around the clock, in mud and rain, in a battle against the rising waters."

Farther downstream along the Mississippi River, memories of the disastrous spring flood of 1927 remained fresh. The Mississippi had breached levees in more than a hundred places, flooding 26,000 square miles and stretching at some points eighty miles across, and left 700,000 homeless and several hundred dead. Since then, a series of levees and spill basins had been built to allow the Corps of Engineers to try to manage the flow of the great river, but as the water surged in from the Ohio, even these were threatened now. "A super flood is on the way," said Lieutenant Colonel Eugene Reybold, the district chief of army engineers at Memphis. Thirteen hundred WPA workers were abruptly pulled from other projects and sent to reinforce the levees along the St. Francis River in southeastern Missouri, where the river lapped within eighteen inches of the top.

On January 18, the Ohio rose over the flood walls protecting Cincinnati. Across from Cincinnati, the northern Kentucky towns of Newport and Covington were inundated a day later. At Louisville, where the huge riverfront hydroelectric plant that supplied the city with electricity was already surrounded by water and rowboats were ferrying workers to their shifts, the river reached flood stage on January 21 and rose an additional 6.3 feet the next day. Cincinnati saw a 6.7-foot rise over twenty-four hours. Downriver at Paducah, the waters had already reached the 39-foot flood stage and flowed over the earthen levee into the streets, flooding homes and stores and boiling up out of the sewers. By January 24, the entire Ohio River was above flood stage, and still the rain, sleet, and snow came down.

On January 25, Howard O. Hunter, the administrator in charge of WPA's Region IV, which included the flood zone, wired Illinois governor Henry Horner and Kentucky governor A. B. "Happy" Chandler, Cincinnati city manager C. A. Dykstra, and Louisville mayor Neville Miller from his headquarters in Chicago to say he was sending WPA engineers and field agents to assist them. "All resources of WPA available to flood-stricken areas," he wrote.

A day later, Hunter wired Harry Hopkins in Washington to say he had ordered administrators outside the flood zone to direct surplus commodities and clothing from WPA sewing rooms to the flood area. These would be shipped in rented trucks to avoid "all present red tape on shipping by rail" and ensure fast delivery. The same day, Ellen Woodward wired her Midwest regional administrator, Florence Kerr, in Chicago to update her on other commodities that were on their way by rail to distribution points close to the flood zone. They included eggs by the carload—12,000 dozen per car—canned beef, evaporated milk, Florida grapefruit, cotton and mattress ticking, overshoes, blankets, heavy underwear, shirts, and galoshes. The Coast Guard shipped boats overland to evacuate flood victims. When there still were not enough boats, crews of WPA carpenters assembled lumber in the streets and hastily built fleets of skiffs.

The river crested in Cincinnati on January 26 at 79.9 feet, in Louisville on the twenty-seventh at 57.1 feet, in Paducah on February 2 at 60.6 feet. From one end of the flood zone to the other, the records of 1884 were broken by eight to eleven feet. A sixth of Cincinnati was underwater, 70 percent of Louisville, all of Paducah. Families in cities across southern Indiana awoke in the middle of the night to the sounds of factory whistles and fire sirens, the signal for invading waters, and soon found themselves on trains steaming north, huddled together with other refugees. Evansville was said to be "near panic." In Jeffersonville, the water on Spring Street measured a depth of twenty-two feet, fulfilling Reverend Branham's vision; inside his Tabernacle, the wooden pews and pulpit floated to the ceiling. Fires raged in a varnish plant and a shoe factory in a riverfront industrial area of Louisville; firemen were kept away by ten feet of water in the streets. The Federal Theatre in Cincinnati sent word to Washington that *It Can't Happen Here*, scheduled for a one-week run starting January 28, would have to be postponed. Parts of southern Illinois were like an inland sea, a fifty-mile swath of water broken only by the highest hills. Shawneetown, the pioneer gateway from the river into Illinois, stood isolated and abandoned; a WPA emergency crew and volunteers were the last human beings to leave, boarding a Coast Guard cutter after they had helped the town's civilian residents onto a river steamer that was their last route to safety.

Cairo, Illinois, notched precariously in the narrow V formed by the

Mississippi flowing down from the northwest and the Ohio from the northeast, was threatened from both sides as the Ohio backed the flood up the larger river. On January 25, army engineers blasted a levee downstream at New Madrid, Missouri, to spill some of the surging Mississippi into a 131,000-acre flood-control spillway basin and take pressure off the town. Breaching the levee stabilized the water levels for a time; then they began to creep up again. The Coast Guard sent twenty-two of its fast river boats to evacuate women and children, and cars and trucks carried more evacuees over the single road link that remained open to the north. Although Illinois was a northern state that had fought with the Union in the Civil War, black refugees were divided from whites and sheltered in separate facilities, one of them a black school in Carbondale, fifteen miles north of Cairo, that had been named for the Revolutionary War hero Crispus Attucks. The evacuation reduced the town's population by two-thirds, leaving 6,000 people in danger from the rising waters.

A sixty-foot-high floodwall, running for two and a half miles along Cairo's eastern riverfront, protected the city on the Ohio side. A similar but longer wall ran along the Mississippi riverfront. On January 25, an army of WPA and CCC workers directed by army engineers began building a three-to-five-foot parapet of earth and wood along the top of the Ohio floodwall. Two thousand men worked merciless long shifts in the cold and rain. Many of them had no proper shoes, and George Augustus Pomeroy, a Cairo riverman who had not been able to afford shoes for his own children until he caught a prize catfish in the Mississippi, took money from his meager savings to buy boots for some of them. Some men were forced to sleep on bags of sugar on a warehouse floor until WPA officials convinced Mayor August Bode to call on the army for cots. Still others slept in the pews of St. Patrick's Catholic Church. When they finished the parapet on January 29, the hungry waters were only eight inches from the top of the original Ohio floodwall, and a crest of sixty-two feet was predicted for February 1. Some of the workers were sent north to stand by for cleanup duty, but others stayed behind in case the waters spilled into the town streets twenty feet below, where they would be trapped like bathwater in a stoppered tub, covering streetlamps and submerging buildings up to the second floor. Just as great a problem was water intruding from below, forced under the levees by great pressure and emerging as "sand boils" in the lower floodwall that were like open faucets. On January 31, the army set up a roadblock on the one road out of town and started to turn able-bodied male evacuees back into Cairo to help the relief workers in case the emergency barrier gave way.

Forty-two miles downstream at New Madrid, the raging Mississippi now threatened to overflow the spillway where its waters had been diverted to save Cairo and inundate surrounding farms and towns. Missouri's WPA mustered hundreds of new workers to the scene. The men gathered under dark skies and awaited orders. Temperatures were in the thirties. Given a signal, they boarded steel barges that ferried them from New Madrid to the spillway's western wall, where they disembarked and started filling and stacking sandbags along the crest of the levee above the rising water. They worked all day on January 31 in unremitting rain and sleet. At day's end, the barges returned to ferry the men back across the brown waters of the spillway to New Madrid, where food and rest awaited. The WPA men were tired, hungry, and cold. A hundred or more of them surged aboard one craft, their weight pushing it lower in the water. When there was no more room inside the barge's dank steel shell, its pilot steered away from the levee and headed out across the spillway in the dark.

The barge had gone only about 150 yards when one of the workers, Leonard Workman, felt it hit a snag. Its nose jerked down and water spilled in over the sides, sinking it within seconds and plunging the exhausted men into the frigid spillway. Another of the WPA men, nineteen-year-old John Selvidge, was still on the levee when he heard the sounds of men struggling and splashing. "I don't think—I know—lots of them were drowned," he said.

Most of the workers managed to reach the safety of the levee, but thirty did not. Searchers using chains and grappling hooks pulled five bodies from the spillway the next day, and ultimately nineteen more. Six men were never found. The government paid compensation of $3,500 to each family. The New Madrid drownings were the deadliest incident in the WPA's history.

As the waters rose at Cairo and recovery workers dragged the New Madrid spillway with chains and hooks for the missing men, Harry Hopkins left Washington to tour the flood region. He went in two capacities, as head of both the WPA and a special flood relief commission named by Roosevelt to assess the damage and recommend what was needed in the aftermath to put the region back together. With him were Major General Edward M. Markham, chief of the army engineers, Surgeon General Thomas Parran Jr., and James L. Feiser, in charge of operations for the Red Cross. Typhoid from contaminated water was among the public health concerns, and with thousands of refugees scattered in more than 100 Red Cross emergency hospitals and 360 temporary camps, some consisting of tents and boxcars and other unheated shelters, influenza and pneumonia were already widespread. The figures eventually rose to 270 field hospitals and 838 camps.

"Fortunately, the WPA is equipped to fight this battle," Hopkins said. "It is the job of the WPA to do all it can to prevent the outbreak of such epidemics as would normally follow in the wake of great disasters." He said that 30,000 workers had been assigned to cleanup and sanitation jobs in West Virginia, Ohio, and Kentucky, where the waters had started to recede.

Hopkins and his party landed at Memphis. Crossing the Mississippi into Arkansas and driving to a camp housing 12,000 refugees, they encountered five miles of hub-deep water and were almost stranded. At the camp, WPA carpenters were hammering together flooring for hundreds of tents and moving in field stoves to provide heat. On February 3, the party boarded a military vessel for the trip upriver to Cairo, churning against waters carrying tree limbs and animal carcasses and other flotsam downstream. They reached the town to find the water only six inches below the top of the floodwall and still rising, if infinitesimally, toward the emergency bulwark erected by the WPA. But there it stabilized. Hopkins vowed to keep workers in the town as long as they were needed, and promised there would be "no red tape or bickering" when the cleanup started.

Next the party went by boat from Cairo to Paducah, which Feiser likened to the streets of Venice, "navigable for miles." Returning to Cairo, Feiser found he could see "none of the familiar river lines. There was nothing but bleakness. Even the cities and towns were without light, electric power, water or heat." But by then the rain and snow had eased and the waters had begun to slowly drop on the Ohio, although the flood crest moving down the Mississippi did not reach the Gulf of Mexico until the end of the month.

As Hopkins and the others moved on to Evansville, Louisville, and

Cincinnati, the falling waters began to reveal the extent of devastation. Almost 500 were dead in the Ohio Valley, including 40 WPA workers who died in the icy waters, most of them in the New Madrid spillway accident. As many as a million were homeless. The countryside was littered with the wreckage of houses and barns that had been swept from their foundations and reduced to kindling. There was no electricity or clean water. Sewer systems, overwhelmed with river water, were clogged and unable to function. Bloated bodies of cattle and horses and pigs rotted in the fields where they had come to rest, creating public health concerns. Thick, gumlike silt coated streets and fouled every home and business the river had invaded. The entire path of the Ohio River was a swath of debris and human misery, with the added threat of contagion lurking in the flood's festering aftermath.

As hard as they had worked in the preceding days, an equal task now began for the workers of the WPA. Hopkins said cleaning up the mess would be "one hell of a job," and promised to deploy 150,000 workers from West Virginia to Memphis. Jennings, the Indiana WPA administrator, said, "The nightmare and uncertainty...has now passed. The heavy task before us now is one of mere mechanics."

The New Harmony (Indiana) Times described the damage more directly: "A heavy deposit of silt has been deposited over the streets, sewers are disrupted, levees are broken, and the inhabitants must be returned to their homes." The work, wrote the paper, "makes Hercules' cleaning the Aegean stables a piker's job."

WPA crews along the Ohio Valley—at their peak numbering almost 200,000 as Hopkins authorized additional workers—performed a thousand tasks. They built sanitary privies over sewer manholes, nailed together wooden catwalks to carry foot traffic over the swamps of mud, and then carried relief supplies over those same catwalks. They cleared refuse from town streets and county roads and hauled away garbage. They set up field kitchens and cooked and served meals to flood refugees as well as to the military and Red Cross personnel with whom they worked. WPA nurses attended to the sick. WPA theater and music groups rolled into the stricken river towns to entertain refugees whose homes had been damaged or destroyed. In Cincinnati, both during the flood and after the waters receded, the Theatre Project played forty engagements to 14,660 flood victims, performing to the light of lanterns and candles in the face of what were often their own losses; two of the clowns entertaining homeless children had lost their own homes in the flood. WPA workers far from the flood zone contributed as well, as Woodward directed more of the output of sewing rooms into the region to clothe and warm the victims.

General Hugh Johnson, the NRA and New York City WPA administrator turned syndicated columnist, wrote of the flood and its aftermath, "Never in our history have one-tenth so many people been affected by a great disaster and certainly never before have affected people been so skillfilly relieved." He called Hopkins "a doer of good deeds, executor of orders, go-getter, Santa Claus incomparable, and privy-builder without peer."

Unusual for a business association, the Evansville, Indiana, Retail Bureau took ads in the *Courier* to praise the work of the WPA in "salvaging property and saving lives, and immediately afterward they handled the cleanup job with such efficiency that many visitors were amazed that there was practically no evidence of the flood left throughout the entire city. All honor and gratitude is due to the rank and file of the WPA for their often almost super-human efforts, always giving their best in the interest of humanity."

2. WPA FIGHTS THE
"FEROCIOUS FIRE DEMON"

By the time the waters were receding along the Ohio and Mississippi, the WPA had achieved near ubiquity across the country. Its rolls were down to 2.2 million in February, below the 1936 peak of 3-million-plus, but there was not a county in the United States that the agency had not touched in some way, and scarcely a possibility for work that had not been exploited.

WPA workers in Boston had made fish chowder for welfare recipients. New Hampshire's WPA had started a medicinal herb farm where digitalis, lemon balm, peppermint, chamomile, and hyssop were among dozens of plants raised for sale to pharmaceutical companies. In Denver, WPA workers restored fabrics and jewelry found after the death of the notorious "Baby Doe" Tabor, widow of the Leadville, Colorado, mine king Horace Tabor, for display in a museum, thereby burnishing the legend of their affair, silver's boom and bust, and the thirty-five years of impoverished widowhood she spent living in a shack outside Leadville's Matchless Mine, which had given up its riches long before. Another legend was Bobby Jones, retired from golf after winning thirteen majors as an amateur, who was brought in by Hopkins as a course consultant; no fewer than 600 municipal golf courses were being built or improved with WPA labor in 1937. The

WPA put stonemasons in Rochester, New York, back to work hand-cutting curbstones. In Skagit County, Washington, elders of the Swinomish Tribe were conceiving a plan under which the WPA would pay Indian wood carvers to depict the tribal history on a cedar totem pole. Gilford, New Hampshire, was ready to host an eastern ski jumping competition at a winter sports complex built by the WPA, and plans were under way in the upper Michigan town of Iron Mountain to build the world's highest ski jump using WPA labor.

In the Appalachian foothills of eastern Ohio, burning necessity drove a project employing teams of coal miners assembled by the WPA. They were fighting a fire that had been raging underground for more than fifty years, consuming a vast fortune in coal. The fire at New Straitsville had defied all previous attempts to put it out.

New Straitsville told the hard story of American coal as well as any place in the country. Prospectors had discovered a "Great Vein" of bituminous coal running through the Hocking River Valley during the Civil War, coal so valuable it was referred to as "black diamonds." In 1869 a speculator named John D. Martin rode through the valley with gold in his saddlebags, looking to buy land. He bought a few thousand acres south of the town of Straitsville, started mining operations, built a railroad spur to take the coal out, and New Straitsville took off. Other booms followed—iron ore in the late 1870s and oil after the turn of the century—but they were short-lived. It was always coal that was the town's pride, and its chagrin.

Mining New Straitsville's coal was child's play, relatively speaking. It was soft and lay just below the surface of the hills. Strong men swinging pickaxes was all it took to get it out, and there were a lot of those. Men from mining regions in the British Isles—Welshmen, Irishmen, Englishmen, and Scots—came to work the veins, married, had children, and stayed on. The plentiful coal brought others, Germans, Italians, Scandinavians, eastern Europeans, and African-Americans. They inhabited not only New Straitsville but also Shawnee and other hamlets that were contained in a section known as Coal Township.

The Coal Township mines, as mines did elsewhere, exploited the miners who worked them. Hourly wages were unheard of. Men were paid for each ton of coal they dug, and veins that were easy to work paid less than ones that were hard. The miners lived in company houses and shopped at company stores, where they inevitably fell into debt for groceries and equipment. The stores were so profitable that mine owners brought in more miners than they needed, which meant less work for each miner and, as a consequence, more debt. For each man, every ten-hour day and six-day week involved a race to fill the tipple cars with coal faster than rent and groceries ate away his earnings, so that he would have something left at the end of the month.

Slumps in the economy, mild winters, the summer letup in the use of coal: all made this precarious existence worse. Owners paid the miners less when demand dropped and prices softened, but prices at the company stores stayed the same. The year 1884 began with a worsening recession. Owners cut the prices they paid miners from $1 a ton to 80 cents in March, then to 60 cents in June. The miners continued to work. But that October, when a crew of coal-smudged workers emerged from the number four shaft of the New Straitsville Coal Company, they were greeted by a sign that read, "Due to economic conditions, hereafter workers will be paid 40 cents per ton instead of 60 cents."

The miners reacted with a wildcat strike that closed the mines around New Straitsville. A small minority, however, was bent on further action. A group of angry men—there were six of them, by most accounts—loaded mine cars with oil-soaked kindling, coal, and lumber, lit them with torches, and pushed them down the shafts at several of the mines.

Days passed before the underground fires were discovered. The frantic owners assembled mine crews who bulldozed dirt into the shafts, flooded them with water, and built clay firewalls called bradishes, but none of these measures worked. Soon the awful realization dawned that the fires could not be extinguished. The coal's high quality and its accessibility, the very characteristics that created the town's coal boom, kept them burning. Fed with air through mine tunnels, ventilation shafts, and innumerable surface fissures, the fires slowly ate away at New Straitsville's "black diamonds" and the work of mining. By the 1920s, many areas were impossible to work because of smoke, heat, and poisonous gases called "black damp." The workable mines that remained had to dodge the fire's advance in order to find new seams of coal, but there were not enough of these to sustain the population. New Straitsville's reliance on coal was largely over.

Mining families packed up their households and left to search for jobs elsewhere, leaving empty houses and shuttered storefronts. New Straitsville had lost some 500 citizens between 1880 and 1920. It lost 500 more in the next ten years.

Of the fewer than 2,000 who remained, many found opportunity in Prohibition. The terrain around New Straitsville, with its deep woods, concealing hollows, and abandoned mineshafts, favored the making of moonshine whiskey, and the smoking hills provided cover of their own. Federal agents couldn't be sure whether they were closing in on a bootlegger stoking the fire under his still or a plume rising from one of the underground fires through a crack in the earth. At the depths of the depression, when Prohibition was still in force, some 175 stills operated in the New Straitsville area. "Straitsville Special" rivaled bonded Canadian whiskey for popularity in Chicago speakeasies and was widely known for quality.

Although the moonshiners prospered during Prohibition, few others did. The town's only bank closed its doors on December 17, 1930. Two brickmaking companies shut down, along with the A&P, two meat markets, a men's clothing store, the citizen-owned cooperative store, and the drugstore. Only the oil companies, Ohio Oil and Gas, Chartiers Oil, Greendale Minerals, and Kachelmacher Oil, kept workers on the payroll.

The underground fires advanced through good times and bad. One winter's day in 1933, the janitor at New Straitsville's only school went to the basement to stoke the furnace. Before he pitched a shovelful of coal into the firebox, however, he realized the basement wall was heated from outside. The school straddled a coal seam that had been kindled by the heat of the furnace, and the students watched from their classroom windows as bulldozers arrived to tear away at the seam behind the school. Workers set dynamite blasts to break the seam, and the explosions hurled rocks against the back wall of the building.

Work crews were successful in quenching the school fire, but the main fires burned as before, creeping along the network of old mine tunnels. After Prohibition ended in December 1933, New Straitsville became less a haven for moonshiners than a magnet for the curious. People came from all around southeast Ohio on weekend outings. Ruth McKee, who lived in nearby New Lexington as a little girl, remembered riding to New Straitsville with her parents in their car. "You could tell when you were getting close," she said. "You'd look out and see smoke coming out of holes in the ground."

Even before the WPA, local and state officials had begged the federal government for help trying to put the fire out. The first response came in November 1934, when the U.S. Bureau of Mines sent its district engineer, Ralph M. Geiser, to New Straitsville to assess the possibilities. Geiser filed his report on November 23, and he was pessimistic. To one mine operator's suggestion that the fire could be stopped by drilling holes into the burning coal and pumping water into them, he noted "the terrible expense." Such an operation would take years of work and might never be completed, he wrote. And even if successful, "the amount of coal saved would be too small to even pay for a small percentage of the cost." Geiser's conclusion was to let it be: "I would recommend that the fire be allowed to burn its natural course. This might require several hundred years but at the present price of coal there is nothing that could be done profitably to either put the fire out or head it off."

But by the time the WPA entered its second year in 1936, new thinking had emerged: if the fire couldn't be extinguished, it could at least be isolated within the thirty-six-square-mile area where it now burned by cutting off the seams that extended to the west, northeast, and southeast. The last of these ran down the Hocking Valley all the way to the Ohio River, a path that exposed perhaps $1 billion worth of coal. Preserving that much coal plus work for several hundred miners made a strong case, and the allotments committee in Washington granted the project $360,000. Early that fall, Bureau of Mines engineer James Cavanaugh arrived from Pittsburgh to assemble crews and start the work. His first hire was Adam J. Laverty, a local mining expert, to supervise the project. When hiring was complete, 340 men stood ready, most of them ex-miners. They would receive the WPA's pay rate for skilled labor in the New Straitsville region: $63 a month.

The WPA was already well established in the town by then. New Straitsville had never had a water or a sewer system. Cisterns fed water to the business section and the firehouse, but residents used wells and outhouses. Age and weather had rotted wood and rusted hinges, leaving the outdoor toilets tumbledown, and WPA workers had been replacing them with sanitary privies built of concrete, too solid for pranksters to tip over, with pitched roofs and ventilation. For the long term, the town was drawing plans for a water system free of acid-laced mine water that it hoped the WPA would be around long enough to build.

While Cavanaugh and Laverty were assembling their work crews, the WPA rented a downtown storefront, nailed up a sign designating it Uncle Sam's Fire Rescue Station, and launched a round of first-aid courses. Fighting the fire was going to be dangerous. Experienced mine rescue crews would be standing by in case of cave-ins or explosions, but local students would make up a second rescue tier. WPA nurses and medical technicians taught them mine safety and rescue basics. Students bandaged their fellow trainees, strapped them to wooden splints with their heads braced, and learned resuscitation methods. The entire town was preparing to wage war against the fire.

On October 10, 1936, as Cavanaugh and Laverty and a group of town officials looked on, a worker at the controls of a large steam shovel broke the earth at a section west of town called Plummer Hill. The plan devised by the Bureau of Mines was to cut across the veins in the same way a firebreak is used to stop a forest fire, but using open trenches and tunnels instead of controlled burn. The miners would remove the coal and replace it with a non-flammable mixture of clay, mud, and rock. The engineers projected three of these firewalls, twenty-five feet thick and ranging in length from 525 feet to almost a mile and a half. When the fire reached them, so the thinking went, it would not be able to burn through to the coal on the other side. This approach had been tried before and failed, but new earthmoving and drilling machines increased the odds of success.

Plummer Hill was a desolate stretch of denuded hillocks west of town where the fire had parched the earth and stunted and killed most of the trees, and smoke boiled from cracks in the earth. Two families still lived there. Parts of David Rush's farm had collapsed into pits excavated by the burning coal. The garden behind his house had gotten so hot from the approaching fire that potatoes baked in the ground. Still, these families felt a strong sense of attachment to their homes. The Rushes and the Willard Andrews family argued that they were used to the fire and didn't want to move.

The Plummer Hill firewall, "Barrier C" in the Bureau of Mines firefighting plan, was designed to be the shortest of the barriers. The coal veins were shallow there, and the power shovels could attack from the surface. But the big machines left traces of coal and oil shale that only men with hand tools could remove, so through the Christmas season of 1936 and the winter of 1937, WPA mine crews followed the machines along the lengthening trench with picks and hand shovels, scouring it free of anything flammable. Other WPA workers sorted useable coal from the scrap and delivered it to families on relief.

The smoking hills, the destructive onslaught of the fire, its unquenchable force, and the danger of the work attracted nationwide publicity. The WPA's information service had a juicy story, and the publicists peddled it adroitly, using fact laced with hyperbole: the fire had been an unstoppable monster. It already had destroyed some $50 million worth of coal and might destroy a billion dollars more if it broke into rich coal fields to the south. If that happened, only the Ohio River stood in the monster's way. Fighting it involved both scientific ingenuity and the sweat and muscle of courageous men. "Theirs is a race against time to determine whether they can reach their objective before the flames eat up the remaining distance and leave their work for nought," reported the *St. Louis Star-Times* on October 26, 1936.

The *Cleveland Plain Dealer,* the *Toledo News-Bee,* the *Dayton Daily News,* the *Columbus Dispatch,* and the *Charleston* (West Virginia) *Daily Mail* all ran sensational picture spreads in early 1937. The stories polished local legends, such as that of the murderer on the gallows who was about to reveal the names of the miners who started the fire when the hangman silenced him forever. And they created new ones, such as the one about the farmer who was driving his horses home from pasture when a fiery crevice opened and swallowed his prize mare, roasting her alive. With each new article, more people within driving distance of New Straitsville got into their cars to have a look at what the *Plain Dealer* called "the ferocious fire demon."

By the spring of 1937, men working three shifts around the clock had completed the Plummer Hill barrier and sealed it at each end with thick rock walls. The flames consuming the coal vein were fifty feet from the barrier in April when Cavanaugh proclaimed the fire "whipped" and turned his attention to the two remaining firestops.

These were deeper and more dangerous jobs. The barrier at Lost Run, to the southeast, would extend for a mile with several doglegs. To the northeast, near Shawnee, the miners would work 200 feet underground to build a firewall 1.4 miles long, also with several ninety-degree turns. The deep tunnels required extreme caution. Moving foot by foot and removing old timbers as they went to take away flammable material, the miners were creating the potential for collapses and cave-ins. Their safety equipment was limited and primitive. The gear included gas masks and oxygen packs that would let them work in the poisonous, methane-laden air, though these in themselves were risky—the packs, which they carried strapped to their backs, weighed thirty-six pounds, and the outfits included battery-powered headlamps from which a loose connection could spark an explosion in the volatile methane. The job to this point had been accident-free. To ward off the chance of a disaster, Cavanaugh and Laverty assembled rescue crews of five men each, equipped them with masks and oxygen, and directed them to stand by around the clock as the action moved to the new barriers.

3. THE COURT-PACKING DEBACLE

After his stunning election triumph, Roosevelt had entered 1937 in a mood, like the mythical Zeus, to throw thunderbolts. The climate seemed to offer him carte blanche: the people had embraced him as they had no other president; the economy was showing a vigor it had not exhibited since 1929, and although it had not yet reached that level, it seemed to contain the elements that would let Roosevelt reestablish a claim on economic orthodoxy. That meant balancing the budget, a nicety not allowed by the vast relief expenditures of the first term. This had been one of the themes of his 1936 campaign. It was intended to be a signal to businesspeople that he was committed to a sound economy in which they could invest—and could support politically. Employment and productivity were now on the rise, and despite the demands made by the flood on the Ohio and its aftermath, and ongoing but relatively small jobs such as the New Straitsville fire fighting, the numbers working for the WPA were declining. Hopkins had testified before a congressional budget committee that they would drop from February's 2.2 million to 1.6 million in June. There were normally more jobs in the summer, but Hopkins said he anticipated "a large and widespread increase in private employment" beyond these seasonal fluctuations. This, in turn, meant less spending.

Yet even though the economy seemed to be responding to his actions of the last four years, as Roosevelt saw it much of that economy
remained unfair. In his inaugural reference to "one-third of a nation,"
he had signaled that he meant to push for further New Deal laws addressing the poverty and exploitation of farmers and workers. But
here he faced an obstacle. Congress had been his willing partner in re-
forming the old system that promoted a marketplace glutted with
goods that no one could buy and workplaces that treated workers in-
humanely. But since 1935 the Supreme Court had been striking down
those reforms. It had thrown out the National Industrial Recovery Act
and the Agricultural Adjustment Act, the president's first efforts to restore sanity to the economy. More recently, it had overturned the
Guffey Coal Act, which established collective bargaining and price
and production controls in coal mining, as well as a New York State
minimum wage law. This brought to eleven the number of New Deal
and other reform measures the Court had invalidated. (Previous courts
had struck down only sixty laws in 140 years.) The last two had come
in five-to-four decisions that left the president and his aides increasingly frustrated.

"Does this decision mean that the United States government has no
control over any national economic problem?" Roosevelt had asked
rhetorically at a news conference after the unanimous NRA decision
back in May 1935. "We have been relegated to the horse-and-buggy
definition of interstate commerce." He used the phrase "horse-and-
buggy" to suggest that the Constitution's commerce clause deserved
an updated interpretation that took into account new national distribution networks, and also as a way of tarring the Court as old and out
of touch.

At the time, the Supreme Court consisted of a conservative bloc
comprising Pierce Butler, James C. McReynolds, George Sutherland,
and Willis J. Van Devanter; a progressive bloc comprising Louis D.
Brandeis, Benjamin J. Cardozo, and Harlan Fiske Stone; and two
moderates, Owen Roberts and Chief Justice Charles Evans Hughes,
one or both of whom had tended to side with the conservatives. Six of
the nine were over seventy years old, and as the Court continued to
strike down New Deal laws the president kept painting them as relics
of a bygone era. Stealing a phrase from the title of a popular book on
the Court by journalists Drew Pearson and Robert S. Allen published

in the fall of 1936, he referred to them as "nine old men," and charged that the Court's defense of corporate liberties had created a " 'no-man's land' where no government—state or federal—can function." Indeed, pro–New Dealers treated the court rulings as an affront to popular democracy itself as voters had expressed it in the landslide of the previous November.

Now, two other vital pieces of New Deal legislation—the National Labor Relations Act and the Social Security Act—were pending review, and the administration feared the Court would continue to block its agenda. Whereas Hoover had been able to appoint three justices in the course of his single term, Roosevelt had appointed none, which increased his frustration.

So in the fullness of his mandate, and with an economy that seemed likely to increase his popularity still more, he hurled a bombshell from the heights of his political Olympus. On February 5, 1937, he submitted to the Congress a plan to restructure the Supreme Court by appointing one additional justice for each current justice over the retirement age of seventy who refused to retire. This amounted to enlarging the Court to as many as fifteen members. It was constitutionally feasible, since the Constitution failed to specify the number of justices on the high court; in fact, the numbers had varied between six and ten until Congress set it at nine in 1869, during the Grant administration. Under Roosevelt's proposal, the same rules would apply to the lower federal courts, as long as the judge had served for ten years and declined to retire within six months of turning seventy, although it also limited the number of jurists the president could choose to fifty overall.

Court reform had been on the White House agenda ever since the NRA and AAA were overturned. Most of the proposals involved constitutional amendments that would limit the Court's power or expand Congress's, or laws allowing the next Congress to repass laws that had been overturned. But the amendment procedure would take too long, and any new or repassed law was itself subject to review by the Supreme Court. Roosevelt believed he was taking the speediest and most effective course, and his election margin suggested he could bring it off.

But it quickly developed that he had overstepped. First, he had shrouded the plan in what one friend and advisor, Harvard Law

School professor and subsequent Supreme Court appointee Felix Frankfurter, called "dramatic, untarnished secrecy." And he had dropped it on Congress's doorstep without even briefing his floor leaders to expect it. The Court's adverse rulings had won it few friends among the president's legislative allies, but even so, his move came as a shock and a surprise. It also shocked the nation. Its bland title, the Judicial Branch Reorganization Plan, was quickly supplanted by a headline-friendly and politically charged nickname: it became Roosevelt's "court-packing" scheme.

Opponents reacted predictably. Colonel Robert McCormick's *Chicago Tribune* wrote that if the plan passed, "the principle of an impartial and independent judiciary will be lost in this country." Its February 7 editorial went on to compare Roosevelt to Mussolini, Hitler, and Stalin: "They are dictators because they write the laws, they put them into effect and there is no independent judiciary to which the citizens can appeal against the autocrat." But even *The Nation,* a liberal weekly that unfailingly supported Roosevelt and the New Deal, described the plan in apocalyptic terms: "What the president is proposing is to dynamite the reactionary judges into retirement." Metaphors abounded: Editorial cartoonists chose themes from sports, depicting Roosevelt as changing umpires and referees and lowering the net in tennis because he didn't like the score. Others showed him as a puppeteer orchestrating a chorus of yes-men.

The president labored to depict the court system as overworked and understaffed, but the subtext was clear. In his message to the Congress, he referred to "aged or infirm judges" and the need for an "infusion of new blood" and "younger blood." "Little by little," he said, "new facts become blurred through old glasses." It was obvious that he simply wanted to be able to appoint judges, and in particular Supreme Court justices, who would go along with his legislative program.

He said as much in a nationally broadcast speech to an audience of Democrats in Washington on March 4. Abandoning the pretense that he was promoting court efficiency, he argued that "the three-horse team of the American system of government" should pull together. If the three "pull as one, the field will be plowed," he said, but "if one horse lies down in the traces or plunges off in another direction, the field will not be plowed."

On March 9, he tried to drum up support in a fireside chat, using language that was both patronizing and fear-mongering. Invoking the economic catastrophe of the depression, he said that laws did not exist to deal with it. "We became convinced that the only way to avoid a repetition of those dark days was to have a government with power to prevent and to cure the abuses and the inequalities which had thrown that system out of joint. The Courts, however, have cast doubts on the ability of the elected Congress to protect us against catastrophe.... We are at a crisis in our ability to proceed with that protection. It is a quiet crisis [that] is far-reaching in its possibilities of injury to America. I want to talk with you very simply about the need for present action in this crisis—the need to meet the unanswered challenge of one-third of a nation ill-nourished, ill-clad, ill-housed."

He went on to say that the Court had been acting not as a judicial body but as a policy-making one, the same charge of judicial activism that would be echoed by conservatives in ensuing years. And again he painted the image of old men lost in the past; he wanted "to bring to the decision of social and economic problems younger men who have had personal experience and contact with modern facts and circum-stances under which average men have to live and work. This plan will save our national Constitution from hardening of the judicial arter-ies."

But Roosevelt had made a rare political misreading, both of his elec-tion mandate and of the people's respect for the delicate balance of powers enshrined in the Constitution. A cartoon in the *Brooklyn Eagle* conveyed this ominous truth: it showed a scowling Roosevelt voter holding a newspaper headlining the court plan, and a caption reading, "I Did Not Vote for That!" Letters to the Congress ran nearly eight to one against it. The president was blistered even by admiring constituents in letters pointing out that the three branches of govern-ment were not supposed to pull together, and that he was not calling for the resignations of his elderly supporters in Congress. Nor did the Court fit his portrayal of it as overburdened, since Chief Justice Hughes was able to inform the Senate in March that the Court was "fully abreast of its work."

Still, Roosevelt pushed the plan forward against gathering legisla-tive opposition. Montana Senator Burton K. Wheeler, a Democrat and longtime progressive, exhibited the extent of this disaffection by lead-ing the resistance in the Senate.

Then an odd thing happened. On March 29, with the swing vote coming from its youngest justice, sixty-one-year-old Owen Roberts, the Court approved a Washington State minimum wage law that was very much like the New York law it had struck down the year before. This decision in *West Coast Hotel Co. v. Parris*—written by Chief Justice Hughes—was completely unexpected, and no sooner had it been announced than the Court surprised observers again. On April 12, in another five-to-four decision with Hughes and Roberts in the majority, it upheld the National Labor Relations Act, also called the Wagner Act for its sponsorship by New York senator Robert F. Wagner. The Wagner Act was anathema to employers, for it outlawed unfair labor practices and guaranteed collective bargaining and the right to join unions.

This victory for labor came in a season of equally significant advances on the picket line. In February, General Motors recognized the eighteen-month-old United Auto Workers as the sole bargaining agent for its workers, ending a six-week strike in which workers had taken over its Fisher Body plant at Flint, Michigan, and shut down its production lines, a relatively new tactic in the labor arsenal known as a sit-down strike. On March 1, U.S. Steel acceded to the unionization of its workers in order to prevent a strike. Big Steel had fallen, although Little Steel, as the smaller steelmakers including Republic and Bethlehem were called, continued to resist the efforts of unions to organize their workers. Nevertheless, it was reasonable to believe that the Court's new majority now recognized that realities had changed.

The administration's biggest victory came at the end of May, five months after the first payroll taxes were collected and the first lump-sum payments had been made, when the Supreme Court upheld the Social Security Act. It ruled in separate cases that both unemployment compensation and the act's system of old-age pensions, each of them funded by taxes on employers and workers, passed constitutional muster. With its minimum wage and Wagner Act approvals, and now Social Security, the Court itself had voided any urgency for Roosevelt's plan to go forward. And by then seventy-eight-year-old Justice Van Devanter, the Court's staunchest conservative and longest-serving member, had given notice of his intention to resign, providing the president with the prospect of his first appointment.

Roosevelt could have gracefully abandoned the idea at this point. In fact, the plan to augment the roster of older justices at the trial and first appeals court levels—the federal district and circuit courts—had already been stripped away. Support for the Supreme Court portion of his plan was moribund; polls showed that even compromise proposals that fell well short of the original enjoyed no more than 35 percent support. But Roosevelt kept pressing ahead, offering his Senate floor leader, Joe Robinson, the appointment to Van Devanter's seat in exchange for the best deal Robinson could steer through the Senate. This was a plan that would allow the president to appoint a coadjutor justice for each justice seventy-five or over, but no more than one such appointment a year. But when Robinson died of a heart attack in mid-July, the proposal died with him, and in August Roosevelt appointed the staunchly liberal Senator Hugo Black of Alabama, a dependable supporter of the New Deal, to the seat Van Devanter had vacated.

The six-month battle had cost the president dearly. It had eroded his public support and emboldened conservatives, including those in his own party, by showing that he was not invincible. One high-profile defector was the vice president, John Nance Garner, who had disappeared to Texas at the height of the debate, leaving Joe Robinson to fight the battle in the Senate. In trying to alter the high court to give New Deal legislation new momentum, Roosevelt lost the momentum he had had, and with it the potential for new legislative possibilities. Far more important, he had lost a measure of trust. Nor was this the only misstep in the first year of his new term. While Roosevelt pursued an ever-smaller slice of victory in the court fight, a greater peril was creeping up on him. The economy that had seemed robust as the year began was weakening, yet he seemed not to notice. He persisted in trying to wring savings out of the federal budget, and this would have implications for all of his programs, especially the WPA.

4. WPA CUTS AND THE "ROOSEVELT RECESSION"

By that summer, as the court plan was in its final throes, the cuts in the WPA rolls that Harry Hopkins had forecast to Congress at the beginning of the year had come to pass. Unemployment had ticked up in March after reaching a depression-low 14 percent, although the warm weather had brought its usual increase in private jobs. Hopkins's fund request for the fiscal year starting in July 1937 reflected an improving job picture: he had asked for only $1.5 billion for the WPA, less than a third of the original work relief appropriation of $4.8 billion just two years earlier. This would allow him to keep WPA employment at 1.65 million, a little above the summer low. The employment situation was far better than it had been. Still, 7 million people continued to be out of work.

Since the death of Roosevelt's close longtime political advisor Louis Howe the year before, Hopkins had grown closer to the president. Howe, gnomish, sickly, and politically astute, had devoted his career to Roosevelt's electoral fortunes ever since his early New York State activities; within the presidential circle only Hopkins offered a similar combination of loyalty and advice untarnished by a personal agenda. Hopkins had tried to warn Roosevelt in advance that trying to sell the court plan on the basis of efficiency would not fly since the court calendars were not that crowded, although afterward he dutifully spoke in favor of it. Now the president would test his loyalty again.

Roosevelt had looked at declining unemployment, industrial production that was almost back to the levels of 1929, and increased farm income and decided from these bellwethers that the depression was on its way to being whipped and it was time to cut relief spending. Treasury Secretary Henry Morgenthau Jr. had a hand in this conclusion. He argued that only a balanced budget and an end to deficits would convince businesses that the economy had regained enough stability to warrant new investment, which would spur a rise in private jobs. More relief spending would have the opposite effect, causing them to hold back because they feared the additional spending would lead to inflation and higher taxes.

Against this policy stood the views of Hopkins and others, including his economic advisor Leon Henderson and Federal Reserve Board chairman Marriner Eccles, that cuts in relief spending would effectively turn off the spigot of pump priming and send the nation into recession. Although the budget theories of John Maynard Keynes were not then widely known, their views reflected Keynesian thought. Hopkins in particular believed that purchasing power in the hands of consumers was a more powerful economic force, at least in the current emergency, than the sound national credit engendered by a balanced budget. He favored continuing deficit spending to stimulate the economy, a case he was arguing more frequently, and vocally, within the administration.

But Roosevelt kept pushing for spending cuts and savings. On top of the reduced WPA budget, he wanted local and state governments to increase their contributions to projects for which they sought WPA-paid labor. "More contributions please!" the president wrote Hopkins, urging that he immediately press project sponsors to shoulder 30 percent of project costs. Some members of Congress wanted it to be even more. Local sponsors had contributed 9.8 percent to the costs of their WPA projects in 1936, and by 1938 it would be up to 20.8 percent. Although Hopkins was beginning to move in the president's direction, he opposed making the local share a strict demand on the grounds that many of the smaller state and local governments could not afford the additional spending; if so, projects would fold and they would have to lay off workers.

Hopkins had gone after his $1.5 billion appropriation for the new fiscal year with a vengeance, lobbying mayors, governors, and sympathetic senators and representatives in a blizzard of phone calls and office visits. The seasonal cuts, and the suggestion in his budget request that these would be more or less permanent, had already set off protests among WPA workers. As usual, the leftist factions concentrated in New York were among the most vocal; 7,000 of them in the New York arts units staged a one-day strike on May 27, 1937. And while Hopkins was reconciled to the lower appropriation and the lower rolls, he was determined to resist cuts that went beyond what he recommended. He did not believe that either the WPA or the country would be served by cutting the employment program even closer to the bone, which set him against an increasingly hostile anti–New Deal bloc in Congress.

He won the day, but his victory came at a cost. His relations with congressional conservatives, never warm, cooled further. When Senator James Byrnes of South Carolina asked Hopkins if he could get along on $1 billion for twelve months, Hopkins snapped, "I can, but the unemployed couldn't." Some members resented the ease with which he moved in and out of Capitol Hill offices, courting those he chose to and ignoring others. Some, especially from the low-wage South, disliked his support for a minimum wage. His sharp tongue, his resistance to patronage appointments in the WPA, and the continuing rancor over the court-packing battle spilled over, and when the House passed its version of the appropriations bill, it added language cutting Hopkins's salary from $12,000 to $10,000.

It was a petty action designed to send a message. The *Baltimore Sun* ascribed the move to "a frantic hatred" of Hopkins caused in part by his opposition to "earmarking" WPA funds—that is, specifying the individual projects on which they could be spent. Earmarking was a thinly disguised effort to turn the WPA appropriation into a feast of pork, in which members of Congress would swap favorite projects among themselves regardless of the local unemployment rolls. Hopkins emerged victorious from this scrape, too; the bill called for the $1.5 billion to be spent in broad categories, and within those categories, Roosevelt and Hopkins had discretion. They included highways, roads, and streets ($415 million); public buildings and other public projects ranging from parks, airports, and utilities to pest eradication and flood control ($630 million); women's and professional projects including the arts programs ($380 million); and the National Youth Administration ($75 million).

And the final bill also restored Hopkins's full salary, although *Washington Post* columnist Franklyn Waltman summarized the extent to which he was accumulating enemies: "It was a pleasant sight," he wrote, "to see someone slap that smartalecky Harry Hopkins down."

It was not a time for Hopkins to gloat, however, for he had devastating matters on his mind. His wife, Barbara, had been diagnosed with breast cancer early in the year, and by the end of June, when Congress approved the WPA funding, the disease was well advanced. Hopkins was splitting his time between Washington and New York, where Barbara was receiving treatment, and a retinue of friends and retainers assisted in caring for their little daughter, Diana. When they learned that her case was hopeless, Hopkins and Barbara left New York for a final late summer stay in Saratoga Springs. They returned to Washington soon after Labor Day, and at the beginning of October she entered Garfield Hospital, where she died early on October 7 with Hopkins at her bedside. Barbara Duncan Hopkins was only thirty-seven, and she was the love of Hopkins's life. They had been together for barely six years, he adored her, and he blamed his various failings for her death. Nor was Hopkins well himself. His duodenal ulcer had developed into something more serious and he suspected cancer, but he had allowed himself no time to confirm this during Barbara's final months.

Members of the administration rallied around him in his grief. Hundreds sent sympathy cards. Florence Kerr, who in addition to heading the Division of Women's and Professional Projects in the Midwest had been his classmate at Grinnell, returned to Washington to help look after Diana. Harold Ickes set aside his hostility and invited Hopkins to spend time at his farm in Maryland, an invitation Hopkins accepted, bringing about a temporary truce between the two. Hopkins apparently moped much of the time that he was there, but as Ickes later told Robert Sherwood, "Harry was an agreeable scoundrel when he wanted to be."

Meanwhile, the economy was not showing the resilience Roosevelt had hoped for, or that Hopkins's budget request had contemplated. Many of the workers laid off in the seasonal cutbacks had been unable to find jobs in the private sector. Pleading letters arrived on the desks of mayors and governors as the cuts took hold. Mayor Robert S. Maestri of New Orleans was a typical recipient, and he dutifully championed the causes of the unemployed with relief and WPA officials:

Mr. Richard R. Foster
Director of Public Welfare
Soule Building
New Orleans, Louisiana

Dear Mr. Foster:

This letter will be handed to you by Mrs. Josephine Maestri [she was apparently unrelated to the mayor], who has been connected with a WPA sewing project as a seamstress' helper. Mrs. Maestri has been dropped because of reduction of funds.

I will appreciate it if you can have this lady reinstated. She is alone in the world and has a daughter to support. The small amount she has been receiving is all that she has to live on. I will appreciate your personal attention in this matter.

Sincerely yours,
Robert Maestri, Mayor

By August, when the rolls dropped below 1.53 million, the cuts had produced more protests. David Lasser, the president of the left-wing union called the Workers Alliance of America, made up of WPA employees and relief recipients, led 2,500 of his claimed 400,000 dues-paying members to Washington, where they camped at the Washington Monument. Hopkins met with Lasser twice in two days, and the meetings probably were more interesting than other events on Hopkins's calendar, since Lasser was a man of many parts. Before he founded the Workers Alliance in 1935 and started agitating for more work and better pay for WPA workers, he had founded the American Interplanetary Society and written a book, *The Conquest of Space,* that proposed rocket-propelled space travel. He turned to labor advocacy after deciding "it is necessary to remake the Earth before delving into life on the moon." But on the subject at hand, Hopkins refused to promise that WPA employment would expand, and Lasser appealed to his members for contributions to a political action fund to take the union's case to voters.

At the same time, the Federal Reserve board was acting at cross-purposes. Although its chair, Eccles, favored a continuation of pump-priming relief spending, the Fed also wanted to ease business fears about inflation, so despite the stagnant job market it tightened credit by increasing bank reserve requirements. This was the opposite of pump priming; it took "some water out of the spout." The new pay-roll taxes for Social Security removed an additional $2 billion from the pockets of consumers, and the WPA job cuts did still more to keep potential buyers away from retail counters.

Industrial production, which had struggled to a peak during the spring, started to fall; by October it had dropped 14 percent. The stock market, after fighting its way to 194.4 in March, also declined, incrementally at first and then more drastically in August and September. The New York Stock Exchange sought to halt trading and close the exchange after a sharp early September sell-off, but William O. Douglas, who had replaced Joseph Kennedy as chairman of the Securities and Exchange Commission, rejected the request. Then, on a single day, October 19, the Dow Jones Industrial Average lost 7.75 percent of its value and the Standard and Poor's index 9.12 percent. More than half a million Americans in private jobs were thrown out of work in that one month alone, 2 million by the end of the year, and what Republicans gleefully called the "Roosevelt Recession" was a fact.

5. THE ROOSEVELTS AT TIMBERLINE

The recessionary signs were deepening, but were not yet acute, when the president and first lady embarked on a two-week trip to the Northwest in early fall. Although 1937 was not an election year and the trip was billed as an inspection tour, it had a political feel. Bloodied in the court fight by a majority of newspapers—he was convinced that 85 percent of them were "utterly opposed to everything the administration is seeking"—and still angry, he wanted to bypass them and their sniping columnists and connect directly with the people. He had called a special session of the Congress for later in the fall to revisit wages-and-hours and other legislation that had stalled during the court battle, and he hoped to generate momentum for the bills he wanted to push through. Perhaps most important, he wanted to call attention to the lavish investment in jobs, public works, and public benefits the nation's citizens had financed with their tax dollars at some major dams and building sites.

The presidential train left Hyde Park on September 22. It reached Iowa the next afternoon and started making whistle stops, the president emerging onto the rear platform to observe that the corn was a "little bit taller" than his corn back in the Hudson Valley and that looking over the country "at first hand...is the right thing for a president to do." The stops continued into Wyoming. In Cheyenne, Roosevelt reminded his audience that the government had spent "a great deal of money in putting people to work" building, among other things, thousands of airports and schools. In Boise, Idaho, after a two-day stopover at Yellowstone National Park, he said meeting the American people gave him renewed strength like Antaeus, the Greek giant of mythology who drew strength from contact with his mother the earth. Indeed, the crowds that gathered seemed to Roosevelt to be larger than ever, and to have lost none of their affection. He gave the glad hand to senators, governors, and local politicians, though he also signaled displeasure with some—Montana's Wheeler was one—who had opposed him in the court fight. There were visits to WPA parks and anti-erosion projects, irrigation projects sponsored by the Bureau of Reclamation of the Department of Interior, and PWA-funded buildings, and then the presidential party headed west to Oregon.

Here he began a series of stops that put the magnificent vision of the New Deal on full display. At eight on the morning of September 28, the train rolled to a halt in Bonneville, on the Columbia River forty miles east of Portland, and the party shifted to a motorcade to inspect the Bonneville Dam and locks, a $51 million joint effort of the Public Works Administration and the Army Corps of Engineers. Bonneville was precisely the value-laden project Harold Ickes envisioned spending work relief money on. Its navigation lock, then the world's largest single-lift lock, would extend shipping 188 miles upriver to the Snake River inside Washington State; it would provide irrigation water for arid eastern Oregon; and its hydroelectric turbines would generate 580,000 horsepower of affordable electricity to feed aluminum plants operating in the area as well as rural consumers in Washington and Oregon. What was more, $3.2 million of its cost had gone into fish ladders that would allow Pacific salmon to reach their upstream spawning beds.

The president spoke of navigation and electricity in his brief remarks at Bonneville. Then the party headed south in a motorcade to Mount Hood, Roosevelt and his wife in an open car wrapped in blankets and robes. It was less than twenty-five miles as the crow flies, but more than sixty skirting the mountain to the west, and by the time they arrived at Timberline Lodge in the early afternoon of September 28 they were cold. Eleanor was ushered to one of the rooms to get warm, while the president chatted with E. J. Griffith, the Oregon WPA administrator, and took stock of the crowd from the balcony above the main entrance. Two or three hundred people were standing around the south front of the still-unfinished lodge, many of them masons, carpenters, and craftspeople who had been working on the structure nonstop since it had gone "under roof" the previous December. More watched from the large dining room windows behind him, and from a viewing platform built for the occasion. Still, Roosevelt probably wished the crowd were larger, given the semi-political nature of his trip and the cost of Timberline. It had ballooned to $1 million and counting when road building and landscaping were figured in and because Harry Hopkins kept saying yes to Margery Hoffman Smith's arts-and-crafts proposals. The president was to give the lodge its formal dedication now, although its opening was still four months away. Just to reach this point had stretched the WPA work crews, and the artists and craft workers, to their limits.

Even after the lodge was roofed, outdoor work had continued. A small crew of quarriers working in snow trenches that were over six feet deep cut granite for the interior stonework and loaded the stones into canvas-tented truck beds. At the lodge itself, carpenters nailed on shingles, clapboard siding, and board-and-batten to complete the exterior walls ahead of the rising snowdrifts. The masons working on the headhouse roof to complete the main chimney labored with only a wooden shelter to protect them.

The jobs of the road-clearing crews were among the most dangerous on the mountain. It was easy to lose men in a blizzard, and back in January two had gone missing. Only after a suppertime roll call came up two names short did the workers turn out to form a human chain to search the road below the lodge. Remarkably, they found the men still alive and brought them back to safety. Down at the camp, Albert Altorfer kept two men and sometimes three busy chopping wood for the cookstoves. His head cook, responsible for rousing the kitchen crew to start the morning meal, discovered that a bucketful of snow was good for waking up men who clung to the warmth of their cots in the predawn cold.

While carpenters, plumbers, and electricians completed their tasks within the lodge, other workers devoted themselves to the architectural and decorative flourishes. Ray Neufer's woodworking shop handled an array of tasks. Men carved old cedar telephone poles into newel posts with eagles, beavers, squirrels, and other animals at the tops. Other carvers shaped ram and buffalo heads that would be part of the exterior decoration. Still others rendered "Native American" petroglyphs to decorate interior doorways; their designs were cribbed from the Camp Fire Girls handbook. Cabinetmakers working under Neufer built most of the lodge's furniture, including tables, chairs, beds, and dressers. In the blacksmith shop, Orion Dawson directed workers, including Henry Moar, as they built wrought-iron gates, lamps, and chandeliers, as well as straps, knockers, and handles for the lodge's heavy wooden doors.

Back in Portland, Hoffman Smith had WPA craft shops humming at full speed, with women hooking and weaving rugs and bedspreads and upholstery fabrics. She also commissioned art to support the frontier and outdoor themes that were part of the lodge's brawny Western beauty. Douglas Lynch, the Portland muralist, would use linoleum to carve and then paint scenes of camping and fishing for the coffee shop walls. Modernist C. S. Price painted large-scale western scenes on canvas. Karl Fuerer, who had spent his career reproducing old-master paintings, did watercolors of local wildflowers for the guest rooms that would bear their names (although the Skunk Cabbage Room would later be renamed to improve its occupancy rate). A room intended for wood storage was turned into the Blue Ox Bar, with art by Virginia Darcé based on the Paul Bunyan legend. When the lodge was finished it would be, inside and out, a salute to the people of Oregon: their ingenuity and their surroundings.

In the days before the Roosevelts' arrival, the Timberline architects had received a new rush commission: based on sketches sent by the White House, they were to build a podium for the president to speak from. Linn Forrest described it as "like an apple box, with a couple of handles for him to hold onto and a seat like a bicycle seat to sit on." This, and the plywood sheeting requested by the White House for the ramp up to the balcony where he would speak, brought home to Forrest the efforts made by the president's team to disguise the extent of his paralysis, a subterfuge at which they were now expert.

Roosevelt made his way to the podium midway through the afternoon, with Eleanor looking on, warm again after the cold ride. It was a clear, sunny day, and before them lay the magnificent fifty-mile view down the Cascade Range to Mount Jefferson. The president spoke briefly, saying the lodge and projects like it would attract more recreational users to the national forests and quoting from the dedication plaque; it was "a monument to the skill and faithful performance of workers on the rolls of the Works Progress Administration" and "a place to play for generations of Americans in the days to come."

Rooms had been prepared for the presidential party. Neufer's woodworking shop had even designed a special armchair for the president, and Griffith tried to persuade them to stay overnight. But the Roosevelts were traveling with their daughter Anna, her husband, John Boettiger, and their two young children, and they were eager to get to Seattle, where the Boettigers lived. After they left, the frantic pace of work continued, so as to ready the lodge for paying guests in February 1938.

And before those first guests arrived for their skiing, and for the views downrange from the dining room where they ate 75-cent veal chops and 50-cent beef jardinière polished off with coffee and 15-cent huckleberry pie, there was a lively party for the WPA-paid construction workers. As they milled around their former workplace they were both awestruck and bereft. It had been an extraordinary experience. "They were doing something that was really creative and they could see the results of it, and it was their building, their lodge," said Hoffman Smith afterward. "A lot of those men cried. I wouldn't have believed they could be so moved but they literally cried, thinking that the project was over."

6. DECLINE AND REVIVAL

The Roosevelts made their way back east, stopping to highlight the massive Grand Coulee and Fort Peck dams and to dedicate a WPA bridge in Chicago, and they were back in Washington by the end of the first week in October. From there, the president witnessed the painful drop in the economy. Before it was to bottom out in March 1938, two-thirds of the economic gains achieved since 1933 had been lost. Industrial output fell 40 percent overall, steel production 75 percent, and corporate profits 80 percent. The stock market as reflected by the Dow fell to 99, losing nearly half its value. By then, 4 million Americans who had regained jobs since 1933 had lost them, and the unemployment rate had jumped back up to 19 percent. Harry Hopkins and the other nascent Keynesians had been correct: the unprimed pump was sucking air.

Equally painful to the president was the failure of his legislative package in the special session to which he called the Congress in November. He had summoned it because he wanted a farm bill to replace the struck-down AAA, the industrial wage-and-hours bill that had so far eluded him, the authority to reorganize the executive branch to give him more flexibility in managing the government, and a plan that would create seven regional planning bodies to develop and manage natural resources as the Tennessee Valley Authority was doing in six states in the Southeast. But the revitalized conservatives were in no mood to cooperate, and when the session adjourned in December after five contentious weeks, it had produced literally nothing on Roosevelt's list.

By the time he delivered his fifth State of the Union address in January 1938, he was no longer talking about balancing the budget in the year ahead. He threw a bone to Morgenthau and the other budget balancers, saying his budget request for fiscal 1939 "will exhibit a further decrease in the deficit." But he added that while he was "as anxious as any banker or industrialist or business man or investor or economist that the budget of the United States government be brought into balance as quickly as possible," he would not permit "any needy American who can and is willing to work to starve because the Federal Government does not provide the work." He hinted that the blame for the shrinking economy lay with businesses that were preventing expansion by withholding investments in new plants. This he interpreted as a politically motivated strike at his economic program. "The selfish suspension of the employment of capital must be ended," he declared.

In fact, there was blame aplenty for the economic plunge, although if a single word could describe the cause, it was probably *confusion*. True, industry was not investing in new production capacity, but whether this was the work of monopolists and profiteers determined to undermine the reforms of the New Deal, or simply uncertainty over how far those reforms would go, was unclear. "We don't know," Lamont du Pont had said in 1937, addressing questions that ranged from the future course of everything from taxation to the advance of unions. Indeed, business was still coming to terms with the new landscape as approved by the Supreme Court: the collective bargaining provisions of the Wagner Act, as well as taxes for Social Security and unemployment compensation. Roosevelt's attacks on what he termed "economic royalists" and "selfish interests" suggested that more, and more drastic, measures might be in the offing. Now that the Washington State minimum wage had been upheld, his push for a national wage-and-hours law threatened to raise business's operating costs, and he made it clear at every turn that he would not rest until it passed. The people favored it "by an overwhelming vote," he had said in the State of the Union address. They wanted "the Congress—*this*

Congress" to install a floor beneath wages and a ceiling over hours. In a similar vein, the vast gains in unionization in the auto, steel, and mining industries had contributed to the nervousness with which business viewed its future prospects.

Blame aside, the first months of 1938 recalled the depths of 1933. The relief rolls swelled in hard-hit industrial cities still trying to regain their economic footing. Cleveland exhausted its relief budget in the first week of the year, leaving 65,000 people without emergency food and clothing. Chicago had no money to keep open its nineteen municipal relief stations. Detroit's rolls of employable relief recipients eligible for WPA jobs jumped a startling 434 percent, and Toledo's rose 194 percent. St. Louis and Omaha foresaw the end of their relief funds, and Omaha cut back to token payments. Many people were once again forced to scavenge for food, and starvation and suicide crept back into the public consciousness.

Hopkins was watching all this from Palm Beach, where he was recuperating from cancer surgery. He had finally mustered the courage to seek a diagnosis of the eating problems that had plagued him for more than a year. Doctors at the Mayo Clinic in Rochester, Minnesota, had confirmed his worst fears and performed an operation that removed the cancer, together with most of his stomach. Around the first of the year, when he was again able to travel, he had accepted Joe Kennedy's invitation to convalesce at his winter home.

But although he was absent from Washington, Hopkins was not silent. He resumed his advocacy of deficits to shore up purchasing power, his allies including Marriner Eccles and Leon Henderson, and when Roosevelt invited him to Warm Springs at the end of March he made his case directly to the president. By then, reeling from the business wipeout and the reappearance of staggering human hardship, and looking ahead to the midterm elections in the fall, Roosevelt had heard enough. He passed his decision on to Hopkins on the train back to Washington: budget balancing was off the table and he would ask the Congress for new spending to try to pump up the economy.

On April 14, he sent a $3 billion spending plan to Congress. It would add money to the WPA, CCC, and National Youth Administration and fund new public works, highways, federal buildings, slum clearance, housing, and flood control projects. He also said he was loosening credit by reducing bank reserve requirements. It had been a mistake, he told the people the same night in a fireside chat, to have tried to reduce spending. One week later, the WPA rolls were back above 2.5 million.

Hopkins was soon on the stump again, touting the rebirth of the WPA. The president was monitoring Hopkins's health personally, having decided that the WPA head was the best choice to succeed him as the Democratic candidate in 1940, and Eleanor had invited him to move into the White House, where Diana had been living since Barbara's death. Although he was in what for him was fine health following his surgery and long recuperation, to Eleanor, his longtime ally on programs for youth, women, and the unemployed, Hopkins now gave the impression of "being hollow" physically. He had always been thin and slumped, but the operation had increased that sense of concavity; his suits hung even looser and his collars gapped around his scrawny neck. He was also in fine fettle; in a nationwide radio broadcast on May 8, he toted up the agency's accomplishments: 43,000 miles of new roads and 119,000 miles of road improvements, 19,000 new bridges, 185,000 culverts, 105 new airports, 12,000 new schools and other public buildings, 15,000 small dams, 10,000 miles of water and sewer lines, and more than 10 million trees planted and improvements on millions of acres of land.

"These things constitute national wealth and national assets. Any private business which builds improvements to its physical plant counts these improvements as assets, and considers itself richer because of them. Government alone counts the cost of such improvements on the red side of the ledger," Hopkins said.

By the end of June, Congress had passed Roosevelt's new spending plan and the Fair Labor Standards Act. This was his wage-and-hours law at last. It banned the employment of workers under age sixteen in industry and established a forty-hour workweek, a minimum wage of 40 cents an hour (phased in over eight years, after starting at 25 cents an hour), and time and a half for overtime. The night before he signed the law on June 25, Roosevelt delivered a fireside chat in which he said that except perhaps for Social Security, it was "the most far-reaching, the most far-sighted program for the benefit of workers ever adopted here or in any other country." But despite these successes, his opposition was solidifying in Congress. This was a result of the continuing fallout from the court fight and the new vigor of conservatives, so the prospect for further New Deal reforms was dim.

That month, Hopkins released a WPA survey that assessed relief needs since 1933. Its conclusions were based in part on an "unemployment census" that Roosevelt had launched with a fireside chat the previous November, seeking data on the skills and locations of those who were then jobless. Unemployment relief is "not the permanent cure," the president had said. But as the recession persisted and deepened and Hopkins gained in influence, the administration's thinking changed. The data now suggested, said Hopkins, that high unemployment "can no longer be regarded as a temporary problem to be treated on an emergency basis."

The report recommended the establishment of a three-part program that included relief, unemployment insurance, and an ongoing government-sponsored work component. "No single program will eliminate the distress from unemployment," it stated.

Time took note of Hopkins's reemerging profile a month later, in a cover story in its issue of July 18. He had last graced the magazine's cover during the CWA's flurry of temporary job creation in the winter of 1934. Now, more than four years later, the WPA was adding 60,000 workers a week. Hopkins's portrait, this time rendered in color, showed him in a typical pose, his hands cupped around a match as he lit a cigarette, his dark, bulging eyes gleaming. The story noted that he was hard at work in his "plebian" office in the Walker-Johnson Building at a time when most of official Washington was on vacation, and elaborated on his view of the need for a permanent work program, which he had been touting in speeches and on national radio. "This new frontier of idle overhead," as he described it in a May radio address, meaning jobless workers, idle machines, and unused capital, had cost Americans $200 billion in lost wages since 1929. With 12 or 13 million still unemployed, he said, only the government had the resources to organize all their "resourcefulness, ingenuity and courage" into a program that would "provide a broad base of purchasing power . . . increasing the stability of the economic system."

Hopkins was less voluble when it came to his personal life. He told *Time* it was "nobody's g——d—— business" whether he was engaged to thirty-three-year-old Dorothy Donovan Thomas Hale, the widow of artist Gardner Hale, who had died in an automobile crash in 1931. The magazine described her as a "beauteous Pittsburgh-born glamour girl" with homes in Paris and Southampton and a résumé that included a Broadway chorus line. In fact, she and Hopkins were not engaged. And his tongue loosened once again when he was reminded of attacks on the WPA by Representative Hamilton Fish, a New York Republican. Fish had applied to the WPA an often-used damnation of corruption orginally attributed to eighteenth-century Jacksonian Party representative and Senator John Randolph of Virginia, that "like a dead mackerel in the moonlight, it stinks and shines and shines and stinks."

"They can call names just so often," Hopkins said. "I know a lot of adjectives myself and I am going to start in pretty soon."

It was not an idle threat. The WPA was demonstrably not corrupt at the national level. Hopkins still rejected patronage in WPA hiring, and pressuring workers to support a favored candidate was a firing offense. But five years in Washington had inured him to the ways of politics. He knew that politicians would lay claim to WPA votes if they could. He also knew that jobs translated into votes without a lot of prompting, and rolls that increased before elections sent a message. So did pay raises, such as the across-the-board wage hikes that had gone through in Kentucky and Oklahoma after pro–New Deal senators Alben Barkley and Elmer Thomas, who were fighting tough renomination battles, were attacked by opponents who pointed out that WPA workers in neighboring states made more than they did. The primary election season that was now under way before the midterm elections in November found many of the administration's friends under pressure from the right. Reform remained a part of the Roosevelt agenda, and Hopkins, especially now that he had entered the inner circle, was committed to pursuing that agenda. Between his hopes for a permanent WPA and a new interest in his own electoral possibilities, he was more than ever the politician, ready to do battle with the administration's enemies.

Meanwhile, the agency continued its resurgence. By late August 1938, the numbers of men and women working for the WPA had surpassed the previous high reached in February 1936, and they continued to climb toward 3.3 million, more than double the 1,435,169 of one year earlier. The agency, as if reflecting the thrust of its own study, was showing undeniable signs of permanence.

7. BUILDING ROADS IN NORTH CAROLINA (JOHNNY MILLS)

Now three years old, the WPA had embarked on and completed a wide array of projects. False starts such as the Florida ship canal and the occasional dry lake notwithstanding, there was much to be proud of. The agency had to its credit masterpieces small and large, from Art Project murals and structures built by hand of native stone and wood to the imposing array of art, craft, and architecture that was the Timberline Lodge.

But the largest component of the work program was, as Hopkins had pointed out, road building. WPA crews built and repaired roads and streets in cities, often joining works already under way. In San Francisco, for example, the majestic Golden Gate Bridge had been started with bond financing in 1933, prior to Roosevelt's inauguration, but before it was completed and opened in May 1937, the WPA had contributed by building one of its approaches. The agency built new roads through remote areas, its workers living in field camps far from home. Its major aim from the beginning had been to improve the more than 2 million miles of dirt and gravel roads that were the main links between farms and market towns. The work, which included clearing right-of-way, digging and clearing drainage ditches, building culverts and small bridges, widening and scraping roads, and often resurfacing them with gravel or crushed stone made on the spot with rocks dug from the roadside, gave paying jobs to many farmers who for a variety of reasons could not force a cash income from their farms. One of these was Johnny Mills.

Mills lived in a one-industry county in the hardscrabble mountains of western North Carolina. That industry was paper, its one plant the Mead Paper Company factory in the Jackson County seat of Sylva. It spewed from its smokestacks a vile mixture that hung over the hills like thick white wool and smelled like rotten eggs. He had gone through the sixth grade in school and done odd jobs since. He met Shirley Shuler at her sister's wedding party in 1936. He was a ropey five-nine with a head of jet-black hair, she was a brunette with a beautiful smile, and it was not long after the party that they started to talk of getting married. Mills was twenty-one but Shirley was only sixteen, which was why, when the day came—April 17, 1937—they had to drive the forty miles from Sylva across the state line to Clayton, Georgia, to get married. It was no spur-of-the-moment elopement, though. Shirley wore a blue silk dress and Mills a blue serge suit he'd bought for $16 at the Sylva Supply Company; Judge Frank A. Smith, the Clayton County ordinary, read the vows; and Shirley's mother put on a wedding supper in their honor when they got back home.

They moved in with Shirley's grandfather, a widower who needed help keeping up his ninety acres in the Willets community north of Sylva, on the way up Balsam Mountain. They ate what the cornfield and the garden and the chickens and hogs and a single milk cow produced; Shirley churned butter, canned vegetables, and preserved fruit, and Johnny continued to pick up the day work that bought the flour and shortening and coffee and sugar and lamp oil that the land could not provide. He hoed corn, he picked apples across the ridge at Barber's orchard, he went into the woods and felled and hauled the blight-killed chestnut trees that the Mead Paper Company prized for making paper.

"I worked many a day for a dollar," he said.

But the day work and the land together were not enough to give them a doctor's care when Shirley got pregnant. As her delivery date in April 1938 approached, Mills needed a regular job, and there was only one prospect: the WPA. From their spot on the mountain, he could walk down to the road to pick up a bus or flag down a south-bound train. The bus ride cost 20 cents and so did the train, so his preferred ride to town was one he could hitch for free aboard one of the log trucks hauling wood to "the Mead," as locals called the paper factory. Sylva was a single long main street of stores crowned by the Jackson County courthouse atop a hill at the west end, with a parallel lower-level street behind the stores that ran alongside the railroad tracks and Scott's Creek, a tributary of the Tuckaseigee River. The WPA office was on the main street.

Mills made the trip to town with some trepidation. He was a Republican. There were a number of them in the mountains of this southern state, descendants of the pro-Union strain that had survived since the Civil War in the areas of the South where there were no plantations and no slaves. As a Republican, he worried that the WPA would not be open to him. This was the way it worked with state jobs controlled by Democrats. He had seen the evidence the year before, when Roosevelt had passed through Sylva on his way from the Great Smoky Mountains National Park to Asheville, and the Democrats had shut the schools and county and town offices to line the streets with a show of election-year support. The president had gone straight through without stopping on a warm September day, waving from the open window of the car.

Hopkins himself had confronted this very fear in his first news conference back on the job in Washington after his convalescence. Reporters had greeted him with questions about the relief situation and politics in Pennsylvania, where charges were flying that WPA workers had been told their jobs depended on a certain way of voting.

"These things crop up every year at election time," Hopkins said wearily. "I have said often before, and I repeat again that I do not care how these people on WPA vote. They can vote for anybody they please, and nobody will lose his job or be penalized in any way because he votes for this man or the other man. Furthermore, if any official of the WPA is found doing any funny business on political fronts... he will be fired at once, and I do not have to ask anybody about whether I shall fire him or not. I do not intend to tolerate any political interference in the WPA."

Apparently the Jackson County WPA supervisor, Cary Henson, had taken Hopkins's words—and frequent memoranda to the same effect—to heart. "He was a good fellow," said Mills. "He was a Democrat, but he wanted to be fair. He'd lived up in the mountains and he knew how it was. The politics didn't matter to him."

Mills was certified and put on a road crew. Like state highway departments across the nation, North Carolina's had seized on the WPA to improve its road system, specifically those linking farms to market towns. In western North Carolina, as elsewhere, these roads were rarely paved and seldom even graveled; paving was reserved for federal highways and the state roads linking county seats. The rest—again reflecting the country as a whole—were descendants of horse tracks and wagon trails, widened over the years to meet the needs of motor vehicles but still likely to swim with mud during rainy seasons and harden into washboards of red clay when it was dry. Indeed, of the 351 miles of rural and secondary roads in Jackson County, less than half a mile was paved. Road work was not the WPA's only focus in the county, where it had spent $175,000 through January 1937; the WPA sewing room in Sylva employed about twenty women; and a rich supply of native mica-flecked granite had gone into a school building in the Webster community and a gymnasium on the campus of Western Carolina Teachers College in Cullowhee, where two other WPA buildings were also on the drawing board. Still, here roads were the WPA's primary work.

Mills began a routine that started at around four in the morning, in the darkness before dawn. He groped his way into his overalls, stumbled into the kitchen, where he lit a kerosene lamp and pulled on his boots, then plunged out the door into the chilly air, his lantern illuminating his path to the barn. Once he had milked the cow, he returned to the house, where Shirley was now up, frying eggs and making biscuits for their breakfast. Then he pulled on a coat, tugged his hat down, and took the lunch she had made—usually a sandwich of fried pork or chicken, more biscuits, and maybe a piece of pie or cake since she would rather bake than cook, all wrapped in wax paper or folded in a piece of flour sacking—and walked the mile down to the highway, where he waited for a state truck that would carry him and the other men on the road crew to the job site.

The day's work varied with the roads and their condition. Specifications called for widening all roadbeds to twenty feet in anticipation of greater future traffic flow; in the mountains, where the roads often were cut out of steep hillsides, this meant digging away the embankments on the high side to gain width and dumping the dirt onto the low side to stabilize the roadway. "Shovels and wheelbarrows is what we used," Mills said, "and we cleaned ditches out, and worked like that."

Where graveling was called for, the men broke rocks and loaded them into trucks, and then unloaded the rocks into portable crushers that would reduce them to gravel. "A road hog crusher, it was called," he remembered. "We dumped the rock there in that crusher and it come out with a man on either side, spreading that gravel on the road." They would cover a section of the road and then move to another section and repeat the routine.

Certain levels of disability did not bar a man from working on a road crew, at least in western North Carolina. Shirley's father, who had lost his left arm to blood poisoning from an infected cut, had learned to hoe a corn row with his right by rigging a metal loop to a leather belt that he wore outside his overalls and fixing the hoe handle in the loop. When Mills was assigned to a crew working on Yellow Mountain near Cashiers, a resort town about twenty miles from Sylva, he found his one-armed father-in-law distributing water from a milk can he carried on his hip to the men who were hauling rocks and spreading gravel.

Unlike the big-city road crews and the crews that worked out of camps assembled from a statewide labor force, Mills knew most of his fellow laborers. "There wasn't hardly anybody in Jackson County you didn't know," he said.

The money he earned from the WPA—he recalled making about $44 a month, the rural rate for unskilled labor—paid for the doctor who attended Shirley when she gave birth. Patricia, their first child, was born without complications at home on April 8, 1938, with Sylva's Dr. D. D. Hooper in attendance. Mills continued on the WPA for two more years, through the birth of their second child, joining road crews when new projects got the green light and stacking his shovel when they were waiting for approval.

Mills found it strange that some people were ashamed of working for the WPA, and that others criticized men like him as idlers: "When people talked about, you know, leaning on the shovel, well, we did a whole lot of work. And a whole lot of hard work. I guess there was some that thought you was on relief, but I know I was working for money when I was doing that. It wasn't no different than no other job. You earned the money. You know, it was for the needy people. Good people, they can't always help hard times, tough luck. I always figured I tried to make a living for my family. And it was a help to us."

8. KENTUCKY ARCHAEOLOGY
(JOHN B. ELLIOTT)

Archaeology and the WPA had proved to be the perfect match of dovetailing necessities: archaeology that needed labor to excavate prehistoric sites and the WPA for providing that labor. The Smithsonian Institution was well aware of the expanded possibilities the jobs program was providing, and pursued them eagerly. Marksville, Louisiana, where digging for a town swimming pool had shifted to excavating a Hopewell Indian village, was the first dig to use relief labor under FERA, but Smithsonian archaeologists were alert to other opportunities. When the CWA was created in the winter of 1933–34, the Smithsonian moved quickly, applying for grants and then setting up digs in warm-weather states where work could proceed without breaks for snow and cold and frozen ground. CWA excavations employing about 1,500 workers were set up in Georgia, Florida, North Carolina, Tennessee, and California under the Smithsonian's supervision. The largest of these was an extensive mound site on the Ocmulgee River outside Macon, Georgia, and it and several other digs continued under FERA and then the WPA.

At the same time, the Tennessee Valley Authority recognized that its plan to flood vast parts of the river valleys in the Tennessee River system in order to build hydroelectric dams had archaeological implications. Major sites in Alabama, Tennessee, North Carolina, and Kentucky would be lost forever to archaeology once the dam flood-gates closed and water crept up over the land, so by early 1934 the TVA had developed a program that was employing more than 1,000 CWA workers to excavate and remove Indian artifacts below those dams.

The head of TVA archaeology was William S. Webb, who by the WPA's third year must have been the busiest archaeologist since Howard Carter discovered King Tut's tomb. A physicist who had turned an amateur's passion for archaeology into a career, Webb had chaired the University of Kentucky's Department of Anthropology and Archaeology since its creation in 1927. In addition to that post and the TVA, in the summer of 1937 he shifted his attention long enough to submit a proposal for a major archaeological program in Kentucky. He and his colleague William D. Funkhouser had already redefined what was known about Native American cultures in the Southeast, which ranged from simple hunting, fishing, and gathering to moder-ately evolved societies that lived in villages, farmed, fired pottery, made weapons and tools of stone and flint, and constructed elaborate burial mounds. The valleys of the Ohio and its feeder rivers were par-ticularly rich grounds for exploration, with evidence of cultures known as the Hopewell, Mississippian, Fort Ancient, and Adena all represented. Since relief labor continued to be available, Webb now envisioned excavations of sites throughout northern Kentucky. When the WPA approved his plan in August, Webb started sending cables and making phone calls.

He recruited a group of young archaeologists as supervisors, choos-ing those with field experience if he could find them. The man he put in charge, William Haag, had a master's degree in geology from the University of Kentucky and a year of graduate work in vertebrate pa-leontology, and he had worked on TVA projects for three years. Webb's plan was to have Haag organize a dig, then turn it over to one of the other supervisors, and move on to organize another. Late in the year, Webb contacted a young Chicagoan named John B. Elliott.

Elliott was among the fortunate students whose families could af-ford to keep them in college during the depression. His father was an engineer with the American Bridge Company and unlike the majority of engineers had retained his job. Elliott had earned an undergraduate degree in archaeology from the University of Chicago in 1933 and was working on his master's when he contracted colitis. He was sick for a year, then transferred to the University of Illinois to study agriculture; his family owned land in New Harmony, Indiana, and he saw farming as something he would do eventually. But when his course of study was completed a year later, he realized he wasn't ready to start farming. Archaeology remained his first love, but no jobs beckoned. Time passed and Elliott, spare and wiry and now twenty-five, found himself managing one of the Childs chain of restaurants that were popular in Chicago and New York, and wondering if he would ever find work in his chosen field.

His fiancée, Josephine Mirabella, was impatient, too. Like Elliott, she had graduated from the University of Chicago. She spoke French and Italian fluently, but had to take a job as a file clerk for an insurance company until her degree in languages finally landed her a job teaching French in the Chicago schools. When Chicago could again afford to pay its teachers, she made about $70 a month, as did Elliott. It was an income that many Americans caught in the depression would have envied, but not what the young couple thought they needed to get married.

Then, one night in early December, Elliott phoned Jo at home. His voice was quivering with excitement. He told her that a Western Union messenger had shown up at his parents' door earlier that day with a telegram addressed to him. It came from a big-time archaeologist named William Webb. Years later, Jo remembered that John had sounded "as if the moon, sun, and stars had fallen in his lap." As he reminded her, the two summers he'd spent at the University of Chicago's archaeology field school in southern Illinois were the happiest times of his life. Now, not only did he have the chance to work in archaeology, but Webb was offering him the grand sum of $160 every month as a non-relief field supervisor, more than the two of them were making together. They would be able to get married.

Elliott spent $400 of his savings on a new Ford pickup truck. He celebrated Christmas at home, then left for western Kentucky without waiting for the new year, driving south through the winter countryside. He crossed the Ohio River at Evansville, Indiana, and continued south until he reached Calhoun, Kentucky, the McLean County seat.

Calhoun lay on the Green River, which meandered west and north from central Kentucky and spilled into the Ohio near Evansville. The town was the rough center of a scattering of prehistoric villages arrayed along the river. These villages were marked by shell mounds that their inhabitants had used as tombs and garbage middens, and Webb was interested in what they might reveal about Native American cultures during the Archaic period, roughly 8000 to 1000 B.C. He wanted to see how they compared with mounds already excavated in the Wheeler River basin in north-central Alabama under the TVA archaeology program, which were consistent with the Mississippian sites found throughout the Mississippi River valley.

Calhoun turned out to be a sleepy town, suspicious of change and wary of outsiders, especially those who had come to dig in the mounds. Its citizens thought of the mounds as their own: not only their heritage but also a potential source of income from the pots and other artifacts that an enterprising digger could sell on the open market for hard cash. This information Elliott learned from his dour, elderly landlady, who had carved two rooms out of her house and turned them into a makeshift apartment that she rented for $15 a month. She complained about the digging. "Doesn't the WPA have better things to spend the government's money on?" she demanded of her lodger. Nonetheless, she was happy to collect his rent in that winter of renewed recession.

There were half a dozen mound sites on the Green River in McLean County. When Elliott arrived in late December, work was just starting on one of them, the Read Shell Midden. Among the others were Indian Knoll, the Carlson Annis Mound, Chiggerville, and the Cypress Creek villages. He observed the efforts going on at Read, then in February 1938 moved to Cypress Creek to get the work under way there.

The Cypress Creek villages were a collection of several sites, as the name implied. Elliott was to start at Ward, named for the nearest community of any consequence. The site stood at the end of a rutted dirt track that gave way to an open knoll, part of a ridge that overlooked a valley two miles wide. Elliott assembled a crew of some twenty-five men, most of them farmers and out-of-work miners certified for WPA relief jobs. He needed to cover a lot of ground in a few months. Webb and Haag wanted to reveal the village structure, so they had ordered him to do a comprehensive excavation. But Elliott's first test was to impress on the men the need to dig carefully, making sure they destroyed none of the artifacts that the excavation might reveal. The process was exacting. The men couldn't dig as if they were sinking postholes; they had to "shave" the soil with light horizontal sweeps of the shovel in order to uncover any protruding artifacts. At that point, diggers took over whom Elliott had briefed on the special techniques of finer work. They used small trowels and even smaller tools for the painstaking work of extracting what they had found. Working through a cold winter and a rainy spring, his WPA crew picked up the archaeological work quickly. They impressed him from the beginning.

Weapons, tools, vessels, and bones—human and animal bones from ritual burials, bones shaped into crude fishhooks or spear and arrow points, a spear launcher called an atlatl, even bones that were the remnants of meals—would add detail and color to the archaeological picture. Elliott handled all these objects carefully, for removal later to the laboratory at the University of Kentucky. From them Webb would be able to determine that the Indians who had inhabited the site hunted deer, rabbits, wild turkeys, raccoons, and opossums, and gathered roots and berries. He guessed that they had lived there roughly 1,000 to 2,000 years before, during a transition from the hunting-and-gathering Archaic period to the more evolved mound building of the Mississippian, a time known as the Woodland Period.

Elliott worked at the Ward site into the summer. In July, when the school year ended for Jo, he returned to Chicago for their long-awaited wedding. Her Italian family almost succeeded in derailing the plan because of their objections to her marrying a Methodist who didn't even go to church. But the couple fell upon the mercies of a sympathetic priest, Father Molinari, who married them in his offices at St. Michael's, the Roman Catholic church in the Mirabella family's West Side neighborhood. In exchange, Jo promised that she would raise their children in the Catholic Church.

Back in Kentucky, the newlyweds felt crowded in the two rooms that had been large enough for Elliott when he was on his own. His work routine governed their lives. Each weekday morning, they woke in the dark, and he dressed in his archaeologist's wardrobe of khakis and work boots while she cooked breakfast. Her breakfasts—all her meals, in fact—were an adventure in those early stages of their marriage, since she had grown up in a wealthy home and never learned to cook. The landlady provided additional distraction, sometimes joining their breakfast conversations from her side of the door and indicating some resentment at no longer being asked to make Elliott's lunch. Jo did it now, usually a sandwich that she wrapped in wax paper and put into his lunchbox. Carrying this, a thermos of coffee, and a large milk jug of water, he would climb into his truck and set off as the clock struck six.

He was gone for twelve hours on most days, and then he came in carrying the results of the day's excavations. With space at a premium, he would roll up the findings in a blanket and store them under the bed, and after dinner, he would write up his field notes. Jo got used to the idea of sleeping over Indian bones.

But she did chafe at the lack of social life in Calhoun. The days were long and she had little to do, and when the weekends came he wanted to relax from his week's labors while she wished that the small town had at least a movie theater. Church socials seemed to be the only diversion, but the Elliotts had not turned into churchgoers overnight. And while Owensboro, a larger town with theaters and a bowling alley, was less than twenty miles away, there was the cost of gasoline to think about. Jo was saving $60 a month from her husband's salary.

Thus their chief social opportunities came on the one weekend a month when the field supervisors from the Green River and other Kentucky digs traveled to Lexington to report to Webb and Haag and present the artifacts they had unearthed for lab analysis.

They usually left for these weekends on Friday morning unless Elliott wanted to get in another half day of work, in which case they couldn't count on reaching Lexington until well after dark. Kentucky's rural roads, even those that had benefited from the WPA's improvements, were twisty two-laners, and the drive in the pickup was slow and rough. Once in Lexington, they would throw their bags into the spare bedroom of whichever member of the archaeology faculty they were staying with that month. Nobody had money for hotels. Jo remembered sitting around kitchen tables talking with other archaeologists' wives, happy to have a conversation that didn't involve bones and arrowheads, while the men talked shop.

On Saturdays the field supervisors and faculty came together for all-day discussions of the prior month's findings and what they signified. Then, after a large communal dinner—sometimes the group would splurge and eat at a restaurant in one of Lexington's hotels—and one more night in the various guest rooms, the field men and their families would drive back to their scattered outposts.

Elliott finished his work at the Ward site in September and moved on to Kirkland, another site in the Cypress Creek villages group. Rather than hiring new workers whom he would have to train, he took most of his WPA crew to the new site with him; it was close enough to allow them to commute. Kirkland was another large dig, and he worked it from September 20 until after the elections in November before moving to a third site.

All the while, the Cypress Creek sites he and the other field supervisors were unearthing, and the artifacts they carried to Lexington, were helping Webb and Haag to enlarge and sharpen their picture of the life lived by the ancient Indians in what was now Kentucky. As they noted when they wrote of the site at Chiggerville, where a shell midden was excavated earlier in 1938, it could have been done only partially or not at all if there had not been WPA labor. With it, "it was possible to excavate so considerable a portion of this site that its whole history was revealed."

9. HURRICANE!

On the morning of Wednesday, September 21, 1938, coastal residents of Long Island and New England were enjoying lingering end-of-season warmth and thinking of storing their beach chairs and umbrellas. The skies were clear and the winds calm. The Eastern States Exposition in West Springfield, Massachusetts, was open for another day of agricultural exhibits, midway games, and shows, and four huge Ferris wheels were lined up side by side among the rides luring children and adults alike. The *New York Times* looked at the state of weather forecasting and pronounced it good. An editorial lauded the role of "an admirably organized meteorological service" in informing the world about the approach of hurricanes.

But to the south, the ships and scientific stations that comprised the warning network the *Times* referred to were being taken by surprise. A hurricane in the South Atlantic, rather than drifting out to sea, had swung on a path that paralleled the coast. Squeezed between two high-pressure systems, it was barreling north at sixty miles an hour and gathering strength from the warm waters of the Gulf Stream. The hurricane passed Cape Hatteras, North Carolina, at seven in the morning. By noon it reached New Jersey.

The blow that struck New Jersey was a glancing one, wrecking the boardwalk at Manasquan, fatally weakening the bridge between Atlantic City and Brigantine, and ruining much of the unharvested tomato and apple crops. New York City too was inconvenienced more than harmed. Sixty-five-mile-an-hour winds tore through Manhattan's streets, ripping down awnings and shop signs and forcing pedestrians to clutch their hats. Heavy rains flooded cellars and roadways, blocking traffic and disrupting subway and rail service. One man drowned when he tried to swim from a swamped car near the Queens waterfront at Whitestone Landing and two more were lost at Throgs Neck in the Bronx after rescuing residents from the rising waters of Long Island Sound. The force of the wind against the high sides of the arriving French passenger liner *Ile de France,* 791 feet long, was so great that it took twelve tugboats instead of the usual six to wrestle the ship into its berth at a Hudson River pier. Heaving seas plunged the rail of one of the Staten Island ferries under a dock protrusion, where the vessel locked; it was halfway to capsizing with 200 passengers aboard before tugs could pull it free.

Farther east, conditions were far worse. At one-thirty in the afternoon, a barometer reading taken on the exposed south shore of Long Island showed 29.78 inches of air pressure. By three o'clock, the barometric pressure was 27.43 inches, a stunningly steep drop that prefigured a drastic change. The wind increased steadily from forty miles an hour to ninety. Blowing sand burned the skin raw.

As the hours passed, the wind kept rising, and circled so that it came directly off the ocean. Waves that had been glancing along the shoreline now came from straight offshore. In the late afternoon, people with a view of the beach looked out to sea and saw what they thought was a low fog bank headed toward the shore. When they realized it was not fog but a wall of water bearing down on them, for most it was too late to run. The huge wave crashed across the fragile barrier islands that protected the South Shore, burrowed channels through the dunes, and ripped through the residential areas behind them, sweeping homes off their foundations and carrying the nail-spiked wreckage inland to smash more houses as it went. Residents scrambled to their attics only to have their houses crumble under them. Others swam for their lives. Very few made it. Among the victims was twenty-one-year-old Thomas Fay of Quogue, the captain of the Colgate University golf team; his body washed up at Hampton Bays six days later.

The resort communities of Fire Island were decimated—Ocean Beach lost 300 homes, Fair Harbor and Saltaire at least 100 each. At East Hampton, a Long Island Rail Road train tumbled off the tracks where the surge had undercut the roadbed. On Long Island Sound, hundreds of yachts lost their moorings and were wrecked along the North Shore of the island. The manager at Greenport's Metro Theater evacuated the house minutes before the wind blew the building down. At Sag Harbor, the 125-foot steeple of the Old Whalers' Church was ripped from the roof and fell into the churchyard.

The hurricane reached Connecticut, Rhode Island, and Massachusetts with no warning whatsoever. Its speed, together with the downed telephone and telegraph wires that lined its destructive path, wiped out communications. At first people thought they were experiencing one of those blows that seemed to arrive every year around the autumnal equinox. But as the wind increased and drove rain past tightly sealed doors and windows, the realization dawned that New England was in for something worse.

Coastal residents at Charlestown-by-the-Sea, Rhode Island, between Newport and Stonington, Connecticut, said the wave coming off the ocean was sixty or seventy feet high. This was surely an exaggeration, but not by much. At Watch Hill, a few miles to the west, the surge arrived in disastrous conjunction with the astronomical high tide. It crashed across the Napatree Point peninsula, swept away every one of the forty-four summer cottages on the narrow, curving strip of sand, broke the local yacht club in two and carried the debris across Little Narragansett Bay to the shoreline of Connecticut. E. L. Reynolds, the assistant fire chief, said, "Some of the houses just blew up like feathers."

The surge roared past Newport and up Narragansett Bay. At the island town of Jamestown, at the entrance to the bay, seven children drowned when the wave swept their school bus off a causeway and into deep water. In Providence, workers left their offices to head for home and found eight feet of water in the streets and a paralyzed transportation system. By then the water was rising so quickly they had to scramble up fire escapes to save their lives. At the Rhode Island Hospital Trust Building, a plaque marking the high-water mark in an 1815 storm was submerged under three feet of water. At the busy waterfront, the wave tore workboats from their moorings and slammed them into bridges, docks, port offices, and warehouses.

In the ports and coastal resorts and islands of Connecticut and Massachusetts, the big wave decimated workboats, fishing fleets, and yachts, smashed dwellings large and small, and took the lives of the rich and poor alike. Actor James Cagney lost only a few trees at his Martha's Vineyard home but reported that the fishing fleet at Menemsha had been destroyed. The flood short-circuited electric wires at New London, Connecticut, an hour after the surge passed, and fire broke out in a four-block section of the downtown business area. Firemen fought the blaze in water up to their necks, directing their hoses toward the flames only to have the wind blow the hose water back into their faces until a wind shift finally let them gain control.

At the Eastern States Exposition, Connecticut governor Wilbur L. Cross had laid the cornerstone of his state's building along the Avenue of States—the fairground's main drag with replicas of each New England statehouse—just the day before. The midway offered the usual collection of carny shows and come-ons; the four huge Ferris wheels invited riders to view from high above the panorama that included a racetrack where Jimmy Roach's Hell Drivers skidded and spun through a repertoire of death-defying high-speed auto tricks. Exhibitor S. G. Hyatt, the H. D. Hudson farm equipment company's New England representative, was set up in a large tent showing off the company's poultry and dairy barn equipment, crop sprayers, garden tools, and ventilators. The display featured the latest in cow-watering devices and poultry incubators.

As the wind rose, the operator of the Ferris wheels emptied the rides and removed the seats as a precaution. Without them, he said, the wind would simply blow through the open frames of the wheels. This prediction was as accurate as the forecasts that failed to anticipate the storm. Fairgoers watched as the wheels began to sway and tip, until the first toppled onto the second and they all fell like dominos into a pile of twisted steel. At the H. D. Hudson tent, a dozen baby chicks peeped on a bed of straw under a warming lightbulb in their brooder until the winds collapsed the tent into a mound of sopping canvas. Hyatt crawled under the pile, retrieved the chicks, and took them home in a cardboard box. Afterward, he would say he saved twelve lives. He was one of the few who were able to speak easily about the storm.

The water from the storm surge receded almost as quickly as it had come. But along the Connecticut River, the crisis was just beginning. The rain falling on already saturated earth loosened the roots of trees, which fell by the thousands in the wind. And as the river rose during the night, the first news of the disaster, spread by teams of young ham radio operators, began to reach the outside world.

President Roosevelt was still in bed at six-thirty on the morning of Thursday, September 22, when his press secretary, Marvin H. McIntyre, told him of the extent of the devastation. By nine o'clock, the WPA, along with the Coast Guard, the army and navy, the CCC, and the Red Cross, had field agents headed to Long Island and New England. Hopkins, in California, telephoned to say he was cutting his trip short and would take the first available plane headed east. Meanwhile, his deputy, Aubrey Williams, instructed Ray Branion, now the WPA's regional administrator for New England after his transfer from California, to muster every available worker for flood rescue in Hartford and elsewhere on the Connecticut River, and for body searches along the coast. Williams also ordered the WPA's acting chief of engineers, Major B. M. Harloe, to fly over the hurricane zone to map out a rehabilitation plan. Before the day was out, he was briefing the president on the WPA's plans for debris removal and the restoration of roads, bridges, and public health facilities.

As the storm clouds moved north, leaving their trail of destruction, among the structures that stood tall and strong amid the ruins were some of the works of the WPA. WPA-built seawalls along coastal beaches had withstood the brutal storm surge. A bathing pavilion at Scarborough State Beach at Narragansett, Rhode Island, built by the WPA the year before, stood in solitary relief on a beach where everything around it had been reduced to rubble. Flood control dams on the Connecticut and Nashua rivers, installed by WPA crews after the floods of 1936, were yet to be tested.

The hurricane winds and rain disappeared as quickly as they came. Hartford residents awoke on Thursday morning to a soft autumn day with hazy sun and puffy clouds. Hartford itself, west of the Connecticut River, was disheveled, with fallen trees and wind damage, but dry. But across the river in East Hartford, the river had overflowed and inundated businesses and rail yards. And it was still rising, threatening the west bank residences and the central business district, including the Colt arms factory and offices two blocks from the river. Factory workers frantically moved machines and supplies in threatened areas to higher ground and boat patrols were mustered to evacuate residents. Forecasters revised their predictions of high water ever upward. By the afternoon, WPA workers mobilized from throughout the region, along with CCC campers, world war veterans, college students, and other volunteers, descended on the southeast section of the city in the attempt to save homes and protect the semi-industrial area, which had been severely damaged in the flooding two years earlier.

By Thursday night WPA and other laborers were filling sandbags and loading them into trucks. More WPA men stacked the bags on dikes along the river and at the ends of streets that stopped at the river's edge. From where they worked along the sandbag barriers, the men could look out toward the river and see the Bartlett-Brainard Construction Company building with water halfway up its windows. And the water continued to rise at a rate of almost two inches an hour.

The WPA's local representative, Thomas F. Foley, directed the operation while the state administrator, Vincent J. Sullivan, was fighting his way over debris-blocked and flooded roads from New Haven to Hartford. Working without sleep out of the Colt offices, Foley paused between urgent phone conversations to hobble outside on a sprained right ankle to monitor weak spots in the dike and keep track of the flood's rise. In charge of a thousand men, he worked them into Friday night, when the water finally peaked within inches of the tops of the last sandbags and began to slowly fall. When Sullivan arrived at last, he set up refugee centers in the schools, and within them stocked playrooms with toys and games for children left homeless by the storm. He organized a radio appeal for more toys, and bands from the Federal Music Project played popular music for children and their parents at the refugee centers.

East Hampton, Connecticut, well away from the river, also had to cope with rising waters. Lake Pocotopaug had spilled over a company dam and filled the local streets; a breach of the dam would wipe out the town. For forty-eight hours, WPA workers, along with CCC men and volunteers, fought non-stop to save the dam. They won the fight, but the waters receded so slowly that on Saturday, four days after the hurricane, a local man was still able to catch a seventeen-and-a-half-pound carp on Main Street. More WPA men worked in the town of Ware, Massachusetts, making emergency repairs on three vital bridges over the Ware River. Elsewhere in Massachusetts, in Springfield, Holyoke, Amherst, Southbridge, and Fitchburg, the WPA joined workers from the CCC and the military to stack sandbags against flooding, evacuate residents from flooded neighborhoods, carry invalids from hospitals to higher ground, repair bridges and clear them of debris, and restore order during states of emergency when looting broke out in some of the devastated areas. In Manchester, New Hampshire, the WPA labored to raise walls of sandbags against the Merrimack and Piscataquog Rivers.

Meanwhile, the WPA-built flood control dams on the Connecticut and Nashua withstood the worst the downrushing waters had to offer until the crests finally receded and the rivers settled back toward their normal levels.

WPA workers marshaled to the coast of Rhode Island found their work grim. There, thousands of men from the WPA and CCC, joined by volunteers, searched low-lying areas for bodies. Windblown and waterborne debris hampered their work, and in some places sand was several feet deeper than it had been before the hurricane. More WPA workers waited alongside bulldozers and tractors that were disassembling the wreckage of houses and boats where bodies might lie hidden.

WPA workers also joined the search for the dead at New Bedford, Massachusetts, where the seaside community of Crescent Beach had been swept by a wall of water that destroyed a mile-long stretch of waterfront and left only five houses standing.

By Friday morning, there were 100,000 WPA workers in the field on Long Island and throughout New England. Even as search-and-rescue efforts were giving way to cleanup, one crew in Rhode Island found a man alive buried under eight feet of wreckage where the storm had passed forty hours earlier. Hopkins, back from the West Coast, summoned the governors of the devastated states to a meeting in Boston to review their needs for help. Throughout the region, WPA sewing rooms put aside their other work to produce clothing for flood victims. WPA nurses and nutritionists staffed refugee centers at schools and infirmaries, and kindergarten teachers set up children's playrooms.

On Sunday, Hopkins toured the area by air and car from Providence.

There were 260 dead in Rhode Island with the body count still rising, 10,000 homes had been destroyed or damaged, and losses were estimated at $100 million. Hopkins saw WPA workers digging through the ruins, talked to eyewitnesses of the hurricane, and returned from his day-long tour with a terse assessment. "From what I've seen today, I would say the situation is very bad," he said. He estimated that the WPA could spend $25 million rebuilding the region "without wasting a penny," and added, "We will do whatever needs to be done."

The eventual death toll from the New England hurricane reached 682, with 1,700 injured. Almost 9,000 homes and other buildings were destroyed and another 15,000 damaged. Some 2,600 boats, from working and fishing boats to yachts, were lost and another 3,300 damaged. And then there was the decimated landscape, with countless trees that had been blown down or otherwise uprooted now being reduced to sawdust by the workers of the WPA in their fast-moving cleanup. But so swift and efficient was that recovery work that by late November, the storm debris had largely disappeared and much of New England was looking forward to a normal winter. Red Cross chairman Norman H. Davis credited the WPA among the agencies contributing to "one of the most amazing disaster recoveries this organization has ever known."

PART VII

A government agency, supported by public funds, has become part and parcel of the Communist party.
—REPRESENTATIVE J. PARNELL THOMAS

I must express my ... disappointment over the very un-American way in which the committee has handled charges against this project.
—ELLEN S. WOODWARD, DIRECTOR, WPA WOMEN'S AND
PROFESSIONAL PROJECTS

1. WAR AMONG THE DEMOCRATS

The fury of the New England hurricane was short-lived compared to the turbulence that had been roiling the Democratic Party since the summer, when Roosevelt had launched a battle for its soul and in the process, the New Deal's legislative prospects. After the failed special session of Congress at the end of 1937 that left him empty-handed, his opponents had trumpeted their new power in a "Conservative Manifesto." This document, produced by a bipartisan coalition led by southern Democrats with the tacit support of Vice President Garner, denounced the sit-down strikes in the steel and auto industries, called for tax cuts and a balanced budget, condemned federal intrusion on states' and employers' rights, and warned that agencies such as the the WPA would lead to a permanent welfare class.

Although the wage-and-hours law and the farm bill had been passed by the following summer, the president remained unsatisfied. As he saw it, an "uncompromisingly liberal" platform had brought about the Democratic landslide of 1936, yet the Seventy-fifth Congress produced in that election had not responded fully to this mandate. In a June 24 fireside chat, Roosevelt had gone on the attack.

"Never before have we had so many Copperheads among us," he said, alluding to the Democratic appeasers who had opposed the Civil

War and urged Lincoln and Congress to give up the fight against seces-
sion as the price for peace. They had their modern equivalent, he said,
in the legislators who now would cave in to "that small minority
which, in spite of its own disastrous leadership in 1929, is always eager to resume its control over the Government of the United States."
Democratic primary voters should ask themselves which side a candidate was on. "An election cannot give the country a firm sense of direction if it has two or more national parties which merely have
different names but are as alike in their principles and aims as peas in
the same pod," he warned.

But the protests that flooded the White House after the broadcast
ranged from discomfiture to outright anger. A Methodist minister
from Kokomo, Indiana, wrote, "No great leader can ever afford to
stoop to do what you proposed regarding your opposition. This is a
democracy and it is *healthy* to have a strong opposition. No man is always right. You need criticism for your own good." A Cincinnatian
used a telegram to lambaste the president's single-mindedness: "I RE-
SENT BEING CALLED A COPPERHEAD BY ONE WHOSE EGO-
TISM FAST APPROACHES MANIA."

Obviously, he also received messages of support, but when he set
out in the summer and early fall 1938 primaries to campaign against
Democrats he considered obstructionist, including Senators Ellison
"Cotton Ed" Smith in South Carolina, Walter George in Georgia, and
Millard Tydings in Maryland, the voters resisted. There was a racial
component in these southern races; Smith was a virulent racist who
had walked out of the 1936 Democratic National Convention in
Philadelphia when a black pastor rose to deliver the invocation, say-
ing, "By God, he's as black as melted midnight. Get outta my way.
This mongrel meeting ain't no place for a white man." George and
Tydings were less coarse, at least in public, but as implacably segrega-
tionist.

In fact, Roosevelt had already conceded to the southerners over
race, heeding the warning of North Carolina senator Josiah Bailey
early in his first term that "no administration can survive without us."
With Bailey's words ringing in his ears, he had refrained from strongly
endorsing an anti-lynching bill that had been offered by Senators
Robert Wagner of New York and Edward Costigan of Colorado in
1934. It followed a rash of twenty-eight lynchings, primarily in the

South, the year before. These killings were public spectacles of racist bloodlust. Mobs snatched their victims from jails under the noses of the police and sheriff's deputies who were supposed to be protecting them, often tortured them before hanging, and then dragged their bodies behind cars or burned them. Photographs of bodies dangling from tree trunks, surrounded by spectators, routinely appeared in local newspapers. The pressure to speak out mounted after a particularly grotesque lynching in Maryland of a black man accused of attacking a white woman; it was followed by the murder of two white men who were taken from a jail and hanged in San Jose, California. Roosevelt spoke up at last, condemning lynching as "a vile form of public murder" and decrying those in "high places or low who condone lynch law." But this was as far as he was willing to go. If he supported the Wagner-Costigan bill, southerners elevated to power by the congressional seniority system would "block every bill [he proposed] to keep America from collapsing." "I did not choose the tools with which I must work," he said in May 1934, and in the years thereafter he kept his silence despite entreaties from black leaders and from his wife to support similar bills introduced in every single session of Congress.

Yet this deference had not paid the desired dividends. The bipartisan "Conservative Manifesto" signaled a newly cohesive resistance to the New Deal's push to make the central government a regulator and protector. The Liberty League had spoken for the bankers and industrialists starting in 1934, and the Republican National Committee for the party faithful rendered powerless by the elections of 1932 through 1936. But neither had been able to do more than express anger and frustration until the manifesto. It was different; it erected a bulwark against the kinds of progressive laws that had swept through Congress in the president's first term and, with Hugo Black now replacing Willis Van Devanter and the moderates moving to the left, were being upheld by the Supreme Court. Indeed, it was this southern and rural conservative strain, with racism as its subtext, that waved the flag of individualism, sided with business against unions, and favored states' and property rights over government controls. It was to animate the political divide into the next century.

Whether or not Roosevelt foresaw saw the depth and tenacity of these divisions, he clearly felt an urgency about advancing his agenda. He had asked his fireside chat listeners for "all the help I can get."

They should reject "outspoken reactionaries" who "have fought against progress with tooth and nail." Instead, they should favor liberals who saw that new conditions required new, government-provided remedies. Thus the battle for primary votes was not to be restricted to the South or aimed solely at southerners. He did urgently want to lift wages in the South and erase the economic disparities between the region and the rest of the nation—he had called the pittance southern farm workers received an example of a "feudal economic system." But he took aim at all Democrats who had joined Republicans in opposing New Deal reforms, or who promised to do so when running against New Deal supporters in Democratic primaries.

As Roosevelt was stumping against his party's conservatives in and out of the South, longtime anti–New Deal fanatics were in full cry. Among the loudest, as usual, was Robert McCormick, publisher of the *Chicago Tribune*, who opened the 1938 midterm election season in September by running a scurrilous attack on the WPA in a sixteen-part series that mixed vitriol with thin reporting.

"In a little more than three years the Works Progress Administration has grown into a vampire political machine that has engulfed three million Americans and their families," it began. "More than 12 million people are dominated by this monster of the Roosevelt government. It has grown vast and powerful on their hopelessness and in many cases their shiftlessness." The series voiced the usual complaints: that the president was using jobs to buy votes; that social workers, not businessmen, were in charge of the vast spending program; and that corruption and malingering were rife.

Three years into the WPA, these accusations were of course old hat. But this time the *Tribune* went further. One article claimed, according to its headline, that "Green Pastures of WPA Entice Negroes to City," and lamented that boatmen along the lower Mississippi River could no longer hire black freight handlers for a quarter. Clifford Blackburn, the author of six of the articles, charged that the WPA had created an American peasant class. "The peasant of Europe is a hopeless, beaten fellow," Blackburn wrote. "The deadening influences that have made him what he is now have been brought to bear upon his American cousin." The influences to which he referred boiled down to "the evils of the dole" and "dumb and hopeless poverty."

Blackburn, it turned out, was a former WPA worker who, according to an extensive rebuttal released by Howard O. Hunter, the agency's regional administrator in Chicago, had been fired "after repeated reprimands and suspensions for intoxication and inefficiency." It took twenty-five pages for Hunter to deal, almost line by line, with the allegations in the series. His response, after an investigation, charged that aside from "editorialized gossip and vicious propaganda...every statement published by the *Tribune* was found to be false." Every single one.

Needless to say, the paper did not acknowledge Hunter's countercharges. There were, however, other accusations being made against the WPA that were more credible than the *Tribune*'s. These had to do with the use of the WPA as a political machine. Hopkins had always insisted that this was not the case, but from time to time events occurred that seemed to contradict him. In June, soon after Roosevelt's call for a Democratic Party shakeup, deputy administrator Aubrey Williams had made headlines with a speech to the Workers Alliance, the WPA union. He had praised the president's remarks and was quoted as urging union members to vote to "keep our friends in power." He later denied he had said exactly that, but the Senate Committee on Campaign Expenditures called his words "unfortunate," warned government officials against "unwarranted political activity," and threatened to set the Justice Department on the union if it tried to raise campaign funds from its members.

Hopkins and Roosevelt both spoke out against soliciting contributions from WPA workers. "What they need to do is spend their money on food and clothing and shelter," said Hopkins. But this restriction was harder to enforce at the local level than at the national level. The hotly contested Democratic senate primary in Kentucky was an example. In this race, majority leader Alben Barkley was trying to fend off a challenge from the conservative governor, A. B. "Happy" Chandler, who accused the WPA of allowing its 70,000 workers in the state to be pressed to contribute to and vote for Barkley. (Chandler's own campaign, in turn, was accused of manipulating state records governing Social Security eligibility to buy votes for his side.) Hopkins's investigation showed that one district director had turned over lists of WPA workers to the Barkley campaign, and said publicly that he was "deeply grieved to find even one such case." Nevertheless, it was charges like these, and the extent to which Hopkins and the WPA had become a lightning rod for conservative outrage, that prompted Jim Farley, the Democratic strategist, to pull Hopkins off the campaign trail.

And indeed, when the primary votes were in, across the Democratic spectrum the New Deal had managed only the barest of victories. Kentucky's Barkley had withstood Chandler's challenge. Elmer Thomas was renominated in Oklahoma, as was Senator Robert Bulkley in Ohio. In Texas, the liberal young congressman Lyndon Baines Johnson won his renomination race. New Deal Democrats prevailed in New Mexico after Hopkins fired that state's WPA administrator for allowing local politics to intrude in the agency's business. But in the races where the president himself had stumped, his candidates failed. He had gone to Maryland six times to campaign against Tydings, but Tydings won handily. In Georgia, which Roosevelt called his "adopted home state" because of the time he spent at Warm Springs, he had said he and George did "not speak the same language on most issues" even as George looked on in shock. George responded by comparing the president's campaign to Sherman's ruthless march from Atlanta to the sea, and he won without breaking a sweat. "Cotton Ed" Smith won his primary in South Carolina. Back in Texas, liberal stalwart Maury Maverick—whose grandfather's refusal to brand his cows had given the dictionary a new word for stubborn independence—was defeated for renomination after two terms leading the progressive bloc in the House of Representatives.

Roosevelt's intervention in New York did manage to defeat conservative House rules chairman John J. O'Connor, a Democrat, in his bid for renomination to his House seat, but under the contorted election rules of New York City that allow candidates to run on multiple party lines, O'Connor won the Republican nomination.

And on November 8, the midterm elections reverted to their customary results, with losses to the party in power. A week after the underdog Seabiscuit bested Triple Crown winner War Admiral in a horse-racing matchup that captivated the nation, the once lowly Republicans performed a comeback of their own. The GOP gained eighty-one seats in the House, eight seats in the Senate, and eleven governorships. Roosevelt's sole face-saving consolation was the defeat of O'Connor in New York.

In the aftermath, the Democrats still held large majorities in both houses, and the president remained vastly popular among the rank and file of voters. But arrayed against Republicans and conservatives of their own party, the party's progressive wing no longer had the votes to put the reform agenda forward. There had been advances. The worst abuses of unfettered laissez-faire were neutralized. Homeowners, factory workers, farmers, the unemployed, the elderly, child laborers: all had reason to thank the urgent experiments of the New Deal for injecting order, safety, and security into their lives by way of government. But apparently the taste for reform had soured now, and the nation chose to catch its breath. It was certainly clear beyond all doubt, if it had not been clear already, that the New Deal was at an end. Now the new power of the conservatives would be arrayed against, among other targets, the WPA.

2. THE RISE OF THE RED-BAITERS

In 1930, a young lawyer named Martin Dies Jr. had followed his father into the House of Representatives from Texas's Second District, in the east Texas oil patch around Beaumont. A tall man with a gunslinger's swagger and eyes that squinted like a cowpoke scanning the range for a lost steer, at thirty he was the youngest member of the Congress, and when Roosevelt first entered the White House, Dies joined his fellow Democrats in supporting the New Deal. By 1937, however, under the mentoring guidance of his fellow Texans Vice President Garner and House Majority Leader Sam Rayburn, he had joined the growing ranks of conservative defectors whose goal became to dismantle the New Deal coalition. These southern and rural conservatives, allied with Republicans, implacably opposed unions, wage-and-hours legislation, and the third term that they had now begun to suspect Roosevelt desired.

The following spring, Dies found a new springboard for the pursuit of this agenda, and for enhancing his own political reputation. Up to that point his notoriety, such as it was, rested on his unofficial chairmanship of a loose gathering of House members who loved to hear themselves talk and called themselves, only half in jest, the "Demagogues Club."

Congressional investigating committees had had a largely positive effect on American political affairs and, on occasion, on the reputations and political fortunes of their star performers. Senator Thomas Walsh, Roosevelt's choice for attorney general until he died on his way to the inauguration in 1933, had revealed corruption at high levels of the Warren Harding administration in hearings on the Teapot Dome oil leasing scandal in 1923 and 1924. Investigator Ferdinand Pecora, working under both Republican and Democratic chairmen of the Senate Committee on Banking and Currency, had exposed practices that led to several banking and securities reform laws in 1933 and 1934. Since 1936, Wisconsin Senator Robert La Follette had chaired a committee examining the methods used by employers to squelch unions and collective bargaining. These ranged from workplace spies to private police forces to gangs of strikebreaking thugs. Its title was a mouth-clotting gruel of Washington verbiage—the Subcommittee Investigating Violations of Free Speech and the Rights of Labor—but most people called it the La Follette Civil Liberties Committee, and its hearings produced evidence that was cited on behalf of the wage-and-hours law before it was passed in 1938. As a matter of course, each of these committees took testimony from both sides of the issues it was studying, and allowed witnesses to have their lawyers present.

But investigative committees also presented temptations that were hard to resist, especially when patriotism could be invoked. In 1930 and 1931, Republican representative Hamilton Fish of New York had toured the country as the chair of a committee investigating Communist activities in the United States, and after hearing from 275 witnesses in fourteen cities introduced bills to suspend the rights of free speech for Communists. These failed to pass, and the committee's overheated report was dismissed as witch-hunting: professional patriotism. The dawn of the Hitler era brought another House committee into being. Chaired by Massachusetts Democrat John W. McCormack, it was charged with investigating Nazi and other forms of propaganda. This committee took 4,350 pages of evenhanded testimony but then lost credibility because of the anti-German rants of one of its members, New York Democrat Samuel Dickstein, on the House floor, after which an irritated Congress let the committee die.

McCormack's had been the first committee to have a title that specified its the task as investigating "un-American activities," and early in

1938, two incidents led to its revival. That April, on East 86th Street in New York City, in the middle of a neighborhood of German immigrants called Yorkville, a hundred or so Jewish members of the American Legion mingled with the crowd of 3,500 entering the Yorkville Casino for a special event. The German-American Bund, an obstreperous group of pro-Nazi ethnic Germans formed in 1936 and headed by a dedicated anti-Semite named Fritz Kuhn, was throwing a party to celebrate Hitler's birthday. Young men in the audience were clad in gray storm trooper uniforms bedecked with eagles, iron crosses, and swastikas, which they also wore on goosestepping weekend marches through the neighborhood. When the program in the casino started, German-speaking orators harangued the crowd with recitations of Nazi Germany's accomplishments. Finally one of the Legionnaires rose and shouted out a pointed question: was this crowd German or American? "Storm troopers" hauled out billy clubs and descended on the questioner. The Legionnaires stood up, put on the blue overseas veterans' caps they had been hiding in their pockets, and waded into the fight. By the time the police broke up the melee, seven were injured, and two Bund members and two Legionnaires were in jail on riot charges.

The fight at the Yorkville Casino occurred after earlier reports about a German spy ring operating in the United States. What with Nazi spies and the Bund's would-be storm troopers parading on the streets of New York and other cities with large German populations, Congressman Dies saw his opportunity.

Soon afterward, he rose in the House to argue that an investigative committee be appointed. He stressed the need to monitor the Nazi threat. "I am not inclined to look under every bed for a Communist," he said, "but I can say to this House that there is in my possession a mass of information showing the establishment and operation of some thirty-two Nazi camps in the U.S., that all of these camps have been paid for, that they claim a total membership of four hundred and eighty thousand...that in these camps men are marching and saluting the swastika." He also charged that among the Nazis' aims was assassinating Roosevelt.

Dies offered no source for his "mass of information," and the *Public Opinion Quarterly* ascribed "heated inaccuracy" to his claim that there were almost half a million Nazis in the country. Nevertheless, the House approved Dies's resolution in a voice vote on May 26, 1938, and the Committee to Investigate Un-American Activities was reborn. The leadership, still displeased with Dickstein's harangues, left him off the new committee and named Dies chairman. Its charge was to investigate the extent and character of anti-American propaganda and subversion, whether of foreign or domestic origin. This last distinguished it from the original McCormack committee that had been authorized to look only at foreign-generated activities, and it gave the new committee freer rein. Nor was it aimed specifically at Nazis, though that was clearly the intent when it was formed.

Five of the committee's seven members were conservatives. Two of these were Republicans: J. Parnell Thomas of New Jersey and Noah Mason of Illinois. The Democrats, in addition to Dies, were Arthur Healey of Massachusetts, Harold Mosier of Ohio, John J. Dempsey of New Mexico, and Joe Starnes of Alabama. Only Healey and Dempsey could be termed even remotely liberal. After almost three months of preliminary interviews, Dies convened hearings in August. They were closed to the public, but open to reporters and photographers. He announced as the hearings began that the committee would not permit them "to become a three-ring circus. Neither will we permit any individual or organization to use the committee as a sounding board to obtain publicity or to injure others." The investigation would be "fair and impartial," and witnesses would not be permitted to smear innocent people, make reckless charges, or indulge in character assassination. "The chair," he said, "wishes to make it plain that the committee is not 'after anyone.' "

Indeed, Dies made a brief stab at investigating Nazi agitation. The committee's first subpoena went out to George Sylvester Viereck, a German-born poet and writer who had been an apologist for German causes since before the world war. After the ascension of Hitler and the Nazis, the German consulate in New York paid him to promote the German point of view, which he did through magazine articles, friendships he cultivated with isolationists in Congress, and advice to German officials on American attitudes. Viereck initially defied the subpoena, saying he was booked to sail for Europe where, according to Dies, he was going to meet with Hitler at his retreat in the Bavarian mountains. Then he agreed to meet with the committee, and Dies consented to his departure after reaching a "gentleman's agreement" in

which Viereck promised to testify on his return. A single day followed
in which two other witnesses—a committee staffer and a former member of the Chicago chapter of the Bund—testified about the activities
of Nazi groups. But thereafter, the Dies Committee largely abandoned
its original emphasis on right-wing sedition and shifted its focus to
Communism and labor organizing. Despite its chaiman's initial
promises, the hearings rapidly degenerated into anti-Communist hysteria, paranoid rantings, and political and personal score settling.

None of the fevered testimony the committee heard was substanti-
ated, and none of it was contradicted by opposing witnesses. The sheer
volume of its accusations was astounding. A few days of testimony
produced charges that 483 newspapers, 280 labor unions, and 640 organizations, including the Boy Scouts, the Camp Fire Girls, and various Roman Catholic groups, were "Communistic." The parade of
colorful and high-strung crackpots and the lurid fantasies they related
produced a bumper crop of headlines. The columns of the *New York
Times, Washington Post,* and other major dailies swelled with coverage of the hearings. The *Times* alone devoted more than 500 column
inches to the committee in August and September.

Much of this torrent of accusations targeted Roosevelt and the
members of his administration who were most outspokenly opposed
to Dies's tactics, notably Harold Ickes and Labor Secretary Frances
Perkins. But one committee member had the WPA, and especially its
theater and writing projects, in his gunsights. These most politically
oriented of the arts projects had in all but a few cases operated under
the assumptions Hopkins had created with his promise of a "free,
adult, uncensored" theater. But where playwrights, producers, and
writers saw art and drama in the struggles of human beings and institutions in society, politicians saw Marxian class warfare. And while
the arts project administrators believed—naively—that art stood on its
own apart from politics, the warriors of the right admitted to no such
distinction. They saw only sedition on the march, and they went all
out to stop it. Thus when HUAC—the committee was often referred to
by its initials or its sounded-out acronym—declared war on these projects in the late summer and fall of 1938, the administration and the
WPA were unprepared. They failed to take the opposition seriously
until it was too late.

3. THE "RUNAWAY OPERA"

The turmoil of the year before had lingered in the memories of conservatives. When the New York arts units took to the streets with strikes and protests against the pending job cuts in 1937, it had hardened the conviction that those projects had to go. The obvious sin was that they were radical hotbeds that flaunted their radicalism under the protection of the Congress itself, in the form of the rule—ironically designed mainly to ensure that Republicans had access to WPA jobs—that said no one could be barred from working for the WPA because of political affiliation. They also exemplified the ever-present dilemma confronting publicly funded arts: the tension between creative free expression and political sensibilities.

This tension had been present in one form or another in the theater and writing projects, and to a lesser extent in the art project, since their beginning. Hallie Flanagan had learned early on of the Federal Theatre's vulnerability to oversight when she was forced to cancel the Living Newspaper *Ethiopia* over its depiction of Mussolini. But Flanagan was the least likely of WPA administrators to shrink from a fight. The "wild little woman" described by producer John Houseman was unafraid to stand foursquare behind her conviction that the theater might become a force for social change in the public interest. She was "a fanatic," Houseman wrote, meaning it kindly. Under Flanagan, the project had continued to produce plays and Living Newspapers that saw the issues of the day through a lens of New Deal social activism and reform.

The Living Newspapers seemed especially designed to provoke conservatives by their choice of subjects, if not their very titles. *Power* told the story of the TVA, presented as a case of government aiding consumers in a region ignored by private power companies. "Some people will say it's propaganda," Harry Hopkins enthused after seeing it. "Well, I say what of it? It's propaganda to educate the consumer...It's about time." *Injunction Granted* reported on the American labor movement in pro-labor terms that even Flanagan objected to, sending its writer and director a letter saying, "I will not have the Federal Theatre used politically." Still, she called for no changes in the script. *One-Third of a Nation* looked scathingly at slum life, deploying its actors on a stage overhung by fire escapes and battered garbage cans in a mute statement of what it meant to be, as the president had put it in his 1937 inaugural address, "ill-housed." *Spirochete,* a production of the theater project in Chicago, told the story of syphilis and the fight, in those days before the availability of penicillin, to bring the deadly venereal disease under control.

Social reactionaries were not the only ones who bridled at these treatments, although some of the responses could not have been foreseen. *Spirochete,* for which Surgeon General Thomas Parran and noted *Microbe Hunters* author Paul de Kruif had helped supervise the research, was supported by doctors, public health systems, and the press everywhere it opened. But the Knights of Columbus chapter in Philadelphia protested the play's mentioning the introduction of syphilis to Europe by Christopher Columbus's crewmen returning from America, and lobbied successfully to have his name omitted.

It was the musical *The Cradle Will Rock,* however, that so inflamed conservatives against the arts programs that it brought to a head the ongoing war between the WPA's creative workers and its politically wary administrators. In the process it also provided one of the singular moments in the theatrical history of the United States.

The play was the story of a steel strike. It was as current as any of the Living Newspapers, and so were the passions it stirred up. Marc Blitzstein had written it in 1936, but the following winter and spring had brought an uncanny reality to his imaginings. In March 1937, when U.S. Steel recognized the steelworkers union, smaller steel producers had continued to fight the union with strikebreakers, private police, and guns. The United Auto Workers had unionized General Motors with its six-week sit-down strike, and strikes had also shut down the Chrysler and Hudson auto factories. Union sentiment was at a high, but so was the outrage of conservatives over the sit-downs, plant takeovers that they viewed as crimes against property. Blitzstein's play took the union view. His none-too-subtle characters included a grasping steel baron named Mr. Mister; a poor steel-town woman, Moll, forced by hunger into prostitution; and a labor hero, Larry Foreman. Houseman and Orson Welles, who had moved from the Negro theater to the classical theater in the New York project, decided that same March that *The Cradle Will Rock* would be their next production and cast it.

If *Cradle* dramatized the labor-management divide, the WPA itself was being torn by similar issues. The job cuts brought on by the mirage of an improving economy and the ensuing protests had galvanized the ever-busy Communists. Already represented in the leadership of the Workers Alliance, where Communist Herbert Benjamin was the secretary-treasurer, they now used the fear of pink slips to step up recruiting for both the party and the union. In fact, president David Lasser was fighting a losing battle against the Communists' growing influence on the union's executive board. The May 27 one-day strike of arts project and white-collar workers in New York idled not only actors, writers, artists, musicians, and dancers, but also architects, engineers, and teachers, a total of some 10,000 workers. Individual performance units conducted their own sporadic strikes, which often morphed into all-night sit-downs in the company of their sympathetic audiences. The dance unit of the theater project concluded a recital at the Nora Bayes Theatre on West 44th Street by occupying the theater overnight and mingling with audience members in the seats and on the stage, while other arts workers and supporters picketed outside, forcing police to close the street. Flanagan told the American Theatre Council that the project workers were "striking for what was once described as life, liberty, and the pursuit of happiness." Actions like these drew press coverage that helped to paint WPA workers as ingrates who were not sufficiently thankful for their public jobs. People who never liked the arts programs to begin with now saw their dislike vindicated. Meanwhile, Houseman and Welles speeded up the pace of their rehearsals.

As May ended and June began, tensions on the labor front escalated further. On Memorial Day 1937, the Chicago police shot striking workers at the Republic Steel plant in South Chicago. (Ten would die, and the La Follette committee hearings would reveal that seven of them had been shot in the back.) Five thousand protesters shut down the business district of Lansing, Michigan, over the arrests of union pickets. Johnstown, Ohio, was placed under martial law after a night of riots. Akron, Ohio, and Pontiac, Michigan, had already experienced labor riots. In those days before the passage of the wage-and-hours law, both sides were battling not only for a stake in the economic recovery that appeared to be at hand but also for their starkly different versions of what was best for the country. And as they fought, rumors began to circulate in Washington that *Cradle* was a dangerous play.

In the second week of June, cuts caused by the new lower WPA appropriation were announced. The arts projects across the nation were taking a 30 percent hit that would eliminate entirely the theater components in Delaware, Rhode Island, Nebraska, and Texas. Seventeen hundred New York theater project workers received pink slips. In Harlem, a Lafayette Theatre audience joined the cast and crew of a Negro Theatre production in an all-night sit-in. A Brahms concert at the Federal Theatre of Music, put on by the music project, ended similarly. Houseman and Welles redoubled their efforts to finish their production, assuming that if they were able to open before the end of June, they would be spending this fiscal year's money, so would not be affected by the cuts. They set June 16 for the first of two weeks of public previews, with the official opening two weeks later, on July 2. The official opening would trigger reviews, but in all other respects the performances would be the same.

On June 12, after more than 14,000 tickets had been sold, an announcement from Washington stunned all the arts projects. Citing the budget cuts and ensuing reorganization, it barred "any new play, musical performance, or art gallery" from opening before July 1. The ban included *Cradle*'s previews.

Flanagan viewed this as "obviously censorship in a different guise."

Indeed, she said, it was "more than a case of censorship. It marked a changing point of view in Washington," and one that she feared would prove disastrous.

Cradle had by then absorbed a large investment in rehearsal time and in the construction of Welles's elaborate sets. Flanagan appealed for an exception, but to no avail. Houseman opened the Maxine Elliott Theatre on June 14 and rounded up an audience for the final rehearsal. The next day WPA guards sent by Colonel Brehon Somervell, the New York administrator, moved in and cordoned off the theater. This was followed by a flurry of regulations, from both the administration and unfriendly unions, that seemed designed specifically to keep *Cradle* from being seen.

But Houseman and Welles were determined to mount the play regardless of the consequences. They sneaked past the WPA "cossacks" guarding the Maxine Elliott and set up a war room in a downstairs powder room. From there, using the still-open phone lines, they tried to find another theater while reassuring the theater clubs and others who had purchased tickets that they would open somewhere. Meanwhile, another bombshell dropped. Actors' Equity, the theatrical union, ruled that a company that had rehearsed a play for one producer could not take the stage for another producer without permission from the first. Houseman and Welles were the new producers by default; the Federal Theatre had been the old one and was not likely to grant permission, effectively keeping the cast of *Cradle* off the stage. The ruling said nothing, however, about the actors singing or speaking from elsewhere in the theater. The powder room war council decided this meant they could perform as long as they did not take the stage.

On the afternoon of June 16, the audience gathered outside the theater, along with reporters and the simply curious, and everyone waited. Houseman gave an assistant $10 and sent her out to rent a piano and find a truck to bring it to a destination that had yet to be determined.

Alternative venues fell through one by one. All seemed lost until, at 7:40, twenty minutes before curtain time, the distraught group in the powder room finally focused on a theatrical real estate agent they had been ignoring. He had been trying to offer them the Venice Theatre, twenty-one blocks north on Broadway. Houseman snapped it up for $100 for the night, and the troupe, the audience, and the growing crowd of curiosity seekers began making their way north by cab, the subway, and on foot.

At the Venice, the piano arrived, the curtain time was pushed back to nine o'clock, and monumental exercises in improvisation began. The lead actors—Will Geer as Mr. Mister and Howard da Silva as Larry Foreman—were part of the small non-relief contingent who didn't need their jobs in order to eat. Houseman had told the cast members who were on relief that he would understand if they took the safe course and chose not to perform their parts, even though they were technically within their rights as long as they weren't onstage. At a little after nine, before a standing-room-only crowd, the performance began.

Blitzstein sat at the piano on an otherwise bare stage. He was prepared to be the entire show, playing and singing and reading the stage directions. But as he laid down the first bars of the opening number and started to sing, the audience gradually realized with a shock and a thrill that he was not singing by himself. The spotlight moved into the audience and settled on a frightened redhead wearing a green dress. It was Olive Stanton, the young relief worker playing Moll, standing at her seat. Houseman recalled that she was "glassy-eyed, stiff with fear, only half audible at first in the huge theatre but gathering strength with every note." When Blitzstein caught on, he shut up and let her sing. Her bravery braced her fellow actors. The audience applauded the end of her number and Blitzstein had uttered only the next stage cue before Stanton's partner in the next scene rose and spoke his part from ninety feet away. From that uncertain opening the momentum gathered, with actors rising in the orchestra, the balcony, the boxes. Blitzstein still had to speak some parts, and some actors filled in for others, but the chorus sang, and even the union accordionist, who had been part of the orchestra now barred from performing, began to play along with Blitzstein while staying carefully out of sight. At the end, with Larry Foreman's triumph over the corrupt and frightened Mr. Mister lingering in the fading strains of the title song, the curtain fell. For a beat: dead silence. Then the crowd, 2,000 strong, went wild.

The standing, cheering ovation might have been expected. In the pro-labor audience, Blitzstein had in effect been preaching to the choir. But the crowd was applauding more than the experience of seeing its own convictions brought to life. The play's renegade performance had transcended its content to become an event in itself, with the supreme irony that it also exposed conflicts between management and labor.

The "runaway opera" made all the city's front pages the next day. The publicity allowed Houseman and Welles to stage a two-week run of *Cradle* privately, performed by the same WPA actors on the maximum two-week leave they were allowed before they lost their relief status. Later, Houseman and Welles mounted the production successfully at their new Mercury Theatre, formed after Welles resigned from the FTP and Houseman was fired under a new rule which said that only American citizens could work for the WPA. (Art Project painter Willem de Kooning, who had arrived in the United States as a stowaway from Holland, was forced to resign as a result of the same rule.)

But the adage that there is no such thing as bad publicity did not hold true for the Theatre Project and the WPA's other arts programs, because *Cradle* and the drama surrounding it caused conservatives to train their guns more squarely on these projects.

4. SACCO AND VANZETTI

The FTP was not alone in provoking the attentions of the right. The Federal Writers' Project also helped cement the notion among conservatives that the arts projects were overly influenced by Communists and leftists of all stripes. Whatever truth there was to this, it was not initially the case.

After Vardis Fisher won his race in January 1937 to make Idaho's the first state guide of the American Guide series to be published, the Writers' Project went on to produce a series of state and city guides that met with great acclaim. The Washington, D.C., guide, which project director Henry Alsberg had hoped would precede Idaho's, appeared that April. It was bound in black cloth, was 1,141 pages long, and weighed five and a half pounds. Jokes about its size were irresistible. Hefting it, Hopkins observed that it would make an excellent doorstop. Roosevelt, not to be outdone, asked, "Where is the steamer trunk that goes with it?"

Yet despite its intimidating bulk, *Washington: City and Capital* got reviews that echoed the praise for the Idaho guide. The lengthy gestation period now seemed to be worthwhile; reviewers such as the *New York Times'* R. L. Duffus wrote that the guides, "taken together, will enable us for the first time to hold the mirror up to all America."

New England was the next to weigh in, not initially with the state guides but with a piece that fell into the project's lap by accident. *The Cape Cod Pilot* was an idiosyncratic, anecdote-filled introduction to Cape Cod that writer Josef Berger had contracted with a local bookseller, Paul Smith, to produce long before he joined the Writers' Project. Smith's intention was to publish it under a new imprint, the Modern Pilgrim Press. Once the Writers' Project hired Berger, he worked four days a week researching and writing content for the project's Massachusetts guide, but spent his remaining time on his own book, which went to the printer in the spring of 1937. Soon afterward, two project administrators dropped in on Berger while he was reviewing his galley proofs, started reading, and then insisted on publishing *The Cape Cod Pilot* under the aegis of the Writers' Project. After an initial protest, Berger agreed, with the stipulation that it would carry his own byline—the pseudonym Jeremiah Digges—and that he, not the government, would earn the royalties. The book appeared that June, met with universal praise, and immediately sold out its first two editions of 5,000 copies each.

Four of the New England state guides—Massachusetts, Vermont, Rhode Island, and Connecticut—appeared that summer and fall. The Massachusetts guide was the first of these, rolling off the press in August, but rather than garnering the praise and sales momentum that the earlier guides had generated, *Massachusetts: A Guide to Its Places and People* generated a storm of controversy. Once again, the enemies of the New Deal in general and the arts programs in particular found ammunition for attack.

Alsberg had inadvertently added to this storm. He had persuaded Ellen Woodward to journey to Boston for a public ceremony announcing the guide's publication. Handing Massachusetts governor Charles F. Hurley a leather-bound copy, Woodward praised the federal government's "helping hand to the development of our cultural resources." Hurley echoed the comments he had made in the introduction, in which he wrote that he was "happy that this valuable work is being made available to the citizens of Massachusetts and the nation."

But this mutual happiness was short-lived, for the next day the *Boston Traveler* published an incendiary story that counted the number of lines the book had given to the notorious Sacco and Vanzetti case. This case of two Italian American anarchists charged with bank robbery and murder had transfixed the nation during the Red Scare of the 1920s. Nicola Sacco and Bartolemeo Vanzetti were eventually convicted and executed in the Massachusetts electric chair, but in the seven years between the crime with which they were charged and their execution in August 1927, their case had become a touchstone for political divisions in America. One side held them to be "un-American," and therefore guilty, primarily because they were radicals who had been involved in labor strikes and other forms of agitation. Progressives and liberals defended them, saying their trial had been flawed and prejudicial, and arguing that they were convicted less on the evidence than on their radicalism. Though all this was history by the time the Massachusetts guide appeared ten years later, the memories and divisions remained. When the *Traveler* wrote that the guide had devoted thirty-one lines to the Sacco-Vanzetti case but only fourteen to describe the Boston Tea Party and five for the Boston Massacre, the anti–New Deal press seized the opening and all hell broke loose.

"Sacco Vanzetti Permeate New WPA Guide," read the *Traveler*'s headline. Others picked up the theme, and before long, an editorial lynch mob was in full cry, demanding that the books be seized and burned. Further readings revealed more "evidence" of the apparent radicalism of the Writers' Project: passages that were deemed pro-labor and anti-establishment. Several Massachusetts mayors banned the book from their cities, and Governor Hurley now demanded that the writers responsible be fired.

Hopkins, who had other matters on his mind that August, when his wife, Barbara, was dying and he feared that he too had cancer, treated the outcry as an annoyance. Asked about it at a news conference, he said, "Lots of people might object to lots of things, but if we turn handsprings every time somebody objects, we could spend all day doing it." He said he doubted he would delete the Sacco and Vanzetti section as requested. "Hopkins Jeers Book's Critics," went the headline in the *Boston Globe*, and the *Christian Science Monitor* soberly pronounced the matter a "melodramatic comic-tragedy."

Dora Thea Hettwer, Alsberg's secretary, suggested several changes in her red-penciled copy of the Massachusetts guide. One would have changed the reference to the "notorious" Sacco and Vanzetti trial to the "celebrated" trial, and another proposed eliminating references to the lack of indoor plumbing in Boston tenements, but most of her suggestions simply softened mentions of episodes in the state's labor history. Few of these changes made it into print, however, and the guide sold out its 10,000-copy first edition and two editions more.

Still, the damage was real. The uproar over the Massachusetts guide drew attention to the struggles of the New York Writers' Project office to retake its own project from its collection of opinionated, vocal radicals. Most of them were Stalinists and Trotskyites, and each group disdained the commitment of the other to class struggle. As a result, they warred incessantly, haranguing each other with pamphlets and invective. Each time a new manager tried to bring them into line, they found reasons to protest his politics. Indeed, they spent all their time objecting and none producing copy.

This esoteric foolishness was highlighted by other hijinks that told the public the project was not only radical, but also undisciplined and prey to the more common vices. Orrick Johns, the poet and former newspaper reporter who was hired to head the New York project after arguing that it took a radical to manage one, made the news in the fall of 1936 when a jealous husband caught Johns with his wife, beat him, doused his wooden leg with brandy, and set it on fire.

Johns recuperated and returned to work, but he was never able to bring peace among the warring factions, and he soon joined the ranks of those dismissed for ineffectiveness. The office's main project, the New York City guide, was nowhere near completion. It would not appear until 1939. The New York State guide was even more hopelessly behind. It was being compiled by the state project office operating out of Albany, which was a dumping ground for political hacks who couldn't write. Still, the guides that did appear continued to generate good press. So did the fiction and creative writing published in book form under the title *American Stuff* by the handful of serious writers in the New York project who worked on their own and reported to the office once a week with the tacit approval of Alsberg. Among these were Maxwell Bodenheim, Claude McKay, Harry Roskolenko, and Richard Wright, who had moved from Chicago. Eda Lou Walton, writing in the *New York Times Book Review,* said Wright's "The Ethics of Living Jim Crow," about growing up black in Mississippi, was a piece "that hit me squarely between the eyes," and that the collection was evidence "that our WPA writers know their craft and know present-day America." But the attempt to turn *American Stuff* into a New York–based magazine with contributions from WPA writers nationwide fell prey to the same internal divisions that were slowing progress on the New York State and New York City guides. The Stalinists and Trotskyites advanced their own versions of what the magazine should include and what the writing should reflect, and each side took issue with editorial appointments, with the result that the magazine itself was an undistinguished and only occasionally interesting miscellany.

The real result of all of the creative fury, the ideological haggling, and the sideshow distractions that were erupting in the theater and writers' projects was to help arm conservatives against the projects. The view advanced that they were riddled with Communists, that they embraced every left-wing and labor cause, and that even if they sinned in no other way at all, they were at the very least propaganda wings of the New Deal. Vulnerable on so many fronts, they were increasingly subject to attack. By the summer of 1938, when the Dies Committee was ready to begin its hearings, the guns were aimed and ready to be fired.

5. IN THE CROSSHAIRS

Republican Representative J. Parnell Thomas of New Jersey feasted on his hate for the New Deal. An investment banker before winning his House seat in the 1936 election, Thomas viewed its progressive reforms with almost pathological aversion. It was, he said in a 1938 radio broadcast, a plan "to sabotage the capitalist system." Within the administration's far-flung array of programs, Thomas reserved his harshest hostility for the Federal Theatre Project. He hurled his first accusations even before the Dies Committee hearings opened, when it was still interviewing witnesses privately. The theater project, said Thomas, was "a patronage vehicle for Communists," in which "practically every play presented...is sheer propaganda for Communism or the New Deal." He vowed to give it a "thorough cleansing."

Practically alone among the WPA's adminstrators, Hallie Flanagan viewed these rumblings with alarm. When she read Thomas's charge in a New York paper that project workers were required to belong to the pro-Communist Workers Alliance, she issued an immediate denial. But the Dies Committee's potential to do serious damage had not penetrated the WPA's hierarchy because Flanagan had been reined in. David K. Niles, who headed the Information Division and advised

Hopkins on press matters, had told her that only his office was to respond to press reports. At this point the WPA's official policy on the Dies Committee was apparently to laugh at it or ignore it altogether.

But as Flanagan wrote later, "It never seemed funny to me." Indeed, as the committee opened hearings and immediately shifted its focus from Nazis to Communists, Dies trotted out a parade of witnesses hurling charges against the theater project and completely ignored suggestions that he try to balance the testimony by calling project officials or theater experts. Flanagan found it "increasingly incredible" that the WPA let the charges go unanswered.

One early star witness was a woman named Hazel Huffman. Dies announced her as representing "a committee of theatrical workers on relief." Huffman was in fact strongly prejudiced. She had worked in the mail room of the New York project office, where her duties included handling the mail and, unbeknownst to Flanagan, opening her letters and reporting their contents to the New York administrator, Somervell, who was seeking to confirm his own suspicions of leftist influence. Huffman had been discovered and dismissed before her testimony, but Dies ignored this history and her meager credentials, and treated her as an authority on a wide range of project activities. She flung charges far and wide: most of the workers had no theatrical experience, a Communist paper was circulated among employees, she had seen portraits of Lenin and Stalin in a meeting room, and while she could not prove Flanagan was a Communist, the Theatre Project head was "an active participant in communist activities." The proof Huffman offered was that a play of Flanagan's had been described in the Communist magazine *New Masses* as the "best revolutionary play yet produced in America."

Testimony from other witnesses produced more of the same: a "dangerous un-American atmosphere on the project"; Communist propaganda sold on government property; a blond Austrian-born actress who complained that she was asked for a date by a Negro, and that blacks and whites on the project fraternized "like Communists" in pursuit of social equality and race mixing.

Flanagan maintained her public silence through September but wrote Dies asking that she and the six regional directors who made up the project's policy board be allowed to testify. They were the only people, she noted, who could speak to the direction and intentions of the theater project. But she received no reply, the hearings continued, and the WPA continued to officially ignore the wild charges they produced.

Not only was Flanagan concerned by the damage the project was suffering; she was also mystified by the way Thomas interpreted its plays. He had even found fault with *Prologue to Glory,* about young Abraham Lincoln: because the play portrayed Lincoln "battling with the politicians," it was "simply a propaganda play to prove that all politicians are crooked." Flanagan had considered it a patriotic look at the sixteenth president, and when she encountered Thomas on a train from Washington to New York she approached him in the hope that she could decipher his objections. He described a scene in which the Lincoln character had objected to an abstract debate topic—the value of bees versus ants—and suggested instead that "the subjects for debate before this forum ought to be alive—subjects for action, useful for living."

"That is Communist talk," she recounted him saying.

Indeed, Flanagan herself was perplexed by much of the adverse reaction, not just from Thomas but from some project workers, even with plays that had no obvious political content. The New Jersey project was rehearsing *Created Equal,* a drama that retold the history of the Constitution. Half the cast supported the play, but the others claimed it was un-American, and sent Thomas a petition saying it should not be allowed to open. This contingent believed that the play's stress on the roles of ordinary citizens in the revolution, as opposed to leaders, smacked of "collectivism." They also thought that when the characters of Thomas Jefferson, Andrew Jackson, and Lincoln did speak, their lines made them sound like Roosevelt. Ludicrous though charges such as these were, Flanagan could not find much humor in them; their implications for the future of the project were just too scary.

It was little consolation that the Federal Theatre Project was neither the only target of the committee nor the only one being accused with neither documentation of the charges nor a chance to answer them. Colonel John P. Frey, an official of the American Federation of Labor, charged that the AFL's competitor, the CIO—the Congress of

Industrial Organizations—was riddled with Communists. Asked to give a source for a specific charge, Frey said, "I cannot openly give the source of my information." But he assured Dies that he was convinced of its authenticity, and the testimony was allowed to stand. Similarly, a committee investigator charged that Communists dominated the Hollywood movie industry, and that labor organizer Harry Bridges was a Communist guilty of terrorism, crop sabotage, and murder in fomenting labor strife on the West Coast. Bridges's accuser was Edward F. Sullivan, a longtime labor spy who had actively supported anti-Semitic and anti-Catholic activities in the United States. And when the HUAC spotlight turned again to the WPA and one Edwin P. Banta testified to Communist domination of the Federal Writers' Project in New York, he turned out to be a professional informer and a Nazi sympathizer.

Yet it was not until Dies allowed Michigan Republicans to hurl charges against the state's Democratic governor, Frank Murphy, who was locked in a tight reelection battle, that the administration made any response at all. The so-called issue was Murphy's handling of the General Motors sit-down strike in January 1937. Fearing lethal violence, he had resisted calling out the National Guard to remove the strikers. GM capitulated, and much of the auto industry except for Ford had unionized as a result. The parade of politically motivated witnesses against Murphy included Detroit police officials, the Flint city manager, and a judge, all of whom testified to Communist activity in Michigan, Communist control of the unions, Communist links to Murphy, and Murphy's "treasonous" failure to remove the union members from GM property. As usual, Dies called no rebuttal witnesses and did not allow Murphy to respond.

When the polls showed Murphy losing ground, Roosevelt finally struck back. He issued a statement accusing Dies of allowing the committee "to be used in a flagrantly unfair and un-American attempt to influence an election." It had made "no effort to get at the truth, either by calling for facts to support mere personal opinion, or by allowing facts or personal opinion on the other side," he said.

But Dies was unmoved; the administration, he said, was trying to discredit the committee's work with "a well-planned campaign of misrepresentation, ridicule, and sarcasm." He also announced that he planned to investigate Communism among Democratic officeholders in California, Minnesota, and Ohio. The California charges were discredited, and the election had passed before the committee could turn to Minnesota and Ohio, but in a close race Murphy lost.

The reporters and photographers who were the only public witnesses to the sensation-mongering parade were unsure what to make of it. They felt they were being used, yet the charges of Communism in high places were too juicy to ignore. The Dies Committee hearings sold newspapers. Dies shrugged off accusations that he was allowing witnesses to make wild, defamatory, and unsubstantiated charges. He blamed this on the administration-backed leaders of the House, who had given him a budget of only $25,000 to conduct his investigations after he had asked for $100,000. What was more, he said, the WPA and other agencies had ignored his requests for investigative help. The WPA had lent staff to help the La Follette Civil Liberties committee, but Hopkins refused it to Dies on grounds that its most recent relief appropriation had stipulated that its personnel not work for other agencies. Attorney General Homer Cummings declined Dies's request for FBI agents to work with the committee as investigators. The Labor Department under Frances Perkins also turned him down.

"I offered them the chance to put their own choice of attorneys, clerks, investigators, office boys, everything," said Dies. "Without help from the administration...I have still gone on the best I could."

He did acknowledge that the witnesses had shortcomings. "Some of it's no good. I know that. I admit it. I don't believe a lot of the testimony myself." But what could he do? "I haven't the money or the trained men," he pleaded. "I have to rely on the testimony of witnesses who are willing to testify."

And an "unfortunately large number" of them, according to an article in *Public Opinion Quarterly,* were "professional patriots, vigilantes, political stool-pigeons, labor spies, anti-Semites, Nazi-sympathizers, and criminals."

Thus the hearings continued: a riot of false accusations, publicity ploys, and grandstanding. And as the "evidence" from these fusillades against the WPA and the two arts projects mounted, it was countered by nothing at all. Again Flanagan wrote to Dies asking to appear before the committee. She was concerned for the jobs of thousands of theater project workers, she said, and that there was much good to be said about the project, if only the committee would listen. Yet again, her letters were ignored. So were those of playwright Emmet Lavery, the head of the project's Play Bureau, which coordinated the selection and clearance of plays nationally, who told the committee that he had never permitted a Communist play and wished to be heard. Like Flanagan, he never received a reply.

6. HARRY DEPARTS

The planets were realigning over Harry Hopkins in the fall of 1938, though for better or worse it was impossible to tell. Just as fatigue with reform was setting in, so too was an impatience with Hopkins as the most visible and vocal head of a New Deal agency.

Back in September, newspaper reports had tarred him with an outright lie. Frank R. Kent of the *Baltimore Sun,* Joseph Alsop and Robert Kintner of the North American Newspaper Alliance, whose column "The Capital Parade" ran in more than 200 newspapers, and Arthur Krock of the *New York Times* all reported a conversation allegedly overheard at a New York racetrack. Hopkins, they wrote, had told an unidentified companion, "We shall tax and tax, and spend and spend, and elect and elect." Alsop and Kintner wrote that the story was "probably apocryphal," as indeed it was. Hopkins denied he had ever said it. So did two people who were with him, and even the person to whom he was supposed to have made the remark. But it was widely considered, as Krock smugly told a Senate committee, "a concentrated gem of Mr. Hopkins's philosophy." Coming in the run-up to the November elections, the quote was political dynamite, brilliantly confirming the views of New Deal haters.

At the time Hopkins was experiencing a case of presidential fever. He had been encouraged by Roosevelt to think he was his favored successor, although the president had not specifically ruled out seeking a third term. His notes from a conversation in the spring of 1938, after he returned to Washington following his recuperation from cancer surgery, indicate that Roosevelt had considered his advantages and liabilities as a candidate and spelled them out to him in a kind of campaign primer. He noted that Hopkins had been divorced but that previous candidates and presidents had also overcome personal drawbacks: "Cox divorced + Cleveland bastard," Hopkins wrote. Roosevelt thought that his marriage to Barbara would help, but that his own health might become an issue. Doctors at the Mayo Clinic had given him two-to-one odds against a recurrence of his cancer, but Roosevelt noted that the presidency is a killing job, so Hopkins should be fully recovered before he made a presidential run. Assessing other potential Democratic candidates, the president dismissed Secretary of State Cordell Hull, Agriculture Secretary Henry Wallace, Hopkins's nemesis Harold Ickes of Interior and the Public Works Administration, and several others. Of them all, he considered his Postmaster General appointee and Democratic Party chair James Farley the most ambitious and therefore the most dangerous. After running Roosevelt's campaigns in 1932 and 1936, Farley had drifted away from his support for the New Deal and was now aligned with another onetime supporter turned opponent, Vice President Garner. The president told Hopkins he thought he would do the best job of any of these possibilities and offered him "assurances and hopes." Among those assurances was a cabinet appointment. He planned to name Hopkins secretary of commerce, a job that would allow him to mend his fences with the business community, whose support—and donations—he would need.

From that point on Hopkins had taken his presidential aspirations seriously, despite the fact that he had never held elective office. The caustic relief administrator who had always had sharp words for politicians now became a political animal himself. His speeches took on pro-business themes, while at the same time he tried to help Roosevelt purge the Democratic Party of conservatives by supporting a liberal challenger to Senator Guy Mark Gillette of Iowa. It did not bode well for his ambitions that his home state Democrats renominated Gillette overwhelmingly. Nevertheless, he explored buying property back in Grinnell, the idea being to run as an Iowan and a midwesterner and not as the eastern bureaucrat he had been these many years; the harness maker's son would be so much more appealing to the voters. He told a few close friends, sworn to secrecy, that he was planning to run. But when the subject came up in public, he denied it, or hedged, as was the case at a news conference a month after the election.

About a third of the way through the session, the subject turned to rumors circulating in gossip-driven Washington. A reporter asked him if he intended giving up his WPA job "anytime soon."

"No, sir, I certainly do not," Hopkins replied.

A moment later, the question came at him again, this time with a reference to "statements that the White House has been so well pleased with your work here that they would like to elevate you to a job of greater importance. It has even been suggested that you might be elevated to the White House."

"You hear anything you want to hear in this town," Hopkins responded, drawing laughter.

Still, the news conference had a valedictory quality about it, as if everybody in the room knew that Hopkins would soon be leaving the WPA and moving on. He was spent and distracted. His new immersion in politics was stealing his attention from policing the kinds of activities in local WPA offices that had raised cries of election scandal in Kentucky. It is also likely he was bored. By now he had headed the New Deal relief setup for five and a half years and the WPA for three and a half, and the howls of criticism from the right had never eased and never changed. Indeed, with the Dies Committee hearings savaging the Federal Theatre Project and Federal Writers' Project, they had increased. Congress had vindictively tried to cut his salary. Legislation impelled by the Kentucky scandal that would prevent federal employees from engaging in political activity was gathering support in the Senate under the guidance of its sponsor, Democrat Carl A. Hatch of New Mexico. There was also legislation afoot to change the way the WPA was organized, which would limit workers to eighteen months on the job before they were pink-slipped and would require them to take a month off before working again—and then only after they requalified for relief. After building to their peak in November, the rolls were falling again; between 100,000 and 150,000 workers a month were finding private jobs. The WPA still had an energetic and accomplished workforce that was undertaking projects small and large. Work on New York City's first commercial airport was occupying 5,000 men working three shifts a day, as only one example. But Hopkins's dream of a twenty-year WPA, which he had spelled out in September, was dimming. He undoubtedly sensed that the agency's salad days were over, and was eager to pursue the administration's goals in a new way, as well as his own newfound ambitions.

For all of that, he still bristled when the familiar charge that WPA workers were loafing on the job was raised. One reporter asked if the Democratic losses in November were an expression of dissatisfaction with the WPA.

"My answer would be no," Hopkins replied. "After all, you are asking me a thing that is purely a matter of opinion. You might have an opinion about that and I might have one and neither of our opinions would make it a fact."

The reporter persisted. "A week before the election in Pennsylvania, on a small road project on the highway there were seven men working. Four of them were holding flags."

"What do you want me to comment about that?" Hopkins asked sharply. "Are you just making a little speech? Fine."

"What do you think of it?"

"I could say I doubt that it ever happened," Hopkins said. "That kind of statement does not mean anything unless you have all the ramifications of what happened there. You might make an isolated case of eleven people out of three million people working. They might have been shooting off dynamite, and four people were holding flags. Perhaps eight should have been holding flags. It does not necessarily mean anything."

Hopkins also denied manipulating the WPA rolls from Washington to aid Democrats' election chances. Asked if there was any significance to the rolls having peaked at the time of the election, he responded, "If anybody would tell me why we would decrease WPA in Michigan immediately prior to the election and increase it in Alabama for political purposes is beyond me. If we wanted to play politics, we would have increased the WPA in Michigan and not decreased it. We would have increased it in Cleveland, not decreased it, and certainly we would have had no occasion to increase it in all the southern states where no Republican is ever elected to office and where the highest increases in the WPA took place." As for the charges that local supervisors in Kentucky and other states had directed workers to vote or work for favored candidates or exacted contributions, he said he favored a ban—"the stronger the better"—on political activity by WPA workers.

But for all the attention on Hopkins's future, the election, and the old saws and canards attached to the WPA, only one question got at the future of the agency itself. "What part will the WPA play in the national defense program?" one reporter asked.

"Whatever part Congress and the president want us to take," Hopkins answered.

And less than two weeks later, he was gone. At a news conference on December 23, he was asked if he would accept the commerce post if it was offered, and replied, "Don't kid me, boys. This is the Christmas season and I'm accepting anything." Roosevelt announced his appointment as secretary of commerce later the same day.

Hopkins's resignation as WPA administrator was as terse as his responses were when politicians wanted to drag out the process of getting jobs, food, and money to the unemployed. "Dear Mr. President," he wrote. "I hereby resign as Works Progress Administrator, effective December 23, 1938. Very Sincerely Yours, Harry L. Hopkins."

Polls did not ringingly endorse this choice for a cabinet post. In a Gallup poll, two-thirds of those who had an opinion said Hopkins should not be named commerce secretary, but 40 percent of those polled said they simply didn't know. The results of a Roper poll showed him in a better light. While only 10 percent said he had done a fine job at the WPA and should be kept in mind for higher office, another 30 percent agreed that he had handled a difficult job well. His detractors—those who agreed that he had done fairly well but not well enough, and those who believed he had done a bad job and should get out of government—amounted to less than 30 percent. Another 30 percent had no opinion. A few newspapers applauded the appointment, but most attacked it in terms like those used by the normally supportive *Chicago Daily News,* which called it the "most incomprehensible" and "least defensible" appointment of Roosevelt's entire presidency. What these responses showed, if anything, was less about Hopkins as a cabinet choice than about the implausibility of his presidential hopes.

Nevertheless, he was confirmed easily and Roosevelt, seeking a less polarizing choice for his successor, named Colonel F. C. Harrington over Hopkins's alter ego, Aubrey Williams, to head the WPA. Harrington, whose white hair and mustache set amid a florid complexion had given him the nickname "Pinky," was a no-nonsense type from the Army Corps of Engineers who was the WPA's chief engineer in charge of the construction division. He was also an attractive choice because he was serving for his army pay and thus would not have to undergo the Senate's confirmation process.

Hopkins's departure signified an end to the New Deal as much as did the rise of the conservative alliance in Congress. It was more symbolic an end than that one, which had also signaled the end of reform through legislation—but it was no less real. For all of the attention given to what became known as Roosevelt's "Brains Trust"—Rexford Tugwell, Raymond Moley, and the other academic architects of the New Deal's first thrust of government into the banking and securities systems and the agricultural and industrial economies—it was Hopkins who had emerged over the president's term and a half as the face of the government's new concern with the welfare of individual citizens. With his exit, conservatives and the anti–New Deal press lost a political piñata; reporters lost a reliable source of juicy quotes; and his coworkers lost a figure who inspired them, one for whom they were willing to work beyond endurance because he did. Hopkins believed in the fundamental worth of people who were unemployed through no fault of their own. He believed that work brought dignity and meaning to their lives, and therefore that government, by providing work, was rebuilding not just the country and the economy but individuals and families. These beliefs were inseparable from his leadership. His impatience with those who questioned the work ethic and skills of the men and women who labored on WPA projects characterized the sea change that the New Deal represented in American life. Never before had the federal government taken an active role in addressing the employment and health needs of Americans. More than anyone, Hopkins reflected that new role. His willingness to cut red tape and spend money brought a new urgency to human needs. Conservatives hated him so violently because he made no apologies, instead rebuking those who denied the government a role in easing deprivation.

One political cartoon, from the *Parkway Transcript* in Roslindale, Massachusetts, summed up Hopkins's lasting image. It pictured a plaque on the front of the WPA's headquarters building with the words:

TO THE
EVERLASTING HONOR OF
HARRY L. HOPKINS
AN AMERICAN BOY
FROM IOWA WHO
SPENT *9 BILLIONS*
OF HIS COUNTRY'S
MONEY *AND NOT A*
DOLLAR STUCK
TO HIS FINGERS!

And the WPA after Hopkins would remain significant, especially as totalitarianism increasingly gripped Europe and the Far East and America turned to rebuilding its military capability. At the end of 1938, some of its most important and long-lasting projects were still on the drawing board, and even without him, it would stay in the forefront of the war against the lingering depression. It was still an agency with heart, although with Hopkins gone, it had a little less soul.

7. CHANGES IN THE WIND

That Hopkins's successor, F. C. Harrington, lacked this ineffable quality was not immediately clear. But as the WPA struggled to cope with the fallout from the Dies Committee hearings, it would emerge that while the new administrator believed in the overall work program, he found the arts projects a distraction that he was unwilling to defend as Hopkins had.

Dies had kept his committee hard at work investigating "un-American activities," and grandstanding and slandering its targets, into December. By then, after seeing Governor Frank Murphy brought down by Dies's unanswered charges and the president powerless to negate his one-sided scandal-mongering, the administration and the WPA itself began to take the Dies circus seriously at last. Under Flanagan's direction, Emmet Lavery of the Federal Theatre Project's Play Bureau, who was familiar with all the plays mounted by the project, and Ted Mauntz, the New York project's information director, undertook to answer the charges of widespread Communist influence. They broke down the composition of the theater parties that were a large part of the Federal Theatre audiences to reveal that of more than 1,000 organizations that had attended the project's plays, only fifteen were political organizations, and these represented all political parties.

They compiled a list of every play that had been performed, and analyzed those criticized by witnesses and the committee. And they reminded the committee of the Congress-passed WPA rule prohibiting discrimination against employees based on political affiliation, adding that no policy makers in the play project were Communists.

Alsberg and his staff at the Writers' Project also put together a brief answering the charges made against it. These preparations were coordinated with Hopkins's deputy, David K. Niles of the WPA Information Division. Hopkins, with less than three weeks to go before his resignation, was typically defiant. He said that as far as he was concerned, Flanagan and Alsberg could "go up and spit in the faces of the Dies Committee." But in a meeting on December 4, Niles shocked Flanagan and Alsberg with the news that they would not be testifying. Instead, Women's and Professional Projects head Ellen Woodward would make the case for the theater and writing projects. Niles gave no reason for refusing to let the heads of the two projects defend themselves. Woodward's long political experience and the possibility that the committee would defer to her as a southerner were probably among the factors. Flanagan and Alsberg argued heatedly but failed to change Niles's mind. Good soldiers that they were, they spent the rest of the day going over with Woodward the points made in their briefs.

It took only a few minutes on the morning of December 5 to erase the thought that the committee would treat Woodward gently. She entered the high-ceilinged hearing room to find its members decidedly hostile. By now their grandstanding had become addictive. With Dies directing traffic, a smirk visible behind the black cigar jammed in one corner of his mouth, they attacked without letup. None of the committee's friendly witnesses, the ones who told them what they wanted to hear, were subjected to the abuse Woodward received. She put up a good fight. Interrupted at the outset as she began to read her statement, she said, "Would you kindly listen for just a minute?" She expressed deep concern and disappointment "over the very un-American way in which the committee has handled charges made against this project." But when she asked if the members had read any of the plays they had charged were communistic, she earned a rebuke from Starnes of Alabama. "You are not here to ask the committee questions. You are here to answer questions," he said sternly, and forced her to apologize. Moreover, Woodward herself, even after her briefing, could not refute accusations about individual plays or Writers' Project manuscripts because she did not have the details. She faced the committee for a day and a half, then was excused.

Now the committee, bursting with anticipation, looked forward to Flanagan and Alsberg, who were freed by Niles to testify.

Flanagan was called on December 6. She took her seat at the foot of the T in which two long tables had been arranged, with the members arrayed across the top and reporters, photographers, and stenographers on either side. In her initial statement, she observed that while the committee had been investigating un-American activities, she had spent four years fighting un-American inactivity, by which she meant unemployment in the theater world. "The distinction," she later wrote, "was lost on the committee."

Predictably, its members dwelled on the charges of Communism. They managed to see it everywhere. Thomas quoted the statements of witnesses who had said that project employees had to belong to the Workers Alliance. Flanagan explained that most project workers were required to belong to other unions—the stagehands union, Actors Equity, and so forth—which precluded Workers Alliance membership. Starnes questioned Flanagan about her visits to view Russian theater in 1926 and 1931, about whether propaganda was circulated at project sites, about the plays themselves, and about an article she had written for *Theatre Arts Monthly,* a professional trade magazine. Reporting on a drive to set up workers' theaters, she had described their audiences as possessing "a certain Marlowesque madness."

"You are quoting from this Marlowe," said Starnes. "Is he a Communist?"

Laughter rippled through the hearing room. When it died, Flanagan explained that she was referring to Christopher Marlowe.

Starnes persisted. "Tell us who Marlowe is, so we can get the proper references," he demanded.

At that moment Flanagan felt a deep pang of despair for the 8,000 Federal Theatre employees whose jobs were at stake. She gathered herself and with careful patience said, "Put in the record that Marlowe was the greatest dramatist in the period of Shakespeare, immediately preceding Shakespeare."

Starnes, she later wrote, "subsided." But his was not the only display of ignorance or confusion on the part of the committee. Dies questioned Flanagan about the Communist Party membership of Edwin P. Banta, who had worked not for the theater but for the Writers' Project. He confused a Michigan labor leader named John G. Reid with the American Communist and journalist John Reed, for whom the Communist John Reed Clubs were named and who had died in 1920. He had similar difficulty distinguishing between Tom Mann, a member of the British Labor Party, and Thomas Mann, the Nobel Prize–winning German novelist whom he went on to refer to as a Communist. Errors such as these would have been laughable had they not shown its victims the sloppiness, intractability, and stupidity they faced.

The committee dismissed Flanagan at a lunch break. She asked to be recalled to make a final statement, but her request was ignored. "We don't want you back," said Thomas. "You're a tough witness and we're all worn out." He then conceded that she didn't look like a Communist. "You look like a Republican," he joked.

Alsberg was called after the lunch break. He took his seat at the table as an aide wheeled in a cart stacked with Writers' Project publications. Fighting through his initial nervousness and speaking in a low, gruff voice that gained strength as he grew more confident, he gradually won over the committee by recounting his well-documented disillusionment with Soviet-style Communism. He spoke of a book he had edited of letters from Russian political prisoners. He said the book, published in 1925, was "considered the most devastating attack on the tyrannical Russian situation" and lost him many liberal friends. "I suffered. I was blacklisted. I could not get my articles published," he recounted.

He went on to complain about the disruptions caused by the political infighting at the New York project offices. He said he laid the law down after one of the frequent sit-down strikes, issuing an order that the project would shut down if there were any more disruptions. "That is flat," he said. But he said it was still almost impossible to keep the fractious New York writers from agitating for one concession or another: "Every time we drop a man there are delegations. There are protests...wanting to expand the Writers' Project, wanting to do this and wanting to do that."

When Dies asked him about Orrick Johns, whose term as director of the New York project had been marked by the episode in which the jealous husband set fire to his wooden leg, Alsberg pointed out that while Johns indeed had been a Communist, he had been dismissed, and that the three directors who followed him had no Communist affiliations. He said that he had objected in strong terms to the Communists' handing out their pamphlets at the project door. And he agreed that the New Jersey guide, which witnesses had charged with promoting class hatred, had overstated the case for labor but only because uncorrected galley proofs had reached the printer in error. The staff responsible for this had been changed. Meanwhile, said Alsberg, editors in Washington had worked to moderate controversial language in the guidebooks.

All this was in marked contrast to the combative tones taken by Flanagan and Woodward. But the distinction made no difference. The damage had been done. Despite the cordiality Dies accorded Alsberg, the report he submitted to the incoming Congress after the first of the new year condemned the Writers' Project, and it painted the Theatre Project with the same broad brush of damning generalities: "We are convinced that a rather large number of the employees on the Federal Theatre Project are either members of the Communist Party or are sympathetic with the Communist Party. It is also clear that certain employees felt under compulsion to join the Workers Alliance in order to retain their jobs." A single paragraph from the committee's beleaguered liberals took exception to the majority report, pointing out the extent of "biased" and "exaggerated" testimony.

The Dies Committee was now a national phenomenon. During its short life, no institution in the country had ever received as much press coverage. The reams of newsprint that it generated defied any sober assessment of its methods, and the obvious biases of its report. A Gallup poll showed that 60 percent of the country was now familiar with the committee, and three-quarters of those wanted it to continue. No more would Dies have to struggle for appropriations to continue its work. The Seventy-sixth Congress, which took office in January 1939, quadrupled the HUAC budget to $100,000, and the committee, with its rants and excesses, its powers to be abused and feared, was now a fixture of American life.

8. CAN ANYBODY SPARE A HOT SCHOOL LUNCH?

While the Dies Committee peddled sensation and reaped headlines, Congress was following its usual practice of scrimping on operating funds for its fiefdom, the District of Columbia. The District, an economic and political vassal of the Congress, had no self-government, no representation in the House or Senate, and no voting rights; its citizens were not allowed even to vote for president and vice president. This arrangement had long been a source of frustration for D.C. residents, but as a practical matter, as 1938 ended its burden fell most heavily upon the poor children of the District. The funds that paid for WPA-prepared hot school lunches dried up just in time for Christmas.

More than 5,000 children received the lunches daily. They usually consisted of sandwiches, soup, or a hot plate such as meat loaf or spaghetti; fruit; and a dessert of pudding, applesauce, or prunes. Each child also got a third of a quart of milk with the meal. The District school system had intended to keep the program going over the Christmas holiday, which lasted from December 23 to January 3, since most of the families could not afford to provide the same level of nutrition. But not only did funds for the lunches run short, the schools themselves were so broke they could not afford to keep the boilers lighted in ninety of the buildings so as to give the children a warm place to eat the lunches school officials despaired of being able to provide.

"Take that buttery thought with your Christmas turkey," the *Washington Times* editorialized on December 21, criticizing the "$10,000-a-year Congressmen, to whom it has never apparently occurred that you can't control a hungry kid's appetite by a calendar."

Hot school lunches had been a feature of the relief program almost from the beginning. Hopkins had begun the practice of providing them in public schools under the Federal Emergency Relief Administration in 1933. By January 1934, the program was serving 4,000 students in seventy-eight schools in the District of Columbia under the Civil Works Adminstration. Then Eleanor Roosevelt took the project under her wing and pushed to improve the quality of the meals.

Predictably, conservatives protested anything they saw as undermining self-sufficiency. Rufus S. Lusk, spokesman for the Washington Taxpayers' Protective Association, had objected to the earmarking of District relief funds for free school lunches before a Senate subcommittee that was considering the relief appropriation bill in March 1935. "If free school lunches should be furnished," he asked, "why not clothes and shoes?"

Voices that objected to preventing malnutrition in poor schoolchildren were a minority, however. By 1936, the WPA had received so many applications from local parent-teacher associations and boards of education that the program was expanded nationwide under the Division of Women's and Professional Projects, and now included parochial as well as public schools. February 1936 saw the program in the District of Columbia doubled to cover 8,200 students. That March, in Tennessee, Elizabeth Coppedge, the state director of the women's division, announced that the WPA had served 1.25 million hot lunches to rural schoolchildren and that in some counties school attendance had increased by 37 percent. School officials in Minnesota, where the program was serving 7,500 children, called it "the best truant officer the schools have ever had." Indiana tested the program in five cities before taking it statewide in June 1937 and feeding up to 6,000 grade-school children. In Augusta, Georgia, school nurses saw malnourished children gaining weight—an average of five pounds in a group of 1,000 children—and credited the lunch program.

Despite the WPA budget and job cuts in the fall of 1937, the program was set to expand exponentially with the beginning of the school year. Lunches were to be served at the rate of 500,000 a day, and Hopkins said hundreds of thousands of relief families would benefit. The menus were written by WPA dieticians with an eye to filling nutritional gaps in the children's home diets, and prepared and cooked by WPA employees using school facilities if possible. If not, the food was cooked at centralized kitchens and trucked to the schools where it was served. Most of it would be purchased, although in some areas, WPA gardeners and canners using school gardens and workrooms would add their products to the local food supplies.

As part of this WPA health initiative, WPA-paid nurses and doctors had made some 9 million home visits to examine and treat children. Home aides had helped with housework and child care in relief families where mothers had fallen sick. WPA housekeeping aides appeared at the doors of poor families on schoolday mornings to fix breakfast and send the children off to school. The thrust of these efforts, which evolved into one of the underpinnings of the modern welfare system, was to keep relief families together and avoid the expense of institutional care for children who previously would have been sent into orphanages or foster homes.

But in the fall of 1937, with the economy starting to slide into recession, finding local money to support the hot lunch program suddenly became a problem. This was especially true in the District of Columbia, where the Congress parceled out funds to the local government with the reluctance of a disapproving feudal lord. Even before the beginning of the school year in September, the District schools had announced that the lunch program was out of money and would be curtailed.

Washingtonians reacted by starting a self-help program. To keep the lunches going, residents formed the Citizens' Emergency Committee for the Feeding of Hungry School Children and launched a donation drive. They won the support of the district's newspapers, which ran stories about the drive accompanied by boxed displays containing the information that 7 cents would provide one hot lunch, $1 would provide two weeks of lunches, and $13 would feed a schoolchild for a year.

On October 18, District of Columbia police and firemen joined forces to stage a boxing benefit at Griffith Stadium, the home of the Washington Senators baseball team. Thousands crowded the event, the exhibition raised $11,000, and the committee, which had already acted on the advance ticket sales, got the school lunch program restarted the same day. More fund-raisers continued: a lecture on the wonders of the Caribbean, a benefit ball, and a magic show at the Belasco Theater. Sponsors pushed toward the goal of $100,000 to feed over 5,000 children for a year, which was where the program stood until the Christmas vacation cuts loomed at the end of 1938.

In New York, the city was contributing enthusiastically to the program and more than 100,000 children from relief families were eating hot school lunches every day, a number that would increase as time went on. Indeed, by May 1939, a record high of 119,000 New York schoolchildren participated in the lunch program, which employed 3,000 WPA-paid employees and used fifty trucks to deliver the lunches from centrally located kitchens to 846 elementary schools. Despite their hunger, the children's tastes were not indiscriminate. They rejected the dieticians' attempts to prescribe cabbage sandwiches, preferring peanut butter and jelly. They ate bananas at more than twice the rate of apples—2,792,881 pounds of bananas versus 1,273,745 pounds of apples in 1938. They turned up their noses at raw carrots until the dieticians became food stylists, trimming and slicing carrot sticks to make them appetizing.

Nationally, the beginning of 1939 saw the program pass 130 million meals served and more than 1 million children fed by the school lunches. In the face of the rising conservative opposition to the projects of the WPA, it was one of the agency's most enduringly popular programs.

9. THE DEATH OF THE THEATER

Dies and his committee had bloodied the Federal Theatre Project, but the coup de grâce was still to be applied, and the dagger lay in the hand of Representative Clifton A. Woodrum. Woodrum, a conservative Virginia Democrat who chaired the House Appropriations Committee, held the purse strings. He had the potential to do just as much if not more damage than Dies, and he announced his intention to do just that. It was time, he announced, "to get the government out of the theater business." His vehicle was an Appropriations subcommittee that he also chaired. Its charge was to investigate relief spending, a sweeping mandate that allowed the chairman free rein.

Hallie Flanagan was optimistic at first. Here at last, she believed, was an opportunity "to have a real investigation with findings made public." She wrote Woodrum to that effect but his response was the same as that of Dies: she heard nothing.

In fact, Woodrum recycled the Dies Committee's collection of suspect witnesses in hearings that began in the spring of 1939. As had Dies, he concentrated on the projects' weak spots. For the Writers' Project, that meant the troublesome New York office. His attacks against the Theatre Project were broader, but also concentrated on

operations in New York. Unlike Dies, Woodrum had paid investigators at his disposal, but objectivity was not in their job description.

The chief investigator was H. Ralph Burton. He was hired to look
at the accomplishments as well as the failures of both projects, but
those good intentions, if actually meant, quickly deteriorated. He assembled reams of material, which he used in selective and damaging
ways. This was especially frustrating to Flanagan, who was proud of
the fact that in its four years the theater project had been so successful
at attracting audiences that box office receipts, not tax dollars, had
been paying for all its non-labor costs for some time. Theater rentals,
costumes and scenery, and play royalties were funded from the $2 mil-
lion the project had taken in from paying customers, an impressive figure given the top ticket price of 50 cents for most shows. The
government had paid these costs in the beginning, but Burton testified
only that the project cost more than it took in. This was hardly surprising, since its original purpose had been to give work to the unemployed, but he declined to point this out.

Burton's men pored over Writers' Project manuscripts for evidence
of "class-angling" and other "Communist propaganda." What they
didn't find they were willing to plant. Aiming to produce visual proof
of the project's leftist tilt, they visited the empty offices one lunch
hour armed with cameras and some Communist literature they
arranged on desks for an intended photo session. An administrator,
James McGraw, caught them in the act and threw them out before
they could photograph the "evidence."

Only one committee member objected to the parade of unchal-
lenged witnesses. Clarence Cannon, a Missouri Democrat, pointed out
that they were "people who either have been fired or are going to be."
When Burton recycled a charge from the Dies Committee hearings—
that members of the New York Writers' Project were communistic
based on their gift to Edwin Banta, the fired worker who turned out to
be a spy and an informer, of a book signed by Communist leader Earl
Browder—Cannon reminded the committee that discrimination based
on politics was barred in the WPA and cited Mayor La Guardia's statements disavowing any subversive control of New York WPA units. He
also contested their conclusions. When a witness presented as evidence
of communistic intent the fact that audiences had hissed at a police
character in a play called *Life and Death of an American*, Cannon

reacted with unbridled scorn: "So because in a play an audience gets up and hisses a policeman, you think that is sowing the seeds of communism? This is the most ridiculous thing I ever heard of. If that is sowing the seeds of communism, then we have communism all over this country." He called the statement opinion without fact, and "wholly worthless."

But no one else spoke up for the Theatre Project. Indeed, an internal decision had been made to sacrifice it for the overall good of the WPA. Ellen Woodward had resigned as deputy administrator over women's and professional projects back in January, when she was appointed to the Social Security Board. Florence Kerr, one of her regional administrators and a longtime friend of Hopkins from Grinnell College days, was appointed to replace her. With Hopkins's departure in December for the commerce secretary's post, Aubrey Williams had moved to full-time administration of the National Youth Administration, and Howard O. Hunter, Hopkins's Midwest regional administrator, had replaced him as the WPA's second in command. Collectively with Harrington, this new regime judged the theater to be expendable. The numbers talked. Two and a half million jobs were on the line, as against 8,000 in the theater project.

The House Appropriations Committee reported out a $1.775 billion relief bill for the year beginning July 1, 1939. It contained the stipulation that no funds were to go to the theater. Flanagan still believed the project could be saved; she had many supporters, and she knew she could persuade them to descend on Washington. But when she asked Hunter—she had never been given the opportunity to meet with Harrington—who would lead the fight to save the FTP, he told her there would be no fight.

Flanagan fought on regardless. She ignored WPA rules and rallied thirteen House members who agreed to speak for the project. Another promised to introduce an amendment putting the project back into the bill. New York theater critics telegraphed Woodrum as a group disputing his statement that they disapproved of it and urging that it be continued. Brooks Atkinson, the noted drama critic of the *New York Times*, wrote that the project "has been the best friend the theatre as an institution has ever had in the country" and that it "deserves to be rescued from partisan politics."

But as Flanagan wrote later, partisan politics were "booted and spurred." Representatives speaking for the project on the House floor were shouted down, as was the amendment to restore its funding. Having lost the battle in the House, she turned to the Senate. Here Hollywood joined the fight, with James Cagney among those offering to guarantee the non-labor costs in the California project. Lionel Barrymore made a radio speech in which he said that killing any of the arts projects was "almost like taking one of the stripes out of the American flag." Actress Tallulah Bankhead—the daughter of House Speaker William Bankhead of Alabama—visited the Senate Appropriations Committee and pleaded with a catch in her throat, "But actors are people, aren't they? They're *people*!" The attacks set Flanagan to musing. She couldn't accept that the congressmen who called classic plays by Sheridan and Molière dangerous and indecent, or who said that other plays stirred class hatreds, really believed what they were saying. She wondered instead if they were spurred by fear of a more literate public educated by plays on current events such as the Living Newspapers, or by fear of better understanding between blacks and whites, because many politicians found thinking people a risk.

And when Flanagan actually won the battle in the Senate, hope remained. Its version of the appropriation bill retained three-fourths of 1 percent of the total for the Federal One arts projects, including the theater. But hope faded as quickly as it surged. Traditionally, differences between the House and Senate versions of bills each has passed are worked out in a conference committee from both houses. This time, when the conferees met, Woodrum and the other House members refused to yield, threatening to kill the whole relief appropriation. Roosevelt called it "discrimination of the worst type," but he signed the bill rather than bring the entire WPA to a grinding halt.

The Federal Theatre Project went dark at midnight on June 30, 1939, with several successful productions still on the boards. One was the innovative *Swing Mikado*, a jazzy update of the popular Gilbert and Sullivan operetta. Another was *Pinocchio,* Yasha Frank's adaptation of the children's story that had found an enthusiastic audience with children and adults alike. Frank wrote a new ending for the final performance. In it, Pinocchio became a puppet again after a brief life as a boy. With stagehands striking the sets on an open stage before the audience, the actors laid him in a wooden box that bore his epitaph: "KILLED BY ACT OF CONGRESS, JUNE 30, 1939."

10. A DIFFERENT PLAYING FIELD

The Writers' Project survived the onslaught, but only under vastly altered circumstances. The entire WPA was under pressure in the spring of 1939, and when the dust had settled it was a much different organization than it had been under Harry Hopkins in the early days of the New Deal, when the need for jobs was desperate.

In 1937 and 1938, Roosevelt had tried to push through a federal reorganization plan that would give him the power to realign the government's executive agencies into more functional groupings. This was based on a plan submitted by the President's Committee on Administrative Management and was largely free of partisan impact. But in the wake of Roosevelt's failed court-packing plan, Congress had been in no mood to expand presidential powers even in the administrative area. Not until the spring of 1939 did it finally pass a reorganization bill, and it was much weaker than the one the president had originally requested.

It allowed him, among other things, to create three broad departments. A Federal Security Agency grouped departments whose thrust was to promote economic security, including the Social Security Board, the United States Employment Service, the Office of Education, the Public Health Service, the National Youth Administration, and the

Civilian Conservation Corps. The National Youth Administration had originally been a jobs program, albeit one whose purpose was to allow young men and women to pay for schooling. So, too, had the CCC, whose "boys" had been sent into the woods to work on conservation and other projects. Their move into the security agency demonstrated a new emphasis on the long-term goals of training and education rather than just providing jobs and fighting unemployment. Under the aegis of a Federal Loan Agency were the Reconstruction Finance Corporation, the Electric Home and Farm Authority, the Federal Home Loan Bank Board, the Federal Housing Administration, and their associated agencies and boards, as well as the Export-Import Bank of Washington. The idea here, said Roosevelt in his message to the Congress about the new plan, was to stimulate and stabilize "the financial, commercial, and industrial enterprises of the nation."

The third of the new entities was a Federal Works Agency. This grouped the entities that dealt with public works not routinely handled by other departments, and that administered construction grants and loans to state and local governments. It was here that the WPA was now placed, along with the agriculture department's Bureau of Public Roads, the public buildings branch of the Treasury Department's Procurement Division, the National Park Service branch that managed federal buildings in the District of Columbia, the United States Housing Authority, and the Public Works Administration. In fact, the new agency virtually replaced the PWA, and was placed in the charge not of Ickes, who wanted it, but of John M. Carmody, who headed the Rural Electrification Administration, charged with pushing electric service into remote and unserved areas. Under the new umbrella, the function of the WPA remained much the same. Its name, however, changed; it became the Work Projects Administration, which allowed it to keep the same initials. Roosevelt told Congress the new name was "more descriptive of its major purpose." He also said the reorganization would save $15 million to $20 million.

Ickes's Interior Department had lost several of its functions in addition to the PWA, putting him, as he wrote, "very low indeed in my mind." At the WPA, however, Harrington embraced the new structure along with his new title, which had changed from administrator to commissioner. With its construction role unaltered, and the lighter work managed by the Division of Women's and Professional Projects continuing as before, he oversaw much the same organization as Hopkins had.

Harrington's attitude about the arts projects, however, was markedly different from Hopkins's; he viewed them as a distraction from the WPA's construction and service work and a red flag to conservatives in Congress. Indeed, the Woodrum committee's assault on the Federal Theatre Project would affect the writing, art, and music components by removing them from federal sponsorship and forcing them to scramble to find sponsors at the state level. All did just that, cajoling university presses, music societies, art leagues, and the like to step in, and except for the banned Theatre Project were thus able to continue operating. At the Writers' Project, renamed the Writers' Program, Harrington removed his main remaining trouble spot by dismissing Alsberg in September in favor of a more efficient successor, John Dimmock Newsom, who had headed the project's Michigan office and, in the words of Katherine Kellock, was "not given to Greenwich Village dreams of sponsoring genius." He simply wanted to see the American Guide series through to completion, although this itself posed a major challenge: more than half the state guides were still to be published.

And of course, it did not require congressional action to kill individual programs in the arts. That could be done locally. The Art Project's teaching component in New York included a program for mental patients at Bellevue Hospital. Late in 1939, New York administrator Somervell decided to include it in his weekly inspection tour of WPA activities. He collected Audrey McMahon and they proceeded to the hospital, where they looked in on several classes in progress and then moved on to meet some of the adult patients who were among the students. The treatment wards were under lock and key, and McMahon later described staff members unlocking the doors to admit them and locking them inside, unlocking them to let them out again, and repeating the process as they went from one ward to another. At a male ward, the staff coordinator repeated the introductions of McMahon "and the administrator, Colonel Somervell." At the mention of rank one of the patients jumped to his feet, snapped to attention, and saluted. "The trouble," recalled McMahon, "was that he was minus the trousers of his hospital pajamas and his jacket was flapping wide." McMahon could barely keep from laughing, but Somervell was not amused. He turned abruptly and as they left the hospital said, "Mrs. McMahon, that project is closed."

But while the arts received an outsized share of criticism and attention, the WPA's primary purpose continued to be its vast variety of building jobs. In terms of national iconography, none was more important than a twenty-month, $250,000 refurbishment of the Statue of Liberty. For years rainwater had been pouring off the statue's copper sheeting and invading the pedestal on which it stood. Starting in 1937, WPA crews had installed flashing to reroute the water, repaired the masonry, strengthened and painted the steel frame, reinforced the spikes jutting from the statue's crown, put new glass into the torch (which was then lit from the inside), installed a new staircase, added an acre to the Bedloe's Island grounds, and performed extensive landscaping before the statue reopened to visitors in December 1938. In January 1939, San Francisco had christened its $1.5 million, WPA-built Aquatic Park near Fisherman's Wharf on the shore of San Francisco Bay. A center for boating, swimming, and other water sports, the park featured grandstands overlooking the city's only downtown beach, a modernist building housing restaurants and walls of murals that was likened to "a great white ocean liner," and views of Alcatraz and the Golden Gate Bridge. The park employed 782 workers and artists for two years, of whom the *San Francisco News* wrote, "WPA critics will have to eat all their jokes about 'shovel leaners' when they come to Aquatic Park." Down in San Antonio, Texas, former congressman Maury Maverick had turned the tables on the machine that beat him in the 1938 Democratic primary and was now the mayor of San Antonio. True to his New Deal credentials, he had launched a plan of city-wide improvements that encompassed the city's parks, playgrounds, and swimming pools, and even the Mexican and black slums and the red-light district, using WPA labor. The plan's centerpiece was the heart of the city itself, a twenty-one-block stretch of the San Antonio River that meandered through the business district. For much of San Antonio's long history the river had been a flood-prone, litter-strewn nuisance, but plans to beautify it with riverside walkways, landscaping, stairways, and pedestrian bridges had been gathering force after a devastating flood in 1921. Maverick had secured WPA funding for the beautification project while he was still in Congress, and construction of the $400,000 project had gotten under

A Denver, Colorado, student in the WPA's hot school-lunch program. *(Courtesy of the National Archives.)*

WPA workers joined cleanup and recovery efforts after a hurricane hit New England in September 1938. This crew in Cheshire County, New Hampshire, clears felled trees from a road. *(Courtesy of the National Archives.)*

Col. Francis C. Harrington of the U.S. Army Corps of Engineers succeeded Harry Hopkins as WPA administrator in December 1938. *(Courtesy of the National Archives.)*

WPA deputy administrator Aubrey Williams, Women's and Professional Projects head Ellen Woodward, and Music Project director Nikolai Sokoloff. *(Courtesy of the National Archives.)*

Holger "Eddie" Cahill headed the Federal Art Project. *(Courtesy of the National Archives.)*

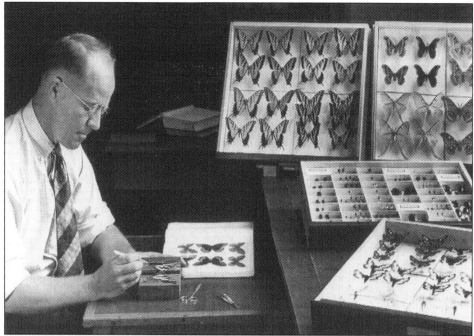

WPA workers like this entomologist at the Natural History Museum in San Diego, California, supplemented staffs at museums and other public institutions. *(Courtesy of the National Archives.)*

Archaeological digs employed WPA labor, including this excavation at the site of the Odessa meteor crater in Ector County, Texas. *(Courtesy of the National Archives.)*

Young divers take the plunge at this WPA-built pool in Carbon Hill, Alabama.
(Courtesy of the National Archives.)

A driving lesson being conducted on the Ohio State University golf course designed by Perry Maxwell and constructed by the WPA.
(Courtesy of the National Archives.)

The WPA Recreation Division conducted fly-casting classes, including this one at a trout stream in California.
(Courtesy of the National Archives.)

A downhill skier photographed above the WPA-built Timberline Lodge.
(Courtesy of the National Archives.)

The WPA's Federal Art Project sponsored community art centers like this one in Lynchburg, Virginia.
(Courtesy of the National Archives.)

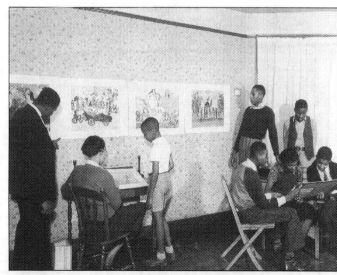

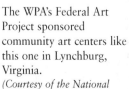

A WPA children's class at the Walker Art Center in Minneapolis.
(Courtesy of the Franklin D. Roosevelt Library.)

The WPA Pavilion at the 1939 New York World's Fair. The mural, entitled
"Work—The American Way," was by Philip Guston. *(Courtesy of the National Archives.)*

Portland artist Douglas Lynch created the murals in the Timberline Lodge coffee shop. The stools were hand-carved by WPA craftsmen. *(Courtesy of the National Archives.)*

WPA muralist Edward Laning and assistants at work on the Ellis Island mural "The Role of the Immigrant in the Industrial Development of America." *(Courtesy of the National Archives.)*

The lobby of Cook County Hospital in Chicago featured murals by Edwin Boyd Johnson, mosaic murals by John Winter, and the figure at center by Charles Umlauf. The polished stone benches were also by WPA craftsmen. *(Courtesy of the National Archives.)*

One of the musicians in Leroy Smith's Detroit Community Dance Band No. 13, sponsored by the WPA's Federal Music Project, takes a solo spot at a night concert. *(Courtesy of the National Archives.)*

The WPA's Federal Theatre Project dramatized current events in plays called "Living Newspapers." This is a scene from *Triple-A Plowed Under*. *(Courtesy of the National Archives.)*

BE LOYAL TO FEDERAL THEATRE

See every Show!
Start the Applause!
Send your Friends!
Talk up our Shows!

KEEP PLUGGING OUR PROJECT

The Federal Theatre responded to attacks from Congress with pleas for loyalty.
(Courtesy of the National Archives.)

The Federal Theatre Project's production of *Pinocchio*, its final play.
(Courtesy of the National Archives.)

Kate Sandwine, the Strongest Woman in the WPA Circus, demonstrating her strength with a volunteer. *(Courtesy of the National Archives.)*

New York City lacked its own commercial airport before the WPA built La Guardia Field, which opened in December 1939. *(Courtesy of the National Archives.)*

The WPA-built San Antonio River Walk converted a crime- and litter-infested area into an attraction for tourists and locals. *(Courtesy of the National Archives.)*

The new Southside Bridge at Charleston, West Virginia, opened in 1937, is one example of the WPA's rebuilding of the national infrastructure. *(Courtesy of the National Archives.)*

The WPA's Federal Writers' Project produced landmark guides to every state and to major cities. They are promoted in this window display in Dawson's Book Store in Los Angeles in 1941.
(Courtesy of the National Archives.)

The WPA turned to defense-related work as the threat of war grew closer. This laboratory worker waters a guayule plant being tested as a possible rubber source at the California Institute of Technology in Pasadena. *(Courtesy of the National Archives.)*

Librarian Dorothea Asher looks on as soldiers at Fort Belvoir, Virginia, check selections at the bookmobile operated by the Fairfax County WPA Library Extension Project. *(Courtesy of the National Archives.)*

Marchers picket the WPA headquarters in Washington, D.C., in 1941 to protest layoffs, and pay that lagged behind the rising cost of living. *(Courtesy of the National Archives.)*

The WPA conducted Americanization classes for immigrants. Mrs. Lola Bierbower, at right, leads a group of women taking the Pledge of Allegiance in San Antonio, Texas. *(Courtesy of the National Archives.)*

The WPA helped the United States solve a shortage of aircraft mechanics as World War II approached. Trainees J. D. Oliver and Charles Steele work with instructor L. P. French at Meacham Field in Fort Worth, Texas. *(Courtesy of the National Archives.)*

WPA construction crews aided the buildup of military installations. These workers are moving dirt for a runway at a military airport in Laredo, Texas. *(Courtesy of the National Archives.)*

The WPA led the introduction of women trainees into defense jobs. Marian Rust, Mary Watson, LaVerne Kersey, and Sally Painter take a break from their aircraft sheet-metal and riveting course at the Dallas National Defense School. *(Courtesy of the National Archives.)*

After World War II began with the Japanese bombing of Pearl Harbor, WPA artists produced posters such as this one urging the conservation of coal in wartime. *(Courtesy of the National Archives.)*

way early in 1939. Architect Robert Hugman, who had drawn the plans, had named it the San Antonio River Walk and columnist Ernie Pyle wrote that it was going to make the Texas city into "a kind of Venice."

But the largest of the WPA's current construction jobs was a twenty-four-hour-a-day whirlwind of work that was transforming a swath of shoreline of the Borough of Queens in New York City into the nation's most modern commercial aviation complex.

North Beach, as the site was called, jutted into the East River between Bowery Bay and Flushing Bay. Beginning in the 1880s, the Gala Amusement Park there had attracted visitors from Manhattan and Long Island. Later North Beach was home to a sportsmen's air park, Glenn Curtiss Airport, where, during the late 1920s, wealthy private pilots had arced over the East River in biplanes and speed racers. The depression grounded them, but aviation dreams floated in the head of Fiorello La Guardia, then a congressman, and once Roosevelt was in the White House and he had been elected mayor, those dreams started to take flight. He objected to the fact that buying an air ticket from another city to New York got a passenger only as far as Newark, New Jersey. That was where New York–bound flights landed, and to the Little Flower it was a breach of contract. On a flight from Chicago in 1934, he insisted on his rights and refused to disembark until the plane carried him from Newark to an actual New York destination, Floyd Bennett Field in Brooklyn. With the New Deal and his own extraordinary success at luring federal public works dollars to New York—the PWA had built the Triborough Bridge, the Lincoln Tunnel, and several other major projects, to say nothing of Robert Moses's WPA-funded parks and swimming pools—La Guardia realized that a major airport was within his reach. Once the WPA approved the project, the mayor kicked it off himself in one of his exuberant forays into the spotlight. On September 9, 1937, as reporters and photographers looked on, he took the controls of a steam shovel and dug a bucketful of earth from a bluff that overlooked the East River and Rikers Island, which itself now sported a new complex of men's penitentiary buildings.

The bluff was an unusual feature of the North Beach shoreline. Most of the shoreline was low and marshy, thus requiring the addition of tons of refuse used as fill. A great deal of this fill was barged from Rikers, which itself had been expanded with the addition of dirt from

New York City subway excavations before the first jail there opened in 1932. Once the 432-acre tract had solid footing, the actual work on the airport began.

The plans envisioned a combined sea and land facility. The great Pan American Clippers and the transatlantic seaplanes of European airlines, including Air France, Royal Dutch, Deutsche Lufthansa, and Britain's Imperial Airways, would set down in Flushing Bay and disembark their passengers at a bayside platform. The seaplane complex would include two hangars, together accommodating twelve to fourteen planes, connected by a tunnel to a marine air terminal. Waiting rooms and baggage facilities would be housed in an administration building that also housed offices for customs, immigration, health, and flight control and navigation.

The land-based companion airport was to be even more expansive. Here on the acres of landfill would be built four runways ranging in length from 3,532 to 4,688 feet, an administration and terminal building, and six hangars to service the planes of four domestic airlines—American, Eastern, Transcontinental & Western, and United—that would use the new airport as their eastern terminus, appropriating that distinction from Newark. A prime feature was an observation deck that would let sightseers watch the planes take off and land.

Costs rose way beyond the original $22 million estimate. Detractors began to mock the frenzied work on the isolated spit of land as "Fiorello's Folly." But the mayor was undaunted. He appeared at the site so often, usually with visitors in tow, that workmen took to handing him their tools. One of the men on the job was Clifford Ferguson. Ferguson, a union carpenter, never turned over any of his precious tools, not even to New York's mayor. He'd had them stolen once, managed to recover them, and after that rarely let them out of his sight. But he would always remember the mayor's visits, his enthusiasm for the job, and the way his energy seemed to give the shift a second wind even when they had been at work for several hours. "He kind of picked you up," Ferguson said.

The airport was Ferguson's first job for the WPA. Earlier in the depression, he had done whatever work he could to make a dollar. He had been around buildings doing odd jobs since he was ten years old, working for his contractor father, and sometimes—he recalled this most vividly of all—working in theaters: never on the sets but offstage, repairing seats and floors. When the stock market crashed in 1929, he was driving a taxicab; and he kept that up off and on for a year. He worked as a night watchman at St. Andrew's Episcopal Church in Astoria, Queens. He mixed concrete for his brother-in-law, who had worked on the subway lines that were being extended into Brooklyn, until he dislocated a shoulder while heaving a 100-pound bag of concrete onto the back of a truck and was unable to work for almost a year. It seemed to him that job interruptions were the norm, whether they were the result of an injury or the lack of a job in the first place. "Nobody ever had work straight through," he said.

Like everyone he knew, Ferguson was familiar with the extent of WPA work going on around him. You couldn't miss the signs, and even if you did you couldn't miss the armies of shovel-toting, wheelbarrow-pushing men, some wearing felt hats and overcoats, who swarmed over the new roads now pushing through the eastern boroughs of the city. Ferguson had seen, and scorned, his fair share of shovel leaning. But he was married, with three sons, and when news of the airport project began circulating through the halls of his union local in 1938, he applied, was certified for relief, and took the job without a second thought.

The brickwork on the administration building had been completed by the time he started work. Ferguson joined a crew of men building the "stairway to the stars," the ascent to the observation deck. Here the city was gambling on the public's fascination with the new aviation age. A visitor who placed a dime in the coin slot of a turnstile would gain admittance to a half-mile promenade that gave a sweeping view of the majestic four-engine flying boats alighting in the bay and the thundering silver Lockheed 10s and the larger Douglas DC-3s swooping in over the East River and touching down on runways that began literally at the water's edge. As the complex came together, its components were best expressed as quantities of cement (1,000 truckloads), asphalt (3 million gallons), underground piping (25 miles), cable (200 miles), and steel (20,000 tons). So frantic was the pace of the construction that it sometimes outstripped the preparation of blueprints, with the result that the hangars did not always jibe with the plans they were based on.

Costs continued to rise, fueling renewed criticism of the airport as a massive boondoggle; it would eventually cost $40 million, of which the WPA's share was some $27 million. But it soon proved to be a powerful business magnet: American Airlines moved its administrative offices from Chicago to North Beach in 1939. And when the public embraced the airport with the same enthusiasm, La Guardia's victory was complete. Officials predicted that 150,000 people would attend the formal dedication on October 15, 1939. Instead a crowd of 325,000 showed up, and more would have attended if all the parking lots had been completed. As it was, lines of cars were backed up for blocks into the streets of the surrounding neighborhoods.

Two days after the dedication, proving still further that La Guardia's vision of the future of air travel was widely shared, 5,000 young women swarmed the new airport offices of American Airlines to apply for twenty available jobs for flight attendants, or air hostesses as they were known then, and within three weeks the airline had opened a hostess training school.

A TWA flight from Chicago was the first to touch down at the new field, just after midnight on December 2. Despite the hour, the twenty passengers aboard were surprised to find themselves greeted by the mayor himself, who shook their hands, welcomed them to New York, and accepted kisses from the stewardesses. Bad weather held up the rest of the day's flights, but at the end of its first full day of commercial traffic on December 3, the airport was the busiest in the United States. Less than a year later, it was the busiest in the world, the New York City Council had joined the Board of Estimate in naming it La Guardia Field after its champion, and Newark Airport, scorned by the mayor as a New York terminus, was closed to commercial traffic.

La Guardia had described his pet project to Roosevelt as "the airport of the New World." Another New World vision was attracting even more visitors just a mile or so away. Flushing Meadow Park was a former dump converted by Robert Moses into a graded and landscaped 1,200-acre site that was home to the 1939 New York World's Fair. Here, too, WPA workers toiled, not only on the site and construction of fair infrastructure but also on the WPA's own building.

The fair opened on April 30, 1939, following by ten weeks a rival global fair across the country: the Golden Gate International Exposition, built on a man-made island in San Francisco Bay. This, too, featured contributions by the WPA, notably a mural, seventy-four feet long and twenty-two feet high, painted by WPA artists under the direction of famed Mexican muralist Diego Rivera. In New York, fairgoers who could pull themselves away from the clean white spike of the Trylon and its companion orb, the Perisphere, the iconic structures at the center of the fair, or the chairs that took them on a fifteen-minute ride across the United States as envisioned by General Motors in its "Futurama" exhibit, could be reminded of the works program. The WPA building sported fluted art-deco–style columns under a tall modernist facade. The familiar old name "Works Progress Administration" marched across the concave brickwork, and above it loomed a huge Philip Guston mural depicting in heroic style the overalled, smocked, and booted workers for whom the WPA had been a godsend: a mason, a sewing room worker, a surveyor, a concrete driller. They leaned intently to their jobs against a backdrop of white clouds, and where flesh showed it was taut and muscled. Guston had called it "Work—The American Way," and it evoked the scenes that Art Project muralists had painted in schools and other public buildings all across the country. A second Guston mural appeared inside, featuring more workers and a mother—or perhaps a WPA home health aide—holding a child.

Inside, the building's exhibits showed off the WPA's work in art and writing, landscaping and conservation, recreation and construction, sewing rooms, and disaster relief, including the 350,000 workers who in various ways were fighting the renewed drought that was then scorching parts of the Midwest. A display made the point that the WPA's building and infrastructure work "helps Anytown USA keep abreast of modern American standards." In case a visitor failed to connect that modernization to his own hometown, another room contained a state-by-state compilation of major WPA projects. One showboard, seeming slightly defensive, told the viewer that "out of every 20 American workers only 1 is on WPA."

The fair's overall theme was "The World of Tomorrow," and its crystal ball forecast a progressive future. "Democracity," another catchword of the fair, implied that the world was evolving toward an inclusive cosmopolitan democracy.

That admirable vision, however, had already fallen into peril, for the dogs of war were on the prowl. Within half a year of the fair's April opening much of the world was at arms, with democracy among the victims. Japan's Imperial Army had surged across large swaths of China in the undeclared war that had raged since 1937. The Japanese had taken Kwangsi province in the south all the way to the border with French Indochina—later Vietnam—and was confronting the Soviet Red Army in Manchuria near the Korean and Siberian borders.

In Europe, Hitler's lust for conquest had proven time and again to be insatiable despite English and French efforts to placate him short of war. Having annexed Austria and blustered and threatened his way to a takeover of the Czechoslovakian border region known as the Sudetenland, he had dropped all pretense of legitimacy and invaded Czechoslovakia in March 1939. In the third week of August, to guard his eastern flank, he signed a mutual non-aggression pact with Soviet Russia. Then on September 1 came the move that brought events full circle. German troops and tanks struck across the border of Poland, the invasion drawing declarations of war from its English and French allies and plunging the European continent back into the nightmare from which it had awakened twenty short years earlier when the world war ended. World War II began.

And with the formally declared war in Europe came debate in the United States. It was not a new one; it was an intensification of the one that had been going on ever since President Woodrow Wilson took the country into the world war in 1917 to make the world "safe for democracy." Afterward, he supported the creation of the League of Nations as a body of world governments whose purpose was to mediate disputes and ideally to bring an end to wars. But these events had stirred a deep strain of American isolationism. Many of its citizens wanted no part of world affairs. The unsettling passions of people who spoke strange languages, worshiped strange gods, and followed strange customs, who massaged their grievances and enshrined the hatreds they had nursed for centuries—these were not for the forward-looking, business-oriented citizens of the United States. Isolationist sentiment said it was better that the country defend its borders and let the rest of the world take care of itself. This sentiment had kept the country out of the League of Nations, and contributed to the defeat of the Democrats in 1920 by a Republican ticket headed by the unimpressive Warren G. Harding, whose slogan was "a return to normalcy." Now, with America's allies again at war in Europe and democracy under renewed attack by fascist powers, the United States was again torn between isolationism and involvement.

The argument would go on for many months. In the meantime, how the WPA would be affected was unclear. If the isolationists had their way, enforcing a strict neutrality, the agency could expect to continue largely as it was, its construction program perhaps shifting to defense work in border and coastal areas, at least until the fitful economy finally started breathing on its own again. Given the performance of the last seven years of New Deal depression fighting, when and even if that might happen was far from certain. It had not been that long ago that Harry Hopkins was talking about a permanent WPA. But if America was able to unleash its industrial strength on behalf of its allies, turning out a range of goods from arms to food supplies, then the unemployed might finally be able to return to private jobs.

Deputy commissioner Howard Hunter, speaking at a news conference in Harrington's absence on August 31, as the German tanks were massing at the Polish border, said it would be "pure guesswork" to predict the effect of a European war on relief employment. How the WPA would reintegrate its workers into a resurgent private economy also remained to be seen. Hunter did speculate that the WPA would of necessity become more flexible, moving workers into jobs where they were needed. "We have a very good index of the people on the WPA as to their training and qualifications, and if any group of industries or any particular industry were in need of either skilled or unskilled workers, I think we could get our people off the rolls into those jobs," he said.

The labor pool to which Hunter referred was several million strong, people who either were currently working for the WPA or had done so in the past. They were a huge resource with a wide variety of skills. They had needed the work provided by the government in order to survive. Now it was possible to think, with war raging in both hemispheres, that they might be called upon to return the favor if dreams of peaceful isolation crumbled and the United States was plunged into a fight for the survival of democracy and, indeed, its very life.

PART VIII

WPA: WAR PREPARATION AGENCY

In the years 1935 to 1939, when regular appropriations for the armed forces were so meager, it was the WPA workers who saved many Army posts and Naval stations from literal obsolescence.

—<u>THE ARMY AND NAVY REGISTER,</u> MAY 16, 1942

1. NO MILITARY WORK

When Congress passed the relief appropriation for the then-
new WPA back in the spring of 1935, the bill contained a
provision against military spending: "No part of the appropriations...shall be used for munitions, warships, or military or naval
matériel."

Republican senator William E. Borah of Idaho was among those
primarily responsible for this provision. A progressive on domestic
matters, he had long ago shed the internationalism that had prompted
him to vote for sending American troops to fight in Europe in the
world war; he was now a leading isolationist. He had voted against
the Treaty of Versailles and the League of Nations on the grounds that
they would entangle America in European politics, and more recently,
he had helped pass the Neutrality Act of 1935, which among other
provisions prohibited arms sales to nations at war, no matter whether
they were the aggressors or were defending themselves against aggression. The embargo received almost unanimous support in the light of
the Senate Munitions Committee hearings that began in 1934 under
Senator Gerald P. Nye of North Dakota. The aim of the special
committee was to investigate charges that arms makers and their
bankers had conspired to draw the United States into the world war. In

ninety-three hearings conducted over a period of eighteen months, the munitions interests were painted as greedy war profiteers bent on filling their coffers with "blood money." Nye failed at his goal of nationalizing the arms industry, but the hearings left lawmakers averse to any overseas commitments, and Congress had renewed the Neutrality Act in 1937 over Roosevelt's objections. Borah, Nye, and their colleagues believed, with most of the country apparently agreeing with them, that denying the government the capacity to make war was tantamount to securing peace. "Fortress America" would defend its borders, but it would not reach out militarily beyond them.

In fact, isolationist sentiment was so strong that in 1937, Representative Louis Ludlow, an Indiana Democrat, introduced a constitutional amendment that would submit a declaration of war to a national referendum unless the country was invaded. Roosevelt protested that this "would cripple any president in his conduct of our foreign relations" and tempt hostile governments to believe they could violate Americans' rights and get away with it. Critics likened it to calling a town meeting before dispatching the fire department to a fire. But national polls showed that 73 percent of the people supported it, and it emerged from committee in January 1938 with strong backing; only some all-out presidential lobbying sent it to defeat by a thin twenty-one-vote margin.

The view that America could ignore the world and isolate itself behind the protective oceans that flanked its coasts alarmed the White House. Roosevelt had sought to dent the appeal of isolationism as early as the fall of 1937, when Hitler and Mussolini were deep into the buildup of their war machines and Japan already had invaded China. Homeward-bound from the northwestern trip during which he had dedicated Bonneville Dam and Timberline Lodge and visited other federal projects, the president appeared in Chicago on October 5. The occasion was the opening of the WPA-funded Outer Drive Bridge, the final link in a thirty-mile boulevard along the Lake Michigan waterfront. But as he addressed the crowd at the noon bridge dedication, the president went beyond the usual script stressing federal largesse and the benefits of public works. Instead, in this heartland where the isolationists were strongest and Robert McCormick's *Tribune* relentlessly attacked all things Roosevelt, he spoke about "the present reign of terror and international lawlessness" outside the United States.

He named no names, but even casual followers of world events would have understood that he was talking about Japan, Germany, and Italy, and even General Francisco Franco's right-wing rebellion against the elected government of Spain, which Hitler had aided that April by raining bombs on Guernica in the Basque country and killing some 1,500 civilians. Such aggressions, he said, had reached the point "where the very foundations of civilization are seriously threatened.

"Without a declaration of war and without warning or justification of any kind, civilians, including vast numbers of women and children, are being ruthlessly murdered with bombs from the air. In times of so-called peace, ships are being attacked and sunk by submarines without cause or notice. Nations are fomenting and taking sides in civil warfare in nations that have never done them any harm. Nations claiming freedom for themselves deny it to others.

"Innocent peoples, innocent nations, are being cruelly sacrificed to a greed for power and supremacy which is devoid of all sense of justice and humane considerations."

Quoting novelist James Hilton's best-selling novel *Lost Horizon*, he raised the specter of " 'a time when men, exultant in the technique of homicide, will rage so hotly over the world that every precious thing will be in danger, every book, every picture, every harmony, every treasure garnered through two millenniums, the small, the delicate, the defenseless, all will be lost or wrecked or utterly destroyed.' "

Speaking directly to the isolationists, he said, "If those things come to pass in other parts of the world, let no one imagine that America will escape, that America may expect mercy, that this Western Hemisphere will not be attacked and that it will continue tranquilly and peacefully to carry on the ethics and the arts of civilization. If those days come," he continued, quoting again from Hilton, " 'there will be no safety by arms, no help from authority, no answer in science. The storm will rage till every flower of culture is trampled and all human beings are leveled in a vast chaos.' " Nor, he added, would there be escape "through mere isolation or neutrality."

He compared the spread of violence to an epidemic of disease: "War is a contagion, whether it be declared or undeclared." The only answer, as in an epidemic of disease, was for peace-loving nations to "quarantine" the aggressors, isolating them to protect the 90 percent of humanity they threatened.

The quarantine speech, as it became known, was front-page news and the beginning of a long campaign by Roosevelt to force the isolationists to look at hard realities. The *Washington Post* called it "perhaps the most momentous utterance of his career." For all of its borrowed eloquence, however, its effect was doubtful. "It's a terrible thing to look over your shoulder when you are trying to lead—and find no one there," he reportedly said later.

But if he seemed ineffective in public, he acted in private. Roosevelt had no doubt that war was on the way and that when it came, airpower would be a key to victory. In March 1938, coinciding with Hitler's annexation of Austria, he sent Harry Hopkins on a closely guarded mission to the West Coast, where America's airplane manufacturing industry was concentrated. Traveling with Colonel Arthur R. Wilson of the Army and Lieutenant Colonel Donald H. Connolly of the Corps of Engineers, who was the Los Angeles–based WPA administrator for southern California, Hopkins toured aircraft factories to assess their capacity to build military airplanes.

His trip resulted from information Major General Henry "Hap" Arnold, the assistant chief of what was then the Army Air Corps, had given to the president. The United States military had fewer than 2,000 planes, most of them obsolete, and only 1,650 pilots. Seventeen B-17 bombers were on order, but they were not due to be delivered until the end of 1938. Germany, Arnold briefed the president, had 8,000 fighters and bombers in its rapidly expanding air force. Moreover, in commanding a roundtrip flight of ten B-10 bombers between Washington and Fairbanks, Alaska, in 1934, Arnold had demonstrated by the distance of the flight that enemy bombers might have a similar range, so America was not necessarily safe from an attack by air.

When Hopkins undertook his mission for the president, he and Colonel Wilson, who was the liaison officer between the Army General Staff and the WPA, already had a working relationship. Hopkins shared the view of Roosevelt and the military that some of its legitimate needs were being denied by Congress. The president had put in his budget request for the 1938–39 fiscal year a request for a billion dollars for a "two-ocean Navy." Even the isolationists could not deny that warships could be used to defend America, and the president got his naval appropriation. But Hopkins later recalled that about the time

Roosevelt sent him to make his California survey, when the president said the country needed to add planes—he set the number at 8,000—as well as battleships, "everybody in the Army and the Navy and all the newspapers in the country jumped on him."

All this meant that well into 1939, American airpower continued to lag far behind Germany's. Not only did the United States have many fewer airplanes, the ones it had did not perform as well. In December 1938, the head of the U.S. Navy's Bureau of Aeronautics pleaded for more research money to develop planes equal to the German Messerschmitt and the new Heinkel fighter; the Heinkel could fly at 440 miles per hour, while no American or English plane could top 400 mph.

But in his last months as head of the WPA, Hopkins had been doing what he could, in public and behind the scenes, to repair the situation. In little-noted remarks in San Francisco on September 20, 1938, he said he would like to see more national defense projects performed by the WPA. Later that same year, after meetings with Wilson and General George C. Marshall, the head of the Army's War Plans Division who was appointed deputy chief of staff in October, Hopkins secretly authorized the use of several million dollars in WPA funds for making machine tools to be used to produce small-arms ammunition.

At the same time, the National Youth Administration, the education and training program within the WPA, was launching a program to help solve a serious shortage of aviation mechanics, who would be vital in wartime. Assistant Secretary of War Louis Johnson had sent a memorandum to Roosevelt on August 12, 1938, saying that War Department studies and conversations with aircraft manufacturers indicated "that one of the most serious problems as regards national defense will be found in a shortage of skilled workmen. Specifically, I anticipate that the shortage of airplane mechanics, both for the construction of aircraft in the civilian manufacturing plants as well as for the maintenance of planes in service with the armed forces, will be perhaps the most difficult problem of all."

Both England and Germany, he wrote, were turning out 5,000 trained aircraft mechanics every year. Here, too, the United States was far behind; airplane manufacturers and airlines would not spend money training more workers than they needed, and aspiring mechanics usually could not afford to pay to attend trade schools out of their own pocket. Johnson asked the president to direct the War Department to launch a comprehensive training program that involved government agencies, including the NYA, the CCC, and the Department of Labor.

Three days later, Roosevelt sent Hopkins a memorandum asking for his recommendations on the matter. By October, he went public, speaking at a news conference about the need for "a very large additional number of aviation mechanics" but adding that he was not yet ready to announce specifics of a training program. Before the end of the month, however, Aubrey Williams had given the White House a proposal to use NYA resources to set up a wide range of vocational training courses that could support military needs. It envisioned a system of schools in urban centers, as well as residential centers that brought together youth from isolated rural areas. The training, Williams wrote, "will include blacksmithing, electric and acetylene welding, sheet metal, simple pattern-making, foundry and machine tool practice, auto mechanics, electric motors and wiring, plumbing, steam-fitting, blue-print reading and draft."

The best students would graduate to regional centers for intensive training in mechanics and the metal trades, and a technical institute for master mechanics would incorporate the needs of the army and navy into its training program.

A feel of urgency accompanied these covert explorations and public pronouncements about the need for more airplanes, more ships, more mechanics, more defense projects. Still, it was not as if the country was starting from scratch to rebuild its military capability, despite the isolationist rule in Congress. Indeed, even with the restrictions placed upon it, from the very beginning the WPA had been working on the military complex to prevent installations from falling into decrepitude and disrepair.

2. THE PICATINNY ARSENAL

Construction at military camps and bases had languished after the American doughboys came home from France and the world war, a victim of the distaste for armed conflict left by 116,000 dead and 200,000 wounded. It was a distaste that would eventually harden into isolationism, and the deteriorating facilities distressed the professional officers who oversaw them. By the time work relief was institutionalized under the WPA, the armed services were poised to take advantage of what for them was cut-rate labor, since they paid only a sponsor's share of the costs, and prohibitions against using relief funds for munitions or matériel did not apply to construction at military bases or other installations.

From the moment the first $4 billion work relief appropriation was announced in 1935, the army's Quartermaster Corps went after a share of the money. By June 20 of that year, even before a single WPA worker was on the job, the corps had been allotted $1,215,772 for work on military posts across the country. In July, following up that early success, the quartermasters came back with a request for almost $20 million for work at facilities in fourteen states ranging from California to New York and Maine to Georgia. On July 12, two days after this request landed at the Division of Applications and

Information, the War Department applied for almost $23 million more in WPA work. Most of it was for construction and repair at army installations, but the navy's Bureau of Yards and Docks had also seen the potential and $676,400 of the request was for improving docking and other facilities. On July 20, the Quartermaster Corps was back again with another $24 million request for sixty-five projects scattered across several states. One of the largest of these requests was for $1,476,364 for "new buildings and other improvements" at New Jersey's Picatinny Arsenal.

Even the most ardent isolationists could not have argued that it was against the nation's interests for the WPA to work at the Picatinny Arsenal, a venerable piece of America's military history. Morris County, New Jersey, had been America's ammunition factory since the Revolutionary War, when Swiss ironmaster John Jacob Faesch supplied cannon, shot, and iron tools to George Washington's Continental Army from his Middle Forge, using a workforce of 250 Hessian prisoners. In 1880, the War Department bought the property on Lake Picatinny where the Middle Forge had been, and established the Dover Powder Depot for the storage of gunpowder used in making ammunition. The name was soon changed to Picatinny Powder Depot, and in 1907 it was changed again, to the Picatinny Arsenal. It became the first powder-manufacturing facility for the U.S. Army.

As the world war approached, the army expanded the arsenal and its activities there quickly. Within the gates that hung from cannon barrel gateposts, officers studied the science of weaponry and researched and developed new forms of ammunition. Handsome officers' homes of stucco and blue puddingstone were erected facing a parade ground; new magazines and warehouses were built of brick and tile. America's entry into the world war brought further expansion. The arsenal added testing and control laboratories and started experimental programs in artillery design and development. Fuse experiments began in 1921. In the years that preceded the depression, the army settled on Picatinny as its main artillery supply facility and increased its capacity to manufacture and load munitions. The number of buildings grew to over 900, many of them linked by a narrow-gauge railroad on which fireless locomotives moved artillery shells from manufacturing to storage or to outside standard rail and road links that would carry them to units at other bases. On adjacent land that had been deeded by the army to the U.S. Navy in 1891, the navy stored shells, high explosives, and smokeless and black powder in forty-four of its own magazines. The navy's ordnance was reserved for defending New York Harbor, just forty-five miles away to the southeast.

On the hot afternoon of July 10, 1926, thunderheads roiled the sky over northern New Jersey. Lightning ripped the clouds and thunder crackled like gunfire. One thunderclap shook the earth and brought people out into the streets of nearby Morristown. Before long, smoke rising over Picatinny Lake revealed that the thunderclap had actually been a massive explosion, caused by a lightning bolt that struck a naval magazine holding 670,000 pounds of high explosives. The detonation set off a chain of further explosions. The next magazine to erupt contained 1.6 million pounds of TNT. When it went up, it leveled the navy's storage depot and destroyed much of the arsenal. Shock waves rocketed out from the site and ricocheted among the hills. They blasted the walls and roofs of arsenal buildings from their frames and left skeletons of twisted metal, and blew away rail cars, leaving nothing but the wheels. Nineteen people died in the explosions and fires that followed, and forty more were wounded. In Mount Hope, Hibernia, and Rockaway, as far as a mile away, shells rained down and citizens ran for their lives. None of the shells exploded, but the shock waves flung cars and trucks around like toys, uprooted trees, and shattered plate glass windows.

When the smoke finally cleared, the Picatinny reservation looked like one of the blasted European battlefields of the Great War. The swath of devastation was a mile wide. Telephone and electrical wires hung limp and tangled from their listing poles. Steel railroad tracks were warped and useless. Huge craters marked the sites of the initial explosions, which had generated heat so great that it melted bricks and turned their sand content to glass. Hundreds of military and civilian workers, their barracks and homes destroyed, took refuge at hotels and the National Guard Armory in Morristown, where residents rushed donations of food, clothing, mattresses, and cots. Secretary of War Dwight F. Davis and three army generals who toured the smoldering ruins the next day were forced to take shelter from still-exploding shells.

Congress speedily appropriated $2.3 million to rebuild the arsenal complex in the wake of the disaster. But in the deceptive peace that followed the Treaty of Versailles, there was little sense of urgency, and the work was far from complete when the crash of October 1929 ended the boom times. Given the depression and the country's turn inward to concentrate on its own problems, the restoration work lagged further. Much of the vast complex remained in disrepair. The lack of storage facilities left the army storing high-caliber artillery shells by standing them on end in open fields, row upon row, without protection from the weather. Still, by 1935 and the advent of the WPA, Picatinny remained the army's primary ammunition research station and was at the forefront of explosives research. Dr. George C. Hale, working there, patented the powerful explosive Haleite in 1935 and developed a processing method for armor-piercing cyclonite. The physical plant, however, continued to be a shabby vestige of the arsenal of the early 1920s.

But just as Robert Moses's corps of engineers and architects had at the ready blueprints that brought an outsized share of WPA funds to New York City, when the time came the army's artillery command had well-developed plans in hand for rehabilitation of the complex. Two years earlier, in 1933, FERA workers operating under the first emergency relief appropriation had surveyed the arsenal's grounds and buildings to assess its physical and engineering needs, from building reconstruction to water, sewer, and flood control improvements. The survey information went into plans drawn by the Corps of Engineers, and those plans, in turn, sped through the Division of Applications and Information and the Committee on Allotments and won Roosevelt's swift approval. On September 19, 1935, even as Harry Hopkins was still trying to clear the bottlenecks that were keeping funds away from some other projects of the new WPA, the agency went to work on Picatinny's resurrection.

Every part of the arsenal complex, which now covered 1,842 acres, fell under the rehabilitation plans. A workforce of a thousand men descended on the Morris County site, skilled workers and laborers alike.

The first goal was to reconstruct the magazines. There were at least sixty-five of these powder, ammunition, and explosives storage buildings at the arsenal, ranging in size from 30 by 30 feet to 30 by 150 feet. Although their walls had been rebuilt following the 1926 explosion, floors and roofs were crumbling; some had been replaced with nothing more than tar paper and corrugated metal after the explosion. WPA crews ripped up rotting wooden floors and poured new ones of concrete, installed new wooden roof trusses and reinforced ones that could be saved, and tore off old roofs and replaced them, all in all providing almost 160,000 square feet of rebuilt storage space.

Security was also tightened. WPA workers used discarded rails from the arsenal's outdated railway system as fence posts, set them in concrete, and erected a six-mile perimeter of climb-proof fence.

The spring floods of 1936 set back plans to upgrade the rail system of narrow- and standard-gauge track when the waters washed the roadbeds out from under long stretches of track, leaving tracks and ties suspended, but by the time the work was finished crews had renewed eighteen miles of existing lines and added some two and a half miles of new construction. The rail cars that moved over the arsenal's lines were also refurbished in a WPA shop where boxcars and flatcars were stripped down to their wheels and given new frames, floors, sides, and roofs.

By the summer of 1937, with as many as 1,300 men working at times of peak WPA employment, the restoration and upgrading of the complex was largely complete. Ten miles of new paved roads wove through the site. There were seven new or rebuilt road and railway bridges. New sewer and water lines ran underground, and the sewage treatment plant had been rebuilt using up-to-date equipment. Steam lines had been rerouted and rehung, wrapped in waterproofing, and painted. A number of new buildings had risen on the campus, including a greenhouse, quarters for company and non-commissioned officers, a variety of storage buildings, a pyrotechnic factory for the production of signal and night-lighting flares, a rock-crushing plant, and a building used for cleaning shells. The experimental fuse plant, where bomb detonation fuses were developed and produced, was almost doubled in size with the addition of a new second floor. When more than a hundred small buildings, some used for hazardous explosives loading processes, were included, the arsenal had a total of 530 new and reconstructed buildings set amid new landscaping.

When Roosevelt made his quarantine speech that fall, New Jersey's Picatinny Arsenal was ready to resume its role as ammunition maker to the United States military. Except for small-arms and machine gun bullets, the plant was capable of making every type of ammunition from .30 caliber to sixteen-inch shells. These last, used in the turret guns of battleships, contained 800 pounds of powder poured by hand into eight-foot bags.

Nevertheless, with America still locked in its oasis of neutrality, the arsenal worked almost like a craft shop, as if it were making fireworks for the Fourth of July. It was not yet urgent to keep the military's weapons loaded. The arsenal produced only 600 bomb fuses in 1938, and all of them were painstakingly handmade.

3. RACE AND ISOLATIONISM

Roosevelt's quarantine speech had been an attempt to alert and educate the country. It was, he conceded, less successful than he had hoped, but he also believed that events would bring the public around to his point of view.

In November 1937, the month following the speech, Italy, Germany, and Japan formed the Rome-Berlin-Tokyo Axis. While not yet the formal military alliance that would be created by the Tripartite Treaty in 1940, formation of the Axis was a declaration of mutual interest and opposition to the democracies.

Nor had there been any letup in the aggression of which the president had spoken in Chicago. Indeed, it had increased and, in one instance, targeted America. Japan's Imperial Army, having invaded China that summer and taken Shanghai at the mouth of the Yangtze River, was occupying large chunks of Chinese territory. By early December, two months after the Chicago speech, Japan was at the gates of Nanking, the Chinese capital, located 150 miles farther up the Yangtze, and China's Nationalist government under Chiang Kai-shek advised Americans to leave the city. Embassy staff, foreign correspondents and photographers, and American businessmen retreated to an American gunboat, the *Panay*, anchored in the river. When the *Panay* was loaded, her crew weighed anchor and moved upstream away from the Japanese lines, anchoring again near three American tankers. All the vessels assumed that the treaty designating the Yangtze as international waters meant they were safe from attack. Moreover, the gunboat was well marked, with American flags painted on its hull and superstructure and its location known, the American embassy in Tokyo having informed the Japanese that it was standing by for a rescue mission, specifically to prevent an accidental attack. But on December 12, Japanese dive-bombers swooped down on the gunboat and tankers, as well as on a British gunboat in the same area, sinking the military vessels and two of the tankers. Then the warplanes strafed the lifeboats heading to shore. Two of the *Panay's* crew and one of the civilians were killed, and many were wounded. Film taken during the attack clearly showed it was deliberate. The isolationists, however, argued that the gunboat had provoked the attack because it was escorting the tankers. Afterward, American opinion stood two to one in favor of getting out of the Far East altogether, meaning missionaries and doctors as well as diplomats and business representatives. Indeed, it was the *Panay* incident that brought Ludlow's referendum-to-declare-war amendment out of committee onto the House floor to be debated. In view of such sentiments, Washington demanded $2 million in reparations and accepted the money along with Tokyo's "profound apology."

When Nanking (now Nanjing) fell, for the Chinese, soldiers and civilians alike, the consequences were far worse than America's loss of lives and property. Japanese commanders unleashed their troops in a bloody orgy lasting over a period of six weeks, in which nearly 370,000 civilians and prisoners of war were killed and as many as 80,000 women and girls raped. American newspapers and magazines carried reports of the atrocities, yet rather than shaking the grip of isolationism, these reports seemed to reinforce it. The stories emerging from Nanking were too terrible to be believed.

Furthermore, to the extent that it focused on foreign matters at all, American attention was fixed on Europe, although there, too, evidence of the brutality to come was being dismissed or ignored. Through 1937, Hitler's war against the Jews had been largely a matter of marginalization and harassment. The Nuremberg Laws, passed in 1935, had reduced German Jews from citizens to subjects. They were prohibited from teaching Germans, could not work as dentists, doctors, or accountants, and had to file papers with the government describing the businesses they operated and register lists of their assets and property.

But it was not until November 1938, shortly after the midterm elections in the United States, that the campaign escalated from official contempt to sanctioned violence. When a Jewish teenager in Paris reacted to his family's expulsion from their home in Hanover by assassinating a minor official with the German embassy, propaganda minister Joseph Goebbels blamed it on "international Jewry," and unleashed gangs of Nazi thugs. They smashed and looted Jewish businesses and synagogues across the country and attacked and murdered Jews in a two-day rampage that was fully endorsed by authorities. Reinhard Heydrich of the SS, the black-uniformed enforcers of Nazi purity known for their intolerance and cruelty, sent a memo to local officers that included these instructions: "Only such measures are to be taken as do not endanger German lives and property (i.e., synagogues are to be burned down only where there is no danger of fire in neighboring buildings). Places of business and apartments belonging to Jews may be destroyed but not looted." The violence demolished 101 synagogues and 7,500 Jewish businesses, 91 Jews died, and 27,000 were arrested and sent to concentration camps. The pogrom, which came to be called Kristallnacht, "the night of broken glass," signaled the onset of genocide.

Yet even as the fascist ascendency continued in 1939, with Germany swallowing Czechoslovakia, Italy occupying Albania, Franco taking Madrid in March to end the Spanish Civil War and bring fascism to Spain, and Japan continuing its rampage across China, most Americans still considered domestic matters their prime concern. Moreover, even as they evinced a desire to turn away from what George Washington had called "the insidious wiles of foreign influence," the home-front waters were being roiled by many of the same ugly hatreds that lay behind these events occurring overseas.

The would-be Nazis of the German-American Bund were the tip of the iceberg, and what festered beneath the surface rendered the Bund members, goosestepping in their storm trooper uniforms, pale by comparison. William Dudley Pelley was a homegrown anti-Semite from

Lynn, Massachusetts, who formed his Silver Legion in the wake of Hitler's ascension to power in Germany. By 1939, he claimed 100,000 members, the "flower of Protestant Christian manhood," who trained in far-flung American camps for the coming worldwide fascist revolution and called themselves Silver Shirts in an echo of Germany's SS. Father Coughlin returned to the airwaves in a new guise: he no longer emoted about social justice, but spoke in favor of the Christian Front, an Irish Catholic equivalent of the Silver Shirts, and at a rally in the Bronx he told his followers, "When we get through with the Jews in America, they'll think the treatment they received in Germany was nothing." The Christian Front and the Citizens Protective League, American Patriots, Inc., the Ku Klux Klan, Defenders of the Christian Faith, the Knights of the White Camellia, and various other more or less organized groups—some 800 of them, according to *Survey Graphic* magazine—stirred a potent brew of isolationism, anti-Semitism, and anti-Communism that boiled over into hate speech and violence. Anti-Roosevelt extremists railed against the "Jew Deal." Youths lurked on New York subway platforms to insult girls they decided were Jewish and provoke their escorts to retaliate so they could beat them up. A Christian Front camp in Narrowsburg, New York, in the Catskills on the Pennsylvania border, had a rifle range where shooters fired at targets made to look like the president.

Insulting the Roosevelts was nothing new, of course. Detractors had been hurling slime since the moment the president took office. Some of them could not even bear to say his name; he was "that man" in parlor conversation. But the calumny aimed at the president was mild compared to that flung at Eleanor Roosevelt, owing among other reasons to her unapologetic embrace of black Americans and their causes and her willingness to welcome them regularly into the White House. The vilest whisperers said that she and the president both had gonorrhea that she had contracted from a black lover.

The racial prejudice and fear this foulness signaled swelled even further with the rise of Hitler and the Nazis. That one of America's greatest heroes walked the path of Nazism and anti-Semitism must have granted some license to these feelings. Charles Lindbergh was an international icon, Lucky Lindy, the triumphant Lone Eagle who had flown into history with the first solo flight over the Atlantic in 1927, then as the victim of his baby son's horrendous kidnapping and death in 1932. Three years later, after a long investigation and a trial in which the accused kidnapper, Bruno Hauptmann, was convicted and sentenced to death, Lindbergh and his wife, Anne Morrow Lindbergh, fled to England to escape the relentless public exposure to which they were subjected. In 1937, they moved to an island off the coast of France, where he pursued an interest in the work of the French scientist Dr. Alexis Carrel, who had won the Nobel Prize for medicine in 1912. Carrel also had notions about racial superiority, and Lindbergh embraced them. It was during this time that the Lindberghs first visited Germany. The American military attaché in Berlin, who suggested this, wanted an assessment of German airpower, and Lindbergh came away impressed not only with the country's rapidly developing and technologically advanced air force but also with the energy and vigor he detected in the German people under Hitler.

In October 1938, Field Marshal Hermann Goering, the head of the German air force, gave Lindbergh the Service Cross of the German Eagle, the highest honor Germany could award a foreign national. The swastika-embellished cross was bestowed for his contributions to aviation, and Lindbergh, having received many honors for his solo flight, accepted it as such. (Henry Ford, another American with anti-Semitic views, was also given the German cross in 1938; it was presented by the German consul in front of 1,500 prominent Detroiters gathered at a dinner to celebrate the automaker's seventy-fifth birthday.)

The deadly rampage of Kristallnacht occurred a month after Lindbergh received the Service Cross. Though he embraced Germany's notions of its racial and military superiority, the pogrom did dissuade the Lindberghs from their plans to move to Berlin. In 1939, they returned to the United States and Lindbergh joined the ranks of the isolationists. Two weeks after Germany invaded Poland that September 1 and France and England declared war on Germany in response, he spoke on nationwide radio to urge that America remain neutral. A war against some "Asiatic intruder" such as Genghis Khan or Xerxes would be a different story, but war in Europe, he said, was "not a question of banding together to defend the white race against foreign invasion," but "one more of those age-old quarrels within our own family of nations." Shadowy powers, Lindbergh suggested in a veiled reference to the Jews, were the ones who wanted America to take sides against Hitler: "We must learn to look behind every article we read and every speech we hear. We must not only inquire about the writer and the speaker—about his personal interests and his nationality, but we must ask who owns and who influences the newspaper, the news picture, and the radio station."

A month later, after Poland had surrendered, he spoke again over the radio, arguing against sending arms to Europe. "I do not believe that repealing the arms embargo would assist democracy in Europe because I do not believe this is a war for democracy," he said. "This is a war over the balance of power in Europe."

The White House knew otherwise. "This nation will remain a neutral nation," Roosevelt had pledged in a fireside chat two days after the German tanks smashed into Poland, and hours after the British and French declared war on Germany. But, he added, "I cannot ask that every American remain neutral in thought as well. Even a neutral has a right to take account of facts. Even a neutral cannot be asked to close his mind or close his conscience."

And American public opinion, aided by photographs and newsreels documenting the harshness of German occupation, showing Poles being ousted from their homes at gunpoint, had finally begun to shift in Roosevelt's direction. Sixty percent of Americans polled favored repeal of the Neutrality Act, and 84 percent wanted to see the Allies win, versus 2 percent for the Germans. In Congress, those who held to the strictest interpretations of neutrality were suddenly on the defensive. Counting votes, the president decided it was time to press for an end to the embargo. He called Congress into special session at the end of September.

In November, Lindbergh expanded his views still further in a *Reader's Digest* article. Accommodating Hitler, he wrote, would erect a "Western Wall of race and arms which can hold back either a Genghis Khan or the infiltration of inferior blood." By now his prejudices, ever more blatant, appealed only to a small minority. They went right on hating, but Lindbergh was winning no new converts to his point of view.

Indeed, by the time the article appeared, Roosevelt had all but won the battle. William Borah and his isolationist colleagues fought on, but both the Senate and the House voted for repeal of the old Neutrality

Act by substantial margins, and on November 3 its worst restrictions were erased. Some limits remained, but under the Neutrality Act of 1939, America could sell arms and grant credits for arms purchases to nations at war. This meant that the United States could start arming the Allies, and an Anglo-French Purchasing Board set up shop in Washington.

4. HOLD THE JOKES, PLEASE

T he furious debate over neutrality had bypassed the WPA. But while it raged, the agency was anything but placid. It was coping with internal problems of its own, and although these lacked the grave import of war and peace, in keeping with the contest between isolation and involvement they did reflect divisions between two impassioned and vocal schools of thought within the country. Some of these were more serious than others.

In the months before war broke out in Europe, the regrowth of the WPA as a result of the Roosevelt recession had triggered a resumption of the wisecracks that had been a feature of the 1936 presidential race. Some went to great lengths to be funny. During construction of the Aquatic Park in San Francisco, jokesters told of WPA carpenters discarding half their nails because the heads were on the wrong end, until supervisors issued instructions to save them since they could be used later when work shifted to the other side of the building. The do-nothing WPA as an example of suspended animation was another popular theme: one old fellow asks another his age. "Eighty-four," says the other. "I would have been eighty-six, but I was on WPA for two years."

This brand of humor persisted in nightclubs and on the vaudeville circuit until it reached the point where the workers who were the butt of the jokes started feeling sorry for themselves. Their complaints reached the American Federation of Actors, which in March adopted a resolution prohibiting its 10,000 members from using witticisms about the WPA and WPA workers in front of paying audiences. "The WPA joke is a very great injustice," said federation executive Ralph Whitehead, and compared it to a joke at a funeral. The heads of Actors' Equity and the Associated Actors and Artistes of America, when asked if they would join the ban, said they sympathized but didn't want to put shackles on their members' humor.

In rare instances the WPA even displayed an ability to laugh at itself. The Theatre Project turned the tables in a lighthearted revue called "Sing for Your Supper," which featured a skit in which the actors sang and danced as they leaned on miniature shovels. But the jokes, of course, persisted, along with other barbs. A year after workers found laugh lines about the WPA unfunny, Louis Armstrong and the Mills Brothers had a hit with a Jesse Stone song entitled "W.P.A.," which rhymed the old shovel-leaning charges and put them to a foxtrot beat featuring Armstrong's trumpet:

> Sleep while you work while you rest while you play
> Lean on your shovel to pass the time away

The three major radio networks banned play of the song on the grounds that it was in "bad taste," and the complaints eventually reached Decca Records, which in the summer of 1940 announced it was withdrawing the record from the market.

But it was certainly hard not to laugh at—and with—some of the more far-fetched projects. The straitlaced Brehon Somervell, head of the WPA in New York City, defended its "record for good work" against the jokes, but in November 1938 he revealed that a $103,339 project to repair fire hydrants in Brooklyn would include painting and stenciling them and topping them off with shiny aluminum domes. "Brooklyn's Fire Hydrants to Be Glorified by WPA," chortled a headline in the *Brooklyn Eagle*.

And how could the law-abiding citizens of Indianapolis be persuaded to visit a local fire station to submit themselves to voluntary fingerprinting by a WPA worker? By suggesting that they might bump their heads and suddenly become amnesiacs, forgetting who they were. That was actually one of the arguments for a joint Indianapolis police–WPA program that had been launched in December 1937. Set up with a $5,453 WPA grant, the fingerprinting scheme sent eighteen relief workers for police instruction, and then to four city fire stations that had been pressed into service for the program. Although some 3,000 "non-criminal" prints already were on file with the police, the early turnout for the WPA program was disappointing.

"Despite invitations to the public to have prints taken and filed, there has been little response," reported the *Indianapolis News*. "Apparently the fact that fingerprinting was developed originally for use in identifying criminals makes it difficult for police to extend the service to people generally."

Nonsense, said Lieutenant Albert G. Perrott of the Indianapolis police bureau of identification, who was coordinating the program with the WPA and had trained the workers. He said criminals had it all over law-abiding citizens because their fingerprints were on file. "If a criminal is picked up dead, they check his fingerprints, find out who he is and ship him home, and he gets a nice funeral—flowers and music and everything. In many cases, the honest citizen loses out completely in a case like this. They may never get the right name on his tombstone, if he ever gets one; he may land in the potter's field or in a lime kiln. I understand they put 'em in a lime kiln in Chicago." After all, 60,000 unidentified bodies were discovered in the country every year.

Criminal and non-criminal fingerprints would not be mixed, said Perrott. And women were reassured that fingerprints would not reveal their age: "Wrinkles may come, hair fall out and teeth disappear, but the fingerprints do not change through the years." The only caution he offered them was that they should refrain from having manicures before they got their prints taken, because it took gasoline to get the ink off "and there goes your nail polish."

Despite the lieutenant's impressive salesmanship and ample local news coverage—"City 'Awhorl!' " read one headline, clearly pleased with itself—that lured volunteers to the fire stations in the program's first days, business quickly fell off, and the WPA fingerprinters, who were on duty from eleven in the morning to nine at night six days a week, were rarely called upon to apply their newfound skills. Other law enforcement agencies, including the New Orleans police department and the New York State Bureau of Identification, also employed WPA trainees to take and classify fingerprints, but none of these tried to lure citizens in to give prints voluntarily.

There were any number of reasons why law-abiding people might have been reluctant to put their fingerprints on file, and within the WPA some of them were especially strong. The FBI's J. Edgar Hoover wanted to establish a national fingerprint index, and in April 1938 he said he thought it should start with workers on the rolls of the WPA. Hopkins strenuously resisted the idea, but it resurfaced after he resigned, and Harrington was a far more malleable figure. To convince would-be critics that he was neither a fire-breathing liberal like Hopkins nor a conservative, he bragged that he had never voted in his life and therefore was free of political bias. By January 1939—within a month of his appointment—he had allowed Somervell in New York City to order all WPA educational workers who came into contact with children to be fingerprinted in order to prevent sex crimes. But many others whose contacts with children were random at most, including carpenters, printers, and clerks, reported to the WPA Teachers' Union that they, too, had been ordered to submit to fingerprinting.

Union executive secretary William Levner called Somervell's order a "trial balloon" for ordering all New York City WPA workers—then numbering 170,000—to provide fingerprints. In turn, he said, that could lead to labor blacklists, police surveillance, intimidation, and potential blackmail.

In Philadelphia, WPA administrator Harry R. Halloran refused fingerprinting for the workers in his education and recreation division after some 200 New York workers were caught in the fingerprint dragnet and fired, many for petty offenses long in the past. One had stolen a single item when he was twelve years old and never committed a crime since. Halloran said he believed that "intelligent selection of competent personnel is far more effective in preventing the possibility of sex crimes than fingerprinting."

Fears that the New York program could be misused were further borne out after Somervell added workers who handled valuable government property to the list of those told to report for "voluntary" fingerprinting. One was Anthony Merendino, a non-relief construction engineer. His fingerprint record revealed that twenty years earlier he had pawned a ring he bought on the installment plan and hadn't finished paying for. For obtaining money under false pretenses, he was convicted and sentenced to a twenty-month jail term, which he served. His WPA career had been remarkably successful. From associate supervisor of a small project, he had worked his way up to a supervising engineer, and at the time his prints were taken he had 4,000 people working under him, was making $2,900 a year, and had a job rating of 100 percent. Merendino, told he was about to be fired, resigned instead.

Both the jokes and the lurking suspicions that led to the push for fingerprinting WPA workers were fostered by the poisons spewed into the political atmosphere by the Dies and Woodrum committees. And many, indeed most, WPA workers faced additional troubles in the months preceding the start of the war in Europe. These stemmed from a drive in Congress to assert stiff new controls over the WPA, adjusting wage scales downward, curbing political involvement, and generally bringing the agency to heel.

5. PINK SLIPS AND PINKOS

Congress was determined to "fix" the WPA in 1939. Several factors contributed to this determination. One was a residue of anger at Hopkins, now removed as a target himself, over the charges that local officials had played footsie with political campaigns in several states in the 1938 elections. Conservatives retained their general distaste for the vast cadre of workers on the public payroll who seemed to favor unions and other forms of "leftist thinking," and that distaste was heightened by the uncountered accusations aired before the Dies Committee. Before the fixing was over, the WPA would face an unsettling array of changes.

The first of these was an absolute ban on political activities by WPA employees. Public Resolution Number One, which went into effect in March 1939, made it a felony to offer a job as a political reward, to threaten to deprive anyone of a job as political punishment, or to solicit political contributions within the WPA. It was also a firing offense (though not a criminal one) for anyone on the WPA payroll to work in or manage a political campaign, or try to influence the outcome of a campaign.

Colonel Harrington, at a March 9 news conference, said the latter portion of the new law covered hundreds of the agency's 35,000 administrative personnel. As a result, he said, "we are having to re-move a number of persons who have been county chairmen, presidents of political groups, or who have occupied other positions of that char-acter." If they didn't quit, he said, they would be fired. Evidence of ac-tivities that violated the criminal portions of the statute would be turned over to the Justice Department.

The ban on "pernicious political activities," to take effect later in 1939, would be widened to include all federal employees under the Hatch Act, of which Democratic Senator Carl A. Hatch of New Mexico was the prime champion.

But these rules were minor in their impact compared with the provi-sions of the new relief appropriation act for the 1940 fiscal year that grudgingly allowed the WPA to continue. Contained within the legis-lation that cut off funding for the Federal Theatre and forced the re-maining arts projects to turn to the states for sponsorship was a far more drastic change. The new relief act forced the abandonment of the prevailing wage system that had governed WPA pay rates from its start, despite attempts to change it. Prevailing wages meant trade union rates in urban industrial areas, and where those wages were the norm, a WPA worker could earn a month's pay by putting in a little over a week's worth of hours. Replacing this happy arrangement was a "security wage" that allowed workers to earn roughly the same monthly pay, but in many cases doubled and almost tripled their hours. Workers and their unions reacted with outrage.

Work stoppages halted WPA projects across the nation early in July when 100,000 workers, mostly skilled tradesmen, walked off the job. In New York, strikes shut down construction of two schools and the new airport at North Beach that would later be called La Guardia Field. One thousand WPA workers in Rochester quit the projects they were working on and signed their names to a petition demanding that Congress return to the prevailing wage system. Employees halted work in Cleveland, Toledo, Detroit, Chicago, and San Francisco. State WPA offices also reported walkouts in New Jersey, Massachusetts, Minnesota, Wisconsin, Florida, Iowa, Kansas, Indiana, Washington, and Mississippi. Most of the job actions were peaceful, but in Minneapolis, a policeman died after a clash with striking workers.

Skilled workers in urban areas suffered most under the new rules. In New York City, on the four-week standard by which the WPA kept its pay records, carpenters who had earned $85.75 by working 48 hours now had to work 120 hours for $85.20. The same $85.20 for 120 hours of work over four weeks applied to plumbers and electricians, who had worked 42 hours for $84; bricklayers 42 hours for $79.21; structural iron workers 44 hours for $84.70; sheet metal workers 46 hours for $85.10; metal lathers 48 hours for $84; and painters 56 hours for $84.

At the middle-skill levels, workers also saw their hours more than double, but they at least received small four-week raises under the new scale. Drill runners, bricklayers' helpers, house wreckers, concrete and cement workers, and asphalt workers, all of whom had drawn pay of between $56.01 and $64.01 for working between 48 and 64 hours, now received $66 for 120 hours on the job.

Common laborers were the largest group affected by the new wage regimen. They had worked longer hours for less pay under the old scale, so were less drastically affected. Already used to putting in 112 hours over four weeks for a $56 paycheck, now they would work 8 hours more for 80 cents less.

Professionals were affected, too. The hours of dentists, doctors, and lawyers on the WPA payroll doubled, from 60 hours to 120, while their pay dropped from $91.08 to $90. Teachers and recreation instructors fared a little better. They had worked 84 and 96 hours, respectively, for $91.06, and under the new scale would work 120 hours for $90.

The WPA took a hard line against the stoppages. Harrington told reporters on July 6 that he didn't consider the job actions a strike, since strikes were intended to lead to negotiations, and negotiations were not going to happen. The WPA's work would benefit from the new arrangement, he said; construction supervisors would find jobs easier to manage with all of the workers on the same schedule. And he suggested that the new wage scale would reduce cheating, since workers frequently used their extra time to hold private jobs under assumed names, a practice the WPA's investigative unit was helpless to stop unless it received reports of violators.

Two days later, Harrington met with a delegation from the American Federation of Labor, which represented 125 unions, and told them that their protests were useless. They were to tell their workers that "the requirement of working 130 hours a month is law [120

hours over four weeks translated to 130 hours a month]; that no official of the WPA up or down the line can change it; that we offer employment under those conditions—working 130 hours a month for a
security wage. The decision as to whether they accept the employment
or not is in their own hands.

"Furthermore, if anyone is off his job for five consecutive working
days without any reason other than that he doesn't want to work, he
will be dropped from the rolls."

Somervell, in New York, echoed this ultimatum, and the city's welfare commissioner said that WPA workers who refused to accept the
new wage scale would be turned down for home relief. Somervell
threatened to file felony charges against anyone interfering with WPA
jobs, even if this meant merely throwing up a picket line.

Most of the wildcat strikes stopped within the five-day limit. Even
with the usual summer uptick in private hiring, the waiting list for
WPA jobs was always larger than the number who were working,
and those already on the rolls were not ready to give up their steady
paychecks even if it meant many more hours on the job. But in
Minneapolis, the work stoppages persisted for two weeks and shut
down much of the WPA construction in the city. Workers who wanted
to go back to their jobs were prevented by union protesters until city
and state police stepped in to protect them. But eventually, even the
most persistent strikes dissolved after Roosevelt declined to back
moves in Congress to restore the union wage scale, and when the
Workers Alliance called a one-day strike to protest the new work
rules, few workers joined in.

An even larger problem for WPA workers followed on the heels of
the revised wage scale. That was a provision in the appropriations act
aimed at preventing "careerism" in WPA employees. It stated that relief workers on the agency's rolls could work no more than eighteen
months in succession. Then they had to give up their jobs for at least a
month and apply to be recertified for relief before returning. This provision, along with the new wage scale, would take effect September 1.
Harrington estimated it would affect at least 600,000 of the 2.4 million employees then on the rolls and hamper a number of projects that
would lose essential personnel. By August 31, with German tanks
massed at the Polish border, WPA employment stood at 1.8 million as
the eighteen-month rule temporarily stripped the rolls.

Yet another new rule landed on the WPA as the result of the new appropriations act, one more example of the Dies Committee's effect upon American political life. It included a requirement that WPA employees now had to take a loyalty oath as the price of their jobs. At its least, this requirement allowed Harrington to scoff at the committee's charges of Communism within the WPA's ranks.

Asked at the same July 6 news conference if he had had to halt "Red activities," the colonel was at first incredulous. "Do you mean that seriously?" he asked the questioner.

Assured that he did, Harrington said, "No, I have not found it necessary to halt Red activities in the WPA. There is a great safeguard now, you know," he continued sarcastically. "They have to take an oath that they do not advocate the overthrow of the government by force or violence." He did not take the charges seriously, he said, and did not think the oath was necessary.

Nevertheless, the anti-Communist outcry had its effect on behavior within the WPA. Even the pro-Communist Workers Alliance told its members they were required to pledge their loyalty to the United States in an echo of the oath required by the relief appropriations bill. "The idea is to answer those who charge we are subversive and against the government," said Willis R. Morgan, president of the New York chapter. He said Communists could take the pledge and still belong to the union. (By that point the union's leadership was almost entirely in Communist hands; founder and national president David Lasser would resign within a year and denounce the Workers Alliance as a Communist front.)

Workers who declined to sign the loyalty oath were summarily dismissed. But very few, no matter how they felt about it, were willing or able to give up their paychecks on grounds of principle. In New York, only 66 of the 103,985 WPA workers in the city failed to sign, some apparently because they were sick and had not been at work. One who refused was Art Project muralist August Henkel, a Communist who had run for Congress and state office on the party ticket.

Henkel had painted aviation scenes for the terminal at Brooklyn's Floyd Bennett Field, but once he was fired and his politics had been revealed, critics looked for evidence of subversion in his murals. The Women's International Association of Aeronautics, the Flatbush Chamber of Commerce, and the Floyd Bennett Post of the American

Legion found much cause for suspicion. The Wright brothers, they said, seemed to be dressed in Russian peasant garb, one of Henkel's planes resembled a Soviet aircraft, the star on a pictured Naval Reserve hangar was red, not the regulation white, and one of his figures looked like Josef Stalin. As far as the Stalin image was concerned, Henkel maintained that he had merely copied a picture of Franz Reichelt, a mustachioed Austrian tailor who dabbled (fatally) in parachuting, having combined an overcoat and parachute that he tested by jumping from the Eiffel Tower and falling to his death. Nevertheless, his Bennett Field murals were ripped down and destroyed in 1940.

6. BEFORE THE DELUGE (VINCENT JAMES "JIMMY" BONANNO)

Jimmy Bonanno was a union man, but he watched the WPA labor strife with no particular concern. Ever since 1933, almost six years now, he had bent over a last at the Columbia Slipper factory at Prince and Crosby Streets in New York City, turning out slippers on a piecework basis that paid him between $27 and $30 a week. He and his wife, Teresa, had one child, Frank, whose birth in May 1935 coincided with the advent of the WPA. They also took care of Teresa's little brother, Gerry, a responsibility for which they received $20 monthly from the City of New York's Bureau of Child Welfare, since Gerry, like Teresa, was motherless, had been abandoned by their father, and so was considered an orphan. The household's combined income, which could approach $150 a month, was good money for the times.

What complaints Bonanno had were related not to his job but to his living situation. Their apartment, on Allen Street between Delancey and Rivington in the heart of New York's Lower East Side immigrant quarter, had gotten too small for them, and bums were a constant presence, sleeping in the building entryway and warming themselves over wood fires built in empty oil drums in vacant lots around the neighborhood. And he was getting tired of paying 3 cents at the public baths across the street when he wanted a hot bath.

"They'd give you soap and a towel, and you'd go in and when the bell rang you had to get out. They'd give you maybe ten minutes," he said. "This was cold-water-flats days." In the middle of 1939, they decided to move to an apartment with hot water in Brooklyn.

Bonanno turned thirty that August. He had been born on the Lower East Side in 1909 but left with his parents for their native Sicily in 1917. After ten years, when he realized that they probably would never return to the United States despite frequent promises to do so, he and his brother Umberto came back on their own. They disembarked from the boat on a Friday in June. Jimmy, who was still called Vincenzo then, was not yet eighteen but already a man, and along with his luggage he carried a box of carpenter's tools. These he took with him on Monday when he went to meet his cousin, Dominic Logalbo, a union carpenter with whom he now began an apprenticeship that lasted, he later remembered, "quite a few years."

Still, from 1927 to 1929, his income as a young carpenter met his needs and more. "I was a rich man," he said. Then came the depression. The work that had been plentiful during the good times began to disappear, and soon he was scrambling—"jumping around," as he put it—to find odd jobs to sustain himself. He lived with his cousin, so the rent was cheap. New York's Lower East Side had always been poor; now it was a virtual showcase for the woes of the depression. A soup kitchen opened a block away, on Chrystie Street near Rivington, and he watched the lines of people shuffle along, buckets in hand to receive steaming bean soup and rice ladled out of garbage cans. Another cousin had a barber shop on East 3rd Street, and one day the talk was all about the older upstairs tenant who had thrown himself off the roof after losing his job and spending the last of his money. There were the men who slept on park benches, one a lawyer who collected empty cardboard boxes and took them to a store on Delancey Street where neckties were made, where he would be paid a nickel for a box, but who refused handouts if he had no boxes to sell. After Roosevelt took office and government relief became a possibility, Bonanno was among those who didn't want it. "To me, relief was a joke," he said. "I wanted to work."

Providentially, work appeared in the form of a job at the slipper factory. Bonanno put away his carpenter's tools, joined the boot and shoe workers union, and began the steady routine of a slipper maker at the factory at Prince and Crosby, in a part of the Lower East Side that would much later take the fancier name of Soho. He rented an apartment on the second floor of the building at 122 Allen Street. Above him lived a taxi driver named Nick Furco, who went out every morning and drove until he had a quarter in his pocket. He would purchase breakfast with the money and bring the food home to his wife and two daughters. When they had eaten together, Furco would hit the streets again.

In his new stability, Bonanno found romance. Teresa Fiore was sixteen. Her mother had done hand embroidery on women's coats, and it was Teresa's job while still a child to deliver the coats back to the factories that had sent them over. This she did, summer and winter, though in the winter she had no coat of her own, only a sweater. After her mother died at Bellevue Hospital of internal bleeding, Teresa and her infant brother fell under the care of an aunt, who took them in grudgingly. Teresa went to work in a non-union garment sweatshop, where she sewed for pay of only $5 a week. This money, said Bonanno, was taken by the aunt and used, among other things, to clothe her own daughter. "The daughter was dressed like a princess. Teresa dressed like a beggar. That was how she was treated," he recalled.

Bonanno courted Teresa for a little over a year. There was family trouble, Bonanno's uncle at his behest complaining to the aunt about her treatment of the girl. The aunt moved out, saying to Bonanno, "You take her. I don't want her." Teresa was then seventeen and Gerry three.

She and Bonanno were married on January 27, 1934. Her uncle accompanied them to city hall and stood up as her father when they applied for the marriage license. The wedding was held at the Church of the Nativity on Second Avenue. Bonanno wore a rented tuxedo and Teresa a rented gown, white, with a long train and a white hat. Her hair was done in marcelled waves, she carried white calla lilies, and lipstick adorned her cupid's-bow mouth. Her rings came from a pawn shop on the Bowery (he would exchange them later for better ones) and the wedding pictures were taken at the M. Ficalora Studios, also on the Bowery. For the reception, they went home to his Allen Street

apartment with the bathtub in the kitchen and its four rooms furnished only with the bedroom and kitchen sets on which he had spent
$300. "It was all the riches I had under my name, but I told her, we
buy on cash, not credit," he said. Workers at the slipper factory passed
the hat and collected $35 as a wedding present. Relatives brought
them towels and lamps and other household items. The sandwiches
for the reception came from Buffa's Luncheonette, where a plate of
spaghetti and meatballs cost a quarter. Friends, among them a man-
dolin player and a singer, provided entertainment. Bonanno's brother
Umberto supplied sodas, as well as copious hard drinks that rendered
the building's super, another cousin, drunk, as well as the cop who
walked the Allen Street beat. The super retired to his own apartment,
while the wedding party undressed the passed-out cop, put him to bed,
and later woke him up in time to get back into uniform and make his
shift change.

The second year of their marriage brought a child, Frank, born on
May 23, 1935. Frank was four when his parents decided to abandon
the teeming Lower East Side for Brooklyn. It was a fateful move.

Two weeks after they moved into their new apartment on West 5th
Street, the Columbia Slipper factory closed its doors at Prince and
Crosby Streets and fled to Pennsylvania, leaving behind a broken
union and fifty jobless workers. One of them was Vincenzo Bonanno.

After the relative comfort of a steady job, Bonanno was now reduced to once again "jumping around" in order to find work. When
his efforts failed and the monthly $20 from the city for the care of
Teresa's younger brother was no longer enough to cover their expenses—their rent was now $30 a month, up from the $14 they had
paid on Allen Street—he turned to the relief he had earlier rejected.
The $11 weekly payments gave them enough to scrape by. More im-
portant, it qualified him for the WPA. In December 1939, with the
summer's strikes a memory, the WPA rolls stood at 2,122,960, down a
million workers from the year before. Harrington attributed the reduction to improving business conditions, but the economy remained
too slack to absorb all the job seekers who weren't working for the
WPA. Its waiting list stood at over a million, and Bonanno joined a
long line of eligibles impatient to move into jobs.

In no time, however, he was working, thanks to the eighteen-month
rule that churned new people into the system as established workers

met the limits of their eligibility. His first jobs were small ones. He remembered that somebody handed him a shovel and he cleared out a vacant lot near his Brooklyn church, Our Lady of Grace. The next assignment was in St. George, on Staten Island, where he built shelving for food storage at the borough jail and added screens against insects. By now he had dusted off the tool box he had brought from Sicily and was rediscovering the carpentry skills he had given up when he went to work making slippers. When he rejoined the carpenters union, the WPA sent him to the airport at North Beach, where crews were working to complete pieces of the infrastructure that remained unfinished when the airport was hurriedly opened at the end of 1939. In March 1940, he was among 380 skilled workmen putting the finishing touches on Hangar Four, a steel-framed structure longer than a football field and half as wide that was to be occupied by Trans-World Airlines. Bonanno was working on a wooden scaffold inside near the roof, building wooden boxes that would route ventilation ducts to the outside. Alongside him worked plumbers and electricians who were installing sprinkler pipes and power cables.

On the afternoon of March 5, he had finished work for the day, hung up his overalls, and stowed his tools in his locker and was about to go home when the crews were ordered to hold at the airport. "My foot was already on the bus. All of a sudden they shut everything down and wouldn't let us leave," Bonanno recalled. Then there was a wail of sirens and he saw a column of smoke rising over the hangar, the middle one of three on one side of the administration building. A fire had broken out inside, and twenty fire trucks roared to the scene as glass in the roof and windows shattered in rifle-shot explosions, the heavy steel beams glowed red and sagged, a section of the roof collapsed, and seven-ton steel doors curled like wood shavings.

The fire was later traced to the workers' paint shed inside the hangar, filled with volatile solvents, where a worker had hung up his overalls leaving a lighted pipe smoldering in one of the pockets. Once the fire broke free of the paint shed, it was fed by the framework of scaffolding. Estimates placed the damage to the $1.25 million structure at $250,000. Bonanno lost his tools and work clothes in the workers' locker room, but the damage assured him of additional work when repairs commenced and the hangar was completed.

By then, however, the kinds of civic improvements that Mayor La

Guardia's pet project signified—public works, which had been the stock in trade of the WPA—were about to be eclipsed by a different kind of work. For Jimmy Bonanno, and for millions of other WPA workers, what was happening in the European war at last turned the nation's attention to the urgent need for defense, and the resulting buildup began to produce something no one had seen in years: more jobs.

7. A "HURRICANE OF EVENTS"

For the first three years of the Great War in Europe, from 1914 to 1917, Germany had fought France and England in the west and Russia in the east. Although Russia withdrew after the Soviet revolution, Hitler was convinced that the demands of this two-front war had contributed to Germany's eventual defeat. Wanting for the moment to concentrate his military attentions on the west, in August 1939 he had his foreign minister, Joachim von Ribbentrop, approach his Soviet counterpart, Vyacheslav Molotov, to arrange a non-aggression pact. The deals that were signed that same month had three components: a relatively straightforward economic segment that would exchange Russian food and raw materials for finished goods from Germany; a ten-year agreement that the two countries would not attack or intervene against each other; and a third, top-secret protocol that allowed each country to expand its sphere of influence. Thus Poland lay divided, its western two-thirds under the heel of Germany and the rest in Soviet hands, along with the Baltic states of Estonia, Latvia, and Lithuania. And on the last day of November 1939, the Soviets took the next step and invaded Finland. The Red Army faced surprisingly fierce resistance from the Finns until the latter finally capitulated. But while British planes were blanketing Germany with anti-Nazi leaflets, western Europe remained free of ground war while Hitler bided his time through the winter and into the spring of 1940. The lull of that first winter brought from Senator Borah, ever the isolationist, the opinion that this new war was a "phony war."

During this period, Roosevelt bided his time in declaring whether he would seek a third term. There was nothing in the Constitution to prohibit it, although no president of the United States had ever done so. These were unusual times, however. A strong majority of Democrats wanted him to run again. Hopkins's presidential ambitions, realistic or not, had succumbed to a combination of opposition from both conservatives and party regulars, who saw him on one hand as too liberal and on the other as politically inept, and his increasing frailty. He was unable to function in the role of commerce secretary, and it took a return visit to the Mayo Clinic to restore him to reasonable health late in 1939.

Three other hopefuls remained: the vice president, John Nance Garner; the secretary of state, Cordell Hull; and the postmaster general, James Farley. Each had displayed some degree of opposition to Roosevelt and to his commitment to New Deal liberalism. Garner, from Texas, had long since distanced himself from the president, beginning with the effort to pack the Supreme Court. He embraced the South's traditional antipathy to organized labor and to legislating wages and hours, and he opposed deficit spending. Relations between the two men had deteriorated to the point where Roosevelt hoped he would stay away from cabinet meetings. Farley was Garner's antithesis, a garrulous New York Irishman whose skill at political fixing and manipulating had served Roosevelt well when Farley was the manager of his 1932 and 1936 campaigns. But he was also the essence of a big-city machine politician, and Roosevelt was convinced he would always choose expediency over principle in deciding what policies he wanted to pursue. From Roosevelt's standpoint, Hull was the least objectionable of the three, although like Garner, the Tennessean had a southerner's reflexive suspicion of the New Deal's big-government cornerstones.

Farley was the most nakedly ambitious of them all. At fifty-one, he was the youngest and could conceivably accept the vice presidential nomination with an eye on a presidential bid four years later. But he could not run with Roosevelt because the Constitution bars presidential and vice presidential candidates from the same state. Garner was hale at seventy-one, but having broken with the New Deal, he was less interested in becoming president than in denying Roosevelt another term. Roosevelt had encouraged Hull, sixty-eight, to believe he was his chosen successor, just as he had Hopkins before him, but Hull believed that campaigning for the nomination was unbecoming for a secretary of state. Besides, all three were effectively prevented from launching a campaign until Roosevelt made his intentions clear.

This the president refused to do. He spoke of wishing to return to Hyde Park to plant trees and tend the land and write, but he certainly did not want an opponent of the New Deal to end up in the White House, and he feared the effects of an isolationist Congress if the progress of the war began to turn against America's British and French allies.

Then for all intents and purposes Hitler made the decision for him. The winter lull of the so-called phony war ended abruptly on the morning of April 9, 1940, when the German army drove north across the border of Denmark and simultaneously the German navy torpedoed Norwegian gunboats and landed troops who within two days captured Norway's main ports. The shaken western Allies parried the German thrust ineffectually and then withdrew.

One month later, German forces were on the move again. Hitler now took aim at western Europe, and on May 10, tanks, armored troop carriers, and infantry crossed the borders of Belgium and the Netherlands while 16,000 paratroopers descended from the skies and screaming dive-bombers pummeled military airfields. This would be no war of attrition between two static dug-in armies, as the first war had been. The assault combined speed with overwhelming force and inscribed the word *blitzkrieg*, German for "lightning war," into dictionaries of military terms from that day forward. Half a million Allied troops moving to counter the attack in Belgium were outmanned and outmaneuvered. No longer could it remotely be believed that the German dictator could be appeased. British prime minister Neville Chamberlain, who had gone that route, resigned, and Winston Churchill, the primary critic of Chamberlain's pre-war policies, formed a new coalition government in London.

In both looks and attitude, Churchill embodied the fighting spirit of the English bulldog. On May 13, in his first address to the House of

Commons as prime minister, he said, "I have nothing to offer but blood, toil, tears, and sweat.

"We have before us an ordeal of the most grievous kind. We have before us many, many months of struggle and suffering. You ask, What is our policy? I say: It is to wage war, by land, sea, and air. War with all our might and with all the strength that God has given us, and to wage war against a monstrous tyranny never surpassed in the dark, lamentable catalogue of human crime. That is our policy. You ask, What is our aim? I can answer in one word. It is victory, victory at all costs, victory in spite of all terrors. Victory, however long and hard the road may be, for without victory there is no survival."

One of Churchill's first communications as prime minister was to Roosevelt. The two had met briefly and unmemorably during the first war, when Churchill served as first lord of the admiralty and Roosevelt was an assistant secretary of the navy. They had begun to correspond in 1939 after the German invasion of Poland, when Roosevelt invited Churchill to keep in touch through sealed diplomatic pouch "with anything you want me to know about." Now Churchill wrote him of the swiftly darkening scene in Europe, of the smaller countries being smashed "like matchwood," of the likelihood that Mussolini's Italy would join Germany in the fighting. And even as he was writing, the Allies' situation worsened. Hour by hour, the Germans drove the French and British backward toward the sea and in the waters of the North Sea and the English Channel inflicted heavy losses on the vaunted British navy. Britain, Churchill wrote, needed ships, planes, steel, and anti-aircraft guns and ammunition.

Roosevelt addressed a joint session of a cheering Congress on the afternoon of May 16. He called for adding nearly $1 billion to the military budget. To keep the isolationists at bay, he did not mention Britain's needs and he spoke not of rearmament but of national defense. The Atlantic and Pacific oceans were no longer adequate defensive barriers in an age of air warfare, he said. "If Bermuda fell into hostile hands, it is a matter of less than three hours for modern bombers to reach our shores." He called for a standing military air fleet of 50,000 planes and for increasing aircraft manufacturing capacity from the current 12,000 to "at least fifty thousand planes a year." He called for updating and modernizing all the equipment used by the army, navy, and marines, and for ramping up factory output to "turn out quickly infinitely greater supplies." He had told reporters earlier that he envisioned munitions and matériel sufficient for an army of 750,000. This day's speech, carried on the national radio networks, won strong public support; Americans were even willing to pay higher taxes to ensure a strong defense, according to a Gallup poll, and the president's request moved swiftly through the Congress.

On May 26, he delivered a fireside chat in which he spoke of "the approaching storm." He asked Americans to donate to the Red Cross to help millions of Belgian and French civilian refugees "running from their homes to escape bombs and shells and fire and machine-gunning, without shelter, and almost wholly without food." He updated his listeners on the state of military preparedness, said the needs of defense were no reason to roll back social gains such as the wage-and-hours law and old-age pensions, and vowed to build the national defenses "to whatever heights the future may require." And in what was clearly another effort to isolate the isolationists, he called for a sense of national purpose against groups who would cause "confusion of counsel, public indecision, political paralysis and eventually, a state of panic."

But those groups were not silent. Lindbergh made a radio address the same day, terming the president's call for 50,000 planes a year "hysterical chatter." Senator Arthur Vandenberg, running for the Republican presidential nomination, called for an "insulated" America. And indeed, while Americans favored improving the nation's defenses even at the cost of higher taxes, they remained wary of sending soldiers into an overseas war. Among a flurry of letters and telegrams Roosevelt received in advance of the broadcast was one signed by 167 students at the City College of New York asserting, "YANKS ARE NOT COMING WE WILL NOT DIE FOR WALL STREET," a version of the "Hell, no, we won't go" chants to be heard thirty years later during Vietnam. A group from Chicago that included a man called Louis Terkel, the birth name of the WPA Writers' Project employee and later author Studs Terkel, sent a telegram (with a flourish that smacked of a writing professional), "WE DO NOT BEG FOR PEACE LIKE SLAVES WE DO NOT PLEAD FOR IT LIKE SERFS WE COMMAND IT."

The president knew he had to proceed carefully. He had told Churchill that the loan of forty or fifty older destroyers the prime minister had requested would take an act of Congress, and the time was not yet right for it. Besides, he noted, it would take several weeks to prepare the ships for service by the British, so he asked Churchill to bear with him. Planes, anti-aircraft weapons, and steel he could provide.

Roosevelt expanded his military request by another $750 million three days later, on May 29. By then, the Belgians had already surrendered to the German onslaught, and the routed Allies were being evacuated from Dunkirk, on the northern coast of France, in a makeshift fleet that included some 800 pleasure yachts and fishing boats along with military vessels, as overhead the Royal Air Force fended off a hail of German bombs and shot down three Luftwaffe aircraft for every British fighter lost. The smallest craft to ferry evacuees across the fifty miles of the English Channel to Dover was an open boat, *Tamzine*, made of wood and less than fifteen feet long, with only oars and sails for power. More than 338,000 soldiers crossed the Channel to England and safety in the weeklong evacuation.

On June 4, when this ordeal was finally over, Churchill gave a speech to Parliament that was heard around the world. The British army had lived to fight another day, he said. "We shall go on to the end. We shall fight in the seas and oceans, we shall fight...in the air. We shall fight on the beaches, we shall fight on the landing grounds, we shall fight in the fields and in the streets, we shall fight in the hills; we shall never surrender." American opinion shifted still further toward aiding the British after the speech was broadcast— delivered this time by an impersonator using Churchill's voice, since he didn't have time to reprise his performance before Parliament. In its wake, Roosevelt ordered that enough rifles, artillery and shells, machine guns, ammunition, and explosives be sent immediately to England to replace the supplies left behind at Dunkirk.

By now only the remnants of the French army stood between the Germans and Paris. It had taken up defensive positions along the east-west line of the Somme River less than 100 miles north of Paris, and it was to these defenses that the Germans turned their attention. They crossed the Somme on June 5. By June 14, they had taken Paris. France surrendered a week later, and continental Europe was now under German control in an uninterrupted swath from eastern Poland to the Atlantic Ocean.

As Churchill had predicted, Mussolini declared war on both France and England, opening up a front not only at the French-Italian border but also in North Africa and East Africa, where British, French, and Italian colonies stood side by side. Roosevelt characterized Italy's entry into the war starkly. "On this tenth day of June, 1940," he said in a radio broadcast, "the hand that held the dagger has struck it into the back of its neighbor."

It was indeed a "hurricane of events," as Roosevelt called it, and in a matter of weeks it radically changed the presidential race, increasing the pressure on the president to make himself available for a third term.

8. RIGID PRIORITIES

T he hurricane swept through the WPA, turning it almost overnight into a virtual adjunct of the military services and civil defense authorities. Defense work became the agency's prime focus. On June 6, Colonel Harrington told his administrators that seventy-three projects the army and navy considered "of first importance" to national defense were to receive precedence. These included work at navy yards, major military reservations, military airports, and civil airports located in strategic areas. The projects anticipated a vast expansion of the military.

"Types of WPA work to be expedited in every possible way include, in addition to airports and military airfields, construction of housing and other facilities for enlarged military garrisons, camp and cantonment construction, and various improvements in navy yards," he said.

As Harrington pointed out, much of the work the WPA had done since its inception had prepared the nation for this sudden and intense move to a military footing. In the five years since it began, he said, the WPA had built 85 percent of all the new airports in the country. Its work on army, navy, and coast guard facilities, costing $420 million, had already contributed directly to national defense, and he forecast that half a million WPA workers would be employed on defense projects costing $250 million during the coming year.

In August, Harrington's deputy Howard O. Hunter underscored this, telling a news conference that "rigid priority is going to be given to WPA projects which may have military value." Airports near America's coasts and borders topped the list. These included as many as twelve new airports in Maine, whose long finger, extending northeast toward Nova Scotia and Newfoundland, could serve as the launch point for the shortest flights from the United States to the European war zone. The Snohomish County Airport in Seattle, receiving $2.5 million worth of WPA work, would serve as a departure point for flights to Canada and Alaska. In nearby Tacoma, the WPA was working on the army flight training facility at McChord Field. California airfields to receive WPA work included those at Ontario, Hemet, Glendale, San Diego, Santa Maria, and Los Angeles; three of them would be used to train new pilots. The San Antonio, Texas, army airfield was on the work list, as well as several others scattered along the border with Mexico. Several existing airfields in Florida were also on the list, as was a major air base south of Tampa, Florida. Work on the Southeastern Air Base, Tampa, later known as MacDill Air Force Base, would begin on September 6.

Airfields in the country's interior were not neglected. Scott Field, in southern Illinois, already tripled in size to over 1,800 acres between 1938 and 1939, was getting twenty-one new buildings and being prepared as a training facility for aircraft radio operators and mechanics. Lowry Field, near Denver, Colorado, was slated for additional runways and extensions of existing ones.

Further, the WPA had reached agreement with the War Department and the Bureau of Public Roads to work on a network of roads necessary for military transportation, building new ones where necessary, widening shoulders and strengthening bridges on existing roads, and doing similar upgrades on roads into military reservations. WPA picks and shovels would see duty on some 75,000 miles of federally aided main highways. Housing at and around military posts was also an acute need, for which the WPA would build infrastructure elements such as stores and sidewalks and install water and sewer lines and communications systems. Hunter upped Harrington's earlier estimate of WPA workers on defense projects to between 600,000 and 700,000 and said they would be kept on for eight months to a year.

The agency also had begun preparing its workers to shift to private jobs. Twenty-five thousand of them were enrolled in training courses for specific war industries. The courses, taught in state vocational schools, were supported by the WPA and the Office of Education under the supervision of the newly revived National Defense Council, and the WPA workers were being paid while in training. The number of trainees would rise to 50,000 by October.

Still, not everyone was prepared to accept the WPA's role in helping to rebuild the military and defense infrastructure. The *New York Times,* in a series of editorials headlined "WPA vs. Defense," wrote that the agency's projects were only incidental to defense and that the "WPA in its present form needs to be completely abandoned" as "an obstacle to the defense program." But the reasons cited in the editorials—the restrictive work rules, limited hours, sponsorship cost requirements, and ceilings on amounts spent for materials on WPA projects—were even then being revised to allow for exceptions for defense projects. Moreover, the newspaper's view was shortsighted.

The military services had languished in the post-war period. The end of the draft that had sent 4 million soldiers to the battlefields of Europe in 1917 and 1918 and the peace that followed that war had left their ranks depopulated. Its installations had crumbled from disuse, a process that accelerated during the depression when Roosevelt cut the army's budget in order to steer money to relief and reduced its manpower below 140,000. As recently as 1938, when Hitler initiated the second of his territorial grabs, claiming the Czech Sudetenland for Germany, the army still had only 176,000 soldiers, and much of their equipment was of world war vintage. When new gear did become available, there was little of it; a year after the army adopted the M1 Garand rifle in 1936 for use by the infantry, the isolationist Congress limited the army's new equipment purchases to 1,870 more of them. With no demand at home and with the neutrality laws preventing them from selling their wares to combatants overseas, arms manufacturers had no significant pool of trained workers to meet what was now a rapidly growing demand. Only the WPA, having employed millions of relief workers for more than five years, had a comprehensive awareness of the skills that would be available in a full-scale national emergency, both for accelerating the refurbishment and construction of military installations and supporting links such as roads and airports and for arms manufacturing itself. As the country began its preparedness buildup, the WPA was uniquely positioned to become a major defense agency.

White-collar WPA workers, however, saw their jobs jeopardized by the emphasis on construction. In San Francisco, they formed a Committee to Save WPA Clerical and Professional Projects and began a letter-writing campaign to restart projects that had been suspended, including a history of journalism, a history of music, and theater research. "Amid the current, feverish preparation for instruments of destruction, help us to preserve such symbols of peace and serenity of living as only the arts can impart," the committee wrote in an appeal.

Some factors were very slow to change. Even as project priorities shifted to defense, political concerns remained focused on supposed threats of sedition. This caused protections against discrimination based on political affiliation to dissolve, at least as they related to Communists and Nazis. As Congress was debating emergency relief spending for fiscal 1941—the budget plan under which the WPA would operate starting July 1, 1940—Representative Howard W. Smith of Virginia pressed forward with a bill to outlaw advocating, teaching, or abetting the overthrow of the government, or belonging to any organization that did this. His legislation also struck at aliens, requiring that all those over the age of fourteen be registered and fingerprinted. Suddenly, sunset was falling on the days when Writers' Project workers could engage in Stalinist-Trotskyite pamphlet wars and take home their government salaries at the end of the day.

Harrington did not wait for this legislation to take effect, nor did Somervell in New York City. The two army men moved forcefully to purge the WPA of Nazis, Communists, and whatever aliens remained from previous bans or who had come onto the rolls since those expulsions. Rather than taking a loyalty oath administered in groups, as workers had been required to do the year before, the new price of job security was a signature on a sworn affidavit attesting that "I do not and will not advocate or hold position in any organization that advocates the overthrow of the Government of the United States, and further, that I am not an alien, nor a Communist, nor a member of any Nazi Bund organization, and that I will not become a Communist or a

member of any Nazi Bund organization during any time that I may be
paid from funds appropriated to the Work Projects Administration."

Somervell was not content to let it rest at that. He said that in New
York, he would match the WPA payroll with Board of Elections registration lists and bring the FBI, the New York Police Department, and
the WPA's self-policing Bureau of Investigation into the affair. He was
also planning to look at the records of the Dies Committee hearings
and the transcript of the 1939 trial in which German-American Bund
leader Fritz Kuhn had been convicted of stealing funds from the organization. Further, since Communists routinely denied their party membership and used false names, he was asking "responsible citizens" to
inform on WPA employees they suspected of subversion. He anticipated some "grudge letters" among the 50,000 reports he expected to
come flooding in, but would endeavor to separate those from authen-
tic information. One thousand of the 101,000 WPA workers in the
city were already under scrutiny, and he assumed at least that many
workers would be dismissed in the purge. When it came down to a
question of who was a Communist and who wasn't—Trotskyists, he
said, were Communists under his interpretation—he would have the
final word.

An orgy of affidavit signing ensued. Harrington had set July 1 as the
deadline for completing the purge. With five days to go, a fifty-seven-
year-old WPA stenographer from the Upper West Side of Manhattan
became the first WPA worker to be fired for refusing to put pen to
paper. Her name was Charlotte I. Long. Looking "matronly" with her
gray hair and black polka-dot dress and glasses, she appeared at the
offices of the Workers Alliance and told reporters she had been born in
Kansas, traced her family's arrival in America to the seventeenth century, and hated fascism "with all my heart and soul," but would not
sign such an un-American document. The job she lost paid $68.90 a
month, and she said it was her sole support.

When the purge ended, the numbers fell far short of those expected.
Nationally, they did not even reach half of the 1,000 dismissals
Somervell had predicted in New York City alone. State-by-state figures
showed that forty-nine New York WPA workers were dismissed
for refusing to sign the affidavit or confessing to one of its banned
activities, a number matched only in Louisiana. Only twelve states
reached double-digit figures. The highly unionized industrial states of

Pennsylvania, Michigan, and Ohio, with thirty-nine, seventeen, and fifteen dismissals, were outdone by Oklahoma and Iowa, with forty-three and forty-one. In all, the purge terminated WPA work for 429 employees, a minuscule percentage of the 1,665,000 then on the rolls. In being fired, they received not the fabled pink slips the WPA had used to let workers know they were being let go, but new notices in green ink on white paper. (The WPA did not invent the pink slip—the term originated twenty years before the agency came into being—but its use of pink dismissal notices cemented it into the vocabularies of millions of Americans.)

Meanwhile, the Alien Registration Act, as the Smith bill was called, passed. Roosevelt signed it into law on June 29, and by the December 26 deadline nearly 5 million aliens had registered under the act's provisions.

9. THE THIRD-TERM EQUATION

The president continued to equivocate on whether he intended to seek a third term, clouding the political landscape for both parties. Republicans gathered in June in Philadelphia without a clear front-runner, and observers were expecting a Democratic-style free-for-all for the nomination. But Roosevelt stole the opposition's thunder on the eve of the convention when he named two Republicans to vital cabinet posts. Henry L. Stimson, who had served in the cabinets of William Howard Taft and Herbert Hoover, became secretary of war, and Frank Knox, publisher of the *Chicago Daily News* and Alf Landon's running mate in 1936, was appointed secretary of the navy, both replacing men whose tendencies were isolationist. The Republicans cried, "Dirty politics!" and then descended into a multiballot contest that was indeed reminiscent of Democratic conventions past. In the end, after six ballots, political neophyte and former Democrat Wendell L. Willkie, an Indiana lawyer and electric utility executive known primarily for waging war against the TVA, beat out two party insiders, Manhattan district attorney Thomas E. Dewey and Ohio senator Robert A. Taft, the son of the former president.

And Roosevelt still refused to declare his preferences. The Democratic delegates, convening in Chicago at the beginning of the third week of July, heard that Harry Hopkins knew the wishes of the president. Hopkins was now living at the White House, having felt ill after dinner on May 10, the day the Germans invaded Belgium and the Netherlands, and been invited by Roosevelt to spend the night. He would end up staying for three and a half years, occupying what had once been Lincoln's study. But even Hopkins, who had become the president's closest advisor and confidant and even had a hot line to the White House in his Chicago hotel bathroom, did not know Roosevelt's intentions.

On the second night of the convention, delegates at last heard a message from the president, delivered by Kentucky senator Alben Barkley. He said the president had no desire to continue in office and "wishes in all sincerity to make it clear that all the delegates to this convention are free to vote for any candidate."

This demurral caused a moment of uncertainty in the convention hall. Then the loudspeakers erupted with a chant: "We want Roosevelt! We want Roosevelt!" These were the words the delegates wanted to hear; joining in, they started an hour-long demonstration that took over the convention floor. The demonstration appeared spontaneous, but it was not; the voice on the speakers belonged to the Chicago sewer commissioner, positioned at a basement microphone by Chicago's Democratic mayor, Edward J. Kelly, to provoke it. Still, this maneuver was less important than the fact that it expressed what the convention really did want: a proven hand at the helm in a time of international crisis, and a proven vote getter at the top of the Democratic ticket. And Roosevelt, too, had gotten what he wanted—a draft that would let him keep the reins of office while allowing him to say he had not sought them. He was nominated the next day by acclamation after demonstrating decisive strength on the first ballot.

But a second fight lay ahead. The president had decided that he wanted Henry Wallace as his running mate. The agriculture secretary was a queer duck politically: he did not smoke, drink, or swear, and glad-handing and small talk were beyond him. Moreover, he was an ex-Republican and a religious mystic who sought spiritual truth "from the pews of mainstream Protestantism to the esoteric fringes of eastern occultism." But as a champion of price supports to control farm output and increase farmers' income, he was popular in the farm belt, where isolationist sentiment remained strong. And he was the dependable liberal Roosevelt had lacked in Garner, an advocate who had traveled, written, and spoken extensively in support of Roosevelt's policies. This last was the key: the ticket would be united in its commitment to the philosophy of the New Deal; there would be no more defections. Party regulars were outraged, but the president had his way, and the ticket was set.

As the summer progressed, Willkie campaigned while Roosevelt devoted his attention to the ticklish prospects for actually aiding England. The challenge was to create a scenario that could be spun as a matter of national defense, thereby neutralizing the isolationists in Congress. Advocates of defensive preparedness were already arguing that the shipments to England to replace the weapons left behind at Dunkirk had rendered America unarmed and vulnerable in case of an attack. Moreover, a majority of the American public believed that England was certain to fall before the German juggernaut, making any arms shipments a double waste since they would end up in enemy hands. Roosevelt's ambassador to England, Joseph Kennedy, formerly the head of the SEC, shared this dim view of British prospects and argued for a British armistice with Hitler. Against these dismal voices, the president now was called upon to meet additional requests from Churchill that were vital to England's survival.

The stunning air war over England known as the Battle of Britain had started on July 10. German Heinkel and Junkers bombers, protected by outriding Messerschmitt and Stuka fighters, began bombarding the island's coastal defenses in preparation for an invasion, which the Nazis had designated with the code name Operation Sea Lion. But the British refused to give up. Their cryptanalysts had broken the German Enigma code, giving British commanders some idea of German plans, and coastal installations employing the newly developed radar technology gave advance warning and location of specific attacks. The Royal Air Force swarmed the skies with Spitfire and Hurricane fighters and continued to bring down approximately three German planes for every loss of their own. In the meantime, the RAF's own bombers were making nighttime raids that targeted German oil depots and aircraft and munitions factories. In mid-August, the air warfare intensified, with the German targets now shifting to England's airfields and aircraft factories. Hitler had decided that he needed to decimate the Royal Air Force before launching an invasion, so for five straight days, between August 13 and August 18, Goering sent the Luftwaffe to England: first 1,400 planes, then 1,800, then 1,700. At the end, the Germans had lost 376 planes, yet failed to break England's air defenses. It was the astonishing bravery of the English pilots that spurred Churchill's famous statement of gratitude: "Never before in the field of human conflict has so much been owed by so many to so few."

Nonetheless, England was in desperate straits. It, too, had lost many planes, and a quarter of its thousand pilots had been killed or wounded. Churchill pressed Roosevelt to announce a deal on the destroyers as much for psychological reasons as for military advantage; the ships in question were outmoded and slow, but the prime minister was certain that it would give Hitler pause to believe that America was actively on England's side.

Still, Roosevelt made no mention of England's needs when he dedicated the Great Smoky Mountains National Park at the border of Tennessee and North Carolina on September 2. Rather, he stressed the need for the ongoing defense buildup and the military draft legislation that was then working its way through Congress. It was not easy to ask men to leave their homes, he said, but "if we are to survive, we cannot be soft in a world in which there are dangers that threaten Americans—dangers far more deadly than were those that the frontiersmen had to face."

A day later, he was back in Washington, where he at last announced a deal on the destroyers: they were to be a quid pro quo for ninety-nine-year leases on British bases in Bermuda, Newfoundland, and the Caribbean that could be said to contribute to America's defenses. It was a deal that barely passed the test of political acceptability, and isolationist Senator David I. Walsh of Massachusetts called it an act of war. Predictably, so did Robert McCormick's *Chicago Tribune*. And in its wake Charles Lindbergh, along with Senator Burton K. Wheeler of Montana, perennial Socialist Party presidential candidate Norman Thomas, and General Robert E. Wood of Sears Roebuck, announced the formation of the America First Committee to resist involvement in the war.

This new spearhead of isolationism drew the bulk of its membership from the Midwest. Its main principles stated that the United States had to build an impregnable defense that no foreign power or powers could successfully attack, that American democracy could be preserved only by staying out of the European war, and that any aid to allies unless war had been declared weakened the national defense and threatened to drag the country into foreign conflict. Underlying these fine sentiments, however, were the whispered slurs of anti-Semitism and conspiracy that were a staple of the Roosevelt-bashing arsenal: the Jews (including the closet Semites Franklin and Eleanor), along with the British and the arms profiteers, were in league to plunge the nation into war. It would be better, they believed—as did Joseph Kennedy—to accommodate Hitler and bring what Lindbergh called "peace and civilization throughout the world as far into the future as we can see."

But by then Hitler had once again shifted the Luftwaffe's priorities. In response to British air raids on Berlin, the German bombs now were raining down on London in a campaign of night bombings called the Blitz (another variation on *blitzkrieg*)—their purpose to kill civilians and spread terror. But these raids lacked the precision of the daytime bombing of British aircraft factories, and those factories were now able to replace more planes than were being lost in combat. Across the Atlantic, Americans who tuned in to nightly CBS radio reports heard Edward R. Murrow in London describing the destructive effects of the Blitz, and saw vivid pictures of that destruction on movie newsreels and in their daily papers. But while Congress and the anti-Roosevelt press may have been against the destroyer deal, in the brief months since May the tide had turned among the public. Americans strongly favored aid to England now, vindicating the president in his decision to bypass Congress on the destroyer transfer. And early in October, whether the result of the message sent by the destroyer deal or of some other factor in the mind of Adolf Hitler, who had now turned his thoughts to invading his erstwhile ally, Russia, the invasion of England planned in Operation Sea Lion was postponed until the following spring.

10. BREATHING SPACE

A fter Labor Day 1940, Colonel Harrington had gone to Connecticut to visit his brother-in-law, William Rayburn, at his summer home. His wife, Rayburn's sister, had died in February 1938, but the two men had stayed in touch. Harrington badly needed a break from the demanding WPA work schedule, and he lacked Hopkins's network of wealthy friends who were able to offer their homes for convalescence. But he had taken ill during his visit and was admitted to a hospital in New London. He underwent an operation for what his doctors called an "intestinal ailment" and was apparently recovering, but his condition worsened at the end of September.

Hopkins learned the news at his suite at the Essex House hotel in New York City. He had resigned as commerce secretary in August because of several factors. As the man with the hot line to the White House at the Democratic convention, he had been identified, erroneously but insistently, as prompting the "voice from the sewers" that had triggered the "draft" of Roosevelt, and though he had had nothing to do with it or the contentious nomination of Wallace as the vice presidential candidate, party regulars aimed their fury at him. Moreover, he had never fully recovered from his own health problems; in fact, in his twenty months as commerce secretary he had not been able to spend more than two months in the office. Hated within the Democratic Party, with no cabinet record to defend, and with poverty—heretofore his strong suit—receding as an issue with the rise of war, he recognized that he was a political liability to the administration. Responding to his August 22 resignation letter, Roosevelt wrote, "You may resign the office—only the office—and nothing else. Our friendship will and must go on as always." Hopkins had left the White House to return to New York, where he thought he would write and perhaps work at the presidential library Roosevelt was establishing at Hyde Park. As it happened, his absence would be short; he would return to Washington and the White House before the end of the year and emerge as the president's closest confidant and emissary to Winston Churchill and the British government. But now, hearing Harrington was ill, he drove to New London and joined Howard Hunter, and Harrington's son and daughter, at his bedside. Harrington died on September 30. He was only fifty-three.

The WPA was far different from the organization it had been when Harrington was named to replace Hopkins less than two years earlier. The non-political West Pointer had resisted controversy almost as strongly as Hopkins had attracted it. He had steered the WPA off the front pages for the most part. Even the reorganization and wildcat strikes of a year earlier, and the continuing accusations of the Dies Committee that Communists lurked within the WPA, lacked the resonance they might have had with a lightning rod such as Hopkins at the helm. By not playing the political card, Harrington had brought attention back to the WPA's building accomplishments and its job of furnishing employment, and these were difficult to assail on any grounds. It was a very valuable contribution, and now, with the country's defense needs taking on new urgency and the WPA drafted as part of the defense effort, the swirl of controversy was largely in the past. Howard Hunter became the acting commissioner, and his permanent appointment some months later was noted with very little comment of any kind. Controversy had moved on to find new targets.

One of these was the new Selective Service System. The Congress had approved the first peacetime draft in the nation's history on September 16. Roosevelt had signed the executive order putting it into effect on September 23, calling it "an orderly, just, and democratic method" of obtaining men for military service. Wendell Willkie also supported the draft; the tousled, rumpled, folksy Indianan, who had already campaigned his way into a state of perpetual hoarseness, was considerably removed from the anti–New Deal Republican orthodoxy that had sent Alf Landon to his epic defeat in 1936. Nor was Willkie an isolationist. He based his early campaign not on criticizing the New Deal itself but on its ineffectiveness in reducing unemployment and on Roosevelt's failure to move earlier to rebuild the nation's defenses. But these positions failed to gain the Republican ticket any traction; if the president had been slow to throw money at the makers of airplanes, battleships, and tanks, he was certainly doing so now, as duly reported in the newspapers and on the radio. And unemployment was dropping; the weekly number of WPA workers leaving for private jobs had doubled by the end of October, and while the rolls rose as expected in response to seasonal employment patterns, the increase was less than the authorized number and below that of a year before. So as the days dwindled before the November election, Willkie shifted his tactics and painted Roosevelt as a provocateur who, despite his promises to the contrary, was likely to send America to war.

The draft system was on prominent display in this attack on Roosevelt as a warmonger who could not be trusted to keep his word. Under the law, all men between the ages of twenty-one and thirty-five were required to register with local draft boards by October 16, and drawing lots for what was then a compulsory year's service was scheduled for October 29. Millions of young men stood in line outside hastily established registration sites—Seattle, Washington, used the sprawling car barn at Fourteenth Avenue and East Jefferson Street that housed its trackless trolley cars—to place their names in the hopper for possible conscription. During the registration period, said Willkie in a Chicago campaign speech, "if his promise to keep our boys out of foreign wars is no better than his promise to balance the budget, they're already almost on the transports." He was more specific in a Baltimore campaign speech: "On the basis of his past performance with pledges to the people, if you re-elect him you may expect war in April 1941."

Roosevelt finally took up the challenge late in October, when the polls showed Willkie narrowing the president's comfortable early lead. His campaign staff worried that he was vulnerable on several fronts, primarily among German and Italian immigrants and the families of draft-age men. Nevertheless, the president himself oversaw the October 29 draft lottery drawing in an auditorium at the War Department building in Washington. He looked on from the onstage podium as Secretary of War Stimson, blindfolded for the occasion with a piece of linen that had covered the chair on which the Founding Fathers sat to sign the Declaration of Independence, reached into a large cylindrical glass jar containing 9,000 cobalt blue capsules and withdrew one. Stimson handed the capsule to Roosevelt, who opened it and read off the number on the slip that was inside: 158.

The men who held the number were thoroughly American in the variety of their origins. In New York, they included the names Cody and Chan, Tsatsaronis and Stazzone, O'Reilly and McDonald, Gonzales and Gerkowski, Wolf and Weisblum. By now the election was a week away, and Willkie kept saying the boys were almost at the boats, but Roosevelt had regained the initiative. He attacked the isolationists as foolish and unrealistic, and assembled three of them—Republican representatives Joe Martin, Bruce Barton, and Hamilton Fish—into a rhythmic catchphrase, "Martin, Barton, and Fish," that delighted his partisan audiences when he tied them to Willkie. On October 31, he announced orders for 12,000 fighters and bombers, and artillery, machine guns, rifles, and tanks for England, orders that would continue to reenergize the nation's once-moribund production lines. But those weapons, he insisted, would not be used in fighting by Americans— and each time he said it, his campaign aides insisted that he repeat it.

"But how often do they expect me to say that? It's in the Democratic platform and I've repeated it a hundred times," he protested to speechwriter Robert Sherwood.

"I know it, Mr. President, but they don't seem to have heard you the first time," Sherwood answered. "Evidently you've got to say it again— and again—and again."

Sherwood put the insistent repetition into a speech that Roosevelt gave in Boston the night that Willkie, earlier in the day in Baltimore, had charged that if "the third-term candidate" was returned to office, Americans would be at war by April. "I have said this before," said the president, speaking to the "mothers and fathers of America," "but I shall say it again and again and again. Your boys are not going to be sent into any foreign wars."

Normally he had added a qualifier at the end: "except in case of attack." But this time he dropped it, reasoning that if America was attacked, it was no longer a foreign war. How much difference the redaction made was something the pundits of the time were left to speculate about and future isolationists to ridicule. But on election day, November 5, with an unprecedented turnout of 49,815,312 voters, Roosevelt compiled 55 percent of the popular vote, 27,243,466, to Willkie's 22,304,755, and a much larger electoral majority, 449 to 82. The third term was a reality, and the hand at the helm in the storm of approaching war was one Americans had learned to trust.

The wars across the oceans continued without letup. Japan had signed the Tripartite Treaty with Germany and Italy in September, pledging with them to fight any American attempts to block their expansion. It now controlled a great swath of northeast China from Shanghai to the Soviet border, and after the surrender of France to Germany had taken positions along the coast of French Indochina. Although Hitler had postponed his plans to invade England in order to concentrate on building up his forces to the east for the invasion of Soviet Russia he now planned, in violation of their non-aggression pact, his Luftwaffe continued to rain bombs down on London and British military targets. German submarines stalked supply and arms convoys crossing the North Atlantic from Canada. (The danger from German U-boats off the coast of North America would eventually force Roosevelt to give up his seaborne vacations aboard the presidential yacht, the USS *Potomac*, in favor of a WPA-built cabin camp in Maryland's Catoctin Mountains; converted to Roosevelt's specifications into a presidential getaway, it is now famously known as Camp David.) The losses to submarine attacks reinforced Britain's dependence on an unstemmed flow of American arms, but by now it had exhausted both its credits and its gold reserves.

On December 29, Roosevelt once again sat before the microphones and spoke to the American people. Freed by his election mandate, by Italy's invasion of Greece that fall, and by a ranting speech by Hitler three weeks earlier in which the Führer declared that fascism and Western democracy stood at odds—"I can beat any other power in the world," he proclaimed—the president spoke more frankly than he had during the campaign. He attacked both Nazi ruthlessness and American isolationists who are "doing exactly the kind of work that the dictators want done." With that, he said America's best defense against the world domination intended by the Axis lay in helping Britain and the Allies with "more ships, more guns, more planes—more of everything."

"We must be the great arsenal of democracy," he said, producing yet another memorable phrase and launching the debate on a new stage of American involvement in the war in Europe—which now, with Italy and England fighting in North Africa, had expanded beyond the boundaries of the continent. The debate continued in his State of the Union address in January 1941, in which he again proved a master of persuasive rhetoric, calling for "a world founded upon four essential freedoms." These were freedom from want, freedom from fear, freedom of speech, and freedom of worship, and together they neatly dovetailed his commitment to the principles of the New Deal with what was at stake in the conflicts threatening to engulf the world. Most important, even before they were turned into icons of Americanism in four paintings by Norman Rockwell, citizens embraced these freedoms as matters worth defending. And when the debate finally concluded in March 1941, the Lend-Lease Act was law.

What this history-changing piece of legislation did, as Roosevelt initially described it, was to "get rid of the silly, foolish old dollar sign" in discussing how to meet Great Britain's war needs. He compared it to lending a neighbor his garden hose to put out a fire. When it was out, the neighbor returned the hose or, if it was damaged, replaced it. In passing Lend-Lease, Congress authorized $7 billion in initial aid to Great Britain, Greece, and China, fulfilling the promise Roosevelt had made to Churchill that England did not stand alone. As soon as it passed, British merchant ships warped up to American docks and took on planes and aircraft parts, artillery and shells, rifles and machine guns, vehicles, food, fuel, industrial equipment, and other supplies to carry back across the ocean. Appropriate to Roosevelt's original analogy, aboard one of the first cargo vessels to brave the U-boat–infested waters of the North Atlantic on its way to England was 900,000 feet of fire hose. And as the president had done in the economic emergency of the depression, when he needed to get relief to his own people, in the military emergency that now faced England he turned to Hopkins to manage the lifeline as his advisor and assistant on Lend-Lease.

11. A FEVER OF PREPARATION

The factories filling England's orders were taking on new workers and pushing unemployment steadily lower; 300,000 new jobs were being created every month. Still, 8 million people remained out of work at the end of 1940, a rate of 14.6 percent, and Roosevelt had rejected calls from his army and navy chiefs to crank up arms factory work schedules to seven days a week with heavy overtime. Holding to the five-day week would continue to spread the work around, even as the arms orders were adding private sector jobs at a fast pace.

The rolls of the WPA had bumped up from the previous summer's usual dip, even though from July 1940 through March 1941, 855,000 workers had left the jobs program. One was Jimmy Bonanno, the Brooklyn carpenter. From his work at La Guardia Field, after the fire that damaged Hangar Four, the WPA assigned him to Fort Hamilton, the historic army garrison on the Brooklyn waterfront that once guarded New York against attack from the sea; it was also where Robert E. Lee, Thomas "Stonewall" Jackson, and baseball inventor Abner Doubleday had served. He was there only briefly, working as part of a crew that did general repairs, before he received a call from the union. A private contractor was hiring carpenters to build housing for defense workers in East Hartford, Connecticut. Bonanno gave his notice to the WPA, packed his clothes and the tools he had replaced since losing his old ones in the hangar fire, and said goodbye to Teresa and little Frank, now five years old. It would be several years before he lived full-time with them again. By the fall, he was one of 11,000 carpenters among a workforce of 20,000 men on upper Cape Cod, tasked to build a huge army training camp. Crews working three shifts around the clock built Camp Edwards using production line methods, finishing 1,200 buildings in 125 days. The first of 25,000 trainees began arriving in January 1941.

But as men such as Bonanno left the WPA for private work, others from the million-strong waiting list were taken on, so the total enrollment remained around 1,900,000. The flow of WPA workers into private defense jobs was complicated, Commissioner Hunter told the House Appropriations Committee in February, by the fact that most of those jobs were in areas where the rolls were thinnest. Meanwhile, 400,000 workers were employed at the WPA's multifarious defense projects, and more were moving into defense-related training, including 50,000 who would be trained to work in hospitals as ward attendants, orderlies, and aides.

By that April, the WPA was working on a large array of new construction projects sponsored by the War and Navy Departments. These included bases and cantonments, airports, hospitals, arsenals and arms depots, and ship repair yards, a majority of them clustered on the northeastern and western coasts, along the Mexican border, and in Florida. The agency was building new civil airports in every state in the nation and military access roads and strategic highways in most of them. It had built or reconstructed 9,241 buildings for the army and navy and 576 armories for state national guards. White-collar workers, meanwhile, were compiling statistics, performing research, and doing clerical jobs for the defense agencies.

The WPA was doing so much defense-related work that Hunter, in an April 15 letter to the president, requested he designate the WPA as a national defense agency. It would strengthen the "patriotic morale among the unemployed," he wrote. Roosevelt declined, since the defense agency designation was used to keep civil service employees from being shuffled among agencies, and WPA workers, who were not permanent government employees, did not fall under civil service rules.

In May, Hunter recommended in testimony before the House Appropriations Committee that the eighteen-month rule and the ban against aliens be dropped. "In the past we have been glad to utilize their skill and special training," he said, referring to non-naturalized immigrants. Since they had to obey the law and pay taxes and were subject to the draft and military service, Hunter said, it seemed unfair to bar them from WPA jobs, especially since they were denied private sector jobs by employers who maintained citizens-only hiring policies. He also suggested the Theatre Project be revived under state sponsorship, in line with the other arts programs, as a means of entertaining military trainees. The committee ignored all three suggestions.

On May 27, 1941, Roosevelt declared an unlimited national emergency. "Common prudence," he said, required instant readiness "to repel any and all acts or threats of aggression." The declaration lent even more urgency to the war preparations, as the president called upon "all loyal workmen as well as employers to . . . insure the survival of the only kind of government which recognizes the rights of labor and of capital."

On June 19, Howard Hunter called a news conference in Washington to tell reporters that the WPA rolls would be pared to around 1 million workers as of July 1. They currently stood at 1,413,000. Until now, in the six-year history of the WPA, there had never been fewer than a million and a half workers on the rolls, and that figure had come in the fall of 1937 before shooting up again during the Roosevelt recession. The availability of private jobs was causing more turnover than the WPA had ever seen, Hunter said, but the defense program would keep the sheer numbers steady at close to 1 million through the end of the year. Even so, the once ubiquitous program was receding; 1,500 of the nation's 3,100 counties would see their WPA projects disappear.

Construction work, much of it on airports and access roads to military installations, continued to provide the biggest share of jobs, but 27 percent of them remained in the white-collar and service areas. These included the arts projects. The Writers' Program still had much of its original work to complete: thirteen of the state guides in the American Guide series remained unpublished at the beginning of 1941. Where writers were not scrambling to finish the guides, they were assigned to produce introductions to the environs of the new military camps springing up around the country, as well as cautionary pamphlets on the dangers of malaria, unsafe drinking water, and un-protected sex. The Music Project's orchestras and bands were in de-mand as morale boosters for draftees undergoing military training. The Art Project's graphic artists were producing civil defense and other informational posters. The rest of the white-collar projects would focus on nutrition, health, recreation, and adult education.

Hunter also said that the number of WPA workers training for arms factory work, which had dropped below 50,000, would rise again. This training had now shifted from state vocational schools to the manufacturing facilities themselves. Bell Aircraft in Buffalo, New York, was training 300 WPA workers. In New Haven, Connecticut, the Winchester Repeating Arms Company had committed to training 1,000 of them.

Three days later, Hitler launched his long-rumored invasion of Soviet Russia, deploying troops and tanks across a 930-mile front from the Arctic to the Black Sea, bombing military airfields, and de-stroying a thousand planes in twelve hours—one-quarter of the Soviet air force. The invasion forced a reassessment of ideological allegiances in the United States. As long as the Nazi-Soviet non-aggression pact had been in force, it was possible to conflate the two vastly different dictatorships as enemies of America and Western democracies. With the invasion came the prospect that the United States, under the policy inscribed in the Lend-Lease Act of furnishing all necessary aid to ene-mies of the Axis as a means of ensuring its own defense, would now be sending military weapons and supplies to Communist Russia. The per-ception was that this surely would be a waste, since military estimates reckoned it would take the German army no more than three months to defeat its Soviet counterpart and occupy its territory as far east as Leningrad, Moscow, and Ukraine. Hitler aimed to feed his troops from the Soviet breadbasket and add its industrial production to his war machine. But he never anticipated that Russian civilians by the many thousands, including women volunteers, would take up shovels (albeit at gunpoint) to help dig anti-tank defenses on the fringes of Leningrad and Moscow, or that the Red Army would prove tenacious and resilient in defending its territory until the winter turned the tide against the invaders, just as it had against Napoleon in 1812.

Hitler's turn to the east added a new leaf to Harry Hopkins's portfolio as Roosevelt's unofficial ambassador to the Allies. By the end of July, after returning to England for new discussions with Churchill, he was on his way by flying boat and transport plane to Moscow to meet with Soviet premier Josef Stalin on the president's behalf. He returned with requests for aluminum, rifles, and anti-aircraft guns. The "arsenal of democracy" was now arming not only itself and the British Commonwealth but its new ally the Soviet Union.

The increasing demands of war production drove unemployment down still further. It would drop below 10 percent for 1941, the first time since 1929 that it had reached single digits. The number of jobless was 5.3 million, down from 13 to 15 million when Roosevelt took office. Hunter spoke to the press again on September 26. He said in opening, "The WPA is really getting out of the news these days."

"Yes. Too much war," said one of the reporters.

The commissioner announced that WPA enrollment now stood at its lowest level ever, 1,034,629 workers in the United States and Puerto Rico. He was operating under a budget of $875 million for the fiscal year that ended on June 30, 1942, a drop of $500 million from the year before and the first time the emergency relief appropriation had fallen below $1 billion. Still, there were more than a million eligible people for whom there were no WPA jobs, and he expected the need to spike again after the first of the year, as it usually did when seasonal employment dropped.

Of the million-plus remaining on the WPA rolls, about one-third— 334,000—were working on defense projects. Some 90 percent of these were construction workers on the still-to-be-completed roads and airports. The white-collar component included teachers called on by the Selective Service System to teach draftees to read and write at the fourth-grade level after the army discovered that some 90,000 of its draftees, primarily from southern states, were illiterate. As Hunter pointed out, WPA-paid teachers had already taught the basics of literacy to 1 million people in its adult education classes, so "90,000 more wouldn't be much of a bite to take." He also noted that a full quota of 50,000 WPA-paid workers were now training in 266 defense-related factories, and while they were eligible for government pay for a training period of up to eight weeks, most were moving off the WPA payroll and onto the plants' payrolls in two and a half weeks.

It was time to give WPA workers a raise, Hunter said. Their pay had not changed since the 1939 reorganization, ranging from $31 to $94 a week depending on the region of the country and the job, while hourly pay for industrial workers had increased 15 percent and weekly pay, factoring in overtime, had increased 32 percent over the same period. This was pushing prices up—7.5 percent in the general cost of living and 15 percent in food costs—and he said he would increase wages 10 percent in the next thirty days.

He made a further point, one that anticipated a sea change in the face of American manufacturing. Paul McNutt, who headed the Federal Security Agency that included the U.S. Employment Service, had pointed out that many of the parts assembly and other jobs at arms plants could be done by women as well as men, but that manufacturers were reluctant to hire them. Hunter concurred. "There are not many manufacturers willing to accept women in defense industries," he said, adding that he wanted to do more to train women and move them into defense jobs. He was not asked about, and did not address, anti-black discrimination by defense contractors, which persisted despite Roosevelt's executive order of June 25, 1941, barring discrimination in the defense industry and the federal government on the basis of "race, creed, color, or national origin."

Six weeks later, on December 7, 1941, the Japanese launched their sneak attack on the American fleet at Pearl Harbor. It was a day, Roosevelt said famously, "that will live in infamy." It was also a day that swept aside many of the assumptions that had existed until then, the resistance to women (though not to African Americans) in defense plants being one. It erased the idea that America could hide behind its oceans; the America First Committee, the last bastion of isolationism, would dissolve within a single week. And with the United States at war, in swift succession, against Japan and then Germany and Italy, it was a day that foretold the end of the WPA.

12. THE LAST HURRAH

Hunter was in his native New Orleans dealing with a host of accumulated medical problems when the Japanese attacked Pearl Harbor. "The goddamned Japs caught me with all my teeth out and a fresh abscess up my rectum—and with a fairly good diverticulitis in the gut I am really working both ends against the middle," he wrote to Harry Hopkins in a December 15 letter. The two had been good friends when Hopkins headed the WPA, sharing both a social work background and a fondness for the horse track, so the tone of the letter was not unusual. Nor was the fact that Hunter sought Hopkins's advice. "Should I stay on in WPA?" he asked. "Or should I wangle around for something else in Washington?"

Hunter was ambivalent because he was chafing under the yoke of the Federal Works Agency, under which the WPA had operated since the 1939 reorganization. He held out hope that General Philip B. Fleming, like the late Harrington a construction-oriented army engineer, would recover from an illness and take over the umbrella works agency. The FWA was currently leaderless, John M. Carmody having resigned in November, and to Hunter's thinking it was "a disgraceful shambles."

Hopkins replied three days later. His short note had an impatient tone, as if he couldn't be bothered with trivia now that he had managed Lend-Lease, served as Roosevelt's personal ambassador to Churchill and Stalin, and was part of the White House inner circle monitoring daily developments in the three theaters of the war. "I think you should stay with the WPA and get your mind off other things," he wrote. "I think it is extremely important that you get yourself in a mental frame of mind where you have made up your mind that you are going to stay here and stick by this job."

In fact, Hunter had already fired off telegrams to Stimson and Knox, the war and navy secretaries, on December 8, offering the WPA's resources for the war effort. "Pending such time as full private employment is possible I assure you that the unemployed want to work for their country on the most essential projects," he wrote. Another telegram went to state and regional administrators: "State of war demands complete cooperation and effectiveness of WPA. War and navy departments have requested acceleration of work on vital projects and possible deferment of others not essential at this time. You are instructed to close off rapidly as possible all construction projects of nondefense nature using critical materials or labor where they can be effectively used in defense activity."

The administrators responded quickly. By Christmas, assistant commissioner Florence Kerr, the head of the old Division of Women's and Professional Projects, now called the Service Division, had turned the toymaking shops that in several cities had built and repaired toys for the children of relief families into sign shops. Paint that had reddened cheeks on dolls now went into arrows pointing to air raid shelters, first-aid stations, and other civil defense emergency facilities. Sewing rooms shifted their output from layette kits for newborns to first-aid packets for shipment to the front. Soon after the new year, the WPA's archaeology projects started to shut down from coast to coast.

By January 13, with the war just over one month old, Hunter had recovered sufficiently to return to Washington, where he addressed the U.S. Conference of Mayors at the Mayflower Hotel. Although his frustrations had continued to mount, he kept them to himself and touted the partnership under which the WPA and the mayors had remodeled their cities. There had been "lasting improvements in every conceivable kind of public facility," he told them, and he quoted from a posthumous award given to Harrington that called the accumulated work "the greatest peacetime achievement in the history of our country."

Ever the New Dealer, Hunter went on to warn that "budget balancers" were claiming that the WPA was no longer essential despite the fact that just over 1 million men and women remained on its rolls. "Are people non-essential?" he demanded. "These people...are not statistics and they are not zombies. They are men and women who are citizens of this democracy. They have not learned how to live happily or patriotically without eating." He said the unemployed still needed "a chance to sweat in honest work as a part of our democracy."

But their ranks were rapidly diminishing. In New York City, Colonel Somervell had returned to army service and, promoted to brigadier general, was overseeing the building of the Pentagon. His successor, Major Irving V. A. Huie, reported in February that the city's WPA was shifting to war work and that the work-relief rolls now stood at 60,684, down from 97,986 a year earlier. Some 20,000 of these were in the Service Division, and by April the division was keying its remaining projects to war and civilian defense programs.

On May 1, the WPA Writers' Program became the Writers' Unit of the War Services Division of the WPA. Only forty state offices remained open, and their employees were a collection of middle-aged men and women who were not candidates for military or industrial work. Untrained as writers, they turned out such products as servicemen's recreational guides to the areas surrounding army training camps. John Dimmock Newsom, the director who had replaced Henry Alsberg, had seen the American Guide series through to completion—the last of the state guides, Oklahoma's, had been published in January—and he would soon resign and join the army. The Art Project became the Graphic Section of the War Services Division. Mural painters turned to designing camouflage patterns for tanks and ships, and graphic artists now turned out posters urging Americans to patriotism, conservation, and discretion. Music Project bands entertained soldiers in training. Holger Cahill now headed all three arts projects, recast as the Cultural Division.

May 1 also saw the departure of Hunter from the WPA. Fleming now headed the Federal Works Agency, but he had insisted on imposing administrative authority over the WPA, increasing Hunter's frustration. He had written Hopkins in March to say the situation "stinks" and that he was unwilling to follow orders from "irresponsi-ble and incompetent people." Hopkins arranged an appointment with the president, at which an anguished Hunter repeated the charges of incompetence and interference, but Roosevelt's attention was else-where. There was no indication at that point that he intended to dis-solve the WPA, but he gave Hunter no encouragement. In his resignation letter, Hunter said it was "embarrassing for me to continue as WPA Commissioner," and called for "major changes" in the FWA.

November brought midterm election losses for the Democrats, who saw their margin in the House diminish to thirteen votes. The low turnout benefited the Republicans, but so did a lack of progress in the war; American marines had a toehold on Guadalcanal in the Pacific but could not dislodge the Japanese, and American forces had yet to engage German or Italian forces anywhere, either in North Africa or in Europe, though an invasion of North Africa was imminent.

At the time of the election, WPA employment stood at 354,619, roughly 10 percent of its maximum in 1938. Unemployment nation-wide was under 5 percent. The WPA had lost the rationale for its exis-tence.

Roosevelt dropped the hammer a month later. On December 4, he wrote to Fleming as Federal Works Agency administrator and acting commissioner of the WPA. They had obviously discussed the letter's contents beforehand. It was valedictory in tone:

> By building airports, schools, highways and parks; by making huge
> quantities of clothing for the unfortunate; by serving millions of
> lunches to school children; by almost immeasurable kinds and
> quantities of service the Work Projects Administration has reached a
> creative hand into every county in this nation. It has added to the
> national wealth, has repaired the wastage of depression and has
> strengthened the country to bear the burden of war. By employing
> eight millions of Americans, with thirty millions of dependents, it has
> brought to these people renewed hope and courage. It has maintained
> and increased their working skills; and it has enabled them once more
> to take their rightful places in public or in private employment. . . .
>
> With these considerations in mind, I agree that you should direct the
> prompt liquidation of the affairs of the Work Projects Adminstration,
> thereby conserving a large amount of the funds appropriated to this

organization. This will necessitate closing out all project operations in many states by February 1, 1943, and in other states as soon thereafter as feasible. By taking this action there will be no need to provide project funds for the Work Projects Administration in the budget for the next fiscal year.

I am proud of the Work Projects Administration organization. It has displayed courage and determination in the face of uninformed criticism. The knowledge and experience of this organization will be of great assistance in the consideration of a well-rounded public works program for the post war period.

With the satisfaction of a good job well done and with a high sense of integrity, the Work Projects Administration has asked for and earned an honorable discharge.

The news was sandwiched between columns of war coverage: U.S. marines fighting the fanatic Japanese for every inch of Guadalcanal; the army linked with British and Commonwealth forces now advancing against Germany's General Erwin Rommel on the sands of North Africa and American bombers targeting Axis targets in Italy; the Red Army in the process of breaking the German siege of Stalingrad. Editorials commended the WPA and said that it should rest in peace, not to be revived. Letters to the White House offered praise and condemnation, as they always had. The Toledo Small Business Men's Association noted "with interest and pleasure your abolishment of the WPA." A hotel owner in Mitchell, South Dakota, wrote that the end of the agency "leaves a good taste in the public's mouths." A WPA recreation supervisor in Independence, Missouri, thanked the president "for the opportunity that I have had of working with some of the finest people that I have ever met or known." A widow in Oxford, Mississippi, also offered thanks "for giving to the little person like myself a chance to work and try and make an honest living for myself and family. Of course I am referring to that wonderful program W.P.A."

It spiraled to its end swiftly. Evidence of its presence began to disappear from the American landscape. This accelerated in February 1943 when Fleming ordered that the familiar red, white, and blue signs that marked its projects be taken down and processed for scrap to aid the war effort.

By May 1 WPA offices had shut down in thirty states and New York

City. The entire project roll then stood at 37,000. The administrative staff, itself once numbering 36,000, was a skeletal 250, and news reports said employees were leaving daily for private jobs or other work in government. And those who remained were tying up loose ends, balancing accounts, and microfilming files that would provide, if anyone ever cared to look, a record of the most extensive and egalitarian jobs program ever seen in a democracy.

EPILOGUE

THE LEGACY OF THE WPA

I am sure that the full accomplishments of the WPA will never be known by any one person. It has simply been too large in figures and volume of things done to get it all in one brief statement.

—HOWARD O. HUNTER,

COMMISSIONER, WORK PROJECTS ADMINISTRATION,

TO THE U.S. CONFERENCE OF MAYORS, JANUARY 13, 1942

In fact, after its final death knell on June 30, 1943, no one would care to look at the WPA again for quite some time. In the heat of war, there was too much else to think about, and the agency closed its doors without fanfare. Two years later, when the war was ending and life slowly began to return to normal, Americans did not want to remember the depression. And its physical legacy, the works of the WPA, were so familiar as to go unnoticed. Their ubiquity rendered them invisible. The post-war generation grew up attending WPA-built schools. It rode on WPA roads, attended games at WPA stadiums, applied for marriage licenses at WPA courthouses, read books in WPA libraries, swam in lakes created by WPA dams, adopted pets from WPA animal shelters. But for some weathered plaques and cornerstones that marked these structures, they might have been there always, and they rarely got a moment's thought.

The accomplishments of the WPA came to be measured in statistics: 650,000 miles of roads, 78,000 bridges, 125,000 civilian and military buildings, 800 airports built, improved, or enlarged, 700 miles of airport runways. It served almost 900 million hot lunches to schoolchildren and operated 1,500 nursery schools. It presented 225,000 concerts to audiences totaling 150 million, performed plays, vaudeville acts, puppet shows, and circuses before 30 million people, and produced almost 475,000 works of art and at least 276 full-length books and 701 pamphlets. Such numbers convey almost no impact by themselves. They are silent on the transformation of the infrastructure that occurred, the modernizing of the country, the malnutrition defeated and educational prospects gained, the new horizons opened.

The workers of the WPA of course moved on.

Grace Overbee, the Kentucky packhorse librarian, moved to a job in a WPA sewing room. When the agency shifted to defense work she and other women working in a building in the Lee County seat, Beattyville, made parachutes and uniforms, and when the WPA shut down she returned to farming and eventually remarried.

Henry Moar, the laborer and blacksmith's helper at the Timberline Lodge, worked on other WPA jobs, was rejected by the draft, and spent much of his post-WPA life moving blocks of ice around the floor of the Northwestern Ice and Cold Storage plant in Portland.

Frank Goodman, the precocious teenager who headed youth publicity for the Federal Theatre Project in New York, followed John Houseman and Orson Welles to their Mercury Theatre. Anthony Buttitta became a private theatrical publicist for performing groups including the San Francisco Light Opera and a memoirist who recounted both the Federal Theatre and his friendship with F. Scott Fitzgerald. Milton Meltzer became an extraordinarily prolific writer with more than 100 books to his credit. Many were for young people, and one covered the WPA arts programs.

Thomas Fleming, the Writers' Project researcher in Berkeley, was pink-slipped in a personnel reduction but got another WPA job with the Agriculture Department conducting botanical research. When the WPA shifted to defense work, he took one of the training courses and went to work at the Kaiser shipyard in Richmond, California, building the lightly armored aircraft carrier escorts that were known as "Kaiser coffins." Near the end of the war, he cofounded with a friend what was then San Francisco's only black newspaper, the *Reporter*.

Johnny Mills, who worked on WPA road crews in the mountains near his Jackson County, North Carolina, home, farmed and worked mining olivine, a green-colored, iron-bearing rock used in manufacturing processses for its heat resistance.

John B. Elliott, the archaeologist, moved in 1939 from the Green

River digs in western Kentucky to explore Adena mound sites in northern Kentucky near the Ohio River. Using a crew of more than fifty men at a site called the Crigler Mounds, he unearthed an Adena "town house" that had been burned, as well as evidence of several log tomb burials. It was a spectacular and chilling discovery, because the cremated remains around the central tomb forced Elliott's supervisor, William Webb, to wonder if the Adena had engaged in ritual human sacrifice. The last spade was turned at the Crigler Mounds on January 5, 1942, when all WPA archaeology shut down. Elliott, then thirty and subject to the draft, joined the exodus to farming that was considered vital work during the war. He and his wife returned to his family lands in New Harmony, Indiana, where their daughter was born in April 1942, and they would continue to farm through the war and beyond.

Jimmy Bonanno, the carpenter, spent the war years working for private contractors doing defense-related work in New England and New York State, returning to his family in Brooklyn only periodically. In addition to the monumental task of building Camp Edwards on Cape Cod in record time—its construction became a model for similar camp projects—he worked in Springfield, Massachusetts, and in Utica and Rome, New York. Eager to return home, he applied for a job at Sullivan Drydock and Repair, a Brooklyn shipyard that was building submarine chasers among other vessels for the navy, and although he passed the test he was never called. Nor was he called up for the draft, since his work was vital to the military effort. When he finally returned home for good after the war in the Pacific ended, he was greeted by a brand-new daughter, Annette Nicolina Bonanno.

Howard Hunter joined the army, made lieutenant, was captured by the Germans, and was interned at a prisoner-of-war camp in Adelboden, Switzerland, until the German surrender in May 1945.

Harry Hopkins married his third wife, the former Louise Gill Macy, at the White House in 1942. After Roosevelt died of a cerebral hemorrhage in Warm Springs on April 12, 1945, less than a month before the German surrender, Hopkins performed one last mission for the government. Although sick and frequently confined to bed, at President Harry Truman's request he mustered the strength to fly to Moscow at the end of May for meetings with Stalin and Soviet foreign minister V. M. Molotov. The talks produced a Soviet concession on voting procedures that salvaged the new United Nations but were less successful at limiting post-war Soviet influence over Poland. At the beginning of July, Hopkins left Washington for the last time and returned with his wife to New York, where they moved into a house on Fifth Avenue and he planned to write about his government experiences. In the meantime, Mayor La Guardia appointed him to arbitrate disputes in the New York garment industry. But his health continued to deteriorate and he died on January 29, 1946, of hemochromatosis, the digestive ailment that had plagued him for years. He was only fifty-five years old.

The great works of the WPA fell victim to neglect and disrepair, its most ambitious initiatives obscured by fading memory.

The Timberline Lodge on Mount Hood was abused by its early patrons, who found the handmade furnishings and art too attractive to resist. They stole watercolors from the walls, stuffed the handmade bedspreads into suitcases, and tossed the wrought-iron lamps with their rawhide shades out the window into the snowbanks, then fished them out and took them home. The lodge closed from 1942 to 1945, reopened after the war, and closed again in 1955 after the electricity was cut off because of unpaid bills. Reopened later the same year, it continued to entertain more visitors than it was built for, and the heavy traffic took its toll on the handmade furnishings that remained.

The WPA turned the San Antonio River Walk over to the city in March 1941. It featured new sidewalks, stone footbridges, stairways from street level, waterside benches, and 4,000 trees, shrubs, and other plantings. Fifty thousand San Antonians came out for the opening and a parade of boats. Then they went away. For almost thirty years, the River Walk languished as a hangout for drunks and derelicts, avoided by most of the city's residents.

Roosevelt tried to resurrect the ill-fated Florida Ship Canal in 1939, at the beginning of the defense buildup, but by then the cost had risen to an estimated $200 to $300 million, and it was again rejected by the Senate. It was revived yet again during the administration of Lyndon Johnson, this time as a shallower barge canal. This, too, was rejected, and today the only sign of its presence are the tidy frame cottages of Camp Roosevelt, now private homes, and two huge concrete pylons, largely invisible in roadside undergrowth, that would have supported a bridge to carry traffic over the canal.

In New Straitsville, Ohio, the coal fires burning underground grew in notoriety even as the WPA mine crews fought to contain them. Journalist Ernie Pyle supplemented his columns about the fire with a radio report for NBC in which he donned miner's gear and went underground with a microphone so listeners could hear the crackling flames. Tom Manning of the *Ripley's Believe It or Not* radio show broadcast from the Lost Run Mine while helpers threw water on the flames to make the fire roar. Mine engineer James Cavanaugh declared the fire licked on January 1, 1940, and the crews packed up and went away.

But beginning sometime in the late 1960s, the work of the WPA gained new attention. It found fresh appreciation and new advocates. San Antonio's international Hemisfair, celebrating the city's 250th anniversary in 1968, sparked a restoration of the River Walk. Today, like the Alamo, it is one of the city's most popular destinations, treasured by tourists and locals alike. In Oregon in 1975, the nonprofit Friends of Timberline formed to bring the lodge's glory back to life. Since then it has painstakingly documented the lodge's art and craftwork, preserved and restored furnishings and decorations and replaced others, including parchment lampshades, hand-woven fabrics, and more than a hundred hand-hooked rugs. It is a measure of the group's success that Timberline Lodge is today perhaps the nation's chief monument to the WPA. The Mendocino Woodlands Recreation Demonstration Area, one of the forty-six WPA-built camping areas across the country, is being restored by the State of California and is still used for family recreation and environmental education. (The Catoctin, Maryland, camp called Hi-Catoctin is, as noted, the presidential retreat Camp David.) Pantheon Books, a division of Random House, reissued the state and major city guides of the American Guide series in the early 1980s in both hard- and softcover editions, complete with new introductions and art deco covers to evoke the 1930s.

There are many other survivors of the WPA's building program, great and small. They include swimming pools, golf courses, tennis courts, parks, zoos, animal shelters, yacht marinas, stadiums, baseball parks, libraries, museums, schools, and too many other examples to mention, but the list goes on. So, too, with the services that it originated. It would be unthinkable today if public-school children were not offered hot lunches at their cafeterias.

Much valuable work was lost, the canvases of the easel art division of the Federal Art Project being the first casualties. Thousands of them were still "unallocated" when Pearl Harbor brought the nation into World War II, meaning that they had not found homes on the walls of government offices as had been intended. In the haste of mobilizing in the emergency of all-out war, they were shipped to warehouses for storage. What happened then—or didn't happen—became the stuff of urban legend in the art world. At some point the paintings were deemed to be expendable. One account had them being auctioned off as scrap at 4 cents a pound. One auction lot of canvases was purchased by a New York plumbing contractor who intended to use them as pipe insulation, but the oil paint on hot pipes "produced an unattractive smell" and the plumbing man sold them to a secondhand store in Manhattan, where artists including Jackson Pollock rushed to buy their works back for $3 to $5 apiece. A *Time* magazine item in 1944 recounted the journey of "bales" of easel paintings from a Flushing, Queens, warehouse to a bric-a-brac shop on Canal Street in Manhattan, where art dealers bought them on the cheap—again, $3 to $5—to clean, mount, frame, and resell. Artist/sculptor Pierre Clerk recounts a story his neighbor on the Bowery, abstract impressionist Adolph Gottlieb, told him in the 1960s. Sometime after the war, Gottlieb, Franz Kline, and Willem de Kooning decided to find out what had happened to their WPA paintings. They pursued various reports and rumors to a plumbing warehouse on Staten Island, where they found hundreds of canvases stacked according to size. They sifted through the stacks until they were exhausted but found none of their own works, and finally retired to the nearest bar in frustration. Barroom tales aside, there seems little doubt that a great deal of the easel art was destroyed. As *Art Digest* editor Peyton Boswell Jr. wrote, some good art was surely among "the thousands of canvasses...sold for scrap by the ton." Audrey McMahon said she was promised that the works would be preserved, and that what happened "is shameful history."

Yet today the government is asserting its rights to the work that it once scrapped. The General Services Administration, the custodian of federal property, is reclaiming WPA pieces that have fallen into private hands. In June 2006 it stopped a Pennsylvania auction house from selling a consigned painting by WPA artist R. A. D. Miller entitled

"House with Fence," valued at $10,000 to $15,000. Ownership records don't count, says the GSA, because the government never sold the pieces in the first place. Relying on tips, it targets works that are advertised online or in auction catalogues as WPA art and that still have the Works Progress Administration labels that were pasted to the back to identify them. A GSA fine arts specialist says perhaps half a dozen pieces a year are reclaimed and placed in public buildings or donated to approved institutions. Private art dealers say that collectors have reacted by removing the labels before trying to sell WPA pieces, despite the destruction of provenance that this represents.

The murals have fared better. They, like other works of the WPA, are being rediscovered and restored at sites from New York to California. The works of Charles Alston, Alfred Crimi, Vertis Hayes, and Georgette Seabrooke at Harlem Hospital in New York City were taken down and restored starting in 2005, for reinstallation in a new patient pavilion by 2009. At Golden Gate Park in San Francisco, at the Beach Chalet across from the Pacific Ocean, the frescoes of Lucien Labault, Primo Caredio's mosaics, and the staircase wood carvings of Michael Von Meyer were cleaned and brought back to their original splendor in 1997 and now anchor the park's visitors' center. In Chicago, an artist and art historian named Heather Becker has spearheaded an effort to locate, preserve, and restore WPA and other early-twentieth-century murals, which has evolved into the country's largest mural preservation program. As a result, the Chicago area now boasts some 437 restored murals in sixty-eight locations, primarily in public schools. Nationally, the National New Deal Preservation Association was formed in 1998 to bring attention to WPA and other New Deal art, construction, and conservation projects.

Looking back, what does the WPA mean? Is it a historic artifact almost lost to living memory, or a model for some sort of future government initiative? Many people wonder if anything like the WPA will ever happen again. The answer to that, at least in terms of the wholesale offering of public jobs, is almost certainly no, despite circumstances such as the aftermath of Hurricane Katrina in which it is possible to imagine the benefits of a vast labor force mobilized by a committed government.

What, then, did it mean for the government to exchange faith with its people in such an unprecedented way? In looking at the legacy of the WPA, the fact that shines through the statistics and the human stories, the administrative dramas and political attacks, is the New Deal's fundamental wisdom of treating people as a resource and not as a commodity. Franklin Roosevelt and Harry Hopkins believed that people given a job to do would do it well, and the fact that their paychecks were issued by the government would make not a whit of difference. They were right. The workers of the WPA shone. They excelled. They created works that even without restoration have lasted for more than seventy years and still stand strong, art that is admired, research that is relied upon, infrastructure that endures. They clothed the threadbare, fed the hungry, taught the illiterate, innoculated the vulnerable. They turned toys that were rich children's discards into poor children's treasures. They fought floods and hurricanes and forest fires with bravery that exists today only in the memory of the fewer and fewer who survive, in moldering newsprint, and in the great memory bank created by the Internet. This history and these stories, great and small, remain to be discovered by those who seek them. Those who do will be enriched by what they learn.

One final accomplishment of the WPA's workers must never be forgotten. These ordinary men and women proved to be extraordinary beyond all expectation. They were golden threads woven in the national fabric. In this, they shamed the political philosophy that discounted their value and rewarded the one that placed its faith in them, thus fulfilling the founding vision of a government by and for its people. *All* its people.

GLOSSARY OF NEW DEAL "INITIALIZED" AGENCIES

AAA: Agricultural Adjustment Administration. Agency established under the Agricultural Adjustment Act, May 1933, to regulate crop and livestock production.

CCC: Civilian Conservation Corps. Created by presidential act March 31, 1933, to employ young men eighteen to twenty-five in conservation work in national parks and forests.

CWA: Civil Works Administration. Temporary jobs program during winter of 1933–34.

FAP: Federal Art Project.

FERA: Federal Emergency Relief Administration. First federal relief agency established under the Federal Emergency Relief Act, May 12, 1933.

FMP: Federal Music Project.

FSRC: Federal Surplus Relief Corporation. Agency that processed surplus food and fuel for distribution to relief clients. Later became the Federal Surplus Commodities Corporation.

FTP: Federal Theatre Project.

FWA: Federal Works Agency. The entity created in Roosevelt's government reorganization plan in 1939. It included the Work Projects Administration and the reduced Public Works Administration.

FWP: Federal Writers' Project.

HABS: Historic American Buildings Survey.

HRS: Historical Records Survey.

NRA: National Recovery Administration. Agency set up under the National Industrial Recovery Act, June 1933, to establish and monitor "voluntary" industry-wide codes setting production levels and employment standards.

NYA: National Youth Administration. Agency established under the WPA to provide part-time jobs for high school and college students to allow them to earn money while continuing to study.

PWA: Public Works Administration. Construction agency set up under the National Industrial Recovery Act to build major public works.

RFC: Reconstruction Finance Corporation. Agency established under Herbert Hoover, January 22, 1932, to make emergency loans to banks, railroads, and insurance companies. Later authorized to make loans to state and local governments to provide jobs.

TERA: Temporary Emergency Relief Administration. New York State relief agency established under governor Franklin Roosevelt, November 1931.

TVA: Tennessee Valley Authority. Multistate public agency created in May 1933 to build hydroelectric dams to bring electricity and development to a large part of the rural South.

WPA: Works Progress Administration. Established by presidential order May 6, 1935, to move unemployed workers from relief to jobs and to rebuild the national infrastructure. Name later changed to Work Projects Administration. (See FWA, above.)

SOME HIGHLIGHTS OF THE WPA
A (Very) Partial List by State

ALABAMA

Birmingham: Vulcan Park observation tower
Brundidge: "We Piddle Around" Theater (formerly Brundidge City Hall)
Sylacauga: Isabel Anderson Comer Museum and Arts Center (formerly B. B.
    Comer Memorial Library)

ALASKA

Ketchikan: Federal Building

ARIZONA

Coolidge: Casa Grande Ruins National Monument
Naco: Turquoise Valley Golf Course club house

ARKANSAS

Jasper: Newton County Courthouse
Mountain Home: Baxter County Courthouse

CALIFORNIA

Clayton: Summit Building at Mount Diablo State Park
Mendocino County: Mendocino Woodlands State Park
San Bernardino County: Asistencia, Mission San Gabriel
San Francisco: Cow Palace, murals at Beach Chalet
San Jose: National Guard Armory

COLORADO

Denver: Bonnie Brae Park
Mesa Verde National Park: historic dioramas
Pueblo: City Park (including Lake Joy, Monkey Mountain, and Monkey
    Island), Pueblo Junior College

CONNECTICUT

New Haven: Chatfield Hollow State Park tower
Norwalk: Oak Hills Park Golf Course; murals at Norwalk City Hall,
    Norwalk Transit District, Norwalk Community College, Norwalk Public
    Library, and the Maritime Aquarium at Norwalk
Stamford: Michael A. Boyle Stadium

DELAWARE

Hancock: Hancock Golf Course

DISTRICT OF COLUMBIA

Washington: murals at Smithsonian American Art Museum

FLORIDA

Tavernier Key: Monroe County Health Department (built as a school and
    hurricane refuge)
Fort Myers: Fort Myers Yacht Basin

GEORGIA

Clayton: nine-hole golf course at Rabun County Golf Club
Macon: Macon City Hall, Ocmulgee National Monument

HAWAII

Oahu and outer islands: civilian and military airfields

IDAHO

Arco: Recreation Hall
Boise: Ada County Courthouse and murals
Idaho Falls: Idaho Falls Airport Historic District

ILLINOIS

Aurora: Phillips Park Golf Course
Brookfield: Brookfield Zoo

Chicago: Zoo Rookery at Lincoln Park Zoo
Dixon: park system bridges and landscaping
Murphysboro: Riverside Park baseball field and band shell

INDIANA

Hammond: Hammond Civic Center
Michigan City: Washington Park Zoo improvements
Mishawaka: Battell Park band shell and rock garden

IOWA

Clinton: Stone Lookout Tower
Dubuque: Eagle Point Park, Shot Tower restoration

KANSAS

Hiawatha: National Guard Armory
Hutchinson: Prairie Dunes Golf Course

KENTUCKY

Ashland: Central Park, Putnam Stadium at Paul Blazer High School

LOUISIANA

Baton Rouge: Louisiana State University's Tiger Stadium addition
New Orleans: Crescent City Golf Course

MAINE

Caribou: Nylander Museum
Portland: Portland Observatory Maritime Signal Tower restoration

MARYLAND

Cumberland: Constitution Park pool
Frederick County: Camp David presidential retreat

MASSACHUSETTS

Danvers: murals at Danvers Town Hall
Haverhill: Haverhill Stadium
Hyde Park: George Wright Golf Course
Melrose: Stone wall in Wyoming Cemetery
New Bedford: New Bedford Municipal Golf Course

MICHIGAN

East Lansing: East Wing and murals at Michigan State University's Kresge Art Museum
Kalamazoo: Milham Park Municipal Golf Course

MINNESOTA

Currie: Beach House and Mess Hall at Lake Shetek State Park
Roseau: Roseau City Hall
St. Paul: Keller Golf Course, Minnehaha Playground building

MISSISSIPPI

Carrollton: Carrollton Community House
Jackson: terminal building at Hawkins Field (airport), castle and Elephant House Café at Jackson Zoo

MISSOURI

Arrow Rock: open shelter and stone bridge at Arrow Rock State Historic Site
St. Louis: picnic shelters at Tilles Park, Grand Staircase at Fort Belle Fontaine Park

MONTANA

Bozeman: Longfellow School
Kalispell: Buffalo Hill Golf Course
Lewiston: Rock ponds and bridges at Big Springs Trout Hatchery
Miles City: Denton Field baseball stadium

NEBRASKA

Lincoln: "The Smoke Signal" sculpture at Pioneer Park
Nebraska City: Stone footbridge at Steinhart Park

NEVADA

Reno: Washoe County Golf Course, Southside School annex

NEW HAMPSHIRE

Laconia: Gunstock Mountain Lodge
Manchester: airport terminal building
Nashua: Holman Stadium

NEW JERSEY

Alpine: Lookout Inn on the Palisades Parkway
Newark: murals at Newark City Hall
Somerset: Great Swamp drainage ditches

NEW MEXICO

Claunch: Old School House
Fort Sumner: mural at De Baca County Courthouse
Magdalena: old WPA gym

NEW YORK

Bethpage: Bethpage State Park golf courses
Buffalo: Buffalo Memorial Auditorium
Bronx: Split Rock Golf Course
Fair Haven: Fair Haven Beach State Park
New York City: La Guardia Airport
West Point: stained glass and painted murals at U.S. Military Academy's
    Washington Hall (cadet mess)

NORTH CAROLINA

Cullowhee: Western Carolina University's Breese Gymnasium
Goldsboro: Old Station 1 fire station
Roanoke Island: Fort Raleigh National Historic Site

NORTH DAKOTA

Bismarck: Edwards House at Camp Grafton (North Dakota National
    Guard)
Linton: Emmons County Courthouse
Minot: Pioneer Bowl

OHIO

Akron: Rubber Bowl stadium at University of Akron
Cleveland: Forest Hill Park
Columbus: Ohio State University Golf Course

OKLAHOMA

Fort Gibson: Fort Gibson Historic Site restoration

OREGON

Eugene: Civic Stadium, Howe Memorial Gates at University of Oregon
Mount Hood: Timberline Lodge
Portland: Stone House at Forest Park

PENNSYLVANIA

Pittsburgh: Stone stairs and bridges at Schenley Park
Philadelphia: reading room at the Philadelphia Museum of Art Library,
    buildings at Fairmount Park
York: WPA Models and Dioramas at Indian Steps Museum

RHODE ISLAND

Barrington: Stone fireplaces at Dr. George B. Haines Memorial Park
Providence: Stone staircase at Neutaconkanut Hill Park

SOUTH CAROLINA

Charleston: Dock Street Theatre restoration
Columbia: McKissick Museum at University of South Carolina

SOUTH DAKOTA

Philip: Philip Auditorium
Rapid City: Dinosaur Park

TENNESSEE

Bristol: Stone Castle Stadium at Tennessee High School
Kingsport, Johnson City, and Bristol tri-cities: airports in Memphis,
    Chattanooga, Knoxville, Nashville, and Jackson
Memphis: Children's Museum of Memphis (formerly National Guard Armory)
Nashville: Fort Negley restoration

TEXAS

Dallas: Dealey Plaza
La Porte: San Jacinto Monument
San Antonio: River Walk

UTAH

Garfield County: Bryce Canyon Airport, between Escalante and Panguitch
Helper: Helper Civic Auditorium
Salt Lake City: rotunda murals at the Utah State Capitol

VERMONT

Montpelier: Recreation Park

VIRGINIA

Fredericksburg: Spotsylvania County Courthouse annex

WASHINGTON

Seattle: Woodland Park Zoo

WEST VIRGINIA

Fairmont: Stone walls at East-West Stadium

WISCONSIN

Hales Corner: Golf club house at Whitnall Park
Milwaukee: Sculptures at Parklawn Housing Project
Milwaukee County: swimming pools, pavilions, Milwaukee County park
   system
Wauwatosa: Murals at Wauwatosa East High School

WYOMING

Casper: Natrona County High School
Dayton: Dayton Community Hall
Newcastle: Anna Miller Museum (building originally constructed for the
   Wyoming National Guard)

A CHRONOLOGY
1929–1946

October 29, 1929: The "Black Tuesday" stock market crash that ushers in the Great Depression.

November 1, 1931: New York State under Governor Franklin Delano Roosevelt establishes Temporary Emergency Relief Administration (TERA), the first state agency to provide assistance for the unemployed.

January 21, 1932: FDR announces his candidacy for the Democratic nomination.

March 1, 1932: Infant son of famous aviator Charles Lindbergh is kidnapped.

March 7, 1932: Four killed by police in march of unemployed on Ford plant in Dearborn, Michigan.

April 7, 1932: FDR "forgotten man" speech.

May 26, 1932: FDR speech at Oglethorpe University calling for "bold, persistent experimentation."

June 16, 1932: Herbert Hoover nominated by Republicans as candidate for second term.

July 1, 1932: Democratic National Convention in Chicago nominates FDR as party's candidate for president.

July 2, 1932: FDR breaks tradition by accepting nomination in person at convention.

July 8, 1932: Dow Jones Industrials hit a low of 41.22, down 89 percent from the pre-depression peak of 381.17.

July 21, 1932: President Herbert Hoover sets aside $300 million in Reconstruction Finance Corporation funds for loans to states and cities to fight unemployment.

July 28, 1932: "Bonus Army" of world war veterans petitioning for immediate payment of a deferred service bonus is evicted from their camps in Washington by army troops under General Douglas MacArthur.

August 11, 1932: Hoover is officially informed of his renomination as Republican presidential candidate, and accepts.

November 8, 1932: Roosevelt defeats Hoover.

February–March 1933: U.S. unemployment reaches 24.9 percent.

February 14, 1933: Out-of-work bricklayer Giuseppe Zangara tries to shoot FDR in Miami, fatally wounds Chicago mayor Anton Cermak.

March 4, 1933: FDR inaugurated, in inaugural address says, "The only thing we have to fear is fear itself." Declares nationwide bank "holiday" starting Monday, March 6.

March 9, 1933: Start of the "Hundred Days" during which the most significant New Deal legislation is passed and signed into law, starting with the Emergency Banking Act.

March 12, 1933: FDR's first "fireside chat" on nationwide radio.

March 13, 1933: Banks reopen.

March 31, 1933: FDR signs bill establishing the Civilian Conservation Corps (CCC).

April 7, 1933: Low-alcohol beer and wine on sale as first step toward ending Prohibition.

May 12, 1933: Congress passes Federal Emergency Relief Act, setting up Federal Emergency Relief Administration (FERA) with $500 million to aid unemployed.

May 12, 1933: Congress passes the Emergency Farm Mortgage Act, allowing farm mortgages to be refinanced.

May 12, 1933: Agricultural Adjustment Act is passed, providing for payments to farmers to limit production.

May 18, 1933: Congress approves the Tennessee Valley Authority to dam rivers and provide electric power to develop the Tennessee Valley.

May 22, 1932: Harry Lloyd Hopkins begins work as federal relief administrator, spends $5 million in two hours.

June 13, 1933: Congress passes Home Owners' Loan Act, allowing home mortgages to be refinanced.

June 16, 1933: National Industrial Recovery Act is passed, setting up National Recovery Administration (NRA) to supervise "voluntary" industrial employment and production codes and providing $3.3 billion for dams and bridges and other large-scale projects under the Public Works Administration (PWA).

October 4, 1933: Federal Surplus Relief Corporation chartered; aim is to provide surplus agricultural products to relief families.

November 7, 1933: Fiorello La Guardia elected mayor of New York City.

November 9, 1933: FDR signs executive order creating the Civil Works Administration (CWA) to provide 4 million jobs over the winter of 1933–34. Puts Harry Hopkins in charge.

December 1933: Twenty-first Amendment to the Constitution ratified, ending Prohibition.

December 15, 1933: Hopkins has placed 2.6 million workers in CWA jobs.

January 1, 1934: La Guardia sworn in as New York City mayor.

January 15, 1934: 4,264,000 working at CWA jobs.

February 19, 1934: Hopkins on cover of *Time* magazine.

March 31, 1934: CWA phased out. Some workers keep jobs under FERA, others go back on direct relief.

August 22, 1934: The anti-Roosevelt American Liberty League announces its formation.

October 22, 1934: Charles "Pretty Boy" Floyd shot to death by federal agents in Ohio.

November 6, 1934: Midterm elections give Democrats overwhelming majorities in both houses of Congress.

January 4, 1935: FDR calls for a "greatly enlarged" work program in his State of the Union address.

January 11, 1935: Aviatrix Amelia Earhart becomes the first solo pilot to fly from Hawaii to California.

April 3, 1935: Aldermanic hearings in New York City produce testimony about "boon doggles."

April 8, 1935: Congress passes and Roosevelt signs the 1935 Emergency Relief Appropriations Act authorizing $4.8 billion for work relief.

April 28, 1935: FDR announces the work-relief program in a fireside chat.

May 6, 1935: FDR signs executive order creating the work program structure, with the Works Progress Administration under Harry Hopkins its operational arm.

May 27, 1935: Supreme Court declares the National Industrial Recovery Act unconstitutional.

June 5, 1935: Passage of the Wagner Act guarantees the right of collective bargaining.

June 26, 1935: National Youth Administration (NYA) created as a division of the WPA.

July 1935: Ellen Woodward, head of women's work programs under CWA and FERA, placed in charge of WPA's newly combined Division of Women's and Professional Projects. Jacob Baker's Division of Professional and Service Projects is dissolved, though Baker stays on to head federal arts projects.

August 2, 1935: Federal Project Number One, the federal art, music, theater, and writing projects, are announced in Washington. Directors of the projects are Holger Cahill, art; Nicolai Sokoloff, music; Hallie Flanagan, theater; and Henry Alsberg, writing.

August 14, 1935: FDR signs bill creating the Social Security System.

August 15, 1935: Humorist Will Rogers and pilot Wiley Post are killed in an airplane crash near Barrow, Alaska.

September 2, 1935: Hurricane strikes FERA work camp employing world war veterans in the Florida Keys, killing more than 400.

September 8, 1935: Senator Huey Long fatally shot in the Louisiana capitol at Baton Rouge. He dies two days later.

September 19, 1935: FDR sets off by telegraph an explosion opening construction of a canal to carry shipping across Florida. The WPA project is killed by Congress before a year is out.

September 30, 1935: Hoover Dam, formerly Boulder Dam, is dedicated in Nevada.

October 10, 1935: George Gershwin's *Porgy and Bess* opens on Broadway.

October 17, 1935: WPA Circus debuts in Brooklyn, marking the Federal Theatre Project's first performance in New York.

October 22, 1935: "W-men," a squad of WPA fraud investigators, announced by WPA administrator Harry Hopkins.

December 14, 1935: Proposal to build a ski lodge on Mount Hood in Oregon with $250,000 from the WPA is approved in Washington.

January 6, 1936: Supreme Court overturns the Agricultural Adjustment Act, passed in 1933.

January 1936: Workers on the WPA payroll reach 2.8 million.

January 27, 1936: Immediate bonuses to world war veterans approved over Roosevelt's veto.

March 1936: Spring floods in New England and the Ohio River valley leave 171 dead and 430,000 homeless; 100,000 WPA workers join rescue, recovery, and cleanup efforts.

March 14, 1936: *Triple-A Plowed Under,* the Federal Theatre Project's first Living Newspaper production, opens at the Biltmore Theatre in New York.

April 5–6, 1936: Tornadoes strike Tupelo, Mississippi, and Gainesville, Georgia, killing more than 200 in each city and spurring WPA rescue and cleanup work.

April 14, 1936: The "voodoo" *Macbeth,* a production of the Federal Theatre Project's Negro Theatre in New York, opens to a sellout crowd in Harlem.

Summer 1936: WPA workers become firefighters as forest fires strike across the upper Midwest.

June 13, 1936: Ground broken on Mount Hood for the Timberline Lodge.

July 11, 1936: The Triborough Bridge, a project of the Public Works

Administration, is dedicated by FDR; the bridge links Manhattan with the Bronx and Queens in New York City.

September 14, 1936: Harry Hopkins visits Timberline Lodge construction site.

October 10, 1936: WPA crews begin effort to quench fires burning in coal shafts under New Straitsville, Ohio, for more than fifty years.

October 27, 1936: Federal Theatre Project opens stage version of *It Can't Happen Here,* by Sinclair Lewis, simultaneously in sixteen cities.

November 3, 1936: Roosevelt defeats Republican challenger Alf Landon, the Kansas governor, by more than 10 million votes and 523 electoral votes to 8.

November 28, 1936: Harry Hopkins dedicates stadium addition at Louisiana State University built by the WPA; LSU Tigers beat Tulane.

January 1937: *Idaho: A Guide in Word and Picture* is the first of the state guides in the Federal Writers' Project American Guide series to be published.

January 20, 1937: FDR inaugurated for a second term, says he sees "one-third of a nation ill-housed, ill-clad, ill-nourished."

January–February 1937: Some 200,000 WPA workers mustered to fight flooding on the Ohio and Mississippi Rivers and join the cleanup afterward. Forty WPA workers are among almost 500 dead in the flooding, including 30 who drown when their transportation barge sinks at New Madrid, Missouri.

February 5, 1937: FDR submits his "court-packing" plan to Congress.

February 11, 1937: General Motors recognizes the United Auto Workers as the sole bargaining agent for its workers, ending a sit-down strike that began on December 30.

February 23, 1937: The Federal Theatre Project's Living Newspaper *Power* opens at the Ritz Theatre in New York City.

March 1, 1937: U.S. Steel permits unionization of workers to prevent a strike.

March 29, 1937: Supreme Court upholds a Washington State minimum wage law.

April 12, 1937: Supreme Court upholds the Wagner Act, also known as the National Labor Relations Act.

May 6, 1937: The dirigible *Hindenburg* explodes at Lakehurst, New Jersey, killing thirty-six.

May 24, 1937: Supreme Court upholds the Social Security Act.

May 27, 1937: Golden Gate Bridge opens in San Francisco. WPA arts workers in New York stage a one-day strike to protest job cuts.

May 30, 1937: Chicago police fire on demonstrators outside Republic Steel, killing ten and wounding many more.

June 16, 1937: The Federal Theatre Project's "runaway opera," *The Cradle Will Rock*, is performed despite WPA efforts to shut it down.

June 22, 1937: Joe Louis knocks out James J. Braddock, the "Cinderella Man," to win the heavyweight title.

July 2, 1937: Amelia Earhart and navigator Fred Noonan take off from Papua New Guinea in their attempt to fly around the world at the equator, and are never heard from again.

July 7, 1937: Japan invades China.

July 14, 1937: Congress kills Roosevelt's court-packing plan, leaving the president politically weakened.

Summer 1937: WPA rolls decline to around 1.5 million as jobs are cut with signs the economy is beginning to improve.

September 8, 1937: FDR dedicates the Timberline Lodge on Mount Hood in Oregon. It will open to paying guests in February 1938.

September 9, 1937: Mayor Fiorello La Guardia, at the controls of a steam shovel, breaks ground on New York City's first commercial airport, to be funded by the WPA.

October 5, 1937: FDR, speaking in Chicago, calls for a quarantine of aggressor nations.

October 6, 1937: Harry Hopkins's second wife, Barbara Duncan Hopkins, dies of cancer in a New York hospital.

October 19, 1937: Stock prices plunge, signaling the start of the Roosevelt recession. Four million reemployed workers will lose their jobs again, and unemployment will rise to 19 percent from a depression low of 14 percent earlier in the year.

December 1937: Harry Hopkins has cancer operation at Mayo Clinic. Much of his stomach is removed.

December 22, 1937: First tube of the PWA-funded Lincoln Tunnel linking midtown New York City with New Jersey opens to traffic.

February 16, 1938: Congress passes the Second Agricultural Adjustment Act.

March 14, 1938: Hitler annexes Austria to Germany.

April 21, 1938: WPA rolls back above 2.5 million.

May 26, 1938: Texas congressman Martin Dies named chairman of the House Committee to Investigate Un-American Activities (HUAC).

June 22, 1938: Heavyweight champion Joe Louis knocks out Max Schmeling in the first round of their heavyweight rematch at Yankee Stadium.

June 24, 1938: In a fireside chat, Roosevelt launches effort to purge Democratic Party of conservatives.

June 25, 1938: Roosevelt signs the Fair Labor Standards Act, establishing for the first time a forty-hour workweek, a minimum wage, and a ban on factory workers under sixteen.

July 18, 1938: Harry Hopkins makes the cover of *Time* for the second time.

August 1938: House Un-American Activities Committee begins hearings alleging Communism in the WPA arts projects. They run through the fall.

September 21, 1938: A hurricane hits Long Island and much of New England without warning, taking 680 lives. Flooding follows. The WPA assigns 100,000 workers to flood control and recovery efforts.

October 1, 1938: German troops begin occupation of the Czechoslovakian Sudetenland.

October 30, 1938: *War of the Worlds* airs on nationwide radio. Many believe H. G. Wells's fictional tale of an attack from Mars is a news report and flee their homes in panic.

November 1938: WPA employment reaches its highest point, with 3,334,594 people on the rolls.

November 1, 1938: Seabiscuit beats Triple Crown winner War Admiral in a match race at Pimlico.

November 8, 1938: Voters rebuff FDR in midterm elections, reelecting conservative Democrats he campaigned against. Republicans add 11 governorships, 81 House seats, and 8 Senate seats.

November 9, 1938: Kristallnacht, "the night of broken glass," signals the beginning of the pogrom against German Jews.

December 23, 1938: Harry Hopkins resigns as WPA administrator and is appointed secretary of commerce by FDR. Francis C. Harrington, an army engineer who has overseen WPA construction projects, is appointed to replace Hopkins.

January 1939: Ellen Woodward, WPA assistant administrator in charge of the Division of Women's and Professional Projects, is named to the Social Security Board. Midwest regional director Florence Kerr succeeds her.

February 18, 1939: Golden Gate International Exposition opens on Treasure Island in San Francisco Bay. The island and its access via the Bay Bridge linking Oakland with San Francisco were projects of the PWA.

March 15, 1939: Germany invades Czechoslovakia.

March 28, 1939: General Francisco Franco's troops take Madrid, ending the Spanish Civil War.

April 30, 1939: The New York World's Fair opens at Flushing Meadow Park in Queens.

June 21, 1939: Congress passes the Emergency Relief Appropriations Act of 1939, making major changes in the WPA and, in a reaction to the HUAC hearings, barring funding for the Federal Theatre Project.

June 30, 1939: Federal Theatre Project gives its last performances.

July 6, 1939: WPA workers strike to protest wage cuts, longer hours. Strike peters out by the end of the month.

September 1, 1939: Germany invades Poland, starting World War II.

September 3, 1939: Britain and France declare war on Germany.

November 30, 1939: Soviet Union invades Finland.

December 2, 1939: La Guardia Field in New York City opens to commercial traffic.

January 1, 1940: WPA declares that it has extinguished the long-burning underground coal mine fires in New Straitsville, Ohio.

April 9, 1940: Germany invades Denmark.

May 10, 1940: Germany invades Belgium and the Netherlands, leading to the evacuation of British and French troops from Dunkirk starting May 29.

June 5, 1940: German troops enter France.

June 21, 1940: France surrenders to Germany.

July 17, 1940: FDR nominated for a third term at the Democratic convention in Chicago. He will face Republican Wendell L. Willkie.

August 22, 1940: Harry Hopkins resigns as secretary of commerce.

September 16, 1940: Congress passes the Selective Service Act, establishing the country's first peacetime draft.

September 30, 1940: WPA commissioner F. C. Harrington dies in New London, Connecticut. Deputy Commissioner Howard Hunter is appointed to succeed him.

November 5, 1940: FDR elected to an unprecedented third term.

December 29, 1940: FDR says the United States must be the world's "arsenal of democracy." With the resulting arms buildup, WPA workers turn increasingly to training for military production. Meanwhile, WPA construction work focuses on military bases, housing, roads for moving troops and matériel, and airports.

January 6, 1941: FDR in State of the Union address calls for a "world founded upon four essential human freedoms." He includes freedom of speech and worship and freedom from want and fear.

May 27, 1941: FDR declares a state of unlimited national emergency.

June 22, 1941: Germany invades the Soviet Union, violating the mutual non-aggression pact Hitler and Stalin had signed on August 23, 1939.

July 1941: WPA employment drops to around 1 million, the lowest it has been since the agency was created in 1935 and the lowest of any of the New Deal work-relief programs including CWA and FERA.

December 7, 1941: Japanese attack U.S. fleet at Pearl Harbor.

December 8, 1941: United States declares war on Japan.

December 11, 1941: Germany and Italy declare war on United States.

January 1942: The last of the American Guide series, *Oklahoma: The Sooner State*, is published.

January 1942 and beyond: Almost all WPA work is defense-related. Arts workers create civil defense posters, writers craft pamphlets for military personnel, and musicians play at military bases, while construction workers continue to improve the military infrastructure.

March 16, 1942: Howard O. Hunter submits his resignation as WPA commissioner to FDR effective "about May 1."

December 5, 1942: Roosevelt orders abolition of the WPA as no longer needed. Only 354,619 are on the rolls as of November 24.

February 9, 1943: WPA orders that its remaining familiar red, white, and blue project-identifying signs be taken down and processed for scrap metal to aid the war effort.

June 30, 1943: WPA goes out of business and returns $105 million in unspent funds to the Treasury and $25 million worth of supplies and materials.

November 7, 1944: FDR elected to a fourth term over Thomas E. Dewey.

April 12, 1945: FDR dies of a cerebral hemorrhage in Warm Springs, Georgia, at age sixty-three.

May 8, 1945: War ends in Europe.

August 14, 1945: War ends in the Pacific.

January 29, 1946: Harry Hopkins dies in a hospital in New York of hemochromatosis. He was fifty-five.

BIBLIOGRAPHY

Allen, Everett S. *A Wind to Shake the World: The Story of the 1938 Hurricane.* Boston: Little, Brown and Company, 1976.

Allen, Frederick Lewis. *Since Yesterday: The Nineteen-Thirties in America, September 3, 1929–September 3, 1939.* New York: Harper and Brothers, 1940.

Alter, Jonathan. *The Defining Moment: FDR's Hundred Days and the Triumph of Hope.* New York: Simon & Schuster, 2006.

Anderson, William. *The Wild Man from Sugar Creek: The Political Career of Eugene Talmadge.* Baton Rouge: Louisiana State University Press, 1975.

Andrist, Ralph K., and the editors of *American Heritage. The American Heritage History of the 20's and 30's.* New York: American Heritage, 1970.

Appelt, Kathi, and Jeanne Cannella Schmitzer. *Down Cut Shin Creek: The Pack Horse Librarians of Kentucky.* New York: HarperCollins Publishers, 2001.

Badger, Anthony J. *The New Deal: The Depression Years, 1933–1940.* New York: Hill and Wang, 1989.

Barber, William J. *From New Era to New Deal: Herbert Hoover, the Economists, and American Economic Policy, 1921–1933.* Cambridge: Cambridge University Press, 1988.

Barry, John M. *Rising Tide: The Great Mississippi Flood of 1927 and How It Changed America.* New York: Touchstone, 1998.

Bauman, John F., and Thomas H. Coode. *In the Eye of the Great*

Depression: New Deal Reporters and the Agony of the American People.
DeKalb: Northern Illinois University Press, 1988.

Bentley, Joanne. *Hallie Flanagan: A Life in the American Theatre.* New
York: Alfred A. Knopf, 1988.

Bindas, Kenneth J. *All of This Music Belongs to the Nation: The WPA's
Federal Music Project and American Society.* Knoxville: University of
Tennessee Press, 1995.

Black, Conrad. *Franklin Delano Roosevelt: Champion of Freedom.* New
York: Public Affairs, 2003.

Bogzevitz, Chris, and John Winnenberg. *Our Journey Continues: The
History of New Straitsville, Ohio.* 2 vols. New Straitsville, Ohio: New
Straitsville Betterment Association and Sunday Creek Associates,
1995–96.

Brinkley, Alan. *Voices of Protest: Huey Long, Father Coughlin, and the
Great Depression.* New York: Vintage Books, 1983.

Brown, Josephine C. *Public Relief, 1929–1939.* New York: Henry Holt,
1940.

Burns, Cherie. *The Great Hurricane: 1938.* New York: Atlantic Monthly
Press, 2005.

Burns, James MacGregor. *Roosevelt: The Lion and the Fox.* New York:
Harcourt Brace, 1956.

Buttitta, Tony, and Barry Witham. *Uncle Sam Presents: A Memoir of the
Federal Theatre, 1935–1939.* Philadelphia: University of Pennsylvania
Press, 1982.

Caro, Robert. *The Power Broker: Robert Moses and the Fall of New York.*
New York: Alfred A. Knopf, 1974.

Charles, Searle F. *Minister of Relief: Harry Hopkins and the Depression.*
Syracuse, N.Y.: Syracuse University Press, 1963.

Cohen, Robert, ed. *Dear Mrs. Roosevelt: Letters from Children of the Great
Depression.* Chapel Hill: University of North Carolina Press, 2002.

Cook, Blanche Wiesen. *Eleanor Roosevelt, vol. 2: The Defining Years,
1933–1938.* New York: Penguin Books, 2000.

Cutler, Leland W. *America Is Good to a Country Boy.* Stanford, Calif.:
Stanford University Press, 1954.

Dickson, Paul, and Thomas B. Allen. *The Bonus Army: An American Epic.*
New York: Walker and Company, 2004.

Edsforth, Ronald. *The New Deal: America's Response to the Great
Depression.* Malden, Mass.: Blackwell, 1999.

Ellis, Edward Robb. *A Nation in Torment: The Great American Depression,
1929–1939.* New York: Kodansha America, 1995.

Federal Writers' Project of the WPA. *New England Hurricane.* Boston: Hale,
Cushman and Flint, 1938.

———. *The WPA Guide to California.* New York: Pantheon, 1984. First published in 1939.

———. *The WPA Guide to Florida.* New York: Pantheon, 1984. First published in 1939.

———. *The WPA Guide to Massachusetts.* New York: Pantheon, 1984. First published in 1937.

———. *The WPA Guide to New York City.* New York: Pantheon, 1984. First published in 1939.

Ferrell, Robert H., ed. *FDR's Quiet Confidant: The Autobiography of Frank C. Walker.* Niwot: University Press of Colorado, 1997.

Flanagan, Hallie. *Arena.* New York: Duell, Sloan and Pearce, 1940.

Galbraith, John Kenneth. *The Great Crash, 1929.* Boston: Houghton Mifflin, 1955.

Gilbert, Martin. *The Second World War: A Complete History.* Rev. ed. New York: Henry Holt and Company, 1991.

Glenn, John, with Nick Taylor. *John Glenn: A Memoir.* New York: Bantam Books, 1999.

Gordon, John Steele. *An Empire of Wealth: The Epic History of American Economic Power.* New York: HarperCollins, 2004.

Griffin, Rachael, and Sarah Munro, eds. *Timberline Lodge.* Portland, Ore.: Friends of Timberline, 1978.

Holmes, Michael S. *The New Deal in Georgia: An Administrative History.* Westport, Conn.: Greenwood Press, 1975.

Hoover, Herbert. *The Memoirs of Herbert Hoover: The Great Depression, 1929–1941.* New York: Macmillan Company, 1952.

Hopkins, Harry L. *Spending to Save: The Complete Story of Relief.* Seattle: University of Washington Press, 1972 [1936].

Hopkins, June. *Harry Hopkins: Sudden Hero, Brash Reformer.* New York: St. Martin's Press, 1999.

Hopkins, Robert. *Witness to History: Recollections of a World War II Photographer.* Seattle, Wash.: Castle Pacific Publishing, 2002.

Hornfischer, James D. *Ship of Ghosts: The Story of the USS Houston, FDR's Legendary Lost Cruiser, and the Epic Story of Her Survivors.* New York: Bantam Books, 2006.

Houseman, John. *Run-Through.* New York: Simon & Schuster, 1972.

Jackson, Robert H. *That Man: An Insider's Portrait of Franklin D. Roosevelt.* (Edited by John Q. Barrett.) New York: Oxford University Press, 2003.

Kennedy, David M. *Freedom from Fear: The American People in Depression and War, 1929–1945.* New York: Oxford University Press, 1999.

Kessner, Thomas. *Fiorello H. La Guardia and the Making of Modern New York.* New York: Penguin Books, 1989.

Klein, Maury. *Rainbow's End: The Crash of 1929*. New York: Oxford University Press, 2003.

Leuchtenberg, William E. *Franklin D. Roosevelt and the New Deal, 1932–1940*. New York: HarperCollins, 1989.

———. *The Perils of Prosperity, 1914–1932*. Chicago: University of Chicago Press, 1993.

Levine, Lawrence W., and Cornelia C. Levine. *The People and the President: America's Conversation with FDR*. Boston: Beacon Press, 2002.

Lyon, Edwin A. *A New Deal for Southeastern Archaeology*. Tuscaloosa: University of Alabama Press, 1996.

Manchester, William. *The Glory and the Dream: A Narrative History of America, 1932–1972*. Boston: Little, Brown and Company, 1973.

Maney, Patrick. *The Roosevelt Presence: The Life and Legacy of FDR*. Berkeley: University of California Press, 1998.

Mangione, Jerre. *The Dream and the Deal: The Federal Writers' Project, 1935–1943*. New York: Avon Books, 1972.

McElvaine, Robert S. *The Great Depression: America, 1929–1941*. New York: Times Books, 1984.

———. *The Depression and the New Deal: A History in Documents*. New York: Oxford University Press, 2000.

McJimsey, George. *Harry Hopkins: Ally of the Poor and Defender of Democracy*. Cambridge, Mass.: Harvard University Press, 1987.

———. *The Presidency of Franklin Delano Roosevelt*. Lawrence: University Press of Kansas, 2000.

Meltzer, Milton. *Violins and Shovels: The WPA Arts Projects*. New York: Delacorte Press, 1976.

Naifeh, Steven, and Gregory White Smith. *Jackson Pollock: An American Saga*. New York: Clarkson N. Potter, Inc., 1989.

O'Connor, Francis V., ed. *The New Deal Arts Projects: An Anthology of Memoirs*. Washington, D.C.: Smithsonian Institution Press, 1972.

O'Connor, John, and Lorraine Brown, eds. *Free, Adult, Uncensored: The Living History of the Federal Theatre Project*. Washington, D.C.: New Republic Books, 1978.

Perkins, Frances. *The Roosevelt I Knew*. New York: Viking Press, 1946.

Phillips, Cabell. *From the Crash to the Blitz, 1929–1939*. New York: Fordham University Press, 2000 [1969].

Rae, John W. *Images of America: Picatinny Arsenal*. Charleston, S.C.: Arcadia, 1999.

Schlesinger, Arthur M., Jr. *The Crisis of the Old Order, 1919–1933: The Age of Roosevelt, Volume 1*. Boston: Houghton Mifflin Company, Mariner Books, 2003.

———. *The Coming of the New Deal, 1933–1935: The Age of Roosevelt, Volume 2*. Boston: Houghton Mifflin Company, Mariner Books, 2003.

———. *The Politics of Upheaval, 1935–1936: The Age of Roosevelt, Volume 3*. Boston: Houghton Mifflin Company, Mariner Books, 2003.

Schomburg Center for Research in Black Culture, New York Public Library. *The Black New Yorkers: The Schomburg Illustrated Chronology*. New York: John Wiley and Sons, 2000.

Selvaggio, Marc S., comp. *The American Guide Series: Works by the Federal Writers' Project*. Berkeley, Calif.: Schoyer's Antiquarian Books, 1998 [1990].

Sherwood, Robert E. *Roosevelt and Hopkins: An Intimate History*. New York: Harper and Row, 1948.

Snyder, Louis L. *Encyclopedia of the Third Reich*. New York: Paragon House, 1989.

Stockbridge, Frank Parker, and John Holiday Perry. *So This Is Florida*. New York: Robert M. McBride and Company, 1938.

Sullivan, Patricia. *Days of Hope: Race and Democracy in the New Deal Era*. Chapel Hill: University of North Carolina Press, 1996.

Swain, Martha H. *Ellen S. Woodward: New Deal Advocate for Women*. Jackson: University Press of Mississippi, 1995.

Terkel, Studs. *Hard Times: An Oral History of the Great Depression*. New York: Pantheon Books, 1970.

Ware, Susan. *Beyond Suffrage: Women in the New Deal*. Cambridge, Mass.: Harvard University Press, 1981.

Watkins, T. H. *Righteous Pilgrim: The Life and Times of Harold L. Ickes, 1873–1952*. New York: Henry Holt and Company, 1990.

———. *The Great Depression: America in the 1930s*. Boston: Little, Brown and Company, 1993.

———. *The Hungry Years: A Narrative History of the Great Depression in America*. New York: Henry Holt and Company, 1999.

White, Nancy Marie, Lynne P. Sullivan, and Rochelle A. Marrinan, eds. *Grit-Tempered: Early Women Archaeologists in the Southeastern United States*. Gainesville: University Press of Florida, 1999.

Wilson, Edmund. *The American Earthquake: A Documentary of the Jazz Age, the Great Depression, and the New Deal*. Garden City, N.Y.: Doubleday Anchor Books, 1958.

———. *The Twenties*. New York: Farrar, Straus and Giroux, 1975.

NOTES

1. The End of Jobs

7   Unemployment figures vary among New Deal histories. Here I rely primarily on Brown, 134, 145. Fifteen million unemployed is used by Manchester, 28.

7   Rise in suicide rate: Galbraith, 133–34. People felt fear...dark, uncertain future: These views are not unique and are expressed at greater length in any number of New Deal histories, but I rely heavily on Barber.

8   Hoover to Fourth Pan American Commercial Conference, Oct. 8, 1931, from the American Presidency Project Web site, www.presidency.ucsb.edu/ws/index.php?pid=22840. Coolidge to the American Society of Newspaper Editors, Jan. 17, 1925, from Bartlett's *Familiar Quotations*, 16th ed., 614.

8   Babe Ruth's salary and quote: Arthur Daley in *New York Times* (henceforth *NYT*), Aug. 19, 1948, 29.

9   Bank failures and unemployment figures: Watkins, *Hungry Years*, 41. New York City unemployment: Caro, 369.

9   3.2 percent unemployment rate: U.S. Dept. of Commerce, Bureau of the Census, *Historical Statistics of the United States, Colonial Times to 1970*, 126. Hoover acceptance quote: *NYT*, Aug. 12, 1928, 2.

9–10   The composite picture of frustrated job seekers is approximated from accounts in many depression histories, as are the composites of the further effects of joblessness below.

10   Children in foster homes and orphanages: *NYT*, June 5, 1932, 17.

10   By 1932, the situation of city dwellers: Watkins, *Hungry Years*, 342–47.

11   And no matter where they lived: ibid., 60–62; 68–70.

12   Americans slow to turn to charity: ibid., 73. Hoover quotes: *NYT*, Oct. 23, 1928, 2.

12   Schoolteacher quote: Bauman and Coode, 78.

12   Elizabethan poor laws: Brown, 3, 13. Chamber of Commerce poll results: ibid., 109. Quote: *NYT*, Dec. 18, 1931, 5.

12   Shrinkage of state and local tax revenues and charitable contributions covered generally in Brown, chap. 5, "The Battle for Federal Relief Begins," 103–23.

12   Winslow Township, N.J.: *NYT*, Jan. 3, 1932, 20.

2. THE PEOPLE ON THEIR OWN

14   Exchange between Thomas Bell and Judge Alfred Coxe: *NYT*, Jan. 7, 1932, 25.

14   Los Angeles "slave market": *NYT*, July 8, 1932, 9. Statewide unemployment rate: Go, Charmaine, U.C. Berkeley, *Unemployment Relief Distribution in the Bay Area During the Depression*. Online at eh.net/Clio/publications/unemployment.html.

15   Letters suggesting decorating and clothes from *NYT*, Apr. 25, 1932, 14, and Feb. 13, 1932, 12. Hoover auto construction quote from *NYT*, Apr. 2, 1932, 1.

15   New Ford price from *NYT*, Apr. 3, 1932, Special Features Section, XX6. Per capita income figures from U.S. Dept. of Commerce, Bureau of Economic Analysis, Regional Economic Accounts, Table SA1-3, http://www.bea.gov/regional/spi/drill.cfm.

15   Apple sellers and shippers described in Watkins, *Hungry Years*, 76. Hoover quote from Hoover, 195.

15–16 Shoeshiners described in Watkins, *Hungry Years*, 76–77. Fuller Brush success from Manchester, 33–34.

16   Larchmont woodcutting from *NYT*, Feb. 22, 1932, 16.

16   White Plains unemployed golf caddies from *NYT*, Apr. 24, sec. II, 1; Apr. 26, 1932, 14; May 18, 1932, 44. St. Louis golfing clothes donations from *NYT*, Oct. 9, 1932, 28.

16   Arizona gold prospecting from *NYT*, May 22, 1932, sec. III, 6; July 3, 1932, sec. II, 6. California gold mining from *NYT*, July 3, 1932, sec. IV, 18. Unemployed making jobs by setting fires from Andrist et al., 179.

16–17 Weed pullers from *NYT*, Aug. 10, 1932, 6; Aug. 12, 1932, 17; Oct. 9, 1932, sec. II, 6. Pittsburgh Plate Glass actions from *NYT*, June 26, 1932, sec. II, 7. Miami auto tax from *NYT*, June 8, 1932, 28.

17   Garden plots from *NYT*, May 9, 1932, 17. International Harvester farms from *NYT*, Apr. 20, 1932, 42. Needy family adoptions from *NYT*, Mar. 7, 1932, 7; Mar. 10, 1932, 23. Savannah fish donations: *NYT*, Aug. 14, 1932,

sec. II, 6. Train station food baskets: *NYT*, Apr. 14, 1932, 18. Al Capone soup kitchen: pictured in Charles, following 122. Watch finder rewarded from *NYT*, Feb. 7, 1932, 22. Eighty-two New York City breadlines from Manchester, 35. Times Square soup kitchens: Watkins, *Hungry Years*, 59.

17–18   Pennsylvania jobless from *NYT*, Sept. 27, 1932, 38. St. Louis relief figures from *NYT*, Dec. 24, 1932, 5. New York City unemployed from *NYT*, Oct. 31, 1932, 1. One in seven in city on relief from *NYT*, June 10, 1932, 21. Lillian Wald entreaty from *NYT*, July 8, 1932, 19. Labor forecast from *NYT*, July 18, 1932, 2.

18   U.S. Steel production figure from Manchester, 34. Spread-the-work movement from *NYT*, Sept. 2, 1932, 1.

18   Thirty-four million with no income from Manchester, 36.

3. Pleas on Deaf Ears

19   Pinchot to Hoover, Aug. 18, 1931, from National Archives and Records Administration, Hoover Presidential Library online, www.ecommcode.com/hoover/hooveronline/text.109.html.

19   Cox bio material from University of Pittsburgh Library System, Archives Service Center online, www.library.pitt.edu/guides/archives/finding-aids/ais695.htm.

20   Cox motorcade from *NYT*, Jan. 8, 1932, 3.

20   Gorky from Manchester, 23. Hoover flood relief role: Barry, 275–89. Hoover quoted in *NYT*, Jan. 8, 1932, 3.

21   Chamber of Commerce quote from *NYT*, May 2, 1930, 1. "…sixty days too late" quoted in Manchester, 26. "The real victory": *NYT*, Jan. 8, 1932, 3.

21   Cox's army did not leave: *NYT*, Jan. 8, 1932, 3. Hearst support for Garner: Black, 219.

21   Home again in Pittsburgh: Carnegie Library of Pittsburgh Web site on the Strip District and Father Cox: www.clpgh.org/exhibit/neighborhoods/strip/strip_n10.html.

4. The Philosophy of "Rugged Individualism"

23   "Rugged individualism": Hoover campaign speech, New York City, Oct. 22, 1928; text from *NYT*, Oct. 23, 1928, 2.

23   Hoover bio material: Barry, 275–89.

24   Umpiring rather than playing: text of Hoover speech, *NYT*, Oct. 23, 1928, 2.

24   "World lives by phrases": Barry, 289. Also see Manchester, 26, for view of Hoover's belief that depression was a public relations problem.

24–25   Col. Arthur Woods and Emergency Committee for Employment: Schlesinger, vol. 1, 169–70.

25   Eight million out of work, doubling previous year: ibid., 171. POUR announcement, Gifford background: *NYT*, Aug. 20, 1031, 1. Hoover radio address, quote: *NYT*, Oct. 19, 1931, 1, 4.

25   The next morning's report: *NYT*, Oct. 19, 1931, 1.

25   Thrill of a great spiritual experience: Brown, 99; also Schlesinger, vol. 1, 173. Will Rogers's joke: H. Hopkins, 62–63.

26   POUR, Gifford haplessness from Schlesinger, vol. 1, 173–74.

26   Business leaders' outlooks from *NYT*, Jan. 1, 1931, 35.

27   Hoover quoted in Schlesinger, vol. 1, 242.

27   Mellon joke quoted in ibid., 245; Manchester, 24.

27   Hoover to Rudy Vallee from Schlesinger, vol. 1, 242; Manchester, 27.

27   Vallee and Crosby versions at number one: Malcolm Macfarlane's Bing Crosby Diary 1930–1939, online, http://community.mcckc.edu/crosby/brother.html.

5. Hoovervilles and Hunger

28   John Glenn recollection: Glenn, 23.

29   Eviction figures: Watkins, *Hungry Years*, 57, 60.

29   Eviction joke: ibid., 57.

29   Rent strikes: *NYT*, Feb. 9, 1932, 18. Farmers' revolt against foreclosures from Leuchtenberg, *Franklin D. Roosevelt and the New Deal* (henceforth *FDR*), 23–24.

29   References to Hoovervilles, etc., appear throughout depression-era histories, including Schlesinger, vol. 1, 245.

29–30   Seattle Hooverville: Online Encyclopedia of Seattle/King County History (www.historylink.org/output.cfm?file_id=741). St. Louis Hooverville: *NYT*, Jan. 17, 1932, sec. III, 6. Youngstown Hooverville from Watkins, *Hungry Years*, 58; Connie Eisler anecdote from family interview; Pittsburgh shantytown from Carnegie Library of Pittsburgh Web site, www.clpgh.org/exhibit/neighborhoods/strip/strip_n10.html.

30   Hard luck on the river: *NYT*, Aug. 3, 1932, 17; Nov. 25, 1932, 3. "Civilization creaking": Kessner, 170. Unemployed carpenter Hollinan and baby buggy home in Central Park: ibid. Hoover Valley: *NYT*, Sept. 22, 1932, 3.

31   Connecticut ocean liner housing petition: *NYT*, Sept. 29, 1932, 3. Los Angeles streetcar housing: *NYT*, July 6, 1932, 2. Houseboats for the homeless on Lake Pontchartrain: *NYT*, July 24, 1932, sec. II, 6. Detroit tent city: *NYT*, Aug. 7, 1932, 8. New York City homeless housing proposals: *NYT*, Oct. 3, 1932, 9.

31   British heir: *NYT*, Oct. 7, 1932, 2.

31   Hoover quoted on starving, hoboes: Schlesinger, vol. 1, 242; also Manchester, 41. Seven-course meals in black tie: ibid., 23.

31–32 Starvation figures are notoriously difficult to confirm, since death often is attributed to other causes. The report of twenty deaths in 1931 comes from the University of Houston's digital history Web site, www.digitalhistory.uh.edu/learning_history/children_depression/depression_children_menu.cfm. The report of 105 deaths in 1932 comes from www.bookrags.com/research/great-depression-timeline-gdnd-01/. *NYT*, June 1, 1934 (25), reports 31 deaths by hunger and 104 by malnutrition in 1932. Mother and daughter starving: *NYT*, Sept. 7, 1932, 13. Starving nurse: *NYT*, Sept. 9, 1932, 42.

32 People no longer overeating: *NYT*, Jan. 2, 1932, p. 12.

32 Farm prices: Manchester, 36–37. Consumer: Morris County, N.J. historic price survey www.gti.net/mocolib1/prices/1932.html; 1932–1933 price list, Mooresville, Ind. (www.todaysteacher.com/TheGreatDepressionWebQuest/1932pricelist.htm).

32 TERA fishing licenses: *NYT*, Aug. 22, 1932, 17; Aug. 26, 1932, 19.

32–33 Health figures: Watkins, *Hungry Years*, 64.

6. The Problem with Laissez-Faire

34 Wealth ownership from Manchester, 44; poverty from ibid., 32.

34–35 Oregon hours: usinfo.state.gov/usa/infousa/facts/democrac/30.htm. Massachusetts minimum wage: Clifford F. Thies, "The First Minimum Wage Laws," *The Cato Journal* 10, 3 (Winter 1991): 716. Online at www.cato.org/pubs/journal/cj10n3-7.pdf. Child labor: www.archives.gov/education/lessons/hine-photos/. Edgerton quote from "An Industrial Leader Who Leads: A Brief Story of How John E. Edgerton, Through a Natural Sequence of Life and Action, Was Called to Lead the Nation's Organized Industry," E5, National Association of Manufacturers archives.

35 Wages and Edgerton quote from Manchester, 38.

35 Speed-up: Watkins, *Hungry Years*, 126–27. Ford quote: ibid., 126.

35 Stretch-out: ibid., 192–93.

36 Liberty of contract and background: University of Missouri at Kansas City law school Web site, http://www.law.umkc.edu/faculty/projects/ftrials/conlaw/libertyofk.htm. Child laborers: Kessner, 169.

36 "Liquidate labor": ibid.

37 Young quote from Andrist et al., 159. McGrady quote: Schlesinger, vol. 1, 176. Illinois Relief Commission and Cermak: ibid., 176, 250.

7. RUMBLES ON THE LEFT

38–39　The origins of socialism and Communism in the United States have been written about widely. Contributions to my discussion include all three volumes of Schlesinger, principally *Crisis of the Old Order*, 210–23, and Watkins, *Hungry Years*, 111–22.

39　Debs arrest, draft cards: *NYT*, June 17, 1918, 6. Conviction upheld: *NYT*, Apr. 1, 1919, 4.

39–40　Hardwick and mail bomb plot: *NYT*, May 1, 1919, 1. Palmer and Roosevelt windows, leaflets: *NYT*, June 3, 1919, 1. Eight cities: *NYT*, June 4, 1919, 3.

40　New laws: *NYT*, May 3, 1919, 1. Palmer raids: Andrist et al., 30; Watkins, *Hungry Years*, 114. Wall St. bombing and initial death toll: *NYT*, Sept. 17, 1920, 1.

40　Election results: 2003 *New York Times Almanac*, 108.

41　8,000 members from Schlesinger, vol. 3, 197; Young quoted in Schlesinger, vol. 1, 176.

41　Tactics of Unemployed Councils from ibid., 219.

42　National Hunger March of Unemployed Councils in December 1931 is mentioned in Schlesinger, vol. 1, 219–20, but the account here comes primarily from newspaper sources, especially *NYT*, Nov. 3, 1931, 3; Dec. 6, 1931, 3; Dec. 7, 1931, 1; Dec. 8, 1931, 1; Dec. 9, 1931, 2; Dec. 10, 1931, 7.

43　St. Louis protests: *NYT*, July 12, 1932, 2. Toledo grocery raid: *NYT*, Sept. 13, 1932, 2. Mob at Associated Charities: *NYT*, Sept. 9, 1932, 42. Crowd at Cleveland mayor's office: *NYT*, Nov. 22, 1932, 9. New York Home Relief Bureau protests: *NYT*, Dec. 6, 1932, 46; Dec. 7, 1932, 2.

43　Unemployed Citizens League: Schlesinger, vol. 1, 251. Philadelphia appeals, protests: *NYT*, Aug. 5, 1932, 2; Aug. 26, 1932, 7.

43–44　Marion Stull: *NYT*, Aug. 23, 1932, 12; Sept. 3, 1932, 28. In Elizabeth, N.J.: *NYT*, Oct. 1, 1932, 20. In Copper Hill, Tenn.: *NYT*, Apr. 28, 1932, 41.

44　George Bratt: *NYT*, Feb. 13, 1932, 14.

44　Willard quoted in Schlesinger, vol. 1, 181.

44　Keller: ibid., 250.

44–45　Brooklyn "holdup": *NYT*, Nov. 29, 1932, 10.

8. THE GUNS OF DEARBORN

46　Accounts of the deadly riot at the Ford plant in Dearborn, Michigan, on Mar. 7, 1932, are included in many depression-era histories. I rely on reports in the *NYT* of Mar. 8, 1932, 1; N.Y. *Daily News*, Mar. 8, 1932, 2; *New York Herald Tribune*, Mar. 8, 1932, 1; *NYT*, Mar. 9, 1932, 3. Also mentioned in Manchester, 10–11 and 26; descriptions of the Ford plant contained in Watkins, *Hungry Years*, 5–8, and the riot, 127–30; McElvaine, *The Great Depression*, 92–93. Brief description of the riot and the workers' funeral contained in Dickson and Allen, 52–53.

9. The Bonus March

50–56   Descriptions of the Bonus March by veterans seeking immediate payment of deferred compensation voted them by Congress are also staples of depression histories. The fullest account to date is contained in a book devoted entirely to the Bonus March and the events surrounding it. This is Dickson and Allen's *The Bonus Army: An American Epic*, published in 2004, which mentions Hoover's meeting with Amelia Earhart on 136. Schlesinger, vol. 1, 257–65, also contains an excellent account of the Bonus March. Other book mentions include Manchester, 3–4 and 10–18; Kennedy, 92; Leuchtenberg, *FDR*, 13–16; Black, 240–42 and 281; McElvaine, *The Great Depression*, 93–94. See also newspaper accounts in the *New York Herald Tribune*, July 29, 1932, 1; N.Y. *Daily News*, July 29, 1932, 1 and 3; *NYT*, July 29, 1932, 1 ff.

10. Roosevelt onto the Stage

57–63   Franklin Delano Roosevelt's personal and political history leading to the presidential campaign of 1932 is well-chronicled in Schlesinger, vol. 1. See Black on Roosevelt's service to and enthusiasm for Wilson (60–65) and return to Madison Square Garden to nominate Smith after polio (164). See also Leuchtenberg, Burns, Kennedy, Manchester, and Caro on Al Smith. While there are dozens of other sources, the above are my primary references, along with texts of Roosevelt's campaign speeches available online. Specifically, the probable beginning of the Roosevelt campaign for the nomination is set in January or February 1931 by Frank C. Walker, who attended a meeting referred to in his autobiography edited by Robert H. Ferrell, 58. Walker, 55–56, is also illuminating on the rift between Roosevelt and Al Smith.

11. The Battle Is Joined

64–67   The Democratic convention that nominated Roosevelt is covered in detail in Schlesinger, vol. 1, 296–314; Leuchtenberg, *FDR*, 7–10; Burns, 134–40; and Black, 230–39. These are my primary sources as to atmosphere and maneuvering. Roosevelt's acceptance speech: *NYT*, July 3, 1932, 8.

12. A New Direction

68   Stock market figures: New York Stock Exchange Web site: www.nyse.com/about/history/timeline_trading.html. Meeting of mayors: *NYT*, June 2, 1932, 1. Detroit emergency rations: *NYT*, Apr. 26, 1932, 42.

New York relief payments: Schlesinger, vol. 1, 250. Fully half of Chicago's workers: ibid., 250.

68   Nationally, only a fourth: ibid., 249.

69   Creation of Reconstruction Finance Corporation: Kennedy, 84–85. "Millionaire's dole": ibid., 85. RFC loans to states and cities: Watkins, *Hungry Years*, 102. Hoover, Curtis, cabinet pay cut: *NYT*, July 16, 1932, 1. Savings of $37,500: *NYT*, July 16, 1932, 1.

69–70 Hoover nomination acceptance: *NYT*, Aug. 12, 1932, 1.

70   Hoover campaign trip to Iowa from Schlesinger, vol. 1, 432; Manchester, 52–53; Kennedy, 94 (in passing).

70–71 Accounts of discontent in the heartland in the months preceding FDR's inauguration include Watkins, *Hungry Years*, 339–52; Schlesinger, vol. 1, 266–68; Manchester, 58–60; Kennedy, 196. Farmers' Holiday Association song quoted in Manchester, 59; also in "Toward the Cooperative Commonwealth: An Introductory History of the Farmer-Labor Movement in Minnesota, 1917–1948," Ph.D. thesis of Thomas Gerald O'Connell of the Union Graduate School, Feb. 1979 (O'Connell cites the *Iowa Union Farmer*, Feb. 27, 1932).

71   "Wild Bill" Langer quoted in Watkins, *Hungry Years*, 350.

71   Reactions to Hoover: Schlesinger, vol. 1, 432; Manchester, 52–53.

71–72 Hoover's speech that night: *NYT*, Oct. 5, 1932, 18. "Hoover smiles": *Des Moines Register*, Oct. 5, 1932, 11.

72   In that final month: Schlesinger, vol. 1, 432, 437; Dickson and Allen, 201.

Part II
Hope on the Rise

1. Jobs from the Sky (and Nowhere Else)

77   New York City weather, snow shovelers: *NYT*, Dec. 8, 1932, 1; *NYT*, Dec. 11, 1932, 1; *NYT*, Dec. 18, 1932, 1, 24; Dec. 19, 1932, 1; Dec. 20, 1932, 3.

77–78 Reconstruction Finance Corporation loan application by Los Angeles and number it would employ: *NYT*, Mar. 10, 1933, 10.

78   72nd Congress lame duck session: Schlesinger, vol. 1, 448–49, 456. Debate on relief: Burns, 146. Sales tax: Schlesinger, vol. 1, 449. Senate Finance Committee: ibid., 4, 457.

78   Unemployment rate of 24.9 percent is widely cited, including in Watkins, *Hungry Years*, 44.

78–79 "Feed the hungry": Schlesinger, vol. 1, 448. Landon and Fish quoted in Manchester, 58. Reed quoted in Schlesinger, vol. 1, 268.

79   Louisiana bank closures and Union Guardian Trust: ibid., 475.

79–80   Bank failures and bank closings in February, March 1933: Manchester, 71–74; Kennedy, 131–33; Senate hearings and effect on depositors' confidence: Schlesinger, vol. 1, 478.

80   McAdoo quoted in Schlesinger, vol. 1, 5, who cites *Time*, Mar. 6, 1933.

2. An Agony of Waiting

81   Hearst quoted in Schlesinger, vol. 1, 467.

81–82   Roosevelt cabinet appointments: ibid., 466–72; also Burns, 148–49. Ickes and Progressive background: Schlesinger, vol. 1, 100–1, 421–22; Watkins, *Righteous Pilgrim*, 277–80.

83–84   Roosevelt cruise and assassination attempt from sources including Schlesinger, vol. 1, 464–65; Black, 263–64; Burns, 147; Kennedy, 116; Phillips, 82. Leona Merrill from her obituary by Kaitlin Keane in *Patriot Ledger* (Quincy, Mass.), Dec. 17, 2005, 52. Zangara execution from *WPA Guide to Florida*, 379.

84   Roosevelt's sense of calm and national anticipation: Schlesinger, vol. 1, 465–66; Kennedy, 116–17.

84–85   Hoover clung to his conviction: Schlesinger, vol. 1, 476–77; Black, 264–67. Hoover letter to Reed: ibid., 265–66.

85   Roosevelt speech preparation: *NYT*, Mar. 2, 1933, 3.

85   Spread of bank closings: *NYT*, Mar. 2, 1933, 8; also see Leuchtenberg, *FDR*, 38–39.

85–86   Roosevelt party to Washington for inauguration: *NYT*, Mar. 2, 1933, 1; Mar. 3, 1933, 1–3; Mar. 4, 1933, 1, 3.

3. Action at Last

87   Inaugural weather, banks closed: *NYT*, Mar. 4, 1933, 1.

87–88   Inauguration day: *NYT*, Mar. 5, 1933, 1 ff; *Washington Post*, Mar. 5, 1933, 1 ff.

88   Atmosphere in presidential limousine from Schlesinger, vol. 1, 2–3; Black, 270. Hoover quote from Cutler, 172. Tea from Schlesinger, vol. 1, 2; Kennedy, 133; Manchester, 75.

89–90   Inauguration and speech from *NYT*, Mar. 5, 1933, 1 ff. Also described in Schlesinger, vol. 1, 1–8. Descriptions of avid listeners: Manchester, 76–77; Schlesinger, vol. 2, 1; Black, 271; Watkins, *Righteous Pilgrim*, 299.

90   If people wanted action now: Schlesinger, vol. 2, 4.

90   Cash shortages, runners: *NYT*, Mar. 5, 1933, 6. Golden Gloves: Manchester, 78.

90–91   First fireside chat, intro by Robert Trout: Black, 276; transcript of interview by Bob Cockrum with Robert Trout, posted by Cockrum, rmc44@sbcglobal.net, to old.time.radio@oldradio.net, seen at members.aol.com/jeff560/am8.html.

91   Will Rogers quote from *NYT*, Mar. 14, 1933; also Schlesinger, vol. 2, 13. Chat quote from fireside chat posted online at New Deal Network (http://newdeal.feri.org/texts/379.htm); also Black, 276–78.

4. Winds of Change

92   Official Washington itself had changed: Schlesinger, vol. 1, 243; Schlesinger, vol. 2, 14.

92   Decision to push forward: ibid., 8.

93   Speakeasies from Andrist et al., 106. Cassidy from Dickson and Allen, 32–33. Chicago gangland murders from Andrist et al., 111.

93   Hundred Days legislation summarized in Schlesinger, vol. 2, 20–21, among others.

94   Le Mars and Denison, Iowa, from Schlesinger, vol. 2, 42–43. White Cloud, Mich., from Tom Lewis, "A Godlike Presence: The Impact of Radio on the 1920s and 1930s," Organization of American Historians *Magazine of History*, spring 1992, online at www.oah.org/pubs/magazine/communication/lewis.html.

94   Lack of jobs, prospects: Schlesinger, vol. 2, 263; Brown, 146.

94   Lack of relief structure: Schlesinger, vol. 2, 263–65, Leuchtenberg, *FDR*, 52, among others.

5. The Passion of Harry Hopkins

95   Harry Hopkins is abundantly described in New Deal literature. Schlesinger, vol. 2, 265–66, provides a general description that is incorporated here; my description also relies on photographs of Hopkins.

95–97 The fullest descriptions of Hopkins's background and early life appear in McJimsey, *Harry Hopkins*, 17–34, 35–43, and 45. Also Sherwood, 14–30.

98   Origins of New York's Temporary Emergency Relief Administration: Brown, 89–94; Sherwood, 31–32. Hopkins's appointment: McJimsey, *Harry Hopkins*, 45–46; Sherwood, 32.

98   1.2 million New Yorkers receiving TERA aid: McJimsey, *Harry Hopkins*, 46. $20 million additional: Brown, 90. November bond issue: McJimsey, *Harry Hopkins*, 47; Sherwood, 33.

98   Components of TERA: Brown, 92–93.

98–99 Hopkins much preferred work: McJimsey, *Harry Hopkins*, 55–56; Charles, 31.

99   80,000 into TERA jobs: *NYT*, Mar. 13, 1932, sec. II, 1. Hopkins appointed chairman: *NYT*, Apr. 22, 1932, 21. Report to legislature: *NYT*, Aug. 1, 1932, 33.

99   Road construction and other work: *NYT*, Aug. 1, 1932, 33. Money for

artists' colony: McJimsey, *Harry Hopkins*, 48. Bond issue approval: ibid., 47.

99–100 Hopkins in Washington: McJimsey, *Harry Hopkins*, 51; Brown, 140–41. Letter to Roosevelt: Schlesinger, vol. 2, 264; Brown, 141.

100 Hopkins and Hodson to Washington: McJimsey, *Harry Hopkins*, 51; Schlesinger, vol. 2, 264.

100 Meeting with Perkins: Perkins, 183–84. Also ibid.; Black, 281; McJimsey, *Harry Hopkins*, 51; J. Hopkins, 161.

100 Plan for relief, FDR choice of Hopkins as administrator: Schlesinger, vol. 2, 264–65.

100–1 Hopkins's style, Roosevelt's view of him: J. Hopkins, 161–62; Sherwood, 32; McJimsey, *Harry Hopkins*, 40. Hopkins's datebook note: Box 51, Harry L. Hopkins Papers, Georgetown University.

101 Cable to Lehman: J. Hopkins, 162. Straus offer: McJimsey, *Harry Hopkins*, 51. Child support: ibid. 52. Pay cut: Black, 282. "Took train to Washington": Box 51, Hopkins papers, Georgetown U.

6. "Money Flies"

102 Hopkins started work: J. Hopkins, 162; McJimsey, *Harry Hopkins*, 52; Sherwood, 45.

102 Hopkins was pleased: Sherwood, 45.

103 Description of Walker-Johnson Building and quote from Sherwood, 62. Insecticide from Phillips, 265. States and grant total from *NYT*, May 23, 1933, 21.

103 "Money Flies" quoted in Watkins, *Hungry Years*, 170; Sherwood, 44–45.

103 "I'm not going to last six months": ibid., 45.

103–4 Hopkins's appointees: Charles, 29–30.

104 "I don't want anybody…to waste…time": Sherwood, 49. Staff of 121 and total salary of $22,000 a month: ibid., 48.

104 RFC transfers: Charles, 28–29.

105 "In more places than could be believed": H. Hopkins, 103.

105 Matching funds and grants: Brown, 148. Family subsistence rising: H. Hopkins, 103.

105 Boy shot while stealing milk: Charles, 28.

106 "made to feel his pauperism": H. Hopkins, 100.

106 Relief investigator's job: ibid., 101.

106 Freedom to spend on beer and cigarettes: ibid., 105.

106 Civilian Conservation Corps: Schlesinger, vol. 2, 337–41.

106–7 Not everyone embraced the CCC: Watkins, *Righteous Pilgrim*, 338, 339. First enrollee, Henry Rich: USDA Forest Service Web site for George Washington and Jefferson National Forests, www.fs.fed.us/r8/gwj/cultural/ccc/index.shtml.

107 A good overall description of the CCC is contained in Watkins, *Hungry Years*, 159–69. See also Schlesinger, vol. 2, 338–39.

108 Black CCC workers and resegregation:
http://newdeal.feri.org/aaccc/index.htm. Fechner to Griffith from
http://newdeal.feri.aaccc/aaccc04.htm.

108 World war veterans return to Washington: Dickson and Allen, 212–16;
Schlesinger, vol. 2, 15; Watkins, *Righteous Pilgrim*, 340. Veterans offered,
accepted jobs in CCC, Dickson and Allen, 216.

108 CCC enrollment: Schlesinger, vol. 2, 338; also Watkins, *Hungry Years*, 162.

109 Two-part legislation for National Industrial Recovery (leading to National
Industrial Recovery Act): Schlesinger, vol. 2, 98–99; wage/hour figures: ibid.,
90; economic planning: ibid., 99.

109 Public works component: ibid., 99.

109 Record of the Hundred Days from, among others, ibid., 20–21.

7. THE DESIRE TO WORK

110 TVA dams from TVA Web site: www.tva.gov/sites.

110 White House conference, FDR quote: Brown, 152.

111 Hopkins address to National Conference of Social Work in Detroit, welfare
a federal obligation: Brown, 152–54.

111 Response to teachers out of work: H. Hopkins, 112–14.

112 Textile workers employed: H. Hopkins, 113–14.

112 Marksville, Louisiana, archaeology: Lyon, 1–4.

113 2 million on FERA work relief: H. Hopkins, 114.

113 Public Works Administration's slow start: Schlesinger, vol. 2, 109. The PWA
projects mentioned are described in many New Deal histories and Web sites,
but I have relied primarily on T. H. Watkins's excellent Ickes biography,
Righteous Pilgrim.

114 Ickes's appearance: Watkins, *Righteous Pilgrim*, 1–2. "Honest Harold":
Kennedy, 178. "Old Curmudgeon": *Time*, Feb. 11, 1952 (Ickes's obituary,
retrieved online). Attention to fine print: Kennedy, 178.

114 Contractor hiring, no relief requirement: Schlesinger, vol. 2, 284.

115 Title I of National Industrial Recovery Act and Hugh Johnson sketch:
Schlesinger, vol. 2, 101–6. "Old Ironpants": *Time*, Nov. 4, 1940, and
Manchester, 51. Role of NRA in job creation: Kennedy, 177–79. Blue Eagle
and "We Do Our Part" from Schlesinger, vol. 2, 114; also Kennedy, 183.

115 NRA a force for stabilization, not expansion: Schlesinger, vol. 2, 109. PWA
too slow: Charles, 47.

8. THE BIRTH OF THE CIVIL WORKS ADMINISTRATION

116 "a stupendous and varied work program.": H. Hopkins, 115.

116–17 Hopkins in Chicago, Kansas City; Williams report from Commons:
Sherwood, 51; Charles, 46–47. *Federationist* report also mentioned: H.
Hopkins, 115.

117   White House lunch and "walk on air": Sherwood, 35–36; 51–52. Roosevelt, Hopkins quotes: Watkins, *Righteous Pilgrim*, 391; McJimsey, *Harry Hopkins*, 58.

117   Hotel Powhatan sessions: Sherwood, 52.

117   Ickes learned about the raid: Watkins, *Righteous Pilgrim*, 391–92.

118   FDR signs order creating Civil Works Administration: Charles, 48.

9. Four Million Jobs

119   Hopkins had high ambitions: Schlesinger, vol. 2, 270. Mayors of Worcester and Lowell: Charles, 48–49.

120   Engineering division, Carmody: Watkins, *Hungry Years*, 179.

120   CWA reviewers processed applications: Charles, 51–52.

120   Workers from FERA; applications in North Carolina, Chicago: Watkins, *Hungry Years*, 179. Bureau of Printing and Engraving: ibid., 179. Veterans Administration disbursement system: H. Hopkins, 120. More than 800,000: H. Hopkins, 117.

120   CWA workers in mid-December: Schlesinger, vol. 2, 270. Field reports: Bauman and Coode, 28–31.

121   Hickok field report from Dickinson, N.D.: Lorena Hickok papers, FDR Library.

121   Hickok reports from Iowa and Wisconsin: Charles, 49.

121–22 There were stories: shoes from Sherwood, 55; Armstrong from Watkins, *Hungry Years*, 181–82.

122   Smith quoted: *NYT*, Dec. 1, 1933, 1.

122   Hopkins quoted: *NYT*, Dec. 2, 1933, 1; also in Charles, 49–50.

122   CWA job types: Charles, 52; see also *NYT*, Nov. 26, 1933, sec. IV, 1. Employment figures: Sherwood, 57.

10. Employment Politics

123   Bulk of CWA money flowed to largest states: Charles, 50. Costigan quoted: Charles, 54–55.

123   McAdoo accusations: Charles, 55–56.

124   Everybody wanted a piece: Charles, 57.

124   Republican National Committee charges: Sherwood, 55.

124   Hopkins quoted: Charles, 58, and Sherwood, 45.

124–25 Hopkins on cover: *Time* magazine, Feb. 19, 1934. Hopkins's fraud investigators: Sherwood, 55. Cases referred, convictions: Charles, 59.

125   Frank Walker's background is summarized from the Ferrell-edited Walker autobiography.

125   Walker's Montana trip: Sherwood, 53–55.

126   The use of CWA workers in New York City parks by parks commissioner Robert Moses is vividly described in Caro, 362–63, 370, 370–71.

127   Winter conditions, 1934: Sherwood, 55. Also Phillips, 270.
127   "Non-manual and professional" workers: H. Hopkins, 123.
127   Borglum quoted: Sherwood, 58.
127   White-collar jobs: Watkins, *Hungry Years*, 180.
128   Hopkins quoted: Sherwood, 57.

11. THE JOBS THAT PAID TOO MUCH

129   Hopkins's success at job making: Charles, 60; Watkins, *Hungry Years*, 179–80; Sherwood, 55.
129–30 Chelsea, Mass.: Schlesinger, vol. 2, 273.
130   Hickok to Hopkins: Hickok papers, FDR Library.
130   CWA wage scale: Charles, 52–53.
130   As little as 5 cents an hour: ibid., 53. See also Schlesinger, vol. 2, 274; Kennedy, 193–94.
130–31 Sketch of Eugene Talmadge drawn from material in Anderson.
131   Johnstone to Hopkins, Sept. 18, 1933: Gay Shepperson papers, Atlanta History Center.
131   Van de Vrede from Shepperson papers. Talmadge–White House exchange: Anderson, 136; Schlesinger, vol. 2, 274.
131   Hopkins on Talmadge: *Savannah* (Ga.) *News*, Jan. 7, 1934, 1.
132   Hopkins federalizing Georgia program, reinstating Van de Vrede: *Macon* (Ga.) *Telegraph*, Jan. 12, 1934, 1.
132   CWA hour/wage reductions: Charles, 52–53.
132   Hickok to Hopkins: Hickok papers, FDR Library.

12. THE BRIEF SHINING LIFE OF THE CWA

133    $950 million and no more: Sherwood, 56. Lehman quoted: Charles, 61. Letters and telegrams: Sherwood, 56.
133   Hickok to Hopkins: Hickok papers, FDR Library.
134   Fear of CWA permanence: Sherwood, 56. Jobs "become a habit": Leuchtenberg, *FDR*, 122.
134   "should be gradually demobilized": *Time*, Feb. 19, 1934. Obeying orders: Sherwood, 56. "You know, this is a great job": Hopkins press conference, Feb. 16, 1934, National Archives and Records Administration, Civil Works Administration papers, Record Group 69 (henceforth NARA, RG 69), Series 737, Box 4 (viewed online at New Deal Network, newdeal/feri.org/texts/787.htm).
135   Key West: WPA and FERA artwork in the Florida Keys Web site, www.keysarts.com/WPA-Spotlight.htm. Palatka: Florida state parks Web site, www.abfla.com/parks/RavineGardens/ravinegardens.html. Montana state capitol, Cathedral of Learning: Black, 315. Coit Tower: Florence Loeb Kellog, "Art Becomes Public Works," *Survey Graphic* 23, 6 (June 1934):

279. Mississippi schools: Hopkins press conference, Mar. 30, 1934, NARA, RG 69, Series 737, Box 4 (viewed online at New Deal Network, http://newdeal/feri.org/texts/791.htm).

135   150,000 privies: Kennedy, 176. Hopkins's quote: Hopkins press conference, Feb. 23, 1934, NARA, RG 69, Series 737, Box 4 (viewed online at New Deal Network, http://newdeal.feri.org/texts/789.htm).

135   Demobilization of 720,000: ibid. Salt Lake City earthquake from *Deseret* (Utah) *News*, Mar. 12, 1934 (www.seis.utah.edu/NEHRP_HTM/1934hans/n1934ha1.htm). New York City parks: Caro, 370–72. Norman Thomas march: Schlesinger, vol. 2, 277. Continuing work: ibid., 277–78.

135–36 Summary of work: Sherwood, 57; Watkins, *Hungry Years*, 180. New York City parks: Caro, 372.

136   Hopkins summarized: Hopkins news conference, Mar. 30, 1934.

Part III
The Dawn of the WPA

1. Toward a Permanent Jobs Program

141   FERA resumed role: Charles, 67–68, 94.

142   Hopkins conversation with Waite: Charles, 97.

142–43 Effects of a works program: Hopkins memo to Roosevelt, Aug. 23, 1935, NARA, RG 69, WPA General Subject Series, Central Correspondence Files, WPA and predecessors, Box 1.

143   Hog and cotton surplus: Kennedy, 204–5; Watkins, *Hungry Years*, 356–57; Schlesinger, vol. 2, 62–63.

143   Milo Reno quoted: Kennedy, 205. Mules beaten, pigs slaughtered: Leuchtenberg, *FDR*, 73.

143   Wallace quoted: Schlesinger, vol. 2, 63.

144   "If there were great food surpluses"; Federal Surplus Relief Corporation: H. Hopkins, 155–57.

144   Dust storms, vomiting dirt: Manchester, 99.

144   Drought zone: www.u-shistory.com/pages/h1583.html. Clouds seen in Albany, N.Y.: Manchester, 99.

145   May 1934 dust storm: Watkins, *Righteous Pilgrim*, 475–76. Heat wave effects in Arizona: Lyle Johnston, *Arizona Journal*, online at http://azjournal.com/pages/areaguide/HolbDrought.html. In Utah: Leonard J. Arrington, "Utah's Great Drought of 1934," *Utah Historical Quarterly* 54 (1986): 245–63.

145   FERA wells and irrigation projects from http://historytogo.utah.gov/drought.html. Food, wool, leather from sheep and cattle: H. Hopkins, 157–58.

145   Several plans drafted: Charles, 94–95.

2. Protests Left and Right

146–47 Sketch of Townsend and beginnings of Townsend Plan: Brinkley, 222–23.

147   State old-age assistance: Brown, 27. Nettie Burk: *NYT,* July 4, 1932, 13.

147–48 Sketch of Coughlin drawn from Brinkley, chapters entitled "The Radio Priest," 82–106, and "Roosevelt or Ruin," 107–23.

149   Coughlin drifting out of Roosevelt orbit: Brinkley, 133–34.

149   Huey Long background from Brinkley, 10–11.

149–52 Political trajectory of Long covered in Brinkley, 8–71.

153   Formation of Liberty League: Schlesinger, vol. 2, 486–87.

153   Liberty League quotes: *Why?* by Jouett Shouse, Shouse Collection, University of Kentucky libraries, online at www.uky.edu/Libraries/libpage.php?lweb_id=474&llib_id=13.

3. "This Is Our Hour"

154   News of Liberty League: *NYT,* Aug. 23, 1934, 1. Pneumonia: J. Hopkins, 134. Europe trip and FDR note to Hopkins: Sherwood, 63; also J. Hopkins, 176.

154–55 SS *Washington* departure: Sherwood, 63. Hopkins on Mussolini: Hopkins papers, Georgetown University, Box 54, Folder 9.

155   Reaction to public housing and social security in Europe: Sherwood, 64. "In an American way": Schlesinger, vol. 3, 191. Townsend still unknown: ibid., 40–41. Social security prelude: Schlesinger, vol. 2, 300–4.

156   Pretty Boy Floyd sketch: www.bugsysclub.com/bugsysclub/content/view/175/121.

156   Election results; White, Krock, and Hearst quoted: Schlesinger, vol. 2, 507.

157   Hopkins quoted: Sherwood, 64–65.

157   Meetings on new work plan: ibid., 65.

157   Warm Springs described: www.fdr-littlewhitehouse.org/01_history/01_a.html. View from hill and tossing ball: Sherwood, 65. Talmadge visit from Charles, 96.

157–58 Stark story: Charles, 95. Clark story: Sherwood, 65.

4. "Work Must Be Found..."

159   Washington weather; Hauptmann; French foreign minister; Vanderbilt marriage: *Washington Post,* Jan. 5, 1935, 1. Fahnestock: *New York Post,* Jan. 4, 1935, 1; also *Washington Post,* Jan. 5, 1935, 1. Perry and Jacobs: *NYT,* Jan. 4, 1935, 29. Basketball game: *NYT,* Jan. 5, 1935, 21.

159   A protester leaped from the crowd: *New York Post,* Jan. 4, 1935, 1.

159   Inside the Capitol: *NYT,* Jan. 5, 1935, 2, 3.

160–62 State of the Union text: *NYT,* Jan. 5, 1935, 2.

162   Crowd response: *NYT,* Jan. 5, 1935, 1–2. Congressional leaders at White

House supper: *NYT,* Jan. 5, 1935, 1. Nesbitt cooking: Black, 1039; also Schlesinger, vol. 2, 578.

162 Townsend, Coughlin, Long, and the status of their movements are taken from Brinkley's detailed chronicle.

162 National Association of Manufacturers: *NYT,* Jan. 5, 1935, 2. Press reaction: *NYT,* Jan. 5, 1935, 3.

163 *Washington Post* editorial: *Washington Post,* Jan. 5, 1935, 8.

5. A Word Is Born

164 Harry Hopkins had greeted the new year: Hopkins diary, Hopkins papers, Georgetown University (henceforth Hopkins diary).

164 Hopkins, Ickes two obvious choices: Sherwood, 67; also Schlesinger, vol. 3, 343.

164 Hopkins most frequently mentioned: *Washington Post,* Jan. 5, 1935, 1. Ickes quoted: ibid., 2.

165 Sunday following the Friday speech: Hopkins diary. Roosevelt quote as related by Morgenthau: Watkins, *Righteous Pilgrim,* 394.

165 Ickes visit: Hopkins diary entries for Jan. 6, 8, 1935; also quoted in Charles, 107.

165–66 House passage of work relief appropriation: *NYT,* Jan. 25, 1935, 1.

166 Hopkins, Ickes testimony: Sherwood, 67.

166–68 Account of "boondoggle" origins at N.Y. aldermanic hearings: *NYT,* Apr. 4, 1935, 1. Hopkins response quoted in Charles, 70–72.

6. The Machinery Takes Shape

169 Senate passage of works bill: *NYT,* Apr. 6, 1935, 1. FDR signed on train: *NYT,* Apr. 9, 1935, 1.

169 Hopkins's diary entry: Schlesinger, vol. 3, 344.

169 Percentage of labor in CWA, FERA budgets vs. PWA: Charles, 123, 137–38, 139.

170 FDR quoted: Schlesinger, vol. 3, 344.

170 Ickes's illusion of control: Watkins, *Righteous Pilgrim,* 397. Structure of work relief apparatus: Sherwood, 69. "Quite a large round table": Sherwood, 69.

170–71 The third unit: Sherwood, 69.

171 Having decided on this structure: Schlesinger, vol. 3, 344.

171 Fireside chat: transcript online at New Deal Network: http://newdeal.feri.org/texts/385.htm.

172 Executive order: *NYT,* May 7, 1935, 13.

172 "Only a brief paragraph": *NYT,* May 7, 1935, 13.

172 Ickes's dislike of name: Watkins, *Righteous Pilgrim,* 397n.

172 The first meeting: Proceedings of the Advisory Committee on Allotments,

vol. 1, FDR Library, FDR Official File OF466f, Box 24; see also McJimsey, *Harry Hopkins*, 79–80; Watkins, *Righteous Pilgrim*, 398.

173   Hopkins's domination of allotment process: Watkins, *Righteous Pilgrim*, 399; also Sherwood, 69. Hopkins news conference, July 3, 1935: transcript on New Deal Network.

173   Sponsorship requirement: Charles, 117.

173   Ickes memo: FDR Library, FDR official files, Ickes to Roosevelt, June 26, 1936.

174   First billion-dollar allocation: *NYT,* May 17, 1935, 1.

7. FULL SPEED AHEAD

175–76 Schlesinger, vol. 3, 263–90, "The Death of NRA," covers the events leading up to and including the Supreme Court's ruling against the NRA. This is the primary source for the summary included here.

176   Second New Deal: Kennedy, 248n.

177   Hopkins, Ickes continued feud: Schlesinger, vol. 3, 345–47; Watkins, *Righteous Pilgrim*, 399–401. Hopkins diary entry, May 13, 1935: Hopkins papers, Box 51.

177   WPA administrators: Charles, 129–30. Hopkins quoted: Charles, 129. Staff occupying nine buildings: Charles, 128.

177–78 Pace of work: Charles, 128–29. Woodward quoted: Swain, 48.

178   Puppy episode: Hopkins papers, Box 54.

178   No way to buy elections: Charles, 175–78.

179   Instructions to administrators: Charles, 132–33.

179   Davey and Langer: Frank P. Vazzano, "Harry Hopkins and Martin Davey: Federal Relief and Ohio Politics During the Great Depression," *Ohio History: The Scholarly Journal of the Ohio Historical Society* 96 (1997): 124–39.

179   National Youth Administration: Charles, 152–53.

179   25 percent of working women professionals: Cook, 87. Woodward's frustration, takes over professional projects: Swain, 47–48.

180   Baker remains over arts: Swain, 104.

180   Westbrook as advisor: 130; Schlesinger, vol. 3, 352. Harrington recruited as chief engineer: Sherwood, 75.

8. "CAN YOU SPEND MONEY?"

181–83 Harry Hopkins's and Hallie Flanagan's train trip to Iowa City, Hopkins's conversation, and Hopkins's speech are recounted in Flanagan, 8–28.

9. THE DIRT FLIES: PRELIMINARIES

185   WPA projects approved (and PWA projects blocked): Watkins, *Righteous Pilgrim*, 399–400. Hopkins quoted: ibid., 400.

185–86 McCarl blocking WPA spending: *Jacksonville Journal*, Sept. 3, 1935, 1; *NYT*, Oct. 6, 1935, 3. McCarl profile from *Time*, Apr. 10, 1939. Florida jobs from *Jacksonville Journal*, Sept. 3, 1935, 1.

186   Hassler trip and quote, Oakland projects approved: *San Francisco Chronicle*, Sept. 15, 1935, 1.

187   In New York City: Caro, 451–54. Roosevelt quoted on La Guardia: Kessner, 336–37.

187   New York City receiving one-seventh of WPA funds: Caro, 453. Treated as forty-ninth state: Kessner, 339. Johnson reluctant appointee: *NYT*, June 26, 1935, 1.

188   Dallas and Dealey Plaza from Web site of the 6th Floor Museum at Dealey Plaza, jfk.org.

188   Texas highway plans: Mark Ansley, "Alphabet Agencies: FDR's Brainstorm," *Borderlands*, Spring 1994, vol. 12:5, online at www.epcc.edu/nwlibrary/borderlands/12_alphabet_agencies.htm.

188–89 Mt. Hood ski lodge: Griffith and Munro. Ft. Myers yacht marina: *Ft. Myers* (Fla.) *News-Press*, Nov. 29, 1936, 1. Hutchinson, Kans., golf course: www.pasturegolf.com/archive/wpa_courses.htm. Idaho Falls airport: Falls Airport Historic District Web site: www.nps.gov/history/nr/travel/aviation/ida.htm.

189   William Webb and the University of Kentucky plans and ultimate use of WPA labor described in Lyons, "WPA Archaeology," 63–122.

189   Black children: author's telephone interview with Love Ingram, Sept. 4, 2001. New Straitsville: "World Famous Mine Fire of New Straitsville," *Journey Through the Years: New Straitsville Centennial, 1870–1970*, 24–38. Hassler: *San Francisco Chronicle*, Sept. 15, 1935, 1; author's interview with Tom Fleming, Jan. 28, 2001. Lack of airport in New York: Kessner, 432; in Washington, D.C.: Jackson, 47.

Part IV
Folly and Triumph

1. DEATH OF A POPULIST

193   The account of Huey Long's assassination is drawn from Brinkley, 249–50; Schlesinger, vol. 3, 339; Manchester, 116.

193–94 FDR lunching with Coughlin, Coughlin quote, Roosevelt's likely reaction to Long's death: Schlesinger, vol. 3, 341; Manchester, 117; *NYT*, Sept. 12, 1935, 13.

194 FDR on Social Security: Schlesinger, vol. 2, 307–9.

195 Opposition of National Association of Manufacturers, American Medical Association: Schlesinger vol. 2, 311–12; Social Security online at www.ssa.gov/history/1930.html.

195 Growing popularity of Townsend Clubs: Kennedy, 225. Signing of Social Security Act and FDR quote: *NYT,* Aug. 15, 1935, 1. Long filibuster: Perkins, 299.

195–96 Social Security collection, payment schedule: Kennedy, 271-73.

2. HOPKINS ASCENDANT

197 Skilled pay: *NYT,* Aug. 8, 1935, 1. White-collar cuts from *NYT,* Aug. 4, 1935, N4.

197–98 Meany strike call: *NYT,* Aug. 8, 1935, 1. Projects shut down: *NYT,* Aug. 11, 1935, E1. Young professionals to clean sewers: *NYT,* Sept. 26, 1935, 5.

198 No home relief: *NYT,* Aug. 10, 1935, 1. Hopkins quote: *NYT,* Aug. 11, 1935, E1.

198 Meany prediction, results: *NYT,* Aug. 13, 1935, 1.

198 Striker, non-striker incidents: *NYT,* Sept. 14, 1935, 1; Oct. 5, 1935, 1.

198 WPA wage tiers: *NYT,* July 30, 1935, 13. Iowa shift from *NYT,* Aug. 11, 1935, p. 14.

199 Compromise to end strike: *NYT,* Sept. 21, 1935, 14; Sept. 25, 1935, 1; Sept. 26, 1935, 15.

199–200 Mick Frank from author interview with daughter Ethel Weiss. Moses, Johnson, La Guardia name-calling over WPA workers: *NYT,* Sept. 11, 1935, 1.

200 Resolution: *NYT,* Sept. 13, 1935, 6.

200 Hopkins-Ickes feud continues: *NYT,* Sept. 11, 1935, 1; Schlesinger, vol. 3, 347–49. Cartoon appeared Aug. 6, 1936, viewed online: http://library.georgetown.edu/dept/speccoll/cex08.htm.

201 Hopkins dominance: Schlesinger, vol. 3, 349.

201 Hopkins's ulcer: Hopkins diary; cruise plan from Watkins, *Righteous Pilgrim,* 408-9.

201–2 Cruise recounted: Watkins, *Righteous Pilgrim,* 417–18.

202 Funding logjam broken: *NYT,* Oct. 23, 1935, 1.

3. HURRICANES AND PIPE DREAMS

203–4 The account of Labor Day hurricane is drawn from sources including *WPA Guide to Florida,* 330; Jerry Wilkinson, www.keyshistory.org; Dickson and Allen, 236.

204 $200,000 for cleanup, Sholtz, Hopkins quoted: *Jacksonville Journal,* Sept. 6,

1935, 1. Reports accurate; Florida Highway Dept. equipment moved: Dickson and Allen, 239, 248. Williams to Florida, "act of God": Dickson and Allen, 243. Hemingway reaction: ibid., 245.

204–7   The rise and fall of the Florida Ship Canal is compiled from newspaper reports including the *NYT*, *Jacksonville Journal*, and *Ocala Evening Star*. Corps of Engineers interviews posted online at the Army Corps of Engineers Web site, www.hq.usace.army.mil/history/index.htm. First payday from *Ocala Evening Star*, Sept. 18, 1935, 1. Vandenberg pipe-dreaming quote from *Ocala Evening Star*, May 30, 1936, 1. Dragline as plaything from author's interview with Ray Cunningham, Ocala.

4. A LODGE AT THE TIMBERLINE

208   The background and history of Timberline Lodge (as well as its later restoration and its collection of art and furnishings) are covered with loving attention in Rachael Griffin and Sarah Munro's compilation of information for the Friends of Timberline, entitled simply *Timberline Lodge*. Their material is a major contributor to my accounts of the various stages of the lodge's development.

208   Lodge origins: Griffin and Munro, 2–3.

208–9   E. J. Griffith background: *Oregon Voter*, July 20, 1935, 10–13.

209   Sponsorship and sale of bonds: Griffin and Munro, 3.

209   Approval and funding breakdown: Portland *Sunday Oregonian*, Dec. 15, 1935, 1.

209–12   The remainder of the chapter describing the beginning of work on Timberline Lodge is drawn from *Griffin and Munro*, 2–6, and from interviews with Linn Forrest and Albert Altorfer in the archives of Friends of Timberline.

5. A NATION AT WORK

213    $7 million on system of dams: statement of Sen. Margaret Chase Smith on the Passamaquoddy Tidal Power Project, July 21, 1953, appendix to *Congressional Record*, A4510.

214   WPA signs: San Diego *Evening Tribune*, Mar. 6, 1936, 1. Moses-Ridder flap: *NYT*, Mar. 13, 1936, 1. Moses allows smaller signs: *New York Herald Tribune*, Mar. 15, 1936, sec. 1, 50.

215   Hopkins quotes: Sherwood, 52. Ernie Pyle column quoted: Sherwood, 61–62.

216   Colonel McCormick and *Chicago Tribune*: Kennedy, 404–5.

216   *Tribune* editorial: Sherwood, 81. Pictured: Sherwood, 82.

216   Hastings-McKellar exchange: *NYT*, Mar. 11, 1936, 10.

216–17 New York *Sun*'s "Today's Boon-Doggle" from National Archives clip files.

217   Randall's Island stadium cost: *New York Herald Tribune*, Aug. 21, 1935, sec. I, 13. Bridge cost: Caro, 392. Moses controls Triborough Bridge Authority in 1934: Caro, 62. Ceremony: Caro, 441–43; *New York Sun*, Aug. 20, 1936, 1.

217–18 Shoe repair criticism, Robinson's response: *NYT*, Mar. 11, 1936, 10.

218   FDR quoted: *NYT*, Jan. 19, 1936, 1.

218   Mt. Airy, N.C., lake: Syracuse N.Y. *Post Standard*, Sept. 13, 1936, 1. Butte ice rink: *Montana Standard*, May 15, 1938, 14.

218–19 Self-policing: Charles, 136. W-men and Dort quoted: *NYT*, Oct. 23, 1935, 6. 4 percent of total spending: *Oregon Journal*, Apr. 7, 1936, 21.

219   FDR State of the Union transcript: New Deal Network, newdeal.feri.org/speeches/1936a.htm.

219   Background of AAA court case, Supreme Court ruling: Schlesinger, vol. 3, 471–72.

220   WPA rolls, Hopkins quote: Hopkins news conference, Jan. 9, 1936, New Deal Network, newdeal.feri.org/workrelief/hop16.htm.

220   "You can pity six men…": H. Hopkins, 111.

6. KENTUCKY'S PACKHORSE LIBRARY

221   Women 22 percent of workforce: Swain, 54–55.

222   Kentucky library spending: Florence H. Ridgway, *Developments in Library Service in Kentucky, A Review* (Berea, Ky.: Kentucky Library Association, Berea College Press, 1940), 8.

222   *Bookmobile* origin dates to 1926 in Merriam-Webster's Collegiate Dictionary, 11th ed.

222   Role of John C. C. Mayo: Jeanne Cannella Schmitzer, *Register of the Kentucky Historical Society* 95, 1 (winter 1997): 62.

222   Role of Fullerton, Nofcier: ibid., 65.

222–26 The account of Grace Caudill Overbee's (later Grace Caudill Lucas) life with Taylor Overbee and as a packhorse librarian: author's telephone interviews with her and her son Richard Overbee, Jan. 3 and 7, 2002.

227   Packhorse librarians, Eastern Kentucky library distribution figures: NARA, RG 69, Series 743, Box 1, WPA Div. of Information, "WPA Traveling Libraries."

227   Extent of WPA traveling library services: Edward A. Chapman, "WPA and Rural Libraries," *Bulletin of the American Library Association* 32, 10 (Oct. 1, 1938): 703, online at New Deal Network: http://newdeal.feri.org/texts/216.htm.

7. THE 1936 CAMPAIGN

228   Veto overturned, $1.1 billion to vets, contrast with Hoover: Dickson and Allen, 253–55.

228   Hoover call for "holy crusade": Schlesinger, vol. 3, 545. Landon "the everyday American": ibid., 601.

229   Democratic convention, FDR acceptance, crowd reaction: ibid., 585.

230   WPA stood for: author interview with Juliet Segal, July 14, 2006. "Comfort shovel" from *The Morning Herald*, Uniontown, Penn., May 21, 1936, 1.

230   Johnny Mills: author's interview, Nov. 30, 2002. Republicans running WPA: Schlesinger, vol. 3, 591.

230–31 Hopkins quote: *NYT*, Aug. 21, 1936, 6. Reduced role in campaign: Schlesinger, vol. 3, 587. "Not one person is to be laid off...": ibid., 590.

231   Landon move further to right: ibid., 623–24. Social Security "cruel hoax": ibid., 614. Conservative papers' treatment of FDR, *Chicago Tribune* banning FDR news from front page, Hearst front-page editorial: ibid., 633.

231   Al Smith endorses Landon: ibid., 618. Coughlin: ibid., 627–30; says drought God's punishment for electing FDR: ibid., 608.

231–32 Crowd booing *Chicago Tribune* press cars: ibid., 633. FDR Chicago, New York quotes: Black, 389.

8. HOPKINS IN LOUISIANA

233–35 Hopkins dedicating WPA addition to LSU stadium and Hopkins speech: New Orleans *Times-Picayune*, Nov. 29, 1936, 1; New Orleans *Item-Tribune*, Nov. 29, 1936, 1.

235   *Charleston News and Courier*, Jan. 14, 1937; *Laurel Leader Call*, Aug. 29, 1936. From NARA, RG 69, Records of the Division of Information.

236   LSU football results: LSU football Web site: LSUsports.net.

9. AT WORK ON THE TIMBERLINE (HENRY MOAR)

237–38 Progress on Timberline Lodge: Griffin and Munro, 1–14. Hopkins visit and comments: *Oregon Journal*, Sept. 15, 1936, 1; *Portland News-Telegram*, Sept. 15, 1936, 3; Wechner and Turner interviews, Friends of Timberline archives.

238   Hoffman Smith plans: interview online in Archives of American Art, www.aaa.si.edu/collections/oralhistories/transcripts/hoffsm64.htm.

238   Addition to Timberline budget: Griffin and Munro, 30, 39.

238   Henry Moar's role in the construction of Timberline Lodge and the details of his life are from the author's interview with Moar, Portland, Oct. 24, 2002.

239   WPA projects in Portland and northwest Oregon: Neil Barker, "Portland's Works Progress Administration," *Oregon Historical Quarterly* 101, 4 (2000). Wilson and Wolf Creek highways: *Oregon Journal*, May 25, 1936, 1.

239 Status of Summit Meadow camp: Altorfer interview, Friends of Timberline archives.

239–40 Various jobs: Griffin and Munro, 6–14.

240–41 Camp menu and cost of meals from Altorfer interview.

241 Progress of construction: Griffin and Munro, 39–40.

241 Andirons described in Hoffman Smith interview, Archives of American Art.

241–42 Visual tricks employed by architects: Linn Forrest interview, Friends of Timberline archives. "Cascadian" described by Griffin and Munro, 5.

242 Race against deteriorating weather and incidents: Gano, Wechner interviews, Friends of Timberline. Masons using stoves: Griffin and Munro, 8.

242 Christmas planning and violinist: Altorfer interview, Friends of Timberline archives.

243 Lodge roofed: Griffin and Munro, 23.

Part V

The Arts Programs

1. The Dilemma of Art and Politics

247 Federal One potential realized: H. Hopkins, 173–77.

247–48 Federal One spending and employees:. "Unemployed Arts," *Fortune,* May 1937. "Usefulness doubted": *NYT,* Sept. 1, 1936, 20.

248 Firebrand arts workers and reaction treated comprehensively in Mangione.

248 Artists' expectations: Lynch and Barnet quotes from author interviews with the two artists, Lynch on Oct. 22 and Oct. 25, 2002; Barnet on Mar. 6, 2002.

248–49 Houseman on Flanagan: Houseman, 174. Cahill sketch from biographical note to Cahill papers, New York Public Library, online at www.nypl.org/research/chss/spe/rbk/faids/cahill.html. Sokoloff sketch: Bindas, 3–14. Alsberg sketch: Mangione, 53–58.

249 Baker belief in decentralization: Mangione, 40–42.

249 Flanagan/Cahill vs. Baker, Cahill quotes: Cahill interview on line, Archives of American Art, www.aaa.si.edu/collections/oralhistories/transcripts/cahill60.htm

2. The Federal Theatre Project: Prelude

251–52 WPA circus opening: *Bulletin of the Federal Theatre Project* 1, 6 (1936): 23.

252 Honest Bill Newton: www.wpamurals.com/wpapools.htm. Elephant reprieve: N.Y. *Daily News,* Dec. 2, 1937, 39.

252 Preexisting units: Flanagan, 59. Gilbert and Sullivan troupe popularity: Flanagan, 79.

252 Flanagan ambitions: Houseman, 174. Centralizing service functions in N.Y.: Flanagan, 63.

252–53 Elmer Rice, N.Y. units set up: Flanagan, 59.

253 Federal pay problems: Robert Asure interview, Smithsonian Archives of American Art online: www.aaa.si.edu/collections/oralhistories/transcripts/asure65.htm. "Stupidity, inefficiency": Flanagan, 61. Theaters reluctant to rent to FTP: Buttitta and Witham, 35.

253 Ticket prices: *NYT,* Jan. 6, 1935, 2nd news sec., N1. Biltmore rental: Buttitta and Witham, 35.

253–54 Unit-theater pairings: Flanagan, 62; Buttitta and Witham, 35. Late October move-in: Houseman, 182.

254 Houseman and McClendon and Negro Theatre units: Flanagan, 62–63. Lafayette condition, restoration: Houseman, 182.

254 Houseman Harlem background: Houseman, 180–84.

255 Welles, origins of "voodoo" *Macbeth:* Houseman, 185–86. Witch doctors: Houseman, 190.

255 Living Newspaper concept: Bentley, 72–73.

255–56 Mussolini invasion of Ethiopia: *NYT,* Oct. 4, 1935, 1. Rejection of selective arms sale ban: Kennedy, 395.

256 Flanagan assumptions regarding politicians: Asure interview, Smithsonian Archives of American Art. White House reaction to script: Bentley, 212.

256 Flanagan call to ER, Baker decree regarding State Department approval, Rice quitting: Bentley, 211–15.

256 *Model Tenement* shelving: Flanagan, 135–36.

3. The Curtain Rises

257–58 Early FTP presentations: Houseman, 186; Flanagan, 69.

258 March offerings: Flanagan, 69–70.

258 *Murder* as "religious ritual," hot ticket, scalper prices: Buttitta and Witham, 46–47.

258–60 Dorothy Sherwood history: transcript of ruling by Court of Appeals of New York re *People v. Sherwood,* July 8, 1936. *Triple-A Plowed Under* description, quotes: Meltzer, 34–35. Reactions to *Triple-A Plowed Under:* Buttitta and Witham, 42–45. Flanagan quote: Flanagan, 184.

4. The Voodoo *Macbeth*

261 The account of the Negro Theatre's *Macbeth* is drawn from Houseman's vivid firsthand account, 189–205; also Buttitta and Witham, 64–65, and Flanagan, 74. Houseman's recollections form the largest part of the account.

261 Troupe size: Houseman, 193.

261–62 Rumors: Houseman, 190–91. Stencils: Buttitta and Witham, 64. Foliage: Houseman, 200.

262 Dress rehearsal: Buttitta and Witham, 64.

262 "not next to Negroes" quoted by Houseman, 198. Scene at Lafayette, furs and jewels, and Flanagan corsage: Buttitta and Witham, 64.

262–63 Gellhorn quoted in Houseman, 201.

263–64 Theatrical workers employed, projects operating, Flanagan quote: *Federal Theatre Bulletin* 1, 4 (March 1936): 5–6. Lancaster: Buttitta and Witham, 51; Cotten: ibid., 78–79; Lumet: ibid., 83.

5. Selling the Theater (Youth Publicist Frank Goodman)

265 Bank description: Buttitta and Witham, 7–8. Bank failure: Kennedy, 67–68.

266 Frank Goodman's account of his early life and the beginning of his tenure with the Federal Theatre Project: author's interviews with Goodman, July 1, 2002; Mar. 12, 2003.

268 William P. Farnsworth: Flanagan, 67.

6. The Art Project: Murals and Intrigue

270 Treasury art programs: Meltzer, 19–20.

271 Asure quote: interview, Archives of American Art.

271 Cahill production quotas: Cahill interview, Archives of American Art.

271 New York City time cards: Meltzer, 60; Cahill interview, Archives of American Art, 11.

271 McMahon: O'Connor, 56.

272 Pollock start on project and Sande Pollock name change: Naifeh and Smith, 274–76.

272 Cahill background: Cahill interview, Archives of American Art.

273 American Scene painting and practitioners from www.artcyclopedia.com/history/american-scene.html.

273 WPA artists: Meltzer, 63–65. "Gloom pervades": *NYT*, June 28, 1936, 22.

274 Mural spaces: Meltzer, 68–69.

274 Laning work at Ellis Island, New York Public Library: Meltzer, 70.

274 Alston work at Harlem Hospital: www.columbia.edu/cu/iraas/wpa/index.html.

274 Michael Lenson background, entry into FAP supervisory role: Lenson interview by Harlan Phillips Nutley, online at www.wpamurals.com/lenstrans.htm. Details of Essex Mountain mural: Essex Mountain Web site. www.mountainsanitorium.net/default.htm.

276 Development of art projects including glassblowing in N.J. and Corning reaction: Lenson interview.

277 Milwaukee handicraft project: *Milwaukee Journal*, Apr. 5, 1936, 16. New

Orleans: *Sunday Item-Tribune*, Nov. 14, 1937 (National Archives WPA clip files, page illegible). Armenians and Turks in SF: www.masreview.org/4403/mlenson_interview.html. Beach Chalet: author's site visit, Jan. 30, 2001.

277   Graphic artists: Meltzer, 76–80.

7. THE INDEX OF AMERICAN DESIGN (AND COMMUNITY ART CENTERS)

278   The origins and execution of the Index of American Design are covered in some detail at the pages devoted to it at the Web site of the National Gallery of Art: www.nga.gov/collection/iad/history/overview.shtm.

279   Cahill approval: ibid.; Meltzer, 81. Harnett, Egyptologist Smith: Meltzer, 83. Delaney quoted: Sam Yates, "Joseph Delaney," introduction to retrospective exhibit, online at sunsite.utk.edu/delaney/retro.htm.

279   Researchers and artists in thirty-five states: Meltzer, 82.

280   Art Project workers as teachers: Meltzer, 84–5. Cahill Chattanooga story: Cahill interview, Archives of American Art.

280   Community art center push: ibid.

280   Number of art centers and attendees: Meltzer, 85.

280–81 Art centers in N.Y.: Meltzer, 87–8; Harlem Hospital WPA Murals Web site, www.columbia.edu/cu/iraas/wpa/index.html. Chicago: www.wpamurals.com/southside.html.

8. THE MUSIC PROJECT: "REAL MUSIC" FOR AMERICA

282   The state of American music at the outbreak of the depression from a variety of sources, of which Andrist et al., 136–37, provides an example.

283   Professional musicians out of work: Bindas, 2–3. Eleven symphony orchestras: Meltzer, 93.

283   Work for musicians under FERA and CWA: Bindas, 2–3. Hopkins's appointment of Sokoloff, reaction: ibid., 3–5.

283   Kiev orchestra: Meltzer, 92. Sale of Sokoloff violin: Bindas, 3.

283   Sokoloff background: Bindas, 3–5.

284   Sokoloff quoted: ibid., 5.

284   Elinor Morgenthau, California state FMP directors quoted: ibid., 5. Sokoloff comparison of swing with funny papers: ibid., 13. Sokoloff "stupid things": ibid., 5. Pattison quoted: ibid., 13.

285   Weber persuades WPA to extend application date: ibid., 6.

285   Sokoloff favoring classical musicians, "no musical ability": ibid., 5. Weber role and Sokoloff capitulation: ibid., 8.

285–86 Advisory committee: ibid., 6. Hopkins's goal for music: Hopkins, 176. Sokoloff's compiling audience numbers: Bindas, 9.

286   Musicians on payroll in 1935: ibid., 8–10.

286   Increase in musicians in 1936: ibid., 8–10. WPA brass band at Pier 58: *NYT,*

Apr. 26, 1936, sec. 1, 29. Federal Civic Opera of San Diego: Peter Mehren, "San Diego's Opera Unit of the WPA Federal Music Project," *Journal of San Diego History* 18 (summer 1972). Audience of 32 million: *NYT*, Oct. 11, 1936, sec. 2, 6.

287 Critics' dilemma: *New York Post*, June 11, 1936, sec. I, 18.

287 Harry Hewes role: Bindas, 11. Sokoloff oversight of radio recording: ibid., 21.

287–88 Sokoloff avoids left-wing sentiment: ibid., 11. Band fired: *NYT*, Jan. 27, 1936, 1. Reinstated: *NYT*, Jan. 28, 1936, 2.

288 FMP playing work of American musicians: Bindas, 10.

288 New works by American composers, "wealth of talent": *NYT*, Nov. 29, 1936, sec. 2, 7.

288 Kentucky Mountain Minstrels: Bindas, 13–14. *Tipica* orchestras in Texas: Bindas, 98.

288–89 Southwestern music: ibid., 97–98. Joint committee on the folk arts: Meltzer, 99.

289 Music copying service: Hopkins, 176; Meltzer, 91.

289 Music education: Hopkins, 176; Meltzer, 97.

289 Largest of the arts projects: Bindas, xiii.

289–90 Frank Gullino: *New York Herald Tribune*, May 19, 1936, 16.

9. THE WRITERS' PROJECT

291 Jerre Mangione's *The Dream and the Deal* covers the Federal Writers' Project in detail from the author's first-person perspective and is the major source for the information and anecdotes contained in this chapter.

291 Writers' lobbying for a jobs program: Mangione, 34–38.

292 Origins of Writers' Project in previous programs: ibid., 46; Selvaggio, 155.

292–93 American guides an idea of Marianne Moore: Federal Writers' Project of the Works Progress Administration of the State of California. *The WPA Guide to California*, New York: Pantheon, 1984 [1939], xvi. Other originators including Kellock: Mangione, 46.

293 Kellock background: ibid., 46, 63–68.

293 Evolution of guide concept, scrapping of other work: ibid., 47.

293–94 Alsberg respected by writers, preferences for company, and background: ibid., 53–56.

295 During the first months, disorder reigned: ibid., 53–93.

295 Baker quote: Baker interview, Archives of American Art: www.aaa.si.edu/collections/oralhistories/transcripts/bakerj63.htm.

295–96 At the California project: Mangione, 137. Roskolenko quoted: ibid., 176. In Chicago: Ibid., 84. In Boston: ibid., 105. Radicalism in New York project office: ibid., 155–90.

296   Eleanor Roosevelt: Alsberg quoted in ibid., 81.

296–97 State directors, interference generally and in Missouri and Nebraska: ibid., 76–77.

297   Named writers: ibid., 97–152, 255–257.

297   Deadline for guide copy, deadline missed: ibid., 92.

297   From the outside: ibid., 92.

10. At Work for the Writers' Project (Researcher Thomas C. Fleming)

299   This material comes entirely from the author's interview with Thomas C. Fleming, San Francisco, Jan. 28, 2001. Recollection of Harlem riots on page 300 supplemented with *NYT* reports, Mar. 20, 1935, 1, Mar. 21, 1935, 1.

11. One Nation, One Play

303   The material in this section comes primarily from Hallie Flanagan's descriptions in *Arena* in the chapter entitled "States United: It Can't Happen Here," 115–29, and from Buttitta and Witham, 79–92.

303   Flanagan quote: Flanagan, 116. Project anniversary, film rights: Buttitta and Witham, 79. Lewis expected even-handedness from FTP: Flanagan, 117.

304   Telegram quoted: ibid., 117.

305   "free, inquiring, critical spirit": ibid., 129.

12. At Work Offstage (Anthony Buttitta and Milton Meltzer)

306   Both Buttitta and Meltzer have written accounts of, or (in Meltzer's case) touched on, their work for the Federal Theatre Project, both of which are listed in the bibliography. The author also has talked with both men. Tony Buttitta was a neighbor in Greenwich Village for several years before his death in 2004. During this time we spoke often about Buttitta's background and his role in the project, which he describes in more detail in his book with Witham. Meltzer's book covers all the WPA arts projects, and my interview with him on Mar. 1, 2002, provided additional details about his background and the circumstances that led to his theater project job.

307   As soon as he arrived: Buttitta and Witham, 7.

307   Flanagan was out of town: ibid., 8–10.

308   Older actors petitioning Flanagan: ibid., 12.

308   Magazine start in November: Flanagan, 63.

308–9 Conversation with Marvin, meeting de Rohan: Buttitta and Witham, 26. Called back: ibid., 32. "Box Score": *Federal Theatre Bulletin* 1, 5 (April 1936): 21.

309 Milton Meltzer background and arrival at FTP: Meltzer, 1–17.
310 Duration of stays at the FTP: ibid., 151; Buttitta and Witham, 239.

13. The American Guides: Idaho versus Washington, D.C.

311 Kellock role: Mangione, 65–66.
312 Contents of California guide: WPA *Guide to California,* viii.
312 The nation seemed determined: Mangione, 360–61.
313 Alsberg decided on Washington, D.C., as first guide: ibid., 201.
313 Fisher working against odds: ibid., 73, 203.
313 Fisher background: Utah History Encyclopedia online, www.media.utah. edu/UHE/f/FISHER,VARDIS.html. Traffic movement: Mangione, 202. Cronyn duties: ibid., 59; Cronyn quoted: ibid., 203.
313–14 Editor to Idaho, Fisher response as described in novel: ibid., 204–5.
314 January publication: ibid., 206. Pages by Fisher: ibid., 203.
314 Reviews and *Saturday Review* quoted in ibid., 207.

14. Layoffs and Protests

315 Unemployment from 24.9 to below 17 percent: McElvaine, *The Great Depression,* 297–98.
315–16 Roosevelt July 1936 cuts: ibid., 297. Hopkins rescinding exemption granted arts projects: Flanagan, 188–89. Arts workers laid off: Mangione, 165.
316 New York protests covered generally in Mangione, 164–66; Buttitta and Witham, 96–99. Also *NYT,* Dec. 2, 1936, 1. Egri quote: telephone interview by author's assistant, Mar. 5, 2001.
316 Writers' Project stay-in: *NYT,* Dec. 4, 1936, 4.
316 Theatre Project shutdown, FBI appearance: *NYT,* Dec. 8, 1936, 1.
316–17 La Guardia and Somervell to Washington: *NYT,* Dec. 3, 1936, 4. Picket line sign: *NYT,* Dec. 10, 1936, 5.
317 Music Project protests: *NYT,* Dec. 25, 1936, 4.
317 Hopkins eases layoffs, Somervell quoted: Buttitta and Witham, 98–99.
317 Inauguration weather from www.weatherwise.org/inaugday.html.
317–18 FDR second inaugural address: New Deal Network, newdeal.feri.org/texts/92.htm.
318 Advisors to argue for spending cuts and deficit reduction: Black, 398.

Part VI
The Phantom of Recovery

1. FLOOD ON THE OHIO

321   Ohio Valley weather: *NYT,* Jan. 15, 1937, 10. Branham:
       www.biblebelievers.org/lohio.htm.
321   Rain drummed down: *NYT,* Jan. 15, 1937, 10.
322   Predictions of flood slowing: *NYT,* Jan. 16, 1937, 19. Increased flooding:
       NYT, Jan. 18, 1937, 3.
322   WPA, other disaster responders marshaling: *NYT,* Jan. 18, 1937.
322   Jennings and Indiana WPA response: Indiana University's Lilly Library, "The
       WPA in Indiana," virtual exhibit online at
       www.indiana.edu/~liblilly/wpa/wpa.html. (The Lilly Library houses the
       papers of John K. Jennings, who later became Indiana's WPA administrator.)
323   Illinois response: Judith Joy, *Illinois,* November 1977, quoted online at
       www.lib.niu.edu/ipo/1999/oi991202.html.
323   1927 Mississippi flood: compiled from Barry. Reybold quoted: *NYT,*
       Jan. 26, 1937, 1.
323   Ohio River flood levels: Bennett Swenson, "Rivers and Floods," NOAA
       Monthly Weather Review, Feb. 1937, 71–77:
       docs.lib.noaa.gov/rescue/mwr/065/mwr-065-02-0071.pdf.
323   Hunter wired offer of WPA help: Hunter wire to Hopkins, Jan. 25, 1937,
       National Archives, NARA RG 69, General Subject Series, Disaster Relief.
324   Surplus commodities to flood zone: Hunter wire to Hopkins, ibid.
       Commodities on way: Woodward wire to Kerr, ibid. WPA building boats in
       street: WPA film *Men Against the River,* Prelinger Archive, 1937.
324   Flood crests: NOAA *Monthly Weather Review,* Feb. 1937, Table 1, 71;
       NYT, Feb. 2, 1937, 10. Status of flood, evacuations: *NYT,* Jan. 26, 1937, 1;
       NYT, Jan. 27, 1937, 1. Jeffersonville/Branham:
       www.biblebelievers.org/lohio.htm. Postponement of *It Can't Happen Here:*
       Federal Theatre Bulletin 2, 4 (undated, 1937), 13. Evacuation of
       Shawneetown from www.illinoishistory.com/hamradio.html.
325   Cairo, Illinois; levee blast at New Madrid; Coast Guard evacuation boats:
       NYT, Jan. 28, 1937, 1. Evacuation of Cairo: author's telephone interview
       with George Pomeroy, June 2005. Population remaining: *NYT,* Jan. 28,
       1937, 1.
325   Cairo work: *NYT,* Jan. 28, 1935, p. 1. Pomeroy buying boots for workers,
       danger from sand boils: author's interview with Pomeroy (grandson of
       subject).
326   New Madrid WPA work, barge pickup: *NYT,* Feb. 1, 1937.
326   Workman quote: *NYT,* Feb. 1, 1937, 2. Selvidge quote: *NYT,* Feb. 2, 1937,
       2.
326   Five bodies recovered: *NYT,* Feb. 2, 1937, 9. Twenty-four bodies recovered

and six still missing; WPA employees, compensation: *NYT*, Feb. 14, 1937, gen. sec., 32.

326   Hopkins departs for flood zone: *NYT*, Feb. 1, 1937, 2.

327   Tour of flood zone: *NYT*, Feb. 2, 1937, 9. Feiser quote: Feiser letter to Red Cross chapter chairs, Feb. 13, 1937, WPA files, National Archives, RG 69, General Subject Series, Disaster Relief.

328   Aftermath of flood, Hopkins quoted: *NYT*, Feb. 4, 1937, 1. Jennings quote: www.indiana.edu/rulibililly/wpa/wpa.html.

328   New Harmony, Ind.: WPA files, National Archives, RG 69, Records of the Division of Information.

328–29 WPA cleanup work: *NYT*, Feb. 9, 1937, 2; Feb. 13, 1937, 28. WPA theater and music groups entertaining flood victims: *Federal Theatre Bulletin* 2, 4 (undated, 1937); Flanagan, 166. Woodward directing sewing room output to flood zone: WPA Files, National Archives, RG 69, General Subject Series, Disaster Relief.

329   Hugh Johnson quoted: Sherwood, 88.

329   Evansville Retail Bureau ad: WPA files, National Archives, RG 69, Records of the Division of Information.

2. WPA Fights the "Ferocious Fire Demon"

330   WPA rolls: Charles, 171.

330–31 WPA work cited: *Boston Globe*, Jan. 26, 1936; *Manchester Union*, Sept. 24, 1936, 8; *Baltimore Sun*, Oct. 4, 1936, sec. 1, 5; *Washington Morning Herald*, Apr. 28, 1936, sec. 2, 21; *Rochester Democrat and Chronicle*, Oct. 15, 1936, 18; *Seattle Times*, Feb. 5, 1938, 5; *Manchester Union*, Mar. 1, 1937, 1.; www.kiwanisskiclub.com/pages/History.htm.

331   The account of New Straitsville, Ohio's colorful history that appears in these pages is drawn primarily from Bogzevitz and Winnenberg. An earlier work of local history, *Journey Through the Years: New Straitsville Centennial, 1870–1970*, covers the fire under the heading "World Famous Mine Fire of New Straitsville," 24–38. The author also interviewed by telephone residents Jack Shuttleworth and Ruth McKee about their recollections of the fire, Feb. 2001.

334   Ruth McKee quote from interview with author.

334   Geiser report: WPA Files, National Archives, RG 69, General Subject Series, Mine Fires.

334    $360,000 granted to fight fire: *St. Louis Star-Times*, Oct. 26, 1936, 11. Cavanaugh and Laverty: Shuttleworth interviews.

334   Outhouses replaced: Shuttleworth interviews.

335   Uncle Sam's Fire Rescue Station: Shuttleworth interviews.

335   On October 10, 1936: *United Mine Workers Journal*, 1939, date and page illegible (from Penn State University archives).

335   Plummer Hill, Rush and Andrews families: *Cleveland Plain Dealer*, Feb. 28, 1937, magazine, 5.

335–36 The Plummer Hill firewall: ibid.

336 The smoking hills: *St. Louis Star-Times*, Oct. 26, 1936, 11.

336 Newspapers cited: WPA Files, NARA, RG 69, Records of the Division of Information.

336 Cavanaugh pronounced fire "whipped": *Columbus Dispatch*, Apr. 9, 1937, 5B.

336–37 Work on two remaining coal seams: *New York Herald Tribune*, Apr. 2, 1938, sec. 2, 1; *Columbus Dispatch*, Jan. 15, 1939, 9A.

3. THE COURT-PACKING DEBACLE

338 Hopkins had testified: Charles, 170–71.

339 Supreme Court history: Schlesinger, vol. 3, 449–52.

339 FDR response to court's NRA decision: FDR news conference, May 31, 1935, New Deal Network, newdeal.feri.org/court/fdr_5_31_35.htm. Analysis of "horse and buggy": Schlesinger, vol. 3, 285–87; Burns, 222–23.

339 Makeup of Supreme Court: Kennedy, 326.

340 Cases pending review and FDR frustration: Kennedy, 330–31.

340 Court "packing" plan and feasibility: Kennedy, 325–26.

340 Court reform on White House agenda: Schlesinger, vol. 3, 490–94.

341 Frankfurter to FDR: Frankfurter letter to Roosevelt, Feb. 7, 1937, newdeal.feri.org/texts/781.htm.

341 *The Nation* quote: Feb. 13, 1937.

341 FDR message to Congress: *NYT*, Feb. 6, 1937, 1.

341 FDR speech to Democratic victory dinner: *Vital Speeches of the Day*: 3, 11 (March 15, 1937): 324.

341–42 Fireside chat on "Reorganization of the Judiciary": www.fdrlibrary.marist.edu/030937.html.

342 Cartoon: *Brooklyn Eagle*, Feb. 9, 1937. Letters to Congress: Black, 409. Hughes's letter to Sen. Wheeler, Mar. 22, 1937: Burns, 301–02.

342 Wheeler opposition: Burns, 301.

344 For thorough treatments of the court-packing battles and its aftermath see Black, 404–21; Burns, 293–316 (Garner's defection to Texas from Burns, 307); Kennedy, 325–38; Leuchtenberg, *FDR*, 231–38.

4. WPA CUTS AND THE "ROOSEVELT RECESSION"

345 Unemployment rate: Brown, 342–43. WPA fund request: Charles, 170–71.

345 Hopkins closer to FDR since Howe's death: Charles, 211.

346 Roosevelt had looked at declining unemployment: Black, 398. Morgenthau on balanced budget: Leuchtenberg, *FDR*, 245.

346 Countervailing views of Hopkins, Henderson, Eccles: ibid., 167.

346 "More contributions please!": Charles, 166.

347 Hopkins had gone after his appropriation: Charles, 161–65. New York arts units strike: *NYT*, May 29, 1937, 6.

347 Hopkins to Byrnes quoted: Charles, 162. Hopkins's salary cut: Sherwood, 90.

347 *Baltimore Sun* quoted: Sherwood, 90. Spending breakdown: Charles, 164–65.

348 Waltman quoted: Sherwood, 91. Barbara Hopkins's illness and death, Hopkins's bereavement and own illness: Cook, 475; McJimsey, *Harry Hopkins*, 117–18; Sherwood, 92. Age, date of death, hospital, Hopkins at bedside: *NYT*, Oct. 8, 1937, 23.

348 Members of the administration rallied: McJimsey, *Harry Hopkins*, 118. Ickes quoted: Sherwood, 93.

349 Maestri letter: Maestri files, New Orleans Public Library.

349 Lasser-Hopkins meetings: *NYT*, Aug. 20, 1937, 8; Aug. 24, 1937, 14. Rolls below 1.53 million: *NYT*, Aug. 20, 1937, 8. Workers Alliance founding and Lasser quote: *Time*, Aug. 10, 1936. Lasser background: www.cgpublishing.com/Author_Bios/david_lasser.html. Political action fund: *Time*, Sep. 5, 1938.

350 "water out of the spout": quoted in Leuchtenberg, *FDR*, 244. $2 billion in Social Security collections: ibid., 244.

350 Economic downturn: ibid., 243–44; Kennedy, 350–53.

5. The Roosevelts at Timberline

351 "utterly opposed": quoted in Burns, 317.

351–52 Itinerary: Official File 200, Western Trip, Box 35, FDR Library. Remarks at Boone, Iowa, and Clinton, Iowa, Sept. 23, 1937: President's Speech File, Box 36, FDR Library. Displeasure with Wheeler: Burns, 317.

352 Bonneville Dam: Watkins, *Righteous Pilgrim*, 384–85.

352 FDR remarks at Bonneville, motorcade to Timberline from Official File 200, Western Trip, Box 35, FDR Library. Scene at FDR dedication: described, Griffin and Munro, 11; pictured, ibid., 12.

353–54 Work at Timberline: ibid.. 6–14; 30–45.

354 Forrest interview: Friends of Timberline archives.

354–55 FDR dedication: President's Speech File, Box 36, FDR Library.

355 Roosevelt party departure for Seattle: *NYT*, Sept. 29, 1937, 16.

355 Menu from Griffin and Munro, 12. Hoffman Smith recollection: oral history interview on line, Archives of American Art: www.aa.si.edu/collections/oralhistories/transcripts/hoffsm.htm.

6. Decline and Revival

356 Remainder of FDR itinerary: Official File 200, Western Trip, Box 35, FDR Library. Recession effects: Kennedy, 350.

356–57 Wishes and results of special session: Kennedy, 340.

357 State of the Union: *NYT*, Jan. 4, 1938, 16.

357 Uncertainty, du Pont quote: Kennedy, 351.

358 Conditions in early 1938: Leuchtenberg, *FDR*, 249; Black, 432.

358 Hopkins operation, recuperation: Sherwood, 92–93.

358 Hopkins's presidential invitation to Warm Springs: McJimsey, *Harry Hopkins*, 119. FDR decision: Manchester, 163.

358 Spending plan: ibid. Mistake to reduce spending: fireside chat transcript: newdeal.feri.org/texts/390.htm. WPA rolls: Hopkins news conference, Apr. 28, 1938: newdeal.feri.org/texts/807.htm.

359 Eleanor Roosevelt quoted in Cook, 477. Hopkins radio broadcast: *NYT*, May 9, 1938, 1.

359 Passage of wage-and-hours law: *NYT*, June 15, 1938, 1. Fireside chat: *NYT*, June 25, 1938, 1.

360 WPA report: *NYT*, June 19, 1938, 8.

360 Hopkins's cover story: *Time*, July 18, 1938, cover and 9. Hopkins's radio address: *NYT*, May 9, 1938, 1.

361 WPA as source of controversy: Charles, 195; Leuchtenberg, *FDR*, 270.

361 WPA rolls: *NYT*, Mar. 5, 1941, 23.

7. Building Roads in North Carolina (Johnny Mills)

362–63 WPA road work: *Better Roads*, Oct. 1936, 42. Johnny Mills's personal history and his account of doing road work for the WPA in Jackson County, N.C., comes from interviews with Mills and his wife, Shirley, by Michele Glover, Apr. 12, 2002, and by the author and Barbara Nevins Taylor, Nov. 30, 2002. Other WPA work in county from Jackson County *Journal*, Apr. 8, 1937. Rural roads paved in Jackson County from N.C. Dept. of Transportation.

364 Hopkins quote: Hopkins news conference, Apr. 28, 1938: newdeal.feri.org/texts/807.htm.

8. Kentucky Archaeology (John B. Elliott)

368–69 Smithsonian and TVA archaeology: Lyon, 30.

369 Roles of Webb and Funkhouser: ibid., 20–23.

369 Role of William Haag: ibid., 62.

369–70 John B. Elliott, Josephine Mirabella backgrounds, Elliott's recruitment and entry into WPA archaeology program: author's telephone interview with Josephine Elliott, Jan. 2, 2002.

371 Webb's interest in Green River sites: Lyon, 98.

371–72 Cypress Creek layout and work: ibid., 100–1. Woodland characteristics: www.cr.nps.gov/seac/woodland.htm.

372–74 Account of Elliotts in Kentucky: interview with Josephine Elliott.

374 Webb and Haag quoted in Lyon, 100.

9. Hurricane!

375   On the morning of Wednesday, September 21: E. S. Allen, 31–36.
375–78 Advance and effects of hurricane described: ibid., 31–93; *NYT*, Sept. 28, 1938, 26; Federal Writers' Project, *New England Hurricane* (henceforth FWP), 23.
378   Personal recollection of Eastern States Exposition: interview and e-mail exchange with Gordon Hyatt, son of exhibitor S. G. Hyatt, Nov. 2005. Ferris wheel wreckage pictured: FWP, 136.
379   News of disaster reaching outside world: Cherie Burns, 203.
379   President Roosevelt was still in bed: *NYT*, Sept. 23, 1938, 19.
379   WPA bathing pavilion: FWP, 52. WPA flood control dams: FWP, 193.
379–80   River rising in East Hartford: E. S. Allen, 100. WPA, CCC workers: *NYT*, Sept. 23, 1938, 19.
380   By Thursday night: E. S. Allen, 100–2.
380   Foley, Sullivan efforts: ibid., 103. Sullivan refugee centers and FMP entertainment: FWP, 121.
380–81   Carp caught: FWP, 115. Ware: FWP, 131. Other Massachusetts WPA work: FWP, 139, 142, 147, 164–65, 193. Manchester, N.H., WPA work: FWP, 196.
381   WPA dams held: FWP, 193.
381   WPA search for bodies: E. S. Allen, 186.
381   WPA work in Crescent Beach: ibid., 299.
381   WPA playrooms: FWP, 121.
382   Dead in Rhode Island, homes destroyed, property losses: *NYT*, Sept. 26, 1938, 1.
382   Death toll: FWP, 218. Hopkins quotes: *NYT*, Sept. 26, 1938, 8; FWP, 188. Damage and quote: *NYT*, Nov. 30, 1938, Resort, Travel sect., 1.

Part VII
The WPA Under Attack

1. War Among the Democrats

385   The growing strength and assertiveness of the Democratic Party's conservative wing, Roosevelt's attempted "purge" of conservative Democrats in the 1938 primaries, and voters' repudiation of Roosevelt at the polls are thoroughly covered among Manchester, 167–71; Kennedy, 339–50; Black, 455–60, 484–86; Leuchtenberg, *FDR*, 263–74; and Watkins, *Righteous Pilgrim*, 630–31. These served as my major sources for the information in this chapter.
385   "Conservative Manifesto": Kennedy, 340–41.
385–86   FDR June 24, 1938, fireside chat: *NYT*, June 25, 1938, 1.
386   But the protests that flooded the White House: Levine and Levine, 257.

386   "Cotton Ed" Smith quoted: McElvaine, *Great Depression*, 192–93.
386–87 Bailey quoted: Kennedy, 342. Lynching: Kennedy, 342–44; FDR quoted, 343. Entreaties from Eleanor Roosevelt: Cook, 243–47. See also *Time*, Jan. 24, 1938.
387–88 Fireside chat: *NYT*, June 25, 1938, 1. FDR "feudal economic system": Sullivan, chap. 2, online at University of North Carolina Press Web site: uncpress.unc.edu/chapters/sullivan_days.html.
388   *Chicago Tribune* series ran from Sept. 2 through Sept. 18, 1938. Clippings from WPA Files, National Archives, RG 69, Records of the Division of Information, page numbers of articles referenced below unclear in reproduction.
388   "Vampire political machine": *Chicago Tribune*, Sept. 2, 1938.
388   "Green Pastures": *Chicago Tribune*, Sept. 15, 1938. "Peasant class": *Chicago Tribune*, Sept. 4, 1938.
389   Hunter response: NARA, RG 69, WPA Papers, Records of the Division of Information, news release dated Sept. 20, 1938, for newspapers dated Sept. 21, 1938. See also *Time*, Oct. 3, 1938.
389   Williams quoted: *NYT*, June 28, 1938, 1. Senate committee response: *NYT*, June 29, 1938, 1.
389–90 Hopkins quoted: *Time*, Sept. 3, 1938. Barkley-Chandler charges: *NYT*, Aug. 1, 1938, 1. Hopkins's findings and quote: *NYT*, Sept. 21, 1938, 30. Farley action: Leuchtenberg, *FDR*, 269–70.
390   Pro-FDR results: *NYT*, Sept. 25, 1938, 1. Anti-FDR results: Kennedy, 348–49.
390   O'Connor results: Black, 459.

2. THE RISE OF THE RED-BAITERS

392   While most depression-era histories treat Martin Dies and the rise of the House Un-American Activities Committee, I found two magazine articles to be most helpful in assessing the Dies committee and its early impact. These were by Raymond P. Brandt in the *Atlantic Monthly* of Feb. 1940 and D. A. Saunders in *Public Opinion Quarterly* 3, 2 (Apr. 1939).
392   Martin Dies's background: Handbook of Texas online, (www.tsha.utexas.edu/handbook/online/articles/DD/fdi13.html). Ascent to committee chair and consolidation of power: Watkins, *Righteous Pilgrim*, 631–36. Physically described: Flanagan, 340. Mentorship: Black, 484.
392–93 "Demagogues Club": Brandt, 234. History of investigating committees: ibid., 233.
393   Fish, McCormack hearings: ibid., 233–34.
394   Yorkville Casino: *NYT*, Apr. 21, 1938, 1.
394   Dies quoted: Watkins, *Righteous Pilgrim*, 632.
394   Dies offered no source: Saunders, 223–25.
395   Committee makeup, schedule, rules: ibid., 227; Brandt, 232–37.
395–96 Viereck subpoena, arrangement: *Washington Post*, Aug. 4, 1938, 4.
396   Various groups described as communistic: Leuchtenberg, *FDR*, 280. 500 inches in *NYT*: Saunders, 224.

396   Ickes and Perkins accused: Watkins, *Righteous Pilgrim*, 633. Focus on WPA: Saunders, 31.

3. The "Runaway Opera"

397–98 Characterization of Flanagan: Houseman, 174.

398   Hopkins quoted: Flanagan, 185. Flanagan on *Injunction Granted*: ibid., 72. *One-Third of a Nation*: ibid., 214. *Spirochete*: ibid., 144.

398   Complaints about *Spirochete*: ibid., 144, 251.

398   *Cradle Will Rock*: Houseman, 247.

399   Benjamin: *Time*, Oct. 3, 1938. Ten thousand on strike: *NYT*, May 28, 1937, 1. Arts projects protests, Nora Bayes sit-in: Houseman, 249–55; Flanagan on the strike: Flanagan, 202.

400   Labor troubles: Houseman, 250. Rumors: Flanagan, 202.

400   Cuts, state projects curtailed: *The Nation*, July 17, 1937, 67–69. All-night sit-ins: Houseman, 254. Previews, opening set: ibid., 255.

400   Ban: Flanagan, 202; Houseman, 255.

400–1 Flanagan quotes: Flanagan, 202–3.

400–2 The description of the events from WPA ban on new productions through presentation of *Cradle*: Houseman, 268–74.

403   Front-page news, two-week run: ibid., 276. Mercury Theatre: ibid., 285. Houseman severance: ibid., 280. De Kooning severance: Meltzer, 71.

4. Sacco and Vanzetti

404   Washington, D.C., guide described, Hopkins's remark: Mangione, 209. FDR quoted: ibid., 11.

404   Review quoted: ibid., 210.

405   Berger, origins of *Cape Cod Pilot*: ibid., 212–13.

405   Four New England guides published: ibid., 216.

405   Ceremony and quotes: Swain, 125; Mangione, 216; *WPA Guide to Massachusetts*, 145, 219, 587.

405   *Boston Traveler*: Mangione, 217. Sacco and Vanzetti as a touchstone case: among many references, an article by Robert D'Attilio posted at the University of Pennsylvania's contemporary writing programs Web site (writing.upenn.edu/~afilreis/88/sacvan.html) provides a summary of the uproar surrounding the case.

406   *Traveler* headline and reaction: Mangione, 217.

406   Hopkins news conference, Aug. 19, 1937: newdeal.feri.org/texts/806.htm. Reactions quoted: Mangione, 218.

406–7 Hettwer notes: Selvaggio, 44–45 and app. D.

407   Stalinists and Trotskyites: Mangione, 175.

407   Orrick Johns: ibid., 83.

407   New York Albany office a dumping ground: ibid., 150–52. Writers reported
       once a week: ibid., 245. Walton quoted: *NYT Book Review*, Aug. 29, 1937,
       2. *American Stuff* magazine: Mangione, 250–51.

5. In the Crosshairs

409   Thomas on New Deal: *NYT*, Oct. 15, 1938, 3. Thomas on theater project:
       NYT, Aug. 10, 1938, 6. Thomas focus on WPA: Saunders, 231.
409   Practically alone: Flanagan, 335–36.
410   Huffman testimony: *NYT*, Aug. 20, 1938, 1. Huffman spying: Buttitta and
       Witham, 188.
410   Testimony characterization and quotes: ibid., 189.
410–11 Flanagan letter, no reply: Flanagan, 336.
411   Thomas on *Prologue to Glory*: ibid., 173.
411   *Created Equal*: ibid., 255.
411   It was little consolation: Saunders, 223–38.
412   Yet it was not until Dies: ibid., 233.
412   Dies answer to accusations: Sidney Olsen, *Washington Post*, Oct. 30, 1938, B-3.
413   Witness characterizations: Saunders, 236.
414   Flanagan's letters unanswered: Buttitta and Witham, 190; Flanagan, 337.

6. Harry Departs

415   Back in September, newspaper reports: Sherwood, 102.
416   Hopkins's presidential ambitions and FDR's encouragement: ibid.,
       94–95.
416   Support of Gillette's opponent: Leuchtenberg, *FDR*, 269–70.
417   Hopkins's news conference, Dec. 8, 1938: NARA, RG 69, Series 737, Box 4,
       Box 5. Viewed online: newdeal.feri.org/texts/809.htm.
417   Hopkins quoted: Sherwood, 105.
419   Resignation letter: NARA, RG 69 WPA files, General Subject Series.
419   Polls: Sherwood, 104–5. *Chicago Daily News* quoted: ibid., 107.
420   Harrington over Williams, Harrington nickname: *Time*, Jan. 2, 1939. Less
       polarizing, serving for army pay: Sherwood, 106.
420   Affection for Hopkins and his beliefs: ibid.
421   Description of cartoon: McJimsey, *Harry Hopkins*, 103; pictured in Charles,
       opposite 123.

7. Changes in the Wind

422–23 FTP response to Dies: Flanagan, 338.
423   FWP response and Hopkins quoted in Mangione, 307–8. Woodward to
       testify and Niles's insistence: Flanagan, 339. Probable factors: Swain, 129.

423–24 Woodward appearance before committee: Swain, 129–30; Flanagan, 339–40.

424   Description of Flanagan testimony: Flanagan, 340–42.

424   Flanagan despair for 8,000 employees: ibid., 342.

424–25 Starnes "subsided": ibid. Other examples of committee's ignorance: Saunders, 237.

425   Thomas quoted: Flanagan, 345–46.

425   Alsberg called, testimony: Mangione, 315.

425–26 Alsberg testimony: ibid., 317.

426   Committee report on FTP: Flanagan, 347. Single paragraph: Brandt, 237.

426   Gallup poll: Mangione, 321. Increased budget: Brandt, 235.

8. Can Anybody Spare a Hot School Lunch?

427   More than 5,000 children: *Washington Times,* Dec. 21, 1938, 20.

428   Eleanor Roosevelt support of school lunch program: Watkins, *Hungry Years,* 265.

428   My reporting about the WPA's hot school lunch program in Washington, D.C., and throughout the United States was gathered primarily from news clippings at NARA, RG 69, Records of the Division of Information, Box 186 (Women's Hot Lunches). I failed, however, to record references to individual papers, dates, and pages except where these are mentioned in the text. I also used speeches written for delivery by WPA deputy administrator Ellen S. Woodward, "The Lasting Values of the WPA" and "Hot Lunches for a Million School Children," both from NARA, RG 69, Series 737, Box 8. These can be viewed online at newdeal.feri.org/works/ wpa01.htm and newdeal.feri.org/works/wpa02.htm.

430   Lunches in New York City schools: *NYT,* May 18, 1939, 27.

9. The Death of the Theater

431   Woodrum position and quote: Mangione, 322.

431   Flanagan optimism, letter to Woodrum: Flanagan, 348.

432   Paid investigators, Burton: ibid., 348–49.

432   FTP income: ibid., 338.

432   Planting evidence about the FWP: Mangione, 323.

432–33 Cannon recounted re: FWP: ibid., 324; re: FTP: Flanagan, 350–51.

433   Relief appropriation bill, no fight for FTP: ibid., 352–53.

433   Flanagan fights on, Atkinson quote: ibid., 354–55.

434   Fight in Senate, Bankhead: ibid., 355–61.

434   House unyielding, FDR signs bill: ibid., 362–63.

434   Last FTP performances, *Pinocchio*: ibid., 364–65.

10. A Different Playing Field

435 Reorganization pursued: Burns, 344–46. Bill passed: *NYT,* Mar. 23, 1931, 1.

435–36 Plan described in FDR message to Congress on "Reorganization Plan No. 1," Apr. 25, 1939: *NYT,* Apr. 26, 1939, 1. Replacement of PWA and Carmody over Ickes: Watkins, *Righteous Pilgrim,* 587.

436 Ickes quoted in Watkins, *Righteous Pilgrim,* 587. Harrington on reorganization: Harrington press conference, Apr. 20, 1939, NARA, RG 69, Series 737, Box 3, online at New Deal Network: newdeal.feri.org/texts/812.htm.

437 Harrington view of arts projects: Mangione, 329. State sponsors, Newsom appointment and aim: ibid., 330–33. Kellock quoted in ibid., 327.

437–38 Bellevue Hospital anecdote: O'Connor, 63–64.

438–39 Statue of Liberty: *NYT,* Aug. 29, 1937, rotogravure sect., 128; Sept. 4, 1938, sect. 11, 1; Dec. 14, 1938, 29. Aquatic Park from *San Francisco News,* Jan. 31, 1939. San Antonio River Walk: "Maury Maverick's San Antonio," *Survey Graphic* 28, 7 (July 1939): 421 (newdeal.feri.org/texts/367.htm). Ernie Pyle: *Washington News,* Dec. 18, 1939, 27.

439 North Beach history: Kessner, 433. La Guardia insistence: ibid., 432. New York City projects: *The WPA Guide to New York City:* 560. Groundbreaking: *NYT,* Sept. 10, 1937, 25. See also La Guardia Airport online fact sheet: www.panynj.gov/CommutingTravel/airports/html/lg_facts.html.

440 Airport construction, features: Kessner, 432–35.

440 Clifford Ferguson from author's interview, Jan. 2002.

441 Materials, figures, and difference between blueprints and actual work: Kessner, 433.

442 Crowd at dedication: *NYT,* Oct. 16, 1939, 1.

442 Jobs for air hostesses: *NYT,* Oct. 17, 1939, 27. Training school: *NYT,* Nov. 7, 1939, 2.

442 First arrival: *NYT,* Dec. 2, 1939, 1. Named by Board of Estimate: *NYT,* Nov. 3, 1939, 18. Newark closed to commercial traffic: *NYT,* May 31, 1940, 17. Busiest in world: *NYT,* Dec. 1, 1940, Travel and Recreation sec. XX1.

442 La Guardia quoted: Kessner, 434.

442–43 New York World's Fair: ibid., 435–39. Descriptions of WPA pavilion: photo files online at New Deal Network: Photo Library, Issues and Events, Exhibitions, New York World's Fair, 1939.

443–44 The onset of WWII and the reign of isolationist sentiment are covered in period histories including Burns, 384–422; Kennedy, 381–464; Leuchtenberg, *FDR,* 197–298.

445 Potential effect on WPA from Hunter news conference: Aug. 31, 1939, NARA, RG 69, Series 737, Box 6, online at newdeal.feri.org/texts/814.htm.

Part VIII
WPA: War Preparation Agency

1. No Military Work

449   No military spending: Schlesinger, vol. 3, 270.
449–50 Borah responsible: ibid. Vote on Treaty of Versailles: Black, 77. Vote on League of Nations: ibid., 343. Passage of Neutrality Act of 1935: Burns, 253–56. Nye hearings: www.senate.gov/artandhistory/history/minute/merchants_of_death.htm.
450   Ludlow amendment: Black, 430; Kennedy, 402–3; Leuchtenberg, *FDR*, 229–30.
450–51 Quarantine speech: transcript in *NYT*, Oct. 6, 1937, 1.
452   "most momentous utterance": *Washington Post*, Oct. 6, 1937, 1. FDR quoted: Kennedy, 406; Manchester, 175.
452   Hopkins mission: Sherwood, 100; Manchester, 178.
452   Arnold flight: www.centennialofflight.gov/essay/Air_Power/Hap_Arnold/AP16.htm. 8,000 planes: Manchester, 178. Needs of military, Hopkins quote: Sherwood, 100.
453   Aviation research money, 440-mph Heinkel: *NYT*, Dec. 18, 1938, Resorts/Aviation/Travel sec., 129.
453   Hopkins San Francisco remarks: *San Francisco Examiner*, Sept. 21, 1938, 28. WPA funds to make machine tools: Sherwood, 101.
454   Johnson to FDR correspondence, FDR to Hopkins, basics of training plan: FDR Library.

2. The Picatinny Arsenal

455   The account of the WPA's work on the Picatinny Arsenal and the installation's history and background is taken largely from John W. Rae's *Images of America: Picatinny Arsenal* (Charleston, S.C.: Arcadia, 1999).
455   Early WPA defense requests: *NYT*, July 11, 1935, 3; July 13, 1935, 4; July 17, 1935, 28; July 20, 1935, 3; Aug. 15, 1935, 6.

3. Race and Isolationism

461   Axis formed: Burns, 353.
461–62 *Panay* incident: Kennedy, 402; Black, 427–28; Manchester, 173–74.
462   Fall of Nanking: Kennedy, 401.
462–63 Nuremberg Laws: www.jewishvirtuallibrary.org/jsource/Holocaust/nurlaws.html. Kristallnacht: Manchester, 178. Heydrich instructions:

http://www.jewishvirtuallibrary.org/jsource/Holocaust/Heydrichkristal.html. Figures: Louis L. Snyder, *Encyclopedia of the Third Reich* (New York: Paragon House, 1989), 201.

463 "insidious wiles of foreign influence": Washington's farewell address, posted online at the Government Printing Office Web site, www.access.gpo.gov/congress/senate/farewell/sd106-21.pdf.

463–64 Domestic anti-Semites: Leuchtenberg, *FDR*, 275–77. Coughlin quoted in Manchester, 176. Eight hundred groups: *Survey Graphic* 28, 2 (Feb. 1939): 113.

464 Slurs on FDR and ER: Manchester, 164–65.

464–65 Lindbergh background, life in Europe, and visit to Germany: PBS American Experience Web site, www.pbs.org/wgbh/amex/lindbergh/sfeature/index.html.

465 German service cross to Lindbergh: Black, 467. To Ford: *NYT*, July 31, 1938, 1.

465 Lindbergh return to United States: PBS American Experience Web site, www.pbs.org/wgbh/amex/lindbergh/sfeature/fallen/html. Radio speech: *NYT*, Sept. 16, 1939, 1; Black, 533–34.

466 Second radio speech: *NYT*, Oct. 15, 1939, 45.

466 Fireside chat: FDR Library, online at www.fdrlibrary.marist.edu/090339.htm.

466 Poll results: Kennedy, 427. *Reader's Digest*: PBS American Experience Web site, www.pbs.org/wgbh/amex/lindbergh/sfeature/fallen.html.

466–67 Neutrality Act repeal: Black, 537; Leuchtenberg, *FDR*, 295; Gilbert, 25.

4. Hold the Jokes, Please

468 Aquatic Park nail joke: *San Francisco News*, Jan. 31, 1939.

468 Two years on WPA joke: *Time*, Mar. 20, 1939.

469 Joke ban: *NYT*, Mar. 8, 1939, 23.

469 Network play ban: *NYT*, July 22, 1940, 22.

469 Hydrants: *Brooklyn Eagle*, Nov. 4, 1938, 9.

469–70 WPA fingerprinting projects: *Indianapolis News*, Dec. 21, 1937, 6; *Indianapolis Star*, Feb. 1, 1938, sect. I, 1; New Orleans *Item*, Mar. 12, 1942, 1.

471 Hopkins's resistance to fingerprinting: Hopkins news conference, Apr. 28, 1938. Never voted: Harrington obituary, *Washington Post*, Oct. 1, 1940, 1.

471 Fingerprint objections: Teachers' Union, *The Nation*, Jan. 21, 1939, 103.

471 Halloran refusal: *Philadelphia Record*, Mar. 12, 1939, sect. 2, 3.

471–72 Merendino: *New York Post*, Apr. 9, 1940, 14.

5. Pink Slips and Pinkos

473 Determination to "fix" WPA: Kennedy, 349; *NYT*, Jan. 15, 1939, 1.

473 Ban on political activities: *NYT*, Mar. 10, 1939, 2.

473–74 Harrington news conference: Mar. 9, 1939, transcript in NARA, RG 69,
Series 373, Box 3, online at New Deal Network:
newdeal.feri.org/texts/810.htm.

474 Hatch Act: *NYT,* Aug. 3, 1939, 1.

474 Security wage attributed to Harrington: *NYT,* July 12, 1939, 1.

474 Work stoppages: *NYT,* July 6, 1939, 1.

474–75 Effects of new wage scales: *NYT,* July 6, 1939, 1.

475 Harrington news conference July 6, 1939: transcript in NARA, RG 69,
Series 373, Box 3, posted online at New Deal Network:
newdeal.feri.org/texts/813.htm.

476 Somervell on strikes and strikes ending: *NYT,* July 8, 1939, 1; July 12, 1939,
1; July 21, 1940, 1.

477 Loyalty oath: *NYT,* June 29, 1939, 12. Harrington response: July 6, 1939,
news conference.

477 Workers Alliance to take pledge, Morgan quote: *NYT,* June 29, 1939, 12.
Lasser would resign: *NYT,* June 20, 1940, 16.

477 Sixty-six not signing loyalty pledge: *NYT,* Oct. 26, 1939, 14.

477–78 August Henkel: *NYT,* July 7, 1940, 4; www.damninteresting.com/?p=321;
Robert Atkins, "Time Line," *Art Journal* 50, 3 (fall 1991): 34; *NYT,* Apr. 9,
2006, sec. 14, 1, 8.

6. Before the Deluge (Vincent James "Jimmy" Bonanno)

479 Jimmy Bonanno's story comes primarily from interviews conducted with
him by the author, Jan. 26, 2002, and July 14, 2004. His account of the fire
at Hangar 4 at La Guardia Field is supplemented by *NYT,* Mar. 6, 1940, 1.

7. A "Hurricane of Events"

485 The events leading up to World War II, and the details of the war itself, are
widely known and in little dispute. I have relied primarily on Martin
Gilbert's exhaustive *The Second World War: A Complete History* for the
details of the conflict provided here and through the remainder of the book.

485–86 Non-aggression pact: Kennedy, 425. Leaflet bombing: Gilbert, 46. Borah
quoted in Burns, 408.

486 Hopkins's health: McJimsey, *Harry Hopkins,* 126–28.

486–87 Garner, Hull, Farley, FDR's third-term calculations, onset of war: Burns,
407–20.

487 Germany's invasion of Belgium, Netherlands: Gilbert, 61. Churchill replaces
Chamberlain: *NYT,* May 11, 1940, 1.

487–88 Churchill speech: online at www.winstonchurchill.org.

488 FDR to Churchill quoted in Black, 532. "Like matchwood" quoted in
Burns, 419. British needs: Black, 551.

488–89 FDR speech: *NYT,* May 17, 1940, 10.

489 Fireside chat: transcript, http://www.fdrlibrary.marist.edu/052640.html.

489 Lindbergh quoted in Black, 552. Vandenberg: *NYT*, May 17, 1940, 15. Telegrams to White House: Levine and Levine, 301, 302.

489 Destroyers: Black, 551.

490 Evacuation: Gilbert, 83. Smallest craft: Association of Dunkirk Little Ships Web site, www.adls.org.uk.

490 Churchill speech, arms to England: Black, 554–55.

490 German advance across Somme, taking Paris, French surrender: Gilbert, 86–101.

491 FDR quoted in ibid., 90.

491 "Hurricane of events" in Burns, 419.

8. Rigid Priorities

492 Harrington to WPA administrators: *NYT*, June 7, 1940, 14.

493 Hunter news conference of Aug. 22, 1940: NARA, RG 69, Series 737, Box 6, posted online at New Deal Network, newdeal.feri.org/texts/817.htm.

494 WPA an obstacle to defense program: *NYT*, June 6, 1940, 24; June 7, 1940, 22.

494 Military undermanned with old equipment: Kennedy, 388; Black, 465. Garand rifles: Manchester, 178.

495 San Francisco Committee: WPA Files, San Francisco Public Library.

495 Rep. Howard Smith bill: *NYT*, July 29, 1939, 3.

495 Harrington and Somervell moving to purge Nazis, Communists: *NYT*, June 23, 1940, 1.

496 Charlotte Long: *NYT*, June 27, 1940, 25.

496–97 Purge results: *NYT*, Aug. 4, 1940, 3. New notices: *NYT*, July 27, 1940, 25.

497 Alien Registration Act signed: *NYT*, June 30, 1940, 5. Registrations from *NYT*, Dec. 28, 1940, 10.

9. The Third-Term Equation

498 Republican convention: Kennedy, 449; Black, 560; Burns, 424.

499 Hopkins stay at White House: Sherwood, 173. Democratic convention and phone in Hopkins's bathroom: ibid., 176–77.

499 Barkley quoted in Burns, 427.

499 Roosevelt demonstration: ibid. Sewer commissioner: Black, 569–70.

499 Wallace as vice presidential nominee: Burns, 427–30; Black, 570–72. Arthur Schlesinger review of *American Dreamer: Los Angeles Times*, Mar. 12, 2000. "Eastern occultism": Culver and Hyde quoted by Schlesinger, above; and others.

500 Joseph Kennedy view of arms to England and English ability to resist Germany: Kennedy, 437, 440, 450–51.

500–1 Battle of Britain: Kennedy, 452. German losses: Gilbert, 119. Churchill quoted: ibid., 120. German planes sent: Burns, 438. RAF pilots lost or wounded: ibid., 440.

501   Great Smoky Mountains National Park dedication speech: The American Presidency Project, www.presidency.ucsb.edu/ws/index.php?pid=16002.

501   Quid pro quo for leases: Black, 578. Viewed as act of war by Walsh, by *Chicago Tribune*: Burns, 439. America First Committee: *NYT*, Sept. 25, 1940, 13; Oct. 31, 1940, 3.

502   Isolationism and anti-Semitic component: Leuchtenberg, *FDR*, 311–12.

502   Shift in American opinion: ibid., 299–300. Operation Sea Lion postponed: Gilbert, 125.

10. BREATHING SPACE

503–4 Hopkins's resignation: Sherwood, 179–80. Roosevelt's letter quoted in ibid., 181. Harrington death accounts: *NYT*, Oct. 1, 1940, 32; *Washington Post*, Oct. 1, 1940, 1.

504   Hunter acting commissioner: *NYT*, Oct. 12, 1940, 11.

504–5 Executive order signed, quoted in *NYT*, Sept. 24, 1940, 1. Willkie support of draft: Black, 583. Unemployment dropping: ibid., 574. Willkie shifts tactics: Leuchtenberg, *FDR*, 320–21; Burns, 448–51.

505   Warmonger: ibid., 443; Leuchtenberg, *FDR*, 320. Quote about "on the transports": *NYT*, Oct. 23, 1940, 1. "April, 1941": *NYT*, Oct. 31, 1940, 1.

506   FDR at draft lottery drawing: *NYT*, Oct. 30, 1940, 1.

506   Names of draftees: *NYT*, Oct. 30, 1940, 1. "Martin, Barton, and Fish": Sherwood, 189–90. Military orders: *NYT*, Oct. 31, 1940, 1.

506–7 "Say it again—and again...": recounted in Sherwood, 191. Election results: Burns, 454.

507   Camp David: "Camp David/A History of the Presidential Retreat" at http://www.infoplease.com/spot/campdavid1.html. England out of money: Black, 604.

507–8 Hitler, FDR "arsenal of democracy" quoted in Burns, 457. FDR address: Black, 607. Transcript of speech online: www.americanrhetoric.com/speeches/fdrarsenalofdemocracy.html. Lend-Lease Act passed: Black, 622.

508   Supplies: Sherwood, 257–58. Fire hose: Black, 622. Role in Lend-Lease: Sherwood, 267.

11. A FEVER OF PREPARATION

509   Unemployment: Bureau of Labor Statistics: ftp.bls.gov/pub/special.requests/lf/aat1.txt. New job creation: Black, 575. Retaining five-day week: Kennedy, 451.

509–10 WPA rolls declining: *NYT*, Mar. 5, 1941, 23. Jimmy Bonanno: author's interviews. Camp Edwards construction: Boston *Sunday Globe*, rotogravure sec., Nov. 10, 1940; http://www.mass.gov/guard/Camp_Edwards/history.htm.

510 WPA enrollment: *NYT*, Jan. 10, 1941, 10. Hunter testimony: *NYT*, Feb. 11, 1941, 14. Hospital training: *NYT*, Jan. 26, 1941, 18.

510 WPA military construction projects: NARA, RG 69, WPA Papers, Records of the Defense Coordinating Section, Misc. Memoranda, Box 1.

510 Hunter letter to FDR, FDR refusal to designate WPA a defense agency: FDR Library, WPA Papers, 1941, Box 10.

511 Hunter May 21, 1941, testimony to House Appropriations Committee: NARA, FDR Library, WPA Papers, Small Collections, Howard Hunter papers.

511 FDR declaration of unlimited national emergency: *NYT*, May 28, 1941, 2 (text).

511 Hunter June 19, 1941, news conference from NARA, RG 69, Series 737, Box 6. Transcript online at New Deal Network, newdeal.feri.org/ workrelief/hun05.htm. Arts projects status: Meltzer, 140–41.

512 Hitler invasion of Soviet Russia: Gilbert, 198–99.

513 Hopkins as ambassador to Stalin: Sherwood, 323–28.

513 Hunter Sept. 26, 1941, news conference: NARA, RG 69, Series 737, Box 6. Transcript online at New Deal Network, newdeal.feri.org/workrelief/hun02.htm.

514 Women in defense plants: ibid.

514 America First Committee dissolves: *NYT*, Dec. 12, 1941, 22.

12. THE LAST HURRAH

515 Hunter-Hopkins correspondence: NARA, FDR Library, Group 24, Harry Hopkins papers, Howard Hunter folder.

516 Hunter to Stimson and Knox: NARA, FDR Library, WPA Papers, 1941, Box 10. Hunter to WPA administrators: FDR Library.

516 Archaeology shut down: Lyon, 77–78

516 Hunter to U.S. Conference of Mayors: NARA, FDR Library, WPA Papers, Small Collections, Howard Hunter speeches.

517 Somervell return to army: *NYT*, Nov. 8, 1940, 23. Huie appointed: *NYT*, Apr. 9, 1941, 20. New York City WPA rolls: *NYT*, Feb. 14, 1942, 35.

517 Writers shift to war service: Mangione, 348. Artists shift to war service: McMahon interview; O'Connor, 74–75. Cahill headed all arts projects: Cahill interview, Archives of American Art.

517 Hunter's departure from WPA, correspondence: NARA, FDR Library, WPA Papers, 1942, Box 10.

518 Election results: Kennedy, 782.

518 WPA employment: *NYT*, Dec. 5, 1942, 1.

518 FDR to Fleming to shut down WPA: NARA, FDR Library, WPA Papers, 1941, Box 10.

519 Letters to White House on end of WPA: NARA, FDR Library, FDR Papers, Gen. Correspondence, Misc.

519 WPA signs used for scrap: Federal Works Agency release, Feb. 9, 1943, from WPA NARA, FDR Library, WPA Papers, WPA Official File.

519–20 May 1 WPA status: *NYT*, May 2, 1943, E9.

EPILOGUE

523 Closing date from *NYT*, July 1, 1943, 9.

523–24 Statistics from Black, 348; Kennedy 252–53; Leuchtenberg, *FDR*, 125–28; Watkins, *Hungry Years*, 263–92; Time, Mar. 8, 1972; "WPA and the War," *Army and Navy Register*, May 16, 1942, 26–28.

524–26 Updates on subjects: author interviews.

525 Howard Hunter interned: Memorandum of Major B. W. Davenport, NARA, FDR Library, WPA Papers, Small Collections, Howard Hunter papers.

525–26 Harry Hopkins's last mission: Sherwood, 883–916. Hopkins in New York: ibid., 917–34. Hopkins's death: *NYT*, Jan. 30, 1946, 1.

526 Timberline Lodge: Margery Hoffman Smith interview, Archives of American Art; Griffin and Munro, 12–13.

526 River Walk opening: the Edwards Aquifer Web site, www.edwardsaquifer .net/sariver.html.

526 Florida Ship Canal: *NYT*, Jan. 18, 1939, 1; May 18, 1939, 1; author's on-site visit.

527 New Straitsville: Bogdevitz and Winnenberg; author's interview with Shuttleworth.

527 River Walk: San Antonio Chamber of Commerce Web site, www.sachamber. org/visitor/riverwalk_history.php. Timberline: Griffin and Munro, vii, 48–59.

528 Fate of WPA easel art: Naifeh and Smith, 453; *Time*, Mar. 6, 1944. Pierre Clerk account: author's interview, Oct. 29, 2005. Boswell quoted in *Time*, Mar. 6, 1944; O'Connor, 75.

528–29 GSA reclaiming WPA art: Robert Kyle, *Maine Antiques Digest*, Aug. 2006, online at http://www.maineantiquedigest.com/articles/aug06/wpa0806.htm.

529 Harlem Hospital murals: Harlem Hospital Web site. Golden Gate Park: author on-site visit. Heather Becker: National New Deal Preservation Association Web site, www.newdeallegacy.org/

ACKNOWLEDGMENTS

This book has been eight years in the making, which gave me the good fortune of being able to talk to actual survivors of the Great Depression and the WPA. By the year 2000 their numbers were small, but to hear from those who were actually there was to give a memorable immediacy to their recollections. Some of their stories appear in these pages; others offered vivid background information. They include Tom Fleming of San Francisco; Jimmy Bonanno and Clifford Ferguson of New York City; Johnny Mills and Early Dietz of Jackson County, North Carolina; Grace Caudill (Overbee) Lucas of Adaville, Kentucky, and her son, Richard Overbee of Milford, Ohio; Henry Moar of Portland, Oregon; John and Josephine Elliott of New Harmony, Indiana; Jack Shuttleworth of New Straitsville, Ohio; Ethel Weiss of New York City and Connie Eisler Smith of Milford, New Jersey; David Cook and Ray Cunningham of Ocala, Florida; and Gordon Hyatt of New York City. Alumni of the WPA arts projects included my late neighbor and friend Anthony Buttitta, Frank Goodman, and Milton Meltzer, all of New York City, who were generous with their time and information, as were Douglas Lynch of Portland, Oregon, Jack Levine of New York City, and Ted Egri of Santa Fe, New Mexico. John Glenn provided vivid memories of his youth during the depression and has been a friend and an advisor.

Some of these people, and many of the specific WPA projects described in *American-Made*, came to my attention by way of local historians and history clubs, whose enthusiasm for the past of their surroundings produced rich troves of material. The Friends of Timberline in Portland, Oregon, and especially Sarah Munro, were most generous, sharing interviews from the files assembled in their long and successful effort to provide the marvelous Timberline Lodge with the record it deserves. The lodge's curator, Linny Adamson, is the on-site keeper of memories and bringer-to-life of Timberline's rich history, and I thank her for providing many necessary details. I also am indebted to the New Straitsville (Ohio) Local History Committee, area historian Connie Dunkle, and John Winnenberg of the Sunday Creek (Ohio) Historical Association for bringing their town, and the WPA's fight against its underground mine fire, to life.

Researchers to whom I owe thanks include F. Kennon Moody, Maria Sliwa, Raina Moore, and Michele Glover; my late friend and writing teacher William Paulk; my sister-in-law Hope Tudanger, who searched files at the Atlanta Historical Society; and my old and good friend Gerry Chambers, who joined me in slogging through countless photographs and files, at both the National Archives in College Park, Maryland, and the FDR Library in Hyde Park, New York, looking for images and information. My cousin Mary Kay McDuffie of Bellaire, Michigan, let me know of WPA projects in her area.

The Internet is an increasingly valuable source of information to both students and researchers of the Roosevelt administration and the New Deal, including the WPA. This owes much to the work of Thomas Thurston, the assembler of the incredible New Deal Network and its first director. (The Network is a project of the Franklin and Eleanor Roosevelt Institute.) Dr. Joseph J. Plaud also helps to keep the New Deal flame alive as founder of the Franklin D. Roosevelt American Heritage Center and Museum in Chicopee, Massachusetts, and the connected New Deal Information Service. Kathy Flynn of the National New Deal Preservation Association, and Heather Becker of its Chicago chapter, have spearheaded efforts to preserve murals and other works of the WPA for future generations.

I thank Gene Morris at the National Archives, whose expertise in the archives' New Deal materials helped me find the right stuff; the staff in the archives' still photo repository for their goodwill and courtesy; and the research room staff at the FDR Library for their patient guidance. The National Park Service staff at the Ocmulgee National

Monument in Macon, Georgia, especially Master Ranger Sylvia Flowers, were generous with contacts and information. Ed McWilliams of the New York Building Trades Council helped me locate members of the carpenters union who had worked for the WPA. Jane Julian at the Kentucky Department for Libraries and Archives provided contacts and information about the WPA's packhorse librarians. New York Assemblyman Jack McEneny offered valuable guidance on New York's WPA projects. Portland, Oregon, city archivist Diana Banning steered me to files chronicling WPA road work in Portland and northwestern Oregon. I'm sure there are others in this pantheon of heroes—librarians, archivists, and curators who have pointed me to the correct filing cabinet or corner of the stacks; or simply interested parties whose zest for the subject and the material reaffirmed my own deep belief that this was a story that needed to be told—whom I should thank by name but can't owing to haste, that crashed hard drive in 2005, or simple human failing. To you I offer apologies, but no less gratitude.

Virtually all works of history stand on the shoulders of previous historians, and among them I am especially grateful to the late Arthur M. Schlesinger Jr., who listened to my early thoughts about this book and recommended sources, among them Robert Hopkins.

There are some people whose contributions test the ability of words to thank them. My editor at Bantam Books, Ann Harris, has been tireless, patient, and firm. Her notes and suggestions have made this a much better book, and her friendship and good cheer make the world of publishing a better place. My agent, Lynn Nesbit, and her partner, Mort Janklow, have been wise counselors in guiding my career.

Finally, to my wife, Barbara Nevins Taylor, go not only gratitude but my deepest love and admiration. She has been unstinting with advice, support, encouragement, and apt criticism during the long gestation of this book. There is no way I can thank her enough for being on—and by—my side.

INDEX

ABOUT THE AUTHOR

Nick Taylor is the author of seven nonfiction books
and collaborated with John Glenn on his memoir.
He lives in New York City.

Printed in the United States
by Baker & Taylor Publisher Services